THE NEW GROVE
HANDBOOKS IN MUSIC

HISTORY

OF

OPERA

THE NEW GROVE
HANDBOOKS IN MUSIC

HISTORY
OF
OPERA

Edited by STANLEY SADIE

MACMILLAN

Parts of this material first published in
The New Grove Dictionary of Music and Musicians®,
edited by Stanley Sadie, 1980

The New Grove and *The New Grove Dictionary of Music and Musicians*
are registered trademarks of Macmillan Publishers Limited, London

First published in the UK 1989 by
THE MACMILLAN PRESS LTD
Houndsmills, Basingstoke, Hampshire RG21 2XS
and London
Companies and representatives throughout the world

British Library Cataloguing in Publication data
Opera. – (The new Grove handbooks in music)
1. Opera to 1985
I. Sadie, Stanley, *1930*– II. The new Grove
dictionary of music and musicians
782.1'09

ISBN 0–333–41730–5

First American Edition, 1990

All rights reserved

ISBN 0-393-02810-0

W. W. Norton & Company, Inc.,
500 Fifth Avenue, New York, NY10110

W. W. Norton & Company, Ltd.,
37 Great Russell Street, London WC1B 3NU

Typeset by August Filmsetting, Haydock, St Helens

1 2 3 4 5 6 7 8 9 0

Contents

*

Contents

Abbreviations

AcM	*Acta musicologica*	*MMR*	*Monthly Musical Record*
AMf	*Archiv für Musikforschung*	*MQ*	*The Musical Quarterly*
AMw	*Archiv für Musikwissenschaft*	*MR*	*The Music Review*
AnM	*Anuario musical*	*MT*	*The Musical Times*
AnMc	*Analecta musicologica*	*MZ*	*Muzikološki zbornik*
BeJb	*Beethoven–Jahrbuch* (1953–)	*NOHM*	*The New Oxford History of Music*,
BMw	*Beiträge zur Musikwissenschaft*		ed. E. Wellesz, J. A. Westrup
CHM	*Collectanea historiae musicae* (in series		and G. Abraham
	Biblioteca historiae musicae		(London, 1954–)
	cultores) (Florence, 1953–)	*NRMI*	*Nuova rivista musicale italiana*
CMc	*Current musicology*	*NZM*	*Neue Zeitschrift für Musik*
EM	*Early Music*	*ÖMz*	*Österreichische Musikzeitschrift*
FAM	*Fontes artis musicae*	*OQ*	*Opera Quarterly*
GfMKB	*Gesellschaft für Musikforschsung*	*PMA*	*Proceedings of the Musical Association*
	Kongressbericht	*PNM*	*Perspectives of New Music*
Grove 6	*The New Grove Dictionary of Music*	*PRMA*	*Proceedings of the Royal Musical*
	and Musicians (1980)		*Association*
HJb	*Händel–Jahrbuch*	*RaM*	*La rassegna musicale*
HMYB	*Hinrichsen's Musical Year Book*	*RBM*	*Revue belge de musicologie*
HR	*Hudební revue*	*RdM*	*Revue de musicologie*
IMSCR	*International Musicological Society*	*RdMc*	*Revista de musicología*
	Congress Report	*ReM*	*La revue musicale* [1920–]
JAMS	*Journal of the American Musicological*	rev.	revision, revised (by)
	Society	*RHCM*	*Revue d'historie et de critique musicales*
Jb	*Jahrbuch*		[1901]; *La revue musicale*
JM	*Journal of Musicology*		[1902–10]
JbMP	*Jahrbuch der Musikbibliothek Peters*	*RIM*	*Rivista italiana di musicologia*
JRMA	*Journal of the Royal Musical*	*RMFC*	*Recherches sur la musique française*
	Association		*classique*
Mf	*Die Musikforschung*	*RMI*	*Rivista musicale italiana*
MGG	*Die Musik in Geschichte und*	*SIMG*	*Sammelbände der Internationalen*
	Gegenwart		*Musik-Gesellschaft*
MJb	*Mozart–Jahrbuch des Zentralinstituts*	*SM*	*Studia musicologica Academiae*
	für Mozartforschung (1950–)		*scientiarum hungaricae*
ML	*Music and Letters*	*SMA*	*Studies in Music* [Australia]
MM	*Modern Music*	*SMw*	*Studien zur Musikwissenschaft*
MMA	*Miscellanea musicologica*	*SMz*	*Schweizerische Musikzeitung/Revue*
	[Czechoslovakia]		*musicale suisse*
MMg	*Monatshefte für Musikgeschichte*	*ZMw*	*Zeitschrift für Musikwissenschaft*

Illustration Acknowledgements

We are grateful to the following for permission to reproduce illustrative material (Every effort has been made to contact copyright holders; we apologise to anyone who may have been omitted): Civici Musei Veneziani d'Arte e di Storia, Venice (figs.1, 60); Biblioteca Communale Ariostea, Ferrara (fig.2); Biblioteca Nazionale Centrale, Florence (figs.3, 6); Metropolitan Museum of Art (Harris Brisbane Dick Fund, 1931), New York (fig.4); Board of Trustees of the Victoria and Albert Museum, London (figs.5, 15, 56b); Österreichische Nationalbibliothek, Vienna (figs.7, 35, 38(right), 41); Theatermusuem, University of Cologne (figs.8, 20–22, 28, 51, 67, 68, 104, 130, 131, 133, 136) (figs.8, 21, 22, 28, 51, 68 Niessen Collection); Bärenreiter-Verlag, Kassel (fig.9); Bibliothèque Nationale, Paris (figs.10, 11, 23 (photo Service International de Microfilms), 77, 80, 81, 102, 110 (photo Jacques Moatti)); Theatermuseum, Munich (figs.12, 55, 71); Herzog Anton Ulrich-Museum, Brunswick / photo copyright Museumsfoto B. P. Keiser (fig.13); Trustees of the Chatsworth Settlement (Devonshire Collection, Chatsworth) (Fig.14); Trustees of the British Museum, London (figs.17, 44); Raymond Mander and Joe Mitchenson Theatre Collection, London (figs.18, 50, 92, 122, 123); Mansell Collection, London, and Alinari, Florence (fig.19); Houghton Library, Harvard University, Cambridge, Massachusetts (fig.24); Civica Raccolta Stampe Achille Bertarelli, Milan (fig.25); Museo Civico, Turin (fig.26); Staatliche Kunstsammlungen, Kupferstichkabinett, Dresden (fig.27); Museo Civico, Varese (fig.29); Music Library, University of California, Berkeley (fig.30); Historisches Museum der Stadt Wien / photo Österreichische Nationalbibliothek (figs.31, 34); Kunsthistorische Museum, Vienna (fig.33); Peter Branscombe / photo University of St Andrews Photographic Unit (fig.36); Internationale Stiftung Mozarteum, Salzburg (fig.38(left)); photo Jean-Loup Charmet, Paris (fig.39); Mary Evans Picture Library, London (figs.40, 78); Soprintendenza per i Beni Artistici e Storici, Bologna (fig.45); Bibliothèque Municipale, Besançon (fig.46); Trustees of the Wallace Collection, London (fig.47); photo Statens Konstmuseer, Stockholm (fig.52); Bibliothèque Municipale, Versailles (fig.54); Harvard Theatre Collection, Cambridge, Massachusetts (figs.56a, 57, 116 (photo Angus McBean)); The Archives, Royal Opera House, Covent Garden, London (figs.56c, 56e, 87a, 91); Richard Macnutt, Withyham, Sussex (figs.59, 61, 75); Stuart-Liff Collection, Port Erin, Isle of Man (figs.62, 87c); Pierpont Morgan Library (Mary Flagler Cary Music Collection), New York (fig.63); Archiv für Kunst und Geschichte, Berlin (figs.64, 76, 100); Karl-Marx-Universität (Universitätsbibliothek), Leipzig (fig.70); Kunstsammlungen zu Weimar (fig.72); Nationalarchiv der Richard-Wagner-Stiftung, Richard-Wagner-Gedenkstätte, Bayreuth (figs. 73, 89); H. Roger-Viollet, Paris (figs.74, 79, 109); Opera Rara Collection, London (fig.82); Theatre and Music Museum, Leningrad (figs.83, 85, 87d); Museum Antonin Dvořák, Prague (fig.84); Society for Cultural Relations with the USSR, London (figs.86, 111, 113); Harold Rosenthal Collection (fig.87b); Historic New Orleans Collection, Museum / Research Center, New Orleans (fig.93 (Acc.No.1974.25.36.21)); Music Division, Library of Congress, Washington DC (figs.94, 126 (*Modern Music* Archive), 138 (Hammerstein Collection, 139); G. Costa, Milan (fig.97); Museo Teatrale alla Scala, Milan (figs.98, 99); Marina Henderson Gallery, London (fig.101); Universal Edition (Alfred A. Kalmus Ltd), Vienna (fig.103); photo Paul Dallüge, Berlin (fig.105); photo Fritz Peyer, Hamburg (fig.106); Ludwig Binder, Berlin (fig.107); Josef Svoboda, Prague (fig.108); Archivio Storico delle Arti Contemporanee della Biennale di Venezia / photo Giacomelli, Venice (fig.112); Music Division, Moravské Museum, Brno (fig.114); Polish Cultural Institute, London / CAF Central Photographic Agency, Warsaw (fig.115); The Britten-Pears Library, Aldeburgh / photo John Garner (fig.117); photo Stuart Robinson, Redruth (fig.118); photo Zoë Dominic, London (fig.119); The Santa Fe Opera, Santa Fe, New Mexico / photo David Stein (fig.120); Glyndebourne Festival Opera, Lewes / photo Guy Gravett, Hurstpierpoint (figs.,121, 135); The Bettmann Archive, New York (fig.124); Bodleian Library (Harding Collection), Oxford / Chappell Music Ltd., London, and Chappell & Co., Inc., New York (fig.125); Billy Rose Theatre Collection, New York Public Library at Lincoln Center (Astor, Lenox and Tilden Foundations), New York / photo Fred Fehl (fig.127); Houston Grand Opera, Houston, Texas / photo Jim Caldwell (fig.128); Bildarchiv Bayreuther Festspiele / photo Siegfried Lauterwasser, Überlingen (fig.132); R.C.S. Sansoni Editore SpA, Florence: from E. Lo Gatto, *Storia del Teatro Russo*, ii (1952) (fig.134); Teatro alla Scala, Milan / photo Erio Piccagliani (fig.137); National Portrait Gallery, Smithsonian Institution, Washington DC (fig.140)

Preface

This volume is one of a series of specialist handbooks arising out of *The New Grove Dictionary of Music and Musicians* (1980) and the methodologies used in that work. It was provoked by a remark in a review of *The New Grove* to the effect that the article under the heading 'Opera' would be useful if available separately.

That article, however, was designed to be read in conjunction with a very large number of other articles, and we felt that it was not suitable for publication as it stood. For one thing, its structure – primarily on a national basis, secondarily by period – was clearly less useful than a more conventional division, primarily by period and secondarily by country. Second, a book on opera needed fuller discussion of the central repertory works where these are discussed under their composers. Third, we felt that there would be advantages in maintaining the national basis of the discussion into the 20th century in place of the systematic approach essayed in *The New Grove*. We took advantage of this restructuring to enlarge very substantially the geographical coverage, incorporating some material from *The New Grove Dictionary of American Music* and commissioning fresh material on other areas not separately treated in *The New Grove*.

We have also supplemented the *New Grove* material with an entirely new discussion of stage movement and opera production generally, an area on which it proved impossible to assemble an authoritative team of writers when *The New Grove* was in preparation. Thus each section of this book concludes with a chapter under the heading 'Staging', made up partly of that material and partly of a revised version of the original *New Grove* discussion of stage design. Some of the material in the glossary is drawn from *The New Grove*.

There is always a danger, in writing about opera, of treating it so primarily as a musical form that other aspects of it – as a social phenomenon, as a convergence of art forms, as a spectacle, as a world of constant financial crisis – may be overlooked. We have accordingly tried in this volume to widen the context of the discussion: first, in the Introduction, which provides a thumbnail sketch of the Western predecessors and non-Western counterparts of opera; secondly, in the Prelude, designed to give a picture of the world of opera; and thirdly, in the series of entr'actes, which attempts to convey something of the changing nature of the operatic experience over four centuries. If these help remind the reader of something of the excitement of opera – the smell of the greasepaint, the rise of the curtain, the thrill of the prima donna's top notes or the castrato's roulades, the sound of the applause or the cat calls – they will have fulfilled their purpose. They are intended to remind the reader that opera is not a matter of books and dusty scores on library shelves but of the enlargement of human experience that this most potent of art forms can provide.

*

I should like to acknowledge the generous help provided by many of the authors who contributed parts of the original *New Grove* article in supplementing their contributions, in many cases very substantially, to render them suitable for this new presentation. I am also grateful to those authors who have helped us round out the picture of the history of opera by supplying new material. Additional help has also been supplied by Curtis Price and Elizabeth Forbes, who have read and commented on particular sections, and by Barry Millington in bringing the section on production up to date.

S. S.

Normally, when any opera is referred to in the text of this book its date and place of first production are given, in the form (1950, London) – not in the form (London, 1950), which is reserved for publication information. Where a place of production is not named and is not obvious from the context, it should be taken to be the capital city of the country or region under discussion.

Introduction

STANLEY SADIE

'Opera' has come to be the main generic term by which we refer to musical dramatic works in which the actors sing some or all of their parts. The term, like the genre itself in the first place, is Italian, meaning simply 'work'; it is derived as the plural of the Latin *opus*. Opera is a union of music, drama and spectacle; these have been combined in a variety of ways and degrees in different countries and historical periods, though usually with music playing a central role. In its generally understood sense, opera originated in Italy at the end of the 16th century.

It is the history of this genre that forms the main topic of this book. But the use of music in dramatic representations is both of greater antiquity and of wider cultural spread than the history of what we understand as opera. It goes back, in Europe, to the Middle Ages and the ancient civilizations; and it appears in many non-Western cultures.

Musical theatre in non-Western societies

The term 'opera' has often been applied by Western writers to musical dramatic events in other societies. Genres of musical drama have been specially cultivated – or at least evidence survives of their special cultivation – in three regions of the world, China, Japan and South-east Asia. They are known in several others, for example in the dance drama of India (the *kathakali*), to which in some regions such as Bengal song is added, producing works based on religious, legendary or historical topics; or in parts of Africa, for example Nigeria, where there are traditions of story-telling to music, vocal and instrumental, sometimes combined with dance; or in Tibet, where there is a history of secular entertainments on a particular range of Buddhist themes embodying a speech-song narration, slow antiphonal chant and choral verses, with dance and mime, performed by some eight actors with two instrumentalists.

Chinese opera has numerous regional variants, which draw in different degrees on four traditional types or systems. Of these types, some of which date back to the 16th century, most originated as popular theatre, performed by itinerant companies and largely improvised; one is more sophisticated, using a written libretto and a delicate, slow-moving vocal style and an accompaniment based on flute tone. Chinese operas, which traditionally are acted by all-male troupes, relate either classic love stories or tales of ancient heroes. The most famous genre is Beijing (Peking) opera, which originated in 1790 and flourished particularly in the early 19th century, again at the beginning of the 20th and, on a new basis of social purpose, in the early years (from 1949) of the People's Republic. Performance involves a highly elaborate, stylized manner of movement and gesture on a sparse stage, involving a complex system of symbolism. Musically, the opera consists of dialogue and solo singing with instrumental accompaniment, chiefly using string instruments (plucked and bowed) and percussion.

The oldest form of music theatre in Japan is *noh*, which was established in the late 14th century or the early 15th, although its forerunners can be traced back as early as the 8th century. It originally had a repertory of about 2000 dramas, of which some 200 survive; its performance traditions have been maintained through a guild, though they have been subject to change in response to the social conditions under which performances took place (achieving, for example, a high degree of formality under the feudal lords of the 17th to 19th centuries). *Noh* performances take place on a stage of standard design, with an entrance ramp, a side stage for the chorus, a pillared main stage, and a back area for the instrumentalists (up to four, playing a bamboo flute and drums). There is no scenery, and the stage props are symbolic. There is a single principal singer, elaborately costumed, who may change roles between acts and whose acting is so stylized as to become dancing; there can be secondary actors and others to provide comic relief. The music consists of solo singing, monologues and dialogues and singing by a chorus of about eight, in unison; these follow one another in a stereotyped sequence, also including dance sections, in some degree linked with the needs of the plot. The melodic line, similarly, is made up of a series of standard units. There are two singing styles, 'soft' and 'strong', each adhering to particular 'nuclear' notes and following strict patterns. The rhythmic patterns, sometimes free and sometimes metrical, are also strictly controlled.

Besides *bunraku*, puppet theatre in which the music is performed by one man and a shamisen (a type of lute), the other main music theatrical form of Japan is *kabuki*. This, freer in style than *noh*, was established in the early 17th century. Traditionally, *kabuki* is performed by all-male companies and draws on a repertory of 18 plays (with local variants) which treat pseudo-historical subjects or tales of plebeian life (today modern plays are preferred as the traditional ones may last for a day or more). Instruments – flutes, percussion and shamisen – are used offstage for illustrative and expressive purposes; onstage music may come from a row of singers, each with shamisen, and *noh*-type drums and flutes, who together provide dance accompaniment or narrative commentary. The soloists may sing, speak and dance. An established repertory of song and instrumental writing exists, with an expressive significance readily understood by its audiences.

The central genre of South-east Asian musical theatre is the Indonesian *wayang kulit*, shadow plays with puppets; its origins lie in Java, in the 11th century. The music has gamelan accompaniment. There are many varieties and sub-genres of *wayang kulit* in Java and other parts of Indonesia, Malaysia, Cambodia (Kampuchea) and Thailand. Dance drama is another widespread genre in this region, existing in forms from the classical courtly Burmese type, dating from the late 18th century and using Buddhist themes, to the ritual type with standard masked figures (the lion, the queen of evil) favoured in Bali. Forms of a more operatic kind, in the Western sense, are found in the folk drama of Thailand, with an oboe-type instrument and varied percussion, and the musical theatre of Vietnam, which goes back to the 13th century and is closely related to Chinese opera (though there also exists a local operetta genre). Attitudes to the tempo of life in this region are reflected in the time that some of the entertainments take to unfold: from nine hours to several weeks.

Early music drama in Europe
It was their understanding of the powerful role exercised by music in Greek tragedy that spurred the Florentine intellectuals of the late 16th century to take steps towards the establishment of what we call 'opera'. We know little more than they did – though we are more aware of the limitations of our knowledge – about the actual music that was used in Greek tragedy. Aristotle talked of speech involving rhythm, metre and melody, though the sense in which he used those terms may be quite different from our understanding of them. But we do know that the Greeks practised choral song and dance, and there is reason to suppose that Greek drama comprehended at least some relics of the choral music used in its predecessor, ceremonies in honour of Dionysus. Moreover, there survives one fragment of papyrus showing what seems to be musical notation against lines for the chorus from Euripides' *Orestes*; some authorities regard these as contemporary or even as composed by Euripides himself. They are, however, beyond decipherment; all we can say about music in Greek drama is that the choruses probably embodied some kind of singing and that it is possible that there may have been elements of musical declamation in solo portions, possibly to some extent improvised. Our knowledge of Roman theatrical music, too, is exceedingly sketchy; dance and mime were popular, but from the 3rd century BC the Roman theatre was much influenced by Greek and, later, by Hellenistic music.

The Roman theatres were destroyed in the 6th century. But some European theatre traditions are likely to have survived during the early Middle Ages, if only in the activities of travelling players and minstrels. The central dramatic forms of the Middle Ages, however, were religious. Medieval music drama falls into two main categories, which existed side by side: the so-called 'liturgical drama', in Latin, and vernacular drama, principally in English, French, German, Italian and Spanish, sometimes known as 'mystery' or 'miracle' plays. From the 13th century onwards secular plays with music are also found.

The Latin repertory, of which some 600 texts survive, was designed for performance within a church ritual, though not necessarily as part of the liturgy. The simplest examples are dialogues introduced into the Mass, the most important being related to Easter and Christmas. A large proportion of the repertory, about two thirds, is for Easter and concerned with the three Marys visiting the tomb of Christ (the standard title for this type is *Visitatio sepulchri*); it may embody antiphons, an Easter chant, hymns and laments as well as dialogue with angels. No generalization is possible about methods of staging or indeed other aspects of perform-ance; but the dramas were performed in churches, in an acting area which might hold structures or platforms symbolizing specific localities, and the acting is likely to have been simple and restrained, often with the performers wearing normal ecclesiastical vestments. The music consisted of liturgical chant or sometimes passages modelled on chant; in some cases instruments (organs, bells, drums, plucked instruments, trumpets) might be used, for example in processional contexts.

In the vernacular tradition of medieval religious drama (a tradition distinct from, and concurrent with, the Latin liturgical one, though the two often come close) music was less central; essentially these works are spoken plays to which music is an adjunct. It might consist of songs, instrumental sections, passages of plainchant or even polyphony (which could be sung in Latin); its role is to assist the action on the stage, sometimes symbolically, and to imitate real-life effects, but not to convey atmosphere or influence the audience's emotions. The actual presenta-tion, while still not naturalistic, with very limited scenery and the simplest of symbolic properties, was less stylized than that of Latin drama, with costumes (contemporary, not historical) and some concern with character. Most performances took place out of doors, in a less formal, less constrained atmosphere than that of liturgical drama. However, the traditions and modes of performance varied greatly between countries, and the sources are mostly uninformative.

Little survives of early secular drama. One tradition derives from the dance-song and other types of lyric (like the *bergerie*, to do with shepherds; or the *pastourelle*, a love encounter; or the *jeu-parti*, a debate); dramas have also derived from satirical comic tales, from mimed monologue and from courtly narrative. The only surviving play with substantial music is *Le jeu de Robin et de Marion*, by the trouvère poet-composer Adam de la Halle. Dating from the late 13th century, it consists of spoken dialogue interspersed with 16 brief songs in a popular courtly style (they may be original or taken from an established repertory). The instruments introduced, bagpipe and horns, conform with the aristocratic stylization of rural life. Two other plays in which music plays a much lesser part are also attributed to Adam; *Robin et Marion* seems to be a fairly isolated phenomenon, and certainly there is no continuity of tradition linking it with later musical dramas.

At the end of the Middle Ages, many of the traditions of religious drama faded, particularly in countries affected by the Reformation. Popular drama of the time, in which music doubtless played some part, includes morality plays, particularly in France and England; in France there also existed a tradition of comic plays in which chansons – either of the standard three-voice type or a 'rustique' single melodic line – played a part. In Italy, pageant-like events, with song and dance, were popular at Carnival time. A new form, the *Schuldrama*, developed in Germany, with an educational purpose influenced by the rise of humanism.

As far as the future development of opera was concerned, however, the most significant types of musical drama that arose at the end of the Middle Ages were those connected with courtly entertainments. These could be mummings or masks, including dialogue, singing and dance; more important as antecedents of opera were the lavish, partly dramatic events such as the Florentine *intermedi* for princely weddings and other court celebrations in the 16th century, or the comparable events at Munich in 1568 and in Paris, notably the *ballet de cour* of 1581 (*Balet comique de la Royne*). With these mixed entertainments, and the pastoral plays of the later 16th century, in which the structure and the patterns of depiction of emotion of the earliest operas are clearly foreshadowed, we reach the point where a new genre was ready to crystallize.

Prelude

STANLEY SADIE

Opera is perhaps the most elaborate of art forms; it may call on the united skills of poet, composer, designer, producer (or director) and choreographer to create a 'complete art work' (or, to use Wagner's term, *Gesamtkunstwerk*). It can offer its creators a breadth or resource unknown in most other art forms, not only because of its simultaneous appeal to so many susceptibilities but also because – as compared with non-musical theatre – the presence of music opens up possibilities of strengthening, subtilizing or inflecting any words that are uttered on the stage, or even of carrying information about words or feelings that are left unspoken.

A traditional and often cited example of the special resources available to the composer of opera comes in the aria for Orestes, 'Le calme rentre dans mon coeur', in Gluck's *Iphigénie en Tauride* (1779), where the accompaniment, characterized by the uneasy, syncopated throb of low violas, contradicts the singer's words and instructs the listener that Orestes' calm is illusory. Examples could easily be multiplied. Wagner, in the closing scene of *Das Rheingold*, gives the orchestra a new, bold theme which tells even the uninformed listener that some grand and momentous idea has struck the central character, Wotan, and in its nature hints at the heroic quality of that idea. Later in the *Ring* the network of motifs, by now linked in the listener's mind with particular characters, objects and concepts, is used to convey information or impressions, sometimes the merest hints but sometimes quite specific (for example in the first act of *Die Walküre*, where Sieglinde is telling the story of the mysterious stranger who intruded on her wedding: the orchestra identifies him for us). The way the motifs are developed and related carries further layers of meaning inexpressible in the text. Wagner's method was, of course, particularly highly developed in this respect, but in all opera music may embody specific information about human relations or bear out those in the words, for example where two characters (usually lovers, though often conspirators) end a duet singing in 3rds, 6ths, unisons or octaves to suggest identity of feeling or purpose; it may also contradict the words, perhaps to imply that they are deceptively uttered or that the sentiments expressed are in vain. Sometimes it may elucidate the emotional relationships between characters in an ensemble, as in the quartet in Verdi's *Rigoletto*. Tonal structures may also carry important dramatic or psychological implications.

The action in an opera tends to move much more slowly than it does in spoken drama. That is primarily because words that are sung require more time than ordinary speech (this is true even of rapid recitative, of a kind that imitates speech patterns). Further, most kinds of opera abound in the musical counterpart to soliloquies – arias, that is – which take considerable time to unfold: large-scale emotion requires a substantial time-frame for its expression and the forms in which arias are cast usually involve much repetition, of words and music equally. Beaumarchais' play *Le mariage de Figaro* had to be severely cut in the course of its adaptation as a text for Mozart's opera; so did Shakespeare's *Othello* for Verdi's.

Part of the librettist's task, in putting together a text for an opera – and this is no less true when he is writing an entirely new work than when he is adapting (for example) an existing play, a book, a plot outline or indeed an ancient myth – is allowing the right degree of scope for lyrical expansiveness. In most operatic traditions, there is a requirement for 'set piece' arias as well as duets and other ensembles. Sometimes these 'numbers' are sharply separated, usually by clear breaks in the musical texture, from their context; sometimes they are welded into a more nearly continuous whole. The extent to which such items should be permitted to expand, at the apparent cost of dramatic realism, has constantly exercised opera theorists and critics and to some extent librettists and composers too. The disputes that run through the history of opera have generally devolved on this question or the closely related one of primacy between words and music. This has even been used as subject matter for operas, for example Salieri's *Prima la musica, poi le parole* (1786) and Richard Strauss's *Capriccio* (1942).

Traditions in this respect differ, both geographically and temporally, and they are closely related to social circumstances and linguistic factors. In Italy, the music has usually been allowed its head, partly of course for temperamental reasons but also because of the susceptibility of the language to treatment equally in speech-like recitative (there is no significant Italian opera with spoken dialogue) and in eloquent musical lines, and because of the concomitant vocal traditions that prevail there. Serious Italian opera in the early and mid-18th century represents an extreme point of formality in the rigid division between recitative and aria. By contrast, opera in France, affected by that country's strong traditions of spoken drama, by the nature of the language and the ways in which it has been nurtured, by the ritual and elaboration of court spectacle and by Enlightenment philosophy, has favoured an idiom that permits the words to carry greater weight and assigns special importance to ballet.

In the more popular forms of French opera, however, as in the vernacular opera that arose – often alongside courtly opera in Italian – in Germany, England and the Iberian countries, most of the early operatic forms were akin to spoken plays with songs, or songs interspersed with dialogue. Such developments ran parallel to the rise of a bourgeois culture.

In all these forms of opera, the main dramatic action took place in the recitative or spoken sections and the arias or songs were essentially statements of a character's reaction to the situation in which he found himself (in court opera, this would often be expressed in elaborate similes, which could widen the range of musical imagery plausibly available to the composer). With the advent of comic opera, which was necessarily more realistic, action began to penetrate the arias and, especially, the ensembles, above all the long and complex ensemble finales to each act (three acts was the conventional number, except in French serious opera, where there were commonly five; towards the end of the 18th century a two-act scheme came to be preferred). The two greatest opera composers who set themselves to 'reform' opera, Gluck and Wagner, both strove for what they considered a more realistic idiom – or at any rate less patently artificial a one (for all opera presupposes certain conventions, most obviously the use of singing as a means of communication), with more continuity of musical texture and stronger emphasis on the treatment of the words: in fact, in Gluck's own words, 'to restrict music to its true office of serving poetry'. Mozart, however, wrote that 'the poetry must always be the obedient daughter of the music'. As the music of these two men to some degree shows, these statements are by no means as contradictory as they at first seem. Gluck was intent on excluding music that was irrelevant to the dramatic sense; Mozart was eager to be provided, by his librettist, with words that gave him the maximum opportunity to use music in expression of the drama. Nor indeed were the objectives of Verdi and Wagner, always seen as opposite poles of operatic thinking in the late 19th century, so far apart: Verdi indeed remarked, as early as 1851 (apropos *Il trovatore*): 'If only . . . there could be no cavatinas, no duets, no trios, no choruses, no finales etc, and if only the whole opera could be, so to speak, all one number, I should find that sensible and right'. That is not to say, however, that the effect of the individual 'number' in a Verdi opera is not of prime importance: an aria here, or in a Puccini opera, is expected, and intended, to provoke immediate applause, which would be unthinkable in a mature opera by Wagner.

Opera, however, has never depended for the forms it takes solely on the artistic preferences of composers or librettists. It has depended on patrons, be they princes or the public. It has depended, since the time of commercial opera houses, on promoters and impresarios, who have put together opera companies of particular capabilities and requirements. It has depended on stage managers, whose machinery and costumes have in some eras represented central attractions to the public, especially in the late Baroque period and in Parisian grand opera of the early to middle 19th century. It has depended, in recent years, on producers (directors, in American terminology), anxious to promulgate new, often strongly politicized styles and interpretations. And it has always depended, perhaps most of all, on singers. Singers, from the times of a Farinelli or a Cuzzoni, in the early 18th century, to those of a Callas or a Pavarotti in the middle and late 20th, have commanded larger publics – and correspondingly larger billings and much larger fees – than composers. Composers from Caccini and Monteverdi to Britten and Stockhausen have planned their operas around particular voices. That includes many of the greatest opera composers, among them Handel, Gluck, Mozart, Rossini and Verdi. In the 18th century no composer would consider writing a new opera without first familiarizing himself with the cast drawn up for the première, partly because it was his job to match the music to the voices on which it was to be heard, and partly because, if the singers were dissatisfied with the music he provided, they would substitute their favourite items from other operas. It was largely for the purpose of presenting singers most favourably in the commercial opera houses that the pasticcio, an opera made up of existing numbers (see Entr'acte I), came into being. At revivals of operas during this period, it was a standard procedure for the opera-house director to adapt, commission or himself compose replacement arias for singers who felt that the existing ones did not show their voices to advantage. Of the operas performed in the 18th century, particularly in public (as opposed to court) opera houses, where it was vital that an audience be attracted, the number containing music by several composers far exceeds that of single-composer works. All these procedures continued well into the 19th century, particularly in Italy but also in other centres with commercial opera houses. To regard such works as an abuse, or in some sense 'inartistic', is to see them in a false historical perspective. Leading composers of the time regularly and unhesitatingly accepted the concept of operas put together from a multiplicity of sources and were happy to contribute to them. This is not, of course, to deny that the single-composer opera remains an ideal.

Opera houses have always been something more than places for performing operas. They have been, and remain, important social centres and meeting places, used for business deals, card games, meals and amorous assignations. From the early 17th century to the late 20th they have been reckoned the natural place at which to entertain distinguished visitors or celebrate notable events. Noblemen owned boxes in the 17th century; business firms now hold regular block bookings. Many of the most famous acts of royal extravagance have been operatic: the performance of Cavalli and Lully's *Ercole amante* in Paris on Louis XIV's marriage in 1662, of Cesti's *Il pomo d'oro* in Vienna on Leopold I's marriage in 1668, of Fux's *Costanza e fortezza* on Charles VI's coronation in Prague in 1723, and indeed the subsidizing by Ludwig II of Bayreuth in 1874. Opera houses have always been enormously expensive to run, and have regularly been under threat, at best, in times of stringency. They require, as no comparable kind of establishment does, several teams of performers – singers, dancers, orchestral musicians, lighting engineers, scene painters, wardrobe staff, stage managers – as well as administrators. The responsibility for supplying the necessary sums of money, once discharged by kings and princes, and for some time assumed in some countries – but rarely with continuing success – by enterprising or speculative commercial impresarios, fell increasingly during the 19th century and almost totally during the 20th, at least in Europe, to government agencies and often to municipalities, proud to maintain the traditions they inherited from local courts and eager to outshine one another. The nature of opera as a luxury art is still seen in the vast subsidies required to support the great opera houses of Europe and the USA.

The distribution of resident opera companies – there are many in the German-speaking countries, rather fewer in Italy, still fewer in France, England, other European countries and the USA – still to some extent reflects the political divisions of Europe in the 18th century and the presence or otherwise of courts with musical traditions at that time. The existence of an opera company does not of itself represent any particular level of activity. The length of seasons, the frequency of performances and the need or otherwise of sharing a theatre with operetta, spoken drama or ballet, are factors. The systems by which repertories are maintained and presented also vary. These, which depend on local factors concerning the existence of resident or part-resident companies, the reliance on guest performers and financial matters, fall into two main types: 'stagione' ('season'), favoured in Italy, in Britain and parts of the USA, whereby each opera has a series of performances concentrated within a brief period; and 'repertory', preferred in the German-speaking countries, under which performances of each opera in a larger repertory are scattered throughout a season. The latter system to some extent depends on the availability of a resident company, particularly as there would otherwise be obvious difficulties over rehearsal. In some houses, like the Metropolitan in New York, a pattern falling between these is preferred, with a 'stagione' system in which some six or seven operas (as opposed to two or three at Covent Garden, London) might be held in the repertory at any one time. Most aim to mount five or six new productions each season.

There are traditionally reckoned to be five opera houses in the world of front-rank importance: La Scala, Milan; the Vienna Staatsoper; the Paris Opéra; the Royal Opera House, Covent Garden, London; and the Metropolitan Opera House, New York. Many more have strong claims, including several in Germany (Hamburg, Frankfurt, the Deutsche Oper in West Berlin and the Komische Oper in East Berlin, where socially aware production was pioneered under Walter Felsenstein and his successors), as well as Rome, Stockholm (nearby is the Drottningholm court theatre, where the complete stage mechanism dating from 1766 remains in working order), Chicago Lyric Opera, San Francisco, Moscow (the Bol'shoy) and Leningrad (the Kirov), Buenos Aires (the Teatro Colón) and Sydney. A few large cities have second opera houses, aiming at slightly different audiences, like the Volksoper in Vienna (specializing in operetta), the Salle Favart (for the Opéra-Comique) in Paris, the English National Opera (performing in English) in London and the City Opera in New York. Several festivals centre on opera, for example Salzburg, Bayreuth, Munich, Florence, Verona, Aix-en-Provence, Glyndebourne and Santa Fé. By the standards of the music profession, the opera industry has always been large and inviting. It has usually offered composers rewards far exceeding those of a safe Kapellmeistership or teaching appointment; it is not exclusively for aesthetic reasons that composers have always vied for opera commissions.

The opera houses of the world have often been described as museums, housing – perhaps fit only to house – the art of the past. Contemporary music plays a modest part, at best, in the repertory of most opera houses; few can afford to perform more than a small proportion of new or recent operas. Until the late 18th century, opera houses normally performed only new or recent works, some freshly composed (or arranged), others brought in by singers or travelling on their own (or occasionally their composer's) reputations. Not until close to the end of the century did a 'classical' repertory begin to form. There had been widespread successes before then, for example of Pergolesi's intermezzo *La serva padrona* (1733), Piccinni's *La Cecchina, ossia La buona figliuola* (1760) and Paisiello's *Il barbiere di Siviglia* (1782) and *Nina* or *La pazza per amore* (1789). But it was the late operas of Mozart, some of Gluck's and (for a time) of Cimarosa's (especially *Il matrimonio segreto*, 1792) that began the establishment of a core repertory, to be supplemented soon by Beethoven's *Fidelio* and several operas of Rossini. Today's standard repertory centres on Mozart, Verdi, Puccini and Wagner, with Beethoven, Rossini, the principal operas of Bizet and Strauss, and works by Weber, Bellini, Donizetti, Gounod, Massenet, Musorgsky, Tchaikovsky and Smetana. Many houses also perform operetta (the younger Johann Strauss, Offenbach, Sullivan). Earlier operas, notably those of Handel and Monteverdi, have only lately come to be considered as serious claimants for professional, repertory revival. Besides those of Puccini and Strauss, some of Janáček's and Debussy's *Pelléas et Mélisande*, few 20th-century operas are regularly given: Berg's *Wozzeck*, Stravinsky's *The Rake's Progress* and Britten's *Peter Grimes* are among the most often performed. New operas continue to be written, but the great cost of staging them and the difficulty of reconciling advanced forms of musical utterance with the requirements of the traditional opera house and its audience – though bold solutions have been essayed by a number of composers, such as Henze, Zimmermann and Stockhausen in Germany, Nono in Italy, Tippett, Davies and Birtwistle in England and Glass in the USA – have induced many composers to turn to chamber opera or other kinds of music theatre susceptible to concert, workshop or experimental production.

PART ONE

Baroque Opera

CHAPTER I

Italy

THOMAS WALKER

Florentine opera and its background

The first operas were only the most comprehensive of a variety of associations between music and spectacle that run through Italian culture from the late 15th century. Signal events (visits, births, marriages) at the leading courts provided occasions for the grandest of these, but there was also an undercurrent of musico-dramatic activity in the more or less formalized associations of intellectuals known as academies, which played a large role in the advancement of learning during the Renaissance.

A chief antecedent of opera was the *intermedio*, episodes or tableaux performed between the acts of plays (mostly comedies) with music and often with machines. The Medici court at Florence was particularly lavish with this kind of entertainment. The *intermedi* for Bargagli's comedy *La pellegrina*, organized by Giovanni de' Bardi as part of the festivities celebrating the wedding of Grand Duke Ferdinando de' Medici and Christine of Lorraine (1589), exemplify the powers of music; and one of them (Apollo's slaying of the Pythian dragon) provided the starting-point for *Dafne*, generally regarded as the first opera.

Also close to the genesis of opera was the pastoral play. Although even the earliest pastoral plays, such as Poliziano's *Orfeo* (?1480), used songs and choruses, the most consequential for opera (and generally) were Tasso's *Aminta* (1573) and Guarini's *Il pastor fido* (published 1589). From them come the obligatory happy endings, the use of comic characters on a lower social level, the affecting depiction of tender passions and indeed a world in which the gap is bridged between elevated speech and song. More specific devices such as the oracle, the echo scene and the use of mistaken identity also have a place here; and in the many fragments of *Il pastor fido* repeatedly set to music lies a conceptual source for the opera aria.

Other parallel developments include a series of short plays, mostly based on mythology and some of them pastoral in character, performed at Venice with presumably madrigalian music from the 1570s until 1605; Gabriele Bombasi's tragedy *Alidoro*, performed at Reggio Emilia in 1568 with pseudomonodic choruses among its musical parts; the dramatized tournaments performed at the Ferrarese court of Alphonse II between 1561 and 1570, with frequent interpolations of vocal as well as instrumental music; a performance of *Edipo re* in a translation by Giustiniani with choruses by Andrea Gabrieli by the Accademia Olimpica of Vicenza in 1585; and the 'madrigal comedies' of Vecchi (e.g. *L'Amfiparnaso*, 1594) and Banchieri (e.g. *La pazzia senile*, published in 1598).

The group or 'camerata' (*c*1570–92) around Bardi who explored the nature and powers of ancient Greek music partly with a view to finding a modern equivalent were less directly involved in the creation of opera than has been supposed. But the writings of Bardi and Vincenzo Galilei (based on ideas of the philologist Girolamo Mei) laid a foundation for the sung recitation of plays with accompaniment; and the compositions of Galilei and Giulio Caccini contributed to the development of the range of monodic procedures on which early opera draws. Bardi's connection with the 1589 *intermedi* has already been mentioned.

Also part of the immediate background to Florentine opera were two (lost) pastorals by Laura Guidiccioni, *Il satiro* and *La disperazione di Fileno*, both produced for Carnival 1590 with music by Emilio de' Cavalieri that probably had more to do with the style of the popular villanellas and canzonettas than with recitative, and the literary and musical debates of the Accademia degli Alterati, of which Bardi was a member. Bardi's group translated the results of their investigations of Greek music only into isolated examples of accompanied monody. The first attempt to discover a stage music comparable in power and intensity to ancient tragedy was made by a later and partly competitive group under the patronage of Jacopo Corsi. Beginning in 1594 Corsi and Jacopo Peri set to music *Dafne* by Ottavio Rinuccini, who like Bardi and Corsi was a member of the Alterati, seeking, in Peri's words, 'a harmony surpassing that of ordinary speech but falling so far below the melody of song as to take an intermediate form'. The surviving fragments of *Dafne* include only one example of the new recitative style which these words describe – declamation, sensitive in its rhythmic flexibility and melodic ambitus to text prosody and affect, over a static bass. The others are songs which rest in part on the traditions for declaiming certain privileged poetic forms.

Close in style and intent to *Dafne* is *Euridice*, the first opera to survive intact. Like many *intermedi* it was an occasional piece, a wedding gift from Corsi to Maria de' Medici for her marriage (by proxy) to Henri IV at Florence in October 1600. Caccini also made a setting, part of which was incorporated into the performance (which was directed by Cavalieri), since some of the singers were under his control. Both versions were published (see Plates 6 and 7), and their prefaces, together with that to Rinuccini's libretto, are vital sources of information about these early contributions to recitative stage music as well as the rivalries that surrounded them. The principal entertainment on the same occasion was Chiabrera's *Il rapimento di Cefalo* with music by Caccini and three other Florentine composers (the music is lost except for a few excerpts printed in Caccini's *Le nuove musiche*, 1601/2); in its elaborate staging, and perhaps in its music, it was closer to the traditions of the *intermedio*.

Besides the more or less fictitious analogies with Greek music that inform its style, *Euridice* (like many of its successors) shows other facets of interest in classical antiquity. The story, from Ovid's *Metamorphoses*, symbolizes the power that the new music would wish to claim for itself. The alteration of Ovid's story so that Orpheus retrieves Eurydice from Hades without conditions, and thus without loss (Tragedy solemnly announces the work's *lieto fine* in the prologue), is an early example of a permissive attitude towards source material that remains characteristic of opera librettos throughout the 17th century and beyond. In the poetry of the choruses which articulate the scenes of the opera are limited examples of the varied poetic metres popularized by Chiabrera (under whose influence Rinuccini stood) and based on the classical emulations of Pierre de Ronsard, leader of the Pléiade. This kind of strophic verse became the poetic basis of the opera aria.

The spread of the new *stile rappresentativo* to other Italian courts began with the performance of Monteverdi's *Orfeo* at Mantua in 1607 as 'a casual entertainment for courtiers' (see Fenlon, 1984). The poem, by Alessandro Striggio, uses the same material as Rinuccini's *Euridice* (there is consciousness both in the parallels and in their avoidance), expanded and with a different ending, initially closer to the myth, but changed in the version of the music that survives. Monteverdi's setting has often been described as the turn from a first, rather amateurish, experimental stage of theatre monody to the creation of 'real' opera. That interpretation sells Peri short. But the music of *Orfeo* embraces a far wider affective vocabulary than that of *Euridice*. It is unique among early operas in the imposition of musical form on unorganized elements in the poetry, a result of Monteverdi's inclination to symmetry and formalization. In Orpheus's aria 'Possente spirto', sung at the first performance by Francesco Rasi, it offers an extraordinary example of early 17th-century vocal virtuosity. The much discussed orchestra of *Orfeo* was apparently larger and more varied than that of the modest *Euridice*, and used in a manner consistent with the colour and symbolism of the Florentine *intermedio*. Both operas had castratos among their casts. In the papal states, where from the time of Sixtus V a ban on the appearance of women on stage was enforced with varying degrees of rigour, castratos regularly sang female roles. There and elsewhere they also performed heroic male roles.

Monteverdi's second opera for Mantua was *L'Arianna* (1608), an attempt by Rinuccini to substitute a tragic theme for the already usual myth-clad pastorale. Ariadne's lament, the only part of the work whose music survives, was said to have moved the audience to tears and remained a model for imitation, in both opera and isolated monody, for half a century. Earlier the same year Marco da Gagliano's *Dafne*, on an altered version of Rinuccini's libretto, was given as a Carnival entertainment preceding the marriage of Francesco Gonzaga to Marguerite of Savoy. The preface to its published score, a mine of information about performing practice, warns against the wanton insertion of vocal ornaments; those pieces such as 'Non curi la mia pianta' that have written-out embellishment make clear that a high level of agility was required. Gagliano's work uses a variety of musical means including prominent choruses, some of them madrigalian in treatment, with episodes for solo and duet.

A comprehensive history of the development of *musica rappresentativa* in the first half of the 17th century has yet to be written. Production of opera performances was sporadic and episodic, following different courses according to the character and traditions of the various courts and towns. At Florence opera played a relatively small part in the constant stream of musical entertainments (balli, *intermedi*, mascheratas, *cocchiate*) in the orbit of the Medici court and was largely confined to the marking of state occasions. In 1619 Gagliano's *Il Medoro* (lost; text by Andrea Salvadori) celebrated the election of Cosimo de' Medici's brother-in-law Emperor Ferdinand II; Francesca Caccini's *La liberazione di Ruggiero dall'isola d'Alcina* (1625, text by Ferdinando Saracinelli), part opera and part ballet, was performed for a visit of Władisłas Sigismund, Prince of Poland; and Gagliano's and Peri's *La Flora* (1628, text by Salvadori) formed part of the festivities surrounding the marriage of Margherita de' Medici to the Duke of Parma. Grandest of all was G. C. Coppola's *favola*, entitled *Le nozze degli dei*, set to music by 'five principal composers of the city' and performed 'without calling in a single foreign musician' for the wedding of Grand Duke Ferdinando II and Vittoria della Rovere in 1637.

Bologna, which had no court, long subsisted on a diet of *intermedi*, such as Girolamo Giacobbi's *Aurora ingannata* (1608, text by Campeggi) or Ottavio Vernizzi's *Ulisse e Circe* (1619, text by Branchi), mostly produced by local academies; the small amount of music that survives shows some penetration of the Florentine recitative style. Indeed Peri's *Euridice* was performed there in 1616, and the following year saw the creation of the first full-blown local opera, Campeggi's *Reno sacrificante*, given in honour of the church authorities, with music by Giacobbi. Similar performances were given less regularly at other towns, including Vicenza and Viterbo, and also at courts such as that of Parma where in 1628 Monteverdi's settings of five *intermedi* by Ascanio Pio di Savoia, and Claudio Achillini's tourney *Mercurio e Marte*, served as response to the Florentine *Flora*. Other isolated examples of experiments in a similar direction include *Il rapimento di Proserpina*, performed in 1611 with music by Giulio Cesare Monteverdi at Casale di Monferrato for the visit of the princes of Savoy. At the Savoy capital, Turin, Marquis Lodovico d'Aglié was responsible for the early, if occasional, importation of recitative style, of which a curious example, Sigismondo d'India's *Zalizura* (performed perhaps in 1623) partly survives in score. At Ferrara, after the fall of the Estense house in 1598, the Accademia degli Intrepedi continued to cultivate chivalric games with dramatic elements, where now 'il recitar cantando' began to play a major role; the culmination of this activity was the sumptuous opera *cum* tournament *Andromeda* (1638, text by Ascanio Pio di Savoia, music by Michelangelo Rossi), which celebrated a Bentivoglio–Sforza wedding. It is probably fair to say that the history of the new recitative style, in its first 30 years of existence, must most often be followed in contexts (*intermedi*, tournaments, banquets and the like) which, while dramatic, elude the traditional definition of opera.

Roman opera

The first dramatic work all in music to be performed in Rome was Cavalieri's *Rappresentatione di Anima, et di Corpo*, an allegorical tale of moralizing intent given in 1600 at the oratory of the Chiesa Nuova. The regular song-like quality of much of its solo music (a response to the monotonous versification of the text, composed almost entirely of rhyming couplets of seven-syllable lines) clearly had less to do with the 'elevated speech' of Peri than with Cavalieri's own pastorales of 1590, by which he claimed to have invented the new genre. Homophonic ensembles and choruses play a dominant role in the work. *Rappresentatione* had no sequel, with the partial exception of Agostino Agazzari's moralizing pastorale *Eumelio* (1606), performed by the pupils of the Seminario Romano. It was not until the 1620s that opera gained a firm footing in Rome.

Stefano's Landi's *La morte d'Orfeo* (published Venice, 1619) is usually taken to be the first secular Roman opera. In its occasionally melodious recitative, affective writing and highly organized ensembles, it stands closer to Monteverdi's *Orfeo* than to Caccini's or Peri's *Euridice*. However, there is no clear evidence that it was written for or performed in Rome. Filippo Vitali's hasty and musically frail *Aretusa*, performed at the house of Ottavio Corsini in honour of the politically powerful Cardinal Scipione Borghese in February 1620, was responsible for introducing to Rome the recitative style of Florence and Mantua, of which its preface gives a potted history. Not only was the composer Florentine, but the scenery was painted by Giulio Caccini's son Pompeo. As the performance circumstances of *Aretusa* suggest, opera developed in Rome under the patronage of wealthy churchmen in the absence of a single formal court. *La catena d'Adone* (music by Domenico Mazzocchi, text by Ottavio Tronsarelli) was given in 1626 at the house of Marquis Evandro Conti; in 1645 Pompeo Colonna, Prince of Gallicano, produced at his palace *La Proserpina rapita*, about which John Evelyn wrote in his *Diary* (its libretto has been wrongly ascribed to Ottaviano Castelli, by then dead).

After the election of Maffeo Barberini to the papacy as Urban VIII in 1623, the Barberini nephews became the principal supporters of opera.

The first work clearly related to them is *Diana schernita* (1629, text by G. F. Parisani, music by Giacinto Cornacchioli). Though performed in the house of Baron von Hohen Rechberg, it is dedicated to Taddeo Barberini and there are other references to the family. *Sant'Alessio* (?1631, music by Stefano Landi, text by Giulio Rospigliosi) was given as the first of a long series of more or less regular performances in the various residences of the Barberini nephews and at the Palazzo della Cancelleria that ran until the family were forced to flee following the election of Pope Innocent X (Pamphili) in 1644. Among the main librettists of the period were the Barberini favourite Rospigliosi, and Castelli, who was also part of the Barberini circle.

Although the Roman repertory includes pastorales such as *Diana schernita* and *La Galatea* (1639, text and music by Loreto Vittori, performed in Naples in 1644 and possibly earlier in Rome), new types made their appearance. *Erminia sul Giordano* (1633, music by Michelangelo Rossi, text by Rospigliosi), *Il ritorno di Angelica dalle Indie* (1628, music possibly by Cignani, text by Tronsarelli) and *La catena d'Adone* drew on the epics of Tasso, Ariosto and Marino. The lives of saints are portrayed in *Sant' Alessio*, *Santi Didimo e Teodora* (1635, composer unknown) and *San Bonifatio* (1638, music by Virgilio Mazzocchi). And *commedia dell'arte*, which already had some influence in *Sant'Alessio*, was the inspiration for the first plainly comic opera, Rospigliosi's *Il falcone* (1637; performed again in 1639 under the title by which it is usually known, *Chi soffre speri*; music by Mazzocchi, probably with Marco Marazzoli). Pirrotta (1968) suggested that the enlarged scope of action in Rospigliosi's dramas may represent an attempt to eliminate the often scurrilous *commedia dell'arte* by equating opera with spoken theatre. Many of these works have a larger number of characters than the older mythological pastorales, and make use of sub-plots and even minor intrigue. One musical consequence is the development of a less melodically sensitive recitative style whose principal function is to quicken the delivery.

The chorus featured prominently in most of the Roman operas, occasionally, as in *Sant'Alessio*, on a grand scale. Solo arias, most of them strophic, are distinguished from recitative by rhythmic regularity and melodic coherence. They often relieve the tedium of the recitative in works such as *La catena d'Adone* (also known for its composer's reference to *mezz'arie*, presumably less formal moments of lyricism), *Sant'Alessio* and *Erminia sul Giordano*; indeed *Diana schernita* is the only opera in which they do not play a considerable role. The extended sinfonias of *Sant'Alessio* and *Erminia sul Giordano*, with elements of the canzona, represent another departure from Florentine practice. Elaborate machinery was on an equal footing with the music in the Barberini spectacles. In *Erminia sul Giordano* the witch Armida conjures up a momentary vision of the walls of Jerusalem to view the progress of the battle. Such developing scenographic techniques played an increasing part in opera, at least in the major centres, throughout the era (see Chapter VI).

Venetian opera

The introduction to Venice in 1637 of opera houses open to the public and with paid admission is a convenient point of demarcation in the social history of opera. Since Venice had no court, nor even as centralized an aristocracy as Rome, the *stile rappresentativo* was late in arriving there. The modest *Proserpina rapita* (music by Monteverdi, text by Giulio Strozzi, performed in 1630 to celebrate a wedding between members of two prominent families) is the earliest recorded example, if one excludes Monteverdi's *Combattimento di Tancredi e Clorinda* (1624).

The troupe that brought opera to Venice, led by Benedetto Ferrari and Francesco Manelli, had associations with Emilia and, more importantly, Rome. Their first productions at the Teatro S Cassiano (*Andromeda*, 1637, and *La maga fulminata*, 1638; settings, now lost, by Manelli of Ferrari's texts) were an attempt to introduce low-cost 'court' spectacle to a new environment. The prefaces to the librettos are clear on this point. Economy was achieved by the doubling of roles and perhaps also by a limited use of machinery. Their success was such that other theatres were immediately opened, mostly financed by aristocratic families on a somewhat obscure variety of models, motivated by a mixture of patriotism, self-indulgence and hope for profit. By 1700 nearly 400 productions had been given in the Venetian public theatres, as many as seven of which were functioning at the same time towards the end of the century.

The complex and contradictory relationship between patronage and public in early Venetian opera is reflected in an instability of content and form in the libretto to the early 1650s. The aura of mythological pastorales present in many earlier court spectacles was maintained in some of the first dramas, for instance in *Le nozze di Teti e di Peleo* and *Gli amori d'Apollo e di Dafne*, set by Francesco Cavalli in 1639 and 1640 respectively. Influential in the production of this sort of work, which sometimes reached extremes of playful erudition, were the members of the sceptical and libertine Accademia degli Incogniti, led by G. F. Loredan. They were also involved in the one attempt to launch a theatre on the scale of that, say, of the Barberini, the short-lived Teatro Novissimo (1641–5). Perhaps the city could not support the expensive machinery of Giacomo Torelli, and perhaps also the outbreak of war with the Turks in 1645 (which probably closed down all the theatres for at least two years) contributed to its failure. A certain Roman influence in the early years can also be seen in the scenographic dependence of *La maga fulminata* on *Erminia sul Giordano*, in the importation of composers (Filiberto Laurenzi, Marco Marazzoli, Filippo Vitali) and singers (Anna Renzi), and in the palpable associations of musical style between the operas of Cavalli and those of the 1630s in Rome.

The subject matter was as wide as that of Rome (with the exceptions of hagiography and full-blown comedy); myth, epic, history (all suitably revised) and free invention were used with little evident discrimination. A connection of Venice with ancient 'history' through the Trojan myth is seen in operas such as Cavalli's *Didone* (1641) and an identification with the Roman republic can be traced throughout, both in the thematic content of opera and in the justification of theatre by its propagandists; despite its inaccuracies, Cristoforo Ivanovich's catalogue of Venetian opera performances, published as an appendix to his *Minerva al tavolino* (1681, 2/1688), is valuable as a survey of repertory and for its discussion of contemporary theatre practice.

The romantic dramas of Giovanni Faustini, mostly set to music by Cavalli (from *La virtù de' strali d'Amore*, 1642, to *Eritrea*, 1652), represent an attempt at a more accessible form than that cultivated by the Incogniti. Their use of elements of intrigue, even though limited, means that plot tensions and release supplant the classical structuring of *Euridice* and *Orfeo*, traces of which can still be seen in the first librettos of Orazio Persiani and G. F. Busenello. These collaborations gave rise to some of the most subtly articulated operas of the 17th century, with Cavalli's affective recitative and fluid arias responding to Faustini's flexible verse forms.

The introduction of a high level of intrigue and comedy, with some influence from the Spanish tradition, was due to the librettist G. A. Cicognini, whose *Giasone* (set by Cavalli, 1649) and *Orontea* (Antonio Cesti, 1649), both first given in Venice, were the most widely performed operas of the 17th century. Intrigue and comedy remained essential ingredients of Venetian opera for nearly four decades in the works of such librettists as Nicolò Minato and Aurelio Aureli. There is otherwise little stability of either theme or form, apart from a number of vestigial elements (lament, sleep scene, invocation), whose treatment varies considerably from one work to another.

From the 1650s operas tended to be a good deal less fluid and more streamlined than those of Faustini. The number of arias, usually of two strophes, grew to 30 or more by the 1660s, and their placement became increasingly standardized to the beginnings and (especially later) ends of the scenes. There was a standardization of form as well: the musical strophe of most arias is constructed as either *ABA* or *ABB'*; the use of arioso became less prominent, and recitative style less melodically coherent. Whereas the scores of the earliest surviving Venetian operas suggest a variety of instrumental usage, the orchestra was reduced by 1650 to a body of foundation instruments (harpsichords, theorbos, lutes) and four- or five-part (usually solo) strings. They played the sinfonias and ritornellos and provided accompaniment to a number of arias, but continuo arias remained in the majority until the end of the century. From about 1670 the trumpet made its appearance as a concertante instrument in the opera orchestra, and other wind began to creep in about 1680 (e.g. *Il Nerone*, 1679, music by Carlo Pallavicino, text by G. C. Corradi) though they did not become a regular feature before about 1700.

Among the principal composers of the 1660s and 1670s were P. A. Ziani, G. A. Boretti, Antonio Sartorio, Carlo Pallavicino, Giovanni Legrenzi and Domenico Freschi. Their arias are still mostly miniatures, and often appear dance-like in character, probably through a close dependence on regular poetic metres. An upsurge in the amount and difficulty of passage-work is not surprising, in view of the well-documented scramble to import famous singers from all over Italy. From the 1670s the motto aria enjoyed great popularity, and by 1680 the da capo, albeit of small dimensions, was established as the dominant form.

Venice also served as a model for the opera repertory of other cities throughout Italy. In this the operas of Cavalli were particularly important. The mechanism for the spread of Venetian repertory was a number of troupes similar to the one that brought opera to Venice in the first place. Ferrari and Manelli took part in fairly regular performances in Bologna in the early 1640s, but the most active were the Febiarmonici and the Accademici Discordati, two nebulous and shifting groups which may have been connected. They were organized on the model of a *commedia dell'arte* company, seeking the protection of a patron in the cities they visited, picking up local musicians where their own forces were insufficient and giving performances with paid admission. Their limited repertory, almost entirely Venetian, included *La finta pazza* (music by Francesco Sacrati, text by Giulio Strozzi), a stripped-down version of the first production at Venice's Teatro Novissimo, *Egisto* (Cavalli–Faustini), and later *Giasone*. They were responsible for introducing opera to many towns such as Genoa, Milan, Lucca and Piacenza, but were also a factor in places such as Florence and Bologna with some prior history of musical spectacle.

The Febiarmonici were the means by which an operatic practice was established in Naples, so much so that their name became a synonym for 'opera singers'. Genoa and Milan were quick to assimilate the Venetian pattern, other towns less so. In Bologna a heterogeneous and largely local repertory of academic inspiration, including exceptional revivals of the Roman spectacles *Sant'Alessio* (1647) and *La catena d'Adone* (1648), co-existed with performances by travelling companies. At the courts of the Farnese (Parma, Piacenza) and Este (Modena) opera remained an episodic and occasional affair (e.g. *Il Coriolano*, 1669, of Cavalli and Ivanovich) until the last decades of the 17th century. In Florence, where despite the visits of troupes opera long remained under the patronage of the Medici family or was produced in the academies assembled around them, the mixture was particularly complex, ranging from the comic *Potestà di Colognole* (1657, music by Jacopo Melani, text by G. A. Moniglia), a work of local reference, to *Hipermestra* (performed 1658), of courtly monumentality but with Venetian music (Cavalli). Even a single occasion such as the marriage of Prince Cosimo de' Medici to Marguerite Louise of Orleans in 1661 could attract pieces as diverse as the Cicogninian *La Dori* (music by Cesti, text by G. F. Apolloni) and the grandiose *Ercole in Tebe* (Melani and Moniglia), which later had to be radically revised in order to suit a Venetian audience. Opera in Rome began to assume a more 'international' character only with the opening of the Teatro Tordinona in 1671.

Comic opera

The 17th century did not witness the development of a coherent and independent tradition of comic opera. There were comic characters in heroic operas, and in the latter part of the century comic scenes placed at the ends of acts not infrequently assumed the proportions of intermezzos, mainly in southern Italy, sometimes employing characters who sang in dialect (particularly at Naples and Palermo). For the rest, comic plots were limited to specific local traditions and tended not to travel: such was the case with the Tuscan dramas of Moniglia for Florence (for example *Il potestà di Colognole*), Rospigliosi's 'cloak and dagger' comedies for Rome, the novelistic librettos of Carlo Maria Maggi for Borromeo's theatre at Isola Bella (Lake Maggiore) and the short pastoral operas which flourished in the 1680s and 1690s, particularly at certain aristocratic villas.

The debt of the 17th-century Italian libretto to Spanish theatre is real if sometimes elusive. An early sign of this is in the correspondence between Lope de Vega and G. A. Cicognini's father Jacopo, himself an author of texts for the musical stage. Jacopo's son was an important adapter of Spanish dramas for the Italian spoken theatre, and that activity left its mark on his four works for the opera house, and thereby on the entire tradition. Two of the librettos which Rospigliosi prepared on his return from a nunciature in Spain were virtually translations of comedies by Antonio Sigler de Huerta and Calderón de la Barca (*Dal male il bene*, 1654, and *L'armi e gli amori*, 1656). Naples, under Spanish rule, was the scene of adaptations of allegorical and mythological plots by Calderón (*La Psiche*, 1683, and *Il Fetonte*, 1685, both with music by Alessandro Scarlatti) and even of an opera in Spanish (*El robo de Proserpina*, 1678, music by Coppola).

The late 17th century

The influence of French tragedy and a corresponding attention to the dramatic principles of Aristotle, as reinterpreted by the Italian humanist tradition, mark Italian opera librettos from the 1690s, most consistently in the five-act dramas of Girolamo Frigimelica Roberti for Venice, but also in works by Domenico David and Apostolo Zeno (Venice), Silvio Stampiglia (Rome and Naples) and, after 1700, Antonio Salvi (Florence). An Italian translation of Lully's *Armide* was even prepared for Rome in 1690. A parallel development was the pan-Italian literary movement of the Arcadian Academy, of which David, Zeno and Stampiglia were members, and which inspired the production of pastorales such as Cardinal Pietro Ottoboni's *Amore eroico tra i pastori*. In most of these works the number of characters is smaller (the Neapolitan librettist G. G. Salvadori, writing in 1691, recommended between four and seven), as is the number of arias, whose placement was gradually standardized at the ends of scenes and the poetic structure of which was made more regular. Plot structure and language were simplified. Comic scenes disappeared from the works of poets such as Frigimelica Roberti, but the separation of comic from serious in Italian opera was not complete until after the first few years of the 18th century.

At the close of the 17th century composers of opera active in the north of Italy (with Venice as a focal point) included M. A. Ziani, C. F. Pollarolo, G. A. Perti, Antonio Lotti, Tomaso Albinoni and Antonio Caldara; in the south Giovanni Bononcini, Bernardo Pasquini and, above all, Alessandro Scarlatti, the dominant figure at Naples and, to some extent, at Rome.

Although the complexity and quality of his invention, and the effective exploitation of pathetic chromaticism, mark Scarlatti off from most of his contemporaries, the principal external features of operatic music were shared by all. By 1690 essentially all arias were in da capo form, and the second strophe had already begun to fall away. From about 1700 most arias had a bipartite *A* section with a clear internal point of tonal arrival; the expansion of da capo form encouraged melismatic passages to blossom, even in otherwise syllabic arias. The traditional accompaniment of continuo, with string orchestra confined to the ritornello, yielded to a more elaborate and continuous orchestral one: in Pollarolo's *Ariodante* (1716), four-fifths of the arias are supported by the orchestra, and continuo arias are entirely absent from Scarlatti's late operas. The variety of orchestral sonority grew to include oboes, horns, trumpets, occasionally flutes, in obbligato as well as supporting roles, and arias without bass. There are notable obbligato horn parts in Scarlatti's *Tigrane* (1715), while *Il Cambise* (1719) and *Griselda* (1721) exemplify the less common appearance of obbligato flutes. By about 1695 the overture settled into the regular three-movement pattern known as the Italian overture.

Italian opera abroad

Italian opera may have been introduced to Paris by the Febiarmonici about 1644–5. Most of the works performed there, however, were a result of Mazarin's cultural politics, from *La finta pazza*, staged with the extravagant machines of Torelli, to *Ercole amante* (music by Cavalli, text by Mazarin's superintendent of Italian artists, Francesco Buti), intended as part of the festivities accompanying the wedding of Louis XIV. The presence of the exiled Barberinis also had a bearing, most directly on Luigi Rossi's *Orfeo* of 1647. *Ercole amante*, commissioned by Mazarin but performed in 1662 after his death, marks the end of Italian spectacle at the court. Gioseffo Zamponi's *Ulisse all'isola di Circe* (1650), for the wedding of Philip IV of Spain and Maria Anna of Austria, was the first opera produced at Brussels, but did not lead to a tradition.

The first inkling of Florentine *stile rappresentativo* in German countries may have been provided by Heinrich Schütz's *Dafne* (1627; see Chapter II). In those German and Austrian centres with strong Italian connections, opera gained a fairly early foothold. It was firmest in Vienna, which maintained a stable group of Italian poets and musicians. Apart from a few early imported examples, the Viennese repertory was indigenous, largely keyed to imperial birthdays, and grand, when the occasion warranted (e.g. *Il pomo d'oro*, by Cesti and Francesco Sbarra, originally meant to celebrate the marriage of Leopold I in 1666). Cesti, P. A. Ziani, G. F. Sances and Antonio Bertali were among the composers who participated in the creation of an Italian repertory, setting the works of court poets such as Sbarra, Minato and others. The principal designer of scenery was the court architect Ludovico Burnacini. A special role was played by Antonio Draghi, who, after beginning as a librettist, composed more than 170 operas and other dramatic works between 1662 and 1699. From the early 1650s until the extinction of the Tyrolean line in 1665, Innsbruck also had a flourishing Italian musical theatre, mostly works by the resident composer Cesti. Some of these (*Argia, Orontea, La Dori*), like several Viennese operas, later became widely known in Italy. Opera was also facilitated at many courts that had Italian *maestri di cappella* such as Dresden (G. A. Bontempi, Pallavicino), Hanover (Antonio Sartorio, Agostino Steffani) and Munich. Any incursions of Italian opera into Spain, Portugal, the Low Countries (Italian operas were given in Amsterdam in 1680 and 1681) and England were few and isolated in the 17th century.

CHAPTER II

Germany and Austria

PETER BRANSCOMBE

Germany

Throughout the Baroque and Rococo eras, opera in the German-speaking lands was, as we have seen, predominantly Italian in its language and Italianate in its musical style. Many of the leading composers of Italian opera held court appointments in Germany (Hasse at Dresden, Jommelli at Stuttgart and Draghi and Caldara at Vienna, for example), and the greatest Italian librettist, Metastasio, was Viennese court poet. If few centres were as decisively Italianate as the court of Dresden up to the time of the Seven Years War (1756), or that of Vienna up to Joseph II's foundation of the National-Singspiel in 1778, attempts to establish opera in the vernacular were for the most part of limited success and brief duration. The one important exception is the famous Theater am Gänsemarkt in Hamburg where, from the late 1670s until the end of the fourth decade of the 18th century, the burghers managed to maintain predominantly German-language operatic performances, despite the opposition of some of the clergy and periodic financial crises. A series of mainly local poets provided the librettos: Lucas von Bostel, Christian Heinrich Postel, Christian Hunold (pseudonym Menantes) and, most important, Barthold Feind. A towering figure, first as tenor soloist, then as opera composer and in his later years as theorist, was Johann Mattheson. All but one of his eight operas were written for Hamburg, between 1699 and 1723. In *Die unglückselige Cleopatra* (1704) and *Boris Goudenow* (1719, to his own libretto) he revealed a distinctive dramatic style, direct, limpid and often folklike, especially in comic scenes. Besides Mattheson, the principal composers were outsiders summoned to Hamburg: Theile (whose Adam and Eve opera, *Der erschaffene, gefallene und auffgerichtete Mensch*, appropriately opened the enterprise in 1678), Strungk, Franck, Förtsch, Kusser, Krieger, Keiser and Telemann; Handel wrote his *Almira*, *Nero*, *Florindo* and *Daphne* while in Hamburg in 1704–5. Easily the most important of these is Reinhard Keiser, in respect both of number (at least 80) and of musical quality; the best of his scores combine melodic freshness, formal variety and bold instrumentation with a real feeling for

27

drama. The arias tend to be considerably shorter and less elaborate than those in contemporary Italian opera, and the choruses are generally simple and straightforward. With few exceptions, Hamburg did without star singers, and castratos were not engaged.

The subject matter of the Hamburg operas was taken principally from the usual sources for the Baroque stage: myth, ancient history and biblical stories. As in the Venetian public operas of the mid-17th century, the introduction of comic servants and peasants became increasingly important and popular, the comic scenes eventually leading to independent intermezzos. Occasionally incidents from German history and local legend were chosen; examples include *Cara Mustapha* (1686, music by Franck, text by Bostel), *Störtebecker* (1701, music by Keiser, text by Hotter) and *Heinrich der Vogler* (1719, music by Schürmann, text by König). Mixed-language performances are attested for Hamburg from at least 1703, when *Die verdammte Staat-Sucht* (*Claudius*: music by Keiser, text by Hinsch) was produced, incorporating Italian arias into its printed libretto. In 1711 Matteson and Hoë included in their *Die geheimen Begebenheiten Henrico IV*, as well as Italian arias, a chorus in Spanish; often recitatives were sung in German and arias in Italian (or, rarely, another foreign language). Many of the Hamburg operas were adaptations or translations of works imported from other centres. Predominantly comic operas were rare until the last years of the Hamburg operatic enterprise; examples are Telemann's *Der geduldige Socrates* of 1721 (performed before his engagement at Hamburg) and *Pimpinone oder Die ungleiche Heyrath* of 1725, and Keiser's *Der lächerliche Prinz Jodelet* of 1726. These comic works have a melodic freshness and an engaging liveliness of utterance largely lacking from the serious operas, qualities especially marked in Telemann's surviving examples. From 1722 until its closure in 1738 he was director of the opera, for which he wrote about 20 works (most of which are lost). The comic operas and intermezzos demonstrate his mastery of popular forms and the early *buffo* style. There are numerous ensembles, and his scores reveal considerable variety in mood and situation, highly original instrumentation and clever satirical and parodistic touches.

Apart from the 60 years of German operatic activity in Hamburg, numerous courts and other centres flirted with opera in German for a longer or shorter period – for example Weissenfels, Brunswick-Wolfenbüttel (where Schürmann was the outstanding opera composer), Nuremberg and Stuttgart, and also smaller courts like Durlach. Schütz's lost opera *Dafne*, a setting of Rinuccini's libretto in a translation by Martin Opitz, was written for a court wedding at Torgau in 1627, and in 1644 Staden's setting of G. P. Harsdörffer's *Seelewig* (a 'sacred sylvan poem') was performed at Nuremberg; text and music were published there in an edition of the poet's works (*Frauenzimmer Gesprächspiele*, iv, 1644). An early product of Germany's slow recovery from the Thirty Years War was the opera *Die Hochzeit der Thetis*, probably set by Philipp Stolle, performed at Halle in 1654. From this time onwards the number of operatic settings of

German-language librettos is considerable (for a valuably extensive list, though neither complete nor absolutely reliable, see Schletterer, 1863, pp.216ff, and Brockpähler, 1964). Few of these many works are of great value, poetically or musically; not until the Singspiel settings by Hiller and others of the librettos of C. F. Weisse in particular, in the mid-18th century, was there any sustained and successful effort to write German operas.

Among other centres of operatic activity, Munich enjoyed periods of operatic distinction, notably in the mid- and late 17th century, when Kerll, the Bernabeis and Steffani wrote many Italian works for the Bavarian court, and early in the following century when Pietro Torri was active. The history of opera in Berlin began modestly under the guidance of Queen Sophie Charlotte around 1690, but the period of its fame was to come only under Frederick the Great, in 1740; his Kapellmeister Carl Heinrich Graun, who had the experience of German (or mixed German and Italian) opera at Brunswick-Wolfenbüttel, wrote a series of Italian operas for the royal theatres at Potsdam and in Berlin between 1741 and 1756. The cult of opera at the Saxon court of Dresden is inseparable from the name of Johann Adolf Hasse, whose long career took him to Brunswick, Naples, Venice and other Italian cities, and Vienna. It was however at Dresden and the nearby residence of Hubertusberg that most of his elegant, melodious operatic scores were written and performed.

Austria

Isolated performances of opera at the Viennese court are attested from the 1630s (though sources are contradictory); intensive cultivation of the genre began with Bertali, who became Hofkapellmeister in 1649. The first of his eight operas for Vienna, *Il rè Gelidoro*, dates from 1659; the last is the famous equestrian opera-ballet *La contesa dell'aria e dell'acqua*, performed on the Innerer Burgplatz on 24 January 1667 as part of the celebrations of the wedding of Leopold I to the Infanta Margarita of Spain. Also written for this wedding, but not performed until 1668 (Prologue and Acts 1 and 2, 12 July; Acts 3–5, 14 July) was *Il pomo d'oro*, arguably the grandest and most famous of all Baroque operas; the score, apart from some numbers by Leopold himself, is by Cesti, to a libretto by Sbarra. Ludovico Burnacini's splendid designs for the two dozen sets give an excellent idea of what the opera must have looked like (see Plate 24), and with the recent discovery and publication of an outline of much of the music for Acts 3 and 5, long presumed lost, it is now possible to form a tolerably complete impression of the music.

Viennese court opera continued to be almost entirely Italian, composed – with the notable exception of Fux – mainly by Italians. Statements that German-language operas were given in Vienna (e.g. by Schletterer, pp.217f) are presumably due to the widespread practice of printing parallel or simultaneously published librettos in Italian, the language in which the work was written and performed, and German, the native language of most of the audience. Occasional, isolated occurrences of the vernacular in Italian operas in Vienna are different in kind and in principle from the widespread use of mixed languages roughly contemporaneously at Hamburg. In Vienna, German, when it was used at all, was used mainly for comic effect. Thus for a court entertainment in 1686, Leopold I wrote an aria that includes phrases of Italian in its predominantly German text: 'Ma sempre betrüben/ist nixnutzes Lieben'. The near-operas lavishly presented in the Jesuit theatre similarly used German in comic scenes, doubtless as a relief to many in the audience for whom the Latin dialogue was difficult to follow. A further example of the use of the vernacular is the traditional German nightwatchman's call in *Il Perseo* (1669, music by Draghi, text by Amalteo; see von Weilen, 1917, p.49).

Although no music for their works has survived before the mid-1750s, the comedians who performed Singspiels and intermezzos in the Kärntnertortheater from 1710 onwards enjoyed great popularity. There can be no doubt that the *Verse* in the plays of Stranitzky and his followers were sung, nor that their attitude towards the works performed at court was parodistic – the down-to-earth attitudes of Hanswurst and the other comic characters contrast sharply with the high-flown Baroque attitudinizings of the emperors, tyrants, princesses and mighty men of valour who dominated the action of the court operas. But the popular comedies with songs that dominated the Kärntnertortheater repertory were not parodies of specific and contemporary court operas; in more general terms they mocked the heroic convention and set in its place the healthy scepticism of ordinary people.

CHAPTER III

France

JAMES R. ANTHONY

The beginnings

The first operas given in France were Italian ones, imported for the French court by Cardinal Mazarin in early 1645, partly in connection with his political aims. To accommodate French tastes, they were often supplemented with ballet music and panegyric prologues, both provided by French composers, and lavishly staged; few were successful other than for their spectacle and ballets. Mazarin did not live to witness the performance of Cavalli's *Ercole amante* (1662), which inaugurated Vigarani's ill-conceived 'Théâtre des Machines' but ended the era of Italian opera in France.

The earliest French operas were pastorales: *Le triomphe de l'Amour* (music by Michel de La Guerre, text by Charles de Bey) was performed, probably in concert form, in January 1655 and staged two years later; Pierre Perrin supplied Robert Cambert with texts for the so-called *Pastorale d'Issy* (1659) and *Ariane, ou Le mariage de Bacchus* (1659, music lost). It was in the 1660s and 70s that true French opera emerged, influenced by several existing genres, by the love of spectacle and dance at the French court (for which all the early operas were written), by the traditions of the French spoken theatre in the age of Racine, Corneille and Molière – and above all by the powerful personality of the Florentine-born composer Jean-Baptiste Lully. The principal form of the French opera was the *tragédie*, more often called the *tragédie en musique* or later *tragédie lyrique*; other associated genres, with stronger ballet elements, were the *opéra-ballet*, the *ballet héroïque*, the *pastorale héroïque* and the *comédie lyrique*. French opera has always been strongly institutionalized: thus serious, all-sung opera is inseparably linked with the court and the Opéra or Académie Royale de Musique (which until the Revolution enjoyed monopolistic rights for all-sung dramatic works), while opera with spoken texts is associated first with the Théâtres de la Foire and then with the Opéra-Comique; these divisions began to break down only in the late 19th century.

After his collaboration with Cambert on the pastorales of 1659, Perrin convinced the king's minister Colbert that France should have her own opera. On 28 June 1669 he received a 12-year privilege to establish 'Académies d'Opéra' in the realm for the performances of operas 'in music and French verse'. The Académie d'Opéra in Paris was inaugurated on 3 March 1671 with a production of the pastorale *Pomone* by Perrin and Cambert, which ran for 146 performances. In spite of this success, Perrin's Académie was short-lived. He was compelled to sell his privilege to Lully, to whom it was formally transferred by Louis XIV on 13 March 1672. This gave Lully the sole right to the Académie Royale de Musique. A series of oppressive patents consolidated his absolute control over all aspects of French stage music. After Molière's death he was given the theatre of the Palais Royal (28 April 1673), the principal home of French opera from 1673 until it burnt down in 1763. The time was now at hand for the creation of French serious opera.

Lully's tragédie lyrique

As conceived by Lully and his librettist, Philippe Quinault, the *tragédie lyrique* is a synthesis of elements judiciously arranged and expanded from earlier and co-existing stage genres. All its principal characteristics have prototypes in the *ballet de cour*, the pastorale, the *comédie-* and *tragédie-ballets*, the *tragédie à machines* and the Italian opera: its scenes of sacrifice and combat; its sleep scenes (*sommeils*) and funeral ceremonies; its *merveilleux*, served by Carlo Vigarani's (after 1680 by Jean Berain's) spectacular machinery; its mixture of comic and pathetic characters (disallowed after Lully's *Thésée* by the Académie des Inscriptions et Belles-Lettres as a violation of the unity of action); its use of short binary and rondeau *airs*, small ensembles and large choruses; its prominent divertissements of songs and dances; and even its politically inspired prologues and its overtures. It differs from earlier genres mainly in its principle of subordination of the purely decorative elements to a dramatic unity and in the central importance it assigns to the recitative. It overshadowed the earlier attempts of Perrin and Cambert to establish a national opera. 'The *grand Opéra, Cadmus*', wrote J. N. de Tralage(1687), 'made it easy to forget the operas *Pomone* and *Les peines et les plaisirs de l'amour*' (see Lacroix, 1880).

Quinault's 11 librettos (or *livrets*) for Lully each resulted from a threefold collaboration between the poet, the composer and the Académie des Inscriptions et Belles-Lettres. The significance of the libretto in Lully's *tragédies lyriques* was summed up in Abbé Malby's comment that 'an excellent Poem is absolutely essential for the long range success of an Opera. The Music, considered by itself, can have only a passing vogue' (*Lettre à Madame la marquise de P. . . . sur l'Opéra*, 1741). The subject matter of the *tragédie lyrique* derived either from mythology (*Cadmus, Alceste, Thésée, Atys, Isis, Psyché* (livret by Quinault, T. Corneille, Fontenelle), *Bellérophon* (livret by Corneille, Fontenelle, N. Boileau-Despreaux), *Proserpine, Persée* and *Phaëton*) or from legends of chivalry (*Amadis, Roland,*

Armide). The dramatic format remained fairly constant: the intrigue of an amorous couple and one or more rivals (often including at least one god or goddess) and, in the earlier operas, a parallel intrigue involving personages of lesser rank. Gods and goddesses, magicians and enchantresses compete among themselves and interfere in mortal affairs. In a Quinault *livret* the amorous intrigues of gods and men are generally more *galant* than heroic in tone (a condition which incurred the enmity of the clergy). Only in such later *tragédies* as *Roland* and *Armide* does the Corneille theme of the conflict of 'gloire' and 'amour' receive didactic comment.

Every *tragédie lyrique* has a prologue and five acts. The prologue, which is preceded and followed by an overture, is generally separate from the subject matter of the main action. The prologue of *Thésée* takes place before the palace of Versailles; that of *Persée* alludes to Louis XIV's victories in the Dutch wars. Although the characters of *Amadis* appear in its prologue, it remained for Rameau in *Zoroastre* (1749) to suppress the prologue completely and create a strong dramatic link between the overture and the drama to follow. The scenes of Lully's *tragédies lyriques* take a variety of structures. They may consist wholly of recitatives, or may have chains of dialogue *airs* interspersed with recitatives; they may be dominated by a single monologue *air* (often with an introductory *symphonie*); or they may constitute a divertissement of songs and dances; while action scenes may be composed of *air* fragments, choral exhortations and dramatic *symphonies*.

The *récitatif ordinaire*, devised by Lully, expedites the action of the drama, along with short dialogue *airs*. Chastellux noted three rules governing the *récitatif ordinaire* in *tragédie lyrique* up to Rameau: 'it must not employ a constant rhythm or metre, it must not use an accompaniment that would prevent comprehension of the text in a natural and rapid dialogue, and it must not tire the actor by exploiting his most brilliant vocal sounds' (*Essai sur l'union de la poésie et la musique*, 1765). Lully's repeated visits to the home of French tragedy, the Hôtel de Bourgogne, to hear 'La Champmeslé' (Marie Chevillet) declaim the alexandrines of Racine's tragedies, convinced him that French recitative must spring from the same source. The necessity of placing the strongest syllables (the rhyme syllable and the caesura) on the strongest beats of the bar resulted in the use of fluctuating metres, a constant feature of French recitative from Lully to Rameau. The recitative was accompanied by the continuo and was performed 'quickly, without appearing bizarre' (Le Cerf de la Viéville, 1704–6), and with little or no ornamentation: 'no embellishments; my recitative is made only for speaking' (Le Cerf, quoting Lully).

There is some confusion over the exact metrical relationships to be observed between the constantly shifting metres of the recitatives of Lully and his successors. However, the time value of a beat in one metre should be equal to that of a beat in the other even though the note values are not equal, i.e. a crotchet in ¢ is equal to a minim in ₵. There is some evidence that as long as the 'built-in' conditions of correct prosody were observed, little attempt was made to force a rhythmically precise rendering of the recitative: 'one must not beat time [in recitative], because the actor must be the master of his song and allow it to conform to his expression' (Le Gallois, 1707).

Lully's simple recitative is best seen in the famous monologue from *Armide* (Act 2) in which Armide's inner conflict is evoked as much by musical means as through standard 17th-century declamation. Rests, for example, are not restricted to caesuras in the text but, more importantly, dramatize her hesitation and confusion. Many 18th-century partisans of French opera considered this monologue, in Titon du Tillet's words, the greatest piece in all French opera; Rameau printed it complete in his *Nouveau système de musique théorique* (1726), used it in *Observations sur notre instinct pour la musique* (1754) to answer Rousseau's criticism of French recitative and gave a detailed harmonic analysis of its opening section in *Code de musique pratique* (1760).

Beginning with *Bellérophon* (1679), Lully turned increasingly to accompanied recitative in which, though not neglecting the rules of prosody, he subordinated them to heightened musical expression. This type of recitative often includes extended passages that lack the typical fluctuations of metre of simple recitative, thus producing a musical hybrid. There is no adequate term for this in French; by the late 17th century it was called 'récitatif mesuré', and perhaps the closest counterpart is the Italian 'arioso'.

The French operatic *air* from Lully to Rameau falls into four basic types: dialogue *air*, maxim *air*, monologue *air* and dance-song. Many are in the tradition of short binary and rondeau court *airs*. However, Lully's favoured binary form is the extended type (*ABB'*) modelled more closely on the cantata and opera arias of Venetian and Roman composers of the mid-17th century than on the French court *air*. In basing some of his dance-songs and maxim *airs* (normally sung by secondary characters) on *chansons à boire* and brunettes Lully was courting popular favour. Le Cerf related how Lully was specially pleased when these pieces, sometimes referred to as 'Pont-Neuf tunes', were enjoyed by 'princess and cook alike'. Static monologue *airs* were reserved for moments of deep feeling when, Rousseau said, the 'actor is alone and speaks only with himself' (*Dictionnaire*, 1768). Unlike the aria in an Italian opera, which provides the climax of a scene, the monologue *air* with its long orchestral prelude usually takes up the entire scene. When the dramatic situation permitted, Lully composed monologue *airs* of considerable amplitude, for instance 'Bois épais' (*Amadis*, Act 2) and 'Plus j'observe ces lieux' (*Armide*, Act 2). The sharp demarcation between recitative and aria so characteristic of Italian opera was foreign to the French style, in which the recitative was nourished by the restrained melodic patterns of the *air*, which in turn never completely lost the declamatory bias of the recitative. According to C. H. de Blainville (*L'esprit de l'art musical*, 1754), 'our recitative sings too much, our airs not enough'.

Besides serving as the crowning embellishment of a decorative divertissement, the chorus of the *tragédie lyrique* could also participate directly in the drama (for example 'Toute est perdue' from Lully's *Bellérophon*) or comment upon it (for example 'Atys, Atys luy même fait périr çe qu'il aime' from *Atys*, or the choral fragment 'Alceste est morte' from *Alceste*; the latter, often parodied, is probably the source for Rameau's similar 'Hippolyte n'est plus' from *Hippolyte et Aricie*). The importance of the chorus in the *tragédie lyrique* is the one point of agreement in France between partisans of French or Italian opera. Both found it laudable. Even Rousseau chided the Italians for their 'little choruses . . . not worthy of the name' in a letter to Friedrich Melchior Grimm written in 1750, three years before the better known *Lettre sur la musique française*. The French operatic chorus from Lully to Rameau was divided into a *grand* and a *petit choeur*. Brossard (*Dictionaire*, 1703) described the *petit choeur* as a chorus of the best singers; trio texture was favoured and the voice distribution was normally for two sopranos and *haute-contre*. It is difficult to determine how many musicians sang in the opera chorus during Lully's lifetime. In 1713, according to the Royal Ordinance, the Opéra chorus included 12 women and 22 men. This did not represent maximum strength, for all the actors and actresses, except those in the eight leading roles, were required to sing in the chorus.

Lully's opera orchestra is conservative, predictable and hierarchical; there is little distinctive writing for the individual instruments. The five-part string group formed the core of the *grand choeur*: in Lully's time its basis was 24 string players, and 30 by 1704 (with, from 1700, a double bass), along with wind instruments (flutes, oboes, bassoons), while the *petit choeur* consisted of pairs of violins, theorbos and bass viols with a harpsichord – probably not used in the overture, the dances or most other instrumental items.

Except for the overture, the instrumental music (or *symphonies*) of the *tragédie lyrique* was expected to have some link with the dramatic or choreographic action. Lully's dramatic *symphonies* stand at the beginning of a development that reached a highpoint in Rameau's *tragédies lyriques*. The 18th century regarded the operatic *symphonie* as an example of the expressive power of music when used to imitate nature or, by extension, states of mind. Dubos (1719), a convincing spokesman for an aesthetic theory of the 'imitation of nature', suggested that operatic *symphonies* were 'able to agitate us, calm us, move us; in short, they act upon us in the same manner as the verses of Racine and Corneille'. A more expanded use of the orchestra is apparent in many of the *tragédies lyriques* composed between Lully and Rameau. The great musical frescoes of nature in turmoil, the tempests and earthquakes of Rameau's *Hippolyte et Aricie* and *Zoroastre*, were modelled on the 'tempests' in Collasse's *Thétis et Pelée* (1689), Campra's *Hésione* (1700) and *Idoménée* (1712), Desmarets' *Iphigénie en Tauride* (1704, completed by Campra) and, above all, the most famous 'tempest' before Rameau – that in Marais' *Alcione* (1706), which inspired 'a prodigious number of others: not only in Opera, but also in Cantatas and even in Church Music' (Brossard, *Catalogue*, 1724).

Lully's long apprenticeship as composer of court and comedy ballets served him well in his use of the dance in the *tragédie lyrique*. He viewed dance as an expressive medium and legitimate dramatic agent as well as a colourful part of the divertissement. Quinault's librettos forced a modification of the exclusively decorative entrées of the *ballet à entrées*. Even the italophile François Raguenet (1702) conceded Lully's superiority in the domain of the dance. He mentioned scenes from *Atys* and *Isis* to document a close link between Lully's dance and drama. Indeed, one critical difference between the Lully–Quinault *tragédies lyriques* and those of the following generations is the later proliferation of dances and increased emphasis on the dramatically impotent divertissement. Campra, in his *Achille et Déidame* (1735), was accused of 'drowning the subject in the divertissement'.

The generation after Lully

During the Regency, Lully's *tragédies lyriques* were apparently eclipsed by the popular *opéra-ballet*, a genre more in keeping with the taste of the pleasure-seeking audiences. Yet they held the stage throughout the 18th century: *Thésée*, for example, was performed for 104 years, until 1779. In the 46 years that separate Lully's last opera, *Acis et Galatée* (1687), and Rameau's first, *Hippolyte et Aricie* (1733), 59 different *tragédies lyriques* were performed at the Paris Opéra, 15 more than all other types of stage work combined. Only 14 of these *tragédies lyriques* were revived more than once, and none could match the performance records of Lully's eight most popular operas. These post-Lully *tragédies lyriques* contributed much, however, to Rameau's musical development with their more sophisticated harmonic language, their more highly developed sense of orchestral colour and their expanded musical vocabulary which resulted partly from a greater absorption of Italian influences (for example in the use of the *ariette*, a French 'aria da capo').

Campra in particular was an innovator in his earlier *tragédies*. In *Tancrède* (1702) he gave all the principal male roles to basses and the principal female role to the alto (Mlle Maupin). In *Idoménée* (1712) he wrote for an offstage chorus (Act 2) of 'shipwrecked people who are heard but not seen', 37 years ahead of Rameau's use of this device in *Zoroastre* (1749). In his *David et Jonathas* (1668), composed for the Jesuit College Louis-le-Grand, Charpentier suppressed the typical allegorical prologue with its fatuous verses praising the king. Instead his prologue goes at once to the heart of the drama itself. Destouches' accompanied recitatives reveal a highly developed expressive and dramatic sense. Zoroaster's recitatives from Act 3 of his *Semiramis* with their dramatic pauses and orchestral interpolations prefigure Rameau's own *Zoroastre* of 30 years later. Grimm, in his attack on Destouches' *Omphale* (*Lettre sur Omphale*, 1752), was forced to admit that the composer's recitatives were 'still esteemed'. There is sufficient strength and originality in much of the music from Charpentier's *David et Jonathas* and *Médée*(1693), Destouches' *Omphale* (1701) and *Semiramis* (1718), Campra's *Tancrède* (1702) and *Idomenée* (1712), Desmarets' and Campra's *Iphigénie en Tauride* (1704), Marais' *Alcione* (1706) and Montéclair's *Jephté* (1732) to refute the common allegation that all operatic composers between Lully and Rameau were mere 'imitators of Lully'.

CHAPTER IV

England

CURTIS PRICE

Masque and the earliest opera

The first century of opera in England is marked by several episodes during which native music drama seemed on the verge of a breakthrough to true opera but then retreated back into the play. This refusal to step into the mainstream of operatic evolution, and preference instead for *opera seria* by foreign composers, is puzzling, as England possessed the same ingredients with which Monteverdi created *dramma per musica* in Italy and Lully *tragédie lyrique* in France. Yet before the arrival of Handel in 1710, only three works were produced that can properly be regarded as full-length, all-sung English operas: Davenant's *The Siege of Rhodes* (1656), set by a committee of composers; Dryden's *Albion and Albanius* (1685), with music by the French-trained Spaniard Louis Grabu; and Addison's *Rosamond* (1707), with music by Thomas Clayton. Any other English 'operas', including those of Matthew Locke, John Blow and Henry Purcell, are either isolated miniatures such as *Dido and Aeneas* (1689) or semi-operas such as *King Arthur* (1691), in which the main characters do not sing. Some music historians have therefore viewed Baroque English opera as an impure hybrid born of the national character and of a language supposedly unsuitable for recitative. But most 17th-century English critics, while expressing a preference for opera with spoken dialogue, voiced no strong objection to dramatic characters conversing in music, provided this happened rationally in celebrations, incantations or allegories of the main action.

English drama had been rich in music since the mid-16th century. In the choirboy plays of the 1580s and 1590s, the main characters, who were acted by trained singers from St Paul's Cathedral or the Chapel Royal, often delivered their own songs. Though this practice might appear to be a decisive step on the path to opera, Elizabethan plays almost never allowed music at the dramatic climax, and in the choirboy plays the Lament – the main vocal attraction – usually came during a moment of calm just before the fatal catastrophe.

Of greater operatic potential was the Stuart masque, a lavish court entertainment which included spoken dialogue, vocal and instrumental music and dance. Though symbolic gesture and scenic spectacle always took precedence over plot and action, several of Ben Jonson's masques have coherent dramatic shapes. And they did not lack recitative, an essential ingredient of all Baroque opera. Jonson's *Lovers made Men* (1617) was said to have been set completely in 'stylo recitativo' by Nicholas Lanier, but this crucial information is found only in the 1640 collected edition of Jonson's works, not in the original text, thereby weakening the masque's claim to be the first English opera. In spite of the occasional declamatory air and the bare bones of a plot, the Stuart masque did not ever threaten to sprout the wings of opera, because its aims were different. Italian opera sought to show the audience a mythical or historical world of exalted passions, while the masque, as an extension of court life, attempted to create a fantasy into which members of the audience could enter and rub shoulders with gods and goddesses.

The masque, and more especially its constituent antimasque (a series of scenes for grotesque or low-life characters presented before the masque itself), did, however, exert considerable influence on later works. The Commonwealth entertainment *Cupid and Death*, based on one of Aesop's fables and set by Christopher Gibbons and Locke (two versions, 1653 and 1659), is a series of antimasques. Though still including spoken dialogue, it has a greater proportion of vocal music and a more developed plot than any previous masque. Furthermore, it is the first English music drama for which a complete score survives. Locke's heavily ornamented recitatives (probably composed for the second production) help to give the final entry (or act) a compelling continuity reminiscent of Cavalli.

Forced by the Protectorate's ban on plays to find an alternative medium, the dramatist Sir William Davenant unostentatiously created the first all-sung English opera, *The Siege of Rhodes*, one of a handful of musical entertainments mounted at Rutland House, Charterhouse Square, in the late 1650s. The music, which is lost, was by Henry Lawes, Henry Cooke, Charles Coleman, George Hudson and Locke, who, along with Cooke and Henry Purcell (the great composer's uncle), were members of the cast; the role of Ianthe was taken by Mrs Edward Coleman, probably the first woman to appear publicly on the London stage. Pepys's diary includes allusions to *The Siege of Rhodes*, certain airs from which continued to impress him for several years. With the Restoration, when the ban on plays was lifted, Davenant converted the opera into a heroic play, thereby revealing his true intentions and an indifference towards all-sung opera shared by several succeeding generations of English dramatists. Apart from the awkward handling of the chorus at the ends of acts, *The Siege of Rhodes* is a remarkably good drama; it is unlike nearly all contemporary Italian librettos in being based on a historical event (the siege of the Knights of St John by the Ottomans in 1522).

Early semi-opera

With this sudden subjugation of vocal music by spoken dialogue, English music drama diverged from its continental cousins. Davenant did not invent the semi-opera, but his adaptations of *Macbeth* (1664) and *The Tempest* (1667, with Dryden) were expanded into musical extravaganzas after his death in 1668. Some modern critics have damned these alterations without realizing that under the terms of the royal patent granted him in 1660 he was obliged to 'reform' certain Shakespeare plays before mounting them. The new songs are skilfully incorporated, usually being allotted to characters who already incline to music, such as Ariel in *The Tempest* and the witches in *Macbeth*. In converting the Davenant–Dryden *Tempest* into what is generally regarded as the first semi-opera (1674), the Duke's Company commissioned a substantial amount of new music from Locke, James Hart, Pietro Reggio, Pelham Humfrey and the elder John Banister, but the crucial factor in the transformation was the spectacular scenery provided by the recently completed Dorset Garden Theatre, London's first opera house, opened in 1671.

The dominant influences on the semi-opera were the *tragédie à machines* and the *comédie-ballet*. Stage machinery and costumes were imported from Paris, and in 1673–4 Charles II even founded a Royal Academy of Music in London, tapping the expertise of Robert Cambert, recently ousted from the original Académie de Musique et de Danse by Lully. But this project failed after two or three productions, as did the king's earlier attempt to establish at court a small Italian opera company under the direction of Giulio Gentileschi. The most impressive English semi-opera of the period is *Psyche* (1675), adapted from the French by Thomas Shadwell and with a full score by Locke, his last major work. It is unlike any other semi-opera of the 1670s in that its musical scenes, while somewhat bombastic and inelegant compared with *Cupid and Death*, are carefully integrated into the plot; more important, Venus, the antagonist, both sings and speaks, thus pushing *Psyche* much closer to true opera than any other drama of its kind. Apart from Charles Davenant's *Circe* (1677), with rather feeble music by Banister, semi-opera died with Locke in 1677, not to be reborn until 13 years later.

The age of Purcell

During the 1680s extravagant stage productions were largely curtailed by political upheaval and financial constraints, with one notable exception. In 1683, after the royal succession had been finally resolved in favour of his brother the Duke of York, Charles II commanded a work in the style of Lully to celebrate his reign. After failing to engage the Paris Opéra itself, the king's agents recalled Grabu from exile in France to supply the music for *Albion and Albanius*, a highly allegorical libretto by Dryden, the Poet Laureate. Though this was his first attempt at continental-style opera, Dryden thoroughly understood the form, which he defined in the preface as 'a Poetical Tale, or Fiction, represented by Vocal and Instrumental

Musick, adorn'd with Scenes, Machines, and Dancing'. The king did not live to see the première and, when eventually performed in June 1685, *Albion and Albanius* failed, mainly because Monmouth's Rebellion occurred at the same time. The full score, published two years later, is strictly Lullian in concept and, in some passages, quality. This is its greatest limitation, for Grabu was generally insensitive to the nuances of Dryden's verse, which demanded both more and less than the constantly shifting metres of French *récit*. *Albion and Albanius* is still the most significant full-length opera produced in England before Handel, and the most neglected.

Purcell, the greatest English stage composer of this or any era, wrote only one true opera, *Dido and Aeneas* (1689), first performed at a girls' boarding school in Chelsea where dancing headed the curriculum. Nahum Tate's concise and underrated libretto was based on his heroic play *Brutus of Alba* (1678). Though not in the main English opera tradition, *Dido* was one of several court or school masques mounted in and around London in the late 17th century. It is closely modelled on Blow's court entertainment *Venus and Adonis* (*c*1682). Both works are three-act miniature tragedies with allegorical prologues (though the one for *Dido* is lost), include a prominent chorus and display similar key schemes centred on G minor, which is meant to symbolize death. Probably owing to the circumstances of the first performance, *Dido* has a high proportion of dances, but its most memorable piece is the Lament, which is built over a five-bar chromatic ground bass during whose final variation Dido dies. Many of the features shared by *Venus and Adonis* and *Dido and Aeneas* are found in few other operas – the ornamented and highly charged recitatives, the terse yet plastic airs, the unsentimental tragic endings. Both works are, however, heavily indebted to Lully, especially through the incorporation of choruses and dances into their dramatic structures.

Dido may have made little impression on Purcell's contemporaries (it was not revived during his lifetime), but it obviously opened doors for him at the professional theatre. Within less than a year of the inauspicious première, he was commissioned to write music for *Dioclesian*, a semi-opera based on *The Prophetess* by Massinger and Fletcher. The text was adapted by the actor Thomas Betterton, also the instigator of nearly all previous opera productions in London. This very successful work was followed in 1691 by Dryden's *King Arthur*, originally designed for Grabu in 1684 but then dropped in favour of *Albion and Albanius*. *King Arthur* is Purcell's only semi-opera not based on an earlier play, which perhaps explains its brilliant fusion of music and spoken dialogue, achieved (as Dryden explained) at the expense of the poetry ('my Art, on this occasion, ought to be subservient to his'). In 1692 Purcell composed the grandest of all semi-operas, *The Fairy Queen*, an anonymous reworking of *A Midsummer Night's Dream*. He did not set a single line of Shakespeare, instead confining the music to five self-contained masques, ostensibly performed to entertain Oberon, Titania and other characters in the play. Yet in a metaphorical sense the music replaces the lyric poetry cut from the adaptation.

After Purcell's death in 1695, the Theatre Royal continued to produce one or two new semi-operas each season. The most frequently revived of all semi-operas, Purcell's included, was *The Island Princess* (1699), adapted from Fletcher by Peter Motteux, with music by Daniel Purcell, Richard Leveridge and Jeremiah Clarke (whose famous 'Trumpet Tune' first appeared here as an entr'acte). While musically and dramatically inferior to most earlier works of this type, it was remarkably successful and may have encouraged the rival theatre in Lincoln's Inn Fields to stage the first professional performance of *Dido and Aeneas* (1700), adapted by Charles Gildon as a series of four masques inserted into *Measure for Measure*.

Anglo-Italian opera

Semi-opera was still in its heyday when the first opera 'after the Italian manner' was produced in London at the Theatre Royal, Drury Lane: *Arsinoë* (1705). Clayton, a mediocre composer apparently unimproved by travel in Italy, set Motteux's English translation of Stanzani's libretto of 1678 to a farrago of old Italian arias, a few original songs and (given his modest abilities) surprisingly idiomatic *secco* recitatives. In spite of Clayton's novel handling of the da capo form, wherein many arias were allowed to begin and end in different keys, *Arsinoë* was very popular and helped prepare the way in 1706 for an English-language version of Giovanni Bononcini's *Camilla*. With new recitatives probably supplied by Handel's future librettist Nicola Francesco Haym, but otherwise retaining most of the arias from the first production at Naples in 1696, *Camilla* helped give English audiences a taste for true, if slightly dated, *opera seria*. In fact, it proved to be the most enduring of all Italian operas performed in London during the 18th century.

The success of *Arsinoë* and *Camilla* was achieved at some cost to the English school of serious music drama. The playwright and architect John Vanbrugh, whose Haymarket Theatre (opened in 1705) remained the principal venue for Italian opera in London throughout the century, believed that spoken drama, *opera seria* and English semi-opera could share the same theatre. But as the swelling troupe of foreign singers demanded higher salaries, the Lord Chamberlain, who was empowered to license all public entertainments, realized that only a separation of operas and plays could prevent the collapse of both enterprises and restricted actors to Drury Lane and singers to the Haymarket. This sensible division nevertheless precipitated the extinction of the still popular semi-operas which, requiring both singers and actors, could not be performed at either theatre. Attempts at all-sung opera in English were not abandoned, but Clayton's *Rosamond* (1707), on a tolerably good libretto by Addison, was an abject failure, and John Eccles's setting of William Congreve's *Semele* (1706–7) was left unperformed in the wake of intense political manoeuvring. This was unlucky, for Eccles had single-handedly invented a viable English alternative to *opera seria* by adding the da capo to his repertory of aria types and by adapting *secco* recitative naturally to his mother tongue; but he also retained the measured, decorated recitative and the simple binary air styles of Purcell.

The Italianate operas that succeeded *Camilla* were pasticcios concocted by local theatre hacks and fitted with arias selected by visiting musicians such as the castrato Valentino Urbani and Haym. At first they were sung in a mixture of English and Italian; as more singers arrived from abroad, Italian predominated. *Thomyris* (1707), with a libretto by Motteux and music tastefully selected and arranged by Johann Christoph Pepusch, offered a wide variety of recent arias by Alessandro Scarlatti, Bononcini, Steffani, Albinoni and Gasparini, executed by some of the finest continental singers. Yet critics such as Addison, who were steeped in a tradition that revered dramatic unity and authorial integrity, ridiculed these polyglot pasticcios for their allegedly poor match between the music and its new English verse. They exaggerated. Motteux had a particular knack for fitting appropriate words to old arias, many of which had already come adrift from their original texts. But the lack of a presiding genius was also sorely felt, and in 1707 a committee of aristocrats headed by Lord Halifax invited Bononcini to leave Vienna for London. The composer of *Camilla*, which many English theatre-goers regarded as the epitome of Italian opera, declined the invitation.

The age of Handel
Similar importuning by the Duke of Manchester, British ambassador to Venice, may have persuaded Handel to travel to London in late 1710, though the exact circumstances behind the momentous invitation are unknown. It was a daring step to be taken so soon after the outstanding success of his Venetian opera *Agrippina*, for Handel was joining an inchoate and disorganized opera house fundamentally different from any he had encountered on the Continent. Without a significant government subvention and only token royal patronage (even after the accession of George I), Italian opera in London was forced to compete with well established and normally solvent acting companies, fiercely proud of their roots in Shakespeare. The friction generated by the two genres – intensified by a moralistic attitude, unknown elsewhere in Europe, that opera was essentially a business venture which had to pay its way – helped to form a distinctly English species of *opera seria*. In their best London works, Handel and other foreign opera composers discovered how to accommodate the audience's ignorance of the Italian language while simultaneously satisfying a desire for sophisticated plots and highly developed characters.

Handel seems at once to have appreciated that the style of *opera seria* then prevailing in Italy – with plots all but shorn of spectacle and comic elements, roughly equal measures of *secco* recitative and da capo arias, fashionable, flimsy and plainly orchestrated – would be unsuitable for London audiences. In general, he drastically reduced the proportion of recitative, even if the result was a patchy and incoherent plot. To his arias, which were already more richly scored and used more sophisticated ritornello structures than those of most of his Italian contemporaries, he gave even greater weight, to reflect actions and emotions which might have been more conventionally conveyed by recitative. Handel's first visit to London also felicitously coincided with a refinement of his harmonic language – a purging of 'irregular' dissonance and purple chromatics, mannerisms which were also shed by Scarlatti and other Italian composers at about this time. The arias in *Rinaldo* (1711), Handel's first London opera, regardless of their intrinsic quality, would have sounded clean and fresh compared with the rather stale fare offered by the pasticcios.

Rinaldo was shrewdly conceived and produced by the playwright Aaron Hill, one of the managers of the Haymarket theatre in 1711. Though it observed all the conventions of *opera seria* and was sung completely in Italian (to verses by Giacomo Rossi, a librettist of little merit), *Rinaldo* resembles a semi-opera in its scenic spectacle and magical effects; in fact several scenes are reminiscent of *King Arthur*. Handel drew extensively on works he had written in Italy, particularly *Rodrigo* and *Agrippina*, but most of the arias are thoroughly reworked and adapted to radically different verses and contexts. As in almost all his operas, there are a few unremarkable arias; but Handel stands above his contemporaries in consistently investing the dramatic highpoints with the finest music.

Rinaldo brought Handel instant celebrity but did little to lessen the precariousness of Italian opera on the London stage. Nicolini, Valentino, Pilotti and his other leading singers had short-term contracts, and they departed for continental spas at the end of each season with no assurance of re-engagement. While Italian opera was now acknowledged, even by its severest English critics, as providing a better synthesis of music and drama than was possible in Purcellian semi-opera, the newcomer had not found its niche on the London stage. This unsettled state of affairs is reflected in the choice of librettos for Handel's next four operas, a series of experiments to find an optimal format for presenting Italian opera to an English audience. The unsuccessful *Il pastor fido* (1712) is a pure pastoral, a genre that had never found much favour in England except when laced with satire; *Silla* (1713) is a political allegory, probably composed for private performance, and a rare musical failure; while *Teseo* (1713) and *Amadigi di Gaula* (1715) are both based on French librettos – the former, which recalls the magical-heroical style of *Rinaldo*, is a virtual translation of Quinault's *Thésée* and thus Handel's only five-act drama.

The Haymarket enterprise began to crumble in 1716. No Italian opera was offered in London between June 1717 and April 1720. Instead, English opera, which had made a promising but ultimately unsuccessful comeback in the form of Johann Ernst Galliard's *Calypso and Telemachus* in 1712 at the Haymarket, now enjoyed a more significant resurgence at Drury Lane and Lincoln's Inn Fields – theatres to which Handel himself was to retreat during the crises of the 1730s and 1740s. Purcell's semioperas were revived, and Pepusch composed a series of masques 'after the

Italian manner', of which the most important were *Venus and Adonis* (1715) and *The Death of Dido* (1716). (Handel's *Acis and Galatea*, composed in 1718 to words mainly by John Gay for performance – whether concert or staged must remain uncertain – at the Marquis of Carnarvon's country house at Edgware, belongs essentially to this tradition.) Bononcini's evergreen *Camilla* returned in early 1717, now hailed as 'an English opera'. Pantomime, musical interludes and afterpieces also developed during the temporary absence of *opera seria*. Coupled with plays, these 'monstrous medleys' or 'proto-ballets', as they have been variously described, sustained the native musical theatre until the advent of ballad opera in the later 1720s.

Under the auspices of the Royal Academy of Music (1719–28), an association of noblemen supported by the king, Handel produced a succession of great *opere serie*, the finest of the century. The new company was planned along different lines from continental opera houses, which were dominated by grand impresario-librettists, such as Pietro Metastasio in Vienna, who initiated productions, commissioned composers and engaged singers. While some members of the Royal Academy probably suggested themes and subjects and helped recruit singers, Handel was in overall control of his own works, almost all of which were based on much earlier librettos adapted and reworked under the eye of the composer himself. Apart from continuing to reduce *secco* recitative to a barely intelligible minimum, Handel made few concessions to the English audience. The librettist of the acknowledged masterpieces of the series – *Radamisto* (1720), *Ottone* (1723), *Flavio* (1723), *Giulio Cesare in Egitto* (1724), *Tamerlano* (1724) and *Rodelinda* (1725) – was the cellist, composer and erstwhile impresario of Italian opera in London, Nicola Francesco Haym. Whether he was instigator or merely amanuensis, these operas are sometimes admired for their frequent interruptions of the repeating pattern of recitative–da capo aria–exit. Accompagnatos, cavatinas, colourful symphonies and other inspirations often help to reinforce moments of dramatic intensity. In reality, these deviations from convention are probably no more frequent in the Royal Academy operas than in those of Gasparini, Vivaldi or Vinci. But Handel's genius for capturing every aspect of heightened emotion in melody, underpinned with rich and imaginative orchestration, naturally appealed to an audience that was largely incapable of following the verbal intricacies of a Metastasian drama. The operas set to librettos of Paolo Rolli – a talented but overbearing poet in the grand, continental tradition – are generally less successful. But even when yoked to this unsympathetic collaborator, Handel rarely failed to discharge the principal duty of any *opera seria* composer: to exploit the strengths of the available singers, as in *Alessandro* (1726), where the delicate balance which had to be maintained between the rival prima donnas Cuzzoni and Faustina happily influenced the plot.

Even so prolific a composer as Handel was not to be expected to supply all the works required for any one season; accordingly, the Royal

Academy also engaged Attilio Ariosti and (at last) Giovanni Bononcini, though Handel retained the right to direct and arrange the works of others not resident in London. Any notion of unpleasant rivalry between the house composers was largely in the minds of the opera-loving (and -hating) literati, though their different styles were topics for discussion. Bononcini, whose *Astarto* (1720), *Crispo* and *Griselda* (both 1721) were each more popular than any of Handel's Academy operas, was regarded as a master of the tuneful, pastoral style; Handel was admired for his heroics, particularly the portrayal of tyrants (though his operas span the gamut of characterization); and Ariosti, famous for his dungeon scenes, was considered to have a genius for *miserere*.

Undeterred by the failure of the Royal Academy in 1728, a result of internal squabbling and a loss of financial confidence on the part of the directors, Handel quickly formed a new company in partnership with the Swiss impresario J. J. Heidegger, who had been manager of the Royal Academy. In spite of many setbacks, the so-called Second Academy produced *Orlando* (1733), perhaps Handel's greatest opera. But he now faced internecine competition from the so-called Opera of the Nobility, founded in 1733 as a direct challenge to his dominion. Building the company round the great castrato Senesino, who had quarrelled with Handel, the Nobility directors engaged Nicola Porpora, one of the most celebrated opera composers of the time and, unluckily for Handel, an exponent of the new *galant* style. The Opera of the Nobility favoured Metastasian librettos, though somewhat tempered to suit English taste: for example, *Arianna in Nasso* (1733), the most successful of Porpora's London operas, had a higher proportion of accompanied recitative than did his continental works. When the legendary castrato Farinelli joined the Nobility troupe in 1734–5, Handel the opera composer was nearly vanquished, and both ventures failed in 1737. Though he wrote no more operas after *Deidamia* (1741), Handel's Italian arias, especially those which, in Burney's words, stand 'out of the reach of time and fashion', continued to be introduced into pasticcios until the end of the century.

Handel's gradual and reluctant withdrawal from *opera seria* was necessitated by financial worries, changing taste and the rise of the oratorio. He did not heed Aaron Hill's impassioned plea of 1732 to write an opera in English, and his setting of *Semele* (1744), in spite of any success with which this and other great oratorios have been transferred to the stage in the 20th century, must be regarded, with its added arias and choruses, as a disfigurement of Congreve's original libretto. The closest Handel ever came to contributing to the native tradition which his early London operas had nearly destroyed is the incidental music for Smollett's lost and unperformed play *Alceste* (1749–50), which was to have been an attempt to revive the Purcell–Dryden style of music drama – the true English opera.

CHAPTER V

Spain

JACK SAGE

Spanish opera grew, from the 1620s onwards, out of Italian models along lines similar to those in France. One particular reason for this was the presence in Madrid from 1625 to 1629 and again from 1644 to 1655 of the leading librettist in the Barberini circle in Rome, the papal nuncio to Philip IV, Giulio Rospigliosi (later to be Pope Clement IX). Another more general cause was the 17th-century clamour for novelty and excitement ('admiratio'). A third was the growing pressure on the monarchy, especially by the Conde Duque de Olivares, on the young Philip IV, to use the command play (in practice a *comedia de tramoyas*, 'machine play') as a means of promoting Spain's international prestige on the one hand and national solidarity on the other, for both diplomatic and socio-economic purposes. Lavish palace theatres, built of political necessity as perceived by ministers of the crown, and nurtured by Philip IV's evident belief in the value of the arts, soon gave rise to a stream of spectacular plays with music produced by nobles for predominantly aristocratic audiences, among them *La selva sin amor* (1629, text by Lope de Vega, composer unknown), an *égloga pastoral* in seven scenes, said to be the earliest Spanish drama completely set to music. Distinguished Italian designers and scenery engineers were bought in, occasionally with Italian composer-directors (as probably in the case of *Fortunas de Andrómeda y Perseo*, 1653).

The growth of Spanish opera, then, is inextricably tied up with the development in the court of partly sung music drama, the so-called zarzuela. In these command plays, whether designated as, for example, 'fiesta de la Zarzuela' or 'fiesta en el Buen Retiro' (the difference was at first one of locale, not of genre), music soon came to be regarded as an indispensable part of the apparatus of *admiratio*, although only about one tenth of the text was sung. Not surprisingly, therefore, the libretto of Spain's first wholly sung opera, *La púrpura de la rosa* (1660, libretto by Calderón, composer unnamed), a version of the Venus and Adonis legend, was later printed as a 'fiesta de la Zarzuela'. Plays with enough of the original music surviving to give an adequate idea of such 17th-century

47

zarzuelas are *Fortunas de Andrómeda y Perseo* (1653, librettist Calderón, composer unnamed) and Juan Hidalgo's *Los celos hacen estrellas* (1672, libretto by Juan Vélez). This and other extant material suggests that zarzuela music was from at least the mid-17th century Italianate, after the style of Cavalli, with a mixture of recitative-like monodies, duets and homophonic choruses (the lament on a ground bass did not find favour). As with the music for the one surviving full-scale 17th-century Spanish opera, Hidalgo's three-act *Celos aun del aire matan* (1660, libretto by Calderón), there are recitative passages leading to an aria or arioso and sometimes whole scenes in recitative style. Popular songs seem to have been used for the interludes between acts rather than worked into the music drama itself.

Composers and musicians involved in these command plays, though paid more as the century wore on, were less highly rated than the scenery engineers or the actor-managers. The instruments used, like those drawn upon for the performances of Venetian operas of the 1630s and 1640s, included violins, viols, theorbos, cornetts, high trumpets, sackbuts, shawms, drums and flutes; the instrumentalists were nearly all Hispanic. The librettist's job too stayed safely in the hands of Spanish writers, though both Lope de Vega and Calderón felt the need to protest at the way they found their texts mauled by the court's spectacle manufacturers. One playwright, Gabriel Bocángel, even had occasion to complain of being commissioned to write verse for a command play (*El nuevo Olimpo*, 1648) to pre-existing music. Such protests, grafted no doubt on to similar complaints by musicians, bore fruit: by the time full-scale opera was tried out on the Spanish court in 1660 (*La púrpura de la rosa* and *Celos aun del aire matan*), composers, librettists and producers, notably Hidalgo, Calderón and the Marquis of Heliche, had clearly managed to have their way severally and jointly. Consequently, for all the importance given to the visual side, in the end the names that most deserve to be inscribed on the foundation stones of Spanish opera are undoubtedly those of Calderón and Hidalgo. As *Celos aun del aire matan* shows, Hidalgo's music is as apt and impressive as Calderón's libretto is discriminating and thoughtful.

There can be little doubt that operatic music was well received by many at courtly and other social levels in 17th-century Spain: partly sung zarzuela, with its operatic type of music, proved a clear success throughout the 17th century (and beyond), and also there is evidence that long excerpts in recitative style were copied in songbooks as samples of popular songs. Nevertheless, apart from its one brief flourish in 1660, full-scale opera failed to catch on in Spain until the 18th century. Calderón blamed this on the Spanish 'choler' or temper, alleging that his countrymen found wholly sung opera boring and that they demanded the variety afforded by sung-spoken drama as in zarzuela.

CHAPTER VI

Staging

MANFRED BOETZKES, ROGER SAVAGE

1. Design

The early Italian perspective stage

The modern stage originated in the 15th and 16th centuries. It was indebted in many ways to ancient and medieval types of theatre; but its development can be fully explained only by reference to Renaissance culture. Humanism, in opening up a science and an art related to reality, made an essential contribution to the growth of the secular theatre alongside the sacred. The theatrical and musical interludes at the court festivities of the ruling families (farces, ballets, *intermedi* and concerts) did not yet require a stage set; but with performances of the classics or of works inspired by them there emerged an event aesthetically distinct from the other activities and necessitating a set as a separate unit of décor. Four factors are decisive in this: the influence of the staging of religious plays; the study of the ancient theatre, in particular that of Vitruvius (1st century BC), and his use as a model, for example for Palladio's Teatro Olimpico at Vicenza (completed 1585; see Plate 19); the discovery and practice of central perspective in the early to mid-15th century; and the theory and practice of contemporary drama.

Central perspective had a decisive effect on stage design by providing a scientific method of reproducing physical reality. It was distinguished from the perspective representation of antiquity and the Middle Ages by its central vanishing-point and the mathematical regularity of its 'visual pyramid'. Brunelleschi is considered its inaugurator, and its laws were first formulated in L. B. Alberti's *Della pittura* (1436). From illusionist painting a technique of large-scale perspective painting developed, notably the work of Bramante, facilitating the growth in the early 16th century of the painted backcloth, which could both depict a segment of reality and provide an image of an absolutist courtly social order. Based on central perspective, it revealed its full effect only to the occupants of the royal seats, who thus became the focal point of the performance.

The development of the perspective stage was influenced by the growth of an Italian dramatic art which, though dependent on the Latin classics, had also developed an aesthetic seeking to combine rational humanism with the realities of court life through a system of poetic rules. The conception of the perspective stage was favoured by the concept of 'plausibility', which linked the theatre with aesthetic and social norms. The rule concerning unity of place presupposed the existence of the perspective stage which, significantly, came into use in comedies conforming to the new aesthetic. Pellegrino da Udine painted perspective views of towns for plays by Ariosto given early in the 16th century at the court of Ferrara; similar town scenes were created by other artists.

Under Horace's influence, late Renaissance drama was grouped into three theoretical genres, each corresponding with a particular social stratum: tragedy (ruling classes), comedy (middle classes) and the pastorale, which developed from the satyr play (peasant classes). This related to Vitruvius's three types of décor; thus theatrical décor too was affected by a class hierarchy. Illustrations from *c*1540 represent scenes for tragedy and comedy as architectural backcloths showing aristocratic and middle-class buildings respectively and that for the pastorale as a landscape.

The Italian transformation stage
Attempts were made early in the 16th century to expand the painted perspective background into an illusionistic area containing the action. By the 1530s, perspective painting was extended from the back-cloth to four angular wings at the rear of the stage, marking the diagonal axes of the perspective. A next step was the use of rotating triangular prisms, painted on all sides, with a larger prism at the rear; by rotation, three different painted scenes could be presented, emphasizing the depth of the stage (see Plate 20). This was subsequently improved by the invention of machines for transformation effects. With the use of horizontally movable flats instead of prisms, the technique of stage transformation reached its peak at the beginning of the 17th century.

The advances in illusionist techniques also influenced the structure of court theatre halls. While perspective backcloths required merely a wooden scaffold at a suitable distance from the prince and the rest of the audience (generally in rising tiers), the more complicated transformation stages necessitated a proscenium frame which screened the theatrical machinery from the spectators and partly hid the lighting apparatus (candles, oil lamps). With the erection of a proscenium arch, as early as the 1560s, the spatial separation of the audience area from the stage was achieved, underlined by the curtain. Early 17th-century theatre architects made a space for the orchestra in front of the stage (Florence, 1622; Parma, 1627–8) and, following the example of the Renaissance courts enclosed by multi-storey galleries and tournament theatres, conceived the audience area as a construction of rows of boxes built vertically to each

Teatro Grimani a S Giovanni Grisostomo, Venice, built by Tomaso Bezzi for Carlo and Vincenzo Grimani and opened in *(renamed Teatro Malibran in the 19th century): engraving*

Interior of the Teatro Obizzi, Ferrara, after its reconstruction in 1660: engraving

3. Jacopo Peri's costume for the role
in the fifth intermedio for the comedy '
grina' by Girolamo Bargagli: sketc
nardo Buontalenti (Biblioteca M
Centrale, Florence)

4. Set for the second intermedio of the series framing Bargagli's comedy 'La pellegrina' performed in Florence in 1589 in hon
marriage of the Grand Duke Ferdinando I of Tuscany and Christine of Lorraine: engraving (1592) by Epifanio d'Alf
Bernardo Buontalenti's design

The first intermedio in 'La liberazione di Tirreno e d'Arnea' performed at the wedding of Ferdinando Gonzaga, Duke of antua, and Catherine de' Medici on 6 February 1617: engraving by Jacques Callot after Guilio Parigi

6. Peri's 'Euridice': prologue and beginning of the first chorus (p.2 of the printed score; Florence, 1600)

7. *Title-page of Caccini's 'Euridice' (1600), published in Florence by Giorgio Marescotti*

8. Design by Jean Berain for Lully's 'Armide' (Paris, 1686) in the Institut für Theater-, Film- und Fernsehwissenschaft, University of Cologne

9. The final scene from Lully's 'Triomphe de l'Amour': engraving by Daniel Marot after Jean Berain

...raving for Cambert's pastoral 'Pomone' from ...général des opéra', i (1703)

...ormance of Lully's tragédie lyrique 'Alceste' in the ...Marbre at Versailles on 4 July 1674: engraving ...by Jean Le Pautre

12. Design by Gaspare and Domenico Mauro for Steffani's 'Servio Tullio' (Munich 1686): engraving by Michael Wening

13. Stage design by Johann Oswald Harms for the first production of Keiser's opera 'Störtebecker und Jödge Michaels' (Ha 1701): pen and wash drawing (Herzog Anton Ulrich-Museum, Brunswick)

Prospect of Mount Philermus, designed by John Webb for 'The Siege of Rhodes' (Act 4 scene i), produced in 1659 by ...iam Davenport, London: pen and ink drawing

...awing by Sir James Thornhill for Act I scene i of Clayton's 'Arsinoë', London, Drury Lane, 1705; pen, ink and watercolour

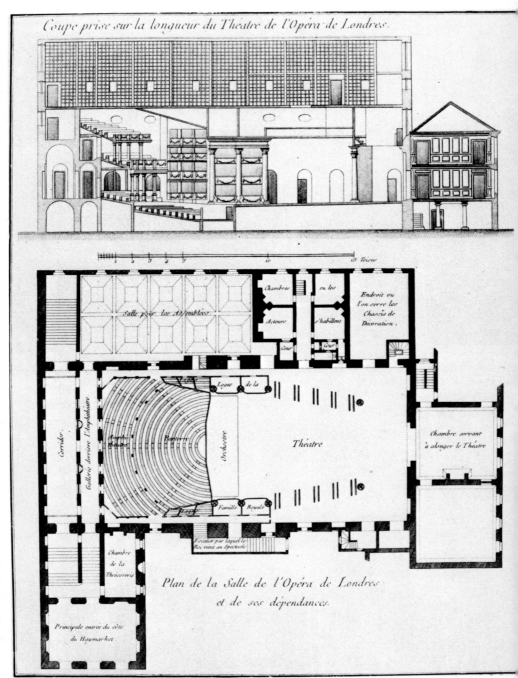

16. *Plan and cross-section of the first King's Theatre, London: engraving from 'Parallèles de plans de plus belles salles spectacles d'Italie et de France' (1774) by G. Dumont*

of a series of stage designs
Devoto which may have
missioned for the first pro-
of Handel's 'Ezio' at the
Theatre, London (1732)

scene from Handel's 'Flavio'
to show Gaetano Berenstadt
with Senesino and Cuz-
graving by J. Vanderbank

19. *Interior of Palladio's Teatro Olimpico, Vicenza*

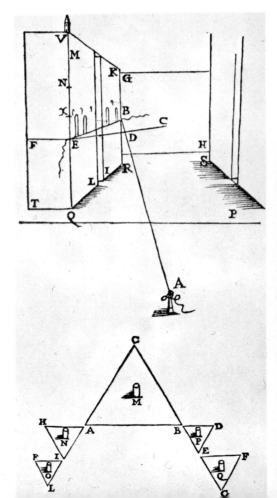

20. *Method of painting and shifting scenes with the use of five 'periaktoi' (rotating triangular prisms) as shown by two stage diagrams by Egnatio Danti in Barozzi da Vignola's 'Le due regole della prospettiva pratica' (Rome, 1583)*

Set for Landi's 'Sant' Alessio', probably designed by
Lorenzo Bernini, Rome, Palazzo Barberini, 1632
1634: engraving by F. Collignon from the libretto
4)

22. 'Camera' for Cavalli's 'Hipermestra' (Act 1 scene
ix) designed by Ferdinando Tacca, Florence, Teatro degli
Immobili, 1658: engraving by S. degli Alli from the libretto

23. *Moving cloud scene (with stage machinery, right) from Legrenzi's opera 'Germanico sul Reno', first performed at the Teatro S Salvatore, Venice, in 1676: pen and ink drawing, with wash, in the Bibliothèque de l'Opéra, Paris*

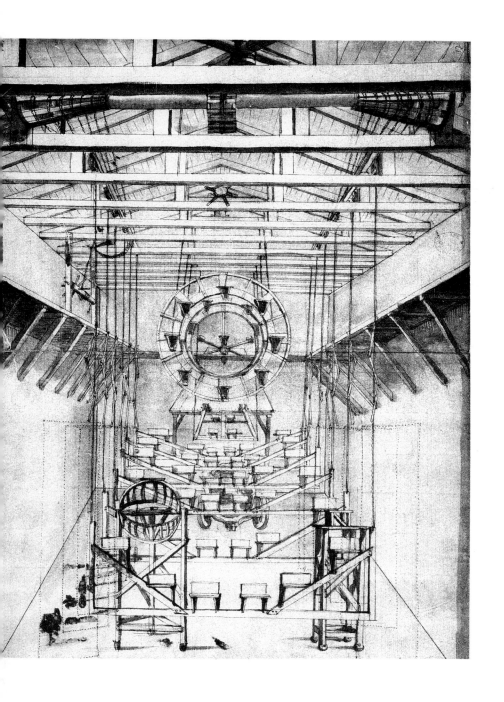

24. Engraving by Matthæus Küsel after Burnacini's design for prologue of Cesti's 'Il pomo d'oro' (first performed 1 July 1668)

25. Interior of the theatre in Vienna built for the marriage of Leopold I and Margherita of Spain, during the performa Cesti's 'Il pomo d'oro' in 1668: engraving by F. Geffels

other, on a groundplan at first right-angled and later horseshoe- or bell-shaped (see Plates 1 and 2). This emphasized the privileged position of the princes, on the central axis of the perspective, and the 'parterre noble' around them. Stage design and theatre construction were discussed in numerous 16th- and 17th-century books that elucidated and refined the laws of perspective and their application.

In the evolution of theatrical machinery, Italian scenography attempted to do justice to a dramatic art which in the late 16th century increasingly suppressed plausibility in favour of the 'marvellous'. To display a 'marvel' – something contrary to nature but also credible and even, with divine intervention, plausible – was seen as the essence of drama from the mid-16th century. It was only logical that writers should thereafter ascribe the introduction of the catharsis in drama primarily to the stage marvels produced by the designers and machine technicians. The prestige of the 'marvellous' in late 16th-century theatre was based on its appropriateness in absolutist courts, where mythological and allegorical subjects mirrored the social structure. The main vehicle for the 'marvellous' was the musical *intermedio*, which accompanied dramatic presentations at court and became a spectacular genre which impressively communicated the rulers' power; this is exemplified in Buontalenti's décor, machines and costumes for the Florentine *intermedi* of 1586 and 1589. Corresponding with the Platonist texts by Bardi and the music by members of the Camerata, Buontalenti drew on mythology to pay homage to the Medici, creating a sequence of symbolic stage sets (temple, garden, forest, sea coast, underworld, Mount Olympus) metaphorically linking court life with the life of the gods.

Opera, developed shortly afterwards, was staged according to the same principles. The performance of Caccini's *Il rapimento di Cefalo* in the Teatro Uffizi (1600; décor by Buontalenti) showed that the *stile rappresentativo* could easily be combined with the ostentatious style of the *intermedio*. Offering a conjunction of all the arts cultivated at court festivities, opera took over the representative function of the *intermedio* at many Italian courts during the early 17th century. It brought on to the stage pastoral and romantic subjects, even themes from the lives of the saints; and an extension of the principles of scenography was introduced, using new motifs of architecture and landscape, in the stage sets of Ludovico Cigoli (Peri's *Euridice*, 1600, Florence), A. M. Viani (Monteverdi's *Orfeo* and *Arianna*, 1607 and 1608, Mantua), Giulio Parigi (Marco da Gagliano's *La regina S Orsola*, 1624, Florence), Alfonso Parigi (Gagliano and Peri's *La Flora*, 1628, Florence), Francesco Guitti (Monteverdi's *Mercurio e Marte*, 1628, Parma; Michelangelo Rossi's *Erminia sul Giordano*, 1633, Rome, and *Andromeda*, 1638, Ferrara), Alfonso Rivarola (Sances's *Ermiona*, 1633, Padua), G. L. Bernini (Landi's *Sant'Alessio*, ?1631, Rome; see Plate 21) and G. F. Grimaldi (Cecchini's *La sincerità trionfante* and Marazzoli's *La vita humana*, 1638 and 1656, Rome). Despite the concern for greater variety, operatic stage design in the early 17th century clung to the concept of unity between court auditorium and stage: its 'marvels' remained firmly tied to the world of the court and to iconographical tradition.

With the opening of the first public theatre (S Cassiano, Venice, 1637), opera production entered a new phase. It became a commercial enterprise counting on the interest of the prosperous middle classes; composers such as Monteverdi, Sacrati, Cavalli, Cesti and Legrenzi created a form of drama that endeavoured to cater for the new public with subjects not previously treated, mostly taken from history. The spectacular success of Venetian opera was based also on the contributions of stage designers and machine technicians such as Alfonso Rivarola, Giuseppe Alabardi, Giovanni Burnacini and Giacomo Torelli. Most of these artists had worked at court and adapted its methods to the new conditions of production, which differed in the diminution of the role of machines and the 'marvellous' to a merely entertaining function. Venetian stage design brilliantly varied the traditional formal principles and exploited the artistic possibilities of central perspective focussing at infinity. At the same time its importance for European stagecraft lay in its ingenious innovations, above all the technique (developed by Torelli) of simultaneous scene changes and the creation of indoor scenes, suiting the small ensemble at the Venetian opera. This type of acting area, already used by Torelli and Burnacini, became for the younger generation – Francesco Santurini, Ippolito Mazzarini and the Mauro brothers – a basic but variable means of construction, and increased in importance as mythology and machine-produced effects largely lost their meaning. Contributing to a more precise representation of court society, the atriums, halls, cabinets and bedrooms reflecting contemporary court interiors indicate a new level of realism, although in Venetian opera historical subjects, like the mythological ones, still served to exemplify courtly virtue. The bounds of scenic realism were also determined by the economic conditions of operatic production: a paying public not only made possible a more realistic stage representation but also enforced (in the sets, the music and the libretto) a reduction of expressive means to the 'typical'; the opera impresario had to regard his theatrical outfit – a supply of universally applicable sets and costumes – as a fundamental business requisite in order to offer a maximum of entertainment and splendour at an acceptable price.

In Italy, stage designers, notably Ferdinando Tacca, Gaspare Vigarani, Giacomo Cipriotti and Girolamo Fontana, took up the ideas suggested by Venetian practice and developed them in the context of court theatres. As a feature of absolutist courtly culture and of the Jesuits' Counter-Reformation propaganda, the Italian perspective stage spread throughout Europe in the late 16th and early 17th centuries; by 1650 at the latest it was well known, even outside princely residences, as numerous popular graphic publications, like the illustrations in J. A. Comenius's *Orbis sensualium pictus* (1654), indicated.

North of the Alps
In France, after a few early experiments (Andrea Nannoccio, Lyons, 1548; Cosimo Ruggieri, Nantes, 1596), the perspective stage was successfully adapted for the *ballet de cour* by the Florentines Tommaso and Alessandro Francini from about 1610 and further developed by Georges and Denis Buffequin. It was given decisive new impetus by Torelli, who went to Paris in 1645 with Mazarin's opera troupe. Torelli's successor Gaspare Vigarani (in Paris from 1659 and the co-beneficiary of Lully's operatic privilege from 1672 to 1680), with his son Carlo, inaugurated the characteristic stage design of Louis XIV's Académie Royale de Musique; as opposed to Venetian opera's gestures towards realism, it sought to preserve the domination of the 'marvellous' with formalized architectural and landscape backcloths and with accomplished mechanical artistry; this conservative conception of the theatre also influenced Vigarani's successor Jean Berain, who designed over 80 productions from Lully's *Cadmus et Hermione* (1673) to Campra's *Les fêtes vénitiennes* (1710).

The princely residences of the German-speaking countries may have been familiar with the Italian perspective stage by the late 16th century. It began to flourish with the cultivation (delayed by the Thirty Years War) of Italian opera in the 17th century. Often German artists who had worked in Italy introduced new ideas: J. W. Baur, who in 1627 presented the most recent Italian stage techniques at the Viennese court; Joseph Furttenbach of Ulm, a pupil of Parigi; and the writer G. P. Harsdörffer, whose *Frauenzimmer Gesprechspiele* (1646) contributed to the popularization of the new type of stage among the middle classes. In 1651 Giovanni Burnacini, one of the most important Venetian designers, went to Vienna. His son Lodovico, active at the imperial court for over 50 years, inaugurated a style of stage presentation using a Baroque multiplicity of forms and stupendous machines; among his most notable designs were those for Cesti's *Il pomo d'oro* (1668) and Draghi's *La monarchia latina trionfante* (1678).

As a result of the willingness of Venetian stage designers in Germany such as Francesco Santurini, the Mauro brothers and Tommaso Giusti, and German designers such as Kaspar Amort, J. A. Gumpp, Elias Gedeler and J. M. Kletzel, to meet the representational requirements of the courts, this style became obligatory for Italianate musical theatre at German princely residences in the late 17th century. Only in the northern and central German opera houses with strong middle-class influence (Hamburg, Brunswick, Wolfenbüttel, Hanover, Leipzig etc) could a realistic type of design be developed, together with German opera, towards the end of the century; its most important representative was Johann Oswald Harms, who designed sets for numerous operas by Kusser, Steffani, Krieger, Keiser (notably *Störtebecker und Jödge Michaels*, 1701, Hamburg), the young Handel and others.

While on the Continent the perspective stage was used in public theatres, in Jacobite and Stuart England it remained a court preserve. In 1605, for a performance in Oxford of a pseudo-antique sequence of dramas for a visit by James I, Inigo Jones designed for the first time in England stage décor painted in perspective. Subsequently he adopted the perspective stage in his court masque designs where, especially after his journey to Italy (1613–15), he conceived the stage as an illusionistic space on the Italian model, realized with stage machinery that he developed to suit the genre. In the pared-down, topographically precise stage designs of his pupil John Webb for the operatic ventures of Davenant (*The Siege of Rhodes*, 1656), the puritanical spirit of the Commonwealth was manifested (see Plate 14). Stage design in the Restoration period, of which the chief representatives were Isaac Fuller, Robert Streeter and Thomas Stephenson, developed both at court and in most public theatres a largely French-influenced theatre of machines which, judged by visitors from abroad, came up to current European standards.

Like stage design, costumes were adapted to formalist aesthetics, summarized by Michel de Pures (*Idée des spectacles anciens et nouveaux*, 1668) in the concept of 'convenance': costume designers were not only referred to the symbolism of contemporary allegorical iconography but were also bound to a typification corresponding to the social status of the person represented; this proved to be fruitful and stimulating. The costumes of the Florentine *intermedi* and operas, the Piedmontese court ballet, the *ballet de cour*, the English court masque and the German court ballet, masquerades and operas show that the court theatre of the 16th and 17th centuries depended much for its effect on the ostentatious display, variety and originality of its costumes. The move towards historical subjects led in the later 17th century to social typification increasingly becoming the central requirement of 'convenance'; it was natural that court dress, primarily on the French model, should become the basis of the hero's costume. This could be modified by historical additions and accessories to suit the taste of the wearer, but it appeared in only three basic forms: the 'Roman' (for ancient history and mythology), the 'Spanish' (for more recent subjects) and the 'Turkish' (for exotic subjects).

2. Production

Princely opera: the 1590s to the 1640s

The courtly Italian opera of the 1590s to the 1640s saw itself as a multimedia entertainment. 'In such affairs the music is not everything', as Gagliano put it as early as 1608 in the preface to his *Dafne*; it had to be unified pleasurably with plot, language, musicianship, gesture, dance and décor. If the show that resulted was to move the audience's passions as it should, each of these things needed to be excellent in its kind: something stressed also by Alessandro Guidotti in his pioneering preface to Cavalieri's *Rappresentazione di Anima, et di Corpo* (1600). Success could be achieved only by careful preparation, which might be lengthy (Monteverdi claimed that his *Arianna* was five months in the rehearsing from the day the cast had their music by heart until the first performance, in 1608) or much brisker (Vitali stated that the libretto for *Aretusa* was not even begun until 44 days before the opera's première in 1620).

For such a complex enterprise to be entirely harmonious and successful called arguably for the universal genius of a Gian Lorenzo Bernini, whom the diarist Evelyn described in 1644 as having supplied the words, music, scenery, stage machinery and even theatre design for one opera (Bernini was a skilled actor who would rehearse his own comedies by demonstrating all the roles to his casts). Failing that, an early opera in rehearsal required either someone on the spot to organize and integrate the talents of the various artists involved or someone to have supplied clear written precepts as to how it was all to be done. There were venerable precedents for such organizers and preceptors: in the theatre of the ancient Greeks, for example, where (according to Athenaeus) Aeschylus had taken the whole management of his tragedies on himself; in the sung Latin liturgical dramas of the early Middle Ages, with their rubrics for costume, gesture and psychological states; and in later vernacular religious plays, their performance often rigorously controlled by *maîtres de jeu* like Jean Bouchet of Poitiers or such *conducteurs de secrets* as the compilers of the detailed performance-book for the Mons *Mystère de la Passion* of 1501.

Among other early forebears were the Mantuan stage manager and lighting expert Leone de' Sommi, who wrote dialogues on his craft in the 1560s; the dancing-master and violinist Balthasar de Beaujoyeulx, who conceived a *Balet comique* at the behest of Queen Louise of Lorraine, contracted out its versification, music and décor, and then supervised the staging at Paris in 1581, also writing the official record of the event; Angelo Ingegneri, who because of his 'aptitude at arranging and directing tragical matters' was put in charge of the production of *Edipo re* (with Andrea Gabrieli's music) which opened the Teatro Olimpica at Vicenza in 1585, and who in 1598 published the essay *Del modo di rappresentare le favole sceniche*, taking *Edipo* as its chief example; and Cavalieri, who as overseer of arts and artists to the Medici supervised the practical realization of the influential Florentine *intermedi* of 1589, as well as choreographing to his own music their final *ballo*, the steps of which are minutely documented in an account of the occasion.

Operatic production grew from all this. Cavalieri himself almost certainly saw to the stagings of *Euridice* in 1600 and of his own *Rappresentazione* the same year, as well as passing on instructions for 'those who want to stage this work or others like it' through Guidotti's preface to the latter. It was in this tradition that the princely operas of the 17th century were mounted; Gagliano's detailed but undictatorial suggestions for subsequent stagings of *Dafne* included in the preface are similarly steeped in this tradition, as are the various sections treating operatic production (notably Chapter 15) that appear in an anonymous manuscript treatise *Il corago*, dating from about 1630 and tentatively ascribed to Ottavio Rinuccini's son Pierfrancesco. (The treatise defines a *corago* as someone charged with coordinating, advising and animating all the artists necessary for the successful staging of a dramatic work: something of a blend of the modern impresario, director and stage manager. *Coragi* occasionally appear in other Italian stage treatises over the next hundred years, and find their transalpine equivalent in the *maître de l'ordre*, the functionary whose activities M de Saint-Hubert, in *La manière de composer et faire réussir les ballets*, 1641, sees as vital to the success of the *ballet de cour*.)

If the organization of early operatic production followed a tradition, so in all likelihood did opera's earliest staging techniques. To exemplify from Monteverdi's *Orfeo* (1607), precedents for its visual and histrionic aspects are to be found in various late 16th-century Italian entertainments: the courtly ceremonial and choric movement of its Act 4 underworld scene could be traced back to the Vicenzan *Edipo re*; its rustic costumes and dances to Renaissance humanist pastoral dramas like the several staged at Florence in the early 1590s; its movable scenery, infernal costumes, practicable boat for Charon and descending cloud for Apollo to the 1589 *intermedi*; its lighting effects (if it had any) to the work of de' Sommi at Mantua; and its style of acting in dramatic monody to a tradition of performance to be seen, for instance, in the musical interludes of Bombasi's spoken tragedy *Alidoro* of 1568, where one performer came to the front of the stage and sang in a persuasive manner closer to speech than to song, 'altering the expression in her face and eyes, and her gestures and movements, to accord with the changes in the meaning of the words she sang'.

Just how detailed and sensitive early operatic acting could be may be gathered from Gagliano's suggestions for the staging of the prologue to *Dafne*: the singer's movements unfussy but pointful, relating clearly but not mechanically to the music. Vitali's tribute to the histrionic skills of the singers in his *Aretusa* – their faces expressive of sincere passion, their vivid, graceful and natural gestures embodying the meaning of the libretto – underlines the fact that true acting (as the late Renaissance understood it) was required from opera singers, not mere standing and chirruping: acting moreover that could range in its mode from the hero's tragic soliloquizing in the last act of *Orfeo* to the antics of such *commedia dell'arte* clowns as Zanni and Coviello in the Roman *Chi soffre speri* of 1639. Ingegneri and de' Sommi had both stressed the importance of expressive movement and eloquent gesture in spoken drama, and the author of *Il corago* maintains that this applies equally to performers in opera, who should regard any specific operatic skills as additions to such things, not substitutes or alternatives. The specifics of opera in his view include the two rules (both breakable if need be) of making an unhurried entrance to downstage centre before first singing, and of subsequently moving about the stage during instrumental ritornellos and continuo flourishes, not while one is singing. He adds recommendations to keep gesture as broad and slow as the music requires, to position oneself on the stage naturally rather than forever gravitating towards the centre, and to avoid looking so directly at one's interlocutor that one's face cannot be seen by the audience. He sees more operatic potential in good actors with passable voices than in expert singers with little acting talent; but he allows a role for the latter as supernatural beings, since as such they will have had most of their stage movement done for them by the machinist who devises the descending clouds, airy chariots and mechanical monsters they ride on. This would leave the stage floor free for such really skilled principals as those singled out for praise earlier in the century: artists like Antonio Brandi, the omnicompetent shepherd-messenger in Gagliano's *Dafne*; Guidobaldo Bonetti, the castrato noted for his *travesti* impersonation as the chaste nymph Flora in *Aretusa*; and Virginia Ramponi, the actress from a *commedia* troupe who took over the role of Monteverdi's Ariadne at the last moment and melted all hearts in her Lament.

Supporting the principals were the *comparse* (silent supernumeraries), the chorus and the décor. The *comparse* are much in evidence in the accounts of the proto-operatic *Edipo re* of 1585 (when there were over 60 of them), while in *Il corago* they are sometimes vividly engaged in battle scenes, which they have been taught by a fencing-master, and sometimes graciously granted ample stage space by principals playing royalty in ceremonial scenes. Cavalieri, Gagliano and the author of *Il corago* also follow on from *Edipo* in their treatment of the chorus: its size ranging from four to 24, its acting respectful and responsive to the principals, its movements often synchronized carefully and forming geometrical patterns but executed with a graceful naturalness avoiding any suggestion of a regimented *corps de ballet*. As for the stage machines and perspective scenes, care was needed to relate these properly to the action. With scenery, opera singers must have tried to follow de' Sommi's advice not to linger near the illusionistic perspectives as that destroyed their verisimilitude; while with machines Cavalieri insists that they should be moved only in conjunction with music of an appropriate tempo, and *Il corago* stresses that they should move very slowly when the supernatural beings aboard them are singing. Décor was nevertheless much honoured by early writers on opera as an integral part of the multi-media show, whether on the small scale of Gagliano's congratulating Cosimo del Bianco for devising an easy way for Apollo in *Dafne* to wreathe a laurel crown on stage, or on the grand scale of the tribute to the machinist Francesco Guitti in the preface to the printed score of *Erminia sul Giordano*: 'a gentleman whose excellence in inventing, ordaining and operating machines and scene changes was attested by universal amazement and applause'.

The Venetian and Parisian axes: the 1640s to the 1690s

The expansion of Italian operatic activity in the later 1630s to include the public and commercial had its shop window in Venice, where a paying citizen found himself for the first time able to see production methods long established behind private courtly doors. Accounts of the Venetian *An-*

dromeda of 1637 and *Bellerofonte* of 1642, for instance, celebrate their spectacular scenic *changements à vue* and machine apotheoses, glittering costumes and stylish acting, *travesti* impersonations of goddesses and nymphs by castratos alongside the acting of female roles by women, their crowds of well-dressed, well-drilled *comparse*, their frighteningly realistic monsters and sophisticated dance interludes. For the next 40 years, intrigued visitors to Venice like John Evelyn, Robert Bargrave, Philip Skippon and Limojon de St Didier were to write of the opulence of the grander opera houses, the number of operas being staged at one time, the outstanding voices of the 'select eunuchs and women', the cries of 'cara' and 'benissimo' from the boxes, the impudence of the gondoliers in the pit, the common practice of buying a libretto at the door and a candle to follow it by (without which 'even those of the country would hardly comprehend anything of the composition'), the 'antics and masquing dances', the 'incomparable apparitions and motions in the air', the 'curious representations and fair perspectives', and the shock of finding how coarse and tawdry the scene painting and costume jewellery could look from close up when they had been so convincing 'at a good distance and by candlelight'.

In these 40 years commercial and courtly opera, from Naples to Vienna and beyond, developed a wide spectrum of scale and finesse in performance: from the productions by small companies who toured the Italian cities much in the manner of itinerant *commedia dell'arte* troupes to grandiose and prestigious events like Melani's *Ercole in Tebe* at Florence in 1661 (where 40 pages of the souvenir word-book are taken up with a breathless account of its many splendours, among them a well-conducted battle between two 30-strong armies of *comparse*, all named) or Cesti's *Il pomo d'oro* at Vienna in 1668 (where the 24 souvenir engravings of Burnacini's sets during performance illustrate the culmination of the 17th-century tendency to impose a strong axial symmetry on performers as well as scenery; see Plate 24). Yet a unified approach to acting in opera – and one the author of *Il corago* would have approved – probably continued in favour until at least the 1670s. The 'sung-play' nature of Monteverdi's Venetian operas and of many by the Cavalli–Cesti school, with their brisk action, mercurial moods, complex plots, flexible monodies, functional airs, telling ritornellos and strong forward movement, still presupposed a cast of performers for whom good acting of a sort appropriate to contemporary spoken drama was as important as good singing.

However, 'the bizarre tastes of the city and the extravagant temperaments of the singers', about which the librettist Aurelio Aureli complained in 1673, had begun by then to add to the length, complexity and potential for vocal display of the arias and consequently to threaten the homogeneity of the acting style and reduce the librettist's firm hold over the composition. In 1699 the Sicilian dramatist Andrea Perrucci points out in his *Dell'arte rappresentativa* that librettists have only a minor share in operatic glory, the greater part going to the machinists, dancers and singers of arias. But he goes on to stress that, apart from voice production and note learning, an opera singer's craft is just the same as a speaking actor's. Perrucci is as insistent as earlier preceptors on the expressive use of head, eyes, arms and body (deriving much of what he says from the teachings of classical rhetoric), and on a clear frontal presentation of character as the performer advances from the wings. In discussing his particular phobia of collisions in the wings between actors making entrances and those making exits, he suggests that one of his two preferred ways of avoiding these – entrances from behind an upstage flat, exits as close as possible to the proscenium arch – is of special value to the opera singer, who can thus leave from the front of the stage just after the last words of an exit aria. His other idea for avoiding collisions is that someone, doubtless the *corago*, should number the entrance spaces between flats and provide each performer with an accident-proof, personal sequence of numbers. It is a system which appears earlier in a surviving manuscript of Rospigliosi's libretto for *Dal male il bene*, along with very detailed notes for scene changes, props and sound-effects, all presumably for the use of Rospigliosi's nephew, who collaborated backstage at the Roman première in 1654.

There are few glimpses of a fully-fledged director figure in action in later 17th-century Italian opera. This is presumably because *coragi*, stage crew and prompters coped unobtrusively with most backstage *minutiae*. Singers now needed little basic instruction in presenting the sort of roles they were likely to be called on to perform; machinists could connive directly with the singers who used their machines; dancing- or fencing-masters took charge of any complicated ceremonies, battles and the like; and the composer and librettist were probably on hand at rehearsals to give any further needful advice. Librettists were certainly involved with staging, and a function like the modern director's might well be included *ex officio* in the librettist's. Printed librettos could be full enough of directorial points to serve as a blueprint for performance: Matteo Noris's text for Legrenzi's *Totila* (1677), for example, averages three to four directions per page on matters of movements, asides, emotional states, props and machines. Significantly, among the published records of Rospigliosi's extensive activities as librettist and man of the theatre in Rome, there is only one clear reference to anyone acting as 'the director who instructed everyone at rehearsals' for any of his operas, and this is to his nominee Lodovico Lenzi in connection with the première of *La comica de cielo* in 1668, by which time the librettist had become Pope Clement IX and was presumably too busy directing Christendom to be involved.

By contrast, the presence of the director at his most absolutist is strongly felt in French opera in the 1670s and 80s, working to the greater glory of the absolutist Louis XIV. While Lully did not quite have the universal genius of a Bernini, he put a great deal of the genius he did have – 'un talent extraordinaire pour tout qui appartient aux spectacles' (Le Cerf de la Viéville) – into opera. He directed his operas at the Palais Royal theatre both musically and dramatically. By the time he acquired control of the Académie in 1672, Paris had for several years been enjoying a golden age of tragic and comic playwriting and acting in the spoken theatre. Lully was clearly determined that opera should not suffer in comparison, and to this end he seems to have pushed one stage further the techniques of rehearsal by firm instruction and practical demonstration (which his former colleague Molière depicts himself using in his *Impromptu de Versailles*, 1663). According to Le Cerf, Lully would instruct his casts as to their entrances, moves and proper deportment, sometimes showing a performer every gesture of his role and demonstrating in person the pantomimic parts of his inset ballets. Only people with specific jobs to do in areas beyond even Lully's competence were admitted to rehearsals, during which the composer would teach and rebuke his performers, 'staring at them with his hand over his eyes to help his short sight'. As for the style of acting at the Palais Royal, it is likely that Lully urged his casts to study the grave momentousness of the tragedians in Racine at the Hôtel de Bourgogne, since he is said to have modelled his recitatives on the declamatory accents of one of them, 'La Champmeslé' (Marie Chevillet).

The subtle construction of Lully's operas, with their symmetrical use of ceremony, celebration, machine epiphany, orchestral symphony, weighty declamation, brief *air* and (in the earlier ones) light relief, arguably required a firmer and heavier single hand in the staging than would have been used for operatic production in Italy at the time. That structures almost as complex could be staged without such extreme centralization, however, is demonstrated by the part-spoken 'semi-operas' or 'dramatick operas' of the English Restoration, especially the collaborative *Tempest* of 1674 and the four produced between 1690 and 1695 with music by Purcell. Three of these latter were mounted at the Dorset Garden Theatre in London by a company headed by the actor Thomas Betterton, with Purcell in charge of music, Josias Priest as choreographer and Betterton himself (who had seen Lully's theatrical work in Paris) as animator and presumably general coordinator. The company consisted of actors, of whom most had some singing ability, and their fairly friendly rivals the tribe of Restoration stage singers and dancers, accustomed to taking small supernumerary parts in spoken comedies and tragedies as well as doing inset turns of their own. English theatre companies were kept on a fairly loose rein by their managers in rehearsal, though they were prepared to take advice from authors when this was available and sometimes bowed to an authority figure set over them. For instance, Betterton himself (who is credited with the elaborate 'Art of Playing' which appears in Charles Gildon's biography of 1710) was once paid 50 guineas by the managers of the company to look after rehearsals 'in the nature of a monitor in a school' and a further £50 'for his care and trouble to get up *The Indian Queen*', Purcell's last semi-opera. But an awful warning against too dictatorial a production method was on hand in the Duke of Buckingham's comedy *The Rehearsal* (1671), where all the attempts of the protagonist Mr Bayes to dominate the staging of his own mixed-media extravaganza only serve to make a bad thing worse.

However, Lully's centralization of Parisian opera did establish a major, long-lasting tradition of the mounting of a fixed canon of pieces, something barely known in Italy or England. By securing a copyright, insisting on uncut performances, having his scores printed, staging revivals and training a generation of performers, he made his work a national institution and monument. His most distinguished leading lady, Marthe le Rochois (who created several Lully heroines as well as appearing in the premières of works by Charpentier and Campra) can stand as the *fin de siècle* opera singer *par excellence*. Though not especially prepossessing in her appearance offstage apart from her large and fiery eyes, she was able to rivet spectators in performance as much by her sheer presence, physical control and *jeu muet* as by her voice. The rich emotional variety she brought to her roles was especially apparent in Lully's *Armide*, where she held audiences breathless in her scene in Act 2 with the sleeping Renaud. One English theatre-goer thought her 'not inferior to Mrs Barry herself', Elizabeth Barry being one of the greatest actresses of Restoration spoken drama, admired by Betterton for her way of 'living' a part on stage. That Le Rochois' approach also involved a degree of identification with the characters she played ('Tâchez de vous figurer que vous êtes ce que vous représentez', as Molière put it) is illustrated by the anecdote of her trying to convince a pupil of the need to dig deep psychologically when rehearsing *tragédie lyrique*. 'What would you do', she asked, 'if you were abandoned by a lover you adored passionately?' 'Take another', was the pupil's reply. 'In that case, mademoiselle', said Le Rochois, 'we are both wasting our time'; and the lesson was terminated.

Entr'acte I

STANLEY SADIE

It may be useful to consider, at this point, something about the expectations of someone attending an opera during the 17th century or the 18th, and in what ways his experience in the theatre would differ from ours today.

First, of course, he must gain admittance to the theatre. That was not always simple. In Venice, from 1637 onwards, or in Naples during much of the late 17th century, or in Hamburg from 1678, he could simply buy a ticket. But many opera performances in this period were private, and he could be admitted only as a guest of a princely patron or of a member of the court, or by special invitation. In France, the Parisian could pay to hear the operatic performances to which, at Fontainebleau or Versailles, only the court was admitted; or, by the early 18th century, he could pay much less and hear lighter works with spoken dialogue done at the Fair Theatres. The Londoner could buy tickets to attend the twice-weekly performances at the main opera theatre, where Italian opera was given; if he was a rich and well-connected person he might be a subscriber, with a right to seats at every performance. At the more middle-class English one he could simply buy a ticket at the door. The division between types of theatre persisted throughout the 18th century: court theatres that were wholly or largely private; court-run theatres, at which anyone correctly dressed (in some cases) or ready to pay (in others) would be allowed entrance; and public theatres, run by impresarios – optimistically – for profit.

Our imaginary opera-goer would be drawn to the opera house partly to hear the performance and partly because it was an important social centre. He might have been attracted by the handbills, which would tell him the title of the opera and possibly the name of the librettist and composer, or by the reputation of the singers. As he entered the house, he would have the opportunity to buy a little book (*libretto*) containing the words of the opera – probably rather roughly and hastily printed, as the book would have been produced quickly to serve each run of performances. In it he would find a title-page and probably a dedication to a patron, then a prefatory essay with an 'argument' (*argomento*) that explained the background to the plot and might include the librettist's apology for adjusting historical fact to make a better story. There would also, as in a modern programme booklet, be a list of the evening's singers (but no producer or director would be named: the role was unknown). Then would follow the text of the opera. Some words might be shown with inverted commas (and accordingly called *versi virgolati*) to indicate that, although part of the poet's text, they would not be sung. Where the words were not in the local language, it was normal for the book to show the sung text and a translation on opposite pages. Opera houses were illumined by candles, which were kept burning throughout the performance, and often there were individual candles by the seats so that members of the audience could readily follow the text (many surviving librettos show candlewax marks). This also enabled the listener to see in advance when his favourite singers would be appearing, so that he could absent himself (perhaps for a conversation or a meal) during the passages he did not mind missing. We know, from contemporary sources and the habits of seat ownership and usage, that many opera-goers would go to hear the same opera several times over. This was partly because opera-going was a social matter, and the opera house an important centre for meeting and talking to friends; also, it was only through repeated attendance that the opera-goer could deepen his knowledge of the music (unless he was a performer, in which case he could buy and sing, or play on the keyboard or the flute, the 'favourite songs' from the opera, which for a reasonably successful one would at once be published, at least in the main commercial centres). In any case, no two performances would be quite the same, particularly as, in many types of opera, the leading singers were expected to embellish their music, and part of the attraction with a good performer was to hear him or her do it afresh each night.

Once inside the opera house, the opera-goer might note its size – seating 400 or fewer in a small, court opera house, perhaps close on a thousand in a large public one and double that or more by the end of the 18th century. Most of the seats would be in tiers of boxes, with a fairly modest-sized open area, the pit (where the orchestra stall would be today), containing some seats or benches. The cheapest seats would be in the gallery or the pit; in some theatres it was customary to admit the waiting footmen there for the last act of the opera. Not all houses follow this pattern; Drottningholm, the Swedish court opera house built in 1766, has few boxes but many rows of benches.

There was rarely a sunken orchestra pit. The orchestra sat at the main floor level, hard by the stage. In the early days it might be very modest in size: in Venice, in the 1660s, Cavalli had five string players with three keyboard instruments and two plucked continuo instruments. But Lully, in Paris, had six violins, twelve violas and six cellos, five woodwind, two trumpets, drums and harpsichord in the 1670s and 80s (increased by 1704 to 35 strings). A Milanese theatre early in the 18th century had strings approximately 9.9.8.3.3, with six oboes, two bassoons and harpsichord, while Handel in London had approximately strings 12.10.2.3.2, with woodwind 2.2.0.3, two horns, two harpsichords and a lute. The Naples theatre orchestra in the middle of the 18th century also had a strong violin complement, with strings approximately 14.14.5.2.4, woodwind 0.4.0.2, with trumpets as needed, drums and two harpsichords; Hasse, though Neapolitan-trained, had a quite different balance at Dresden, 8.7.6.3.3, with woodwind 0.5.0.5, two horns, trumpets and drums as needed, and two harpsichords. At the same time the Paris Opéra orchestra had strings 8.8.6.7.5, woodwind 4.4.2.8, and pairs of horns and trumpets with drums and one harpsichord. The preference for two harpsichords in Italian opera is explained by the use of one for recitatives and the other for the *maestro* in the arias and ensembles; also, recitative dialogue may have been paralleled by dialogue between the harpsichords. The arrangement of the orchestra varied according to local preferences (and acoustics), but most commonly there were rows of players across the width of the theatre, usually one with their backs to the audience facing another with their backs to the stage; one harpsichord would be to the left and one (the director's) central, with bass instruments close to each.

What sort of work would the opera-goer expect to hear? In a court opera house, it would probably be a newly-composed work, possibly by the chief court composer, or perhaps by a visitor. It would have been written for the specific team of singers who were performing it. If originally composed for some court celebration, such as a name day, a birthday, a birth or a wedding, it might well be not what we would call an opera but rather a *festa teatrale*, *azione teatrale* or *serenata*, a work with a modest amount of dramatic action, probably of an allegorical kind (praising the prince by comparing him to a classical hero, for example, and perhaps embodying some reference to the event being celebrated). It would be sung in Italian, unless we were in Paris. If it were a true opera, it would probably be on a mythological or classical historical theme, or possibly one from medieval history or based on the writings of Tasso or Ariosto (occasionally, in Germany especially, religious themes are found). Early Venetian operas, before the last quarter of the 17th century, usually incorporated comic scenes for servants (the elderly, amorous nurse, sung by a tenor in *travesti*, was a favourite) or peasants; so did opera elsewhere in Italy up to the turn of the century, and in Germany rather later, when as a result of 'Arcadian' reform operatic texts acquired a more literary quality. The comic scenes were expelled, but found their way back as intermezzos to divert the audience in intervals. Ballet was an alternative diversion, preferred especially in France.

By the 18th century, however, comic elements had more important a place in public opera houses than in court ones. Here commercial factors dictated that a maximum audience be attracted. The opera-goer in Venice, Naples or London, during much of the 18th century, would expect to hear on most of his visits to the theatre not an integral work by a named composer but a composite one, a 'pasticcio', put together in such a way as to include several favourite arias well suited to the available singers. This could be made up by the house music director from an existing work, by the substitution of a number of arias; or it could be a collection of the singers' favourite pieces with new items supplied by the house music director; or it could be an assemblage of arias to which a house librettist would fit a new text; or it could be based on a given plot outline, into which existing arias would be fitted at appropriate points and new ones supplied by the house composer where none could be found. The pasticcio dates back to the late 17th century; one opera given at Milan in 1694 has 27 named composers. With the repertory of standard texts that had developed by the 1740s through the ascendancy of Metastasio, the procedure became easier, and the domination exercised by singers at that time, castratos especially but also sopranos, fostered it. For smaller, provincial opera houses using visiting singers, the pasticcio including popular arias offered obvious benefits. Among the opera houses outside Italy where pasticcios were particularly favoured, besides London, were those at Hamburg, Brunswick and Brussels.

In the retrospective light of today's aesthetic, the pasticcio may seem an inartistic genre, at best. But the public of the 18th century accepted it without demur, as indeed did all the most eminent composers of the time, as a fact of theatrical life – Handel, Vivaldi, Hasse, Gluck, Haydn, Mozart and numerous others were in some way involved with pasticcio procedures. The unity of an opera was neither guaranteed by its being a work of one composer nor precluded by its being the work of several; and a good pasticcio, artfully assembled, could satisfactorily embody the kinds of characterization, contrast and balance that should belong to any opera.

The pasticcio process was applied most usually to *opera seria*. It was common too in the intermezzo, increasingly in *opera buffa* and in non-Italian genres. The English ballad opera and the French *comédie mêlée d'ariettes*, which incorporate popular melodies, are akin to the pasticcio though not strictly examples of it. The pasticcio flourished during most of the 18th century, but died out early in the 19th, except as an occasional procedure, in the face of the establishment of a standard operatic repertory and the aesthetic outlook of the Romantic era.

Our opera-goer in a commercial or provincial theatre, then, might well expect to hear a work including music by several composers. His first interest, however, was likely to be in the singing. If the opera was a serious one, in Italian, he could expect to hear a cast of about six or seven, of whom at least two would normally be castratos; there might be no true male voices at all, though the tenor became popular in the early 18th century (usually as a king or a father) and there are many minor roles for bass (generally as a military man or a confidant, occasionally a villain). The audience's main interest focussed on the primo uomo and the prima donna (usually in that order), who commanded far higher fees than the supporting singers and sang more, more varied and more virtuoso arias; the number assigned to each singer had to be carefully calculated by librettist and composer according to his or her place in the hierarchy.

Audiences seem to have been unconcerned as to whether a male part was sung by a man, an emasculated man or a woman in *travesti* (and occasionally, notably in Rome where women were periodically banned from the stage, whether a female role was taken by a castrated man). The roles of heroes or lovers were almost always taken by castratos, the best of whom – like the incomparable Farinelli, or Senesino (Handel's Julius Caesar) or Guadagni (Gluck's Orpheus) – had voices of remarkable power, penetration and agility and great intensity of expression. Tenors were not normally assigned heroic roles until late in the 18th century, when the castrato was beginning to fall into disfavour in some parts of Europe.

In comic opera, the singers, at least in the early part of the century, were regarded as less important, at least in purely vocal terms; acting ability, however, counted certainly for no less than it did in serious opera. The patterns of casting were less rigid. A comic opera would normally include a *primo buffo* (a baritone) and a *prima buffa* (soprano), and probably a tenor (in a comic role or as a lover); castratos appeared in some Italian *opere buffe* but played a part much less central than in *opera seria*, and were unknown in comic opera in languages other than Italian. In the *dramma giocoso* type of opera that developed soon after the middle of the century, mainly from the example of Goldoni and Galuppi in Venice, there were serious parts (*parti serie*), usually a pair of noble lovers, as well as *parti buffe* and sometimes also in-between roles (*mezzo carattere*, 'half character'), usually assigned to a soprano or mezzo-soprano and a baritone. Mozart, asking in 1783 for a comic libretto, specified seven characters, including two female ones, one *seria* and one *mezzo carattere*, of equal importance, and a third that could be entirely *buffa*, as could all the male parts.

The patterns found in Italian *opera buffa* are to some extent reflected in the vernacular comic forms found elsewhere in Europe. French serious opera, however, did not follow the Italian *opera seria* patterns. In France, castrato singing was abhorred and stricter ideas of dramatic verisimilitude prevailed: male voices – including that of the *haute-contre*, a high tenor or countertenor – were always used for male roles, and, in a country (and indeed a musical style) where vocal skills were much less readily isolated from dramatic ones, there was no place for the rigid vocal hierarchy of Italian opera which could be so inimical to the drama.

The main Italian forms of opera, both *seria* and *buffa*, dominated the opera houses of Europe except in France – though even there the primacy of French opera was repeatedly challenged by visiting Italians throughout the 18th century, most notably (or most noisily) in the pamphlet war known as the 'Querelle des Bouffons', involving such men as Rousseau, Diderot and Rameau, provoked by the performances in 1752 of Pergolesi's *La serva padrona* by a visiting troupe. Serious opera, as a matter of course, was in Italian in the German-speaking countries (though there exists a handful of serious German-language operas), England, the Iberian peninsula, Scandinavia, Poland and Russia. Many of the leading

Italian opera composers wrote works for Vienna, London, Dresden or St Petersburg as well as for the main cities of their own country. During the second half of the century *opera buffa* tended to overtake it in importance, but outside Italy local, vernacular comic genres were by that time well established: Singspiel in Germany and Austria, comic opera in England and zarzuela in Spain, as well as *opéra comique* in France. *Opéra comique* had older traditions, and had from time to time been exported – to a number of German courts, to the Bourbon court at Parma, to Vienna under Maria Theresa (where Gluck had been involved in the performance and composition of *opéras comiques*) and to Catherine the Great's court at St Petersburg. The plots favoured in these vernacular forms were all of much the same general type, related, or similar, to those of the *commedia dell'arte*: many treat such stock figures as the oldish man duped by the sharp young girl he desires and her young lover, or the townsman or village squire who vainly tries to seduce the virtuous village girl. The rural flavour, reflected in the music, is attuned to the prevailing, idealized Enlightenment view of Nature and the good, simple life. Many comic operas also embody parody of court opera, with its stilted characters and conventions; frequently, too, there is a marked element of social criticism, directed at the behaviour of the ruling classes (the treatment of Count Almaviva in Mozart's *Le nozze de Figaro* is an obvious example) and the manners of *nouveaux riches*.

The 18th-century opera-goer could be fairly sure that he would leave the opera house happy. The convention of the *lieto fine* ('happy ending') was almost universal, in serious opera and *tragédie lyrique* as well as the lighter forms: lovers are regularly reunited, villains are frustrated, clemency is exercised, poisoned heroes or heroines are discovered to have drunk the wrong (or right) draught and return to life. It was not merely a matter of leaving an audience in a state of contentment. Rather it had to do with reflecting the essential optimism of the society and reinforcing its values: its belief that noble and honourable behaviour should be duly rewarded and that justice should prevail, either at the hands of a benevolent ruler or by divine intervention (the *deus ex machina*) – thus encouraging a continued faith in both the institution of monarchy and established religion. There are of course exceptions: it was beyond even Metastasio to find a way of making a happy ending out of Aeneas's abandonment of Dido (the subject of one of his most admired librettos), though it did prove possible with the tale of Orpheus, in Gluck's opera, through a second divine intervention (which to us may seem rather lame). It is of course significant that, while serious court opera was bound to support the existing institutions, spiritual and temporal, through its allegorical meanings – sometimes made explicit in a final *licenza* (usually an extra aria in praise of the qualities, analogous to those of the hero of the drama just enacted, of the prince or other patron) – the more popular forms of opera often embodied a subversive political flavour in their depiction of the ruling classes.

PART TWO

Pre-classical and Classical Opera

CHAPTER VII

Italy

DANIEL HEARTZ, CHARLES TROY, MICHAEL ROBINSON

1. *Metastasian serious opera*

Dramaturgy

The *opera seria* libretto originated in the Arcadian neo-classical reform of Italian literature of the late 17th century. By purging the libretto of comic elements and its Baroque extravagance of characterization, expression and incident, and by imparting to it a regularity of construction (such as the observing of the three unities and the function and placing of the arias), the reformers sought to subject the libretto to the rules governing and distinguishing the classical literary genres, defined by the neo-classical theorists. Since no classical genre existed for opera, this 'reform' was in fact an attempt to force opera into the genre of tragedy. In this it was only partly successful: frequent scene changes and the use of amorous intrigues as important plot elements, for example, were too deeply ingrained to be removed, but the attempt, by forming the libretto along primarily literary lines, resulted in the restriction of the music's role in dramatic development

The early manifestations of this reform appear in the work of Zeno and other poets at the beginning of the 18th century, and came to fulfilment with Pietro Metastasio (1698–1782). Educated in the milieu of the Arcadian Academy at Rome, Metastasio was imbued with the classical ideals of clarity, dignity and purity of style and with an essentially optimistic and conservative view of a hierarchic social order. His rational approach to the libretto, beginning with *Didone abbandonata* (1724), dealt the final blow to the 17th-century extravagances of plot and language (see the comparisons in Burt, 1955) and produced a greater concentration on diction and characterization. That meant relying not on myth and fable but on historical subjects – those of the ancient world. Yet scarcely more than the names of his heroes and heroines came from history, for they nearly all became involved in the same *galant* intrigues, with resulting moral dilemmas, in situations concocted by the poet; with few exceptions, they emerged triumphant and purified. Metastasio's critics charged that he merely rewrote the same drama over and over again under different names, but that judgment disregards his success in creating an individual poetic tone in his best works, for example the Arcadian pastoral ambience in *L'Olimpiade* (1733).

With regard to dramatic structure, Metastasio merely capitalized on the situation he found. Economic conditions in the mainly commercial houses of Italy militated against any great outlay of funds for spectacle. Opera had become a vehicle for great singers; their vocal abilities were of paramount interest to the public, a situation that encouraged composer and librettist alike to concentrate on their arias. The result could as well be called 'aria opera' as 'opera seria'. It was Metastasio who, following Zeno's example, standardized the position of the aria at the end of the scene, invariably culminating in the singer's exit (although minor characters could leave the stage without an aria or remain after having sung one). The rhythm of the drama thus settled into an alternation between recitatives in *versi sciolti* (freely intermixed, unrhymed seven- and eleven-syllable lines), for argument and action, and arias in strophic verse for reaction, reflection and peroration. Given these conventions the poet's musical-dramatic options were narrow. All the more astonishing therefore is the virtuosity with which Metastasio rang the changes on audience expectation. For example, the first word in *Artaserse* is 'Addio!', spoken by the hero Arbace to his beloved Mandane and arousing the expectation that after their recitative dialogue he will take leave of her with an aria – but the last word of the dialogue, another 'Addio!' is had by Mandane, who then sings the aria and makes her exit.

There were usually six or seven characters, consisting of the trio of primo uomo (castrato), prima donna and tenor (for the parts of fathers, kings etc), on whom the most and best arias were lavished, and a secondary group, the secondo uomo (also a castrato), seconda donna and whatever other voice or voices the plot required. These singers, usually less well paid than the first group and of considerably lesser vocal ability and interest to the audience, had to be satisfied with fewer arias and less dramatic weight. It was the poet's task to space out the arias for each singer (four or five in the case of the leading parts) and to ensure that ones in the same style did not follow each other. Here again Metastasio's virtuosity far exceeded that of his predecessors or successors. The da capo aria was inseparable from *opera seria*, constituting its very touchstone. Repetition of the entire main section, da capo, after a shorter subsidiary section provided an opportunity for singers to show their skill in improvised ornamentation, culminating in a grand final cadenza. The musical form thus developed in answer to the needs of the time.

Metastasio's position as the greatest Italian dramatist of his age, reinforced by his standing as the greatest Italian poet, by the stability of the society that his works reflected and by the absence of any serious rival, led to his domination of *opera seria* until near the end of the century, although most of his important works were completed by 1740. Paradoxically, this popularity helped bring about a neglect by audiences of the dramatic side of opera. The fashionable part of the audience, who customarily owned boxes or rented them by the season, attended night after night. Since the season consisted of a few works, each given a continuous run of up to several dozen performances, the audience could scarcely have been expected to take a close interest in the action after the first few; and since the literate part of it knew Metastasio's dramas virtually by heart, they could dip in and out, interrupting the social intercourse to attend to the most affecting scenes or the favourite arias of the leading singers. From this resulted the audience's noisiness and inattention, so often remarked by foreign visitors.

Metastasio's most popular librettos were given new musical settings by dozens of composers in successive generations. Stylistically, these composers can be separated into three groups, constituting three ages of *opera seria* (by analogy with Vasari's three ages of Italian painting).

1720–40

Although *opera seria* acquired its definitive literary and dramatic form only during the 1720s, many of its musical characteristics were present earlier. Alessandro Scarlatti had led the way in the development of aria forms, and by simplifying his accompaniments, so putting more emphasis on the melodic line. This he did while continuing to intermix many arias in the older style. The transition is evident from a comparison between two of his operas, *Ciro* (1712, Rome) and *La Griselda* (1721, Rome). In the former, minor-mode arias with rapidly changing harmonies predominate, and the binary key scheme that was to underlie the *A* sections of the later da capo aria still had only a weak hold in the major-mode arias. In the latter, the old style co-exists with a newer type characterized by static bass lines and a slower rate of harmonic change.

Excluding Handel, whose operas, written mainly for London (see Chapter IV), lie off the mainstream of the Italian tradition and had little or no influence, the dominating figures of the first age were Vinci, Leo, Porpora, Hasse and Pergolesi, who followed Scarlatti (if indeed the older of them did not teach him) in pursuing the new, more clearly articulated melodic style. Their style was perceived as a departure at the time and long afterwards; its success carried their music not only all over Italy but also throughout Europe. Vinci was credited with a major role in forming the new style, especially as regards periodic melody, with balanced (often three-bar) phrases; this legend grew around him in the decades after his death. His settings of Metastasio for Naples, which began with *Didone abbandonata* for Carnival 1725 and concluded with *Artaserse*, completed shortly before his death in 1730, proved epoch-making. The dimensions of his arias were modest compared with what came later, and in perfect harmony with Metastasio's mellifluous verses. Algarotti (1755) praised the last act of *Didone* for its wealth of obbligato (or orchestrally accompanied) recitative, including the final lament, and recommended it as worthy of emulation. Vinci coined the *abb'* phrase (Weimer, 1984).

Hasse, who set *Artaserse* for Venice during the 1730 Carnival, when Vinci's was composed for Rome, invites comparison with Vinci. Hasse was then the more adventurous, in his use of ritornellos, his fondness for subdominant harmonies and his accompaniments, which struck contemporary listeners as richer (though he rarely departed from the prevailing three-part texture). Although best known for his limpid cantabile, Hasse was also a born dramatist. His inserted scene for Artabano to end Act 2 of *Artaserse* raised the expressiveness of orchestral commentary to new potency in the obbligato recitative, which was also closely tied to the aria by motivic and harmonic means.

Pergolesi's setting of Metastasio's *L'Olimpiade* (1735, Rome) is the Arcadian opera *par excellence*. The passionate aria 'Se cerca, se dice', which also illustrates his mastery of periodic phrase structure, long remained popular, while the degree of lyric intensity that Pergolesi attained in the love duet at the end of Act 1 was as consequential for its genre as his much better-known successes in the comic style. Dent (1906–7), contrasting Leo's *L'Olimpiade* (1737, Naples) with Pergolesi's, found Leo's textures more solid and old-fashioned and his melodies, while well constructed and remarkably free of *fioritura*, lacking the tuneful charm and theatrical sense of Pergolesi's.

For all these composers the primary problem in putting together an opera of 25 or more arias was that of contrast. Metastasio's fine control and subtle variety of moods helped solve it. Departures on the composer's part, such as the dropping of the ritornello, as well as the singer's improvised decorations, accomplished still more. Instrumental colour remained fairly uniform and minimal. Metric variety was limited. The keys used rarely went beyond three accidentals, resulting in recurrences of the more popular ones (e.g. D major for bravura, D minor for rage, E♭ for pathetic affects, G minor for lyrical yearning, G major for pastoral tone, A major for amorous sentiment, etc). The result was a loose stringing together of many individual numbers, rather than an organic unity; efforts in achieving the latter were made only slowly and fitfully.

1740–70

The second age of *opera seria* was similarly dominated by Jommelli, Hasse, Galuppi, Traetta, G. F. de Majo, Perez, Terradellas and J. C. Bach, most of them Neapolitan or Neapolitan-orientated. The careers of Gluck and Graun ran parallel with it. Several of the most important composers worked outside Italy, and this period was marked by the diffusion of *opera seria* and its associated styles throughout Europe. Hasse carried the perfected form to Germany in the 1730s and was long *maestro di cappella* at Dresden. In 1749 Jommelli and Galuppi, at the turning-points of their careers, were called to Vienna, Majo and Traetta later to both Vienna and Mannheim. Jommelli began his long reign at Stuttgart in 1754.

In adapting their style for foreign courts, these composers resorted to increasing elaboration of the basic ingredients, still supported by Metastasian dramaturgy. Somewhat more use was made of obbligato recitative in place of the simple continuo-accompanied kind (*secco* or, properly, *semplice*). The arias became longer and more complicated. Instrumentation and dynamic contrast became more varied and important. Metastasio himself remonstrated with Jommelli on the luxuriant growth of display.

Jommelli, the commanding figure, was already transforming *opera seria* during the 1740s, before his foreign visits. The first act of his *Merope* (1741, Venice) ends with a scene including chorus, obbligato recitative and ballet. The main characteristics of his later style were present in his early operas: the introduction of declamatory elements into the arias, the exploration of orchestral sonorities (including four-part textures) and the development of the crescendo and other dynamic contrasts.

Towards the middle of the century a greater prominence began to be given to ensembles, tending to diminish the number of arias but without threatening their preponderance. Ensembles were often created by telescoping several aria texts. When Galuppi, perhaps the only composer of this period as gifted, as prolific and as widely recognized as Hasse and Jommelli, set *Artaserse* for Vienna (1749), the last five scenes of Act I were collapsed into a single quartet, a dramatic action piece in F minor – the first of a new breed. When *Artaserse* was given at the opening of the new opera house at Padua in 1751, Galuppi scrapped this quartet and restored the arias. He may have been unwilling to chance such a departure with the Italian public; but more probably the singers would not tolerate an ensemble in place of their arias. The well-regulated and varied operatic theatre that Algarotti sought to promote was much more possible, as he himself noted, in the great authoritarian capitals – the court-sponsored spectacles of Berlin, Dresden, Vienna, Paris and St Petersburg – than in the mainly civic enterprises of the Italian towns or London, where circumstances often favoured the use of composite works.

The most important operas of Majo and Traetta came after 1760, as did the operas of J. C. Bach. Traetta seems to have gone further than any of his contemporaries, except Gluck, in controlling long time-spans by a careful marshalling and contrasting of tonalities. His more important works were created outside Italy or for Italian courts where French influence was strong (Parma, Turin), and, as with Jommelli, a trend towards incorporating features of *tragédie lyrique* can be discerned. Calzabigi and Gluck depended so greatly on French traditions in their reform operas that these works cannot be considered as Metastasian serious opera. Where the Metastasian aria plan remains the basis, albeit revised and updated by the addition of choruses, ensembles, orchestral tone-paintings, ballets etc, the rubric remains appropriate: thus Mozart's *Mitridate, Lucio Silla, La clemenza di Tito* and even *Idomeneo* still qualify. In his catalogue of works Mozart described *Tito* as an 'opera seria reduced to a true opera by Signor Mazzolà' (who revised Metastasio's original).

Parallel with the relaxation of Metastasian structure was a gradual modification of da capo form; the use of 'dal segno' often indicated only partial repetition of the main part. The fashion for the da capo waned at different times in different places. When J. C. Bach wrote his two operas for Naples in 1761–2 he depended exclusively on the full da capo; writing for Turin (*Artaserse*, 1760), he also used various abbreviated forms. In Hasse's last collaboration with Metastasio, *Ruggiero* (1771, Milan), only six of the 16 arias used the full da capo. The arias necessarily became fewer, for their average length had more than doubled since the days of Vinci and Pergolesi.

1770–1800

Around 1770 a stylistic break is apparent on several levels, one that condemned most of the mid-century composers to rapid oblivion. The last works of Hasse and Jommelli, composed for Italy in the early 1770s, were not particularly successful, while Galuppi wrote his last serious opera in 1772, 12 years before he died. Traetta spent most of his years after 1770 in St Petersburg.

The major figures replacing them were Piccinni, Sarti, Sacchini, Anfossi, Salieri, Paisiello and Cimarosa, and, among non-Italians, Naumann, Haydn and Mozart. There was some overlapping of generations: Piccinni, for example, had long been active. These composers were melodists in a more modern style, using a greater variety of aria forms including a new popular favourite, the expressive rondò (a two-tempo aria, slow–fast). A change to longer but simpler melodic periods went together with a certain blandness of rhythm and harmony, changes clearly calculated to please mass audiences. Grandiose orchestral and choral effects were increasingly cultivated.

The interpenetration of elements from *opera seria* and *opera buffa* can be found throughout the century. Another source of alloy, deleterious or serving to strengthen through diversification, according to one's point of view, was French opera, which continued to make inroads during this period. Until the last decade of the century the dramas of Metastasio prevailed, but to serve these new trends they had to be extensively revised and provided with ensembles, choruses and more spectacle. Further, one may note in their musical settings an increasing falling out with the spirit, and even the sense, of Metastasio's simple aria texts. His genius had lain in fitting the musical idiom and formal proportions of the generation of Vinci and Pergolesi with poems that matched them to perfection. By the late 18th century the music of the average aria had become so long as to make for an intolerable amount of verbal repetition. Some Italians working outside Italy had early adjusted their methods to please their mainly Gallic-orientated patrons, notably Jommelli and Traetta.

Salieri's *Armida* (1771, Vienna) also illustrates this revisionist approach to Metastasian dramaturgy. It has only four characters and a mere ten pieces that can be firmly identified as arias; some of these include choral responses. The music reflects many lessons learnt from Gluck, but Piccinni may also have been one of the models, particularly for the blurring of the boundaries between aria and recitative. Most of these recitatives are obbligato, although *recitativo semplice* is still used, throwing the obbligato into relief. The dances interspersed throughout the score suggest that the choreographer, Noverre, must have controlled the stage production in the French manner, not just the entr'actes as in Italy. Several musical features however reflect the pure Italian tradition, including an *aria di bravura* in D major for the bass and the use of Eb major with its full Neapolitan pathos and sensuousness.

Sarti's *Giulio Sabino* (1781, Venice), one of the most successful operas of this period and one of the few to be printed in full score, shows how composers when writing for an Italian public continued to rely mainly on the aria and on Metastasian principles. There is no chorus; ensembles are restricted to a duet at the end of Act 1, a trio at the end of Act 2 and the traditional 'coro' of soloists to end the opera. Most of the dialogue remains in simple recitative, although Sarti made good use of obbligato recitative at points throughout the score. Each singer has one full aria in Act 1 and one in Act 2; the keys do not go beyond three accidentals, and little large-scale tonal planning is evident. Most of the arias are in binary form, and some are quite short. Multi-tempo arias with a stringendo effect occur several times, following the fashionable rondò; as was usual, Sarti allowed rondòs only to the primary characters, here the *prima donna* and *primo uomo*, reserving the *primo uomo*'s for the penultimate scene, where it forms the dramatic and musical highpoint and turns into a short *presto* duet.

Opera seria continued to enthral the Italian and many other publics during the 1780s and 1790s, and even after; conditions, however, were rapidly changing. The hold of Metastasio's librettos weakened in the 1780s and by the 1790s they were no longer dominant. A steady supply of new librettos was now required, and one of the main sources was found in French librettos and plays. The increasing attraction of the 'merveilleux' of French-style subjects was evident even in conservative Naples in such works as Cimarosa's *Oreste* (1783) and Paisiello's *Fedra* (1788). A concomitant penetration of French musical techniques, probably by way of Gluck, is seen in these and similar works, while the enormous vogue of ballet in Italy during the last third of the century opened another avenue by which French personnel and dance music reached Italian awareness. This influence coincided with the social and political turmoil produced in Italy by the French Revolution, culminating in the French invasion of 1796 and engendering a climate in which Metastasian opera in anything like its original form was ever more out of place. At the same time the principal composers of the preceding period – Cimarosa, Sarti, Paisiello, Guglielmi – were dying or falling silent, replaced by a group of new and mostly lesser names, like Mayr or Generali. No real break in continuity can be pointed out, but a new era in Italian opera had begun.

2. Comic opera

The intermezzo

The term intermezzo was used in the 18th century, generally in its plural form *intermezzi*, for the comic interludes sung, in the intervals between the acts of an *opera seria*. Works of this kind played an important part in the diffusion of the Italian comic style in France around 1750.

Although the form and content of the operatic intermezzo were not fully standardized before about 1700, the practice of emphasizing the division of acts with musical and scenic interludes in the manner of the Renaissance *intermedio* figured in the earliest monodic dramas of the 17th century. As the century progressed, *intermedio* ballets and associated scenic spectacles became increasingly grotesque, often including participation by an opera's comic servants. By about 1700, however, as a result of the Arcadian reform of opera librettos, scenes involving comic characters began to decline in number and gravitate towards the ends of acts in *opere serie* at Naples and elsewhere in Italy (except, significantly, in Venice, where such episodes had declined by about 1670). These comic scenes, true ancestors of the 18th-century operatic intermezzo, most often consisted of bawdy horseplay resulting from the efforts of one of the opera's stock characters, a lascivious old nurse (frequently played by a tenor), to force 'her' attentions on another operatic stereotype, the young manservant. Just before 1700, less grotesque – if no more varied – plots appeared, in which an old man pursues a younger woman with amorous intent. Music for comic scenes from operas dating from about 1700 by Alessandro Scarlatti and others already exhibits hallmarks of the Italian *buffo* style – lively declamation, constant repetition, elements of parody, musical onomatopoeia and patter songs.

Gradually the comic scenes, rather than the dancing and scenic transformations sometimes associated with them, came to be labelled 'intermezzi', although the designation 'scene buffe', together with the incorporation of the comic servants into the opera's principal action, persisted at Naples until after 1720. More common elsewhere was the practice of separating completely the subject matter and *dramatis personae* of the *opera seria* and those of the intermezzo, so as to permit the latter's performance with a variety of serious works. The first substantial quantity of such dramatically independent comic intermezzos was published at Venice from 1706, including a number of subsequently popular librettos such as Pietro Pariati's *Pimpinone* and *Parpagnacco* (both 1708) and the anonymous *Zamberlucco* (1709). Attributions in the surviving scores indicate that their music was by the composer of the opera with which they were first performed. If this reflects the general practice, the most important composer of Venetian intermezzos at that period would have been Francesco Gasparini, with whose operas several frequently revived works had their first performances, including *Melissa schernita* and intermezzos of Lisetta and Astrobolo (both 1707); other important intermezzo composers active at Venice would have included Lotti (*Le rovine di Troja*, 1707) and Albinoni (*Pimpinone*, 1708).

In contrast with the Venetian practice, the Neapolitan custom during the first two decades of the 18th century was to incorporate comic scenes into nearly every new opera; local composers, including Giuseppe Vignola, Francesco Mancini, Francesco Feo and Leonardo Leo, added the traditional 'scene buffe' to works first produced elsewhere without them. After 1720, when the comic elements finally gained independence from the *opera seria* libretto, the Neapolitan intermezzo entered a golden age, exemplified in the works of such composers as Domenico Sarri (intermezzos of Brunetta and Burlotto frequently revived under the title *La capricciosa e il credulo*, 1720), Hasse (*La contadina*, 1728), Pergolesi (*La serva padrona*, 1733) and Giuseppe Sellitti (*La vedova ingegnosa*, 1735). Neapolitan librettists of that time include Bernardo Saddumene, G. A. Federico and Tommaso Mariani.

Substantial contributions to the intermezzo repertory were made by the Bolognese composer G. M. Orlandini, whose works, including the enormously successful *Il marito giocatore*, had their first performances in different Italian cities and seem to belong to no particular local tradition. Important figures active outside Italy include Francesco Conti (Vienna) and Telemann (Hamburg).

The text of an intermezzo typically consists of two or three short parts (the third seems generally to have been performed as the penultimate scene of a three-act opera). Each part customarily contains one or two arias for each of the two singing roles (one or more mute roles frequently appear) and a terminal duet. In addition to its boisterous realism, a striking contrast to the artificial elegance of Metastasian verse, the poetry of the intermezzo differs from that of contemporary *opera seria* mainly in its greater irregularity and in having more rhyme in the recitatives and lengthier aria and duet texts.

Apart from Molière's comedies, at least six of which were adapted as librettos for intermezzos (e.g. Antonio Salvi's version of *Le bourgeois gentilhomme*, published at Florence in 1722 as *L'artigiano gentiluomo*), the most obvious model for poets of the intermezzo was the *commedia dell'arte*. Its influence is apparent in the loosely woven plot, quasi-improvisatory dialogue, use of dialect and garbled foreign languages to establish character, disguises and slapstick humour. Still more striking is the appearance under their traditional names of stock characters from the *commedia dell'arte* in popular intermezzos. By far the most common of the stock types is the cunning servant girl, widow or shepherdess who, despite her humble station, through feminine wiles tricks her male partner or ensnares him in matrimony. Often the soubrette's name indicates her sharp cunning, as, for example, Serpina ('little snake') in Federico's *La serva padrona* or Vespetta ('little wasp') in Pariati's *Pimpinone*. Other common themes include the supernatural, probably deriving from the close connection between the comic characters and transformations of the *intermedi* in 17th-century opera, and satire directed at the *opera seria* (e.g. Metastasio's *L'impresario delle canarie*, his only contribution to the genre). Some of even the most popular 18th-century intermezzos remain anonymous because librettos cite the names of their poets only infrequently.

The intermezzo exhibits nearly as rigid a standard musical format as contemporary *opera seria*. Typically, each part contains two or three arias and a final duet, all in da capo form and separated by *secco* recitatives. Accompanied recitative appears infrequently and usually in a parody context, while overtures and other types of independent instrumental music are lacking altogether or confined to short, concluding dance pieces. Stylistically, it is more progressive: its simple harmonies, homophonic accompaniments, general melodiousness and symmetrical phrase structure are clear harbingers of later 18th-century Classical style. A type of realism is also a prominent feature; scores furnish abundant examples of written-out portrayals of laughter, sneezing, weeping, the palpitations of a lovesick heart and the like. Other characteristics of the *buffo* style exemplified in the intermezzo include a lively, frequently disjunct vocal line; constant repetition of short, balanced phrases; parody directed mainly at the musical conventions of *opera seria*; and – above all – absolute fidelity of music to text, frequently manifested by extreme changes of tempo and style within an aria or duet. As a contrast to the prevailing *buffo* style, composers sometimes introduced mock-pathetic numbers and arias modelled on dance rhythms; the latter were sometimes actually danced by the *parti buffe*, whose favourite step seems to have been the minuet.

During the first half of the 18th century, travelling singers, among them the Mantuan bass G. B. Cavana and the celebrated team of Antonio Ristorini and Rosa Ungarelli, spread the intermezzo repertory throughout Italy and to nearly every European city that supported Italian opera. Intermezzos performed between the acts of *commedia dell'arte* plays at Moscow in 1731 preceded by five years the earliest *opere serie* heard in Russia. Intermezzo performances by itinerant troupes are recorded as early as 1716 in Wolfenbüttel, 1717 in Brunswick and Dresden, 1724 in Prague, 1726 in Mannheim, 1727 in Breslau and 1737 in London. The process of diffusion continued with the tours of Angelo and Pietro Mingotti's opera companies in Austria, Germany and Denmark between 1737 and 1760 and in conjunction with the pantomimes presented by the impresario Nicolini's troupe of Piccoli Holandesi (Dutch children) in central Europe between about 1745 and 1750. Perhaps the most significant of the intermezzo's extraterritorial conquests was Paris. Performances of *opere buffe* and intermezzos there during the seasons of 1752–4 by a troupe of singers brought from Strasbourg by Eustache Bambini precipitated the Querelle des Bouffons, a literary polemic which inspired a rash of musical parodies and imitations that opened a new chapter in the history of French opera.

By 1750, ballets had almost completely supplanted intermezzos as the principal entr'acte diversions in *opere serie*, although works by such composers as Rinaldo da Capua, Gioacchino Cocchi, Niccolò Piccinni and Baldassare Galuppi were occasionally given in the Italian prose theatre throughout the remainder of the 18th century. Because of the size of their casts (up to seven), which permitted large-scale ensembles and concerted finales, these intermezzos (or 'farsette') differ little from contemporary *opere buffe* except in length and function. Many, in fact, were simply versions of full-length comic operas shortened to fit between the acts of a play and reduced to fit the number of available singers (e.g. *Il filosofo di campagna*, an *opera buffa* by Goldoni and Galuppi, 1754, Venice, and *La serva astuta*, a condensed version performed as an intermezzo at Venice in 1761).

Opera buffa

Italian 18th-century comic opera, or *opera buffa* as it is generically termed, was distinguished from comic opera in most other languages by the fact that its text was set to music throughout; it had no spoken dialogue. 18th-century Italians used several terms to describe it including, besides *opera buffa*, 'dramma comico', 'dramma giocoso' and 'commedia in musica' (or 'per musica'). The term chosen was more a matter of local custom than a serious attempt to classify sub-species of the same genre.

Opera buffa plots were much affected by contemporary ideas of the role of comedy in theatre. Italian theorists made no distinction between the social function of comic opera and that of any other kind of comic drama: all comedy should morally instruct the audience through the art of caricature. The human foibles thought most suitable for caricature included vanity, miserliness, stupidity, cowardliness and affectation; against these, Planelli wrote (1772), 'Laughter is the most powerful and effective antidote'. The personification of these and other foibles is to be found in certain character types which appear repeatedly in comic opera of the period, many of which, as in the intermezzo, were similar to the traditional characters of the *commedia dell'arte*. The elderly gentleman of *opera buffa* may, like Pantaloon, be miserly or flirt with the ladies; may, like Doctor Graziano, parade his bogus knowledge; or may, like Tartaglia or Pasquariello, be a mere simpleton. The servants may be dull-witted, like Pulcinella in some of his manifestations, or shrewd, like Coviello. Both the *commedia* and *opera buffa* introduced characters from the professional classes like the military or the medical profession for the sake of caricature. Both also introduced a pair of young lovers, whose path to marriage was blocked by some ban or misunderstanding and whose role was generally to exploit to their own advantage the foolishness of their seniors.

The popular assertion that *opera buffa* evolved from the intermezzo takes no account of the fact that *opera buffa* appeared almost contemporaneously with the intermezzo. It also fails to explain the many differences – in scope and size, for example – that distinguish the two. One line of ancestry for *opera buffa* can be traced back to those rare Italian 17th-century comic operas that contained types of character similar to those described above. Jacopo Melani's *Il potestà di Colognole* (1657) and Stradella's *Il Trespolo tutore* (c1677) are among the outstanding works of the kind. One reason why such works were rare in the mid-17th century is that contemporary audiences found enough comedy to satisfy them within the other types of opera then being offered. Librettists of the period commonly mixed tragic and comic elements in the same plot and included characters representing both high and low classes, the latter of course providing the comedy. At the turn of the century, however, such 'reforming' librettists as Zeno began to remove the lower-class characters from their texts as part of their effort to elevate opera to the status of true tragedy. The emergence of both *opera buffa* and the intermezzo as popular entertainment coincided roughly with this reform, which suggests that these genres arose as a reaction against the recent exclusion of comedy from the musical theatre.

A few *opere buffe* appeared during the second and third decades of the 18th century in north Italian cities, Venice and Bologna in particular. But the first place where Italian comic opera firmly took root as a popular entertainment was Naples. In 1709 the management of the Fiorentini theatre in Naples mounted its first comic opera, *Patrò Calienno de la Costa* (music by Antonio Orefice); this work proved so successful that the theatre abandoned its policy of presenting *opera seria* and promoted comic opera instead. By the mid-1720s Naples had no fewer than three theatres presenting comic opera exclusively. Theatre managements in other Italian cities did not at once follow the Neapolitan lead, continuing to prefer tragic opera, which was popular with the ruling class and the intelligentsia. By the mid-century, however, many managers had come to recognize that *opera buffa* held equal attractions for audiences, and there was a marked increase in the number of *opera buffa* productions throughout Italy about that time. Roman audiences, for example, had the opportunity to see comic operas each Carnival time from the late 1730s onwards. In the 1740s comic opera became normal fare in the Venetian theatrical calendar. At the same time the first moves were made to promote *opera buffa* abroad; it first appeared in London, for instance, in 1748. The immense success of *opera buffa* had a number of effects. Intellectuals, who had always regarded it as an inferior art form, began to reappraise their attitude, and a number of them came to admire it for its vivacity, expressiveness and naturalness, in the sense that it dealt with real human emotions as opposed to the lofty, artificially contrived ones found in *opera seria*. They also realized that the singers of *opera buffa*, lacking in most cases the virtuoso singing techniques of their counterparts in *opera seria* (who often turned their parts into senseless displays of vocal exhibitionism), acted with more sense of the propriety of the drama, much to its benefit. As intellectual attitudes began to change, so did those of the European sovereigns and aristocratic classes. The swing of taste resulted in increased promotion of *opera buffa* in those court theatres that until then had been the chief bastions of *opera seria*. By the 1780s very few opera houses still patronized *opera seria* exclusively.

One of the strong points of *opera buffa* was that it was always receptive to trends in drama and literature. As the century progressed, so it embraced an increasingly wide range of types of subject matter; these included sentimental dramas (often drawn from contemporary writings, like Piccinni's popular *La Cecchina, ossia La buona figliuola*, 1760, Rome, an adaptation by Goldoni of Richardson's *Pamela*), escape dramas and fantasies reminiscent of stories from the Arabian Nights, as well as plots of the more traditional 'comedy of errors' kind that relied heavily on burlesque. Librettists were far from agreed upon what material they should use. No single writer, not even the great Goldoni, whose texts were much set by Galuppi and others, was able to corner the market for comic librettos as Metastasio did in the realm of *opera seria*. That is an important reason why *opera buffa* shows such a multiplicity of facets.

Comic opera texts of the 1720s onwards, however, do show one common preoccupation of librettists: how to temper burlesque and caricature in such a way that they acquired a degree of gentility and sophistication commensurate with what was then considered essential in 'art'. The librettists' common method of overcoming the problem was to divide the cast into two: alongside the traditional comic characters (*parti buffe*) was set a group of serious characters (*parti serie*). A *parte seria* was basically a character of a kind who might also have been suitable for inclusion in *opera seria*. His sentiments and feelings (he would probably be a lover rather than a heroic figure) were expressed in a relatively refined manner; he did not participate in large numbers of silly escapades; he was polite enough not to argue vehemently with anyone else in an ensemble. (He might however be involved in dealings with servants and other inferiors, and possibly in amorous intrigues, in a way that his *opera seria* counterpart would not.) His colleague, the *parte buffa*, was more open to ridicule. He expressed himself in coarser language, got into scrapes through his own stupidity, and sang at cross-purposes during the ensembles.

The appearance of *parti serie* did two things. First, their more genteel manners tended to affect the behaviour of the cast as a whole: thus the mockery and clowning characteristic of the earliest operas gradually gave way to a type of comedy relying on a gentler wit and a gentler representation of human foibles. Secondly, they added variety to the cast and a breadth of characterization unknown in any other branch of Italian opera in the 18th century. Something of this variety can be gauged by a study of Mozart's *Don Giovanni*, in which *parti serie* like Donna Anna and Don Ottavio participate along with *parti buffe* like Leporello, Masetto and Zerlina. At this level and by this date (1787), however, the serious and comic are not readily distinguished: roles like Don Giovanni himself have comic as well as serious elements, as does the Count in *Le nozze di Figaro* (1786), and in the latter opera the comic roles of Figaro and Susanna have serious elements. (For a fuller account of Mozart's operas see p. 98.)

Most early *opere buffe* were set to music by composers born or trained, or both, in Naples, like Vinci, Leo and Logroscino. These men wrote their *opere buffe* for the home market, since there was little demand for them elsewhere. Few contemporary north Italian composers attempted to make a name for themselves in the same genre, though one who did, apparently with some success, was the Bolognese G. M. Buini. With the spread of comic opera in the mid-century, however, the situation changed. More and more non-Neapolitan composers moved from writing exclusively *opera seria* to writing *opera buffa* as well. The first of these composers to make a major contribution to the genre, partly because of his close collaboration with Goldoni, was the Venetian Baldassare Galuppi. As the demand for comic opera increased, so impresarios had to look ever further afield for successful composers to supply new works of the kind for the coming season. Composers therefore began to receive commissions for comic operas from cities at home and abroad and travelled in response to these commissions to an extent unimagined by their predecessors when comic opera had been confined to a few centres like Naples. This was one of the signs that *opera buffa* was being transformed in the mid-century from a local into an international art, composed by Italian and then too by non-Italian composers in response to a growing demand on a European scale. Just how international it had become by the last decades of the century is demonstrated by the fact that some of its finest examples were now by non-Italians like Haydn and Mozart – although several of its leading exponents were still Neapolitan, Paisiello and Cimarosa outstanding among them; the former's *Il barbiere di Siviglia* (1782, St Petersburg) and the latter's *Il matrimonio segreto* (1792, Vienna) were only the most famed among their numerous works that were given in many cities in Italy and abroad.

Composers set *opera buffa* on the general assumption that the music should reflect swift changes of dramatic action, the gestures of the actors and even minute changes of meaning in their dialogue. It was not a type of drama that benefited from long periods of inactivity on the stage. Over the years, therefore, composers sought for musical structures that would allow the action to move forward without check or hindrance. They chose to use almost exclusively simple recitative, reserving the slower-moving accompanied recitative for a few scenes involving the *parti serie*. They abandoned the da capo form in their arias around the mid-century, that is, 20 years before they did so finally in *opera seria*, because the da capo did not propel the action forward. In particular, they developed a type of structure that permitted them to string together an indefinite number of dramatic events in a relatively naturalistic way within a single ensemble. This requires further comment.

An ensemble was obligatory at the end of every act of an *opera buffa*.

Those at the ends of Acts 1 and 2 were by custom comic ensembles, containing much jostling and sparring among the *parti buffe*. Early examples of these comic ensembles or finales are all short, and their music is often in a simple binary or ternary form. In the course of the century, however, the comic finale expanded out of all recognition. It began to spread backwards from the end of the act to embrace not just one but several events within the action. More and more characters (both *buffe* and *serie*) participated in it. Composers – Galuppi already by the early 1750s and Neapolitans like Piccinni by the early 1760s – responded to the challenge of writing ever longer finales by dividing the music into sections, each section with its own individual style, its own speed and time signature. Where one section ended and the next began depended upon the dramatic context; as this varied from one finale to another, there could be no absolute formula for the number of sections or the degree of looseness with which they were joined together. The result was that composers had a considerable degree of flexibility in the way they constructed their finales, and this was then extended to most other lyrical items in *opera buffa* as well and then even to certain items in *opera seria*.

The development of the finale is symptomatic of the progressive nature of *opera buffa*. The fact that this genre was not hidebound by either too much theory or too much tradition, and the fact that it was popular with most of the opera-going public, encouraged its fast growth and evolution. Its humour, its music responsive to the needs of the drama and its generally wide scope helped lead it, at least in the second half of the 18th century, in the hands of such composers as Piccinni, Paisiello, Anfossi, Guglielmi and Cimarosa, to represent much of the best in Italian dramatic art.

CHAPTER VIII

Germany and Austria

PETER BRANSCOMBE, STANLEY SADIE

1. The Singspiel

The rise of Singspiel

The German Singspiel – in the normal sense of that term, an opera, usually comic, in German with spoken dialogue – was developed from a variety of predecessors. Apart from medieval mysteries and church plays, important sources of the Singspiel are to be found in secular plays of all kinds. The tragedies and comedies of travelling troupes frequently contained a number of songs (often with many verses, and sung to a popular melody) as well as a variety of instrumental music – dances, marches, flourishes for royal entrances, battles, hunting scenes. The songs were usually given to the principal comic character (Jean Potage, Jack Pudding, Pickelhäring, later Hanswurst), whose part was in the early days often taken by the only actor fluent in the language of the country where the performance was taking place. The *commedia dell'arte* exercised a twofold influence, through the visits of Italian companies to theatrical centres in Austria and southern Germany in particular, and through the mediation of the Comédie-Italienne in Paris which, in the localized form of the Théâtres de la Foire in the early 18th century, exerted a marked influence, especially on the Viennese theatre.

Baroque opera at the great Austrian and German courts set a standard of magnificence that the popular companies were unable to emulate, though their adaptations and parodies brought at least something of the splendours of the opera to the people. Occasionally, broadly comic musical entertainments and intermezzos were put on at the Viennese court that have close similarities to the world of Hanswurst in the Kärntnertortheater. Other forms of court entertainment, including pastorales and ballets, both mounted and danced, left a mark. The dramatic performances put on by religious orders are also of great importance in the rise of the Singspiel. In particular the Jesuits staged musico-dramatic performances of a magnificence to rival or even surpass the grandeur and lavishness of court opera. In Vienna the use of German songs, parody and even mixed-language verse, as well as extensive musical sequences, helped to break down the barriers between the various art forms and prepare the ground for the plays with music of the comedians in the Kärntnertortheater who, from the beginning of the second decade of the 18th century, represent the oldest unbroken popular theatre tradition in the German lands. Theirs are the earliest works that deserve to be labelled 'Singspiel' in its usual sense.

Where German was normally or often the language of operatic performances (Hamburg, Brunswick etc, but not Vienna or Munich), the musical style was seldom markedly different from that of the Italian operas written for Austro-German houses, or the French models that to a more limited extent exerted an influence in Germany. But the use of the vernacular was certainly an encouragement to the German Singspiel writers, and the music of the peasant and servant scenes frequently has a frankly popular touch that assured its success and its survival – the melodies of many of the songs in collections like Speronte's *Singende Muse an der Pleisse* (Leipzig, 1736–47) had their origins in more sophisticated musical forms, mainly of French origin, but they also included music by Bach, Handel, Telemann, Keiser, Vivaldi and others. In turn Speronte's collections were plundered by actor-dramatists like Kurz-Bernardon in Vienna. On the whole, however, operatic works by German composers had little success or influence in Austria. Handel and Graun were hardly known in Vienna, and later Hiller's Singspiels were seldom performed there, or were given as spoken dramas. Indeed, of the north German Singspiel composers only Benda had any success in the Austrian capital, primarily with his melodramas.

North Germany
Contrary to generally held opinion, the north and central German Singspiel of the mid-18th century arose only after a lusty and prolific Viennese genre had become firmly established. This was some time after Baroque opera had disappeared from the repertory of all but the most reactionary of German theatres. Writing in the fourth edition of his *Critische Dichtkunst* (1751), Gottsched prematurely congratulated the Germans on their taste and good sense in abandoning opera; the brief and dismissive sections on operetta and the intermezzo give no sign of awareness of the gravity of the new danger to what he considered good taste: the emergent Singspiel.

The main sources of the north German Singspiel were the French *comédie mêlée d'ariettes*, an offshoot of the Comédie-Italienne given with great success at the Foires St Germain and St Laurent after the banishment of the Italian comedians from Paris in 1697, and precursor of the true *opéra comique*; and the English ballad opera. The popularity of the Gay–Pepusch *Beggar's Opera* and its successors in London in the late 1720s and early 1730s did not go unnoticed in Germany. C. W. von Borck,

Prussian envoy in London, translated Coffey's *The Devil to Pay*, which was performed in Berlin in 1743, probably with the original English tunes. The era of the German Singspiel proper opened with Standfuss's setting of C. F. Weisse's translation of *The Devil to Pay*, which under the title *Der Teufel ist los, oder Die verwandelten Weiber* was performed by G. H. Koch's company at Leipzig in 1752. Despite its success (not least in sparking off a battle of pamphlets – Gottsched and his adherents objected to what they considered its coarse and tasteless nature), its sequel, *Der lustige Schuster* (based on Coffey's *The Merry Cobbler*), was not given until 1759, in Lübeck; Standfuss's third and last Singspiel, *Jochem Tröbs*, was given at Hamburg on 17 September 1759. It is not without significance that these two works were first performed in north German ports with close trading links with Britain: in the 18th century Hamburg was the principal point of entry for English cultural influences in Germany (Borck translated Shakespeare's *Julius Caesar* as well as Coffey's *The Devil to Pay*).

Once the Hamburg operatic venture had foundered in 1738, the only German-language Singspiel venture with a permanent home was the Hanswurst company at the Kärntnertortheater in Vienna. For the rest, operatic performances of a popular nature and in the vernacular were given by wandering troupes. This helps account for the short-breathed and usually simple nature of the early German-language Singspiels: most of the casts were actors and actresses who could also sing, as opposed to fully trained musicians, and the expense of maintaining even a moderate-sized orchestra and a repertory of large-scale works was beyond the reach of almost all the companies. But several troupes in the third quarter of the 18th century gave notable performances of Singspiels; Anton Seyler's performed at Weimar and Gotha for some years with Anton Schweitzer and later (in Dresden) C. G. Neefe as musical directors and composers, and from the late 1770s G. F. W. Grossmann directed what was probably the most important opera troupe in Germany, with Neefe as Kapellmeister. Yet for all they achieved these companies only briefly enjoyed the settled conditions of a semi-permanent home; the establishment of a tradition of sustained excellence of ensemble was impossible.

The most important figures in the rise of the German Singspiel are the dramatist and poet C. F. Weisse (1726–1804) and the composer J. A. Hiller (1728–1804). All but four of Hiller's 14 Singspiels are settings of Weisse librettos; his first attempts were adaptations of the two Coffey–Standfuss works, for which Weisse had arranged the texts. In most of his Singspiel texts Weisse leant on French originals, mainly by Favart, though in *Der Aerndtekranz* (1771) he wrote an original German libretto. The principal features of Hiller's Singspiels are typical of the new genre (though it should be noted that Singspiels are not always comic; the Gotter–Benda *Walder* of 1776 is an example of the 'ernsthafte Operette'). The story tends to be about lower-middle-class people or artisans, and is frequently pastoral (or at least rural) in vein, as well as comic. A firmly satirical attitude may be taken towards the upper classes or foreigners who threaten the simple idyllic life of the principals. Romantic interest nearly always plays a prominent part. The action is carried forward in spoken dialogue, normally in prose, with music reserved for introductions and emotional highpoints; dances, marches and narrative songs are frequent; recitatives occur only occasionally, normally in addition to the dialogue rather than in place of it; the vocal numbers tend to be fairly simple and often strophic songs, though there are some ambitious arias, usually but not invariably for upper-class characters; choruses and extended ensembles are infrequent in early Singspiels, though straightforward vaudeville finales are often found; marches, recruiting songs and other military touches reflect the Seven Years War through which Germany had recently passed.

The high quality of books and music kept the Weisse–Hiller *Lottchen am Hofe* (1767), *Die Liebe auf dem Lande* (1768) and *Die Jagd* (1770) in the repertory for several decades; many of the songs soon achieved the lasting popularity of what were shortly to be called 'folksongs'. Despite their excellent qualities – high spirits, melodic charm, pathos, pleasing instrumentation – there is something rather monotonous about them, especially by comparison with the livelier Viennese Singspiels. Georg Benda however achieved in his theatre scores a remarkable range and depth of musical characterization, variety of effect, humour and occasional elegiac power and elegance that make Mozart's profound admiration for his melodramas entirely understandable. The best of the Singspiel scores of his contemporaries – André, Neefe, Reichardt, Wolf and Zumsteeg – would also repay occasional revival.

Two composers of more serious opera in German should be mentioned here. Ignaz Holzbauer wrote most of his operas to Italian texts, though as early as 1746 he set a German farce by Weiskern. His most important stage work is *Günther von Schwarzburg* (1771, Mannheim), to a libretto by Anton Klein on a German historical subject. The scoring is imaginative and the expressive accompanied recitatives were greatly admired; Mozart was struck by the fire and spirit of the music when he heard it in autumn 1777. The case of Anton Schweitzer is very different, in that his 20 or so stage works were virtually all written to German texts. Historically the most important of these are *Alkeste* (1773, Weimar) and *Rosemunde* (1780, Mannheim), both to librettos by Wieland; their partnership represented a then rare collaboration between a major German poet and composer, though musically and dramatically Schweitzer did not depart far from Neapolitan *opera seria* practice.

The attempts of major literary figures to raise the tone of the Singspiel by the provision of superior texts had only limited success; neither Wieland nor Goethe added to his reputation or to the permanent repertory of the Singspiel with his contributions (in Goethe's case particularly numerous) to the genre, and Reichardt with his Liederspiele likewise hardly achieved the hoped-for union of a libretto of high quality with music of popular appeal and distinction.

By the early 19th century the borderline between the Singspiel and opera with dialogue is far from distinct. Whereas Weber subtitled *Abu Hassan* 'Singspiel', *Der Freischütz* is a '(romantic) opera' and *Oberon* a 'romantic fairy-opera', notwithstanding very similar proportions between sung and spoken elements in the three works. In general it is probably fair to say that the term Singspiel in Germany as well as in Austria was frequently avoided by those wishing to make exalted claims for their works. There are inevitably many exceptions, yet on the whole a Singspiel made less exacting demands on the performers than did an opera; at least in the early days of the modern German Singspiel, the travelling companies could cope more readily with the demands of the play with songs.

Vienna

Although the term Singspiel was seldom used by Viennese librettists and composers in subtitling their own works, there can be no doubt that the works themselves are most clearly described by this term. The combination of music and comedy was already firmly established by the court operas and the Jesuit dramatists and composers long before the popular Singspiel tradition had begun. It grew directly from these two Viennese theatrical forms, but also from the 17th-century tradition whereby strolling players used music as an added attraction in their works.

It was long held that music played no part, or at most a very restricted part, in the performances of Hanswurst-Stranitzky's company that took over the Kärntnertortheater in Vienna in about 1710. Numerous songs, dances and even complete ballets were performed by this company, as well as incidental music. The texts survive of some 16 Haupt- und Staatsaktionen (plays about historical or mythical characters, with a liberal larding of coarse comic scenes) by J. A. Stranitzky, in which an average of a dozen or 15 arias were sung. After Stranitzky's death in 1726, the musical components of the Viennese popular comedies were extended yet further. H. Rademin's *Runtzvanscad, König deren Menschenfressern* of 1732 includes four choruses, five duets and two dozen arias; and after 1744, with the establishment in the company of Joseph Felix von Kurz (whose guest appearances in central and southern Germany enriched the northern repertory), music began to play a still more important part. Even if the total of musical numbers in a typical Kurz work is lower than in *Runtzvanscad*, there was sometimes a remarkable preponderance of ensembles. The nine musical numbers of *Das zerstöhrte Versprechen des Bernardons* (probably from the late 1740s or early 1750s) comprise three quintets, a quartet, a trio, two duets and a mere two arias. By comparison, Kurz's libretto for Haydn's *Der neue krumme Teufel* (probably printed in 1758) includes as many as 32 arias and only one duet, one trio, one extended solo number and three choruses among its 38 numbers.

The earliest surviving music definitely composed for the Viennese popular theatre dates from the mid- or late 1750s (the so-called *Teutsche Comedie Arien*: published in vols. lxiv and cxxi of Denkmäler der Tonkunst in Österreich); the composer of some of the numbers may well be Haydn, whose puppet opera *Die Feuersbrunst* (*Das abgebrannte Haus*), probably dating from 1776–7, was rediscovered in the late 1950s. Among other composers named on librettos or in contemporary account books as writing music for the popular theatre are Holzbauer (*Arlekin, ein Nebenbuhler seines Herrn*, 1746), and the otherwise unknown Eder, Fauner and Ziegler.

The most important period of the Viennese Singspiel began in 1778, with Joseph II's institution of the 'German National-Singspiel', which was intended to encourage native poets and composers to produce works in the vernacular for the benefit and improvement of lovers of German rather than Italian or French art. Despite the emperor's good intentions and the competence of J. H. F. Müller, the National-Singspiel's first director (he went to Germany in search of good new artists), the encouragement of the best native talent failed to produce the hoped-for results. Year after year, the principal public successes in the court theatre were translations of foreign originals rather than German-language plays, and the same happened with the opera. Two companies, those of Johann Böhm and J. C. Wäser, performed operatic works in the Kärntnertortheater in spring and summer 1776. Böhm's repertory consisted entirely of French operettas, badly translated and poorly performed, which had no public success; and Wäser too failed to please, though he gave a number of original German Singspiels. It was against this background that Joseph II went ahead with his plan to establish a German Singspiel company in Vienna, and many of the works it later performed were revivals from the Böhm and Wäser guest seasons.

The work chosen to open the National-Singspiel venture, Umlauf's one-act opera *Die Bergknappen* to a libretto by Weidmann, was first heard on 17 February 1778 and received 30 performances in four years; the second new Singspiel, *Diesmal hat der Mann den Willen*, was also by a native composer, Ordonez (born in Vienna, despite his Spanish name); but thereafter translations once again preponderated. Seven of the 15 scores given in the opening season were original German works, yet only Ulbrich's *Frühling und Liebe* and Benda's by no means new *Medea*, apart from *Die Bergknappen*, were to attain ten or more performances, compared with four of French or Italian provenance that averaged some 25 performances each. In later seasons the discrepancy was more clearly marked, the only native successes to rival the most popular importations being Umlauf's *Die pücefarbenen Schuhe, oder Die schöne Schusterin* and *Das Irrlicht*, Gluck's *Die Pilgrime von Mekka* (itself a translation from its French original), and Mozart's *Die Entführung aus dem Serail* (with around 40 performances by the final night of the venture, it was the most successful work written for the National-Singspiel; in absolute terms Gluck's *Pilgrime* and Grétry's *Zemire und Azor*, with 56 performances each, were the most often heard). The company closed its doors on 4 March 1783, though a second extended season ran from autumn 1785 until 4 February 1788, including among its few native successes Dittersdorf's *Der Apotheker und der Doctor*

(*Doctor und Apotheker*, to a libretto by Stephanie). It was first heard on 11 July 1786. The comment that its success eclipsed Mozart's *Le nozze di Figaro*, first performed on 1 May 1786, is at best based on unjust comparison: circumstances and criteria differed considerably between the German company that gave Dittersdorf's work and the Italian company that gave Mozart's.

The final closure of the National-Singspiel in February 1788 left Vienna without any theatre specifically catering for vernacular opera. Karl Marinelli, the director of the theatre in the Leopoldstadt suburb, seized the opportunity. In Wenzel Müller he already had a highly gifted young composer who had shown his abilities in Singspiel; with Ferdinand Kauer and other competent musicians to assist him, the Leopoldstadt ensemble was soon able to mount a series of very popular, unexactingly tuneful Singspiels, the best of which held their place in the repertories of Austrian and many German theatres for several decades and ran up some 200 and more performances in the Leopoldstadt alone. Martín y Soler, Schenk and Gluck (*Die Pilgrime*) were the most successful of the 'court' opera composers whose works were taken into the Leopoldstadt repertory (Gassmann, Salieri and Dittersdorf were less successful in this respect), though none of them could rival the best of Müller's own works in popularity. The return to Vienna of Emanuel Schikaneder in summer 1789, when he took over the direction of the Freihaus-Theater auf der Wieden, soon provided Marinelli with a dangerous rival in Singspiel, though Schikaneder did not have house composers quite of the quality or resilience of Marinelli's. Nevertheless Schikaneder's series of 'Anton' Singspiels (with music mainly by the singers Schack and Gerl) enjoyed great popularity, and the performances he gave of works by Mozart, Süssmayr, Seyfried, Henneberg, Winter, Wranitzky and others added greatly to his reputation at least until megalomania clouded his judgment and led to ever more lavish stagings of third-rate new works or revivals of old favourites.

Apart from Mozart, the best of the Viennese Singspiel composers of any pretension was Dittersdorf. Although his indebtedness to Gluck and Mozart is obvious, he was experienced in the Italian idiom, and he also showed himself prepared, as was Hiller (whose Singspiels were seldom performed in Vienna and unpopular there), to include solo numbers ranging from simple songs to full-scale coloratura arias. Dittersdorf's greatest successes – *Der Apotheker und der Doctor*, *Betrug durch Aberglauben*, *Die Liebe im Narrenhause*, *Hieronymus Knicker* and *Das rote Käppchen*, all from the years 1786–8 – were Singspiels, though he sometimes favoured the description 'komische Oper'. All contain thoroughly attractive melodies, skilful scoring (with quite rich use of wind instruments) and lively, well varied ensembles. By any standard other than comparison with Mozart, his feeling for musical characterization and humour is exceptional, and the ensembles (for example the two act finales in *Der Apotheker und der Doctor*) are both extensive and well developed. If he was content to accept the large proportion of non-dramatic arias and songs provided by his librettists, these numbers are undoubtedly neat and pleasing; and in this respect he was more adept than Mozart at providing the public with what it wanted.

Among the other successful exponents of the Viennese Singspiel at the end of the 18th century and the beginning of the 19th a few stand out: Johann Schenk, whose *Der Dorfbarbier* (1796) was one of the most successful of all stage works for two or three decades, Peter Winter with *Das unterbrochene Opferfest* (1796), Joseph Weigl with *Die Schweizerfamilie* (1809) and Adalbert Gyrowetz with *Der Augenarzt* (1811); Schubert's Singspiels however have neither in the composer's lifetime nor since enjoyed the success that the beauty of their music merits. Beethoven's only operatic work, *Fidelio* (1805, rev. 1806 and 1814), hovers uncomfortably between the light, unpretentious world of the Singspiel and the melodramatic world of the 'rescue opera' for quite half its length, and for all its positive virtues and importance in the later history of opera its influence was not wholly beneficial (Weber's dramatic arias often contain exactingly unvocal writing of a kind that can be traced back to *Fidelio*).

The supreme example of the Viennese Singspiel is the Schikaneder–Mozart *Die Zauberflöte* (1791), though it was not mere pride or pretension that led librettist and composer to sub-title it 'eine grosse Oper' or 'deutsche Oper' rather than 'Singspiel'. Despite the extensive scenes of spoken dialogue, most of the musical numbers are of a size and complexity that left the world of the average Singspiel far behind (the same is not true of settings of Schikaneder's later librettos, for singularly few of which was he content to use the modest subtitle of Singspiel). The enormous and lasting success of *Die Zauberflöte* (223 performances in the Theater auf der Wieden alone before Schikaneder moved to his new Theater an der Wien in 1801) led Schikaneder to try ever more desperately and vainly to emulate it; scores from Süssmayr, Mederitsch and Winter, Wölfl, Henneberg and Seyfried all enjoyed at best ephemeral success while failing signally to add anything original to the recipe that had worked so superbly in *Die Zauberflöte*.

Whereas most of the Singspiels given at the court theatres in Vienna from around 1800 tended to reduce the number of solo arias and songs and increase the number of ensembles, the emphasis in the popular suburban theatres continued to lie in the solo song – initially *buffo* or sentimental lieder, later the satirical *couplet* perfected by Nestroy and his composers. Early in his career Wenzel Müller had occasionally written act finales of a length to rival those of *Die Zauberflöte*; but in his later works he and Ferdinand Kauer and the other principal composers for the Theater in der Leopoldstadt tended to limit the number of concerted pieces and place the musical interest firmly on simple solo songs with the occasional more challenging aria. This tendency does not exclude simple choruses and other numbers for more than one singer, but it is rather rare to find even duets that are more than mere alternating strophes. The term *Posse* (or *Posse mit Gesang*) is sometimes attached to such works, especially those of a farcical kind. The twilight of the Viennese popular Singspiel extends from Müller's later scores of the period after his return from Prague in 1813, until the late years of Adolf Müller, the principal purveyor of scores to the Theater an der Wien and the Theater in der Leopoldstadt from 1828 until the late 1870s. The advent of the Viennese operetta in the 1860s, following the vogue of the French vaudeville and the more recent arrival of Offenbach's Parisian operettas on the Viennese stages, may be held finally to have ended the era of the Viennese Singspiel.

2. Classical Viennese Opera

Gluck

The confluence of traditions in the Vienna of the second half of the 18th century produced as remarkable a flowering in the field of opera as it did in that of instrumental music. The city, capital of the Habsburg Empire from which much of north Italy and most of central Europe were governed, had long traditions of Italian opera. It had been cultivated there since the 1630s, particularly assiduously under Leopold I (see Chapter II), and under Charles VI (reigned 1711–40), whose court composers included F. B. Conti and Antonio Caldara and who appointed Metastasio court poet in 1729. Around the middle of the century, under Maria Theresa (1740–80), there was a more French orientation at the court, which manifested itself musically in the introduction, under Chancellor Kaunitz and the opera Intendant Count Durazzo, of *opéra comique* as a court entertainment; Gluck at first adapted, and later composed, *opéras comiques* for performance in Vienna and at the court residences nearby.

The first of Gluck's so-called 'reform operas', *Orfeo ed Euridice* (1762), had a number of precedents, both in theory – notably Algarotti's *Saggio sopra l'opera* (1755) and the writings of the French Encyclopedists – and in practice. As we have seen (Chapter VII), several of the Italian operas of Jommelli, written for Stuttgart, and Traetta, written for Parma, reflect the French orientation of those courts, for example in their use of the chorus and their treatment of orchestral recitative; and Gluck's own ballet *Don Juan* (1761), to a scenario by Raniero de' Calzabigi, with choreography by Gaspero Angiolini and designs by G. M. Quaglio, embraces the approach of the *ballet d'action*, discarding virtuoso elements and formal traditions to achieve a more flexible and expressively natural style in which all the components play a part.

This applies equally to *Orfeo*, created by the same team. Although written for a festive court occasion – generically, it is strictly an *azione teatrale* rather than an opera – *Orfeo* repudiates the Metastasian traditions. That much is clear as the curtain rises, on a French-style *tombeau* as Eurydice's death is mourned in a chorus (through which the voice of the bereaved Orpheus rings); this is followed by a strophic song, each strophe more elaborate than the last, with impassioned orchestral recitative in between. The opera includes no da capo arias, nor simple recitatives. The musical texture is relatively continuous, with orchestral recitative, arioso, short arias and ensembles, choruses and ballets in smooth progression: this enabled Gluck to build up long and texturally varied scenes of a kind precluded by the traditional *opera seria* structure, and is of a piece with his objective of focussing the audience's emotions on a single theme – here, Orpheus's love for Eurydice – and discarding the usual sub-plots with intrigues, disguises and the like. The new, not exclusively aristocratic audiences of the age of sensibility could identify more readily with such an approach. The second act of *Orfeo* in particular, with its succession of Furies' ballets and choruses calmed by Orpheus's pleas, and its climax as he enters the Elysian fields (to the exquisitely evocative strains of 'Che puro ciel!') to be reunited with Eurydice, has a dramatic conception and concern for timing of a kind foreign to the Metastasian tradition. The conventional overture and the French-influenced vaudeville-style finale can be seen as products of the court occasion for which the opera was written; but the time had not yet come for the abandonment of the *lieto fine*, central to the ethic of 18th-century opera.

Orfeo is an exceptionally concise work (less so in its Paris version of 1774, with the part of Orpheus changed from alto castrato to tenor, or in the various compromise versions used from the 19th century onwards). *Alceste* (1767), again written with Calzabigi but choreographed by Noverre rather than Angiolini, is more extended and, again following the principle of a simple, single theme to the plot, musically less concentrated. *Alceste* was published in 1769 with a dedicatory preface in which Gluck's 're-formist' principles are declared:

When I undertook to write the music for *Alceste*, I resolved to divest it entirely of all those abuses, introduced into it either by the mistaken vanity of singers or by the too great complaisance of composers, which have so long disfigured Italian opera and made of the most splendid and most beautiful of spectacles the most ridiculous and wearisome. I have striven to restrict music to its true office of serving poetry by means of expression and by following the situations of the story, without interrupting the action or stifling it with a useless superfluity of ornaments; and I believed that it should do this in the same way as telling colours affect a correct and well-ordered drawing, by a well-assorted contrast of light and shade, which serves to animate the figures without altering their contours. Thus I did not wish to arrest an actor in the greatest heat of dialogue in order to wait for a tiresome ritornello, nor to hold him up in the middle of a word on a vowel favourable to his voice, nor to make display of the agility of his fine voice in some long-drawn passage, nor to wait while the orchestra gives him time to recover his breath for a cadenza. I did not think it my duty to pass quickly over the second section of an aria of which the words are perhaps the most impassioned and important, in order to repeat regularly four times over those of the first part, and to finish the aria where its sense may perhaps not end for the convenience of the singer who wishes to show that he can capriciously vary a passage in a number of guises; in short, I have sought to abolish all the abuses against which good sense and reason have long cried out in vain.

I have felt that the overture ought to apprise the spectators of the nature of the action that is to be represented and to form, so to speak, its argument; that the concerted instruments should be introduced in proportion to the interest and the intensity of the words, and not leave that sharp contrast between the aria and the recitative in the dialogue, so as not to break a period unreasonably nor wantonly disturb the force and heat of the action.

Furthermore, I believed that my greatest labour should be devoted to seeking a beautiful simplicity, and I have avoided making displays of difficulty at the expense of clearness; nor did I judge it desirable to discover novelties if it was not naturally suggested by the situation and the expression; and there is no rule which I have not thought it right to set aside willingly for the sake of an intended effect.

The actual musical style of *Alceste* is in fact rather less consistent than that of *Orfeo*; there is even some continuo-accompanied recitative. But the noble, impassioned manner of Alcestis's music and the elegiac power of the choral scenes represent further steps towards a more natural, more truthful representation in opera of human feeling. *Alceste* too was adapted for production in Paris, in 1776, and substantially strengthened in its dramatic structure by Gluck's revisions.

Gluck composed only one more opera for Vienna, *Paride ed Elena* (1770), also with Calzabigi. In it he did not aim at 'the strong passions suitable to tragedy' but rather at depicting 'the different characters of two nations, Phrygia and Sparta, by contrasting the rude, savage nature of the one with all that is delicate and soft in the other'. Again there is a single theme, Paris's ardent wooing of the austere, resistant Helen, but it is hard put to support an entire opera without some diversionary ballet and choruses. Gluck's remaining reform operas were composed for Paris and essentially belong to the tradition of the *tragédie lyrique* (see Chapter IX). Because several of his innovations – innovations, that is, as far as Italian and German traditions were concerned – were derived from French sources, his operas had rather less novelty in Paris than they had in Vienna, except in their pruning of subsidiary characters and sub-plots and in their classical concentration on the principal characters and their predicaments. In this Gluck's intensity of style, his capacity for achieving strong effects by simple means – indeed he lacked a powerful or wide-ranging compositional technique as such – and his command of dramatic timing served well, most of all in *Iphigénie en Tauride* (1779; given in Vienna, in German, in 1781).

Haydn

Until the late 20th century, Gluck's operas were the earliest to be fully recognized as part of the standard repertory. Their long-term influence was great, notably on Berlioz and Wagner. By contrast the operas of

Haydn, mostly composed for the princely opera house at Eszterháza and only rarely given in larger centres, were little known in his own time or indeed for long thereafter, and unlike his symphonic and chamber music they have exercised no influence. Apart from some short works (some of them surviving only fragmentarily) from his early years, his chief period of operatic composition was between 1768, when his *Lo speziale* was performed for the opening of the opera house at Eszterháza, and 1783. From 1775 until he left Eszterháza in 1790, Haydn was much concerned with the musical direction of the opera house, which involved not only the organization of performances but adapting operas by other composers as well as composing his own.

Most of Haydn's earliest operas are in the lighter genres, including marionette opera and Singspiel. From the late 1760s he favoured the Goldoni-type *dramma giocoso*, and he set three Goldoni texts, *Lo speziale*, *Le pescatrici* (1769) and *Il mondo della luna* (1777); it may be a commentary on the singers available to Haydn, or the Esterházys' taste, or Haydn's own inclinations, that the serious roles were almost entirely omitted. Comic scenes with the stock characters of Italian comedy, like the duped, amorous old man and the impoverished young lovers, predominate in most of these operas, though there are essays at more serious characterization in *L'infedeltà delusa* (1773), to a libretto by Coltellini, and *La vera costanza* (c1778), written for Vienna though not in the event performed there. *Il mondo della luna*, though based on Goldoni's largely farcical play, includes some of Haydn's freshest and most imaginative operatic music, particularly in its ensembles. His last work of the *dramma giocoso* type, *La fedeltà premiata* (1781), though handicapped by a poorly motivated and thinly characterized plot, contains a variety of aria types, with several powerful scenas and sustained ensemble finales.

By this time Haydn seems to have been turning towards more serious forms – again, whether through his patron's directives or his own inclinations we do not know – and it may be that the decision in 1779 to set Metastasio's *L'isola disabitata* came about because of external circumstances (the burning down of the Eszterháza opera house and the need for a work that could be staged in a simple style or given in concert form). This work uses a continuous musical texture, based on arioso and orchestral recitative. Haydn's last two Eszterháza operas are the heroic-comic *Orlando Paladino* (1782), in which magical, heroic and comic elements are juxtaposed, not wholly successfully and *Armida* (1784), the closest Haydn came to composing a true *opera seria*. In 1791 he wrote an opera on the Orpheus myth, *L'anima del filosofo*, intended for London but not performed; it contains music of exceptional imaginative force, including several numbers for chorus – the resources of a large opera house offered him new opportunities – but is fatally undermined by the weakness of its dramatic structure.

That Haydn elected to accept librettos that were inconsequential and poorly motivated speaks for itself. His treatment even of the texts he chose often suggests a limited view, at least as compared with the leading musical dramatists among his contemporaries, of the potentialities of musical drama. The music of his operas is varied, attractive, often distinguished and always technically assured, and it follows the conventional language of Italian opera of the time (with which Haydn, who mounted at Eszterháza operas by such composers as Cimarosa, Anfossi, Paisiello and Sarti, was amply familiar), with rather fuller, Austrian-style orchestral writing. Its sense of character, however, is limited and its dramatic timing is uncertain. Many movements unfold at the pace of symphonic music, irrespective of situation; the sustained ensembles rarely show cumulative energy; and opportunities to provide music that might vividly shed light on character or situation are passed by. Haydn valued his operas highly, but was always conscious that, composed for a provincial opera house, they might not serve adequately in one with more sophisticated audiences. Their static quality has always militated against their establishment in the repertory.

Mozart

The operas that Mozart composed during his youth, in Vienna, Italy and Salzburg, show no particular departure from the standard Italian or Austrian styles of their day, though there are isolated scenes, notably in *Lucio Silla* (1772, Milan), that carry hints of exceptional dramatic powers. It was with *Idomeneo* (1781, Munich) that he first disclosed his full powers as a musical dramatist. With a French source, a libretto written for Campra in 1712, the opera avoids the rigidity of Metastasian *opera seria* in favour of a freer structure in which the chorus (representing the Cretan populace) takes a central role. This might be seen as a mark of the influence of Gluck, with whose Viennese and Parisian operas Mozart was familiar; indeed the appearance of an oracle with the accompaniment of wind instruments (although enjoined on Mozart by his father) suggests *Alceste*, as does the noble gravity of Mozart's ceremonial sacrifice scene in the temple, but such features could equally be put down to the Paris operas of Piccinni, whose *Roland* Mozart had heard there. The richness of scoring – Mozart took full advantage of the presence of the former Mannheim orchestra at the Munich court – and the powerful use of orchestral recitative may also show some debt to Holzbauer's *Günther von Schwarzburg*, with which Mozart had lately had opportunity to acquaint himself at Mannheim. In the orchestral recitative, which is used with unusual urgency, he employed certain patterns of phrase with consistent reference to particular characters and their emotions, for instance Ilia's grief and Electra's jealousy; there are also some well-defined relationships between keys and dramatic context. Bravura singing is not banished: rather, it is used to dramatic ends, notably where Idomeneus parallels the storms in his breast with the raging of the seas.

A happy accident of circumstances – that during the composition of *Idomeneo* Mozart had to communicate with his librettist, G. B. Varesco, by correspondence through his father, in Salzburg – has resulted in the existence of a series of letters that provide valuable insights into the way the work took its final shape. There are also some fascinating letters regarding his next opera, *Die Entführung aus dem Serail* (1782), throwing light on Mozart's attitudes to the expression of drama through music. He refers to a rhythmic figure representing the throbbing heart of the ardent hero, Belmonte, to key changes portraying anger, and to sacrificing one of the heroine's arias to the singer's 'flexible throat'; he also remarks – in sharp contradistinction to Gluck's observation in the *Alceste* preface about music's serving the poetry – that 'in an opera the poetry must be altogether the obedient daughter of the music . . . when music reigns supreme and one listens to it, all else is forgotten'.

In *Die Entführung* music 'reigns supreme' to a degree new to the Viennese Singspiel. It is much more than a spoken play with songs, as indeed is made clear at the opening, where the overture and the first aria are musically integrated. The colourful janissary music and the songs and ensembles for the servants (such as the parody scenes for the Pasha Selim's steward Osmin or the 'Moorish' ballad for Pedrillo) represent no real departure, but the extended, richly scored and often deeply felt arias for the serious characters are on a different plane. Constanze's 'Martern aller Arten', the aria sacrificed to the throat of the singer, is an extreme case, with its 70-bar introduction involving concertante music for four instruments and its bravura vocal writing, which is not however without dramatic function. It is noteworthy, however, that the ensemble finale to Act 2 does not, like those in *opere buffe* of the time, carry forward the external action; also characteristic of the Singspiel, such crucial scenes as those of the lovers' intended elopement and the Pasha's pardoning them are not set to music but conducted in spoken dialogue.

It is in the three comic operas written with Lorenzo da Ponte that Mozart's most famous and most influential contributions to operatic history reside. In writing the librettos for these, *Le nozze di Figaro* (1786), *Don Giovanni* (1787, Prague) and *Così fan tutte* (1790), the astute Da Ponte must have sensed the particular nature of Mozart's gifts, providing him with texts that offered greater opportunity for the musical portrayal of complex character, motivation and emotion than he (or other librettists) commonly did for the generality of Italian opera composers.

The model for *Le nozze di Figaro* was Paisiello's *Il barbiere di Siviglia* (1782, first performed in St Petersburg but popular in Vienna and elsewhere), to which it forms a sequel in the original Beaumarchais plays. Da Ponte, because of the Viennese censorship, had to prune some of the political elements in the original and at least mute the expressions of social resentment; but the social tensions remain, coupled with sexual ones to provide the mainspring of the plot. They are manifest in, for example, Figaro's aria 'Se vuol ballare', with its tone of anger at the Count's sexual threat to his betrothed, Susanna, and (in the opposite direction) in the Count's Act 3 aria when he contemplates his servant's enjoying the sexual privileges from which he himself is debarred. Other arias that extend the expressive range of *opera buffa* include the two in which the Countess bewails the loss of her husband's love, Cherubino's evocations of adolescent passion (particularly 'Non so più', in Act 1) and Figaro's cynical tirade against womankind in the final act – this last devised by Da Ponte to stand in place of Beaumarchais' great monologue in which Figaro rails against aristocratic privilege in all its forms.

The alliance between music and dramatic action is enriched and tightened, especially in the ensembles. In the Act 3 Letter Duet it is charmingly done, with the repetition of phrases and a condensed recapitulation used to portray the act of dictation and reading back. In the Act 1 terzet, where Cherubino is discovered by the Count in supposedly suspicious circumstances in Susanna's room, a sonata-form musical structure is neatly managed to support and reinforce the sense of what is happening on the stage, with witty implications of irony in the music repeated by Don Basilio. The two main finales – to Acts 2 and 4 (the opera is in four acts) – are long, multi-section ensembles in the tradition established by Goldoni and Galuppi, with changes in tempo, metre, tonality and orchestration designed to reflect and propel the drama. Mozart carries this procedure beyond what was customary. Each finale is in a closed tonal scheme, beginning and ending in the same key; several of the sections are themselves formally closed units. There is a good example in the Act 2 finale (the B♭ Allegro, in 6/8, beginning at bar 167), where the Count is questioning Figaro about the paper (Cherubino's commission) that has been found in the garden: the music ranges through various keys as Figaro, searching for the answers, tries to wriggle out of the trap, and returns to B♭ only when he finally provides a plausible answer, to the Count's frustration and fury; the music forms a perfect analogue to the dramatic action. In the Act 4 finale, passing modulation is strikingly used to mark out dramatic incident, and the mock pleas of love from Figaro to the 'Countess' (Susanna in disguise) are paralleled in the parodistic nature of the music.

After the success in Prague of *Le nozze di Figaro*, at the beginning of 1787, Mozart was commissioned to write a new opera for production there: this was *Don Giovanni*, for which Da Ponte drew his libretto from a familiar story, used by Tirso de Molina, Molière, Goldoni and others, basing his text in particular on one by Giovanni Bertati, set by Gazzaniga for Venice early in 1787. Gazzaniga's setting is in one act; Da Ponte both tautened it (by cutting down the number of roles and strengthening the motivation) and expanded it. Generically, as we have seen (p. 83) the work is a *dramma giocoso*, in which there are serious roles (*parti serie*), intermediate ones (*mezzo carattere*) and comic ones (*parti buffe*), in the Venetian, Goldonian tradition. Donna Anna and Don Ottavio fall into the first category, Donna Elvira and Don Giovanni into the second and Leporello and the peasants into the third.

A difference of approach between *Don Giovanni* and *Figaro* is at once noticeable in the long, tonally unified scene that opens the opera: the overture (D, minor and major), a *buffo* aria for Leporello (F major), an ensemble (B♭ major) as Anna pursues the fleeing Giovanni, with a scene (modulating) as Giovanni fights and kills the Commendatore, then a recitative (first simple, then orchestral) leading to the duet (D minor) where Anna demands that Ottavio swear vengeance. In the more conventionally *buffo* material that ensues, the normal pattern of alternate simple recitative and lyrical music reappears; this includes music for the peasants and two numbers establishing Elvira's tragi-comic situation as a jilted woman, with exaggeratedly dramatic leaps and pauses. But with the return of the more serious side of the work, at the quartet 'Non ti fidar', another tract of near-continuous music begins.

What follows – including scenes for the peasant couple, the extended Act 1 finale, the mock-seduction of Elvira, all three of Giovanni's arias and the Act 2 sextet after which Leporello evades his pursuers – is interposed as compared with the Bertati model. But Da Ponte and Mozart cleverly devised what is essentially episodic material in such a way that it would enrich the characterization and maintain the thrust of the drama, driven by Giovanni's manic pursuit of women and Anna's thirst for vengeance. The division of characters by class, corresponding closely to *seria* and *buffa* types, is particularly well illustrated in the Act 1 finale, first in the deeply serious tone of the music sung by the masked trio, Anna, Elvira and Ottavio, as they approach the festivities at Giovanni's palace, and secondly by the three simultaneous layers of music heard and danced in the ball scene: an aristocratic minuet, a middle-class contredanse and a German dance for the peasants.

The main thread of the plot is resumed with the scene in the cemetery, where Giovanni invites the statue of the Commendatore to supper, and in the supper scene, where after diverting music from other operas (including *Figaro* and works by Martín y Soler and Sarti), the stone guest arrives and consigns the unrepentant Giovanni to hell in music of unprecedented power for a comic – indeed even a serious – opera: the original tonic of D minor is at last reached (to music heard at the beginning of the overture), and to hieratic dotted rhythms, the sound of trombones, and harmonies of extreme chromaticism and irregularity of movement Giovanni is overcome by the flames. But this is still an *opera buffa*, and cowering under the supper table throughout this scene is Leporello, proffering advice and the common man's wry or facetious observations, just as he had when Giovanni killed the Commendatore and planned the cruel deception of Elvira: comedy subsists alongside serious drama. Similarly, at the end of the opera, the surviving characters cheerfully draw the moral and plan their future in a sextet – a movement which was commonly omitted during the 19th and early 20th centuries to allow the opera to end on a note of high seriousness. No opera until Wagner's time has exercised such a degree of fascination among audiences and intellectuals or given rise to so extensive a literature, critical, interpretative or purely fanciful.

After works as complex and far-reaching as *Figaro* and *Don Giovanni*, it would have been inconceivable that Da Ponte and Mozart should have written a trivial comedy. That, however, is how their third opera, *Così fan tutte*, was long understood. Even quite shortly after its première, the change of temper of the times led to its theme, a wager on feminine fidelity, being looked at askance; both Beethoven and Wagner expressed shock at Mozart's choosing to treat such a topic. The theme has precedents in classical mythology and Renaissance literature; this most original and most subtly constructed of Da Ponte's three librettos for Mozart probably has a main source in Ariosto. Again, this is a comic opera, but the seriousness of the music makes it plain the the issues it deals with are real and deep and not to be lightly regarded.

The opera's plan and the make-up of its cast lend themselves to symmetrical patterns in the treatment, with three women (two sisters and their maid) and three men (two officers – the sisters' fiancés – and their friend). Each has at least one aria in each act, and the ensembles are devised so that the four principals are kept in their pairs and allowed little individual identity until well into Act 2. In the early part of the opera, the emotions expressed are largely conventional: the sisters' first arias, expressing respectively grief at parting and determination to remain faithful, are in a faintly grandiose, pretentious *opera seria*-like manner which embodies an element of self-parody, a musical counterpart to the girls' over-dramatized protestations. In Act 2, as each of the main characters is touched by stronger emotions, the music becomes more personal in tone and the arias' messages no longer simply the conventional ones. The two sisters and the two officers are increasingly differentiated, in a way that lends logic to the original couplings (in their disguises, the officers woo each other's fiancées). Thus the dilemma of the sterner sister, Fiordiligi, is conveyed in the deeply felt, heroic music of her 'Per pietà' (the only aria of the slow–fast rondò type); Dorabella, who has more readily capitulated and joined in a sensuous duet with Guglielmo, is now assigned a playful aria. Similarly, the quicksilver emotions of Ferrando – represented in the contrasts in his aria 'Tradito, schernito', and particularly in the expressive implications of its key scheme (C minor–Eb–C minor–C major, very rare in Mozart) – are contrasted with the cynicism and the bitterness of Guglielmo, expressed in his aria but especially in the canonic quartet for the supposed wedding toast: here Mozart characteristically made a virtue of necessity by assigning different music, and words to match, to the baritone, who could not join in the canon at a pitch apt to sopranos and a tenor. The pain of Fiordiligi's eventual capitulation, at the climactic point in her duet with Ferrando (note the piercingly chromatic oboe phrase), is unmistakable. It is, then, hard to see the opera as a frolic demonstrating merely the fickleness of womankind; it may rather be interpreted as a parable on the strength and uncontrollability of amorous feelings, on the recognition of human frailty and the importance of mature self-knowledge. Such an interpretation of *Così fan tutte* would make clear its place between the earlier Da Ponte operas and *Die Zauberflöte*.

Before proceeding to Mozart's late operas, however, we should briefly consider in what ways the music of Mozart's *opere buffe* differs from that of his contemporaries'. Comparison with such works as Paisiello's *Il barbiere di Siviglia* or Cimarosa's *Il matrimonio segreto* – the two most popular Italian *opere buffe* of the time – shows first that Mozart used much richer orchestral textures, as one would expect of an Austrian: arias accompanied by strings alone, or even strings with oboes and horns (very common in Italian music), are rare, and touches of woodwind colour are constantly used in allusive or emotionally suggestive ways. Second, Mozart's arias and ensembles tend to be longer and formally more complex and developed: often their structure is clearly related to their dramatic purport. Third, he used a much larger harmonic vocabulary. The criticisms allegedly uttered by Joseph II – 'too many notes' (of *Die Entführung*) and 'too tough for the teeth of my Viennese' (of *Don Giovanni*) – are significant even if apocryphal: a simpler, more direct style, with less distraction from the voice, was widely preferred. But Mozart's achievement in this medium of an emotional depth to which no other composer laid claim – and this was fully recognized and understood in his own day – and his Shakespeare-like ability to transfigure comedy, or to deal powerfully with central human issues while wearing the comic mask, depended on his purposeful deployment of the full arsenal of musical resources.

In his two late operas, the Singspiel *Die Zauberflöte* and the *opera seria La clemenza di Tito* (both 1791), Mozart did not go beyond the Da Ponte ones in terms of alliance between music and drama. The latter, written for coronation celebrations in Prague, makes use of a long-favoured Metastasio libretto, 'ridotto a vera opera' ('reduced to a true opera', to quote Mozart's own thematic catalogue: see p.75) for the occasion. By this he meant that it had been reshaped (by Caterino Mazzolà) in line with current ideas: by the insertion of ensembles and choruses, in particular a substantial concerted finale to the first act of the kind habitual in *opera buffa*, by a reduction in the number of arias, by the substitution of aria texts of a more direct character, and by simple curtailments. The result is a text attuned to the mood of the neo-classical revival that was gaining ground at the time in the German-speaking countries; Mozart's setting, with restrained, almost austere orchestral writing, smooth and broad vocal lines and relatively brief numbers, is an appropriate response. Only the *prima donna* and *primo uomo* are assigned full-length arias (each has one of the rondò type). The Act I finale, unlike the *opera buffa* model, moves from a fast tempo to a slower one, as the principals on the stage bewail the betrayal of the Roman emperor Titus, with the groans of the populace heard in the background as the city burns.

La clemenza di Tito was composed for a court audience in Prague, in contrast with *Die Zauberflöte*, designed for a popular Viennese audience at a suburban theatre run by the actor-manager Emanuel Schikaneder, who supplied Mozart's libretto (and played the leading comic role of

Papageno; see Plate 38). Firmly based in the traditions of Viennese popular theatre, it also draws on fairy-tales of the time, on literature about ancient Egypt and its rituals, and on freemasonry and its philosophical background. It is above all an opera of the Enlightenment. In it, the forces of darkness and light are counterposed: the former in the person of the Queen of Night and her entourage, the latter in that of Sarastro and his priestly community, which erects temples to Wisdom, Nature and Reason and has something of the character of a masonic lodge. The victory of light over darkness is seen in the outcome of the quest undertaken for the Queen, the rescue of her daughter Pamina from the clutches of Sarastro, by the prince Tamino: he chooses the path of enlightenment, is taken into Sarastro's community and, after they have undergone certain trials, is united with Pamina. The comic element in this is provided by Papageno, the bird-catcher who is Tamino's companion and serves to supply the common man's down-to-earth observations on the proceedings.

In *Die Zauberflöte* Mozart did much the same for Singspiel as he had done for *opera buffa* in the Da Ponte operas. He wrote musical numbers that were longer and more complex, including extended scenes at important junctures in the action (while retaining the traditional popular tone for Papageno's music). He brought a new tone of solemnity, closely akin to that in his masonic cantatas, to the ritual music for Sarastro and his priests. The Queen of Night is assigned brilliant coloratura, Tamino and Pamina a more direct, lyrical manner. There is no attempt to draw characters with the richness or human realism of those that inhabit the Da Ponte operas: that would be out of place in a pantomimic allegory. Tamino and Pamina represent ideals, not real people; it is significant that they sing no love duet. There are parallels between their quest and the theme of self-knowledge treated in *Così fan tutte*. More broadly, the opera is susceptible to interpretation in the light of the background to 18th-century freemasonry as referring to the human soul's search for inner harmony and enlightenment; this may help explain why a work in which the ridiculous is so generously mixed with the sublime should appeal on so deep a level. Goethe is among those who tried to supply it with a sequel; Bernard Shaw called it 'the music of my own church'.

Mozart was not a deliberate reformer of opera. He instituted no real changes in the theatrical forms of his day, and the influence on him of Gluck and other reformers of the third quarter of the century was modest. As his correspondence abundantly shows, however, he had a high degree of sophistication and percipience about his fellow human beings. This human insight, combined with his readiness to apply current symphonic techniques to operatic composition, enabled him to bring to the operatic stage a new depth of characterization and urbanity of manner.

Beethoven

Beethoven's place in operatic history rests on a single work, *Fidelio*. It is a Singspiel, with spoken dialogue; but its ancestry belongs less in German opera than in French and in particular that class of post-Revolution *opéra comique* known as 'rescue opera'. The original version of the libretto, by J. N. Bouilly, was written for Pierre Gaveaux, whose opera was given in Paris in 1798; there are also settings, in Italian, by Ferdinando Paer (1804, Dresden) and Giovanni Simone Mayr (1805, Padua). Beethoven's first version, now often known (as he wished it to be) as *Leonore*, was given in Vienna in 1805, but was unsuccessful, partly because of the unfortunate timing (the French armies had just occupied Vienna and most of Beethoven's admirers were out of the city), partly because it was found ineffective and repetitious. Beethoven was induced to make alterations and the opera was presented the next year with cuts and other changes, but Beethoven withdrew it after a dispute with the theatre management. It was revived again in 1814, now more drastically revised: it is in this form that it is normally heard today.

The opera treats the story of a young woman (Leonore) who, disguised as a youth (Fidelio), takes employment in a prison from which she rescues her husband (Florestan), unjustly incarcerated there because of his reformist politics. In the earlier version, there are extensive domestic episodes in the gaoler's house; Beethoven reduced them, but some stylistic discrepancy persists between the Singspiel banter of these sections and the high heroic and visionary music later. Mozart had bridged a similar gap in *Die Zauberflöte*, but in *Fidelio* the more selfconsciously lofty nature of the topic makes it additionally difficult. Beethoven's revisions of 1814 were directed towards producing not only a more succinct and better balanced work but also one more generalized in its tone as a plea against wrongful oppression and as a statement about marital devotion. There is indeed some sacrifice of drama and characterization to these ends in the opera's last scenes. Florestan's dungeon aria, which opens the last act (Act 3 in 1805, Act 2 in 1806 and 1814), has an altered ending, involving a vision of his wife, to replace an expression of defiance; and in the 1814 version Florestan and Leonore merely sing of their joy after the act of rescue whereas, in the earlier one, they are left uncertain as to their fate and have a long and moving recitative before the passionate expression of delight at their reunion – the same duet, changed only in detail, but carrying a different significance.

Yet it is the very nature of *Fidelio* as a generalized statement about courage, freedom and the human spirit that gives it its unique appeal. This is manifest not only, indeed not primarily, in what follows the rescue scene (the finale, where the evildoer, Pizarro, is exposed and arraigned, and in which the prisoners are restored to their families, is set to fairly conventional, jubilant cantata-like music). The most powerful expressions come in the noble aria for Leonore – given a new prefatory recitative in 1814, 'Abscheulicher, wo eilst du hin?' – which, akin to the 'rondò' of Mozart's time, takes the slow–fast form, and indeed may owe its heroic horn writing and its key (E major) to 'Per pietà' from *Così fan tutte*; in the Prisoners' Chorus, music of great poignancy; and in Florestan's aria already referred to. Other remarkable features include the canonic quartet 'Mir ist so wunderbar', where different emotions of great intensity are expressed to the same music (the tradition of canons in such contexts is mentioned above, apropos the *Così fan tutte* finale); and the melodrama (spoken words against music) in the gravedigging scene, one of several features that hint at the influence of Cherubini, whose music Beethoven much admired. But the spirit of idealism and deep seriousness which pervade the work, and lend it so powerful an appeal, are entirely Beethoven's own.

CHAPTER IX

France

JAMES R. ANTHONY, MARTIN COOPER, DAVID CHARLTON

1. The tragédie

The five surviving *tragédies lyriques* of Rameau represent the most important French serious opera of the 18th century up to the time of Gluck. Inaugurated in 1733 with *Hippolyte et Aricie*, they are built on the pattern evolved by Lully and Quinault: operas in five acts, each act containing an interlude or divertissement of singing and dancing which the librettists usually contrived to integrate into the action. The drama is carried on mainly in recitative, generally melodic even when declamatory; from time to time there are more tuneful passages (*petits airs*). Far from excluding melody, Rameau condemned a slavishly accurate imitation of natural declamation. The gradual merging of recitative and melodic passages, typical of his dramatic discourse, tends towards a quasi-Wagnerian continuity. Thanks to its subtlety it renders, as it were, the contour of the sentiment, its delicate changes as well as its massive ones, to a degree unknown to Lully or later to Gluck.

Rameau's solos show great diversity. Some are free and arioso-like; others have an opening ritornello and resemble the da capo aria (though the middle section in Rameau's *airs* is as long as the main one). The vocal line often remains close to recitative. The accompaniment may be elaborate and concertante in style, with the instruments and the voice competing almost on equal terms. The freedom increases in Rameau's later works where the *airs* blend increasingly with their context.

Rameau also wrote set pieces, duets and trios; these should be distinguished from the dramatic scenes where two or more characters sing together. The true set pieces may occur in dramatic scenes (the great Fates' trios in Act 2 of *Hippolyte et Aricie*, for example) but are commoner in divertissements: a well-known example is the trio of Dreams in Act 4 of *Dardanus* (1739).

The choruses, as important as they were for Lully, contain some of Rameau's most forceful writing: they too procure tension and release and, by punctuating the scenes, make up for the lack of contrast between *airs* and recitative. Many are bound up with the drama and are themselves action, for example those for the demons guarding Hell in Act 3 of *Castor et Pollux* (1737) or the contending good and evil forces in Act 5 of *Zoroastre* (1749). Rameau's most expressive outbursts of passion are attained in some of these action choruses, such as the second one for the Magicians in Act 2 of *Dardanus*, where relentless vigour is linked with a boding sense of danger. Action choruses have their counterpart in action dances, and in *ballets figurés*, such as the worship of a divinity, where the music accompanies and underlines dumb show.

It is however in his *symphonies de danse* that Rameau is at his most individual and most markedly superior to those who used similar forms. His dances are rich in both choreographic gesture and emotional significance, and often display remarkable felicities of orchestration, mixing wind and string textures in highly original ways (often with a prominent role for the bassoons). His overtures are formally original: the earliest keep to the slow–fast pattern inherited from Lully, but the faster sections become progressively less contrapuntal. Often his overtures carry a programmatic significance, and several are linked to the action that ensues. Rameau was 50 years old before his first opera reached the stage, at the Paris Opéra, and he began his operatic career with a work outstanding for its tragic grandeur. The libretto of *Hippolyte et Aricie*, by Simon-Joseph Pellegrin, draws on Racine's *Phèdre* and has deeper ancestry in Seneca and Euripides; it is notable for the opportunities it provides for characterization, for the placing of dramatic set pieces and for the integrated management of the divertissements. The opera's title notwithstanding, the two central characters are the tragic figures of Theseus and Phaedra. Pellegrin and Rameau devote the whole of Act 2 to Theseus's journey (on his friend's behalf) to Hades, his pleas and his trial at Pluto's court; in Act 3, he is compelled by his loyal subjects' joyous welcome back to earth (in a divertissement) to suppress his reactions to what he supposes to be an attempt by his own son on his wife's honour. His eventual outburst – after a remarkable modulating section expressing his uncertainty, a sustained and intense 40-bar arioso, 'Puissant maître des flots', an impassioned appeal to Neptune, the voice mingling with a turbulent violin line – gains extra force from the delay. (Surprisingly, Rameau altered the order of scenes when he revised the work, in response to misguided criticism.) No less powerful, and amply worthy of Racine, is the scene where Phaedra reveals her guilty love for her stepson; her expression of remorse at causing his (apparent) death is among the great moments of French opera.

Yet *Castor et Pollux* was generally regarded in his own day as Rameau's crowning achievement, at least from the time of its first revival in 1754. Its topic was unusual for French opera of the time: not romantic love but the fraternal love of the twins Castor and Pollux, one mortal, the other immortal. Telaira's 'Tristes apprêts' stands as a classical expression of grief, avoiding rending chromaticisms, suspensions or the minor mode, but moving simply with a broken fall from tonic to subdominant and thence to tonic – a characteristic example of Rameau's application of his theories about the expressive force of melodic intervals and harmonic progressions. The stark bassoon obbligato adds to its force. *Dardanus*, though musically rich and dramatically spectacular (Rameau heavily revised it for its 1744 revival), and *Zoroastre* suffer from defects in their librettos and both depend heavily on the supernatural. Rameau's last *tragédie* was *Les Boréades*, written when he was in his late 70s and intended for staging in 1764 (but not in fact given until the 1970s); it is remarkable for its vivid invention and especially its telling representations of storms and whirlwinds (the plot involves Boreas, god of the north wind, and his descendants).

The supremacy of musician over poet in Rameau's *tragédies lyriques* lay at the core of the often bitter arguments between the Lullistes and Ramistes which divided the Paris musical scene after 1733. While Campra expressed a professional's awe and respect for Rameau ('there is enough music in this opera [*Hippolyte*] to make ten of them: this man will eclipse us all'), the aestheticians saw in his music a dangerous and intolerable compromise of the sacrosanct role of the poet in the *tragédie lyrique*. Whether Rameau was attacked through his *tragédies lyriques* for his too complicated harmonies, his difficult melodies, his lack of interest in the text or for his Italianisms, 'all these could be reduced to one basic reproach: too much music' (Masson, 1911).

By the middle of the 18th century, as the quarrel between the Lullistes and the Ramistes gave way to the Querelle des Bouffons, attacks against the traditional *tragédie lyrique* multiplied. During the 25 years that separate Rameau's *Zoroastre* (1749) from Gluck's *Iphigénie en Aulide* (1774), only 11 of the 49 stage works performed at the Paris Opéra were *tragédies lyriques*. Before the arrival of the Italian comic troupe known as the Bouffons in 1752, Rameau, at the height of his career as a dramatic composer, was exempted from direct attack by the reformers; even Grimm had nothing but praise for him in his *Lettre sur Omphale* (1752) and carefully aimed his polemic at the earlier *tragédie lyrique*.

Many of the operatic reforms that culminated in Gluck's preface to *Alceste* (1769; see p.96), and indeed that charted the course of French serious opera throughout the rest of the century, were a result of the European intellectual climate of the 1750s and 1760s. During his sojourn in Paris Calzabigi, the future librettist of *Orfeo* and *Alceste*, had opportunity to familiarize himself with Rameau's *tragédies lyriques*, especially *Castor et Pollux*. In his *Dissertazione . . . sulle Poesie drammatiche del Signor Abate Pietro Metastasio* (1755), Calzabigi paid tribute to the spectacle that 'the celebrated Quinault had invented', regretting only the lack of 'purely human actions' to motivate the characters. It cannot be doubted that he was also influenced by Algarotti's *Saggio sopra l'opera in musica* (1755), which appeared in French translation in the *Mercure de France* of 1757. Algarotti decried the abuses of the da capo aria, and suggested that the overture be considered part of the drama, that the dance be related to the plot and that accompanied recitative be substituted for simple recitative. At the same time the Encyclopedists, led by Diderot, d'Alembert and Grimm, called for the simplification of operatic subject matter: Greek tragedy was regarded as the ideal source.

Others experimented with historical and exotic subjects. The plot of *Ernelinde* (1767) by Philidor to a libretto by Poinsinet is drawn from medieval Norwegian history; *Adèle de Ponthieu* (1772) by La Borde and Rezins de St Marc and *Sabinus* (1773) by Gossec and de Chabanon are both based on the history of ancient Gaul. These works are important forerunners of such historical operas as *Péronne sauvée* (1783) by Dezède and de Sauvigny, *Arvire et Evelina* (1788) by Sacchini and Guillard, *Pizarre ou La conquête du Pérou* (1785) by Candeille and Duplessis and *Fernand Cortez ou La conquête du Mexique* (1808) by Spontini and de Jouy.

For the first of his Paris 'tragédies-opéras', *Iphigénie en Aulide* (1774), Gluck and his librettist, Du Roullet, turned to Racine's tragedy, reinterpreting however the classical myth in terms of Enlightenment humanity. Though here, as in his other French operas, Gluck does not so strongly pursue the notion of a single theme to the opera, as in his Italian 'reform' works, there is still a powerful focus, on Agamemnon and his dilemma when as leader of the Greek army he is called upon by the gods to sacrifice his daughter; his agony is made plain in his tortured monologues, the climaxes of the opera. The ostensibly happy ending, when the gods intervene, is partly belied by the stark octaves and the minor tonality of the finale. *Iphigénie en Aulide* was followed the same year by a French version of *Orfeo* (*Orphée*), expanded with additional numbers, especially ballets, and with the castrato role adjusted for a high tenor (the versions favoured since Berlioz's time generally represent a compromise between the Italian original and the French revision, using a contralto as Orpheus but retaining much of the extra Parisian music, including the famous flute solo). In 1776 a similarly altered version of *Alceste* was given. *Armide*, to the libretto by Quinault that Lully had set, followed in 1777; Gluck regarded it later as perhaps his best work, saying that in it he sought to be 'more painter and poet than musician' and that he 'found a means to make the characters speak in such a way that one would at once know from their mode of expression whether it is Armide who speaks, or an attendant, etc'. Whereas *Alceste* must 'call forth tears', *Armide* must 'produce a voluptuous sensation': here Gluck was referring to the music of love and enchantment for Renaud in the magic garden of the sorceress Armide, and to the other love music in the opera, which is orchestrated with uncommon richness. But the most powerful of Gluck's Paris operas, indeed arguably of all his operas, is *Iphigénie en Tauride* (1779, the year also of the unsuccessful *Echo et Narcisse*). For this he created two of his most moving characters: the unhappy Iphigeneia, priestess in a distant land, whose suffering is so nobly portrayed in the long, seamless lines of her 'O malheureuse

Iphigénie' (where the avoidance of exact repetition recalls such a through-composed monologue *air* as Renaud's 'Plus j'observe ces lieux' from Act 2 of Lully's *Armide*); and her brother Orestes, in deepest despair and haunted by the Furies after slaying his mother to avenge his father. The overture represents a storm at sea, analogous to the turbulence in the hearts of the main characters; the musical representation of the friendship of Orestes and Pylades, and of the rival groups of Greeks and barbarian Scythians (pursuing the 'racial characterization' of *Paride ed Elena*) are further features of this noble score.

Gluck's Paris operas met many of the Encyclopedists' requirements. Their musical debt to the earlier *tragédie lyrique* must be acknowledged. The 'programme' overtures of *Alceste* and the two *Iphigénies* have origins in Rameau's overtures to *Zoroastre* and *Naïs*, a *pastorale héroïque* of 1749; accompanied recitatives of ample proportions had existed in French opera from Lully's final period, as had the liaison of chorus and dance with the dramatic action. Gluck's French reform operas assimilated the most dramatically viable features of earlier models, from Lully to Rameau, and subjected all to a rigorous process of simplification (see, for example, the elimination of the role of Alcestis's confidante, Ismene, in Roullet's reworking of Calzabigi's original libretto for *Alceste*). Gluck also extended the dramatic function of the orchestra, subordinated the *merveilleux* and dance to dramatic concerns and, in synthesizing French monologue *air* and Italian aria, created an extended 'air de situation'.

Not everyone found Gluck's simplification of drama (and music) to his liking; the *Mercure* of September 1774, for example, complained about the 'too simple' dramatic action of *Orphée*. Simplification was the essential feature of the subsequent conflict between Gluckists and Piccinnists, at least as regards serious opera. Piccinni's librettist, Marmontel, found Gluck's operas too severe and lacking in variety in their avoidance of spectacle. As early as 1759, Marmontel had declared himself a partisan of Italian music, but at the same time he suggested Quinault's librettos for operatic subject matter (*Mercure de France*, July 1759). He later provided Piccinni with librettos based on Quinault's *Roland* (1778) and *Atys* (1780), and Philidor with his version of Quinault's *Persée* (also 1780). Although Marmontel reduced these librettos from five acts to three, he retained most of the divertissements in the originals, occasionally changing a 'troupe de fées et d'ombres de héros' to a more realistic 'troupe de Chevaliers et de dames françaises' (final scene of *Roland*). The music of Piccinni's *tragédies lyriques* is in fact stylistically close to that of his great rival, in spite of Piccinni's occasional reversions into Italianisms (see, for example, Médor's *air* at the end of Act 2 of *Roland*). The close relationship is especially evident in the 'pompe funèbre' from Act 3 of *Didon*.

The term *tragédie lyrique* embraced many different genres in the last quarter of the 18th century. The work of a single librettist such a Guillard includes adaptations of Greek tragedies (Gluck's *Iphigénie en Tauride*, 1779; Lemoyne's *Electre*, 1782; Sacchini's *Oedipe à Colone*, 1786), operatic versions of Corneille's plays (Sacchini's *Chimène ou Le Cid*, 1783; Salieri's *Les Horaces*, 1786), revisions of earlier French *tragédies lyriques* (Sacchini's *Dardanus*, 1784) and historical operas (Lemoyne's *Louis IX en Egypte*, 1790; Sacchini's *Arvire et Evelina*, 1788). Perhaps it was this loss of identity that stimulated Beaumarchais' comment, in the preface to his libretto for Salieri's *Tarare* (1787): 'Opera is neither tragedy nor comedy, but it partakes of each and may embrace all genres'.

2. Opéra-ballet and related genres

The *opéra-ballet*, cultivated during the period between Lully's death in 1687 and the first performance of Rameau's *Hippolyte et Aricie* in 1733, was a work consisting normally of a prologue and three or four acts or *entrées*, each with its own set of characters and independent action, relating loosely to a collective idea expressed in the work's title. Each *entrée* includes at least one divertissement of songs and dances. The form of the *opéra-ballet* resembles that of the earlier *ballet à entrées* and such stage ballets as Lully's *Le triomphe de l'Amour* (1681), Lalande's *Ballet de la jeunesse* (1686) and Collasse's *Ballet des saisons* (1695).

In the hands of its creator, Campra, and his followers, Mouret and Montéclair, the main contribution of the *opéra-ballet* to the French lyric stage was the introduction of flesh-and-blood characters in recognizable, contemporary settings. The mythological and allegorical figures of the earlier ballets and *tragédies lyriques* were eliminated or confined to the prologues. 'L'opéra' from Campra's *Les fêtes vénitiennes* takes place in the theatre of the Grimani Palace in Venice, 'Les ages rivaux' from his *Les ages* is set in Hamburg, and Marseilles is the location of Mouret's 'La fille' from *Les fêtes ou Le triomphe de Thalie*.

Cahusac saw in the *opéra-ballet* a musical parallel to 'pretty Watteaus' and characterized the first one, *L'Europe galante* (1697), as the 'first of our works for the lyric stage that bears no resemblance to the operas of Quinault [and Lully]' (*La danse moderne et ancienne*, 1754). From *Les fêtes vénitiennes* (1710) onwards, comic intrigue was exploited with great skill. *Les fêtes ou Le triomphe de Thalie* (1714) had a *succès de scandale* because of the humiliating defeat of Melpomene (the muse of tragedy) by Thalia (the muse of comedy) in its prologue whose setting, the stage of the Paris Opéra, was in itself a bold choice. There was an increasing effort to mirror the social and cultural mores of court life during the declining years of Louis XIV and, after 1715, the Regency. Rémond de Saint-Mard (1741) clearly understood the appeal of the *opéra-ballet* for a public grown weary of the heroic gestures of the *grand siècle*: 'We have reached the point, Monsieur, where one desires only Ballets [*opéras-ballets*] ... Each act must be composed of a fast-moving, light and ... *galante* intrigue ... You will also find there the portrait of our mores. They are, to be sure, rather vile [*vilaines*], but they are none the less ours'.

The flexible format of the *opéra-ballet* invited experimentation on the part of librettist and composer. New *entrées* were often substituted for those that had elicited only a fair audience response: for example, from June to December 1710 a total of eight *entrées* had been composed for *Les fêtes vénitiennes*. Innovation extended to musico-dramatic features as well. In scene ii of 'Le bal' in that work, obviously modelled on the *maître de musique* and the *maître à danser* scenes in Molière's *Le bourgeois gentilhomme*, Campra parodied extracts from famous operas of the day to illustrate the power of music and dance. He did not identify his quotations, but many members of the audience could have recognized the 'Tempête' from Marais' *Alcione* and the 'Sommeil' from Destouches' *Issé*. The libretto to Mouret's *Les fêtes ou Le triomphe de Thalie* (1714) indicates that this was the first opera in which female performers were 'habillées à la françoise'; in the *entrée* 'La Provençale', added in 1722, Mouret introduced Provençal melodies sung in local dialect.

The most productive period of the *opéra-ballet* closed with the regent's death in 1723. It was superseded by the *ballet héroïque*, which restored many trappings of monarchial opera. From Collin de Blamont's *Les fêtes grecques et romaines* (1723) to Rameau's *Les surprises de l'amour* (1748), the *ballet héroïque* substituted heroic or exotic characters for the lively *petits maîtres* and amorous ladies drawn from the social milieu of the Regency that characterized the *opéra-ballet*.

It was probably no accident that *Les fêtes grecques et romaines*, the first *ballet héroïque*, coincided with the end of the Regency and the return of a king (even if a boy king) to the French throne. According to the *avertissement* of the librettist, Fuzelier, this was 'a completely new type of Ballet . . . that brought together all the best known Festivals of Antiquity which appeared to be the most adaptable to the stage'. By the time of Mouret's *Les amours des dieux* (1727), any pretence of avoiding a return to mythology was cast aside, although the *avertissement* says that, despite mythological characters, the work is 'absolutely in the heroic genre'. The rare use of comedy in the *ballet héroïque* (see, for example, Destouches' *Les stratagèmes de l'amour*, 1726) demanded explanation in the *avertissement*: 'The public has decided that, if Comedy is allowed on stage, it may be only a noble Comedy which bears the character of Antiquity'. The musical highpoint of this genre was reached in the six *ballets héroïques* by Rameau (*Les Indes galantes*, 1735; *Les fêtes d'Hébé*, 1739; *Les fêtes de Polymnie*, 1745; *Le temple de la gloire*, 1745; *Les fêtes de l'Hymen et de l'Amour, ou Les dieux d'Egypte*, 1747; and *Les surprises de l'amour*, 1748).

Single *entrées* from the more popular *opéras-ballets* survived into the second half of the 18th century as parts of *fragments* (known also as 'spectacles coupés'), a curious genre in which a new production was formed from three or four acts plucked arbitrarily from different *opéras-ballets*, one-act operas or *actes de ballet* (one-act ballets). Thus in 1759, 'Les devins de la Place St Marc' from *Les fêtes vénitiennes* formed part of a *fragment* that also included Rousseau's *Le devin du village* and *Ismène*, an *acte de ballet* by Rebel and Francoeur.

Another genre that co-existed with the *opéra-ballet* and the *ballet héroïque* is the so-called 'comédie lyrique'. Works that fall under that heading use the same kind of contemporary material as the *opéra-ballet* and similarly emphasize the divertissement of songs and dances. The distinguishing feature is that in a *comédie lyrique* the plot is continuous throughout, no matter the number of acts. 'Comédie lyrique' is a modern term; during the period itself the terminology in libretto and score alike is loose. Thus *Aricie* (La Coste, 1697), *Les festes galantes* (Desmarest, 1698) and *Le Carnaval de Venise* (Campra, 1699) were labelled simply 'ballet'; *Le carnaval et la folie* (Destouches, 1704) and *Platée* and *La princesse de Navarre* (both Rameau, 1745) were labelled 'comédie-ballet'; and *Don Quichotte chez la Duchesse* (Boismortier, 1743) was labelled 'ballet comique'. Mouret's *Les amours de Ragonde* (1742), a revised version of *Le mariage de Ragonde et de Colin* (1714), was referred to as a 'comédie en musique' in the libretto of 1742, as a 'divertissement comique' by Moncrif in his 'approbation' at the conclusion of this libretto and as a 'comédie-ballet' in the score. The range of subject matter in the lyric comedy is broad. A light comic intrigue is found in *Les festes galantes* and *Les amours de Ragonde*; *Platée* and *Le carnaval et la folie* border on buffoonery; and *Le carnaval de Venise* is a romantic comedy in which the course of true love is frustrated by jealous rivals.

No survey of French stage music of the *grand siècle* would be complete without mention of the *pastorale héroïque*. The pastoral is a dominant strain in French opera from its inception through the *tragédie lyrique* to the *opéra-ballet*, from the magic scenes in Rameau's *Dardanus* (1739) to the shepherd Lysis with his *carmagnole* and red turban in Grétry's *La rosière républicaine* (1794). Lully's first opera, *Les fêtes de l'Amour et de Bacchus* (1672), is a *pastorale pastiche* and his final stage work, *Acis et Galathée* (1686), is a *pastorale héroïque*. For Pierre-Jean-Baptiste Nougaret the *pastorale héroïque* was a 'Drama whose subject is more serious than simple and whose dénouement is sometimes tragic' (*De l'art du théâtre*, 1769). *Pastorales héroïques* given at the Opéra before Rameau include works by Gatti (*Coronis*, 1691), Destouches (*Issé*, 1697), Bertin de la Doué (*Le jugement de Paris*, 1718), Villeneuve (*Princesse d'Elide*, 1728), Rebel (1730) and Collin de Blamont (*Endimion*, 1731). Rameau's four *pastorales héroïques* – *Zaïs* (1748), *Naïs* (1749), *Acante et Céphise* (1751) and *Daphnis et Eglé* (1753) – lack the sustained dramatic tone of his *tragédies lyriques* and place greater emphasis on the divertissement; they are 'heroic' only in that they happen to involve the actions of heroes and gods.

Although he wrote many pastorales (for example *Actéon*, 1683, *La couronne de fleurs*, 1685 and *Il faut rire et chanter*, 1684–5), Charpentier composed two of what Hitchcock labels an 'operatic divertissement' – *Les plaisirs de Versailles* (early 1680s) and *Les arts florissants* (1685–6); sung throughout, they are in fact operas in one act.

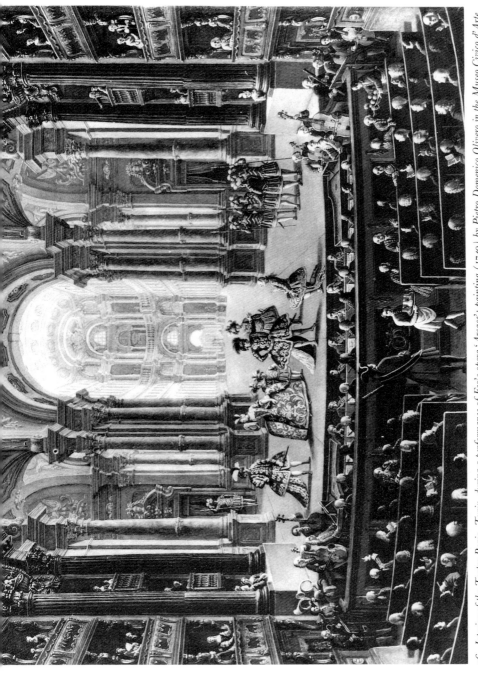

26. *Interior of the Teatro Regio, Turin, during a performance of Feo's opera 'Arsace': painting (1740) by Pietro Domenico Olivero in the Museo Civico d'Arte Antica, Turin*

27. *Engraving after a stage design by Filippo Juvarra for Alessandro Scarlattis 'Il Ciro', first performed at the Palazzo della Cancelleria, Rome, in 1712*

28. *'Reggia magnifica' designed by Pietro Righini for Vinci's 'Medeo' (Act 3 last scene), Parma, Teatro Farnese, 1728: engraving by Martin Engelbrecht*

Stage design by Bernardino and Fabrizio Galliari for the garden scene from Piccinni's 'Tigrane', first performed at the Teatro Regio, Turin, in 1761 (Museo Civico, Varese)

Sarti's 'Giulio Sabino': illustration of Act 2 scene x, from the printed full score (Vienna, c1781)

32. *St Michael's Square, Vienna, with the Burgtheater (right foreground) and the Spanish Riding School (behind it): engraving (1783) by C. Schütz*

...rior of the Schönbrunn Sch-
...er, Vienna, during a per-
...e given in the presence of the
...nily: painting by an artist of
...nese school (18th century) in
...oss Schönbrunn, Vienna

...rior of the Theater an der
...uring the first performance of
...e first two versions (1805 or
...of Beethoven's 'Fidelio':
...g

35. *Ignaz Umlauf's 'Die Bergknappen' (1778), scene iv: drawing and engraving by Carl Schütz*

36. *Title-page of the first edition of the vocal score of J. A. Hiller's 'Der Aerndtekranz' (Leipzig: J. F. Junius, 1772)*

Title-page of the first edition of the vocal score of Mozart's 'Die Entführung aus dem Serail' (Mainz: chott, 1785)

Playbill (right) for the first performance of zart's 'Die Zauberflöte' (Vienna, Theater auf der den, 1791) and Emanuel Schikaneder (left) as ageno: engraving (1791) by Ignaz Alberti

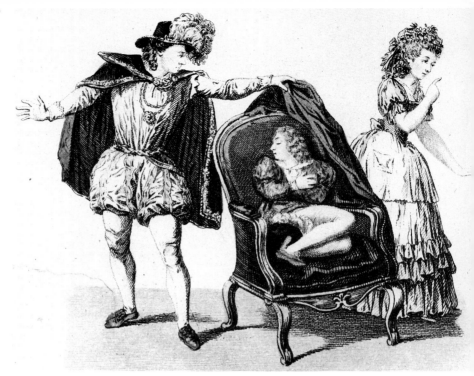

39. *Scene from Act I of Beaumarchais'*
Mariage de Figaro': engraving (late 1
tury) in the Bibliothèque de la Comédie F

40. *Luigi Bassi in the title role of Mozar*
'Don Giovanni': engraving by Medard T
1787

41. *Playbill for the first performance of M*
opera 'Cosi fan tutte', given at the Burg
Vienna on 26 January 1790

42. *Frontispiece from the piano score of M*
'La Clemenza di Tito': engraving showin,
from the opera (Leipzig, 1795)

43. Rameau's 'Castor et Pollux' (Pa...
Opéra, 1737): costumes for Phoebe, Poll...
Telaira, Castor (left to right, top to botto...

44. Scene from Hilverding's revival (175...
of 'Le turc généreux' from Rameau's 'I...
Indes galantes': engraving (1759) by B...
nardo Bellotto

Le Turc Genereux

45. *Stage design by Fabrizio Galliari for Act 2 of Gluck's 'Alceste', first performed at the Burgtheater, Vienna, in 1767: pen and ink drawing with wash, in the Pinacoteca Nazionale, Bologna*

46. *Sketch by Pierre-Adrien Paris of the 'palais enchanté' in Gluck's 'Armide', Versailles, Grand Théâtre, 1784: pen and ink drawing*

47. Scene at the Foire St Germain, Paris: miniature (1763) by Nicholas van Blarenberghe in the Wallace Collection, London

48. Interior of the Hôtel Bourgogne, Paris, during performance by the Opéra Comique: drawing (1767) P. A. Wille (the younger) the Bibliothèque Nationale, Paris

Rousseau's 'Le devin du village'
(1752): engraving (1779) by P. A.
Martini after J. M. Moreau

'The Beggar's Opera' (Act 3
Scene ii) by Gay and Pepusch:
engraving of the painting (1729) by
William Hogarth

Rame 22.

66

51. Courtyard seen fr
angle, illustrating 'oper
67a: Per disegnare le
vedute per angolo' in
inando Galli-Bibiena's
chitettura civile' (I
1711): engraving by un
artist

52. Design by Loui
Desprez for J. G. Nau
opera 'Gustaf Wasa' (
in the National M
Stockholm

three drawings from Franz Lang's 'Dissertatio de actione sceanica' (1727) showing (from left to right) examples of 'the position *of limbs, arms and fingers'; 'how to make an entrance'; and 'how to express feelings in silence'*

ical disposition of singers, dancers and the orchestra for the performance of an opera at the Grand Théâtre de Versailles in 1773, *with the name of each performer: watercolour by François Metoyen (one of the bassoonists in the orchestra) in the Bibliothèque de* 's

3. Early opéra comique

Terminology, antecedents, origins

The term 'opéra comique' is traditionally used, in the discussion of French opera, to signify opera with spoken dialogue, of the kind favoured at the Théâtre de l'Opéra-Comique (as distinguished from 'opéra', with continuous music, as preferred at the Opéra). It does not mean 'comic opera': an *opéra comique* may be heroic, like Grétry's *Richard Coeur-de-lion*, romantic-historic, like Meyerbeer's *L'étoile du nord*, or tragic, like Bizet's *Carmen*. The term is not, in this sense, strictly historical. It was used in the 18th century (before the foundation in 1801 of the Théâtre de l'Opéra-Comique), but as one of a number of alternatives, depending on the genre and tone of the entertainment. Works mainly using traditional tunes were 'vaudevilles' or 'pièces en vaudevilles'. Comedies using composed music in the second half of the century could be designated 'opéra comique', 'opéra bouffon' or 'comédie mêlée d'ariettes' (comedy mixed with arias). But since 'comédie' also meant simply 'play', 'comédie mêlée d'ariettes' also designated more serious subjects, together with other labels such as 'comédie lyrique'. The English-influenced moralizing drama in a realistic setting (*drame bourgeois*) affected *opéra comique* of the 1760s, giving rise to analogous musical works, designated 'drame lyriqe' or 'comédie mise en musique' etc. By 1784 *opéra comique* encompassed many of the sub-genres, dramatically speaking, known to it in the 19th century.

The figures of the Italian *commedia dell'arte* (who appeared in France during the 16th century) and their French equivalents, found in the figures of the medieval *sottie* – the old father Cassandre, Colombine or Isabelle his daughter, the lover Arlequin, the lazy and greedy servant Paillasse – were almost certainly the stock characters in the entertainments given at the big Paris fairs. The Foire St Germain (February to Palm Sunday) and the Foire St Laurent (mid-June to September) offered theatrical entertainments apt to their large number of floating and mostly disreputable visitors drawn from all levels of society. Music was only an accessory, but the latest popular song, or vaudeville, might be introduced as an apt allusion or simply hinted at by humming the music of the first line or the refrain. By degrees a whole repertory of these stock musical allusions came into being, and many vaudeville tunes became common property, to be fitted with new words by any enterprising actor. The words of the refrain or of the first line, by which the tune was known, was called the *timbre*, the music itself the *fredon* (an obvious allusion to the time-honoured humming of the comedian).

If the sideshows of the big fairs provided one of the origins of *opéra comique* in France, the court itself provided the other. As we have seen (Chapter III), when the Italian Cardinal Mazarin succeeded Richelieu as first minister in 1642, he introduced opera into France, and in the 1650s Lully was composing *comédie-ballets* for the court. When Lully's *tragédies lyriques* began to appear during the next decade, their noble and stilted style was soon picked on as a subject for parody by the fair performers, who competed with the Italian troupes at court for the favour of the sophisticated as well as the rowdier elements of the public. In 1682 the Italian troupe at the Hôtel de Bourgogne gave a performance containing *symphonies*, *airs de danse*, vaudevilles and French and Italian *airs*; but the Italians were expelled in 1697, probably for having lampooned Mme de Maintenon in a piece called *La fausse prude*. The popularity of opera parodies developed fully only later, but its eventual extent may be gauged by the fact that no fewer than seven different parodies of Lully's *Atys* were given between 1710 and 1738. Meanwhile the fair players had to contend with the legal monopolies exercised by the Comédie-Française and the Académie Royale de Musique, and they were proscribed in 1707, 1709 and 1710. Their response was to observe the letter of the law by executing their pieces in dumbshow and miming on the stage, with posters or placards (*écriteaux*) displaying the text suspended from the ceiling, and a claque stationed in the audience to lead the singing of the vaudevilles. These *pièces en vaudevilles* became exceedingly popular. In 1716 the Opéra permitted the Théâtres de la Foire to give 'spectacles mixed with music, dance and *symphonies* under the name of Opéra-Comique' (this term had first appeared on publicity notices in 1715).

1715–50

With the death of Louis XIV in 1715 the tone of society changed, and the licence of the Regency was reflected in the *opéra comique* of the next 15 years. The Opéra-Comique, while dodging the various temporary restrictions imposed on it, continued to assemble a repertory in which music was an essential part. Rameau, newly arrived from Clermont, was engaged to write six pieces of original music for Alexis Piron's play *L'Endriague* (1723; now lost), including a ceremonial scene, a magic scene and dances. In 1726 he provided several danced movements for *La robe de dissension*, also by Piron. Already the orchestra could contain some ten to 15 players. Other composers in this period included Jacques Aubert, Pierre-Philippe L'abbé and, especially, Jean-Claude Gillier.

New figures made their appearance alongside the stock characters of the old comedy – the young buck, the *grande dame*, the priest, the boasting Gascon and even such bourgeois figures as lawyers and doctors, with a sprinkling of ill-defined peasant types. The chief writers for the *opéra comique* from 1724 were Le Sage, d'Orneval and Fuzelier, and they incorporated music for overtures, dances, descriptive *symphonies* and vaudeville finales. In 1726 the comedians presented *L'obstacle favorable*, introducing the new character of the *ingénu*, the country simpleton, and his equally simple girl. The peasant figures of Molière had been wholly conventional, a Blaise or a Lucas introduced to raise an easy laugh by their country oaths and their bad grammar. The *ingénu* soon became the stock vehicle for the refined indecencies that fashion demanded. The *double entendre*, always popular, now took on a new importance, and the quandary of Daphnis and Chloë was spun out into literally hundreds of variations. The most popular of these plays, which had 200 performances in its first year, was Favart's *La chercheuse d'esprit* (1741).

It was Favart who, between 1732 and 1750, was responsible, in Voltaire's words, for 'first making a decent and ingenious amusement out of a form which, before you, did not concern polite society. Thanks to you it has become the delight of all decent folk'. Favart's plays at their most characteristic include rustic characters, usually with a pair of thwarted lovers, but his rustics are the elegant, beribboned ones of Boucher's pictures, and the nature of their love is not very serious.

In 1716 the Regent brought back the Italian players, who resumed performances in the theatre of the Hôtel de Bourgogne. They were named 'Comédiens Italiens Ordinaires du Roi' in 1723; their repertory took in French plays, ballets and musical pieces. During the time of Mouret, their composer-director from 1717 to 1737, the orchestra could consist of nine strings, three woodwind, trumpets and timpani. The company gave Pergolesi's *La serva padrona* in 1746; the public liked the music but the show was ousted by a long-popular play, *Le prince de Salerne*. Favart wrote some vaudeville plays for the Italians, but worked mainly for the Opéra-Comique; indeed, in 1743 he was employed by Monnet, the new director of that company, to revise its repertory. At this juncture its musical directors were Blaise and Boismortier; the orchestra now consisted of some ten strings and the usual six wind instruments (two players doubling flutes and oboes, two bassoons and two horns). Monnet's lease was suppressed and performances stopped from 1745 to 1751, but in 1752 the company resumed under his control, showing off a new and richly decorated theatre he had had built at the Foire St Laurent.

1750–62

This period was a turning-point in the history of *opéra comique*: the many interrelated cultural and political forces at work were complex in their effects. One cultural landmark was the appearance of the first two volumes of the great *Encyclopédie* (1751–2), a work which focussed many minds on the reforms of musical theatre in the age of Enlightenment. Another was the first performance of Rousseau's *intermède* with recitatives, *Le devin du village* (Fontainebleau, 18 October 1752), which held the Parisian stage until 1829. This was significant in several ways. The product of a single creative mind, it exemplified the requirement for unity in opera, as opposed to the heterogeneous Baroque approach; it contained a pantomime featuring the fable of a reprehensible courtier who tries to buy the favours of a village girl; it used the Italian 'dialogue' form of duet; and it deployed a quite un-Baroque, unpretentious melodic style. This struck a balance between simple memorability and natural declamatory response to the words (rise and fall, rhythmic stress and patterning). The whole breathed a dignified simplicity and helped establish a useful matrix of *opéra comique* plot: the temporary disruption of a relationship by a third party of socially superior rank.

The Querelle des Bouffons exploded in 1752–4, when a small Italian troupe led by Eustache Bambini gave a series of intermezzos and operas at the Opéra. The public welcome accorded to Pergolesi's *La serva padrona* was boosted by the Encyclopedists' pamphlets in support of Italian opera against French. Rousseau himself inveighed against 'French music' (*Lettre sur la musique française*, 1753), but the real targets of the reformers were the hidebound material and performing practices at the Opéra, which were also a symbol of the absolute monarchy. Soon some important hybrid works arose which coupled real Italian *buffo* music, adapted to French words, and new dialogue: the Opéra-Comique put on *Bertholde à la ville* (*Bertoldo in corte*), *Le chinois poli en France* (1754) and *Le diable à quatre* (1756), while the Comédie-Italienne mounted *Ninette à la cour* (1755) and translations of Italian opera, for example *La servante maîtresse* in 1754 and *La bohémienne* (*La zingara*) in 1755. These proved that French words could satisfactorily be sung in the new *galant* style, and indeed Philidor is traditionally credited with some of the music of *Le diable à quatre*; other of its pieces are derived from such composers as Galuppi, Giuseppe Scarlatti and Duni.

It was a natural step for Monnet to invite an Italian to the Opéra-Comique, and Duni arrived in 1757 with the first of his successes, *Le peintre amoureux de son modèle*. This was followed by long-popular works: *Mazet* (1761), *Les deux chasseurs et la laitière* (1763), *La fée Urgèle* (1765) and *La clochette* (1766). During this period popular vaudevilles still found a place in *opéra comique*. Intense public interest in this genre led to great rivalry between the two companies. Duni wrote mainly for the Opéra-Comique while Favart now worked more for the Comédie-Italienne.

Another cultural force appeared in this period: Diderot as playwright and dramatic theorist. He had already contributed a few writings at the time of the Querelle. In *Le fils naturel* (1757) he demonstrated the possibility of domestic bourgeois subjects as an alternative to current modes of tragedy and comedy, while in its accompanying 'conversations' (the *Entretiens sur Le fils naturel*) he called for a unified type of opera, for 'true tragedy, true comedy': in opera, for the conditions of men to be dramatized, for mime to be exploited and for grouped scenes (tableaux) to be constructed, with their implication of simultaneity and the use of the ensemble. Diderot not only sketched a *Plan d'opéra-comique*; he also helped authors by criticizing and improving their works. In this way he later influenced, for example, the text of Masson de Pezay's *La rosière de Salency*, set by Grétry. Most of Diderot's prescriptions were eventually realized in the theatre.

Among the writers influenced by Diderot, and ambitious for the role of music in *opéra comique*, was Sedaine, whose influential career extended to 1791. His *Le diable à quatre* was merely pasticcio work; he was never again to write without a single collaborating musician (first Philidor, then Monsigny, then Grétry). Sedaine reduced pre-composed vaudevilles to the absolute minimum and soon excluded them. He was inspired by the potential of the musical ensemble, accompanied by action; by music's ability to deal with vital scenes; and by the notion of specifying exactly what an actor should do as well as say. *Opéra comique* in his hands extended in scope and content. *Le roi et le fermier* (1762) was written in deliberate competition with five-act plays at the Comédie-Française. After three (very different) comedies for the Opéra-Comique in 1759–61 Sedaine never returned to this genre pure and simple. He disliked the pastoral mode and was more interested in themes portraying trials of justice and the righting of wrongs.

The years 1759–62 saw a burst of activity involving Sedaine, Philidor and Monsigny, among others, while Favart and Gibert staged the immensely durable *Soliman II* (1761). The farcical one-act *Blaise le savetier* (1759; Philidor and Sedaine) is extraordinary for the length and humour of its duets and ensembles; *Le jardinier et son seigneur* (1761; Philidor and Sedaine), also in one act, sees the range of characters expanded and opportunity for social satire; and *On ne s'avise jamais de tout* (1761; Monsigny and Sedaine), though again in one act, contains no fewer than 17 vocal items. These formed a singular musico-dramatic design, assigning the weight of musical character development to the middle of the work and musical action in ensembles towards the end.

The musical organization of these works is already varied. Arias are often in types of ternary form, but rondo, binary and irregular constructions also occur. Philidor was the most forward in essaying simple sonata structures. The *romance* (partly emulating one in *Le devin du village*) was a regular solo feature, sometimes with pizzicato accompaniment evoking the guitar. All *opéras comiques* included one or more duets, and most had a trio, if not also a quartet, while Philidor's *Le soldat magicien* (1760), as well as *Le jardinier et son seigneur* and *On ne s'avise*, contains a quintet. (Larger ensembles were introduced later.) Ways were already being found to conclude a work in a solidly composed manner. Philidor's *Le maréchal ferrant* (1761) and *On ne s'avise* have an ensemble coda following their final vaudeville statement. Such codas were sometimes designated 'Choeur', even though no actual chorus in the modern sense existed as such within the Opéra-Comique. By March 1761 the *Mercure de France* could say that 'La musique . . . est devenue la partie intéressante d'un opéra-comique'.

Whether simply because of financial losses at the Comédie-Italienne or because the king's advisers also felt that the Opéra-Comique was artistically too successful, a merger was ordered: from 3 February 1762 the best five of the latter's singers and its repertory were taken over by the Comédie-Italienne.

1762–9
Although the Comédie-Italienne thus became the only official troupe

presenting musical stage works besides the Opéra, it was still legally obliged to maintain the use of spoken dialogue (brief recitatives were allowed), and it was not intended that it should be permitted to present Italian opera, even in French. This practice continued to a limited degree. Up to 1759–60 its orchestra was no larger than previously noted; after the merger ten violins were on the regular payroll, with two violas, three cellos, a double bass and six wind players.

The period was characterized by more variety of length, material and musical means in *opéra comique*. *Le roi et le fermier* (1762), with three acts, its just king, its royal hunt and storm (portrayed within an entr'acte) and its English source (Robert Dodsley's play *The King and the Miller of Mansfield*), set the style. Monsigny's music is ingenious and well proportioned to the scale of events. Other English sources informed Duni's *L'école de la jeunesse* (1765), after George Lillo's *The London Merchant*, and Philidor's *Tom Jones* (1765), after Fielding. Favart and Duni's *Les moissonneurs* (1768) showed honest humanity in the paternalist working milieu of the countryside; and in *La fée Urgèle* (1765) the same authors created the first four-act *opéra comique*, which, for all its supernatural strain, ambitiously showed the 'court of love' of Queen Berthe, supposedly in the 7th century, and thus prefigured the 'troubadour' vogue of the 1780s and beyond.

Philidor's *Le bûcheron* (1763), including the first comic septet, two quartets and a trio, continued the farcical tradition. But his *Le sorcier* (1764) was more important, both for its mixture of comic and half-serious material and for the way that it exemplified musically what might be called the 'aggregation tendency' of the 1760s: the tendency for set numbers to run into one another to produce more continuous, ambitious musical items. For example, its opening solo turns into a partial duet and then a fully-fledged duet as an exactly calculated dramatic device. Another characteristic was the 'narrative-descriptive' aria, used by Philidor in particular. It made use of prominent musical description in the orchestra in order to illustrate a character's past adventure or their conditions of work. Humorous vocal techniques were often employed, as in the imitations of an ass and a horse in *Le maréchal ferrant*; the hunting narration in *Tom Jones* even used string harmonics.

In his three *opéras comiques* of this period, *Le tonnelier* (1765), *Les pêcheurs* (1766) and *Toinon et Toinette* (1767), Gossec showed efficient familiarity with recent techniques but did not add new ones. Like Monsigny and Philidor, he ended final acts with an ensemble movement; that to *Les pêcheurs* is a sonata-form structure for six voices, with only vestigial traces of vaudeville elements. This is 83 bars long; the final 'Choro' of *Tom Jones*, again for six voices, is 90 bars long. Monsigny's *L'isle sonnante* (privately staged, 1767) ends with a sectional ensemble in *ABAB'* form, with contrasting tempos.

All these tendencies were drawn together in *Le déserteur* (1769; Monsigny and Sedaine), which had probably the greatest success of any *opéra comique* to date on a world scale. Inspired by Shakespeare's methods,

Sedaine offset the potentially tragic and often moving main story by juxtaposition with the tipsy bravado of Montauciel. The soldier Alexis, who is to be executed for deserting, is rescued by his fiancée, Louise, who petitions the French king. Music was called on to span large contrasts of emotional expression. There are arias in F minor and D minor, a duet in G minor and a trio in C minor. Act 1 ends with an ensemble scene (Alexis and four soldiers, representing an embryonic chorus) and Act 3 with an aggregation of musical items: aria–obbligato recitative–offstage acclamation–ensemble and chorus. The last section is through-composed and maintains dramatic continuity, eschewing any final moralizing. However, the company was still a small one and did not possess the resources for more than one singer per part in the last scene.

1769–90

During the two decades preceding the Revolution, Philidor's works attracted less support and (for reasons of health) Monsigny became less prolific. Monsigny's output closed with *La belle Arsène* (1773) and *Félix* (1777), the first a magic opera, the second a social morality. New composers in the 1770s included Dezède, J. P. A. Martini (Schwarzendorf) and Grétry. The first teamed up with J. M. Boutet (called Monvel) who favoured rustic settings combined with moral lessons of a piquant kind, generally preaching liberalism and humanity. Martini's *L'amoureux de quinze ans* (1771) fell into an adjacent category. Dezède wrote in a suave, Viennese idiom; Mozart's Variations K264/315d are based on his melody 'Lison dormait' from *Julie* (1772), an *opéra comique*. In 1774, on the accession of Louis XVI, Martini and his librettist Farmian de Rosoy took the opportunity to give their *opéra comique Henri IV* a historical authenticity (it is set in 1590) as well as a kind of educative significance. Rosoy subsequently published an important *Dissertation sur le drame lyrique* in which he declared that *opéra comique* was the ideal medium for a modern 'theatre of history', modelled on Shakespeare, and should forgo the purely comic genre. The score of *Henri IV* contains an exceptional entr'acte during which the battle of Ivry was depicted in military music. Rosoy also provided the text of Grétry's *Les mariages samnites* (1776), a fable about duties to one's kin and to one's society, set in Roman times. It was staged with appropriate costumes and scenery.

Grétry was the dominant *opéra comique* composer of the period. He wrote many works, most of which – up to the later 1780s – were very successful. He sought to expand the genre in some way with each new production; he had a secure technique and was acquainted with the latest Italian works, from the time of his studies in Rome (to 1766); and he perfected a declamatory style that reflected the meaning and prosody of his poetry while being faithful to fine melody and purely musical principles. He also had the knack of giving his characters life through music. In his use of form Grétry was equally original, being at home with such schemes as sonata, ternary and rondo, but gradually developing a 'non-repeating' style for those situations where any surface recurrence of music was undesirable. Musical unpredictability was a characteristic, in fact, and Grétry, well served by successive librettists, found formal inspiration from the dramatic situation at any given point. He exploited the 'narrative-descriptive' aria only in early works, developed the virtuoso concert aria in his middle period and, later, the ditty or popular song style. None of his works used pre-composed vaudevilles, though he sometimes alluded to 'vaudeville structure' as part of a closing scene: verse–refrain–verse–refrain. He also made uniquely important advances in the development of musical 'local colour'. Various of his works explore the possibilities of Spanish, Russian, Swiss and medieval colouring, using 'authentic' thematic material derived from literary or even oral sources.

His output can be divided into three parts, up to 1791: the eight *opéras comiques* up to and including *Zémire et Azor* (1771), five of whose librettos were by Marmontel; the eight up to *Les événements imprévus* (1779), the last three of which were in collaboration with d'Hèle (Thomas Hales); and the ten to *Guillaume Tell* (1791), a sequence dominated by the late works of Sedaine: *Aucassin et Nicolette* (1779), *Richard Coeur-de-lion* (1784), *Le comte d'Albert* (1786), *Raoul Barbe-bleue* (1789) and *Guillaume Tell*. During the two decades in question, *opéra comique* again saw a broadening of scale, dramatic ambition, political reference and musical style.

The size of the company increased notably in 1783 when it moved to a custom-built theatre, the Salle Favart. At last 14 violins and five cellos played in the main orchestra, with a much reduced group accompanying vaudeville comedies, twice a week; extra players were hired if clarinets or trumpets were required (salaried clarinettists and trumpeters entered the payroll in 1790). In spite of difficulties of training and discipline, a choral subgroup was established of singer-actors, which had risen to 16 in 1790. The scale of the works themselves stabilized: one-act comedies became exceptional and two- or three-act comedies were the most frequent, while three acts was the norm for serious or semi-serious works. However, *Zémire et Azor* was in four acts, as were the first versions of *La rosière de Salency*, *Aucassin et Nicolette* and others. The broadening of cultural ambition was perceptible in the way that the literary sources of *opéra comique* came, through the use of adaptations, to embrace a whole range of experience. The bucolic worlds of Favart and those derived from La Fontaine were supplemented emotionally, as in *Silvain* (Marmontel's adaptation of Gessner), with the issue of peasant farmers' rights. Marmontel's short stories and the librettos derived from them addressed the more thoughtful Parisian bourgeois on his own home ground. Alien moralities were evoked in *Aucassin et Nicolette* and *L'amitié à l'épreuve*. Moral content tended to become mythic content in *Raoul Barbe-bleue* – derived from Perrault, but containing significant allusions to Psyche and Pandora. Voltaire's fictional and historical writings were adapted (*Le Huron, Pierre le Grand*). The use of the chorus became increasingly prominent, both in musical and in dramatic terms, allied to the 'local colour' proper to the work in question.

Special mention should be made of Grétry's use of thematic or motivic recollection. This evolved from the early comedies through to *Richard Coeur-de-lion* and on to *Guillaume Tell*, where it is primarily motivic. Recollection was used in no single way, but was originally a literal device, becoming an ironic and then a symbolic one. In *Richard* the nine hearings of the *romance* melody, 'Une fièvre brûlante', are spread through the three acts, sometimes disguised and always in a different outer clothing. Because it is first played by Blondel on stage in his role as troubadour, it was consciously modelled on a melodic tradition probably going back through *Le devin du village* to actual trouvère pieces by Thibaut of Navarre, which had been published in Paris in 1742.

The most important new composer in the 1780s was Dalayrac, who produced a stream of generally successful works from 1782. His librettos were varied in quality, but broke new ground in *Nina* (1786), *Azémia* (1786) and *Sargines* (1788). *Nina* is a lachrymose working of the tale about Maria de Moulines, a character in Sterne's *Tristram Shandy* (vol.ix) and *A Sentimental Journey*; *Azémia* is an adventure story on a desert island; and *Sargines* is a pro-monarchist work set in 1214, during the reign of Philip II (Philip Augustus) of France. These works helped to bring the fruits of the Classical style to bear on 'modern' subjects. The full force of modern orchestration, the forceful styles of music illustrating combat, the resources of well-trained voices: all were in place and adopted even by Grétry before the French Revolution. These conditions were thus ready for exploitation in the works of Berton, Méhul and Cherubini.

Opéra comique was regularly exported beyond Paris, not only to such provincial centres as Bordeaux, Lyons and Rouen but also to important European centres. Indeed, Grétry's own interest in it had been kindled by performances given by a small troupe in Geneva in 1766. *Opéras comiques* were performed in French-speaking Brussels and Liège (Grétry's birthplace), but also in Amsterdam, St Petersburg and notably Vienna. Gluck, as musical director of the Burgtheater there from 1754 to 1764 mounted some 30 such productions. His role in supplying new arias in early hybrid settings remains unclear. But his pen is well established in works from *La fausse esclave* (1758) to *L'ivrogne corrigé* (1760), *Le cadi dupé* (1761) and *La rencontre imprévue* (1764), this last being his most successful opera with the public.

Vienna also saw works by Duni, Monsigny, Philidor, Gossec, Grétry, Dezède, Martini and Dalayrac; the Kärntnertortheater put on many in the 1770s and 80s, and the practice continued into the age of Beethoven, who left an account of seeing Spontini's *Milton* in a letter (7 January 1809). In northern Germany the many French works performed by Abel Seyler's travelling company proved influential from 1771 (Weimar and Gotha periods): *opéras comiques* by Duni, Monsigny, Philidor and Grétry were included in the repertory over many seasons and inspired many German dialogue operas. The Bonn court theatre staged works by Philidor, Monsigny, Grétry, Dezède and Dalayrac; in the 1770s these performances involved Beethoven's father as singer and from 1783 Beethoven himself as instrumentalist. In Berlin works by Duni, Philidor, Monsigny and Grétry were given at the Behrenstrasse theatre during the 1770s, continuing in the 1780s. Grétry was a favourite on the Hamburg stage. The Berlin National Theatre turned to *opéra comique* in the early 1790s; Königsberg followed suit. Other cities where *opéra comique* was acted include Berne, Stockholm, Moscow, New Orleans and Philadelphia. Even in Italy, the *opéras comiques* of Grétry were reportedly well received in 1776 in Florence, given by a French travelling troupe.

CHAPTER X

England

CURTIS PRICE

During the second half of the 18th century opera was in greater demand in London than in any other European court or city. After Handel, England continued to attract distinguished composers: Gluck, J. C. Bach, Galuppi, Haydn, Martín y Soler, Sacchini and others, such as Paisiello, who although he never crossed the Channel wrote an opera specially for London. Until the Rossini revolution of 1818–19, Italian *opera seria* was always in the ascendant, a fact which has been obscured by the satirical abuse heaped upon this 'exotic and irrational entertainment' by the best literary minds of the century. Pope, Swift, Lord Chesterfield, Walpole, Johnson and Goldsmith, while eloquent in their opposition to foreign opera, rarely condescended to give compensatory support to native music drama. English opera, which with a few exceptions had spoken dialogue instead of recitative, peacefully co-existed with Italian opera for much of the period, the two types appealing to essentially the same audience. And in the second half of the century there was much cross-fertilization and sharing of conventions, singers and even music between them.

The most radical innovation in 18th-century English music drama was so-called ballad opera – a misnomer, since it is more akin to the play than to opera. The first example is John Gay's *The Beggar's Opera* (1728), in which the spoken dialogue of criminals and other low-life characters is interspersed with songs sung by the actors themselves; the overture and accompaniments were provided by J. C. Pepusch. It was a sensational success. Although the idea of a rapid alternation of speech and song to advance the plot was genuinely new, the roots of ballad opera can be found in Thomas Durfey's parodies of Restoration semi-operas and, more immediately, in Richard Estcourt's *Prunella* (1708), in which the actors apparently sang bowdlerized versions of arias in Giovanni Bononcini's *Camilla*, the work it parodies. Ballad operas drew their tunes from many sources: broadsides, folksongs, Purcell's anthology *Orpheus Britannicus* (1698), even contemporary Italian operas, which they often satirized. Other butts included the legal and medical professions and politicians; in fact Gay's next effort, *Polly*, intended as a sequel to *The Beggar's Opera*, was banned as too close to the knuckle and was not performed until 1779. Established and aspiring dramatists alike capitalized on the vogue: Colley Cibber's *Love in a Riddle* (1729) is a pastoral ballad opera, Henry Fielding's *The Intriguing Chambermaid* (1734) is an amorous farce, Charles Johnson's *The Village Opera* (1729) is the prototype of rural comic opera and *The Mock Doctor* (1732), also by Fielding, is based on Molière. None of these imitations, however, compares favourably with the homespun original, whose brilliance rests squarely on Gay's unerring choice of tunes, which give the drama a powerful, almost savage impetus.

The musical legacy of ballad opera is slight; it threatened to turn good composers such as Pepusch and Thomas Arne into hacks. Its success was not so much a blow to Italian opera, which it only temporarily eclipsed, as an unprecedented boon to more ambitious English music drama. New theatres opened, and in 1732–3 seven full-length English operas were produced. Only Henry Carey's *Amelia* (1732), set by the German J. F. Lampe, and William Hatchett and Eliza Haywood's burlesque *The Opera of Operas* (1733), with music by Arne, enjoyed much success. J. C. Smith, the son of Handel's amanuensis, also composed two operas during this period; and in 1733 Arne reset Addison's *Rosamond*. The general failure of all these works to establish a national school of through-composed opera cannot be easily understood, because little of the music survives; but clearly English audiences preferred to have dramatic music in their own language interlarded with spoken dialogue. In 1737 Parliament passed the notorious Licensing Act, which limited the number of theatres in Great Britain to the three London houses with royal patents, Drury Lane, Covent Garden and the Haymarket, while imposing strict censorship on all theatrical production. This was a crippling blow to the development of English drama (new plays were not encouraged and political satire, in which Gay and Fielding had excelled, was virtually eliminated), but the Act proved a great boon to theatre composers: managers turned to music for novelty, introducing interludes and afterpieces of tuneful and unchallenging sentimentality. At Drury Lane Garrick nurtured his house composers, the most famous of whom, William Boyce, produced remarkably successful all-sung afterpieces such as *The Chaplet* (1749) and *The Shepherd's Lottery* (1751).

After the double collapse of Handel's Italian company and the rival Opera of the Nobility in 1737, foreign opera seemed to have run its course in London. But with a solid core of aristocratic support, a splendid opera house in the King's Theatre, Haymarket, and perhaps the finest pit orchestra in Europe, Lord Middlesex organized a new company in 1741, engaged a troupe of first-rank singers and appointed Galuppi as music director. In spite of a succession of shady and incompetent managers, Middlesex's company established a more economical, scenically modest production style which lasted well into the next century; it introduced the first comic operas to London (1748–9) and hired the young Gluck as resident composer for the 1746–7 season, though he made little impression.

Apart from the absence of a truly great composer after Handel, Italian opera evolved in London much as it did on the Continent – in its gradual shift from *galant* to Classical, the growing dominance of natural male voices in leading roles and the eventual triumph of *opera buffa*. The most important distinguishing characteristic was a heavy reliance on pasticcios: the resident music director, himself a composer, adapted arias from various earlier operas to a new or reworked libretto, and the recitatives and other linking pieces were freshly composed. During the second half of the century, London productions of serious pasticcios far outnumbered those of single-author operas, whether *seria* or *buffa*; and of some 250 operas produced between 1760 and 1800, only about 15 per cent were new.

The predominance of the pasticcio was partly due to the commercialism of the London stage. While Italian opera never broke even, its managers and composers were often deluded by Garrick's prediction that 'the Opera House would prove a mine of gold, if conducted with ability'. Under tremendous pressure to keep the deficit to a minimum, they had to react quickly to adverse newspaper criticism by cutting recitative and substituting arias, even whole scenes. While obviously lacking the coherence of an opera by one composer (though musical consistency mattered less than unity of action, especially in *opera seria*), the pasticcio was designed to facilitate adjustments after the première. It also was an ideal medium for experimentation. London became a clearing house for all that was new and fashionable in opera. Charles Burney, who chronicled the history of opera during the second half of the 18th century from personal experience, thus described the coming of the Classical style not as a fundamental change in the fabric of music but as a piecemeal introduction of lighter melodies with novel embellishments, accompanimental figures and exotic wind orchestration. But the pasticcio, which could readily assimilate the latest Roman or Neapolitan whim, paradoxically also contributed to the underlying conservatism of English taste in opera. Even at the end of the century, the latest works nominally by Paisiello, Sacchini or Guglielmi might also include arias by Piccinni or even Handel, introduced at the insistence of singers, the music director or the business manager.

The London opera establishment, which demanded more works per season than any Italian opera house, suited a mediocre composer such as the Neapolitan Gioacchino Cocchi, whose pasticcios of the late 1750s were generally successful, better than a fine one such as J. C. Bach, whose first solo commissions for the King's Theatre, *Orione* and *Zanaida* (1763), were coolly received. Bach's relations with the management were not good; and his vocal lines, it was claimed, were instrumentally conceived. In spite of the rich orchestration, which included prominent parts for clarinets, Bach's London operas also seem to lack real substance, partly because of his recent abandonment of the da capo aria, which disappeared from all new London works during the 1760s. While undoubtedly quickening the pace of the drama, the new periodic and binary aria forms had little scope for exploiting non-dominant key areas and often lack the contrast and tension inherent in the da capo. And with no opportunity for ornamentation in the repeat of an *A* section, composers were inclined to provide arias that would astonish through continuous embellishment. London remained in the vanguard of *opera seria*, a thinning and tattered battalion; but, because of the flexibility that the pasticcio allowed both composer and singer, was largely unmoved by more fundamental reforms on the Continent.

Comic opera developed late in London; stylized stage humour rarely travels well, and the Italian language proved a greater barrier than it had to *opera seria*. The first real inroads were made by Galuppi's *Il mondo della luna* and *Il filosofo de campagna* in 1761, but their impact was insignificant compared with that of Niccolò Piccinni's *La buona figliuola* (given in 1766). This was one of the greatest operatic successes of the century, though Piccinni did not go to London and the King's Theatre was merely capitalizing on its universal appeal. The company was now forced to carry two troupes of singers, one for *opera buffa* and another for *opera seria*, though a few singers, typically the *seconda donna buffa* and the *primo mezzo carattera*, reserved the right to perform in both types. Castratos persisted in comic operas until as late as 1784, an anachronism encouraged by the undying popularity of *La buona figliuola*. This and a few other Italian operas were translated into English, but in conformity with native comic operas of the period, such as *Lionel and Clarissa* (1768) by the prolific Charles Dibdin, the translations had spoken dialogue instead of recitative.

Because of the prejudice against recitative in English, which seemed to intensify as the century progressed, it is extraordinary that the single example of an all-sung serious opera by a first-rate native composer should have proved so successful: Arne's *Artaxerxes* (1762), set to Metastasio's libretto which the composer himself translated into plain English (Arbaces: 'I hope Mandane's Wrath will now subside; For I have sacrific'd my only Son, To satisfy her Vengeance'). Its success was undoubtedly aided by the performance of the great castrato Tenducci (Arbaces), for whom Arne wrote superb bravura passage-work, but the music must also have added to its appeal; the arias are consistently good, ranging in type from full-blown allegros with oboes, horns and strings for Tenducci and Miss Brent (Mandane) to simple English ballads with plaintive flutes or clarinets. The recitatives do not survive, and the loss of the accompagnatos, all of which occur at crucial dramatic moments, is especially regrettable.

During the last quarter of the century English comic opera began to resemble *opera buffa* in form, though always with spoken dialogue instead of recitative and airs gathered from a wide range of sources. Dibdin and Samuel Arnold, who dominated London stage music for several decades, were little more than arrangers. More gifted was William Shield, promoted from violist and harpsichord tuner to house composer at

Covent Garden in the early 1780s. But even his most popular work, *Rosina* (1782), was assembled much like a ballad opera, the composer's own folklike melodies mixed in with old ballad tunes and even a Sacchini aria. The only English composer who might have taken up the torch of English opera from Arne was the Italian-trained Stephen Storace, whose *opere buffe* had been popular in Vienna. But when he returned to London in 1787 with his sister Anna, Mozart's favourite *prima buffa*, he wrote only one Italian opera for the King's Theatre, was then shut out by a political clique and spent the rest of his career at Covent Garden providing music for dialogue operas, such as James Cobb's *The Siege of Belgrade* (1791), a vehicle for his sister and their friend the Irish tenor Michael Kelly, and *The Pirates* (also Cobb, 1792). These are essentially melodramas with as much speech as music. But the *dramatis personae* do their own singing and the music is worked into the plot in various ways, ranging from naturalistic outbursts of emotion to humorous excuses for patently irrelevant songs, not unlike the witty transitions in Gilbert and Sullivan. As in *opera buffa*, the ends of acts are made up of long stretches of continuous music. Storace borrowed many of the airs and ensembles from Italian opera (Sacchini, Sarti, Paisiello and others) or arranged movements from contemporary symphonies and chamber music. At its best, Storace's style is distinctly Mozartian, though the often graceful airs retain a strong strain of English ballad – a limitation in finales, because their predictable tunefulness prevents harmonic excursions and hampers motivic and thematic expansion.

Italian opera struggled financially during the 1780s. Besides having to employ two troupes of singers, the King's Theatre also carried a full complement of dancers. Ballet had occasionally been incorporated into operas since Handel's day, but by the early 1770s every opera included intermezzos and substantial pantomimic ballets which were the envy of Paris. Principal dancers and choreographers, such as Noverre, Didelot and Dauberval, commanded salaries equal to those of the great castratos, and the joint opera-ballet company sagged under heavy debts and chaotic management.

The destruction by fire of the Haymarket theatre in 1789 precipitated a bizarre episode in the history of Italian opera in London. The leaseholders of the Haymarket site, who had begun to rebuild almost immediately, hoped to open the new house with Haydn's Orpheus opera *L'anima del filosofo*, commissioned as a douceur for his first London visit. But upon arrival, Haydn found that the Haymarket theatre, to which he was contracted, had lost its royal patent; his new opera (perhaps to his relief and certainly to his advantage as a symphonist) could not be staged. The patent had been transferred to the rival Pantheon theatre in Oxford Street, whose manager, encouraged by the Prince of Wales, invited Mozart to become house composer for the 1790–91 season. The invitation was not accepted or even acknowledged; instead, the Pantheon engaged Paisiello as composer *in absentia*. His comic opera *La locanda* (1791) sustained the new theatre until it too burnt down in early 1792. The Haymarket then re-acquired the patent (though too late for Haydn) and in 1793 appointed Da Ponte as poet-in-residence. For the next five years Mozart's former collaborator wrote librettos for such composers as Martín y Soler and G. B. Bianchi, though his chief task was to revise old works and to supply verses for substitute arias.

During the second half of the 18th century, Italian opera gradually ceased to be regarded in London as the exotic excess it had been in Handel's time. As early as 1735 so staunch a xenophobe as Colley Cibber wrote the libretto of Porpora's *Mitridates*, and in 1744 F. M. Veracini composed an aria which incorporates the Scots tune 'The Lass of Patie's Mill' for his opera *Rosalinda*, itself based on Shakespeare's *As you like it*. Later, most English musicals and medleys featured arias adapted from contemporary Italian operas. The invader had at length triumphed over the bitter attacks of writers who, appalled at the enormous salaries paid to singers and unable to comprehend how vocal music in a foreign language could possibly appeal to any true Englishman, failed to notice that Italian opera had greatly enriched their own culture.

CHAPTER XI

Spain and Portugal

LIONEL SALTER

The advent in Spain of the Bourbons in 1700 halted any development in native music theatre. As the court was entirely under Italian influence and the country had an Italian prime minister, Spanish took second place as the language of polite society; Italian opera troupes brought to Madrid staged lavish productions, and for seven years no new lyric-dramatic works in Spanish were given in the capital. For a short time Spanish opera was more lively in the New World. To mark Philip V's 18th birthday, the viceroy in Peru commissioned from Torrejón y Velasco a setting of Calderón's *La púrpura de la rosa* (1701, Lima), which was sung throughout: this is the earliest New World opera whose score survives. The next viceroy, who had literary aspirations, himself wrote the libretto for *El mejor escudo de Perseo*, which was magnificently presented in his palace gardens in 1708 with music by Ceruti, an Italian who was eventually to dominate the colony's musical life. In 1711 *Partenope*, a three-act opera by the Mexican composer Manuel de Zumaya (to the same Italian libretto as was later set by Handel), was mounted in the viceregal palace in Mexico City. After Ceruti's death another Italian, Bartolomé Massa, produced in Lima a number of operas to Spanish texts.

In Spain itself there was an occasional flicker of activity from native composers. Among the surviving zarzuelas by Antonio Literes, the two-act *Accis y Galatea* (1708), contains more music than usual in relation to speech; he also wrote a three-act zarzuela *Júpiter y Danae* and the one-act *Los elementos*, an 'ópera armónica al estil italiano'. A similar appellation was given to *Amor es todo ymbenzion, o Júpiter y Anfitrión* (1721) by Giacomo Facco, an Italian who spent some 30 years in the royal service, and to *Con amor no hay libertad* (1731) by Francesco Corradini, a Neapolitan. Even such Spanish champions of nationalism as the prolific and highly successful José Nebra felt obliged to adopt an Italian musical style, although he diluted this by including spoken dialogue and folk elements. But for the first half of the 18th century Italian composers ruled the roost, particularly Corradini (who nevertheless wrote zarzuelas and comedies as well as *opere serie*), Mele and Corselli (three of whose *opere serie* were the favourite fare of Philip V and his celebrated castrato Farinelli): all three, however, sometimes set texts in the vernacular on native subjects. Under Ferdinand VI, Conforto (like Mele, a Neapolitan) wrote half a dozen Metastasian operas (including *L'eroe cinese*, 1754, and *Nitteti*, 1756) which were sumptuously produced at court. In the Madrid Teatro Príncipe, Nebra was fighting a determined rearguard action. He scored a resounding success with his zarzuela *De los encantos de amor la música es el mayor* (1725), which marked a departure from the usual mythological subjects; although he returned to them in *Cautelas contra cautelas* (1745) and *Achiles en Troya* (1747), in the latter he poked fun at the mannered Metastasian style by having two characters dance a seguidilla before the walls of Troy.

By the middle of the century, public outcry against Carlos III and his hated foreign ministers forced the king to make concessions to popular traditions and tastes: the two-act *sainetes* (comic scenes originally performed as postludes to theatrical entertainments) of Ramón de la Cruz conjured up Goya's Madrid, and were to inspire the *tonadilla*, a form that carried everything before it (originally a solo song with guitar, usually of a topical nature, and appended to theatrical interludes). By the early 1750s the *tonadilla* was developing in the hands of Antonio Guerrero into a sung sketch in one act, akin to the Italian intermezzo. It was usually satirical or political, and either for a single character (frequently a woman) or for up to about five. Later this number was occasionally exceeded, as in Jacinto Valledor's *La plaza de palacio de Barcelona* (1774), which calls for 12 singers. The genre exploited national dances and folk-type melodies, and dealt mainly with lower-class popular life, particularly that of the *majos* and *majas* immortalized by Goya, along with peasants, gypsies, innkeepers, barbers, priests etc. It was always colourful, mostly broad in its humour (for which regional characters often provided the butts) and predominantly picaresque, though a romantic element was also common. Luis Misón, a facile melodist who is sometimes (wrongly) credited with the creation of the *tonadilla*, established the mould (already used by Guerrero) which became customary for the solo form: an introduction which brought on the character and set the scene; the *coplas* (verses) which told the story; and a final sung dance, either a seguidilla or, later, a *tirana* or polacca. Small orchestras gradually replaced the guitar accompaniments, as in Misón's *Los jardineros* (1761).

There was a brief spell in which the zarzuela seemed about to take root again, thanks to the combination of de la Cruz's texts and music by Antonio Rodriguez de Hita. After a couple of conventionally mythological or heroic subjects, the turning-point came with their very successful *Las segadoras de Vallecas* (1768), the first piece to deal with Spanish country life. It was a zarzuela, though also called an opera: this confusion of nomenclature was a constant factor until well into the 19th century. Of even greater artistic significance was its successor *Las labradoras de Murcia* (1769), in which, to prevent silkworms dying of fright at the sound of thunder (such is the local belief), the workers rush in with a *jota murciana* to drown the noise of the storm; this scene uses a *rondalla* (street band) on stage, a feature that remained characteristic of the zarzuela and was drawn on even by Martín y Soler in his *Una cosa rara* (1785, Vienna), which culminates in a jota and seguidilla. Other composers who collaborated with de la Cruz were Fabián García Pacheco (*En casa de nadie no se meta nadie*, 1770); Pablo Esteve y Grimau (*Los jardineros de Aranjuez*, 1768, and *Los zagales del Genil*, 1769); Antonio Rosales, whose *El licenciado Farfulla* (1776) contains an abundance of folkdances; and José Palomino, whose *tonadilla El canapé* (1769) became immensely popular and whose one-act *La mesonerilla* (1769), which inaugurated the form later to be called the *género chico*, contains no fewer than six seguidillas. It is worth observing that Italian musicians in Spain also collaborated with de la Cruz, notably Brunetti and Boccherini (whose *La Clementina* was privately produced in 1778 and at the palace of the Benavente-Osuna family in Madrid in 1786), and that de la Cruz converted operas by Piccinni, Sacchini and Paisiello into zarzuelas.

On de la Cruz's death, in 1794, there was no one to carry on his tradition, and the zarzuela again all but vanished for half a century: its defeat was hastened on the one hand by Italian opera, which had been reinstated in Madrid in 1787, and on the other by the public's insensate craze for the miniature and ephemeral *tonadillas escénicas*, sung sketches of everyday life. From about 1770 to 1810 a spate of these, few surviving longer than a week, was produced in Madrid: some 2000 manuscripts have survived, and even this probably represents only part of the output. The principal composers were Esteve y Grimau, who wrote over 400 examples, including *La parmesana y las majas* (1765), commemorating the visit to Madrid of the Princess of Parma, the topical *Las delicias del Prado* and *El juicio del año* (1779); the resourceful and skilful Blas de Laserna, who wrote over 700 examples, many of which shed light on theatrical conditions of the time and whose *Tirana del Trípili* achieved European fame, thanks to its being borrowed by Mercadante; Rosales (*El recitador*, 1775); and Valledor, whose elaborate burlesque *La cantada vida y muerte del General Malbrú* (1785), which quotes the song 'Malbrouk s'en va-t-en guerre', calls for an unusually large orchestra. Dances from Spanish colonies in Latin America and other exotic sources also found their way into *tonadillas* alongside Spanish folkdances and gypsy music.

In Portugal the accession of John V in 1706 had given the arts an enlightened and enormously wealthy patron, who as well as bringing performers and composers from Italy (the most famous being Domenico Scarlatti, who wrote several serenatas for the court) sent Portuguese musicians to Italy to study. The best known of these is Francisco António de Almeida, whose *La pazienza di Socrate* (1733) is probably the first opera by a Portuguese composer, although *La vida do grande Don Quixote*, the first of a handful of tragi-comedies in the vernacular by António José da Silva, was also produced that year. The great earthquake of 1755 destroyed not only most of Lisbon but the evidence of much of its culture. Between 1762 and 1797 Luciano Xavier dos Santos wrote several well-constructed Italian operas to texts by Metastasio or the court poet Martinelli. The tradition of royal patronage was continued, one of its beneficiaries being João de Sousa Carvalho, notable not only in his own right for more than a dozen Italian stage works, mostly to librettos by Metastasio and Martinelli, but as the teacher of two leading opera composers, António Moreira and Marcos Portugal. The former began by writing a number of *opere serie*, some for royal wedding celebrations, but on becoming music director of the newly built S Carlos opera house he wrote two farcical works to Portuguese texts, *A sàloia namorada* (1793) and *A vingança da cigana* (1794). He then reverted to Italian; *Il disertore francese*, his last *opera buffa*, was performed in 1800 in Turin and Milan. The most considerable native composer of the period, however, was Portugal (Moreira's brother-in-law), who wrote at least six comic operas in Portuguese that predate Moreira's; of these *A castanheira* (1787) gained wide popularity. He later spent eight years in Italy, producing in its major centres 21 operas in the Neapolitan tradition, both *seria* and *buffa*: *Le confusioni della somiglianza* (1793, Florence) was extremely successful not only in Italy but in Dresden, Vienna and Berlin; and *Fernando nel Messico* (1799, Venice) was taken to London by its star, Elizabeth Billington.

CHAPTER XII

Staging

MANFRED BOETZKES, ROGER SAVAGE

1. Design

Despite the 17th-century trends towards realism, the domination of the theatre of machinery did not end until the early 18th century, when Stampiglia and Zeno sought to blend the ideology of court absolutism with bourgeois rationalism and to banish not only the comic elements of later Venetian librettos but also all 'marvellous' subjects. With *opera seria*, the fruit of this compromise, came changed conditions of production, with more commercial companies and increasingly middle-class audiences, catered for by the adoption of elements characteristic of the Enlightenment (notably by Metastasio); but in the last resort *opera seria* remained a courtly work of art. Its rationalist structure in text, music and affects, formalized in a courtly manner, was matched by a scenic framework that translated feudal ideology, not by machines but with the calculated effects of illusionist architectural painting, inclined towards the expression of the monumental and making refined use of *trompe l'oeil*. Its basic techniques – angular perspective, diagonal viewpoint (providing a view of several subsidiary areas) and worm's- and bird's-eye views – were borrowed from quadrature painting, especially the Bolognese school of Dentone, Mitelli and Colonna.

By the late 17th century some Bolognese artists were apparently beginning to transfer this procedure to stage design, but the first to use it systematically in the theatre was Ferdinando Galli-Bibiena in his designs for Sabadini's *Didio Giuliano* (1687, Piacenza). He expounded the mathematical requirements for angular perspective and other quadraturist techniques (see Plate 51), which were to become an art of perspective that spread through Europe with *opera seria* and considerably enlarged the theatre's imaginative potential. Besides the Galli-Bibiena family, the most important representatives of this style were Pietro Righini (see Plate 28), G. D. Barbieri, G. B. Medici and the brothers Giuseppe and Domenico Valeriani. Such technically brilliant scene painting was effectively

complemented by elegant costumes, delineating the standardized characters who wore them and essentially adhering to the courtly dress and the
typology of the 17th century.

With the decline of feudalism and the development of bourgeois
culture, courtly *opera seria* declined. In bourgeois drama (exemplified in
plays by Lillo, Diderot and Lessing), in the new types of musical theatre
(*opera buffa, opéra comique, ballet d'action*, ballad opera, Singspiel) and in the
'reform operas' of Gluck and others, the central concern of bourgeois art
was evident: the overthrow of courtly formalism and the approach to
individual and social existence through the natural and the universally
human. Plausibility no longer consisted in the endorsement of traditional
aesthetic and social norms but rather in its concordance with empirical
nature – which however was reproduced not in its plain appearance but in
a typical, idealizing selection that raised theatrical art above 'common
reality'.

A vital aspect of the new aesthetic was the coordination of the theatrical
arts: stage designer and costume designer were both expected to produce a
truthfulness of representation corresponding to the work being performed. The adoption of this concept by the musical theatre (J. G. Noverre: *Lettres sur la danse*, 1760) meant the end of the formalistic brilliance of
Galli-Bibiena's school, and though the operatic theorists of the second half
of the century – notably Algarotti (*Saggio sopra l'opera in musica*, 1755),
Planelli (*Dall'opera in musica*, 1772) and Arteaga (*Le rivoluzioni del teatro
musicale italiano*, 1783) – acknowledged the great significance of Ferdinando Galli-Bibiena's innovations in the art of perspective, with the exception of Planelli they cited the lack of plausibility in attacking the
bizarre architectural fantasies of his followers. Furthermore they supported the idea of a pictorially composed stage communicating moods and
local colour; such an art had already emerged in the first half of the
century in the work of Filippo Juvarra (for example in his sets for Alessandro Scarlatti's *Il Ciro*, 1712; see Plate 27). This tendency is also evident in
sets designed by others like Antonio Jolli and Luigi Vanvitelli in Rome
and Marco Ricci and Bernardo Bellotto in Venice; and with the Piedmontese brothers Fabrizio and Bernardino Galliari it began to characterize Italian stage design as a whole (see Plate 29).

In spite of compromises with court traditions, these designers reflected
the current processes of change in musical theatre. Genre scenes from the
comic theatre constituted much of the artistic output and furthered
interest in appropriate representation. Enthusiasm for Nature (even in
opera seria) and the new feeling for the aesthetic qualities of landscape led to
the displacement of the architectural scenes which formerly had dominated the stage, and reinforced the tendency of designers to provide visual
counterparts of the intentions of the text and the music. The generation of
the Galliari brothers largely shared the ideal enlightened artist whose
'imagination was guided by erudition' (Algarotti, 2/1763, p.57). By the
adoption (if superficially) of historical and exotic stylistic features to

characterize the scene of the action, it embodied – at least in principle – the requirement for historically correct stage representation, evolved above all by Algarotti, Noverre and F. Milizia (*Trattato completo formale e materiale del teatro*, 1771).

Artists such as L.-R. Boquet, Noverre's collaborator, and Leonardo Marini, the Galliaris' partner in Turin, applied these principles to their costumes. Though they often retained the courtly style, by using elements of contemporary and historical popular and national dress they created costumes of a variety and expressiveness hitherto unknown. This appearance of more realistic décor and costumes reflected middle-class cultural needs, though despite the universality sought in the theatre the art of classical antiquity remained the central point of reference, the republican traditions of the Greeks and Romans increasingly forming an ideal contrast with the contemporary weakening of feudal and absolutist monarchies. This romantic version of classicism was influential in musical theatre and had important scenic interpreters in Italy, notably Pietro Gonzaga, Francesco Fontanesi and Carlo Caccianiga.

The German princely residences, where *opera seria* had become an essential element of courtly self-representation, was in the first half of the 18th century the centre of the Galli-Bibienas' activities. In the few centres of German opera, designers such as Tobias Querfurt (Brunswick) affirmed an attitude of greater realism, and in the mid-18th century the scenographers of Italian opera troupes came round to a similar position. During the second half of the century G. P. Gaspari, Jacopo Fabris, Innocente Colomba, Giovanni Maria Quaglio the elder, Bartolomeo Verona and Lorenzo Sacchetti arrived at scenic solutions fundamentally similar to those of the Galliaris, but the dominant role of architectural scenery long remained a feature of German theatre. In the designs of Lorenzo and Giulio Quaglio, J. H. Zimmermann and Joseph Platzer, the genre-type themes of the Singspiel came to the fore along with classical subjects.

In France, Jean Berain the younger, as scenic director of the Académie Royale de Musique, continued his father's tradition, which had meanwhile fossilized into convention. An important artist such as Claude Gillot (the elder Berain's assistant from about 1697) could threaten this monopolistic situation but not break it down, and only after Berain's death (1726) did French stage design renew its links with international developments in the perspective art of G. N. Servandoni, who, as the Académie's leading stage designer (1726–44) and the organizer of *spectacles de décoration* in the Tuileries (Salle des Machines, 1738–58), combined the tradition of the French theatre of machines with the Italian innovations in perspective. His successor as scenic director to the Académie (1744–8) was François Boucher, the principal master of the Rococo in France, who had been responsible for opera designs from about 1737. His picturesque landscapes and genre scenes translated the world of *fêtes galantes* on to the stage, although they were not always well adapted to the requirements of contemporary musical theatre. The criticism levelled by the Encyclopedists at the theatrical dilettantism of 'peintres de chevalet' was doubtless aimed at Boucher, yet his influence on French stage design was great, extending (despite the classical tendencies of the Slodtz brothers and C. M.-A. Challe) far into the second half of the century. Boucher influenced the production style of Jean Monnet's Opéra-Comique; and during the 1760s he again produced many design sketches for the Académie. Only with Gluck's reform operas did the Rococo style cease to predominate in French stage design: in the designs of J.-M. Moreau, F.-J. Belanger and P.-A. Paris there appeared a classicism (see Plate 46) which was to spread far beyond France, above all in its romantic interpretation by Louis-Jean Desprez in Rome and Stockholm; his atmospheric landscapes and effective tableaux, as exemplified in his sets for J. G. Naumann's *Gustaf Wasa* (1786; see Plate 52), foreshadow principles that were to be developed in Romantic opera design.

In late 17th-century England a form of stage design evolved in the public theatres which, while unpretentious compared with continental practice, was characterized by a bourgeois realism that influenced Italian opera production in London, apparent as early as the simple design sketches of James Thornhill for Clayton's Italianate *Arsinoë* (see Plate 15). Subsequently Italian designers brought the perspective art of the Galli-Bibienas, particularly angled perspective, to England, but the most important designers working for the King's Theatre, such as Marco Ricci (1708–16), Servandoni (1720–21), Antonio Jolli (1743–8), Innocente Colomba (1774–80) and Michaele Novosielski (1777–95) did not follow the formalism associated with court theatres. A more important part was played in the development of a realistic type of stage design, however, by the popular genres of musical theatre such as English-language opera, burlesque and pantomime; their parodies of courtly opera and mythology found in the pseudo-Baroque stage designs of John Devoto (*fl* 1708–52) a form of visual expression that was apt – with picturesque genre scenes, topographical views and fairy-tale or exotic sets – to their themes of everyday life, current political events or romantic incidents. With the effect-conscious depictions of Nature by P. J. de Louterbourg and Robert Carver the scenic realism of the 18th century, though primarily throwing romantic subjects into relief, reached its apex.

The evolution of a more realistic style necessitated a modification of the 17th-century stage structure, with its symmetrical wings, soffits and backcloth. The adoption of quadraturist techniques by Galli-Bibiena had made the backcloth the main medium of illusion, laying the foundations for a primarily 'painterly' art of stage design, though at the same time the construction of the 'cut close' had created the possibility of plastic effects (F. Galli-Bibiena: *Direzioni della prospettiva teorica*, 1732, operazione 69). The favourite theatrical aesthetic formula of the Enlightenment, in which the stage is described as a 'living painting' (Cahusac, Noverre), signifies not the restriction of the scene to two dimensions but a realistic art corresponding to contemporary landscape and genre painting. Even more thoroughly than Galli-Bibiena, Juvarra attempted to achieve this by often asymmetrically placed wings and by a backcloth broken up into juxtaposed (and in part perforated) smaller units of décor, thus giving an effect of greater depth and plasticity. In the second half of the century the concept of a 'natural' stage area was further developed, above all by the Galliari brothers, who staggered the acting surfaces with draped trestles, stairs, platforms and other props while retaining the basics of the wing, soffit and backcloth system. It was perfected, at least in landscape scenes, by Loutherbourg with his naturalistically shaped cut closes, movable scenery and floor-pieces. On the other hand, the application of 'naturalness' to the construction of interiors barely passed the experimental stage; difficulties of lighting precluded widespread dissemination of the 'box set' introduced in Hamburg in the early 1790s by F. L. Schröder.

The various traditional methods of stage lighting were combined during the 18th century in a single cohesive system, comprising four basic factors: chandeliers, mainly for the audience area but also for the stage; footlights; hidden top lights behind the proscenium arch and between the soffits; and side lighting on stands behind the side turrets and in the wings. This system, operating by means of tallow lights, wax candles and oil lamps, had deficiencies – insufficient and uncontrollable brightness, distortion of the actor's gestures by unnatural shadows, smell and fire risk – that made it inadequate for a realistic stage. An improvement in lighting, the central concern of theatrical reformers, became apparent only from about 1780, when a new kind of oil lamp (by A. Argand) made available a relatively bright source of light which neither flickered nor smoked and which could be further concentrated by the use of a concave mirror (developed by A. Lavoisier).

Theatre architecture remained under the influence of courtly traditions far longer than did stage design, and only in the late 18th century were attempts made to modify theatre design to suit changed social conditions, at least to the extent of making the prince's box and the 'parterre noble' less prominent. It was mainly in France, in the years before the Revolution, that an architectural style evolved embodying a democratically organized audience area and a construction expressing the theatre's social function (Bordeaux, 1775–80; Besançon, 1778–84; Théâtre Feydeau, Paris, 1791).

2. Production

Introduction

The 18th century inherited from the 17th a concept of opera as a multi-media entertainment, the creation and staging of which called for the integration (or at least the convergence) of many skills. Part of the legacy, however, was a preparedness to let solo singers, choreographers, designers and the rest get on with their own work with a considerable degree of independence, in the expectation that this of itself would produce a sufficiently harmonious spectacle. But from the later 17th century onwards in Italy and from the earlier 18th in France, the situation differed in one important factor from that during the first flowerings of Venetian public opera and of Lullian opera in Paris: this was the steadily increasing emphasis being placed by composers, singers and audiences on sheer vocal virtuosity as a prime means of operatic communication. In the French tradition this factor is apparent in the remark attributed to Rameau in the 1730s that, whereas Lully's operas needed actors, his needed singers. In the Italian it accounts for the contrast between the view implied in the treatise *Il corago* in the 1630s that one should choose a fine actor with only passable vocal skills in preference to a fine singer of small acting talent, and Tosi's view in his *Observations on the Florid Song* 90 years later that, though the ideal for a performer in opera is a double perfection of singing and acting, in the real world of conflicting demands and divided interests it is the perfecting of one's voice that should have the prior claim.

From this change sprang a new tribe of vocal virtuosos much esteemed in the opera house although their histrionic skills were rudimentary: singers like the castrato Farinelli, who was for 15 years the toast of operatic Europe for all that his acting (according to J. J. Quantz among others) was perfunctory, or like Jélyotte, golden-voiced principal tenor of the Paris Opéra in Rameau's time – 'chanteur unique, mais il n'a ni figure ni action'. However, an approximation to acting (and in Paris rather more than that) was required even of such songbirds. When the *prima donna* Gertrud Mara, on hearing her stage performance criticized, asked in hurt tones whether she was supposed to sing with her hands and feet too, many 18th-century opera-goers would have answered Yes. The perfect opera singer was generally deemed to be one who (in the words of the intendant of the royal opera at Lisbon in the 1760s) possessed 'buona voce e grande estensione di corde, buona figura e buona azione'. And the style of *azione*, in serious opera at least, continued to be close to that of spoken tragedy, with its strong frontal presentation of the actor, its bold language of expressive gesture, and its concern that groups of performers should 'dress the stage' in harmonious patternings (semi-circles being much favoured). As in the 17th century also, principal singers gravitated to the front of the stage as the place where acoustics were at their best, contact with the orchestra was at its greatest and direct light from chandeliers and footlights at its brightest. They continued to perform for spectators equipped with copies of the libretto (including a translation *en face* if the language was not the audience's own). And they continued to be part of an operatic scene which (with the partial exception of Paris) was dominated for most of the century by the first-running of new works: either wholly new operas or new settings of admired librettos or new pasticcios of admired arias. This 'tradition of the new' made for conditions of production considerably removed from those of the revival-dominated operatic scene of today.

Opera seria

The staging of *opera seria*, the dominant form of European opera from the 1690s to well beyond the middle of the 18th century, was relatively simple in organization. The strong segmentation of the form did not require the firm hand or creative vision of the equivalent of a modern producer or director to make it work in the theatre. Such a producer would have found little to do at an *opera seria* rehearsal. As there was a *maître de danse* and sometimes an associated fencing-master seeing to any ceremonies, ballets and battles, a machinist advising performers about any theatrical *coups* they might be involved in (descents of airy chariots, magical transformations, collapsings of city walls and the like), and a designer independently ringing the changes on a limited range of scenic motifs, the function of a hypothetical producer would be to instruct the principal singers in their motivations and moves and to remind the pages and other supernumeraries (the *comparse*) of their duties in attending decorously and decoratively on the principals. However, given the formalized nature of the characterization and movement, to say nothing of the marked independence (not to say ungovernability) of so many singers, he might well find that this was little more than the cipher of a function. So it is not surprising that, though the most detailed libretto-cum-programme-books of Italian operatic performances at court in the 18th century give the names of cast, composer, librettist, choreographer, fencing-master, costumier, set designer and machinist, they mention no figure directly corresponding to the modern producer. When Signor Sospiro, the *maestro di cappella* in Calzabigi's comic libretto *La critica teatrale* (or *L'opera seria*, set by Gassmann in 1769), lists the complete personnel of a commercial company during an aria of eternal enmity to all impresarios, producers do not figure along with the 'singers, dancers, poets, composers, instrumentalists, designers, painters, prompters, ticket-sellers, costumiers, pages, candle-snuffers, scene-changers, supers, carpenters, machinists, locksmiths and copyists'.

It does not follow from this that the stage rehearsal of an *opera seria* by its principals was necessarily anarchic or primitive. For one thing, there were the stage directions in the libretto to be observed: not only for entrances and exits but quite often for characters' moods and stage business as well. For another, performers could apply to their recitatives the age's basic courtly stage deportment, which they might learn from their singing teachers or pick up from acting manuals or their own opera-going: a deportment complementing the theatrical recitative style Tosi described as 'a certain natural imitation which cannot be beautiful if not expressed with that decorum with which princes speak (or those who know how to speak to princes)'. Again, since the staple of *opera seria* was a spectrum of general emotions expressed one after another in a series of arias, an experienced performer coming to a new opera would almost certainly have given formal histrionic expression to all its emotions before – sometimes in exactly the same words (since multiple settings of successful librettos were common), sometimes even, if the new piece were a pasticcio, in the same music. Finally, the standard practice of designing arias for specific singers may well have involved the composer's taking account of the singer's stage manner as well as his or her vocal characteristics, so that aria fitted performer like a musico-dramatic glove.

All these things helped any performer of *opera seria* with a basic theatrical gift to give a strong stage performance after limited rehearsal time and without the assistance of a masterful producer. Indeed, a group of competent principals might in a few days achieve a fluent, decorous, pointed and telling staging of an opera (in all but any spectacular or balletic parts) with no external help, or with no more than was necessary in establishing which wings should be used for which entrances and exits, in assigning retinues of *comparse* and pages, and in resolving any disputed points of princely stage etiquette or clashes of artistic temperament. The person responsible for providing such help in practice seems to have been whoever in the company was most serviceable in a given situation: the manager sometimes, or the *corago*, or even the *maestro di cappella* (who might anyway be the opera's composer). But most often it was the theatre's resident poet, in which case he might take a rather more consequential role on himself at rehearsals.

Maccario in Goldoni's comedy *L'impresario delle Smirne* (1761) typifies this breed of poet. Armed with the works of Metastasio and Zeno, some old plays and a rhyming dictionary, he practises his specialities of writing new librettos, adapting old ones for new settings, fitting new words to old music, instructing the singers in acting, directing the scenes, attending the ladies in their boxes, looking after the *comparse* and blowing the whistle for the scene changes. In his *Mémoires* (1787), Goldoni recalled that his own duties as poet to a Venetian opera house in the 1730s included responsibility 'for directing and coaching the performers'; and Marcello's *Il teatro alla moda* (*c*1720) implies that a librettist worth his salt should explain his dramatic conception and intentions to the performers in rehearsal, advise them on costumes, gestures and the proper sides of the stage for their entrances and exits, and insist on a clear enunciation of his text.

Marcello's implied ideal, Goldoni's Maccario and Goldoni himself have much in common with the master librettist, Metastasio. Though it was not humanly possible for him to rehearse all the settings of his librettos in person, his letters from Vienna (see Brunelli, 1943–54, iii) show him to have been a careful producer. They include his recollections of 'blocking' an especially touching scene of his *Demetrio* in such a way as to make even bears weep (12 January 1732); references to significant scenic details in the staging of his *Issipile* which he did not choose to incorporate into the printed libretto (19 January 1732); simple but comprehensive diagrams of how he disposed the characters in each scene of his own production of *Demofoonte* (10 February 1748); a recommendation that the detailed analysis of the principal character of *Attilio Regolo* he sent Hasse at Dresden should be passed on to Hasse's leading singer (20 October 1749); and a covering note to go with a sheet of stage business for *Alessandro nell'Indie* suggesting that this might perhaps be of use in Farinelli's Madrid production (4 February 1754). Significantly, these letters are not addressed to theatre poets – they did not have a monopoly of stage supervision – but to composers, singers managing companies and intendants; they are diffident and undogmatic in the way they offer information and advice. The letters reveal that what Metastasio pictured at his desk while writing the librettos or devised in the theatre while rehearsing a setting of it was just one possible way of doing things. They also reveal that, however formalized the stage action may have been in *opera seria*, the genre's leading librettist was convinced that telling theatricality in the communication of feeling was the essence of staging, not formula or protocol (21 February 1748).

Also evident in his letters (e.g. 8 January 1734) is Metastasio's nostalgia for the rough and tumble of Italian operatic life, however serious the opera in hand. He caught this aspect of the operatic scene vividly in his libretto for the intermezzo *L'impresario delle canarie* (1724), a text which helped establish the sub-genre of comic libretto on life backstage; later examples include such pieces as Calzabigi's *La critica teatrale* (see above) and Casti's *Prima la musica, poi le parole* (set by Salieri in 1786), with their audition and rehearsal sequences in which leading ladies pointedly ignore the suggestions of librettists, grab inkwells as substitute poison phials in suicide scenes, and arrange composer, poet and various pieces of furniture into a mock-up family tableau to enhance the pathos of a grieving-parent aria.

'Show dignity, and don't move till I've finished', Casti's *prima donna* instructs her conscripted antagonist before another aria in *Prima la musica*, thus bringing together two grand principles of *opera seria* acting. In many respects such acting was no different from acting in spoken tragedy. According to Rémond de Sainte-Albine (*Le comédien*, 1747), if the aim both of tragedy and of serious opera is to touch the heart, the rules for acting the one must apply equally to the other. An opera singer would have found much apt advice in this treatise and in others like it such as Franz Lang's handbook for Jesuit drama teachers (the *Dissertatio de actione scaenica*, 1727; see Plate 53), the works of Luigi Riccoboni and his son Antonio Francesco, and J. N. S. d'Hannetaire's *Observations sur l'art du comédien* (1764). These books and several others like them preach an acting technique for serious drama of composed stance, deliberate gravity, rhetorically eloquent gesture and expressive face-play. Acting is described as something directed unswervingly out towards the audience (in dialogue, for instance, d'Hannetaire recommends that one stands with one's body facing the pit and head half-turned towards one's interlocutor 'almost as though one were conversing with someone while on a walk') and they stress that intensity of characterization must never be allowed to compromise the comeliness and seemliness of 'la belle nature'. Study and emulation of classic sculpture and of painting in the grand style are recommended by Lang and others in this respect, which recalls Richard Steele's praise of Nicolini's operatic acting ('there is scarce a beautiful posture in an old statue which he does not plant himself in', *The Tatler*, 3 January 1710). But at the same time Lang warns against allowing this idealized formal and frontal portraiture of a role to breed any lack of concentration by the performers, any lapse in rapport with colleagues on stage, or any involvement with the spectators that conflicts with character portrayal. The tendency for such warnings to be ignored was satirized by Marcello in the 1720s and several decades later by Algarotti, Arteaga and Grétry in their digs at performers taking the opportunity of someone else's aria to bow to the boxes, smile at the orchestra, fiddle distractingly with a watch-chain or leave the stage entirely to suck an orange.

Two aspects of *opera seria* might seem at first to fall outside the sphere of spoken tragic performance: the presence of castratos and the cult of the virtuoso da capo exit aria. But the gap was not a wide one. There is little indication that, apart from a glandular tendency to ponderousness on stage, the castratos as a breed were worse (or better) as actors than other sorts of singer. Though opera-goers from England and France often felt called upon to make cases for or against them (some, like the English journal *The Prompter*, obsessed by what it saw as the sick grotesquerie of a smooth eunuch impersonating Caesar or Alexander; others, like François Raguenet, enthusiastically contending that a castrato's tones are more apt to poetical love-making than a 'hoarse, masculine voice'), Italian audiences cheerfully accepted the convention of castrato as virile warrior or great lover for the various artistic rewards it could bring, much as French audiences for the same reason accepted ancient heroes in spoken tragedy tirading in rhymed alexandrines. (One of the indirect theatrical rewards of the castrato's making the treble clef a viable male register was that it enabled operatic actresses to pass quite plausibly for men, either in disguise sequences during feminine roles or throughout entire performances as specialist professional male imitators. And of course in opera houses where all-male casts were *de rigueur* for moral or social reasons, for example in Rome or Lisbon, castratos dressed as women were a *sine qua non* if operas of high amorous intrigue were to be performed at all.)

Performance of the ubiquitous da capo arias seems to have been not unlike the classical 18th-century actor's spoken delivery of a tirade or soliloquy. Given the slow pace and composed stances of contemporary serious plays, a fairly static yet sculpted delivery of an aria, visibly embodying one strong emotion (with sometimes another for the central section), would have been wholly acceptable; and the analytic, demonstrative nature of spoken acting, that 'just delineation of the passions' which allowed a strong sense of the performer as craftsman to be felt and relished by the audience as part of his total performance, had a counterpart in the operatic audience's untroubled double awareness of the predicament of the character portrayed (which might induce tears) and the vocal prowess of the singer portraying it (which might almost simultaneously provoke applause). Two of the elements that distinguish the da capo aria from the soliloquy – the physical demands made by complex melodic writing and the recurrence of lengthy orchestral ritornellos – called for special care. The best performers cultivated a plasticity of the face and a controlled bearing of the neck and chest which disguised the efforts involved in virtuoso singing (some practising before a mirror to monitor this), while for the ritornellos they seem to have hit on a golden mean of deportment between the blockish and the fussy which enabled them, when necessary, to move several momentous steps before striking an apt new attitude for the next vocal paragraph. Their less capable colleagues were criticized throughout the century (by Marcello, Algarotti and Arteaga among others) for breast-heaving, neck-twisting and spitting in the vocal sections of their arias, and in the ritornellos either for standing rooted to the spot in inapposite calm, hand stuck in sword-belt, eyeing the musical director for the cue, or for fussing with fans, gloves and trains, holding mimed conversations with antagonists, wandering aimlessly about the stage, scrutinizing the scenery, even vanishing into the wings for a pinch of snuff.

There is no reason to assume that the spitters or snuff-takers were in a majority. True, many of the most vivid surviving accounts of *opera seria* are gossipy, scandalized or satiric, evoking a world of preening eunuchs, squabbling *prima donnas*, *comparse* shuffling about in tatty liveries so far upstage as to clash with the proportions of the scenery, and a perfunctory acting-to-numbers before audiences too busy with their cabals and games of chess to notice more than the odd *aria di bravura*. But there was more to the form in performance than that. Many audiences were attentive in their varying fashions, and some (especially in the north European court theatres) quite silent; large regiments or retinues of smart and stylish *comparse* could dress stages that were subtly lit and backed with grand scenic perspectives *per angolo* symbolizing mighty structures of public order radically askew from the individual characters' predicaments; international stars could work harmoniously together, a considerable number of them manifestly 'born for singing and acting', as Quantz put it of Faustina. Some, indeed, as Joseph Addison said of Nicolini (*The Spectator*, 14 June 1712), were object lessons in eloquent movement and expressive face-play to the tragedians of spoken drama. It was this ideal of a theatre for *opera seria*, on occasion brilliantly realized, that kept major creative intelligences like Handel and Metastasio in its thrall. Even Marcello's *Il teatro alla moda*, the greatest operatic satire of the age, is not an attack on the ideal: rather it is an affirmation of it and of the desirable relationship between poet, composer, singer and impresario; through a mock celebration of the absence of this ideal, Marcello wittily expressed his view of the operatically benighted Venice of Antonio Vivaldi.

The Paris Académie

Paris was one of the few major cities in Europe to which the writ of *opera seria* did not run in the 18th century; but though the native *tragédie lyrique* and its various offspring, notably *opéra-ballet*, were strong enough to resist foreign invasion, foreign visitors to the Académie Royale de Musique – the 'Opéra' – did not find the methods of staging they encountered there enormously strange (though some found its theatre at the Palais Royal surprisingly small). Techniques of scenography, lighting and gesture at the Opéra were largely international ones, and whatever effect a French piece might have on a visitor's ears, he would probably consider it a 'paradise to the eyes' (as Goldoni did) and be 'dazzled with machinery, dresses and dances' (as Burney was).

Such differences in staging as there were grew mainly from the formal differences between French and Italian opera. The Parisian operatic tradition set great store by the *merveilleux*, which led to greater emphasis on the vertical axis of the stage – infernal trap-doors, celestial descents and the like – than was called for in the more historical (or pseudo-historical) *opera seria*. True to that part of its origins which lay in the *ballet de cour*, the Parisian tradition also insisted on the incorporation into the action of frequent dance sequences: hence the presence of a *corps de ballet*, which not only danced the formal and symmetrical *fêtes* for an opera's principal characters but was also the resource for any troupes of warriors, priests, genii and the like that might be required. In these latter roles the dancers were the counterparts of the non-dancing Italian *comparse*: the choreographed battles, ceremonies and visions which resulted at the Opéra seemed to francophiles to be more elegant and eloquent than their mimed equivalents in *opera seria*, while to italophiles they were merely more effete and unnatural.

Nature seemed to be more firmly on the side of the French where their principal singers were concerned. For one thing, the French tradition of solo writing emphasized a close integration of declamatory monody and *air*, which called for a more seamless acting style than would suit the dualistic Italian stage, dominated by the alternation of recitative and aria, action and reflection, verbal primacy and musical primacy, clock-time and arrested time. For another, the distaste of the French for the castrato, coupled with their fondness for a wide range of voice types in opera, allowed – or so some French theorists maintained – for character impersonation that was more 'natural, just and modest' than the Italian. However, the fact that the characters portrayed at the Opéra were vocally more realistic than many of their *seria* equivalents, as well as being less subject to dizzying switches of mood and identity (including sexual identity), did not guarantee that the portrayers were histrionically up to their parts. Indeed, in the same decade (1700–10) that Nicolini was beginning to impress even the wary English with the brilliance of his tragic acting, the loudest champion of the operatic superiority of France, Le Cerf de la Viéville, was forced to acknowledge that the acting of French singers had reached a low ebb for want of a few sharp rebukes from the late great theatrical disciplinarian, Lully. (Even then, however, Le Rochois, the finest of Lully's tragédiennes, was training effective leading ladies for the future.)

The other vital distinguishing feature of Parisian opera was its commitment to a major role for a sizable chorus. The entry of the chorus in *tragédie lyrique* at the Palais Royal was a spectacular moment, its richly dressed members advancing in two ranks, one from each side of the stage, to take up their positions in an elegant U-formation recalling the choric half-moons of the earliest Florentine and Mantuan operas. By framing the activity of principals, dance troupes and theatrical machines in this way, the chorus helped to produce a stronger axial symmetry than obtained in 18th-century Italy, which may partly explain the rarity on the French stage (outside the work of Servandoni) of the relatively asymmetric *scena per angolo* so popular in stagings of *opera seria*.

The rich counterpoint of various arts characteristic of French operatic performance appealed to sophisticated Parisian taste. As one critic put it at a revival of Rameau's *Hippolyte et Aricie*, 'I love to watch Mlle Camargo enter to joyful music and wipe away the tears that Theseus has made me weep'. If such a show were to work well, it was doubtless helpful for each artist involved to have some knowledge of the other arts on display. An aspiring opera composer, said Rameau, needed to study also the stage, actors, movement and dance, and there are stories of specialists assisting in spheres outside their own: the principal baritone Claude-Louis de Chassé advising on military verisimilitude during rehearsals of the siege scene in *Alceste*, for example, or Rameau himself demonstrating a dance step to fit the final chaconne of his *Indes galantes*. But in the main, the preparation, rehearsal and performance of *tragédie lyrique* and *opéra-ballet* in the first half of the 18th century seem to have involved not so much an organic, chemical compounding of the arts as a benign convergence of them. In the performance itself, for instance, principals sat graciously out of harm's way during the inset *fêtes*; the dancers often wore masks, which set them apart from all other performers; and once settled into their U-formation, the chorus rarely moved, even when the words they were singing might be thought to demand some physical agitation, if only the unfolding of their much-folded arms.

By mid-century, discontented spirits like Noverre and some of the Encyclopedists were arguing that there should be much more creative consultation between librettist, composer, choreographer, designer and machinist at the planning stage of an opera and a greater integration of performing arts during the show itself. That such discontent had not been expressed earlier and that the convergence of the arts had been as benign as it had was largely due to the presence at the Opéra of a potent controlling phantom, that of Lully. Lully in a sense directed the staging of Campra's and Rameau's works from beyond the grave. His comprehensive and autocratic creation in the 1670s of a complex art form in which the various design and performance elements could mesh smoothly; his laborious teaching of an acting style to his company ('geste pour geste' where necessary); his quite un-Italian insistence on the publication and revival of his operas; his canny linking of all this to the glory of the French crown: these things had ensured that for the next three generations his works were both classics and yardsticks, that there was a strong (though not inflexible) tradition of staging them, and that the company structure necessary for so doing was at the disposal of subsequent makers of operas, always provided that their works – however much more virtuoso musically, cosmopolitan scenically or *galant* in mood than Lully's – fitted the Lullian mould in their stagecraft.

The company structure itself was rationalized by the royal ordinances of 1713 and 1714 (see Chapter III). Significantly, these edicts (which held in large measure for most of the century) required that the company keep a rehearsed Lully opera in reserve in case of need; and it is significant too that, though they deal with several matters relevant to operatic staging (the size of the company, salary gradations, the need for a performer to accept the roles and costumes he is assigned, the teaching of the vocal music and dances, the doubling of small solo parts with chorus work), they say nothing about inter-departmental liaison in the opera house. Nor do they list any figure corresponding to the modern stage director among those company members drawing salaries: singers, dancers, instrumentalists, orchestral and choral conductors, choreographers, dance trainers, designers, machinists, copyists and tailors. Making sure that there was at least a bare sufficiency of liaison was presumably the responsibility of 'le syndic chargé de la régie du théâtre', one of the two active syndics the edicts created (the other being concerned with stores and finances).

The syndic *de la régie* in the ordinance of 1714, his every move needing the approval of the inspector-general to the company (a royal appointment), dealt with artistic planning and with casting (in consultation with the composer, if alive), and oversaw all rehearsals and performances, during which the theatre staff, stage crew and performers were answerable only to him. It is a moot point how far his role in the staging of an opera, and the role of the 'directeurs' who followed him, was a creative and how far a diplomatic-administrative one; but clearly the drawing of the strands together by such figures made for many memorable performances at the Palais Royal, as audiences sometimes acknowledged. ('One cannot praise enough the troubles *MM. les Directeurs* have taken to make the show as brilliant and satisfying as it could be', wrote the *Mercure de France* of the first revival of Rameau's *Dardanus*, enthusing over the contribution of words, music, casting, décor, costumes, choreography and execution.) Even more performances, doubtless, were memorable for individual triumphs. For example, Casanova wrote in his memoirs of being infected by Parisian enthusiasm for the perfect grace of Louis Dupré's dancing as displayed in *Les fêtes vénitiennes*, though his feelings were tempered by what seemed to him to be the datedness of Campra's music, as well as by the scenographer's presenting a grand prospect of the Venetian Piazzetta which reversed the positions of St Mark's and the Campanile. And even Rousseau, whose caricature of an Opéra performance in *La nouvelle Héloïse* (1761, II.xxiii) is the most vividly cruel thing written about that institution in the 18th century, was impressed enough by Chassé's acting there – he created the roles of Theseus in *Hippolyte et Aricie*, Huascar in *Les Indes galantes* and Pollux in *Castor et Pollux* – to cite him in the *Encyclopédie* as everything a good operatic performer ought to be: never dropping his character to become merely a singer; forever interesting, even in silence; conspiring by steps, looks and gestures to make his audience feel that the music rising from the orchestra pit was rising from his soul.

Comedy and new tendencies
While Nicolini wrestling with the lion in *Idaspe fedele* and Chassé captaining his choric army in *Castor et Pollux* are apt vignettes of *opera seria* and *tragédie lyrique* in effective performance, their counterpart in the changing operatic world of the later 18th century is Gaetano Guadagni as Gluck's Orpheus mourning Eurydice's second death (Burney said that his 'attitudes' and 'action' earned as much applause as his singing in 'the simple and ballad-like air 'Che farò'). Indeed, Guadagni's whole career can stand as representative of the ethos of operatic staging which was one aspect of the new age of Sensibility, Sublime Simplicity, Enlightenment, fresh respect for the arts of comedy and growing concern for theatrical realism. He gained early experience as first *amoroso* in a *buffo* company: a novel way to prepare for a serious career at the time. He was formed as an actor by David Garrick, high priest of the twin cults of Shakespeare and Nature. His acting is said by Burney to have been as distinguished in operatic comedies of genteel life (for instance Piccinni's *La buona figliuola*) as in the sublimities of Gluck. He had strong views about total impersonation of roles; and Burney's tribute suggests that he reversed in a significantly neo-classic way the old exhortation to a player to imitate idealized painting and sculpture: 'his attitudes and gestures were so full of grace and propriety that they would have been excellent studies for a statuary'. It is apt that he should have created the role of the new Orpheus.

Guadagni's early involvement with *buffo* acting came at a time when the *buffo* manner was growing in its appeal to serious opera lovers. The tiny, often two-person troupes performing the farcical intermezzos set between the acts of *opera seria* and the rather larger companies giving the more extended *opere buffe* had developed a style of acting – part Molièrian, part *commedia dell'arte* – which was brisker, saltier and more immediately alluring, though probably not a great deal less governed by convention, than that seen in loftier opera. The unpretentiousness of this style and the leeway it allowed for sharp observation of contemporary life endeared it to such observers as de Brosses and Arteaga, who saw its vivacity and 'air of truth' as rebukes to the traditional high-operatic stage's tendency to stiffness and frigidity. At a time when the extended ensemble as a form was moving upward from *opera buffa* to the opera of myth and history – a time also when Garrick was influentially shifting the norm of serious acting in spoken theatre away from weighty declamation towards a more energetic, pantomimic mode – it is likely that some of the more seemly aspects of the *buffo* style, along with some Garrickian traits, were sharpening the immediacy of serious operatic acting and increasing its air of truth.

Garrick was a model to several of the new men of theatrical Europe in the mid-18th century: not least Noverre, to whom he was 'the Proteus of our time', his versatility among the dramatic genres and his chameleon-like ability to 'become' a remarkably wide range of characters being inspirations behind Noverre's campaign to unmask the dancers in operatic ballet and so increase their histrionic potential. But if Garrick was a Proteus, it was Gluck who tended to be seen as the modern Prometheus, bringing life to inert operatic clay. To the extent that the new opera of the mid-century associated with him was a blending of *tragédie lyrique* and *opera seria*, it risked compounding the stasis of the French chorus – 'ranged motionless like so many organ pipes', one critic said – with the stasis of the fully-blown *seria* aria, of which it was coming to be felt (by Algarotti, Arteaga, Marmontel and Grétry among others) that the ever-lengthening ritornellos and *fioriture* jeopardized any chance of proper dramatic continuity. Both these stases 'chilled the action'; so the slimming of aria form in the work of Gluck and his like-minded contemporaries and their composition of chorus parts which further developed Cahusac's attempts at the Opéra around 1750 'to get the chorus to act in conformity with what they sing' (*La danse ancienne et moderne*, 1754) were hailed as theatrical revitalizations. An article in the *Journal de politique et de littérature* in the 1770s describes Gluck as having to deal at first with principal singers whose acting was either lifeless or grotesquely mannered and with 'a collection of *mannequins* called a chorus'; but 'Prometheus shook his torch and the statues came to life', the principals realizing that the eloquent and expressive idiom of Gluck's music only needed to be felt to bring strong, true stage impersonation along with it, while the chorus members in his operas were 'amazed to discover that they were actors'.

Of course, it should not be supposed that Gluck alone was responsible for theatrical change at this time or indeed that everything was darkness before him. This encomium nevertheless provides a frame in which to set such things as the poet Verazi's stagings of his own librettos in the 1760s and 1770s, noted as they were for their treating the chorus 'as actors, not statues'; his printing of those librettos with stage directions for elaborate, character-revealing business even during da capo arias; the increasing trouble taken by composers like Jommelli over the construction of *buffo* ensembles which would permit 'natural' acting throughout by everyone involved; the growing tendency for operatic stage space to be characterized by chiaroscuro in lighting, local colour in décor, and asymmetry in the deployment of supernumeraries, dancers and scenery; the praises heaped on the acting of such singers as Sophie Arnould at the Opéra for its nobility, tenderness, elevation, energy, soul, sentiment and sensibility; and the determination of Guadagni himself to identify so fully with his roles that he would refuse to acknowledge applause after an aria or to take encores.

Personal vanities, audience enthusiasms and the staying power of the traditions and conventions of *opera seria* all dictated that few singers went as far as Guadagni in this; but his ideal – Burney called it 'propriety of character' and listed it with musico-dramatic simplicity and 'theatrical effects' as one of the three tenets of the Gluck–Calzabigi sect in Vienna – chimes well with a concept of opera as a form involving a conscious and carefully monitored synthesis of theatrical arts, all blending together to present a heightened virtual actuality which will enthrall, elevate and edify. The concept attracted growing support in the later 18th century, though there were differing views as to who should do the careful monitoring. Conscious integration of the arts, as opposed to the tradi-tional *laissez faire*, was urged influentially by Algarotti and Noverre. Both insisted that the librettist (the 'poet') should, as the begetter of an opera, be its monitor, the guardian of its wholeness, and that it is for the other theatre artists to strive to embody the poet's unifying imaginative conception. Noverre further emphasized the need for the executive quintet (composer, designer, machinist, *maître de ballet* and costumier) to work closely together, and for the librettist to be on call throughout. This was certainly an authority structure assured of some success in court theatres where the librettist (or at least the drafter of operatic scenarios) was the local prince himself: Frederick the Great at Berlin and Potsdam, for instance, or Gustavus III at Stockholm and Drottningholm. Else-where, and more humbly, it might be the court's resident theatre poet who would 'stage the performances with good intelligence and good order', as it was put of Gaetano Martinelli at Lisbon in the 1770s, directing the complicated operas he had written with the absentee *maestro di cappella* Jommelli. Elsewhere again, the *maestro* might be in control of the whole proceedings, as was Jommelli himself at Stuttgart and Ludwigs-burg in the 1750s and 1760s under the watchful eye of Duke Karl-Eugen of Württemberg. Jommelli, according to Christian Schubart (1806), confidently revised librettos before setting them, then employed his knowledge of singers, instrumentalists, audiences and theatre acoustics, plus the close cooperation of designers, machinists and choreographers, 'to move and uplift the coldest listener's heart and soul with one great totality [*ein grosses Ganzes*]'.

In other places a close-knit committee was jointly responsible for conceiving, preparing and rehearsing a new work; this was the case with Gluck, Calzabigi, the choreographer Angiolini, the scenographer Quag-lio and the intendant Durazzo for *Orfeo*. During the last three decades of the century the idea of a specialist stage director also began to take root: neither intendant, impresario or company manager on the one hand nor a theatre artist of any of the traditional sorts on the other, but rather someone whose sole function was to see that things were done properly and that they contributed harmoniously to the 'great totality'. This figure – his most direct forebear the *corago* of 17th-century Italy – is described in such works as Antonio Planelli's *Dell'opera in musica* of 1772, Ernst Dressler's *Theaterschule* of 1777 and the anonymous *Instruction für den Regisseur des Schauspiels* drawn up at Stuttgart in the 1790s. His functions in these treatises include regulating all the specialist theatre artists (from poet and composer to costumier), scheduling rehearsals, training the singers in acting, designating entrances and exits, blocking individual scenes, and (in the words of the *Instruction*) 'balancing all the individual details to create the overall effect'. However, where such directors existed in opera houses at this time, their role seems to have been an enabling rather than a dominating one. They did not see themselves as all-powerful puppet-masters – unless, of course, that is literally what they were, as in the case of the puppeteers Pauersbach and Rauffer, who ran the celebrated marionette opera at Eszterháza in the 1770s, where the performers under their direction were said to act 'très naturellement'.

It was against the background of these new tendencies, mingling with the persistent traditions of *opera seria* and *opera buffa*, that the operas of Haydn and Mozart were first staged. In the later 1770s and the 1780s, Haydn found that a major part of his duties as Kapellmeister at Eszterháza lay in operatic work for the princely theatre. There the day-to-day running of the opera was, for much of the time, in the hands of a triumvirate – Haydn himself as musical director, adapter and resident composer; Pietro Travaglia as principal scenographer and lighting designer; Philipp Bader first and later Nunziato Porta as theatre manager – with Prince Nikolaus shaping artistic policy, holding the purse strings and having an important say in the casting. The prince's instructions of 1779 (analogous to Louis XIV's ordinances for the Opéra of 1713–14) require that the musical director be responsible for everything connected with singers and instrumentalists (plus the prompter) once they have been hired, while the scenographer supervises the stage crew and the manager sees to everyone else. Porta's life was a busy one of house management, drawing up costume lists, ordering printing work, approving invoices, copying parts, negotiating over librettos (to say nothing of translating, adapting and writing them) and organizing supernumeraries. One of the principal singers would sometimes arrange the stage battles and other set pieces required of these *comparse* – at Eszterháza they were largely the prince's grenadiers – but generally this was Porta's headache; and a real headache it must have been, as for instance when the first Eszterháza performance of Sarti's *Didone abbandonata* was separated from the second by two day-long additional fencing rehearsals for the 24 grenadiers who impersonated the Moorish and Trojan armies. As for the seasoned Italian principals hired by Prince Nikolaus, one must assume that they were experienced enough histrionically and were cast sufficiently to type to direct themselves in the main, though with the help of Haydn, his prompter and any librettist – Porta or other – who might be on hand.

Assumptions are again called for where the first stagings of Mozart's operas are concerned, since the surviving evidence (as often in the 18th century) is so slight. It is very likely that his librettists were involved in rehearsals when that was physically possible. Schikaneder clearly was in the case of *Die Zauberflöte*; and Da Ponte states in his memoirs that he 'stayed in Prague for a week in order to direct the actors' before the première there of *Don Giovanni*. But it is also likely that Mozart himself was actively concerned with stage characterization at rehearsals as well as with the notes of the score. He regarded himself as 'a composer who understands the stage'; and plausible anecdotes survive to the effect that he was in favour of friendly theatrical give-and-take between creator and performer: the story of his sudden assault on Caterina Bondini to increase the intensity of Zerlina's off-stage scream in *Don Giovanni*, for example, or Michael Kelly's recollection of the composer's bowing to his insistence that, as Don Curzio in *Le nozze di Figaro*, Kelly should stammer consistently like a *commedia dell'arte* Tartaglia all through the role.

It is only with *Idomeneo* that we have many details of the preparation and rehearsal of a Mozart première. The composer's letters to his father in Salzburg during the three months leading up to the première in 1781 suggest a careful collaboration in Munich between Mozart, Seeau the court intendant for music and drama, Cannabich the conductor, Quaglio the scenographer and Le Grand the choreographer. Mozart agreed with Quaglio that the king's disembarkation scene in Act 1 was theatrically far-fetched and needed changing; he settled the action and grouping of the big choric scene of flood, fire and the supernatural at the end of Act 2 with Le Grand, who put their plan into practice; and he rethought the lead into the Act 3 sacrifice scene (presumably in consultation with Quaglio and Le Grand) to make it smoother and scenically more vivid. Much concern was expressed over the proper printing of Varesco's Italian libretto with, if possible, a decent German translation on opposite pages and with scenic descriptions to reflect Quaglio's final arrangement accurately. Yet all this was done without the presence in Munich of Varesco himself, who like Leopold Mozart was detained in Salzburg (and who was contacted through Leopold about needful cuts and rewrites of his text). The lack of a librettist on hand to advise the singers about stage action and no hint of the presence of a new-style stage director suggest that the principals were expected to be largely self-reliant and to use appropriate modifications of well-tried *seria* and Guadagnian techniques, for all that one of their number had, to Mozart's chagrin, never set foot on any stage before, while another acted 'like a statue'. (This led to the composer's insistence that an expository scene between the two be 'shortened as drastically as possible'.) However, the principals almost certainly had theatrical advice from Mozart in his role of composer-répétiteur, with his earnest concern that recitative should be fast-moving, spirited and fiery in performance and his guiding conviction that the best criterion for librettists, composers and performers alike was theatrical effectiveness. 'Consider it carefully', he said during a discussion of the Subterranean Voice in Act 3 (taking a sideswipe at the prolixity of the ghost of Hamlet's father as he did so); 'picture to yourself the theatre . . .'.

Entr'acte II

We should not, Donald Tovey once warned, talk about the French Revolution when we ought to be talking about music. In talking of opera, it is hard to avoid the French Revolution, or at least the social and political changes in the late 18th century of which it was the most spectacular manifestation. Opera was profoundly affected by these changes: internally, as operas came increasingly to treat of topics concerned with or reflecting the great political and military events of the day, and externally, as opera-house managements and audiences were affected by the changing times. Some of the court opera houses of central Europe – those in Vienna, Berlin, Dresden and Munich, for example – maintained their situation, with some degree of royal patronage and royal governance, for another century or more. Not, however, those in Paris – the centre of operatic development for most of the first half of the 19th century – where from the time of the Revolution onwards the theatre, like that in London, was wholly commercial. Because of its wealth, Paris – and almost equally London (as well as New York in the last decades of the century) – was a great magnet to singers: that is why Verdi, in Italy, often had to be content with second-raters.

In Italy (where the research of John Rosselli has so much illuminated the workings of the opera industry), the court theatres survived, as centres of patronage and influence, but their power waned and many new, non-royal theatres were built, stimulated by local rivalries. During the troubled times of the Napoleonic wars, the theatres generally remained active, encouraged by authority (be it French military men or Austrian governors) because the events there represented a harmless diversion which kept the educated classes occupied. The opera houses – which in these secular times had overtaken the churches as the most important local centres of musical life – were patronized not only by the nobility but also by the middle classes. Some opera houses were owned by the local ruler; others belonged to noble families, or groups of noblemen and professional people, or municipalities. Often individual boxes within the houses were privately owned.

Operatic activity in Italy was closely monitored by government. Officials, sometimes working in groups with local nobles and people from the professions and business, concerned themselves with the choice of libretto, of composer and of singers, and made efforts to ensure that the seasons were lavish yet at the same time not excessively costly and also that performances were in no way damaging to public order. Audience behaviour and censorship fell within their purview. These groups, working with impresarios, planned the seasons, of which the most important and fashionable, in the majority of houses, was the Carnival, beginning on 26 December and ending on Shrove Tuesday. There were others during the spring and autumn, but local custom varied, and by the 1830s many houses were giving opera virtually the year round. Normally, two operas were given in a season, but a third would have to be mounted if one turned out to be a failure. Many members of the audience attended nightly, sometimes up to five times in a week; they would not only listen to performances, or those parts of them they were keen to hear, but would also eat (if they were in boxes, servants could prepare their meal in an adjoining room), meet and talk to friends, and – until they were banned in most houses, during the early 19th century – play at the gaming tables.

Most opera houses retained the traditional architecture by which the seats were arranged chiefly in tiers of boxes, sometimes as many as six, of which the second – the 'piano nobile' – was the most comfortable, fashionable and expensive, used by the nobility. The further one sat from the second tier, the cheaper were the seats and the less exalted the social class of their occupants. Officials, professional men such as doctors and lawyers, people in business and commerce, priests and students might be able to afford boxes, or they could sit on the benches in the orchestra stalls, some of which might be reserved for officers and others occupied by the senior servants of the nobility. Lower servants, soldiers and skilled workmen might be found in the top tier.

Serious opera, with its links to an aristocratic past, enjoyed more prestige than any other form of theatrical entertainment. It would occupy the most important seasons as well as predominating at the leading houses; indeed some theatres, such as S Carlo at Naples and La Fenice at Venice, rarely gave anything else. It was however costly to put on, demanding lavish costumes and the best singers. In the smaller theatres and at lesser centres, the house had to be shared not only with comic opera but also with spoken plays and other, lower kinds of theatrical entertainment. The major opera houses generally offered about five new productions each year, three of them new, specially commissioned works; smaller houses had to be more dependent on revivals of new works heard elsewhere and of their own old productions. The leading Italian operatic cities in the early 19th century were Milan, Venice (especially in comic opera), Bologna (a traditional centre for the study of singing, as of other branches of music), Rome and Naples. Milan, the centre of Austrian and then of Napoleonic government, gradually came to be the most important of these, with La Scala becoming recognized by the 1830s – the previous decade had been a fruitful one for opera in Italy, with more money and less political pressure – as one of the foremost houses in Europe.

The winds of intellectual change, however, which had blown so fiercely in France at the end of the 18th century, were gentler in Italy, and later in coming. It was Paris, in the years after the Revolution, that was the crucible of operatic change in Europe. The classical historical or (more persistent in France than elsewhere) mythological dramas favoured for the Académie Royale under the *ancien régime*, by Gluck, Piccinni, Salieri and other visitors as well as Frenchmen, gave way to operas dealing in a more immediate and realistic way with historical subjects. This was to lead to the tradition of Parisian grand opera, through such works as Spontini's *Fernand Cortez* (1809) and *Olimpie* (1819), Auber's *La muette de Portici* (1828) and Rossini's *Guillaume Tell* (1829) – these last two, especially *Guillaume Tell*, are usually regarded as inaugural and prototypical – to the massive works of Meyerbeer and Halévy of the 1830s and 40s. Donizetti too subscribed to this tradition in his French operas, as indeed did Verdi in *Jerusalem* (1847), *Les vêpres siciliennes* (1855) and ultimately *Don Carlos* (1867) – and the grand opera tradition was profoundly to affect the mature works of both Verdi and Wagner. The leading grand opera librettist was Eugène Scribe, whose first text for the Opéra was *La muette de Portici* and who supplied several further texts for Auber and others for Meyerbeer and Halévy. His verse was not in itself distinguished but he was a master at devising librettos that exploited the new stage devices that were becoming available, such as gas lighting and the diorama; he met the mood of the moment by treating large-scale historical themes, often concerning the fates of religious groups, tribes or even entire nations, susceptible of spectacular scenic effects involving processions, battles, massacres and catastrophes, natural as well as man-made.

Closer to the time of the Revolution, however, there had arisen the type, generally more modest in scale – and soon prevalent in *opéra comique* and all-sung opera alike – which later came to be called 'rescue opera' or *pièce de sauvetage*. It was a natural outgrowth of the spirit of the times. As uncomplicated in its ethics as a Western or a World War II adventure film, with good and evil sharply delineated – the moral dilemmas that appealed to the audiences of Metastasian, or Racinian, opera were altogether lacking – the rescue opera invariably had as its climax the last-minute saving of the hero from a cruel, oppressive enemy or (occasionally) from natural danger. The parallels with older forms of serious opera, when an analogous 'rescue' might be performed by a *deus ex machina* or a benevolently merciful monarch, scarcely need emphasis; nor indeed do the differences, when the rescuing agent here could be, for example, the favourable outcome of a battle, the advent of relieving forces or, most popularly, the arrival of a message from (or the person of) a minister of justice. Another, not unrelated variety was the 'bandit opera', typified by Le Sueur's *La caverne* (1793), where a band of virtuous men are compelled by an oppressive regime to live as outlaws. Relics of this type are found as late as Verdi's *Il trovatore* (1853) and even Bizet's *Carmen*

(1875). Both kinds could give scope for the massed choral singing and wind-band music of the stirring kind associated with the French Revolutionary hymn. Other operas too can be related to the Revolution and the Terror: Cherubini's *Médée* (1797) is open to interpretation as an allegory about the oppressed becoming in turn the oppressor.

Cherubini was one of the leading exponents of the rescue opera, along with such men as Méhul and Le Sueur. The solemn, almost austere 'neo-classical' style (there are ready analogies in the other arts, most obviously in the work of Jacques-Louis David), partly inherited from Gluck and his followers, and noticeable too in such German or Italian operas of the time as Mozart's *La clemenza di Tito* and Cimarosa's *Gli Orazi ed i Curiazi*, found a natural home in such works as these, written for an audience anxious to put behind it the decorative manner of *ancien régime* opera and dealing with serious issues and the potential nobility of the ordinary man. Not all the heroes were, in fact, ordinary men; often they were noblemen themselves, as in Pierre Gaveaux's *Léonore, ou L'amour conjugal* (1798), the libretto of which was re-used for Beethoven's *Fidelio*. It is said to have been based on a real occurrence; the critical point is less whether it was than that it could have been, and that the situations are of a kind that meant something to an audience of the time, as the doings of the remote historical or mythological heroes and heroines of the previous era did not.

The hero of *Fidelio* is a nobleman, but its other characters include ordinary working people, whose emotions and utterances are not taken too seriously by the composer or the audience. Here again is the mixture of *seria* parts and *buffa* ones, as in the Goldonian *dramma giocoso*; and indeed the two Italian settings of the same text, by Ferdinando Paer (1804) and Simon Mayr (1805), are described respectively as *dramma semiserio* and *dramma giocoso*. Such intermediate types had become increasingly popular towards the close of the 18th century concurrently with the partial erosion of the distinctions between *seria* and *buffa* styles (or at least the increasing interchange between them). Another favoured type in this category was the *comédie larmoyante*, or 'sentimental comedy', traceable back through Piccinni's *La buona figliuola* (1760) to the English novel, in which the domestic, familial virtues are celebrated and shown to be rewarded. While composers still used old librettos – Mayr and Paer, for example, continued to set Metastasio texts well into the 1820s, and Rossini's *Il barbiere di Siviglia* (1816) is to the libretto Paisiello had set more than three decades before – the relaxation of categories led to composers' and librettists' casting their net wider for models.

Some turned to literature of high quality, of recent or more remote times. For political-historical topics, Schiller was a possible source: Auber and Rossini used his *Wilhelm Tell* (Grétry's opera on this theme is not based on Schiller), Donizetti his *Marie Stuart*, and Verdi, later in the century, was to compose four operas on his plays, including *Don Carlos*. Plots drawn from Shakespeare's comedies had occasionally been used in the 18th century, mainly in England; now the Romantics' rediscovery of his tragedies led to their use – often heavily adapted, but that is beside the point – as the basis for operas, among them Dalayrac's, Steibelt's and Zingarelli's versions of *Romeo and Juliet* in the 1790s and Bellini's version of the same play (1830), Rossini's *Otello* (1816) and Mercadante's *Amleto* (1822). The young Wagner, Balfe and Berlioz were also to write Shakespeare operas, but again it was Verdi who was to meet the author on something closer to his own terms and his own level.

If the use of Shakespeare as a source is significant, still more so is the use of Walter Scott, whose novels and poetry evoked a mysterious, chivalric past in the remote Scottish Highlands that was deeply attractive to the Romantic temperament. The verse of the supposed early bard 'Ossian' (James Macpherson) had already kindled interest in the romantic mystery of the Highlands, drawn on by Méhul in his *Uthal* (1806). Operas based on the writings of Scott, beginning with Henry Bishop's *Guy Mannering* (1816) and Rossini's *La donna del lago* (1819), and including Donizetti's *Lucia di Lammermoor* (1835) and several works after *Ivanhoe* and *Kenilworth*, are numerous. Italian composers, however, rarely tried to evoke the specific spirit of a place; distance and mystery were enough. Equally symptomatic of the Romantic attraction to a remote past is Bellini's choice of Gaul in Druidic times for *Norma*, which is based on a plot akin to that of Spontini's finest opera, *La vestale*. Both deal with priestesses impelled by love to break their sacred vows of chastity: Spontini, in 1807, found a happy resolution, but Bellini did not, and it is instructive to reflect on the differences between the conflict, and its resolution in a funeral pyre, with those that characterize the serious operas of the 18th century, with their rationally ordered, and accordingly happy, outcome.

Norma, to a libretto by Felice Romani, dates from 1831. It was only during the preceding few years that Italian audiences had come to accept (as French and German audiences had for some time) the unhappy ending. This Italian conservatism seems to be a product of social and political circumstances as much as a matter of taste; it is notable that only after the crucial year 1848 did the great issues such as political or religious freedom (long since central to French grand opera) begin to appear with any frequency on the Italian operatic stage. Conservatism is evident too in the Italian retention of the castrato voice on the stage well into the 19th century, long after it had been rejected elsewhere. The last operatic castrato, G. B. Velluti, retired in 1830. The Italian liking for the high voice in male parts led, during the years when the castratos were falling into disfavour, to the use of female contraltos in heroic roles, for example in Rossini's *Tancredi* (1813) and *Semiramide* (1823) or Bellini's *I Capuleti e i Montecchi* (1830).

German opera followed many of the tendencies we have seen in France and Italy: heroic rescue opera, as in *Fidelio*, sentimental, domestic comedy, as for example in the Singspiels of Joseph Weigl in Vienna, and Romantic opera about the distant past, as in Marschner's *Der Templer und die Jüdin*

(1829), after Walter Scott. More specially characteristic of German opera was an interest in the supernatural, typified by E. T. A. Hoffmann's *Undine*, of 1816, and Spohr's *Faust* (not after Goethe) of the same year. The greatest opera exploiting dark forces is Weber's *Der Freischütz* (1821). Here Weber developed the leitmotif technique – the use of a theme, susceptible of modification, to stand for a person, an object, a concept or almost anything else throughout an entire opera; it had been foreshadowed by several composers, in particular Méhul, at the end of the 18th century, and was to be applied more richly and more functionally by Wagner, to draw together into a symphonic fabric the music of an entire evening (or in the case of the *Ring* four evenings).

The other successful opera of Weber's maturity, *Euryanthe*, was first heard in Vienna. But the operatic primacy that Mozart had bestowed on Vienna, at least in historical retrospect, faded in the early 19th century. Rossini was admired above all, and the city's Italianate taste was reflected in the Habsburg emperors' readiness to hand the running of the court opera house over to Italians, among whom Donizetti was briefly Kapellmeister in the 1840s. During the middle years of the century the most important Viennese première was that of Flotow's *Martha* in 1847. The increase of national consciousness in Germany, which had begun two generations before, created a will to oust Italians from their long dominion over German opera houses; the story of Weber's years in Dresden and his constant battles with the Italian establishment there are symptomatic, as was his concentration, as musical director, on the French repertory in which he saw the way forward for German music. His successors at Dresden included Marschner and Wagner, several of whose early works had their premières there. Dresden's great days as an operatic centre returned in the period of Ernst von Schuch's directorship, 1882–1914, with a series of Strauss premières in the early years of the 20th century. Leipzig, a city with no court, had a tradition of middle-class music; in the late 18th century it had been a home of the Singspiel and in the 19th too light German opera prevailed. Most of Lortzing's operas had their premières there.

In Berlin, during the late decades of the 18th century, Singspiel had been given at the Schauspielhaus by the National Theatre while at the Royal Opera House the court company (whose performances were not open to the ticket-buying public until 1789) favoured serious opera in Italian. The two companies came under joint management early in the next century but the distinction of repertory remained – typified in 1821 when *Olympia*, a German version of an opera composed in French by Spontini, the Italian general music director, was given in the Royal Opera House, followed after five weeks by the première of Weber's *Der Freischütz* in the Schauspielhaus: the former to a fashionable and noble audience, the latter to a bourgeois audience including Heine, E. T. A. Hoffmann and Mendelssohn. Works by non-German composers, French as well as Italian (and among the latter particularly Rossini), continued to prevail at the Royal Opera, although Meyerbeer's appointment in 1842 as Spontini's successor affected the situation. In spite of conservative policies – two Wagner premières were turned down in the 1840s, and as late as 1900 the rejection of Strauss's *Feuersnot* led that composer to refuse any future premières to Berlin – the house in Unter den Linden enjoyed a high reputation throughout the century. In the late years of the century numerous German towns built their own theatres, mostly municipally financed and giving spoken drama and operetta as well as opera; they vary greatly in capacity according to the size of the towns, many taking as few as 800 or 900 and even in the larger cities rarely more than 1400 or 1500. The most important new house of the era was of course Wagner's, built specifically for performances of his own works at Bayreuth; seating 1800, it has resemblances to a classical amphitheatre and was the first to have a covered orchestral pit (which had important acoustical consequences). Another innovation of Wagner's was to have the house lighting extinguished during the performance, compelling a greater degree of attention, and preparation, on the audience's part.

Operatic life flourished in London during the century, on a commercial basis; prevailing taste was strongly Italianate but also conservative. The pasticcio-type opera persisted longer in London than elsewhere, particularly in the work of Henry Bishop, who made alarmingly free with the operas of Mozart and Rossini and adapted Shakespeare plays to music with scant regard for their original texts. Only rarely were visiting composers invited to write new works for London: examples are Weber's *Oberon* (1826), which owes its strange form to London taste for exotic spectacle at the time, and Verdi's *I masnadieri* (1847). In the late years of the century New York assumed its place as a leading operatic centre. Italian opera had reached the city in 1825 and the first opera house had opened seven years later, followed by several others, all short-lived; the Academy of Music, lasting from 1854 to 1886, presented leading singers from Europe in Italian and Italianized French operas, but in 1883 it was succeeded as the leading opera house in the city by the Metropolitan Opera, which initially specialized in German (and even Germanized Italian) opera. In South America, Rio de Janeiro and especially Buenos Aires became significant operatic centres late in the century. The only composer from the Americas to make a wider mark was the Brazilian, Carlos Gomes, who had works done at La Scala. Looking eastwards, the nationalist sentiments that began to assert themselves in Slavonic and neighbouring cultures early in the 19th century were strongly manifested in opera: established Italian and German traditions in St Petersburg and Warsaw, Prague and Budapest, all began to accommodate vernacular ones during the first half of the century.

One factor in the beginning, early in the 19th century, of the consolidation of an international repertory was the growing ease and speed of travel, which meant that singers could readily appear in their favourite roles in different houses. For the singer remained at the centre of the stage of operatic life: many of the main roles of Italian opera throughout the century were designed for, and built to fit the voices of, particular singers. This is less true of German opera or French, where vocal prowess as such was less central; and as a core repertory developed and composers came to think increasingly in terms of posterity, rather than immediate and exclusively short-term success, roles came to be composed more for voice types than for specific voices.

The early 19th century, for this reason and others – the demand for heroic singing and for a new kind of expressiveness and the enlargement of opera houses and orchestras – saw important changes in vocal art. By the middle of the century greater volume and carrying power, more brilliant top registers and more resonant low ones, would be the rule; but during the *bel canto* era of Rossini, Bellini and early Donizetti the call was for singing that was florid, graceful and expressive. A generation of singers arose to meet these demands and to satisfy them internationally. Among them were such sopranos as Giuditta Pasta (Bellini's first Amina and Norma, Donizetti's Anne Boleyn) and Isabella Colbran (nine roles in the operas of her sometime husband, Rossini), the contralto Geltrude Righetti (Rossini's original Rosina and Cinderella), and such *tenori di grazia* as Manuel García (creator of Rossini's Almaviva in Rome, Paris, London and New York), Andrea Nozzari and Giovanni Davide – all high tenors moving smoothly into falsetto at the top – as well as Giovanni Battista Rubini (creator of several Bellini and Donizetti roles). These men had taken the place of the castratos, now falling into disfavour – though as we have seen the tradition of the high-voiced hero had died hard and several operas call for mezzo-sopranos in male heroic roles.

The next generation's need for bigger voices was met by such singers as Giulia Grisi, who graduated from Bellini's Adalgisa and Elvira to Verdi and Meyerbeer, and Wilhelmine Schröder-Devrient, who sang not only Rossini and Bellini but Beethoven, Weber and Wagner (she created three of his roles, including Senta). Their male counterparts were the new *tenori di forza*; Domenico Donzelli bridges the gap, moving from a florid Rossini tenor to heavier roles, and others were Adolphe Nourrit, creator of Auber, Meyerbeer and French Rossini roles, and his successor Gilbert-Louis Duprez, the first Edgar in *Lucia di Lammermoor* and also a Verdi singer. By the middle of the century, and middle-period Verdi, the *tenore robusto* had taken the Italian stage (as early as Ernani, continuing up to Othello and beyond) and the *Heldentenor* the German one (from Tannhäuser to Tristan, but above all Siegfried). Among sopranos, the Verdi parts now demanded the so-called *lirico spinto* (literally 'lyrical pushed') voice, powerful and incisive. The French counterpart was the 'Falcon', named after Cornélie Falcon, creator of Meyerbeer and Halévy roles, while in Germany the heavier Wagnerian soprano, with brilliance at the top, staying power and the capacity to carry across a large orchestra as well as to convey strong emotion, was beginning her reign.

Developments ran parallel in the lower-pitched voices. Among women's, there was a move from the florid, heroic Rossini mezzo roles to such sinister figures as Verdi's Azucena and Ulrica or Wagner's Ortrud, demanding dark, full tone and generous resonance, alongside the traditional confidantes, nurses and mother-figures, of which Wagner's Erda was a new kind. The classical baritone of the Bellini era was Antonio Tamburini; in the next generation Felice Varesi, who created Verdi's Macbeth and Rigoletto, was unhappy with the lyrical demands of Germont in *La traviata*; some of the finest Verdi baritones were Frenchmen, such as Jean-Baptiste Faure (the first Posa) and Victor Maurel (Iago and Falstaff), though the French tradition favoured lighter, more lyrical baritone singing. The baritone required by Verdi covers a wide range of character types and needs a strong, warm voice, with a touch of heroic quality, eloquence and a forceful top register. The Wagner baritone, typified by Sachs or Wotan, is heavier and deeper, requiring impeccable enunciation and command of nuance as well as warm tone (the term 'Bayreuth bark' has been applied to those who sacrifice tone too much to sense). The 18th-century *basso buffo* survived into the 19th, in Rossini and Donizetti, though those composers and Bellini also wrote florid bass music (Assur in *Semiramide*, Oroveso in *Norma*; Luigi Lablache, creator of Don Pasquale, was a classic interpreter of such roles). The natural link between authority and deep, resonant voices remained: fathers, aged kings and priests are almost without exception cast as basses (until the enfeebled, croaky tenor of Puccini's Emperor in *Turandot*, in the 1920s). Verdi combines all three in the masterful *Don Carlos* bass duet scene for Philip II and the Grand Inquisitor: Philip is father as well as king, and indeed a fourth tradition, that of the bass villain, is implied too since the Grand Inquisitor may well be seen in that light. Other villains include the Mephistopheles of Berlioz and Gounod and Wagner's Alberich. In Russia, where many deep bass voices are found, the classic roles include Musorgsky's Boris Godunov and Tchaikovsky's Prince Gremin (*Eugene Onegin*). The term *basse chantante* and its Italian equivalent *basso cantante* have been applied to bass singers of the lighter, bass-baritone or even baritone type; such other classifications as *basso profondo* or *basse-noble* are self-explanatory.

The large and eloquent voice was not obligatory in every type of opera house. Where vernacular light opera was performed, acting ability could rank above beautiful singing. This was particularly true in the new world of operetta, which arose in the 19th century from a number of antecedents in light opera with spoken dialogue. It was designed for a broadly based public, although the leading operetta theatres were modest in size: Offenbach's Bouffes Parisiens seated 820, and the Theater an der Wien, where most of the stage works of the younger Johann Strauss were given, 1232. The element of social commentary in this repertory is important; but it was through its verve and its immediacy of appeal that operetta came to flourish, and in due course to lead to other genres of widely appealing music theatre.

PART THREE

Romantic Opera

CHAPTER XIII

Italy

JULIAN BUDDEN

Neo-classical and Revolutionary period

During the latter part of the 18th century many factors, as we have seen, combined to bring the *seria* and *buffa* genres closer, ultimately producing the *semiseria* species that contains elements of both. In the same period *opera seria* began to take on a choral dimension, to vary the round of solo arias with ensembles and at times to use a simpler, more direct manner of expression. This is due partly to the influence of Gluck – minimal in Italy itself – and more directly to that of Traetta, whose example in setting Italian translations and imitations of French *tragédie lyrique* was increasingly followed. In setting Metastasio's *La clemenza di Tito* (1791), Mozart had felt obliged to have the libretto altered by Caterino Mazzolà to the requirements of a 'real opera'. Accordingly the revised text provides for choruses, duets and trios and an elaborate central finale: a structural feature borrowed from the sister genre which was to remain indispensable to *opera seria* throughout most of the following century.

The neo-classical vogue, already discernible in Mozart's last opera, became increasingly evident during the decade in works such as Paer's *Achille* (1801, Vienna) and Cimarosa's monumental *Gli Orazi ed i Curiazi* (1796, Venice) in which, unusually, the tragic end of Livy and Corneille is preserved. Indeed during the Napoleonic Wars French influence on Italian opera was strong and far-reaching, hence a wealth of *opere semiserie* which are mostly Italian equivalents of the Revolutionary *pièces de sauvetage* (or 'rescue operas'): Paer's *Camilla* (1801, Vienna), *I fuorusciti di Firenze* (1802, Dresden) and *Agnese di Fitzhenry* (1809, Ponte d'Attaro); Mayr's *Le due giornate* (1801, Milan), *Lodoiska* (1796, Venice) and *L'amore coniugale* (1805, Padua). Sentimental comedies such as Paer's *Griselda* (1798, Parma) and *Sargino* (1803, Dresden) also fall into the *semiseria* category. In fact *comédie larmoyante* had an early representative in Italian opera in Paisiello's *Nina* (1789, Caserta), with its pathetic treatment of female madness. In general *opere semiserie* are more expansive than their French counterparts, as well as being vocally more ornate. As hitherto on the Italian stage, recitative took the place of spoken dialogue.

During the reign of Murat in Naples (1808–15), productions of Gluck and Spontini at the S Carlo inaugurated the practice, soon to be followed throughout the peninsula, whereby simple recitative was accompanied not by keyboard but by full orchestral strings – a small but important step towards that integration of the lyrical and the declamatory that was to be achieved during the course of the 19th century. About the same time the *opéra comique* tradition of formal numbers linked by spoken dialogue gained a slender foothold in certain of the lesser Neapolitan theatres, instances being found up to the middle of the century, including the first version of Bellini's *Adelson e Salvini* (1825) and Luigi Ricci's *La festa di Piedigrotta* (1852). But this type of opera seems to have been confined to Naples, and invariably included at least one character who spoke in Neapolitan dialect. Outstanding among the serious operas of the period is Mayr's neo-classical *Medea in Corinto* (1813, Naples), which combines Italian melody with German skill in instrumentation, and the classical poise of Gluck with anticipations of the Romantic era.

The age of Mayr and Paer, however, remains essentially one of transition. The rise of the German symphonists, and the establishment of conservatories north of the Alps more than equal to those of Bologna and Naples, were among a number of factors that led to Italy's loss of the musical hegemony that it had enjoyed for 200 years. Paer wrote his most successful operas for performance abroad. Cherubini and Spontini found French opera a more congenial field for their talents. In Italy the star singer reigned supreme, though the all-powerful castrato was now giving place to the female contralto (who also took over his title of 'musico'). Display arias and grand duets written in old-fashioned concerto style alternated with simpler, more periodic structures as the staple units of operatic form; and in general the new variety afforded by the tendency of the genres to merge resulted in a certain amorphousness. Harmonically conservative, unaffected by symphonic developments in Germany and central Europe, the prevailing idiom inclined to monotonous mellifluity.

The age of Rossini, 1813–30

It was Rossini's supreme achievement to have given Italian opera a new identity – albeit a strictly national one – partly through an unerring instinct for form, partly through the unique force of his musical personality. Already in *La cambiale di matrimonio* (1810), the first of a series of one-act *farse* written for the Teatro S Moisè in Venice, an original gift for comedy is apparent through the largely conventional material. The amiable, uneventful flow of post-Paisiellian *opera buffa* is revitalized by a forceful rhythmic current in which the natural inflections of everyday speech are caught and pointed up – witness the duet 'Va taluno mormorando' from *L'inganno felice* (1812, Venice), the melodic contours of which reflect the ironic cut-and-thrust of a duel of wits. To the languors of the serious style Rossini brought a formal stiffening and precision, evident as early as the duet 'Questo cor ti giura amore' from *Demetrio e Polibio* (composed 1806; revised and performed 1812, Rome). In the overture to *La scala di seta* (1812, Venice) a personal style of scoring has already crystallized.

Not however until the double triumph of *Tancredi* and *L'italiana in Algeri* (both 1813, Venice) did Rossinian opera achieve its full definition in the serious and comic genres respectively, and with it a groundplan to be modified according to the demands of the text. In 1815 the composer entered into a long-term contract with the Neapolitan theatres where a galaxy of star singers and an enlightened management permitted him to explore in a number of directions; hence *Elisabetta, Regina d'Inghilterra* (1815), his first essay in continuous opera without *recitativo secco*; the partly Shakespearean *Otello* (1816), with its uncharacteristic tragic ending; *Armida* (1817), with its voluptuous love-duets; the solemn, biblical *Mosè in Egitto* (1818); *Ricciardo e Zoraide* (1818), in which the independently directed stage band makes its first appearance; and *La donna del lago* (1819), Rossini's nearest approach to the nature poetry of Walter Scott. His two most enduring successes, however, were attained outside Naples, in theatres where the available talent was less specialized: *Il barbiere di Siviglia* (1816, Rome), which, after an initial fiasco, won acceptance as a classic comedy of all time, and *La Cenerentola* (1817, Rome), a sophisticated treatment of Perrault's fairy-tale.

With *Semiramide* (1823, Venice) Rossini ended his Italian career, having bequeathed to his successors a mould that was to last, with modifications, to the middle of the century and even beyond. Under the 'code Rossini' the basic languages of comedy and tragedy are one, as may be seen from the fact that the same overture often served for both – e.g. for *La pietra del paragone* (1812, Milan) and *Tancredi*, and for *Elisabetta, Regina d'Inghilterra* and *Il barbiere di Siviglia*. They are in the nature of personal visiting-cards, all of a similar design: slow introduction, followed by an Allegro of traditional symphonic cut, but with development omitted and a crescendo after the second subject. In an age of vocal virtuosity Rossini curbed the singers' licence not only by writing out in full the kind of embellishments that the star singer might be expected to devise, but by making them integral to his musical thought. The result is a style ornate and complex on the surface, simple, strong and yet supple below. With Rossini the basic formal unit was no longer the separate formal number but the scene (i.e. the period during which the same number of people remain on stage), including however the preliminaries to the entry of the dominating character. Each scene had one or more formal numbers embedded in it. A few characteristic patterns may be cited:

(*a*) 'Introduzione e cavatina'. Opening chorus with possible intervention by a secondary character; entrance of principal character with declamatory recitative followed by slow, lyrical movement of essentially periodic structure in two parts; a further chorus with possible intervention of principal; final fast movement (to be known as 'cabaletta'), also periodic, stated twice with intervening ritornello and coda, both fortified by chorus.

(*b*) 'Scena e duetto'. After a dialogue in recitative, both parties proceed to an *allegro* movement, in which each has a musically identical double quatrain, thematic in character but of irregular design, in which the melodic emphasis shifts from voice to orchestra and back again, formal equilibrium restored by an emphatic cadential phrase. The movement then modulates, with the singers (in dialogue) reaching a half-close in a new key. This launches a second, lyrical movement during which the voices become linked in chains of 6ths and 3rds, though as a rule each participant expresses his or her own thoughts. The final movement – sometimes following an intervening transition during which something occurs to alter the singers' moods – is a species of cabaletta, with the melody sung by the two singers first in succession and then, following a ritornello, together, either in unison, harmony or with each phrase in dialogue.

(*c*) Finale. This can be in several movements, of which the last four are laid out as follows. First, a rapid movement consisting of 'parlanti' (i.e. declamation against an orchestral melody) during which the action moves forward; this is usually based on an instrumental figure that develops sequentially. Suddenly the action halts and the music develops a 'largo concertato', a multiple soliloquy of complex part-writing, sometimes in the form of a 'false canon', sometimes led by one singer with the rest entering at the end of the first stanza. After the final cadence the first movement is resumed, and with it the dramatic action. The final movement is again static in character, but noisy and brilliant where the concertato had been slow and expressive.

As in all living conventions (e.g. 18th-century sonata form), no one instance is exactly the same as any other. In Rossini's *Otello* the 'introduzione e cavatina' pattern is expanded by a march, while Othello himself has a cavatina in three movements. In *Il barbiere* the tenor cabaletta serves to complete the *andante*, and the scena concludes with a separate chorus with interventions from the principal. The aria in two contrasted movements (referred to as a 'cavatina' if it marks the character's first appearance) is mostly the rule where a principal is concerned, though the single-movement 'romanza' (sometimes, confusingly, called a 'cavatina' in Rossini's time but never subsequently) can also be found. Most aria movements are periodic but occasionally the more irregular design associated with the first movement of a grand duet can be found (e.g. in Argirio's first aria in *Tancredi*). At first only the second half of a cabaletta would be repeated, as in Rosina's 'Io son docile' from *Il barbiere*; by the 1820s the restatement is invariably complete. The opening recitative to a cavatina may be integrated with its first movement by an orchestral motif common to both, as in the case of Arsace's 'Eccomi alfine in Babilonia' from *Semiramide*. Among the personal mannerisms bequeathed by Rossini to his contemporaries and successors are: a brilliant, prismatic orchestral style with noisy, opaque tuttis and patterns of contrasted wind colouring; a habit of beginning an aria with a succession of ornate flourishes interspersed with pauses, which at first mask the regularity of its construction (e.g. Isabella's 'Pensi all patria' from *L'italiana in Algeri*); and the ubiquitous crescendo placed not only in the overture but very often in the stretta of a finale or in the middle of a cabaletta where it serves to bridge two statements.

Rossinian opera is essentially an isolated phenomenon in music history. With its conscious artificiality, so beautifully self-parodied in the comedies, it represents a Classical, not to say Baroque, survival into the Romantic age, reaching its apogee in *Semiramide*. Its ruling principles are balance and contrast. The abundant floridity, extending to all voices and carrying the tenors into a falsetto range, acted as a brake on emotional expression. Dramatic moments were underlined not with unusual harmonic effects but rather with bold modulations or key-jumps (e.g. where in *Mosè in Egitto* the Pharaoh's son is struck dead). No less suited to the demands of rapid production than the *opera seria* of the previous century, the tradition sustained many a lesser composer. Outstanding examples other than Rossini's include Mercadante's *Elisa e Claudio* (1821, Milan), Meyerbeer's *Il crociato in Egitto* (1824, Venice) and Donizetti's *L'ajo nell'imbarazzo* (1824, Rome).

Romantic period, 1830–50
During the fourth and fifth decades of the century the basic forms of Rossinian opera remained unchanged. If anything, they became more stereotyped, as did sonata form after Beethoven; but they did become suffused with a Romantic spirit. The impulse came principally from Bellini, whose *Il pirata* (1827, Milan) opened up a new world of sensibility (as expressed in the famous sally of the French critic Blaize du Bury: 'Rossini fait l'amour; Bellini aime'). In the revised *Bianca e Fernando* (1828, Genoa) and *La straniera* (1829, Milan) Bellini moved ever further away from *fioritura* to an almost syllabic manner of word-setting which earned him some criticism; but in *I Capuleti e i Montecchi* (1830, Venice) the trend is reversed, to reach a perfectly balanced synthesis in *La sonnambula* (1831, Milan) and his classical masterpiece, *Norma* (1831, Milan). Bellini was a master of the long-breathed, elegiac melody (for example 'Casta diva ch'inargenti' from *Norma*; 'Ah non credea mirarti' from *La sonnambula*; 'Qui la voce sua soave' from *I puritani di Scozia*, 1835, Paris). Under his influence the progress was away from ornament and Rossinian rhetoric to a more lyrical and dramatic style, the gradual abolition of florid writing in the male voice parts, and a vocal delivery based on the natural accents of feeling, which caused Bellini, Donizetti and above all Verdi to be accused by conservatives of ruining the art of singing. Because of his greater dramatic urgency the tenor now definitively replaced the contralto as the hero, while the *basso cantante*, soon to develop in Verdi's hands into the dramatic baritone, assumed the role of father or villain. By contrast, the full *basso profondo* emerged; rarely a principal, he usually played a monk or hermit. Only the *prima donna* retained much of the floridity of the earlier period; but the effect of this was now to enhance the aura of purity and unattainability, even of fragility, that surrounds Romantic womanhood. Plots on the theme of star-crossed lovers gained ascendancy; mad scenes for the heroine abounded; and the happy ending, usual in Rossini's day,

became exceptional in Bellini's. The Largo concertato became a moment of lyrical transformation, dissolving the tragedy in an outpouring of sad, sweet melody.

Another effect of Bellini's influence was the weakening in Italian opera of that tonic–dominant polarity on which musical construction depended throughout Europe in the 18th century and which persisted in German musical thought. Bellini's melodies, though long, rarely modulate in the conventional way, if they modulate at all. His world was nearer to that of Chopin, some of whose melodic and even harmonic traits he anticipated. His units are large and often surprisingly complex; yet their dominant characteristic is a lyricism that extends even to the recitatives. His contemporary Donizetti, on the other hand, furthered dramatic pace and tension, often modifying the inherited symmetry of the various forms to that end.

More prolific and resourceful than Bellini, if less strikingly original, Donizetti attained general recognition with *Anna Bolena* (1830, Milan). His subjects range from the neo-classical *Fausta* (1832, Naples) and *Belisario* (1836, Venice) to the powerful, Hugo-based *Lucrezia Borgia* (1833, Milan); from the more delicate bloom of *Lucia di Lammermoor* (1835, Naples), long treasured as a unique moment in the history of Italian Romantic opera, to the Gothick *Maria di Rudenz* (1838, Venice). A pupil of Mayr, he had declared for reform as early as 1828, but his gift was for varying and manipulating the conventions as they existed. Like those of his contemporary, Giovanni Pacini, his cabalettas show a remarkable variety of style and character. Hybrid forms abound, such as Leicester's 'Ah rimiro il bel sembiante' from *Maria Stuarda* (1835, Milan), half duetto, half aria, or Guido's 'Questo sacro augusto stemma' from *Gemma di Vergy* (1834, Milan), part cantabile, part narrative chorus.

In an age of rapid production, Donizetti showed particular skill in recycling his less successful music and adapting it to new contexts without the slightest sense of incongruity. Donizetti's musical style owes much to Bellini, especially after 1830, while retaining stronger links with that of Rossini (he never entirely forsook the Rossinian declamatory flourish as Bellini did). Two fingerprints may be noted: a fondness for phrase endings that descend from the fifth to the third degree of the scale; and a tendency to evolve melodic periods from simple 'conjugations' of a single rhythmic pattern (see 'D'un pescator ignobile' from *Lucrezia Borgia*). No composer knew better how to exploit the individual qualities of star singers, the dramatic gifts of a Pasta or the technical bravura of a Tacchinardi; while with the tenor voice his touch is especially sure. Despite the haste with which he wrote and which shows itself in the often perfunctory conclusions (e.g. that of *Torquato Tasso*, 1833, Rome), a steady progress is discernible; in his last operas, such as *Maria di Rohan* (1843, Vienna) and *Caterina Cornaro* (1844, Naples), a new compactness of form and concentration of musical thought is evident.

In general, the more unusual the plot, the more original the musical

treatment, as in *L'assedio di Calais* (1836, Naples); but throughout the trend is towards greater continuity. In the duets, first movements in dialogue came to prevail over the parallel stanza favoured by both Bellini and Rossini; Donizetti's final cabalettas sometimes allotted different themes to each soloist. Similar departures can be found in the mature operas of Mercadante, who in the late 1830s announced a programme of reform giving more scope for dramatic development and exemplified in such works as *Il giuramento* (1837, Milan), *Elena da Feltre* (1838, Naples), *Le due illustri rivali* (1838, Venice) and *Il bravo* (1839, Milan); subsequently, however, he fell back into prolixity and self-repetition (to the end of his career he would continue to write florid music for baritone).

Although most of the outstanding operas of the period are tragic, including, besides those already mentioned, Donizetti's *Roberto Devereux* (1837, Naples), *Poliuto* (composed 1838, performed 1848, Naples) and *Maria di Rohan* (1843, Vienna), Pacini's *Saffo* (1840, Naples) and Federico Ricci's *Corrado d'Altamura* (1841, Milan), *opera semiseria* with a heavy pathetic bias flourished in Donizetti's *Il furioso all'isola di San Domingo* (1832, Rome), *Torquato Tasso* and *Linda di Chamounix* (1842, Vienna), Luigi Ricci's *Chiara di Rosenbergh* (1833, Milan) and Federico Ricci's *La prigione d'Edimburgo* (1838, Trieste); while in *L'elisir d'amore* (1832, Milan) Donizetti created a pastoral comedy that fulfils the Romantic ideals of its day as perfectly as did Rossini's *Il barbiere* the taste for inspired artifice of an earlier generation. It was in this genre, too, that he was to reach his musical apogee, recovering in *Don Pasquale* (1843, Paris) much of the heritage of Mozart. Here for the first time *secco* recitative is replaced by freely floating conversational lines punctuated by string chords. With other composers, however, the older convention prevailed for many years to come. As before, the language of tragedy and comedy were the same in essentials; but the forms of *opera buffa* were generally shorter and simpler and there was a greater abundance of 'parlanti' because of the presence of at least one *basso buffo*, whose main vocal talent consisted of rapid syllabification against an orchestral melody.

The arrival of Verdi on the national scene with the success of his third opera, *Nabucco* (1842, Milan), coincided with the swift rise in patriotic feeling that was to culminate in the unsuccessful 1848 revolt against the Austrians. This 'risorgimentale' spirit found its most powerful operatic expression in large choruses, which during the 1840s were to distend the post-Rossinian forms. In Verdi's early works the tone is direct and popular, sometimes brutal; but it was basic to his own sturdy idiom. In the works of Mercadante, his main rival after the retirement of Donizetti, and in many a lesser composer of the period, it took on a monumental, neo-Baroque quality which eventually stifled the spirit of Romanticism that gave vitality to the tradition in which they wrote. Composers such as Federico Ricci and Pacini rarely rose above a style that could be described as 'sophisticated Bellini'.

If Verdi alone was able to find a way forward, the reason lies mainly in his determination from the start to treat each opera as a separate artistic proposition. None of his predecessors was so particular about the choice of subject nor so concerned to bring out the character of the original source as far as the conventions of the time would allow. Of the successors to *Nabucco* each has its own musical colour ('tinta', to use Verdi's own term). *I lombardi alla prima crociata* (1843, Milan), based on an epic poem by Tommaso Grossi, diversifies the choral manner of *Nabucco* with episodes of varying quality. Both remain essentially operas of peoples rather than individuals – remote descendants of Rossini's French operas, already circulating in Italy in translation – and therefore outside the mainstream of Italian operatic development.

With *Ernani* (1844, Venice), his first encounter with the work of Victor Hugo, Verdi's early style is fully crystallized. The drama is articulated in a succession of powerful confrontations, in which the special properties of the male voice-types – tenor, baritone and bass – are exploited as never before. The scoring is plain and functional; extremes of emotion are conveyed by vocal contour rather than harmonic colour. The forms are basically traditional but so tailored as to sustain the dramatic momentum; and there is a tendency in the duets and ensembles to favour different thematic entries for each participant. Characteristic are the heavy accompanimental patterns which lend emphasis to the broad, long-limbed melodies. *I due Foscari* (1844, Rome), based on Byron's closet drama, essays a gentler, more intimate vein with a novel use of labelling themes; but in *Giovanna d'Arco* (1845, Milan), *Alzira* (1845, Naples) and *Attila* (1846, Venice) Verdi returned to the grandiose, poster-ish manner.

He struck out later in an entirely new direction with *Macbeth* (1847, Florence; revised 1865, Paris), an almost revolutionary work for its day, in which the sombre power of Shakespeare's tragedy is caught with as few concessions as possible to the prevailing conventions. Even in their original form the 'dagger' monologue, the scenes of Banquo's ghost and of the apparitions, and above all that of Lady Macbeth's sleep-walking, are without parallel in contemporary opera. *I masnadieri* (1847, London) and *Il corsaro* (1848, Trieste) revert to more familiar procedures, though the latter shows a new degree of thematic concentration. In *La battaglia di Legnano* (1849, Rome) the fruits of a two-year sojourn in Paris are manifest in the more polished scoring, sophisticated figuration and in the use of certain French-derived forms such as the ternary aria with modulating episode. With *Luisa Miller* (1849, Naples) and *Stiffelio* (1850, Trieste) Verdi ventured into the sphere of domestic tragedy, further refining his idiom in the process. Here the busy accompaniments begin to fall away; the scoring is lighter, the harmonies more subtle; while the melodic phrases become more flexible and so capable of a certain development.

A still higher level is reached with the so-called 'romantic trilogy' of *Rigoletto* (1851, Venice), *Il trovatore* (1853, Rome) and *La traviata* (1853, Venice), all of which form a central part of the Italian repertory to this day. *Rigoletto*, Verdi's first generally acknowledged masterpiece, derived from Victor Hugo's play *Le roi s'amuse*, continues along the trail blazed by *Macbeth*: a continuously evolving drama of immense range and potency in which the traditional elements of Italian opera are dissolved in a new synthesis. The famous quartet ('Bella figlia dell'amore') shows Verdi's ability to characterize individuals within an ensemble at its most impressive; while the storm scene with its wealth of pictorial motifs approaches the manner of his later years. No less remarkable is his success in conferring tragic stature upon the name-part, an evil-minded, hunch-backed jester redeemed by a pure-hearted love for his daughter. *Il trovatore*, on the other hand, is once more an opera of isolated situations, but presented with a unique theatrical immediacy. Here an extravagant plot set in 15th-century Spain is resolved into an elementary drama of confrontation between two rivals in love who are both antagonists in a civil war and unsuspecting brothers. In the gypsy-woman, Azucena, Verdi for the first time exploits the full potentialities of the mezzo-soprano voice, whose contrast with the heroine's soprano generates much of the melodic variety of the score. In *La traviata* he confronts a contemporary subject – that of the novel and play *La dame aux camélias* by Dumas *fils*. If the portrayal of a 'fallen woman' points the way to the 'verismo' that prevailed in Italy towards the end of the century, the treatment, with its subtle ennobling of the heroine, remains wholly within the bounds of Romantic art. Although the opera was for many years given in 18th-century costume, it remains rooted in the atmosphere of a Parisian salon of the 1840s. In it the intimacy that marks *Luisa Miller* is carried a stage further; while the musical language of the time is pared down to its simplest poetic essence, so bringing the chapter of Italian Romantic opera to a satisfying close.

Compared with German Romanticism, that of Italy was a more pallid, delicate affair, bounded by the pretensions of star singers and the failure of composers to depart from a groundplan which is the product of Rossini's essentially classical mind. If Bellini's harmonic sense was often subtle, if he sustained a mood of poignancy by continually placing discords on strong beats, his tonal range cannot compare with that of a Schubert or a Schumann. The forms of operatic and instrumental music were never further apart than in this moment of Italian musical history. Similarly, the Romantic ideal of the single unrepeatable masterpiece was rarely sought and scarcely ever attained. Even when the practice of printing vocal scores in full and the gradual enforcement of copyright put an end to the self-borrowings in which Donizetti and others had freely indulged, it was still the custom to adapt an already written opera to new singers, providing new music where required. If a singer found that the original aria did not suit him there was nothing to prevent him from replacing it with one that did. With few exceptions, mostly Verdian, the Italian Romantic hero or heroine is a type rather than an individual; and the type is that of the singer rather than the character portrayed.

The mid-century, 1850–70

Practically all that is of value in 1850–70, a confused period of operatic history, resides in Verdi's work. For the average Italian composer the 1850s represented a decade of stasis, during which the iron hand of the censor made itself felt throughout the peninsula and any music that smacked of the Risorgimento spirit was forbidden. The general atmosphere of escapism brought about a revival of *opera buffa*, whose successful products include Luigi and Federico Ricci's *Crispino e la comare* (1850, Venice), Petrella's *Le precauzioni* (1851, Naples) and Pedrotti's *Tutti in maschera* (1856, Verona). All three make use of *secco* recitative, despite the example of Donizetti's comic masterpiece, *Don Pasquale*. That in itself is sufficient indication of their essential archaizing quality. *Don Pasquale* on the other hand was entirely contemporary in spirit and was intended by the composer to be given in modern dress. *Opere semiserie* on the subject of rustic innocence calumniated, such as Mercadante's *Violetta* (1853, Naples), came once more into vogue. Tragic opera had little new to offer, though beneath the conventional surface the tendency towards greater continuity persisted, with fewer symmetrical repetitions and a greater use of dance music and 'parlanti' as a background to the development of the plot. Not until 1860 or thereabouts was there a marked change. The rise of the professional conductor, combining the functions of *maestro concertatore*, who rehearsed the singers, and the *primo violino direttore*, who gave the beat during the performance, made accessible to Italian audiences the latest works of Meyerbeer and Gounod, under whose influence native composers once more enlarged and diversified their operatic stock-in-trade with forms typical of French opera – the *couplets*, the ternary *air* with modulating episode, the 'characteristic' chorus and even rudimentary leitmotif.

A further stimulus was provided by the writings of the young Boito, a passionate adherent of the North Italian avant-garde movement known as the 'scapigliatura' – the title (literally 'dishevelment') being derived from the novel by Cletto Arrighi, *La scapigliatura e il 6 febbraio* of 1862. Its members set their face against traditional values, both aesthetic and religious, and aimed at enlarging the scope of the various arts by breaking down the barriers that separated them. Their subject matter inclined to the bizarre and even the blasphemous. In the newly founded *Giornale della Società del quartetto* Boito preached the regeneration of Italy's instrumental tradition, and together with Faccio attacked the remaining bastions of post-Rossinian opera. Faccio's *I profughi fiamminghi* (1863, Milan) and more especially *Amleto* (1865, Genoa) – the last with a libretto by Boito which continually departs from the traditional operatic verse-forms of two centuries – are both works of deliberate reform, which avoid cabalettas and aim at truthfulness of dramatic expression without conceding anything to the vanity of singers; but, since Faccio was little more than a careful workman with no original talent, their impact was slight.

In his own *Mefistofele* (1868, Milan), Boito departed so far from the traditional scope and language of Italian opera as to arouse general hostility; but his example had not been without effect, and during the 1860s a split is discernible between the more progressive north and the conservative south, where Petrella continued to cater for the star *prima donna*, sometimes by writing routine cabalettas, sometimes developing the coda of a cantabile into a display piece, while northern composers such as Cagnoni and the young Marchetti approximated more closely to their French contemporaries in harmonic range, the design of their pieces and their use of characteristic orchestral themes to denote people and situations. The Largo concertato and stretta are still to be found in all contemporary Italian opera, but they no longer form part of the same architectural unit; and only the former is still regularly expected for at least one central finale. By the end of the decade, the cadenza that had concluded every slow cantabile since Bellini's day was finally abolished. Yet on lesser Italian composers the lack of a vital tradition bore heavily. Absolved from a fixed code of melodic, harmonic and structural procedures, their music alternated between the stale and the ugly. Among the worthier products of the time are Cagnoni's *Michele Perrin* (1864, Milan) and *Un capriccio di donna* (1870, Genoa) and Marchetti's *Ruy Blas* (1869, Milan).

Throughout the entire period Verdi maintained his power of self-renewal, partly drawing on influences from abroad, in particular Paris, and from his own study of the 18th-century classics, yet not scrupling to make use of the time-honoured conventions where they suited his purpose. His operas remained dramatically functional without any concessions to musical hedonism. In 1857, the year that saw the première of Mercadante's *Pelagio* in Naples, with its ornate baritone lead, he wrote for Venice *Simon Boccanegra*, a gritty political drama of 14th-century Genoa in which the voice parts are almost totally lacking in melisma, the hero has not a single aria, the prologue is confined to baritones and basses with a male chorus, the duets proceed mostly by dialogue with a minimum of ensemble, even where they counter strophe for strophe and in many places declaim on a single note leaving the burden of the musical discourse to be borne by the orchestra. By now Verdi's tendency to throw the main weight of his melodies towards the final cadence has flowered into a characteristic design in which the third and fourth phrase of a lyrical period are run together in a single strain (see Amelia's 'Come in quest' ora bruna'). In total contrast to its predecessor, *Un ballo in maschera* (1859, Rome) presents an interplay of light and darkness, alternating moments of Offenbachian brilliance and humour with high tragedy and the imminence of danger where least expected. Appropriate, sometimes ironic use is made of the French 'couplet' design; and in the most incandescent of all his love-duets Verdi adapted a form usually associated with contrasted emotional phases so as to trace a rising graph of feeling by his manner of linking the three traditional movements. In *La forza del destino* (1862, St Petersburg; revised 1869, Milan) the chief characters attain a further dimension through being projected against a constantly shifting background of ordinary humanity. The effect is akin to that of a Shakespearean chronicle play, all the loose musical threads of the 1860s being woven into a richly varied tapestry.

In all his operas of the period, including the 'new' *Macbeth* and the French opera *Don Carlos* (1867, Paris; revised 1884, Milan), Verdi achieved an ever sharper delineation of character through a widening musical vocabulary in which non-functional harmony begins to play a part. Oscar, the soprano page of *Un ballo in maschera*, is a figure new to Italian opera; so too is Fra Melitone in *La forza del destino*, for whose comic sermon Verdi devised a highly individual style of declaimed melody, neither recitative nor conventional aria. Philip II (*Don Carlos*) remains one of the most telling portraits of a lonely tyrant before Boris Godunov.

The age of grand opera, 1870–90
The impulse towards grand opera on the French model, sometimes called 'opera ballo', came from the increasing importation of foreign works including Verdi's *Les vêpres siciliennes* (1855, Paris) and *Don Carlos*. A decisive event was the first performance in Italy of Meyerbeer's *L'africaine* (1865, Genoa) shortly after its première in Paris; it was played in every major season during the late 1860s and created a new vogue for the exotic, to be reinforced by Goldmark's *Die Königin von Saba* and Massenet's *Le roi de Lahore*, both given in Turin, the year after their premières in Vienna (1875) and Paris (1877) respectively. About the same time, the early Wagner canon established itself in Italy, beginning with *Lohengrin* (1871, Bologna), which soon became an honorary Italian opera. Hence throughout the 1870s and early 80s composers of Italian opera aimed at the grand scale, with varying success. Gomes's *Il Guarany* (1870, Milan), *Fosca* (1873, Milan) and *Salvator Rosa* (1874, Genoa) achieved a temporary acclaim, as did Ponchielli's ambitious *I lituani* (1874, Milan) and *Il figliuol prodigo* (1880, Milan); alone *La Gioconda* (1876, Milan), with its wealth of spontaneous melody, Venetian colouring and its ever popular 'Dance of the Hours' outlasted its composer. With his reduced and revised *Mefistofele* (1875, Bologna) Boito largely redeemed his fiasco of 1868. But as usual the chief honours go to Verdi, who in *Aida* (1871, Cairo) produced a classic of the genre based on an episode supposedly taken from Egyptian history. The plot, unlike that of *Don Carlos* with its tangled web of personal relationships, is unusually simple, presenting the time-honoured conflict of love versus duty in time of war. Nor are the values of a closed society called into question as in the earlier opera. Hero and heroine go willingly to their death. All this is set forth in a score in which the various elements – grandeur, exotic pictorialism and intimate poetry – are held in perfect equilibrium and from which not a single note can be cut.

By 1880 the situation was rapidly changing. The wave of German culture that swept into France after the Franco–Prussian war had also affected Italy, and the revival of instrumental music promoted during the 1860s had combined with a subsequent reform of the conservatories to produce a generation of composers aiming at a more modern conception of opera in which the structural unit was the whole act and in whose organization the orchestra played a more prominent part, without necessarily having recourse to the Wagnerian system of leitmotif. Foremost among the new school were Franchetti, Smareglia and especially Catalani, on whom at first the yoke of 'grand opera' bore heavily, for example in *Elda* (1880, Turin; revised as *Loreley*, 1890, Turin) and *Dejanice* (1883, Milan), but who progressed towards a more delicate, poetic style to achieve his masterpiece in *La Wally* (1892, Milan). All three composers were influenced by Massenet and the young Wagner (not until the first Italian performance of *Tristan und Isolde* under Martucci at Bologna in 1888 did Wagner's mature style begin to impinge).

Meanwhile, Verdi continued on his own, by now lonely, path. His revision of *Simon Boccanegra* (1881, Milan) is a successful adaptation of the original work to the more continuous conception of opera in vogue at the time; while a growing mastery of 'the art of transition' (Wagner's phrase) is reflected in the freshly composed Council Chamber scene and the finale, where the short, somewhat schematic phrases of the first version are welded into long, supple lines. In the rewritten duet for Philip and Posa in the four-act *Don Carlos* (1884, Milan) the dissolution of the closed form can be sensed, single phrases now doing duty for lyrical periods. The summit is reached with *Otello* (1887, Milan), an Everest of Italian opera surrounded only by foothills. Here the musical organization is entirely personal, a blend of old and new transformed by the experience of more than half a century and as little related to the prevailing language as are the late quartets of Beethoven. Motivic development, declaimed melody, dramatic dialogue, a species of bar form, even a faint residue of the cabaletta and of the tripartite grand duet – all are present. But despite its orchestral virtuosity, *Otello* remains a more vocally orientated opera than many written at the time; and however complex the structure of a scene its coping-stone is invariably a plain melodic period (e.g. 'Dio fulgor della bufera' in the opening storm).

Still further isolated from the contemporary scene is *Falstaff* (1893, Milan), a radiant comedy of 'almost Chinese refinement' (Tovey). Here the musical continuity is at last seamless, each idea emerging from its predecessor. Such motifs as recur derive from a line of text (e.g. 'Te lo cornifico'). Aided by the ingenuity of Boito's text, Verdi indulged in musical witticisms, such as the half-minute aria that illustrates Falstaff's slightness when page to the Duke of Norfolk. In general the idiom is plain and classical, heavy Romantic harmonies being reserved for moments of irony, as when Alice reads aloud the flowery conclusion of the Fat Knight's letter. Yet this does not preclude a Windsor Forest scene of the utmost enchantment. Several decades later Alfredo Casella was to describe *Falstaff* as the starting-point of modern Italian music. But in the meantime native opera had taken a very different turning.

CHAPTER XIV

Germany and Austria

JOHN WARRACK

Subject matter

The commonly expressed view that in spirit the 19th century began in
1789 was no less true of Germany than of France. The French Revolution
profoundly impressed the artists of the politically stagnant groups of states
that then formed Germany, and in their search for national unity and for
a sense of growth and direction it was to France that they turned for the
inspiration of a dynamic alternative society. As Otto Nicolai later
observed, 'No art is so closely connected to the character of the nation as
music'; and it was naturally in the opera of the French Revolution that
German Romantic composers first found an example. Several other
strains of thought contributed to the ideas of those who echoed J. G.
Naumann's cry, 'I wish with all patriots that a good German operatic
theatre existed'. Rousseau, venerated in Germany, had drawn attention
to the virtues he saw in simple country people; and in the wake of J. G.
Herder, who not only identified folk poetry and folksong as manifesting
the creative genius of a people but himself called for a German operatic
tradition, there was the newly available material of folksong in the
collections of the early years of the century, of which the most famous was
Des Knaben Wunderhorn, compiled by Arnim and Brentano. There was,
moreover, as we have seen, a strong wish to develop a more popular,
realistic form of opera in reaction to the Italian tradition of *opera seria*
which had long been identified with the courts and the *ancien régime*.

At a very early stage, political subjects became popular. The genre of
'rescue opera' found enthusiastic support, as with Peter Winter's *Das
unterbrochene Opferfest* (1796, Vienna), which proved the most popular
German opera between *Die Zauberflöte* and *Der Freischütz*; and it reached
its apotheosis in Beethoven's *Fidelio*. But the shock wave of the Revolution
affected even the youthful Carl Maria von Weber in his *Peter Schmoll*
(1803, Augsburg), with its treatment of the problem of the émigrés; and
the association of opera with political events was to be a feature of German
Romantic opera for half a century. B. A. Weber celebrated in *Des
Epimenedes Erwachen* (1815, Berlin), to a text by Goethe, the peace after the

181

defeat of Napoleon, and Meyerbeer welcomed the returning troops in his *Das Brandenburger Tor* (1814, not performed). As late as 1843 Heinrich Esser's popular *Thomas Riquiqui, oder Die politische Heirat* (performed Frankfurt) was set in and after the French Revolution; while in 1848 Lortzing attempted, in his unsuccessful *Regina* (not performed until 1899, in Berlin), to match the new wave of revolution with a subject set in 1813.

Other popular themes were to be legends, especially of the North and including those treated by Scott and those attributed to the Gaelic bard Ossian. The European fashion for the Ossianic epics was reflected in several operas in the wake of Le Sueur's *Ossian* (1804, Paris) and Méhul's *Uthal* (1806, Paris), notably Winter's *Colmal* (1809, Munich). The most distinguished German operatic setting of Scott was Marschner's *Der Templer und die Jüdin* (1829, Leipzig; after *Ivanhoe*). Other works, among them Weber's *Silvana* (1810, Frankfurt) and *Euryanthe* (1823, Vienna), indulged the Romantic wish to escape from a mundane present into a heroic, chivalric past. There was a comparable fascination with escape into the exotic, a legacy of the Turkish operas of the previous generation but one given a novel expressive content, as in Spohr's Indian *Jessonda* (1823, Kassel), F. E. Fesca's Persian *Cantemire* (1820, Karlsruhe) and Weber's Turkish *Abu Hassan* (1811, Munich) and Spanish *Die drei Pintos* (begun 1820, but left unfinished; completed by Mahler for its première in 1888).

A more significant characteristic of Romanticism was its emphasis on the supernatural. Romantic philosophy, especially in the ideas of Schelling (which affected his friend Weber), emphasized a spiritual continuum between Man and Nature. Romantic science attempted to support this with experiments demonstrating links between the physical and the spiritual, in the work of Galvani, Lavater and J. W. Ritter; the Romantic arts drew ever closer together, with music at once honoured as the supreme art yet affected by the characteristics of the others. This subtle and often mystic connection which was felt to exist between all the arts, and in turn between them and the natural world, led to subjects chosen for their personification of the supernatural. Often this took the form of a delight in the spooky, most famously and successfully with Weber's *Der Freischütz* (1821, Berlin), but also in the vampire operas of Marschner (*Der Vampyr*; 1828, Leipzig) and Lindpaintner (*Der Vampyr*; 1828, Stuttgart). It might also involve contact between the spirit and human worlds in a more elaborate set of relationships, a theme pursued chiefly for comic effect in the Viennese magic theatre (which influenced many, including Wagner) and showing in operas that included Marschner's *Hans Heiling* (1833, Berlin) and two operas of 1825 on the same subject, Lindpaintner's *Der Bergkönig* (Stuttgart) and Spohr's *Der Berggeist* (Kassel), as well as Weber's London opera, *Oberon* (1826). A potent Romantic symbol of this contact was in the Undine legend used by E. T. A. Hoffmann (1816, Berlin), A. B. Marx (1829, Berlin) and Lortzing (1845, Magdeburg): the subject was essentially Romantic in its tale of the water spirit who attempted marriage to a human, symbolizing the Romantic wish to achieve reunion with Nature (and also a healing of the breach between instinct and reason that was felt to have occurred in the Enlightenment).

The generation of Weber

At first, the methods on to which the new ideas were grafted were those of Singspiel. Many composers attempted to perpetuate Mozartian styles and forms: these included Lortzing (who was, however, an inventive artist) and lesser, more imitative figures such as Carl Eberwein, F. W. Grund and a host of others. A more immediate and potent example was provided by Cherubini, who influenced Beethoven and Weber but also a number of minor composers less able to absorb his characteristics into an individual idiom. Gottlob Bierey, a composer with a successful comic touch, had some difficulty in escaping this in his serious operas, such as *Wladimir, Fürst von Nowgorod* (1807, Vienna). Among many others to turn to Cherubini as a model was Carl Blum, with a series of popular successes in Berlin in the 1820s and 1830s.

Nevertheless, the proportions and content of Singspiel were changing. Broadly, the hero and heroine retained the most important vocal forms, aria and cavatina. The former provided the vehicle for passionate outpourings, accompanied by the most elaborate musical resources of which the composer was capable, and also might furnish a villain with his most impressive number of the opera in a revenge aria. Striking examples of the latter occur, in a line fathered by Cherubini's Dourlinski (*Lodoïska*, 1791, Paris; revised 1805, Vienna), with Beethoven's Pizarro and in operas by Hoffmann (*Undine*), Weber (*Der Freischütz* and *Euryanthe*), Lortzing (his first opera, *Ali Pascha von Janina*, 1828, Münster) and Marschner (*Hans Heiling*). The cavatina, normally given less expressive weight than the aria, tended to be expressive or elegiac: a characteristic example is Röschen's cavatina in Spohr's *Faust* (1813, Prague), and its effect was still vivid when in 1833–4 the young Wagner wrote one for Ada in *Die Feen*.

Other popular forms included the romance, developed from Singspiel and given a more original accompaniment (perhaps using a solo instrument and some enterprising tonality) than the lied, which normally kept to a simple accompaniment and a plain harmonic basis. A common use of the lied was as a working song, perhaps serving to set a scene, provide local colour and introduce a character: from Papageno's entrance song derived many examples, such as those for a cobbler (Görg in Lortzing's *Hans Sachs*, 1840, Leipzig: traces of such a self-contained song remain for Sachs himself in Wagner's *Die Meistersinger von Nürnberg* of 1868) or for other craftsmen, for soldiers or sailors, or for students and drinkers. Yet the hero and heroine might also turn to the lied and give evidence of their simpler side, or (in chivalric operas) of their troubadour nature. It was above all Lortzing who cultivated the operatic lied, developing it from plain origins into a vehicle for some expression of character and narrative (Peter the Great's 'Sonst spielt ich mit Szepter') or of lyrical feeling (Chateauneuf's 'Lebe wohl, mein flandrisch Mädchen', both from *Zar und Zimmermann*; 1837, Leipzig). Other song forms in use included the 'Gebet', sometimes known by the Italian form it took over, *preghiera*, offering a singer a chance to demonstrate his clarity of tone and line in a prayer. The Romantic fascination with the exotic also encouraged certain foreign colourings. Sympathy with Poland's sufferings brought great popularity for the polonaise. The success of the 'Alla polacca' in Act 2 of Hiller's *Die Jagd* (1770) led to many subsequent examples, for instance Suschen's second aria in J. B. Schenk's very popular *Der Dorfbarbier* (1796), an 'alla polacca' that anticipates Weber's Aennchen. The rhythm offered a singer the chance of a lively bravura number, as did Spanish popular exotic dance forms, such as the bolero (in Spohr's *Der Alchymist*, 1830, Kassel) and the *seguidilla* (in Weber's *Die drei Pintos*).

These comparatively simple patterns were to be influenced and then transformed by the impress of Romantic ideas. A tendency of the times was to give the secondary characters music that was more vivid than that allowed the hero and heroine. But from French *opéra comique* also came other features. An essential characteristic of German Romanticism was its emphasis on fluidity and growth, in distinction to the static formality represented by *opera seria*. A new, more fluent, more expressive kind of opera was therefore sought. The expression of more intense emotions placed new importance on harmony, both for sensational effects (wailing chromatics, more startling modulations, the prominence given to sensational chords such as the ubiquitous diminished 7th) and to provide a functional structure in which hero, villain or supernatural forces were associated with their own keys. Similar demands placed greater importance on the orchestra, which acquired a new range of colour in support of wider expressive needs. The wish to show growth and fluidity meant that the old closed forms became less satisfactory; and the move towards music drama and the *Gesamtkunstwerk* began with the loosening of these in various ways.

The finale, already assuming new importance with Mozart, began to grow in length and to absorb separate numbers into its structure as a regular feature. Recitative became gradually more popular than spoken dialogue, which was virtually out of fashion by the middle of the century, though the special effect of melodrama retained its appeal in certain situations. Both Spohr (in *Jessonda*) and Weber (in *Euryanthe*) set an example of melodic fluency ranging between recitative and formal aria. A more declamatory song style developed in response to the more literary and dramatic quality now demanded of opera.

However, with the loosening of forms there naturally arose the need for a new cohesive principle, and this was increasingly provided by motif. The device was an apt one for Romantic ideas, for it combined narrative and illustrative elements (thus connecting with the other arts) with a Romantic fluidity and capacity for growth, at the same time providing the means of achieving new and freer forms. The example of French *opéra comique*, especially the operas of Grétry, Méhul and to a lesser extent Dalayrac, furnished examples observed by Weber and developed by him and by Spohr and Hoffmann in the second decade of the century. Spohr, who moved decisively away from the domination of the lied, made sophisticated use of motif to show conflicting demands on the hero in his *Faust*; and Hoffmann, in *Undine*, used motivic methods, including orchestral colouring, to lend greater unity to the music. Among other composers of the generation who made individual contributions were Poissl, who used motif in *Athalia* (1814, Munich) and was almost alone in his time in writing his own librettos; and Gläser, whose popular *Des Adlers Horst* (1832, Berlin) included Romantic traits that were to impress Wagner.

The importance of Weber's *Der Freischütz* as a landmark of Romantic opera lies in its inventive synthesis of many elements. It includes songs drawing on a melodic style fashioned out of folksong, substantial arias, popular choruses, ensembles using motivic methods, functionally colouristic orchestration and a functional harmonic groundplan; its subject celebrated popular life while at the same time using the Romantic fascination with supernatural horror in the Wolf's Glen (see Plate 72), a scene that takes the operatic finale into new territory in the fluency of its expressive means. Weber was to develop his expressive range further in *Euryanthe*, in his use of motif, his freer melodic manner and his extended harmonic spectrum; but he did not live to benefit to the full from all he had revealed to his generation, for in the last opera before his early death, *Oberon*, he was obliged to satisfy the demands of a totally different genre, English pantomime opera.

The slowness with which Romantic opera spread in Germany was largely due to practical considerations. The decentralization of German life meant lack of organization: the theatre in Germany was long dependent on a structure consisting broadly of Hoftheater, in which aristocratic and normally Italian traditions predominated, Stadttheater or private enterprise theatre (especially in the Hanseatic cities), and small wandering troupes of the kind described by Goethe in *Wilhelm Meister*. In all of these, mixed repertories prevailed, with the leading operatic roles often taken by actors willing to sing rather than trained singers, supplemented by a slender chorus probably drawn from a neighbouring church. Upon these shaky foundations several composers set about building a more individual and dramatic art. Hoffmann at Bamberg and Spohr at Kassel were among those who attempted to improve conditions, but it was Weber at Prague and particularly Dresden who really worked personally on all aspects of operatic production in order to develop a more unified dramatic work of art, what he described as 'the opera the German wants – a self-contained work of art in which all elements, contributed by the related arts in collaboration, disappear and are absorbed in various ways – so as to create a new world'.

It is in the pursuit of this goal that the central tradition of German Romantic opera lies. The operas of Schubert lie to one side of it, since despite the high quality of much of their music they do not have a very strong individual dramatic life; and Meyerbeer, regarded by Weber with affectionate irritation as a traitor to the cause, abandoned Germany for Italy and later Paris, where from 1825 until his death he spent several months each year. There he was to develop the genre of French grand opera (already familiar to Germans from the work of Spontini in Berlin) as pursued by Auber, Rossini and Halévy (see Chapter XV), to the point at which its influence entered German Romantic opera by way of its effect on Wagner. The innumerable smaller composers who made useful contributions to the genre in the years after Weber's death included Lindpaintner, whose *Der Vampyr* draws on various Weberian devices, including a Bridesmaids' Chorus, and uses the familiar devices of aria, cavatina, polonaise rhythm and so on with a considerable fluency, especially in figuration, that was part of the material upon which Wagner built. The more significant Marschner also developed various traits from Weber's world, including the character of the villain with redeeming touches of nobility (Weber's Lysiart influenced Marschner's Vampire as well as Wagner's Telramund). A number of features in Marschner anticipate Wagner, including some dramatic detail, but his Weberian reliance on the orchestra is not supported by Weber's ear for instrumental effect, or by Weber's melodic talent. Nicolai, who was exceptional in his acceptance of Italian influence, has survived in the repertory almost entirely through his elegantly composed, tuneful *Die lustigen Weiber von Windsor* (1849, Berlin).

It is a measure of the force which the new tradition exerted on the Romantics that scarcely a composer resisted the challenge to compose an opera. The young Mendelssohn, who set out with operatic ambitions, saw his *Die Hochzeit des Camacho* fail in Berlin in 1827, an unfamiliar experience for him, and achieved only a private performance of *Die Heimkehr aus der Fremde*, in 1829. Schumann spoke for many when he wrote that German opera was his 'artist's morning and evening prayer'. His own *Genoveva* (1850, Leipzig) follows the example of *Euryanthe* by taking its subject from medieval courtly love, a popular Romantic theme: it is based on free movement between aria, folklike song and passages of dramatic recitative.

Wagner and after

Wagner's genius as the culminating artist of Romanticism lay in his ability to draw creatively on the whole range of the tradition so as to form the 'new world' of which Weber spoke. Many elements contribute to his complex, unified vision, from the Viennese magic theatre to the philosophy of Schopenhauer, from the stage machinery of the Paris Opéra to political theories that conceived of performance at his Bayreuth Festspielhaus as a social ritual as well as the ideal staging of his work; while he also ranged back into German history and legend as well as drawing on the musical example of his immediate predecessors. The latter included not only German composers but French composers of *opéra comique* and grand opera, and he also set more store than was freely acknowledged by the long, elegant melodic line he admired in Bellini and other Italian composers. He was also unique in writing all his own librettos, regarding himself as a dramatist in music rather than a composer setting a text: though he worked through careful stages of prose sketches and verse drafts towards the final text, this was always with the necessary music also forming in his mind, so that to this extent the creative act of writing words and music was simultaneous.

Wagner's first completed opera, *Die Feen* (composed 1833–4; 1888, Munich), takes its example chiefly from German opera, especially Weber and Marschner. Though prolix, and with its ideas less successfully focussed than in later works, it is unmistakably marked with his own personality; and it includes a number of features that were to remain central to his ideas, not least that of redemption through love. This also occurs in *Das Liebesverbot* (1836, Madgeburg), which draws on a wide variety of sources, including French and German opera but also Italian. Wagner was later to regard the work as a deviation from his ideals, but it contributed to his idiom some valuable lessons in vocal melody and in the handling of motif, as well as including some lively and enjoyable music. However, it was the success of *Rienzi* (another opera with an Italian setting and based on an English source) that made him the most talked of composer in Germany after its première in Dresden in 1842. The intention, as with other projects, had been to conquer Paris and the Opéra, then the most influential theatre in Europe and the scene of Meyerbeer's enviable triumphs; in the event, he was rejected by Paris and returned to conquer his native land. Parisian methods are uppermost in the work, though the specific influence of Meyerbeer is less marked than that of the longer tradition of grand opera as it had been cultivated by Spontini, Auber and Halévy, all of them composers Wagner deeply admired and about whom he wrote enthusiastic and penetrating essays.

Der fliegende Holländer (1843, Dresden), especially in Wagner's original one-act conception, returns triumphantly to the style of German Romantic opera, building upon the methods of, particularly, Weber but conferring upon the genre a new fluency and emotional depth. Though specifically Weberian ideas can be identified – for instance, the relationship between voice and orchestra explored in Oberon's first aria, the cut of some of Daland's music, the female spinning chorus, and the sense of natural and supernatural forces intervening in the drama – the imaginative scale is larger. While Daland and Erik have not advanced very far upon Weber, Senta and the Dutchman foreshadow much in the emotional and psychological world of mature Wagner; and the constructive methods which Wagner had to evolve to encompass this enlarged imaginative world led him into a more sophisticated use of motif but perhaps more importantly to the composition of the work in extended scenes rather than in sequences of arias, however fluently linked. *Tannhäuser* (1845, Dresden) and *Lohengrin* (1850, Weimar) develop the genre still further, and contain what are almost the last traces of separate divisions into number and recitative in a free-flowing 'endless melody' that had become Wagner's aim, controlled formally by greater use of motif and given wider scope by his increased range of harmonic and orchestral colour. *Tannhäuser* retains features from German Romantic opera as well as Parisian grand opera, and returns once more to the theme of redemption through love; and despite some banalities, chiefly in the representation of 'sacred love' against which the more musically sophisticated 'profane love' is set, transcends its influences with music of increased imaginative strength.

Lohengrin similarly transcends its influences, absorbing grand opera and some highly Weberian elements: details such as the interrupted wedding (as in Auber's *La muette de Portici*) and the concept of scenes such as the opening ceremony by the river reflect grand opera, while the portrait of Telramund (closely modelled on Weber's Lysiart in *Euryanthe*) and the idea of confronting a virtuous couple with a 'dark' couple (another legacy of *Euryanthe*) suggest the heritage of Weber and his immediate successors such as Marschner. Nevertheless, the finest sections of *Lohengrin* cannot be so neatly accounted for, and in the Grail Prelude Wagner produced music of an abstract yet dramatic beauty that he was not to excel in kind until *Parsifal*. It is none the less possible to regard *Lohengrin* as the culmination of many converging traits – or rather, many traits that Wagner, with his voracious genius, was to select as necessary to his dramatic ambitions. His true claim to greatness rests in the works that lay ahead.

Yet these had been carefully prepared, both half-consciously by Wagner's ability to absorb from existing models what he knew, somewhere in his creativity, to be necessary, and deliberately in his mapping out, quite early in his career, of the subjects that he wanted one day to set. His aims were not achieved without considerable discussion and theorizing, and the years around 1850 formed a period in which he seemed to be gathering his creative reserves together and clarifying his ideas by means of a number of important essays and pamphlets. Though he was to modify or even reject and contradict his views later, important essays that set these out include *Das Kunstwerk der Zukunft* (1849), *Oper und Drama* (1851) and *Eine Mitteilung an meine Freunde* (1851). These outlined ideas of opera as a *Gesamtkunstwerk* ('total work of art'), in which poetry should directly give rise to music in a drama making unified use of all the theatrical resources, moreover a drama that should be given in ideal conditions as something much closer to social ritual than to mere entertainment. That much in these essays had already been foreshadowed or even to some extent explored in practice, and was to be altered later, did not alter their value for Wagner in testing his principles nor their interest for subsequent generations.

The idea for a drama on the Death of Siegfried (*Siegfrieds Tod*) had already been in Wagner's mind by the time Liszt conducted the first performance of *Lohengrin*, together with plans for a special festival theatre dedicated to his works. Finding it necessary to extend his original scheme in order to express his ambitious plan, he added first one and then another preceding work, finally adding a preludial work, or *Vorabend*: thus there were written for music in reverse order the four works that form *Der Ring des Nibelungen*, namely *Das Rheingold*, *Die Walküre*, *Siegfried* and *Götterdämmerung*. *Das Rheingold* was completed by the end of 1854, by which time Wagner was also reviving ideas for an opera on *Tristan* and another on *Parsifal*. The composition of the *Ring* was eventually to extend from 1853 to 1874, with both *Tristan und Isolde* (1865, Munich) and *Die Meistersinger von Nürnberg* (1868, Munich) intervening. Thus, though Wagner was now a fully mature composer, the progress of his idiom can be observed not only in these works and in his final *Parsifal* (1882, Bayreuth), but through the course of the *Ring* itself.

Nevertheless each work, the *Ring* as a totality included, has its identifiable characteristics. The motivic technique which Wagner had evolved from the old 'reminiscence motif' frees the music in *Tristan* from the last vestiges of construction in separate numbers; further, he had by now developed the old German verse device of *Stabreim*, or alliterative front-rhymes, largely out of a wish to avoid the cadencing periodicity that was difficult to separate from conventional end-rhyme. This in turn meant that in *Tristan* he was able to move towards a freely evolving chromatic harmony of a sophistication that had not previously been known in music. These methods, in turn encouraging orchestration of comparable fluency, subtlety and richness, found their ideal creative complement in a story that concerns doomed love finding mystic realization only by a turning away from light and normality into a mysterious, unknown realm of erotic intensity and eventually extinction in death. As always with Wagner, much was drawn into the magnetic field of his creative needs, and in the case of *Tristan* an intense study of Schopenhauer's renunciatory philosophy contributed to the essential ideas of the work.

Die Meistersinger stands in striking contrast to *Tristan*, but in a related contrast: that is to say, more of the ideas in *Tristan* recur in different form in the later work than are immediately apparent. Wagner's assertion that the power of renunciation is still greater than the power of love is at the centre of Hans Sachs's understanding that it is he who must bring about, even at the cost of his own emotions, the true resolution of the plot – which is that the 'new' young Walther, representative of novel ideas in art, shall succeed in winning his bride Eva and thus triumph over the most conservative ideas of the Mastersingers. Yet in a stricter sense, Wagner was here a true conservative, for the opera also celebrates the continuity of tradition by its being refreshed, and takes a stand against its being destroyed either from without by attack or from within by a mindless preservation of rules without spirit. Musically, this conservation by refreshing is manifest in an idiom that remains highly chromatic when necessary but can also be robustly diatonic; diatonic melodies or even Lutheran chorales are set so that their spirit is maintained while their harmonization and treatment are particular to Wagner at this stage of his development. Furthermore, after the virtually total fluency of *Tristan*, Wagner was now in a position to readmit a feeling of separate numbers to his seamless web of music when it was dramatically appropriate, yet without relinquishing his increased mastery of leitmotif as a unifying device.

The opening of Bayreuth in 1876 with the completed *Ring* (conducted by Richter) was an international event, so securely had Wagner won himself a position in the loyalty and the equally powerful hostility of his countrymen, and as the most controversial musician in Europe. The expansion of the constituent works from one to four was necessary not simply as representing the space demanded by the narration of events, but so as to provide a framework for the enactment of a myth and a receptacle for an intricate network of ideas. As we have seen (p.188), Wagner had laid out his theories about music drama in three important extended essays, and the *Ring* sees their fullest realization. He had held up the ideal of Greek tragedy as a unified art form, especially for what he saw as its quality of mythic content and of social and religious significance; and he had argued that there had come about a loss of these values and a separation of the arts, with traditional opera given over to trivialities. The medium that would now encompass a reunification of the arts was music drama; this would draw upon myth and upon musical techniques in which motif, inspired by the example of Beethoven's powers of thematic development, could bring about a new fertilization of music with poetry. He gave examples of how he would apply these techniques; and neither the fact that he could not in the event do so with any consistency, nor the inaccuracy and special pleading of much of his argument, invalidates the importance of these essays for an understanding of his ideas.

His work on the *Ring* was to take him over a quarter of a century, from the beginnings in 1848 to the cycle's first performance in Bayreuth in 1876. For his material, he brought together elements from German and Norse myth, poems and sagas, and legendary characters, using his reading of the Grimm brothers' work on German legend to confer some order on his diverse sources, and making use of Greek example specifically from Aeschylus. His own formidable assimilative powers, and a creative instinct that leapt ahead of his intellectual understanding, enabled him to fashion a many-layered myth of the nature, if not of the kind, he envisaged in his essays. To the immediate eye and ear, the *Ring* is a stirring, humanly appealing narrative of gods, men and women, animals and mythical beasts, magical transformations and the beauty of the natural world, set to music of incomparable power, range and beauty. But lying within this is a work about much in human nature, both noble and corruptible, corrupt and redeemable, and especially about power and the collapse of power when it is not honourably held.

Given the work's long gestation and realization, it is inevitable that Wagner's ideas and methods should have undergone a substantial change during its writing. Motivically, *Das Rheingold* is comparatively straightforward, drawing upon techniques that are often little distinguishable from the old 'reminiscence motif'. But by the end of the cycle, this referential directness has grown into the use of motif capable of embodying either the ideas lying within what is represented, the abstract ideas themselves, or aspects of the characters holding or confronted with these ideas; and in turn as a means for the immediate expression of such ideas, for their recall, or for their adumbration. It further follows that a crucial aspect of Wagner's art lies in the subtle combination of several such ideas so that they gain new depth and meaning from their contact.

An example is the opening of Act 3 of *Siegfried*. Here the musical material is originally associated with the earth goddess Erda (mother by Wotan of the Valkyries), the twilight of the gods, Wotan's spear, his transformation into a Wanderer on the face of the earth, the magic sleep into which he has cast Brünnhilde, and the galloping rhythms of the Valkyries. Thus described, it is a jumble of references. As music – and Wagner's sketches for this passage show that the composition caused him much difficulty – it brings together elements of the story and their accrued meaning into the expression of Wotan's state of mind, as he confronts Erda, before turning to meet Siegfried, the hero who will overthrow him and his order. Wotan's tragic resignation before an event he is nevertheless bound to oppose is but one of many aspects of Schopenhauer's all-pervading influence on Wagner's thought. It also serves to indicate the danger of labelling motifs. Wagner did not use the term *Leitmotiv* (or leitmotif) – preferring, when he did use one, *Hauptmotiv* – and understood well that to refer to his themes by name is to risk limiting with finite words what is essentially musical and therefore subject to change and development. Thus, to speak of the Spear Motif is to acknowledge the physical object, represented in music with a strong scalic downward thrust. But the true meaning of the Spear attaches to the agreements engraved upon it, authorizing Wotan's rule and binding him, and which he infringes only at the cost of his power. Further, by Act 3 of *Siegfried*, the meaning has grown to embrace Wotan's sufferings and his understanding of what must come about. It is in such regions that music expresses what lies beyond the power of words; and this takes us close to Wagner's understanding of what could be achieved by music drama.

It follows that a new relationship must develop between the voices and the orchestra. The vocal lines in *Das Rheingold* are almost excessively plain at times, reflecting Wagner's earlier theories about the relationship between drama and orchestral expression; but by *Die Walküre* practice has overtaken theory, and he is writing vocal lines that are more closely integrated with the orchestra and that of themselves contain a fluent expression of ideas, emotions, references and prophetic allusions in an abundant lyrical flow. It is the avoidance of cadence or period in this manner that earns the vocal line the term *unendliche Melodie*. The demands made upon singers in articulating such lines are enormous, both of sheer stamina but also in the necessity of a close understanding of the issues involved; and it should be emphasized that Wagner himself, in writing for the human voice, never abandoned his admiration for the elegant qualities he admired in a composer far removed from his ideals, Bellini. But the orchestra itself is given new importance. Since the beginnings of German Romantic opera and the lessons learnt from French Revolutionary opera, an increased role had been given to the accompaniment; and now the burden of the expression passes to a greatly enlarged symphony orchestra in which a crucial part of the inner life of the characters is enacted. The complexity of the art Wagner has here developed is part of its richness; naturally it also makes heavy demands upon the listener who is concerned with more than the work's surface. It requires what was in Wagner's day a new approach to opera as a social ritual rather than a socialite's diversion. The *Ring*, like all masterpieces, is capable of renewing its meaning to succeeding generations, who will find new aspects of meaning in its myth; it remains a drama of ideas which will always stand as one of the peaks of operatic achievement.

Like the *Ring*, *Parsifal* turns to myth; however, the sources are much more varied, and are brought together into a creative entity by the most remarkable act of synthesis of Wagner's career. Though the framework of the plot derives from a medieval German poem by Wolfram von Eschenbach, the work enshrines Wagner's most penetrating ideas about, in particular, belief and human structures. No work of his has aroused more resistance or incomprehension, and therefore more conflicting interpretations, some merely absurd. The necessity of belief, and of a structure within which this can be held and ordered, must be indisputably at the centre of *Parsifal*, and the powerful use of Christian metaphor demonstrates at least Wagner's imaginative closeness to Christianity even if much in him could also reject parts of Christianity. It is characteristic of Wagner's subtlety of mind at this late stage of his career that the work can also include, in the person of Kundry, the most extraordinary revelation of his understanding of feminine psychology and of its role in human redemption. In his preparation of the text, he made limited use of end-rhyme, though he was careful to avoid periodicity so as to allow freedom to what can be a harmonic idiom still more far-reaching than that of *Tristan*. Yet there is an exceedingly close correlation between text and music, with a freer use of motif than in the *Ring*; and the orchestration has a subtlety even greater than that of *Tristan*. Conceptually and musically – and it is of the essence of Wagner's art that the two cannot be separated – it is his most advanced music drama, and the one with which he consciously completed his life's work for the stage.

The force of Wagner's personality left no German composer unmarked. Those who resisted his achievement were few, and they tended to find their independence turning into isolation. Of his own immediate circle, some success was achieved by Cornelius, who in reaction to Lortzing tried to give German comic opera new vitality by drawing on Wagnerian methods fertilized by the lightest side of Berlioz: he achieved an enduring popular success with *Der Barbier von Bagdad* (1858, Weimar) before attempting the less congenial grand Wagnerian manner in *Der Cid* (1865, Weimar). Goldmark also won some success with his first opera, *Die Königin von Saba* (1875, Vienna), before being sucked into Wagner's wake with several would-be monumental operas, finally reverting to a simpler manner based on earlier examples. Goetz attempted, especially with *Der Widerspenstigen Zähmung* (1874, Mannheim), to preserve a lineage descending from Mozart through Weber and Marschner independent of Wagner's post-*Lohengrin* achievements. The most ambitious and unabashed imitator of Wagner was perhaps Bungert, who planned two cycles of operas entitled *Homerische Welt* and hoped to establish for their performance a festival theatre on the Rhine (two parts of *Die Ilias* were sketched but never completed; the four operas comprising *Die Odyssee* were given in Dresden between 1896 and 1903). That the lessons of Wagner could be applied with greater success on a modest scale was shown by the enduring success of Humperdinck's *Hänsel und Gretel* (1893, Weimar), which uses nursery tunes motivically and relies on the methods of Wagner's orchestral commentary in well-judged miniature; and by Kienzl's *Der Evangelimann* (1895, Berlin), which adapts similar methods to a folktale. Some Wagnerian traits were also absorbed by Thuille in *Lobetanz* (1898, Karlsruhe) and *Gugeline* (1901, Bremen), though his talent was lightweight and for the merely effective. Wagner's own son Siegfried Wagner turned his father's methods on to more traditional Romantic opera subjects, as in *Der Bärenhäuter* (1899, Munich), with little success beyond the curiosity his name inevitably aroused.

CHAPTER XV

France

WINTON DEAN, DENNIS LIBBY, RONALD CRICHTON

1. Opéra comique

The Revolutionary period

The Revolution convulsed and, for a time, radically transformed the nature of *opéra comique*. The older type, light, graceful, technically unadventurous, with a little romantic sentiment and mild social satire, did not quite die out, as the success of Devienne's *Les visitandines* (1792) and Solié's *Le secret* (1796) bears witness; but it was overshadowed by a new and much more strenuous approach inspired by the political and social idealism of the age. This new school retained the outward form of spoken dialogue with *mélodrame* and songs; indeed this was essential to its purpose of glorifying the common man. Spoken dialogue was the link through which the audience could identify with characters in predicaments not too remote from their own experience. The elements of comedy and parody declined in importance and in many operas disappeared altogether; transmuted, they gave birth to the genre characters, peasants, sailors, fishermen and so on, of Romantic opera. The aim was not so much to entertain and amuse as to edify, exhort and astonish; the *opéra comique* in effect changed places with the serious all-sung opera, which remained in a backwater until the rise of Spontini. This was the direct consequence of the ferment of ideas released by the Revolution: the remote heroes of classical mythology, if they could not supply a model for imitation, became irrelevant or at best diverting. Nothing illustrates this better than the desperate sincerity of Cherubini's *Médée* (1797), whose heroine, in an age preoccupied with the struggle of the common man, fights and dies as a woman, demanding to be judged as an individual and not a chattel, and the same composer's *Anacréon* (1803), with its debilitated charm and climate of relaxed hedonism. The latter was a grand opera; the former, though on a libretto originally intended for the Opéra, was produced with spoken dialogue as an *opéra comique*.

Many early examples of the new *opéra comique* were propaganda pieces of little artistic merit in which martyrs of the Revolution were held up for admiration. They were announced as *fait historique*, a description attached also to later and weightier works based on incidents of contemporary life such as Gaveaux's *Léonore* (1798) and Cherubini's *Les deux journées* (1800). Heroic subjects with a similar didactic purpose were treated in the repertories of both the Opéra-Comique (Grétry's *Guillaume Tell*, 1791, and *Callias, ou Nature et patrie*, 1794, and Méhul's *Doria, ou La tyrannie détruite*, 1795) and at the Opéra, where classical, especially Roman, history was favoured (e.g. Méreaux's *Fabius*, Lemoyne's *Miltiade à Marathon*, both 1793, and Méhul's *Horatius Coclès*, 1794).

More artistically fruitful, and specific to *opéra comique*, were horror stories involving robbers, tyrants, violence and natural catastrophes (Cherubini's *Lodoïska*, Le Sueur's *La caverne* and many more), edifying tales based on principles inculcated by Rousseau (the *Paul et Virginie* operas of Rodolphe Kreutzer and Le Sueur) and romantic subjects from the age of chivalry (Dalayrac's *Léon, ou Le château de Monténéro*, 1798, Méhul's *Ariodant*, 1799, Berton's *Montano et Stéphanie*, 1799). Since these invariably culminated in the rescue of hero or heroine at the eleventh hour by a supreme act of human courage, they are known as 'rescue operas' (this type is not specific to *opéra comique*; the term was invented much later for works often called simply 'drame' at the time). The moral content of the characters became polarized: the darker sides of human nature were explored, partly under the influence of the English Gothick novel, in order to throw the virtuous into sharper relief. Often it is the dynamic villains who dominate the scene, a characteristic that persists into the Romantic age and links up with the wide popularity and fascination of Mozart's *Don Giovanni*. Many of the librettos had a powerful element of realism, and the action was often highly spectacular: fires, avalanches, earthquakes and volcanic eruptions represented on stage added to the stature of the heroes who overcame them and reflected the spirit of France embattled in a desperate struggle against the rest of Europe.

Two further factors contributed to the very large number of *opéras comiques* produced in Paris during the last decade of the century: their encouragement by the various Revolutionary governments, who saw the advantage of whipping up patriotic enthusiasm by theatrical means (though they imposed a censorship and other ordinances, such as the compulsory playing on demand of Revolutionary hymns, including the *Marseillaise*, which provoked frequent riots), and the existence of two flourishing *opéra comique* theatres at the same time. The old Comédie-Italienne in the rue Favart, renamed Théâtre de l'Opéra-Comique National in 1793, met a formidable rival in the Théâtre Feydeau, founded in 1789 as the Théâtre de Monsieur and renamed in 1791. Each had its own composers – Cherubini, Le Sueur and Gaveaux worked for the Feydeau, Berton, Kreutzer, Dalayrac, Méhul and later Boieldieu mostly for the Favart – and they often competed against each other with operas on the same subject: *Lodoïska* (Cherubini and Kreutzer, produced within a fortnight in 1791; the latter, though much the weaker, was more successful in Paris), *Paul et Virginie* (Kreutzer 1791, Le Sueur 1794), *Roméo et Juliette* (Dalayrac 1792, Steibelt 1793), *La caverne* (Le Sueur 1793, Méhul 1795). Further, the Comédie Française was closed for much of the 1790s, so that many of its playwrights turned to writing librettos and the audiences who would have supported it sought entertainment elsewhere. Few new works were written for the Opéra during this time.

Some of the established composers were quick to jump on the bandwagon. Grétry in *Guillaume Tell* (1791) anticipated (and perhaps influenced) Rossini in combining Swiss local colour with mass patriotic fervour, but fell heavily between two stools in trying to adapt the older musical style to new themes. Dalayrac, one of the most prolific and popular composers of the age, from the *ancien régime* right through the Revolution to Napoleon's Empire, was more successful if less ambitious. His *Camille* (1791), on a Gothick horror libretto set in a prison, anticipates that of *Fidelio* in its compound of the sinister, the earthy and the idealistic; the music, despite Romantic anticipations, belongs essentially to the world of Grétry. One of the leaders of the new school, whose influence was even greater in Germany, was (as so often in French opera history) a foreigner, Cherubini.

Cherubini's expert craftsmanship was based on the two techniques in which he had been trained in Italy, ecclesiastical polyphony and Neapolitan *opera buffa*, especially the latter, which had for some time dominated serious Italian opera as well. To these he added a seriousness of approach, strengthened by his study of Gluck and Haydn, and a native vigour that gave substance, if not inspiration, to everything he touched. He expanded the individual movements of *opéra comique*, often writing ensembles and finales of enormous length, and enriched the orchestration. It was chiefly due to Cherubini that an idiom founded on the language of light comedy, buttressed by rhetorical energy, heavy dramatic accents, sforzandos and cross-rhythms, became the foundation not only of Beethoven's style but of the whole of German Romantic opera. In *Lodoïska*, which significantly he called a *comédie héroïque*, he provided models for Pizarro in *Fidelio* and for the emotive treatment of a contemporary political subject (partitioned Poland), and introduced the polonaise to give local colour. Its characteristic rhythm was to become as popular in Romantic opera as the barcarolle, polka and waltz – likewise featured prominently in *opéra comique* – a generation later. *Elisa* (1794) was one of the first operas to exploit the romantic appeal of Alpine scenery. But although in *Les deux journées* he produced a near-masterpiece in which an ethical message, comedy and realism are cleverly combined with the aid of dialect and a particularly skilful use of *mélodrame*, Cherubini never quite resolved the strain set up between the emotional violence of his plots, the classicism of his musical language and the *opéra comique* form. In *Médée*, in which the vestigial comic elements of *Lodoïska* and *Elisa* disappear altogether, he found a subject congenial to his temper but one that comes so near to breaking the mould that the opera is seldom performed in its original form with dialogue and *mélodrame* (Franz Lachner's recitative version of 1855 is a travesty). Cherubini's operas after 1800 show how completely he was left behind by the times.

Of his many contemporaries in France the most important was Méhul, who was much influenced by Gluck. Less technically assured than Cherubini, Méhul was bolder and more original both in design and detail. His first opera to reach the stage, *Euphrosine* (1790), in which the styles of Gluck and Grétry are not yet assimilated, shows him already experimenting with a leading motif that begins the overture and returns at the most important climaxes of the action to symbolize the dangerous power of jealousy. In *Mélidore et Phrosine* (1794) and *Ariodant* (1799) he carried this idea a good deal further. Both have subjects from medieval romance in which the darker passions (incest in the former, obsessive jealousy in both) combine with remote or exotic natural settings to suggest the ambience of the German Romantics, especially Weber and Marschner. But as in all French operas of this period the text is more romantic than the music, which for all its many prophetic touches remains half-shackled to an earlier age. Méhul sought to fuse the spoken dialogue with the musical numbers by means of linking passages (introductions and codas) beginning or ending out of the main key and often incorporating motifs associated with important dramatic concepts.

Like Cherubini, Méhul tended to crack the *opéra comique* mould, for his methods, pushed to their logical conclusion, demand not the breaks imposed by the incursion of dialogue but a continuously evolving musical texture as developed by Weber (in *Euryanthe*) and Wagner; indeed the last act of *Mélidore et Phrosine* goes a long way in this direction. Méhul also experimented with the form of the overture – his examples vary from the free atmospheric prelude (*Ariodant*) to the symphonic poem (*Le jeune Henri*, 1797) and the tonally disorientated overture to *Uthal* (1806), during which the voice of the heroine is heard calling her father in the darkness – and with the orchestra. He treated the horns in a picturesque manner, and employed stopped notes and bells placed one against the other to give an effect of horror and mystery. He sometimes suppressed regular instruments for a dramatic purpose: *Stratonice* (1792) has no oboes, *Uthal*, a nocturnal piece on an Ossianic subject set in the remote, forested scenery of the Hebrides, no violins or trumpets. Méhul also wrote traditional Italianate *opéras comiques*, but his serious works are of much greater interest and power; they influenced his successors in Germany, Weber in particular, but lost their place in the repertory partly because (like Cherubini's) they are comparatively weak in melody and partly because Méhul's technique was not equal to digesting and consolidating his ideas, especially in harmony, where his boldness often verges on eccentricity.

Both criticisms apply to other composers of Revolutionary *opéra comique*. Berton in *Le délire* (1799) sought to depict the derangement of his hero through a motif based on three unrelated major triads, only to suggest that he himself was out of his depth. Gaveaux and Kreutzer were lesser talents, though the former's *Léonore* left a faint mark on the music as well as the libretto of *Fidelio*. Le Sueur, a born eccentric, tackled ambitious subjects in an industrious manner and in *Télémaque* (1796) evolved a curious harmonic and rhythmic system, a kind of personal *Affektenlehre*, based partly on the ecclesiastical modes and what he took to be the principles of ancient writers, partly on 18th-century commonplaces. His reach considerably exceeded his grasp; the elaborate dynamic and descriptive instructions in his scores look like an attempt to convey to readers what his invention was unable to work into the music. The most successful of his three *opéras comiques*, *La caverne* (1793), set throughout in an underground cave inhabited by a band of farouche robbers, combines diverse elements from *opera seria*, *opera buffa* and traditional *opéra comique*. Le Sueur later moved from *opéra comique* to grand opera and produced two of the most massively spectacular works of the Napoleonic period (*Ossian ou Les bardes*, 1804, and *La mort d'Adam*, 1809) before retiring to the Conservatoire, where he left a profound and still audible impression on his most celebrated pupil, Berlioz.

Early 19th century
The Revolutionary *opéra comique* died as suddenly as it began, partly because the rivalry of the two theatres ended in 1801 in the ruin of both (they amalgamated at the Théâtre Feydeau the following year), partly because the genre could be pushed no further without destroying itself, and partly no doubt because Paris audiences tired of strenuous exhortation and example. The political climate too had changed. The decade was by far the most influential in the history of *opéra comique*. For the first quarter of the 19th century its products dominated the opera repertory in Germany, and Beethoven and Weber erected a substantial structure on this foundation. The leading French composer of the next generation, Boieldieu, produced in *Béniowski* (1800) an extreme example of rescue opera in which the entire cast, including the governor of a Siberian prison camp, is delivered from the rigours of the Russian winter; but he soon abandoned this vein for the lighter type of *opéra comique*, in the tradition of Grétry, for which his talents were more suited. He wrote a number of such works for St Petersburg, where he held an official post from 1803 to 1811, including the witty *Les voitures versées* (1808), a skit on provincial snobbery containing some clever parodies. Many of his operas after his return to Paris – *Jean de Paris* (1812), *Le nouveau seigneur de village* (1813), *La fête du village voisin* (1816), *Le petit chaperon rouge* (1818) and especially *La dame blanche* (1825) – were very successful. They are tuneful, unpretentious, artificial comedies, with a mild Romantic tinge (and in *La dame blanche* a little Scottish local colour) but free from the bite of serious satire. Boieldieu's principal rival, the Maltese Isouard, active in Paris from 1800, followed a similarly profitable and unambitious course with *Les rendez-vous bourgeois* (1807), *Cendrillon* (1810) and *Joconde* (1814). The older generation

continued to compose and enjoyed occasional successes – Berton with *Aline, reine de Golconde* (1803), Méhul with *Joseph* (1807) – but their force was largely spent. Spontini, after two one-act *opéras comiques*, *Milton* (1804: a serious piece which ends with the poet sitting down to dictate *Paradise Lost* to his daughter) and *Julie* (1805), abandoned the form for grand opera. *L'auberge de bagnères* (1807) by Catel, a composer with something of Cherubini's solid technique, was condemned as too learned – the charge brought against any *opéra comique* with pretensions to originality up to and including Bizet's *Carmen*.

The next landmark was the introduction of Rossini's comic operas to Paris, beginning with *L'italiana in Algeri* early in 1817, followed in 1824 by the arrival of the composer himself, both to direct the Théâtre-Italien (where he set out to remould the art of singing in France) and to begin a new career in French opera. Although his Paris works, including *Le comte Ory* (1828), were written for the Opéra, his influence was all-pervasive. It appears in the later operas of Boieldieu (especially *La dame blanche*) and all the *opéra comique* composers of the next 30 years, some of whom (like the Neapolitan Carafa, whose successful *Masaniello*, 1827, preceded Auber's setting of the same story, *La muette de Portici*, by two months) were little more than imitators. A less sensational but still important influence was Weber's *Der Freischütz*, produced in debased form as *Robin des bois* in December 1824. Its impact was strongest on Hérold, perhaps the most promising *opéra comique* composer of his generation, who died young without realizing his full potentialities. His first major success, *Marie* (1826), shows more enterprise in harmony and dramatic structure than Boieldieu or Auber and a feeling for nature and romantic sentiment. Its prominent use of barcarolle rhythms, derived perhaps from Rossini's *La donna del lago*, anticipated Auber in *La muette de Portici*. *Zampa* (1831), on an absurdly melodramatic plot, is much more ambitious, and to some extent a return to a more serious conception of *opéra comique*: the motive force, however, came not from the Revolutionary composers but from *Der Freischütz* and *Don Giovanni*. The presence of a supernatural element alien to *opéra comique* tradition and the full and noisy scoring echo the German Romantics, but consort ill with the shadow of Rossini and the ubiquitous polka rhythms. The death of the central character – during an eruption of Etna he is conveyed to Hell by the statue of a girl he has betrayed, thereby combining the dénouements of *Don Giovanni* and *La muette de Portici* – though unusual in *opéra comique*, scarcely constitutes a tragic end; as in Auber's *Fra Diavolo* (1830), it disposes of a criminal who is presented as little more than a painted bogey. Hérold's last complete opera, *Le pré aux clercs* (1832), though it received 145 performances in a single year (more than any other work in the history of the genre), has less vitality and approaches the bourgeois type popularized by Auber and Scribe.

Mid-19th century

The two artists – or businessmen – Auber and Scribe dominated the *opéra comique* for nearly half a century. Between 1813 and 1869 Auber produced 34 works in this form, all but the first four and the last two in association with Scribe. As in grand opera, the librettist found a pattern that exactly hit the taste of the Parisian middle class. It comprised a well-oiled plot, a fair range of amusing situations – some of them, like the heroine's undressing in *Fra Diavolo*, nicely calculated to titillate the palate – but no depth of feeling or character and little dramatic conviction. Auber matched it with lively music that owed a profound debt to the more superficial side of Rossini, for example in its dotted rhythms, glittering orchestration and general bustling activity. It has a certain wit, typically Parisian in its half-cynical raillery and worldliness, and occasional exotic touches, but often declines into a relentless chirpiness. There is little sense of Romanticism or the open air, and no strong emotion; Auber scarcely ever used a slower tempo mark than *andante*. Nor is his structural range wide; the minor mode is rare and his ensembles, though frequent, are seldom extensively developed. His first collaboration with Scribe, *Leicester* (1823), based on Scott's *Kenilworth*, set the pattern – the bouncy theme with triplets for the entry of Queen Elizabeth would have suited any of Rossini's more frivolous heroines – and was followed by a string of successes, particularly *Le maçon* (1825), *La fiancée* (1829), *Fra Diavolo* (1830), *Le domino noir* (1837), *Les diamants de la couronne* (1841) and *Haydée* (1847). Auber achieved his final triumph, not with Scribe but built to the same formula, in *Le premier jour de bonheur* (1868), composed at the age of 86.

Between 1825 and the Franco-Prussian War the *opéra comique* stagnated. Many composers enjoyed success – notably Halévy with *L'éclair* (1835), *Les mousquetaires de la reine* (1846) and *Le val d'Andorre* (1848), and Adam with a series of deftly turned frivolities such as *Le chalet* (1834) and *Le postillon de Longjumeau* (1836) – but they contributed nothing new. Halévy, a man of wide culture who failed to concentrate his gifts, was content to follow the lyrical-sentimental approach of Boieldieu, though with a stronger technique. Adam, with an occasional touch of satire but little feeling for character, was closer to Auber – and to the operetta composers, of whom he was a forerunner. Like a number of his contemporaries he was much indebted to the Rossini of *Le comte Ory*. The lesser figures – Grisar, Maillart, Bazin, Massé – declined into a triviality that cost their audiences no thought and retained their suffrage for decades. The most successful *opéra comique* of the later years of this period was Thomas' *Mignon* (1866), which borrowed from Germany not only its subject but a touch of Schumannesque *Gemütlichkeit* in the music, considerably diluted. Its compound of the picturesque and the sentimental struck much the same chord in the French public as had *La dame blanche* 40 years earlier. A far more distinguished work, Berlioz's *Béatrice et Bénédict* (1862, Baden-Baden), suffers from a strange disproportion between music and drama; while the invention is uniformly brilliant, too many irrelevances are set to music and too much of the main action left in dialogue.

A number of foreigners contributed to the repertory without affecting its course, including Donizetti (*La fille du régiment*, 1840), Balfe, Flotow and Meyerbeer (*L'étoile du nord*, 1854; *Le pardon de Ploërmel*, 1859). So did Offenbach, whose operettas, mostly produced at his own theatre, the Bouffes-Parisiens, were the natural extension of the Parisian taste for the lightest musical fare. His works for the Opéra-Comique, especially *Robinson Crusoé* (1867) and the posthumously produced *Les contes d'Hoffmann* (1881), aimed higher; they contain some of his best music but fall to some extent between the two genres, for *opéra comique* is founded on character (however superficially treated), operetta on caricature (see pp. 213–14 and Chapter XX).

The Opéra-Comique several times changed its residence, moving from the Feydeau to the Salle Ventadour (1829–32), the Théâtre des Nouveautés (1832–40) and the new Salle Favart (1840–87). For some years it had a rival in the Théâtre-Lyrique, founded in 1847 as the Opéra National (the name was changed in 1852), which occupied a number of different buildings. In its attempt to find a middle way between the museum of the Opéra and the puppet-show of the Opéra-Comique it did not insist on spoken dialogue as a pre-requisite, while sometimes using it. Some of its more distinguished productions, which included Berlioz's *Les troyens à Carthage* (1863), Bizet's early operas and several of Gounod's, were nevertheless subsequently taken into the Opéra-Comique repertory. Gounod's very successful *Le médecin malgré lui* (1858) and the original version of *Faust* (1859) were, however, *opéras comiques* in the strict sense. The former, besides a lightness of touch that the composer too often suppressed later, has a melodic and harmonic warmth and a humanity of which the genre was badly in need. *Faust*, converted into a grand opera by the addition of recitatives in 1860, is never performed as first written but might well prove more satisfactory as an *opéra comique* (see pp.210). The higher Gounod aimed, especially when he touched on religion, the more pretentious and empty his music became. Like Bizet, he was at his best in *opéra comique*, but he could not reconcile the pull between his French inheritance and the philosophical and mystical attractions of German culture. The charm and grace of his best music was too often clogged by a rich harmonic idiom to which the absence of rhythmic flexibility imparted an air of enervating complacency. Thanks to the enterprising policy of its director, Léon Carvalho, the Théâtre-Lyrique drew most of the more promising younger composers away from the Opéra-Comique throughout the 1860s; but its financial position was always precarious, and the war of 1870 killed it.

Late 19th century
Camille du Locle, who became joint director of the Opéra-Comique in 1869, tried after the war to revitalize the genre. He was attracted to oriental and exotic subjects, and this may have led him to choose Bizet as his principal agent. Despite some beautiful music whose bold harmonic

idiom shocked the audience, the one-act *Djamileh* (1872) was a failure; so were early works by Massenet and Saint-Saëns. The single success of this period was Delibes' *Le roi l'a dit* (1873). The production of *Carmen* in 1875 carried *opéra comique* to its highest artistic achievement and gave it its death wound. By taking a tragic story of low and almost contemporary life and refusing to soften its impact, Bizet introduced a quality of realism (truth to experience would be a better term) that was implicit in the form but usually evaded. Unlike Méhul and his contemporaries he was able, thanks to his Mozartian command of balance and design within the set numbers, to achieve this without straining the medium. The dialogue is never a hindrance; it is the recitatives composed by Guiraud after Bizet's death, and until recently used everywhere outside France, that distort the work by distancing its immediacy of impact, weakening the plot and obliterating Bizet's vivid use of *mélodrame*. This realism was exploited to sensational ends by less scrupulous later composers, especially in Italy, but in *Carmen* it is held in perfect balance by Bizet's gift of dramatic detachment; he enters into his characters without judging them or using them to browbeat the audience. The murder of the heroine on stage shocked a public accustomed to the superficial repertory of the previous half-century, with its careful avoidance of the deeper and less comfortable emotions, and the opera was a failure in Paris until its revival in 1883.

Carmen is the supreme achievement of Bizet and of *opéra comique*. The musical characterization, especially of José in his gradual decline from the peasant honesty of a simple soldier through insubordination, desertion and smuggling to murder, is masterly. The colour and vitality of Carmen herself need no emphasis; she is redeemed from any suspicion of vulgarity by her qualities of courage and fatalism so vividly realized in the music. The exotic parts of the score were never intended as a literal evocation of Spain but rather to suggest the background for dramatic purposes. He used three themes of Spanish origin, and other parts of the score, notably the 'Seguidilla' and the 'Chanson bohème' in Act 2, make effective use of the procedures, harmonic, rhythmic and instrumental, of flamenco music, to which the augmented 2nds of the Carmen motif perhaps also owe their origin. This motif, which occurs in two related forms, one representing Carmen herself and the other her fatal influence on José, is employed with a notable command of dramatic irony, as also is Escamillo's famous refrain. *Carmen* is unlike any other *opéra comique* in that the main action – and there is much more than usual – is expressed in the music rather than the dialogue, as well as being a *locus classicus* for colour, power and economy of orchestration.

By annexing a serious subject for the Opéra-Comique Bizet upset the artificial distinction that held the two Parisian repertories apart. His successors, unable or unwilling to attain a satisfactory equilibrium within the old confines, soon abandoned spoken dialogue. It survived in a few later works, such as Saint-Saëns's *Le timbre d'argent* (1877), Delibes' *Lakmé* (1883) and Chabrier's *Le roi malgré lui* (1887), but was generally relegated to operetta. Both Delibes and Chabrier owed something to Bizet's vitality and exotic harmonic and instrumental colour; Chabrier and Lalo in *Le roi d'Ys* (1888) also reflected the influence of Wagner, which swept over French musical life in the 1880s and with its emphasis on through-composition helped to bury the *opéra comique* tradition. Massenet composed copiously for both Opéra and Opéra-Comique without much varying the religious-erotic style he inherited from Gounod; but after *Manon* (1884) he ceased to give the title 'opéra comique' to his works for the smaller theatre, calling them instead 'opéra romanesque', 'conte de fées', 'drame lyrique', 'miracle' and so on. The one slender distinction that persisted was the Opéra-Comique's willingness to mount the more experimental works. But little common ground is to be discovered between the realism of Bruneau's *Le rêve* (1891) and *L'attaque du moulin* (1893) and Charpentier's *Louise* (1900), the Wagnerian tumescence of d'Indy's *Fervaal* (1897) and the poetic impressionism and understatement of Debussy's *Pelléas et Mélisande* (1902), all given at the Opéra-Comique.

2. Grand Opera

The genre
The term 'grand opera' was used from early in the history of French opera to designate both the Paris Opéra (the Académie Royale de Musique – sometimes known by other names, such as 'Académie Nationale' and 'Académie Impériale') and the works performed there. Later it tended to be applied more narrowly to the most monumental works performed at the Opéra during its period of greatest magnificence. This, foreshadowed in 1826–7 by French adaptations of two of Rossini's Italian works, as *Le siège de Corinthe* and *Moïse*, began fully with Auber's *La muette de Portici* (1828; libretto by Scribe and Delavigne) and Rossini's *Guillaume Tell* (1829; Jouy, Bis and others, after Schiller), and reached its height in such works as Meyerbeer's *Robert le diable* (1831) and *Les Huguenots* (1836), Auber's *Gustave III* (1833) and Halévy's *La juive* (1835), all with librettos by Scribe (some in collaboration). These set a standard for the genre, which produced examples for several decades, usually to librettos by Scribe (until his death in 1861), notably Meyerbeer's *Le prophète* (1849) and *L'africaine* (1865), several works by Halévy, and others by Donizetti, Gounod and Verdi. Massenet's *Le roi de Lahore* (1877) was the last grand opera to have a great and widespread success. The fruits of the form were however considerable, even if they ripened in alien climates. Grand opera affected Italian opera and in particular, through Verdi's contacts with Paris, his *Aida* and even *Otello*. Although Wagner made grand opera a target of his polemics, its early influence on his work (most evident in the direct imitation of the genre in *Rienzi* and in the Paris version of *Tannhäuser*) was never completely expunged from it, although more or less transformed in the later music dramas. The noblest French opera of the century, Berlioz's *Les troyens* (1863), though never given at the

Opéra in his time (it had a chequered performance history and was not heard in complete form on a single evening until 1957), represents a union of the spirit of Gluckian *tragédie* with the expanded resources of grand opera. With only one opera, the exuberant *Benvenuto Cellini* (1838), behind him, Berlioz built *Les troyens* around the dual tragedies of Cassandra at Troy and Dido at Carthage: an epic work in which classical tragedy is imbued with a Romantic composer's warmth of feeling and passion – 'Virgil Shakespeareanized', he called it.

The grand opera libretto as developed by Scribe was of large proportions, in four or five acts, usually with a historical or quasi-historical background (European settings from the Middle Ages to the early 17th century were favoured), chosen to provide a succession of colourful scenes and the maximum scope for spectacle. It unfolded a drama of passionate human relationships impinged upon, most often with fatal results, by inexorable forces, usually involving the conflict of two peoples, religions or classes and having some relevance to contemporary conditions.

The grand opera might seem to differ most from earlier French opera in its emphasis on historical subjects. In the 18th century, theorists denied the opera libretto the dignity of the tragic genre; French opera was defined primarily as a sensuous, not an intellectual, entertainment, with the fabulous element stressed in order to place the action beyond the realistic and the verisimilar and so make the use of music seem more natural. Marmontel and others saw it as approaching more nearly the epic than the tragedy. Gluck's operas were thus a departure – however much they owed in other ways to older French opera – in playing down the *merveilleux* and moving the opera closer to the spoken tragedy. But the traditional nature of French opera soon reasserted itself. Towards the end of the 18th century, as subject matter taken from classical mythology and Christian epic became *passé*, some librettists turned to history. In the preface to Candeille's *Pizarre, ou La conquête de Pérou* (1785), its librettist C. P. Duplessis wrote:

> When I undertook to treat this subject, the musical stage offered only – in different forms – the unlikely adventures of the strange family of Agamemnon. I thought that history, having the merit of being interesting and able to provide effects as grand as those of mythology or fable, would be a diversion to the amusement of the public.

By the early 19th century tumultuous subjects – the more immediate to an audience who had witnessed the Revolution and its aftermath – were frequently used, but the traditional view of what constituted proper operatic matter continued to condition their treatment. In an *Essai sur l'opéra français* signed by Jouy (*c*1828), the most important French librettist of the period before Scribe (but probably written at least in part by Philarète Chasles), the proper concerns of the serious opera are said to be 'la fable, la féerie et l'histoire dans ce qu'elle a de plus héroïque'; history was admissible only when it approached the fabulous.

This attitude is still reflected in Scribe's librettos. Their larger-than-life approach to their subjects, both simplifying and magnifying them, was deliberate and traditional. Most grand operas lie in the realm of history, but so close to the borders of the supernatural, the allegorical and the exotic that they can slip across them with no sense of disruption, or lie mainly beyond them (like *Robert le diable* or *Le roi de Lahore*) with no discontinuity of genre. The grand opera sought to illuminate neither the historical forces it depicted, in the manner of a true historical drama, nor the psychology of its characters, in the manner of a tragedy. Its dramatic focus was the action of the one on the other, and both were kept simple to increase the impact.

The creation of grand opera
The Opéra had traditionally been the home of spectacle in the French theatre, but developments in the late 18th century had obscured its pre-eminence. With the end of the system of theatrical privilege after the Revolution, many small theatres arose in Paris unencumbered by tradition and avid for novelty. They explored new subject matter, particularly of a melodramatic sort, and new methods of staging it, using the panorama, the diorama and other new *spectacles d'optiques*.

Under the Empire the system of privilege returned. Napoleon tried to ensure the grandeur of the Opéra as a reflection of the grandeur of the state; for him this meant the Opéra's holding to a standard of classical decorum, which may have retarded its progress. Spectacle was emphasized: the triumphal procession became almost a cliché of operas of the Napoleonic period, while Spontini's *Fernand Cortez* (1809; libretto by Jouy and Esménard), as to some extent had his *La vestale* (1807), offered a series of spectacular tableaux that made it a forerunner of the grand opera. These two works were revered by Berlioz, whose essay on Spontini (1852) claims complete originality for the operatic style adopted in *La vestale* and thereafter. In one way Berlioz was right: Spontini's style had no single source. But neither did it proceed entirely from himself alone, although he may be considered an individualistic member of Gluck's school. The style of *La vestale* was a synthesis of French and Italian elements, as its contemporaries clearly saw, and Spontini can be regarded as one of that long succession of Italian émigrés who periodically revitalized French music with transfusions from the Italian. In this synthesis itself lay much of the reason for the success of *La vestale* and for the revolutionary impression that it made on its first audiences.

Olimpie (1819), his last *tragédie lyrique*, was revised (with the tragic ending removed) for its performance in Berlin (1821); its success there was great but short-lived, since it preceded *Der Freischütz* by only a month. During his years in Berlin Spontini produced such works as *Nurmahal* (1822) and *Alcidor* (1825), both of which suggest that he was attempting to compete with German Romantic opera; but they are closer to the traditional French *opéra-féerique*, a genre that was undergoing a new vogue in France at the time, again offering opportunities for spectacle.

But there were few great and lasting successes at the Opéra in the period between the Revolution and the 1820s, and by the early Restoration spectacle was regarded as shabby and old-fashioned; audiences looked elsewhere for up-to-date entertainment.

The production in 1822 of Isouard's *Aladin* (completed by Benincori) marked an important step towards change. This work introduced gas lighting to the Opéra, and was the first collaboration there of the scene painters Louis Daguerre and Pierre Ciceri, who began to apply the scenic techniques of the popular theatres and *spectacles d'optiques*. The arrival of Rossini worked a musical revolution by injecting his style into the serious French opera and by producing a company at the Opéra capable of singing works written in it. The process of change came to fulfilment with *La muette de Portici* (1828); this was Scribe's first libretto for the Opéra.

Famous for his clever construction of lighter works, Scribe applied this talent to his grandiose historical dramas for the Opéra, although their complex mechanism, with the great variety of elements – musical, scenic, dance and so on – that had to be provided for, strained even his ingenuity. Scribe's grand opera librettos are sometimes said to show the influence of the contemporary Romantic drama, particularly in their use of a wider range and variety of tone, incident and characterization than the old classical formulation allowed for; but Scribe had little use for the Romantics or they for him. What he brought new to the Opéra derived more directly from his background in the popular theatres. Hugo, in his manifesto of the Romantic drama, the preface to *Cromwell* (1827), advocated that the stage should make as complete as possible the illusion of reality in the depiction of historical settings and of local colour; but the principle had already been present in the popular theatres, the *spectacles d'optiques* and some of Scribe's own *opéras comiques*. It was to be of primary importance in the grand opera. Local colour was perhaps the greatest single attraction of *La muette de Portici*, with its vivid sets depicting the environs of Naples, supported by Auber's evocative music, with, as climax, the eruption of Vesuvius (a scene that had already figured at the diorama and elsewhere), and rounded off by a shower of stones as the curtain fell (see Plate 74). The Opéra was back in the forefront of Parisian theatrical developments, where it was to remain for several decades with technical innovations (with *Le prophète* in 1849, for example, it became the first Paris theatre to introduce both electric lighting and roller skates).

Although *La muette de Portici* was one of the most long-lived and successful grand operas, Auber remained more at home in *opéra comique*; and although Rossini's music for *Guillaume Tell* contains moments unequalled elsewhere in grand opera, the success of the first production was not complete or sustained, and both music and libretto were too classical in orientation to provide a model for the genre's further development. It was Meyerbeer who became Scribe's musical counterpart and his most successful collaborator. Meyerbeer was a cosmopolitan composer. His thorough German training gave him great technical freedom. He had assimilated the tradition of serious French opera: its exploration of orchestral sonority for dramatic purposes, its methods of organizing the drama into large musical structures that reinforced its effect, its ways of using the chorus both as an element of the background and of the action. From his long and successful experience of composing Italian operas he was able to continue the process, begun by Rossini, of introducing the latest developments of Italian opera into the French.

Meyerbeer has been criticized for the resulting eclecticism of his music, but the serious French opera was musically eclectic by tradition and seemed periodically to need the infusion of new blood from other sources. He also sometimes turned the stylistic diversity of his resources to dramatic ends, as in his use of Italian and French vocal styles as a way of differentiating the dramatic weight of characters. Thus the high soprano part usually represents the love object of the tenor, whom he regards with a purity of devotion that attenuates her to hardly more than a shadowy presence (the regal and remote Marguerite de Navarre in *Les Huguenots* varies the formula slightly). These rather uncharacterized parts tend towards Italianate, often ornamented, vocal writing and, in the early operas, Italianate forms of the cantabile–cabaletta type. The other female character is usually devoted to the tenor – with unrequited passion (Sélika in *L'africaine*), requited passion (Valentine in *Les Huguenots*), maternal love (Fidès in *Le prophète*) or the faithfulness of a servant (Alice in *Robert le diable*). These roles have a more direct part in the action, and their music is usually more energetic and declamatory in the French manner.

Meyerbeer's greatest musical-dramatic strength lay in characterization, including the characterization of local colour, of atmosphere, dramatic situations and conflicts. In this he was aided by his brilliant and innovatory treatment of orchestration and his talent for ensembles and the dramatic juxtaposition of contrasting musical elements. Meyerbeer seems to have influenced Scribe in making the secondary characters colourful, almost caricatured; a notable example, Marcel in *Les Huguenots*, was entirely reworked by him and his former Italian librettist, Gaetano Rossi, when Scribe refused to execute his wishes.

In time the grand opera, like other contemporary genres, moved away from conventionalized formal responses to standard dramatic situations, such as the Italianate stretta finale, and tended to replace large set forms with a more rapid and fragmentary flow of music, a move accompanied in Meyerbeer's case by an expansion of the harmonic vocabulary and elaboration of the recitative. His last opera, *L'africaine*, is musically his richest though, perhaps because of its 30 years' gestation, dramatically his least coherent.

A union of the arts

It had been a commonplace of 18th-century French opera aesthetics that the opera should be a spectacle to which all the arts – music, dance, painting, poetry, each supplied by the greatest artists – contributed as fully as possible; this was the positive counterweight to the denial of its intellectual content. The grand opera carried on this principle with its extended technical resources and its inclination to use them in tableaux designed to produce the maximum effect. A good example is the celebrated scene in *Robert le diable*, the Act 3 finale (see Plate 77), where the demon Bertram, attempting to capture his human son Robert for the side of evil, invokes the ghosts of a convent of nuns damned for their licentious lives (personified by the *corps de ballet*); by their dancing they seduce Robert into picking a bough from the grave of St Rosalie – a talisman conferring magic powers, though its theft brings damnation. (A later echo of this scene can be discerned in Act 2 of *Parsifal*.) The treatment exemplifies the grand opera's typical mixture of tradition and innovation, of the poetic and the bizarre, done with technical brilliance and great expense. Painted by Ciceri, who was famous for such effects, the scene was the gallery of the cloister by moonlight – modelled with typical concern for historical accuracy on an existing cloister, but also typically with changes of detail. The painter's moonlight effects were reinforced by a new subtlety in the gas lighting. 'The white phantoms of the nuns rise from their tombs under the pale rays of the moon, whose light filters through the arches of the cloister' (Allévy, 1938), to the accompaniment of *pianissimo* brass chords, soft gong strokes with double bass pizzicatos and a cello tremolo, and move to the front of the stage as two bassoons play a triplet passage of sepulchral and grotesque effect (a musical equivalent of the visual effect). There follows the usual ballet as the nuns bring out drinks and dice and, in ballet attire, dance a Bacchanale. Led by the abbess, they tempt Robert with drink, gambling and (successfully) love, whereupon thunder is heard, the nuns become spectres and triumphant demons arrive by means of *trappes anglaises*, another new technical improvement at the Opéra. It had long been an axiom of French opera theory that the ballets should be integrated into the action, and two earlier attempts at this are obvious models: Spontini's Bacchanale (1817) for Salieri's *Les Danaides* and the tempting of the knights in Gluck's *Armide*.

Véron, administrative head of the Opéra in the important years 1831–5, tried to analyse the genre's components in his memoirs (iii, 1854):

A five-act opera comes to life only with a very dramatic plot that brings into play the grand passions of the human heart together with strong historical interests; this dramatic action should, however, be capable of being taken in by the eyes alone, like that of a ballet; the chorus must play a passionate role . . . Each act should offer contrasts of setting, of costume and above all of dramatic situation.

Contrast was the central principle of grand opera dramaturgy. Scribe's return to the five-act format allowed for a sizable number of relatively concise scenes, and some scenes were justified solely on the grounds of contrast. Moynet (1873) described the effect in Act 4 of *Le prophète* when the first tableau, depicting a public square 'surrounded by monuments, houses and *praticables*', gave way to the interior of the cathedral for the coronation scene: 'At the change, a part of the flats on stage, instead of leaving their places, are transformed and become part of the cathedral' (this being effected partly by the unrolling of painted canvas); 'everything is done without noise or oscillation'. A few moments after the passionate duet of the previous scene had ended, the famous coronation march would burst forth, introducing a magnificent procession.

The grand opera's emphasis on great effects and contrasts naturally led audiences to expect ever greater ones; Meyerbeer wrote before the première of *Les Huguenots* of 'the public's incredible expectations of magnificence in the production and originality in the music'. This caused the makers of grand operas to be somewhat selfconscious seekers after novelty. The feeling that the grand opera strained after novelty and effect caused some critics to judge it adversely, particularly German ones who felt that works of art should develop only from inner necessity, a view since then widely accepted as an act of faith, although at the time there was a body of critical opinion equally large and serious that judged the grand opera to have raised the musical drama to a new level. As astute a critic as Abramo Basevi saw the path for the development of Italian opera as that of Meyerbeer, not Verdi.

The practical influence of grand opera was immense, and much of what was truly grand in it was absorbed by the stronger and more durable personalities of Wagner and Verdi. Within French opera the predomin-ance, and financial advantages, of the genre sometimes had harmful effects by forcing talents unsuited to its requirements to attempt it, notably Gounod. Serious French opera had its next great period of achievement only when Bizet, Massenet and others developed the possibilities of 'lesser' genres towards the end of the century; Bizet's *Carmen* was composed as an *opéra comique* (with spoken dialogue), and Massenet gave his all-sung opéras titles such as *drame lyrique*. The scale of such works is smaller than that of grand opera and the subject matter and style generally more personal and intimate, tragic love stories replacing the epics of grand opera's heyday.

3. Fusion

The second half of Gounod's operatic career serves to illustrate the confused situation of French opera after the middle of the 19th century. *Mireille* (1864), generically an *opéra dialogué*, expands in mid-stream from Provençal pastoral to rural tragedy; the transition, though not effortless, is on the whole well managed. *Roméo et Juliette* (1867), with the adolescent passions of Shakespeare's drama rubbed down by Barbier and Carré to alabaster smoothness, is more consistent than either *Mireille* or indeed *Faust* (1859), the work by which Gounod first made his name and which remains his most famous.

Faust has long toppled from its former unassailable position as the 'opera of operas', the one all properly educated young persons were expected to begin their opera-going with, performed in opera houses large and small the world over, loved, mocked, parodied, an object of revulsion to young composers like Debussy who regarded the enthronement of *Faust* at the Paris Opéra as a symbol of their frustrations. Now *Faust* has retreated far enough back from the forefront of the repertory to be considered calmly and objectively. One thing becomes immediately apparent, that it is a work of mixed, not to say ambivalent character, closely reflecting its composer's ambiguous nature, torn as he was between worldly if discreetly expressed sensuality and higher things, unable to achieve stylistic certainty. *Faust*, which was commonly regarded as typical 'grand opera', in fact started life at the Théâtre Lyrique as an *opéra comique* with spoken dialogues. Gounod added the recitatives and the big ballet for the Opéra in 1875. From then onwards the long popularity of *Faust* was established.

The additional weight was not all advantage. Towards the end of the score the structure threatens to turn at once flimsy and over-ambitious, with echoes of the world of Meyerbeer. Nowadays one or other of the later scenes is often omitted, usually the ballet (surprisingly enough, those debonair dances add a kind of stiffening). With the passage of time the contrast has grown sharper between the blatancy of such pages as the soldiers' chorus and Mephistopheles' 'Le veau d'or' and the scenes of delicate, intimate lyricism with their skilful setting of the words, especially in conversational exchanges, with the admirably handled to-ing and fro-ing of the two couples in the garden scene. Such things show the best aspect of *Faust*. They are not only very good but quite individual. Those who frown at Gounod's temerity in setting Goethe may not have noticed that their idol's tone in his great philosophical drama, above all in Part One, is not uniformly solemn. It is conceivable that *Faust* will never again become a repertory opera to be depended upon to fill the house even in a workaday performance. It appears now more as a singers' opera in the best sense, demanding and deserving scrupulous classical singing with reliable technique, faultless legato line and expressive diction.

During his stay in England (1870–74) Gounod worked at *Polyeucte* (after Corneille) and *George Dandin*, an attempt to set Molière's prose comedy. Unfortunately he persevered with the former (finally and unsuccessfully performed at the Opéra in 1878) and abandoned the latter. Possibly Molière's rustics need a Musorgsky rather than a Gounod, yet *Le médecin malgré lui* (1858), treated as an *opéra comique*, had brought out the best in Molière's compatriot. The ambiguous Gounod continued to oscillate between lyricism and grandiosity, as if drawings by Ingres or intimate landscapes by Corot could with impunity be blown up to the size of a large canvas by Delacroix or Géricault. Grandiosity won, but the hollowness of the victory was emphasized by the failure of Gounod's last (grand) opera, *Le tribut de Zamora* (1881).

(b)

(c)

19th-century singers: Adolphe
) as Masaniello in Auber's 'La
ortici' (engraving by Maleuvre);
attista Rubini as Arturo (b) and
mburini as Sir Richard Forth (c)
'I puritani' (lithograph by R. J.
A. E. Chalon); Rosine Stoltz (d)
e in Donizetti's 'La favorite'
by Charles Geoffroy); and (e)
the first London production of
'Don Pasquale' at Her Majesty's
June 1843, with (left to right)
Mario (Ernesto), Giulia Grisi
Luciano Fornasari (Melatesta)
Lablache (Don Pasquale)

(e)

57. *Interior view of La Scala, Milan, 1778 (from George Saunders, 'Treatise on Theatres', 1790): engraving by Cherbuin after Sidoli*

58. *Stage design by Alessandro Sanquirico for th[e] Milan performance of Rossini's 'Semiramide' ([Museo] Teatrale alla Scala, Milan)*

ontispiece from the first edition of the vocal score of
'Macbeth' (Milan: Ricordi, c1847)

60. Stage design by Giuseppe and Pietro Bertoja for Act 3
scene i (the encampment of Count Di Luna) from Verdi's 'Il
trovatore' as performed at La Fenice, Venice, 1853–4: pen
and ink drawing with wash (Museo Correr, Venice)

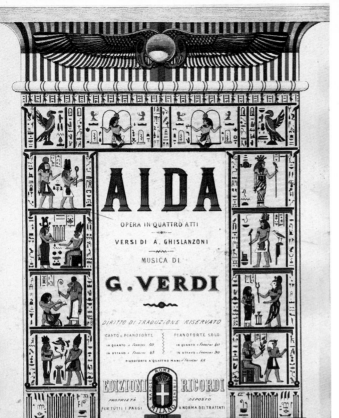

61. *Title-page of the first edition of the vocal score of Verdi's 'Aida', published by Ricordi in 1871*

62. *Teresa Stolz as Aida in the first Ita[lian per]formance of Verdi's opera*

63. *Libretto of 'Aida', Act 2 scene [1? Triumph Scene), with Verdi's annotatio[ns for] staging (Pierpont Morgan Library, Ne[w York)*

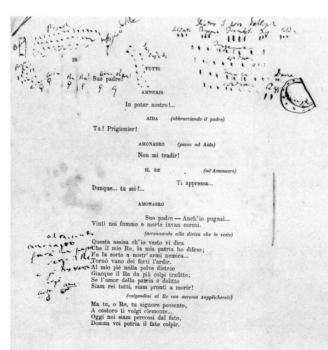

Teatro alla Scala, Milan, built by Piermarini: painting (1852) by Angelo Inganni in the Museo Teatrale alla Scala, ...n

Scene from Act 1 of the first production of Verdi's 'Otello' at La Scala, Milan, 1887: engraving from the Leipzig ...strirte Zeitung' (1887)

66. *Design by Karl Friedrich Schinkel for Act I of Spontini's 'Olimpie', first performed at the Paris Opéra on 22 D* *1819 (Bibliothèque et Musée de l'Opéra, Paris)*

67. *Stage design by Schinkel for Mozart's opera 'Die Zauberflöte' (Berlin, 1816): coloured aquatint (Institut für T.* *Film- und Fernsehwissenschaft, University of Cologne)*

68. *The Queen of Night, design by Simon Quaglio for Act 1 scene vi of Mozart's 'Die Zauberflöte', Munich, Hof- und Nationaltheater, 1818: pen, ink and watercolour*

69. *Stage design by Angelo Quaglio for Act 1 of Wagner's 'Tristan und Isolde', as first performed in Munich, 1865*

70

71

72

Scene from Marschner's opera 'Der Vampyr': engraving (1830) by I. Axmann after Heinrich Ramberg's drawing (from 'hea-Taschenbuch', Jg. 8, 1831)

Scene from Wagner's opera 'Die Walküre': drawing by K. Etwatt

Weber's 'Der Freischütz', the Wolf's Glen scene, as designed by Carl Wilhelm Holdermann for the Weimar production in coloured aquatint by C. Lieber, with figures by Carl August Schwerdgeburth

Wagner's 'Ring', the first production (Bayreuth, 1876): the theft of the Rhinegold in Joseph Hoffmann's painting stage design (above): the Rhinemaidens' trolley (below)

74

75

74. Auber's opera 'La muet[te] [de] Portici' (final scene of Act 5) [first] performed at the Paris Opéra [in] February 1828: engraving aft[er] stage design by Cambon and Th[ierry]

75. Title-page of the first edit[ion of] the vocal score of Rossini's 'G[uill]aume Tell' (Paris: Troup[enas,] 1829)

76. View of the Théâtre [de] l'Académie Royale de Mus[ique,] Paris (the Opéra), built by L[ebas] and opened in 1821: engraving [by] F. Thorigny (1865)

77. Meyerbeer's 'Robert le di[able',] first production (Paris, O[péra,] 1831), P.-L.-C. Cicéri's desig[n for] the Act 3 finale: lithograp[h by] Eugène Cicéri, P. Benoist [and] Bayot

78. Finale of Act 3 of Meyer[beer's] 'L'africaine', first performed [at the] Paris Opéra on 28 April [1865:] engraving from 'L'illustratio[n' (6] May 1865); the sinking of th[e ship] on stage caused a sensation

76

77

78

79. *Bizet's 'Carmen', scenes from the first production (Paris, Opéra-Comique, 1875): engraving by Burn Smeeton and P. Tilly after Lamy (from 'L'illustration', 13 March 1875)*

Poster for the first production of Gounod's 'Faust' in

J. Chéret's poster for the first production of Thomas' ignon' (1866)

82. *Poster by Orazi for Massanet's opera 'Thaïs'*

(a)

(b)

83. Musorgsky's 'Boris Godunov', first production at the Mariinsky Theatre, St Petersburg, 1874: scenes showing (a) the death of Boris: engraving, and (b) the inn near the Lithuanian border, Act 2 scene i: engraving by K. Veyrman after J. Negadayev's painting of the design by I. P. Andreyev (from 'Vsemirnaya illyustratsiya', 9 March 1874)

Růžena Maturová as Rusalka in the first performance
vořák's opera (Prague, 1901)

85. Nikolay and Medea Figner as Hermann and Liza in
the first production of Tchaikovsky's opera 'Pikovaya dama'
('The Queen of Spades'), 1890

The tsar's palace, design by V. M. Vasnetzov for Act 2 of Rimsky-Korsakov's 'Snegurochka' ('Snow Maiden'),
cow, Mamontov's private opera, 1885: pencil and watercolour

87. 19th-century singers: Giovanni Matteo Mario and Adelina Patti (a) in Gounod's 'Faust' at Covent Garden, London
Giuditta Pasta (b) in the title role of Donizetti's opera 'Anna Bolena' (lithograph by Louis-Pierre Henriquel-Dupont); L
Schnorr von Carolsfeld and his wife Malvina (c) as Tristan and Isolde in the first performance of Wagner's opera; and Nikol
Medea Figner (d) as Romeo and Juliet in Gounod's opera

Other composers were more adroit than Gounod at wringing the last drops of success out of an aging formula. Ferdinand Lemaire, Saint-Saëns's librettist for *Samson et Dalila* (1877, Weimar; 1890, Paris), reduced the Meyerbeerian scheme of five acts to three while keeping a reasonable amount of spectacle (and the ballet, carefully integrated) and giving more prominence to the motivation of character. Perhaps if *Samson* had reached Paris sooner, the general public would have been unprepared for it. In the event, when popularity finally came, fashionable opera-goers were swarming round late Wagner and the less popular, finer qualities of *Samson* were overlooked.

Massenet, after Meyerbeer, was the century's most skilful, persevering and successful composer of French opera, as central to the later period as Meyerbeer was to the earlier. Facility and an unfailing sense of the theatre earned him a wide popularity – also the scorn, not unmixed with envy, of more high-minded but less successful rivals. Like Saint-Saëns, he modified the inflated scale of Meyerbeerian grand opera (in *Le roi de Lahore*, 1877, *Hérodiade*, 1881, and *Le Cid*, 1885). Not even Massenet, however, could banish the shade of Meyerbeer for good: *Le roi de Lahore* has something of the perfumed texture of *L'africaine*; and in *Le Cid* Meyerbeerian turns of phrase flicker through the scenes of pageantry, although Meyerbeer would have been hard put to it to match Massenet's skill in setting Rodrigue's soliloquies. Massenet exploited the continuing popularity of exotic subjects in *Le roi de Lahore, Hérodiade, Esclarmonde* (1889) and *Thaïs* (1894). Already in the oratorio *Marie-Magdeleine* (1873, staged 1906) there appears a vein stigmatized by d'Indy as 'discreet and pseudo-religious eroticism', one aspect of the lightly expressed sensuality, part feline, part mawkish, recurring so often in French music that it may be taken for an ingredient of the national style. For displaying this vein so abundantly, Massenet has not been forgiven.

Massenet's most individual contribution, connected with the quality described above, lies in his feminine portraits. The most famous and most typical of these is the heroine of *Manon* (1894), a detailed study of an unheeding, self-centred, irresistible young girl set in a framework of brittle, artificial substance so artfully contrived that, with adroit use of melodrama and smooth interweaving of aria, ensemble and spoken dialogue, almost gives an illusion of through-composition while retaining the pace and sparkle of traditional *opéra comique*.

In *Werther* (1892), after Goethe, Massenet captured an atmosphere of provincial *gemütlichkeit* quite unlike the ambience of his boudoir exercises. In the admirable third act he taps the purest spring of elegiac French lyricism as it is found, for instance, in the closing scene of Gounod's *Sapho* (1851) and in many pages of Bizet. Gounod and Bizet, with Ambroise Thomas, were the most obvious sources of Massenet's style, their influence going deeper than that of Meyerbeer or Wagner. Massenet had a gift for setting conversational exchanges naturally to music; his solos combine melodic sweetness with sprays of cajoling chatter. Whereas Puccini's tunes are hummed by the public, snatches of Massenet are (at least by his compatriots) rarely attempted without the words, so inseparable have notes and text of such phrases as 'N'est-ce plus ma main' and 'Dis-moi que je suis belle' become.

He wrote often with specific singers in mind, taking care not to cover the voices. The alternation in the orchestra of helpfully transparent textures and passionate outbursts lends his scores a feverishness usually justified by the dramatic context. He was as frugal as a French housewife: themes and melodic tags are worked until the tightly stretched musical fabric threatens to crack, yet his theatrical instinct tells him when to stop. With the emergence towards the end of the century of the baritone Lucien Fugère, who was to create a number of leading Massenet roles, the balance shifted from the female voice to the baritone and bass.

As Meyerbeer's star slowly declined, Wagner's rose. The new luminary however was incompletely perceived through clouds of literary vapour. Until the century was well advanced the main Wagnerian influence on French opera composers remained the early operas up to *Lohengrin* (a more serious scandal than the *Tannhäuser* fiasco of 1861 was the delay in the production of *Lohengrin* in Paris until 1887 – it was not given at the Opéra until 1891). The more obvious, Meyerbeerian pages of the first two evenings of the *Ring* were the next stage. *Tristan*, the later evenings of the *Ring* and *Parsifal* waited longer. When their turn at length came they, especially *Parsifal*, bit deep. During the 1880s several French musicians including the composers Chabrier, Fauré, Duparc, d'Indy and Chausson journeyed to Bayreuth or Munich. Passages in Chabrier's *Gwendoline* (1886), whose text is a Wagnerian confection by Catulle Mendès, suggest that Chabrier had experienced *Tristan* at a deeper level than surface excitement, but they mingle with others of an early-Wagnerian cast. The full fruits of Wagner's influence were not to ripen before the turn of the century. After Franck, instrumental and symphonic music made great strides in France, and it was not necessarily on operatic trees that the first fruits were found.

Ironically, one opera which would seem to lie well inside the Wagnerian circle hardly does so. Reyer's *Sigurd* (1884, Brussels), was based by coincidence on some of the legends used in the *Ring* cycle, though drawn from different sources. *Sigurd* was begun much earlier – according to Adolphe Jullien the opera was considered as a possible successor to Verdi's *Don Carlos* at the Opéra nearly 20 years before. Reyer, an experienced critic as well as a composer, admired and supported Wagner up to a point, but his *Sigurd* (to say nothing of his *Salammbô*, 1890, Brussels) owes as much to the grand opera tradition, to Gluck and to Berlioz, of whose music Reyer was a loyal champion, as to Wagner.

Delays in the acceptance and production of operas in any significant way out of the common rut were frequent. Several French works now seen as representative were first given not in Paris but at the Monnaie in Brussels. Hence Paris production dates are an unreliable guide to the gradual fusion between grand opera and *opéra comique*. Yet the appearance as late as 1883 and 1888 of Delibes' *Lakmé* and Lalo's *Le roi d'Ys*, each with one foot in the innocent, fresh and tuneful world of earlier *opéra comique*, implies that the native tradition still offered resistance. The two works illustrate the diversity of 'romantic' opera. *Lakmé* represents the exotic strain perennial in French opera at more than one level. In *Le roi d'Ys* early Wagner (the overture quotes from *Tannhäuser*) mixes unselfconsciously with simpler, folklike strains with the homely but genuine appeal of Grétry or Boieldieu. Their belated appearance underlines the continuing prejudice in the period before Franck against instrumental and particularly 'symphonic' music. Writing of a revival of *Samson et Dalila* in 1903 and recalling the Weimar première of 1877, Fauré observed that in those days no Parisian theatre director would willingly accept an opera by a musician stigmatized as a 'symphonist'.

The question of spoken dialogue is closely connected with the fusion of grand opera and *opéra comique*. As it affected performance of French operas outside France (it was for the Vienna staging a few months after the Paris première that Guiraud provided the recitatives for *Carmen*), this was of more than local importance. While *opéra comique* struggled upwards in a world increasingly dominated by the through-composing Wagner, prejudice against spoken dialogue grew stronger. This was partly due to snobbery, partly to the growing popularity of operetta, which made respectable patrons of such theatres as the Opéra-Comique uneasy. Scribe in his day had written entertaining comic opera dialogue but his epigones had less practised hands. During the Second Empire, at least, operetta dialogue whether represented by the raffish topicality of Meilhac and Halévy or by the zany inconsequence of the scripts provided by various writers for Hervé, tended to be racier than *opéra comique* librettos even when, as occasionally happened, the authors were the same.

After the war of 1870 and the Commune the mood changed. The spirit of caricature in operetta was watered down to something hardly more dangerous than a *Punch* cartoon. This evolution would probably have taken place even without the political upheaval. The tendency is apparent in some pre-war works of Offenbach described as *opéras bouffes* but containing elements of *opéra comique*, for example *La Périchole* (1868) and *Les brigands* (1869). Traffic was two-way. *Carmen* surely owes some of its impact to Offenbach's light but telling touch with 'Spanish' colour not only in operettas with a specifically Spanish setting (e.g. *Les Bavards*) but in some where the flavour is used as an unexpected but spicy ingredient.

The expansion of Offenbach's style from operetta towards *opéra comique* and grand opera, already discernible before 1870, came to partial fruition in his last work, the 'opéra fantastique' *Les contes d'Hoffmann* (1881, Opéra-Comique). Earlier in his career when he was in charge of the music at the Odéon Theatre one of the plays given was *Les contes d'Hoffmann* by Jules Barbier and Michel Carré, based on the stories of E. T. A. Hoffmann, with the German poet as protagonist in his own tales. Offenbach realized that the piece had possibilities for an opera. Later, after Carré's death, Barbier made a libretto out of the play.

Offenbach's opera, not quite finished and only partly orchestrated at his death, is in five acts (or prologue, three acts and epilogue). Each of the central acts represents a fantastic Hoffmann tale in which the poet seeks his ideal beloved but loses her to the supernatural machinations of his evil genius, Councillor Lindorf. In the second act, the girl Olympia is revealed as a mechanical doll, smashed to pieces by an enemy of her inventor-father; in the third, set in Munich, the mortally sick Antonia, who longs to sing, is induced by magic means to do so, overstrains herself and dies; in the fourth, the Venetian courtesan Giulietta deserts Hoffmann for a worthless rival. The prologue and epilogue take place in the Nuremberg tavern where Hoffmann tells his tales and where in the end his real-life beloved, the opera singer Stella (of whom the others are to some extent projections), turns him down for Lindorf. The opera has thus three main settings, distinct in character and atmosphere but held together by a unifying theme; the three principal female roles (Stella is mimed) were written with a single soprano in mind, and the evil-genius roles for the same bass or bass-baritone. It has proved easier to find a bass-baritone to undertake the male roles than a soprano equally suited to the widely differentiated female ones.

The opera was intended for the Gaîté-Lyrique, where it was to be given with recitatives. When that project fell through, *Hoffmann* was accepted for the Opéra-Comique and drastically altered, with spoken dialogue (thus reversing the process that obtained for *Faust* and *Carmen*) and with the Giulietta (Venice) act omitted (though the scene of the Antonia act was switched from Munich to Venice to accommodate the famous Barcarolle, which Offenbach had borrowed from an earlier work); the Giulietta act was later restored, but placed before, not after, the Munich one. Offenbach died in 1880 when *Hoffmann* was in rehearsal; he was in the habit of using final rehearsals, even early performances, for last-minute revisions, ruthlessly tightening the action. His absence at this stage (coupled with theatre fires in Vienna and Paris which destroyed important material) meant that the opera never achieved a definitive form. Fortunately the melodic wealth and picturesque, often sinister atmosphere appeal strongly to the public, unconcerned with questions of what to put in or leave out (two numbers not in their present form entirely by Offenbach, the aria 'Scintille, diamant' and the wrongly-called Septet, are usually included).

Meanwhile, the striking invention and theatrical vigour of the best pages justify for conductors and producers (who should be very much concerned with decisions and choices) the trouble that needs to be taken. The familiar Choudens edition of 1907 is largely discredited. As the climax of research done since World War II, Fritz Oeser's critical edition of 1977 has collated rediscovered material without bringing *Hoffmann* noticeably nearer a final form.

A traditional element in French opera that Wagner's influence did not drive out was the ballet. Wagner himself, in his Paris *Tannhäuser*, supplied what is, with the 'Chasse royale et orage' in *Les troyens*, one of the finest dance scenes in 19th-century opera. Elsewhere the conventional divertissement escaped more or less unscathed. Some care was taken to give the ballet a degree of dramatic justification. In Gounod's *Cinq-Mars* (1877), at a scene in a 17th-century literary salon, dancers take part in a demonstration of Mlle de Scudéry's 'Carte de tendre'. But into his *Polyeucte* of the same period Gounod inserted a 'fête païenne' during which, against a background of Christian martyrdom, the goddess Venus dances a mazurka and a waltz. In *Henry VIII* (1883) and *Ascanio* (1890) Saint-Saëns wrote for his dancers pastiche of a kind now in some disrepute, although it is no more essentially disreputable than pastiche in architecture or the applied arts.

CHAPTER XVI

Russia and Eastern Europe

GEOFFREY NORRIS

Russia up to Glinka

When the writer and philosopher Prince Vladimir Odoyevsky (1804–69) commented that Glinka's *Ivan Susanin* (or *A Life for the Tsar*, 1836) had opened up 'the period of Russian music', his perceptive prophecy could well have applied to the other opera-producing countries in eastern Europe, to Smetana's *Prodaná nevěsta* ('The Bartered Bride') and Bohemian music or Moniuszko's *Halka* ('Helen') and Polish. This is not to say that these were the first operas to be written in their respective parts of eastern Europe, but that they are recognized as seminal works in a period when increasing national awareness was beginning to take a firm hold on Slavonic culture. They achieve a synthesis of national literature, dance, decorative arts and (to a certain degree) music which make them distinctive products of their own countries, and which generated schools of operatic activity that were increasingly imbued with unmistakable national characteristics.

During the 18th century, however, the opera repertory was dominated by Western, and particularly Italian, music in all three countries. In Russia, for example, the first opera ever performed was an Italian *commedia per musica*, Giovanni Ristori's *Calandro*, given in Moscow by the Italian touring company headed by Ristori's father Tomaso in 1731. Araia's *La forza dell'amore e dell'odio* was given at St Petersburg in 1736, the year after he had been appointed *maestro di cappella* to the Empress Anna (reigned 1730–40), thus paving the way for many other foreign musicians whose operas were written for and performed at the Russian court: Traetta, Paisiello, Sarti, Cimarosa and Martín y Soler. It was Araia who composed the first opera to a Russian text, *Tsefal i Prokris* ('Cephalus and Procris'; 1755, St Petersburg), with a libretto by Sumarokov, though the earliest opera actually written by a Russian is thought to be Zorin's *Pererozhdeniye* ('Rebirth'; 1777, Moscow). But it was Sokolovsky's comic opera *Mel'nik-koldun, obmanshchik i svat* ('The Miller-magician, Cheat and Matchmaker'; 1779, Moscow) which, though written in the manner of

Rousseau's *Le devin du village* (1752), marked the first tentative steps away from foreign influence, in that it deals with Russian peasant life and uses Russian folktunes (albeit squeezed into Western harmonizations) for many of its vocal numbers. Spoken dialogue is typical of this genre of opera, and was a feature adopted by such composers as Bortnyansky in *Le faucon* (1786, St Petersburg) and *Le fils-rival* (1787, Pavlovsk), French *opéras comiques* but also tinged with the musical colourings that Bortnyansky's music acquired during his years of study in Italy. Other composers, such as Matinsky, Pashkevich and Davïdov followed more closely in the tradition of Sokolovsky, though their treatment of Russian folksong was subject to prevailing attitudes: by forcing the modal tunes into conventional Western major-minor harmonies, they tended to be no more successful in conveying the spirit of Russian folk music than were contemporary folksong collectors.

Although none of these operas has the musical distinction to make them internationally significant, they can be seen as forerunners of the more emphatically, and more idiomatically, expressed nationalist sentiments evident in opera early in the 19th century. A start was made by the arrival in Russia of another Italian, Catterino Cavos, who quickly found his way into influential positions in the Russian opera establishment, composing, among other things, operas in a deliberately Russian vein, including *Ilya bogatïr* ('Ilya the bogatïr'; 1807, St Petersburg) and the two-act *Ivan Susanin* (composed 1815; performed 1822, Moscow). This latter, written in the wake of the patriotic sentiments engendered by the Napoleonic wars, is based on the same 17th-century heroic incident as Glinka's opera, though the two works have different endings: Cavos's Susanin is rescued by the Russian army from the Poles he has cunningly deceived, while Glinka's is killed by the Poles and thus gives his life for the tsar – so inspiring Nicholas I to suggest the alternative title by which the opera is often known.

Glinka, in common with most of his Russian predecessors, was a dilettante, largely self-taught musician. But his two completed operas, *Ivan Susanin* (1836, St Petersburg) and *Ruslan and Lyudmila* (1842, St Petersburg), display a more sensitive, colourful treatment of folk material and a gift for translucent orchestration lacking in earlier Russian music, combined with certain melodic traits of the Italian *bel canto* tradition and a debt to French opera in the large choral scenes and dance sequences. His influence was such that Tchaikovsky was later to dub him the 'acorn' from which grew the 'oak' of Russian music. The historical and heroic elements of *Ivan Susanin* were indeed taken up, for example, by Borodin in *Prince Igor* (1890, St Petersburg), just as Glinka's treatment of fantasy and comedy in *Ruslan and Lyudmila* were developed, above all, by Rimsky-Korsakov in *Skazka o Tsare Saltane* ('The Tale of Tsar Saltan'; 1900, Moscow), *Skazaniye o nevidimom grade Kitezhe* ('The Legend of the Invisible City of Kitezh'; 1907, St Petersburg) and *Zolotoy petushok* ('The Golden Cockerel'; 1909, Moscow).

Bohemian and other nationalists

While Glinka was producing operas with a distinctive Russian stamp, nationalist schools began to emerge in other east European countries. In Hungary, for example, although the earliest known opera is Ruzitska's *Béla futása* ('Béla's Flight'; 1822, Kolozsvár), it was in such operas as Erkel's *Bátori Mária* (1840), *Hunyady László* (1844) and *Bánk bán* (1861) that an individual Hungarian folklore idiom was more firmly established. *Bánk bán*, his most popular work, is infused with traits of Hungarian *verbunkos* music. As elsewhere in Europe, some Hungarian composers, notably Mihalovich, Zichy and Dohnányi, looked to Germany for their operatic models, but the tradition established by Erkel was maintained by such composers as András Bartay, who wrote the first Hungarian comic opera, *Csel* ('The Trick', 1839), Mosonyi and Hubay. Similar nationalist trends can be observed in Croatia and, a little later on in the 19th century, in Bulgaria; and in the early 20th century opera schools began to emerge in Lithuania, Latvia, Georgia, Armenia, the Ukraine and other areas that now constitute republics of the Soviet Union.

But during the 19th century it was in Bohemia that, second only to Russia, the most colourful and significant nationalist school emerged. Just as it was a major political victory (Napoleon's defeat in 1812) that spurred Russian composers to consolidate a national musical idiom, so it was Italy's defeat of Austria in 1859 and the consequent release of Bohemia from Austrian domination that stimulated Bohemian national awareness. As in Russia, the opera repertory of 18th-century Bohemia had consisted primarily of Italian works, though German ones were given increasingly from 1790; the Estates Theatre in Prague became the home of German opera in 1807. What was in effect the first opera to a Czech text was František Škroup's *Drátenik* ('The Tinker'; 1826, Prague), which makes use of spoken dialogue and interpolated folktune numbers and even includes the new national anthem that Škroup had composed. After the events of 1859 Bohemian culture began to develop more rapidly. The long-felt need for a theatre for Czech opera and drama was realized in 1862 with the opening of the Provisional Theatre in Prague, where Skuherský's *Vladimir, bohů zvolenec* ('Vladimir, the gods' chosen one'), originally written to a German text as *Der Apostat*, was given in a Czech translation in 1863.

Even more important to the history of Czech music was the appointment of Smetana as principal conductor of the Provisional Theatre, a post he held from 1866 to 1874. During his term of office he encouraged the production of new Czech works and strove to improve the balance between the French, German and Italian repertories. His own *Braniboři v Čechách* ('The Brandenburgers in Bohemia'), a reflection of patriotic sentiment, was given in Prague in 1866, but in the same year he achieved a much more lasting success with his vivid folk opera *Prodaná nevěsta* ('The Bartered Bride'), which came to hold a similar seminal position in Czech opera as did Glinka's *Ivan Susanin* in Russian. This work, however, was composed as an interlude, for his chief objective was to write stage works on heroic and epic themes, of which *Dalibor* (1868) and *Libuše* (written 1869–72 and eventually given at the opening of the National Theatre in 1881) were the products. *Dalibor*, on a legendary theme set in the 15th century, has revolutionary undertones in its treatment of a heroic figure who defies authority; Smetana was accused of embracing Wagnerian methods, although his use of thematic transformation of allusive motifs is in fact more akin to the methods of Liszt. *Libuše*, a festival piece and an apotheosis of the Czech nation (it tells of the events surrounding the foundation of the Bohemian dynasty), goes further towards Wagnerian methods with its declamatory writing and its more complex use of associative themes. Quite a different aspect of the Czech spirit is embodied in *The Bartered Bride*, with its picture of village life, using rhythms from Czech folksong and national dances (polka, furiant, *skočna*), with sharp contrasts of mood, colour and dynamics: the result has a naturalness and spontaneity that have ensured its enduring appeal – and, unlike that of Smetana's other operas, beyond the borders of his own country. His later operas, which include *Dvě vdovy* ('The Two Widows', 1874), *Hubička* ('The Kiss', 1876) and *Tajemství* ('The Secret', 1878), also treat aspects of Czech life and show him extending his expressive technique in various ways though without the inventive vitality of his best earlier work.

Smetana was not the only Czech composer to have brought the Czech national heritage into the opera house, though he was publicly the most successful. One other was Karel Šebor (1843–1903), whose *Templáři a Moravě* ('The Templars in Moravia', 1865) and *Husitská nevěsta* ('The Hussite Bride', 1868) in some respects anticipated Smetana's work. The most prominent of those who continued these developments, however, was Dvořák, composer of 13 operas, notably in *Šelma sedlák* ('The Cunning Peasant', 1878), *Čert a Káča* ('The Devil and Kate', 1899) and his fairy-tale opera *Rusalka* (1901); and, also like Smetana, he tackled historical subjects, notably in *Dimitrij* (1882), in a sense a sequel to *Boris Godunov* in tracing the life of the Pretender to the Russian throne after Godunov's death (though Dvořák did not know Musorgsky's opera). Dvořák's dramatic gift was limited, and the most successful of his operas has always been *Rusalka*, the plot of which gives scope for the lyricism and nature poetry that came naturally to him; and its fairy-tale characters such as water-sprites and witches drew more telling music from him than most of his real-life characters. Wagner's influence, in harmony and orchestration as well as the use of leitmotifs, is increasingly marked in his later operas.

Fibich followed in the line of Smetana and Dvořák, for example in *Šárka* (1897), but in such works as *Nevěsta mesinská* ('The Bride of Messina', 1884) he showed an affinity not so much with any folk music idiom as with Wagnerian operatic principles. This further development in Czech opera, absorbed by Fibich into a style of some distinction, places him among the most important operatic composers in his country before Janáček, who raised Czech opera to an altogether more forcefully dramatic and inventive level (see Chapter XXV).

While both Russia and Bohemia show the effects that political events can have on music, this is nowhere more clear than in Poland, which during the 19th century and the early 20th was constantly under pressure from surrounding nations. This extended to the arts, so that the country found it difficult to form any firmly based or continuously evolving operatic tradition. Towards the end of the 18th century Polish culture was enhanced by an artistically aware ruler, Stanisław August Poniatowski, Poland's last king. There is an interesting parallel here between Poland and Russia, for the Empress Catherine II (reigned 1762–96) patronized the arts to an unprecedented degree and, though not by nature a gifted musician, none the less encouraged the performance of instrumental music and the development of opera, making her own contribution by building theatres and even writing opera librettos which were set by the most prominent of the Russian composers of the time and by some of the foreign visitors to the court. In Poland, as in Russia, Italian works proliferated in the operatic repertory in the 18th century, for the Polish court was long linked to the Italianate Saxon one at Dresden; but in 1778 the first Polish opera, Kamieński's *Nędza uszczęśliwiona* ('Misery made Happy') was given at Warsaw, to be followed the next year by two more of his operas, *Zośka* ('Sophia') and *Prostota cnotliwa* ('Virtuous Simplicity'), both now lost. The actor Wojciech Bogusławski translated many foreign texts into Polish and also wrote the libretto for the first important opera dealing with Polish peasant life, Jan Stefani's *Cud mniemany czyli Krakowiacy i Górale* ('The Supposed Miracle, or Krakovians and Highlanders'; 1794, Warsaw). At this time, though, the most consistently successful native composers, both central in the musical life of Warsaw, were Elsner, with *Król Łokietek* ('King Łokietek', 1818) and *Mieszkańcy wyspy Kamkatal* ('The People of Kamkatal', 1807), and Kurpiński, with *Jadwiga, Królowa Polska* ('Jadwiga, Queen of Poland', 1814), *Zabobon* ('Superstition', 1816) and *Zamek na Czorsztynie* ('The Castle of Czorsztyn', 1819).

The further partition of Poland in the early 19th century had a disastrous effect on the development of Polish opera, and it was not until 1848 that Moniuszko produced his *Halka* ('Helen'), at a concert performance in Vilnius (staged 1858, Warsaw); it is now universally regarded as the first important Polish opera and one which, though musically owing much to early Verdi and shot through with traits of other contemporary Italian composers, none the less exudes a local atmosphere both in the occasional recourse to folksong in its vocal numbers and dances and in the setting, a mountain region in the southern part of Poland during the late 18th century. Moniuszko also composed *Hrabina* ('The Countess', 1860) and the four-act comedy of manners *Straszny dwór* ('The Haunted Manor', 1865), one of the first operas to be produced at the Grand Theatre in Warsaw after the revolt against the Russian Tsar Alexander II (1863). But despite the spur he gave to Polish opera, it languished again until the threads of nationalist music were taken up later in the 19th century by Żeleński and in the 20th by Różycki and Szymanowski.

Tchaikovsky and the Five

In Russia, though, operatic ideas continued to be explored earnestly throughout the 19th century, a period which brought Russian opera firmly on to the international stage in the works of Tchaikovsky, Musorgsky, Rimsky-Korsakov and Borodin. Tchaikovsky's enthusiasm for opera was first fired by Mozart's *Don Giovanni* and further coloured by Bizet's *Carmen*; he covered a broad range of subjects in his own operas which, at their best, display an intensity of emotion unparalleled in 19th-century Russian opera. He comes closest to the post-Glinka, 'nationalist' operas represented by Borodin's *Prince Igor* (1890, St Petersburg) and the majority of Rimsky-Korsakov's legend-based works in his *Kuznets Vakula* ('Vakula the Smith'; 1876, St Petersburg), derived from the same Gogol story as Rimsky-Korsakov's *Noch' pered Rozhdestvom* ('Christmas Eve'; 1895, St Petersburg). After a 'triumphant failure' of a first night, Tchaikovsky bemoaned the opera's dense orchestration and the 'meagre' effectiveness of the vocal writing. He found it overloaded with detail and generally unoperatic, lacking 'breadth and sweep', and he revised it in 1885 as *Cherevichki* ('The Slippers', better known in the West as 'Les caprices d'Oxane'), making substantial alterations but retaining the lively Ukrainian atmosphere, evoked musically through the use of folksong and the fairly frequent recourse to the distinctive *hopak*, which sets it decisively in the context of his Second Symphony (the 'Little Russian', 1872) and the incidental music to Ostrovsky's play *Snegurochka* ('The Snow Maiden'; 1873, Moscow). But for all its spirit and dramatic life, the opera is marred by its thin characterization, something that also tends to lessen the impact of such operas as *Orleanskaya deva* ('The Maid of Orleans'; 1881, St Petersburg), *Mazeppa* (1884, Moscow) and *Charodeyka* ('The Sorceress'; 1887, St Petersburg).

But when the facets of a particular character touched a sympathetic chord in Tchaikovsky's own personality he was able to respond with works of such perception as *Eugene Onegin* (1879, Moscow) and *Pikovaya dama* ('The Queen of Spades'; 1890, St Petersburg). In each, Tchaikovsky was able to focus on central figures with whom he could identify from his own experience: Tatyana in *Eugene Onegin*, Hermann in *The Queen of Spades*. In the latter, significantly written between the last two 'Fate' symphonies (the Fifth and Sixth), Hermann's obsession with the fateful (and fatal) power of the three cards similarly enabled him to make a vivid dramatic study of a character crumbling in the face of inexorable forces. In *Eugene Onegin*, Tatyana's unrequited passion for Onegin took on special relevance in the light of Tchaikovsky's experience at the time of his disastrous marriage. Her agitated monologue as she pours out her feelings in a letter is Tchaikovsky's finest operatic scene; and the presentation in the opera of personal passion against backgrounds first of domestic contentment (in the folk-singing at the Larin home) and later of lighthearted or more formal dancing at the Larin and Gremin parties – offering opportunity too for Tchaikovsky's balletic inclinations – has a certain irony, powerfully caught in Tchaikovsky's tautly organized score with its recurrent, four-note motif, capable of assuming a variety of emotional implications in different harmonic or orchestral contexts.

The openness and spontaneity, the depth of feeling and emotional immediacy which Tchaikovsky could bring to such subjects put him inevitably at odds with the notions of 'musical realism' which Dargomïzhsky, in common with such Realist philosophers of the day as Belinsky and Chernïshevsky, was exploring in his music, both in his solo vocal works and his operas. Having already written two full-scale operas – the French-inspired *Esmeralda* (1847, Moscow) and the folky *Rusalka* (1856, St Petersburg) – Dargomïzhsky charted a new course in Russian opera when he conceived the idea in the 1860s of setting more or less word for word one of Pushkin's 'little tragedies', *Kamennïy gost'* ('The Stone Guest'). For this he extended the principle he had been applying to his solo songs of echoing in the contours of the vocal lines the natural inflections of the Russian language: he wanted 'the note to express the word', as did Cui who, around the same time, was advocating the rejection of operatic vocal display in favour of allowing 'each note to reinforce the meaning of the text'. (The piano score of *The Stone Guest* was completed by Cui at Dargomïzhsky's request; orchestrated by Rimsky-Korsakov, it had its première in St Petersburg in 1872.) Since Tchaikovsky's own operatic instincts were at their most acute when he could explore and project in dramatic terms the inner thoughts and emotions of his characters, heightened not through a rigorous adherence to spoken Russian but through a sensitivity to words allied to his own highly individual musical inspiration, it is scarcely surprising that he regarded Dargomïzhsky's notion of expressing 'truth' in music as utterly false. Indeed, in *The Stone Guest* Dargomïzhsky's species of continuous recitative does fail to produce much more than a stubbornly monochrome opera, dogged as it is by weak characterization, a loose construction and a routine treatment of dramatic situation. But his pioneering principle was to have a potent influence on later Russian opera. Some composers even went so far as to follow his lead in setting Pushkin literally: Rimsky-Korsakov in *Motsart i Sal'yeri* ('Mozart and Salieri'; 1898, Moscow), Cui in *Pir vo vremya chumï* ('A Feast in Time of Plague'; 1906, Moscow) and Rakhmaninov in *Skupoy rïtsar'* ('The Miserly Knight'; 1906, Moscow); but none convincingly solves the problem of translating one art form into another, of conveying poetry to be read from the page as opera to be appreciated in the theatre.

Other composers, however, adopted the principle of musical realism as part of their own operatic techniques, Cui's *William Ratcliff* (1869, St Petersburg) and Rimsky-Korsakov's *Pskovityanka* ('The Maid of Pskov'; 1873, St Petersburg, revised 1895) combining declamatory traits with more lyrically melodic writing. This blend was further perfected in Musorgsky's *Boris Godunov*. It was composed in 1868–9, rewritten and then revised before its St Petersburg première in 1874; its spare, even harsh orchestration has drawn arrangements from Rimsky-Korsakov and Shostakovich, but the original is now increasingly preferred. Like Dargomïzhsky, Musorgsky had been working on the expressive possibilities of a declamatory, musically realistic vocal style in his solo songs of the late 1860s, at the same time attempting to find 'an artistic reproduction of human speech in all its finest shadings' in a musical setting of Gogol's prose comedy *Zhenit'ba* ('The Marriage'). Although only the first act was completed (1868), despite its comic astuteness, it serves to highlight the limitations of the technique so far as dramatic representation was concerned. Yet Musorgsky was to find an ideal balance between continuous recitative and the kind of melodic lyricism he explored more fully in the later *Khovanshchina* (1886), also treating a conflict, personal, political and religious, from Russian history, when he composed *Boris Godunov*: in its historical subject, its psychological perception of the decline of Boris's mental faculty, its identification of the haunted Tsar with the sufferings of the Russian people, its vivid portrayal – using such symbols as the traditional idiot, the clang of bells and the old church modes – of the very atmosphere of Russian life, this opera arguably stands at the peak of 'the period of Russian music' heralded by Prince Odoyevsky some 40 years earlier.

CHAPTER XVII

Britain

NICHOLAS TEMPERLEY

In the early 19th century, as in the 18th, opera was patronized by only a small fraction of the British population. The Italian opera house in London was exclusively aristocratic; and the theatres that produced various kinds of English-language musical theatre were places of questionable repute, avoided by most respectable women and by men of religious conviction. By 1900 the public for opera had been enormously increased, by greater general affluence, by the weakening of barriers between the nobility and the middle class, and by a turning away from the sterner religious creeds of earlier times. London was ready to become one of the great world capitals of opera. Even the provinces, which, with the exception of Dublin, had played a subordinate role, were beginning to raise some significant operatic centres. But throughout the century the English never ceased to regard opera as essentially a foreign product. Until the vogue for Gilbert and Sullivan, most sections of the opera public favoured works that were either wholly foreign, or had continental music adapted to an English text, or at the very least, had a plot with a foreign setting. Against that predominant trend, nationalist opera gradually made headway.

Italian opera continued, through most of the 19th century, to command immense prestige in England, and it was the only kind that attracted large-scale royal and aristocratic support. The King's Theatre, Haymarket, which became Her Majesty's in 1837, enjoyed a legal monopoly in the production of Italian operas until the Theatre Regulation Act of 1843. The Royal Italian Opera House, Covent Garden, was opened in 1847, and for many years there were two rival Italian houses: when Her Majesty's burnt down in 1867, the manager, J. H. Mapleson, moved his company to Drury Lane, but it returned to Her Majesty's in 1877 and continued there until its demise in 1887. At Covent Garden the word 'Italian' was dropped from the name of the Royal Opera House only in 1892.

Until the 1880s 'opera' and 'Italian opera' were virtually synonymous in fashionable circles, and a series of operas in Italian was seen as an essential part of the London season. London generally received the most notable successes within a year or two of their premières on the Continent. There was a strict monopoly of language, so that operas in German, French and Russian by such composers as Mozart, Weber, Rossini, Bizet, Wagner and Glinka had to be translated into Italian before they could be performed. Few important premières of Italian operas took place in London: some significant examples are Winter's *La grotta di Calipso* (1803) and *Il ratto di Proserpina* (1804), Balfe's *Falstaff* (1838) and Verdi's *I masnadieri* (1847).

Seasons of opera in German were occasionally given by German companies on tour from 1829 onwards, but it was not until 1882, when the *Ring* cycle, *Die Meistersinger* and *Tristan und Isolde* were given in the original language, that German began to challenge the linguistic hegemony of Italian. Opera in French had a similar history, but the 1860s and 70s witnessed an enormous vogue for French operetta: many of Offenbach's and Lecocq's pieces were given simultaneously at several London theatres, both in French and in different English versions.

Opera in English, including translations, occupied a distinctly lower position in social prestige. The two major theatres in the first part of the century, Covent Garden and Drury Lane, mixed various types of musico-dramatic entertainment into their seasons of spoken drama (in which they too enjoyed a monopoly); the minor theatres, which until 1843 were in effect compelled by law to include some music in every dramatic entertainment they offered, occasionally produced something deserving the name of opera. At various times efforts were made to promote a tradition of English opera: the most important of these were the English Opera, at the Lyceum Theatre (1834–41); the Pyne-Harrison company and its successor, the Royal English Opera (1856–64); the Carl Rosa touring company (founded 1875); and, of course, Richard D'Oyly Carte's collaboration with Gilbert and Sullivan (also beginning in 1875).

In the first three decades of the century, the dominant composer of English opera was Henry Bishop, supported at some distance by a dozen other prolific composers, including Michael Kelly and Charles Edward Horn. Of more than 125 dramatic works for which Bishop provided music, only about 30 can be classified as 'operas' by the definition (founded on the general, though not entirely consistent, usage of the time: see Carr, 1974) that requires the principal roles to have been written for singers. Pieces such as melodramas and burlettas were spoken plays with music, and any singing was done by subordinate characters; a 'musical drama' was somewhere between an opera and a burletta. Even operas were not through-composed, but consisted of musical numbers alternating with spoken dialogue: hence the Savoy operas of the late Victorian period were part of a long established English tradition. Bishop's operas have an overture in several movements; a number of popular airs, ballads and duets, in strophic or simple rondo form; one or two glees or even occasionally a 'madrigal'; a few choruses; and perhaps two or three elaborate scenas for the main singers, with recitative, cavatina and cabaletta. Some 'operas' were merely afterpieces in one act. Only the more ambitious attempted dramatic finales in which the music and the plot advanced simultaneously.

A fair proportion of operas by Bishop and his contemporaries were adapted from continental works, which often had to be considerably altered to bring them within the conventions of English opera. Bishop brought out a version of Boieldieu's *Jean de Paris* as *John of Paris* in 1814, after he had already used parts of the music in *The Aethiop* (1812) and *Haroun al Raschid* (1813). Later he produced *The Libertine* (1817, after *Don Giovanni*), *The Barber of Seville* (1818), *The Marriage of Figaro* (1819), *Der Freischütz* (1824) and *La sonnambula* (1833), in each case with large-scale cuts and interpolations which, however unacceptable to modern tastes, were not unskilful for their purpose. Of Bishop's original operas the most important are *The Maniac* (1810), *The Heart of Midlothian* (1819), *Clari* (1823), *Cortez* (1823) and *Aladdin* (1826). He was an able writer of descriptive music and glees, but his fame naturally rested chiefly on his airs, above all 'Home, sweet home' from *Clari*.

A new phase began with the Romantic operas of Barnett, Loder and Balfe. A precursor was Weber's *Oberon* (1826), written for Covent Garden. Its libretto by J. R. Planché displayed the typical inadequacies of English dramatic writing of the age, but it was transformed by the richness and intensity of the musical score. When in 1834 S. J. Arnold reopened the English Opera House at the Lyceum Theatre, offering a new opportunity to English composers of serious opera, some talented composers came forward. The pioneering works were Loder's *Nourjahad* and Barnett's *The Mountain Sylph* (both 1834). They were followed the next year by Balfe's *The Siege of Rochelle*, at Drury Lane. The success of these operas encouraged the substantial development of English Romantic opera during the next 30 years.

Typically, English Romantic operas were adaptations of French or German plays, operas or ballets whose plots were already familiar to the public. They were set in the age of chivalry, or in some half-magical world of the imagination, and explored exaggerated displays of heroism, love, jealousy and honour. The poetry, by such hacks as Alfred Bunn and Edward Fitzball, was couched in 'Wardour-Street English' of the most banal description. Nevertheless, the music is often passionate and occasionally inventive, though it tends to be episodic: spoken dialogue remained a feature. But concerted movements played a much bigger part than before, and in particular the first-act finale was often an extended sequence of movements that brought dramatic tension to a considerable height. The musical idiom was primarily based on Rossini and Weber, with Meyerbeer as a later influence; some English elements remained, notably the strophic ballad and the glee or madrigal.

The most successful composer of this Romantic school was Balfe, who produced a long series of operas spanning the whole period; above all, *The*

Bohemian Girl (1843) remained on the boards for nearly a century. His pre-eminent position can be attributed to his power of writing a good song: he was indeed a singer himself. Another Anglo-Irish composer, Vincent Wallace, had a very different background. He had made his name as a pianist and violinist, and had travelled the world before his enormously popular first opera, *Maritana*, was performed in London in 1845. The Latin-American scales and rhythms Wallace had picked up on his travels are clearly audible. In their later works Balfe and Wallace developed a bigger choral and orchestral sound along the lines of Meyerbeer, but they remained faithful to the English ballad. Loder's greatest success was *The Night Dancers* (1846), which like *The Mountain Sylph* continued the fairy tradition of *Oberon*; but his most important work, first performed at Manchester in 1855, was *Raymond and Agnes*, the one early Victorian opera with enough cumulative power to sweep a modern audience out of its disbelief.

Somewhat outside the general run of opera composers was the learned George Macfarren, trained at the Royal Academy of Music, who eschewed modern continental influence and sentimentality, resolutely chose English stories for his themes, and modelled his style on Mozart, with an occasional touch of folksong. *King Charles II* (1849) and *Robin Hood* (1860) are his most representative works. The nationalist approach was even more successful in *The Lily of Killarney* (1862), a late effort of the German-born Julius Benedict, who had been a pupil of Weber and had composed for Italian stages in the 1820s and 1830s. Based on Dion Boucicault's *Colleen Bawn*, it can well be called the first Irish opera, though it nationalism is without political overtones – they would not have got past the Lord Chamberlain, who exercised a strict censorship on all theatrical productions throughout the century.

The Lily of Killarney was one of the triumphs of the short-lived Royal English Opera run by Louisa Pyne and William Harrison. The Romantic school continued in the later Victorian period with such works as Cowen's *Pauline* (1876), Arthur Goring Thomas's *Esmeralda* (1833), Sullivan's *Ivanhoe* (1891), McCunn's *Jeanie Deans* (1894, Edinburgh) and Stanford's *Shamus O'Brien* (1896). The tendency now was to write a through-composed or nearly through-composed score complete with accompanied recitatives, and to aim high in the imitation of Gounod, Verdi or even Wagner. *Ivanhoe*, with no spoken dialogue, was a particularly ambitious score, but the Royal English Opera that was formed around it disappeared after one season. *Shamus O'Brien* continued Benedict's vein of Irish nationalism, and this time with greater knowledge: Stanford had made a careful study of Irish traditional melodies. In *Jeanie Deans*, Scottish nationalism made its operatic début.

The one enduring group of English operas from the 19th century is the set of 13 collaborations between Gilbert and Sullivan, ranging from *Trial by Jury* (1875) to *The Grand Duke* (1896). They are often known loosely as the 'Savoy Operas' because, beginning with *Iolanthe* (1882), most of them received their premières at the Savoy Theatre, London. It is generally agreed that the unprecedented success and staying power of these works is due to the complementary natures of the two geniuses who created them: Gilbert's cold logic, biting wit and verbal acrobatics; Sullivan's intuitive flair, warm lyricism and underlying earnestness.

The Savoy Operas were products of the native English tradition. All except the one-act *Trial by Jury* retain spoken dialogue, in which Gilbert's immense superiority to his predecessors is revealed. To this is added Sullivan's technical brilliance, founded on a thorough German training that his rivals could not equal, and incorporating the influences of Mendelssohn and Schubert. Finally, there were elements from French operetta – the patter song, the question-and-answer dialogues between singer and chorus, the limpid melodies over repeated chords and the brilliant 'medley' overtures with an interpolated *andante* before the main sonata-form movement

Both Gilbert and Sullivan were separately supported early in their dramatic careers by the entertainments initiated by Thomas and Priscilla German Reed at the Gallery of Illustration, Regent Street. These semi-theatrical productions virtually created a new public by providing respectable and innocuous pleasure in a building free of the disreputable associations of the theatre. Gilbert and Sullivan from the start continued this policy by publicly setting themselves against the *risqué* humour of burlesque and French operetta. The Savoy Operas broadened the possible range of subject matter for light opera. They appealed to sophisticated tastes by satirizing English institutions and customs (*Iolanthe*; *Ruddigore*, 1887) or exploring topical issues such as feminism (*Princess Ida*, 1884), the merit system in public appointments (*H.M.S. Pinafore*, 1878) and the aesthetic movement (*Patience*, 1881). This was Gilbert's achievement; Sullivan's was to supply the genuine feeling that Gilbert conspicuously avoided, and to exert his formidable talents to satisfy audiences for whom many emotional outlets were barred by social custom. The masterpieces of the series, *H.M.S. Pinafore*, *The Pirates of Penzance* (1879), *Iolanthe*, *The Mikado* (1885), *The Yeomen of the Guard* (1888) and *The Gondoliers* (1889), have never failed to delight Anglo-Saxon audiences from late Victorian times to the present.

CHAPTER XVIII

Iberia and Scandinavia

LIONEL SALTER, JOHN HORTON

1. Spain and Portugal

By the first decade of the 19th century the Spanish *tonadilla* had lost its freshness and was in decline. The treatment of its subjects, once natural and unpretentious, was turning towards allegory, and a moralizing tone was creeping into its texts; and musically its national character was being sapped by the recently renewed influence of Italian opera. The last famous name in the history of the form was that of Manuel García, who wrote, besides numerous *tonadillas*, over 40 operas and operettas, the first of which was *El seductor arrepentido* (1802). The *polo* (Andalusian dance-song) in *El poeta calculista* (1805) was borrowed by Rossini in *Il barbiere di Siviglia* (in the première of which García sang Almaviva): another *polo* by him in *El criado fingido* (1803) formed the basis of the entr'acte to Act 4 of Bizet's *Carmen*.

In the same way that Spain had been dominated by *opera seria* in the previous century, in the 19th what operatic activity there was – for this was Spain's blackest period, with French invasions, tyrannical regimes, political turmoil, national humiliations and civil war – was totally in the grip of Rossini, Donizetti and Bellini. While succumbing to Italianate style and using Italian librettos (five of them by Romani), Ramón Carnicer, a Catalan, chose national subjects in his *Don Giovanni Tenorio* (1822, Barcelona) and *Cristoforo Colombo* (1831). His pupil Baltasar Saldoni wrote one operetta (*El triunfo del amor*, 1826) that was privately performed in his native Barcelona before he turned back to *opera seria*. Both these musicians were professors at the newly founded Madrid Conservatory, opened by the queen in 1831. In choosing an Italian singer as director and imposing Italian as the language of instruction, she may have wished to put Spanish singers on an equal footing with outsiders, but inevitably this was not seen as any encouragement to native composers: nor even was a government grant to Genovés y Lapetra after the success of his *Enrique y Clotilde* (1831), which sent him to Italy for further study, since he then stayed there and wrote his most important operas (such as *Luisa della Vallière*, 1845, Milan) for Italian theatres. Hilarión Eslava, who taught composition at the conservatory and later became its director, also wrote Italian operas – in his first, *Il solitario del monte selvaggio* (1841, Cádiz), introducing the Spanish *palmada* (rhythmic hand-clapping) in one chorus – before forsaking the stage to devote himself to a massive anthology of Spanish sacred music.

A growing tide of frustrated nationalist feelings began to manifest itself about halfway through the century. Another pupil of Carnicer, Espín y Guillén, in 1842 founded the first Spanish musical magazine, *Iberia musical*, in which he vigorously championed native efforts: he himself wrote an opera on a historic subject, *Padilla*, which was praised by both Rossini and Verdi but of which only one act was ever performed (1845). Saldoni, who became director of the Teatro Príncipe in Madrid in 1848, was one of a group of composers who deliberately set out to promote truly Spanish operas: they included Barbieri, Gaztambide and Arrieta, all of whom found a solution in their espousal of the zarzuela, whose less highflown subjects and more populist style immediately secured a warm public response (see Chapter XX). Arrieta had previously tried his hand at opera with *Ildegonda* (which reached Madrid in 1849 after a Milan première in 1845) and *La conquista de Granada* (1850, revised as *Isabel la Católica*, 1855); but despite his choice of subject in the latter, he could not free his musical thinking from its thorough Italian schooling. Even his vastly successful zarzuela *Marina* (1855), which by supplying with recitatives and adding a third act he turned into an opera in 1871, was entirely Italianate. Barbieri (again a Carnicer pupil), the pre-eminent figure in the history of the zarzuela, was convinced that 'our much-desired Spanish opera' needed to be varied and picturesque and to include comic or popular elements even in the most serious subjects. Though he constantly hankered after writing an opera, the nearest he came to this was in his three-act *zarzuela grande*, *Pan y toros* (1864).

Ruperto Chapí made far less impact with his operas, of which the most considerable was the three-act *Roger de Flor* (1878), than with his numerous zarzuelas, some of which (particularly *La tempestad*, 1882) were hailed as heralding a new era in the musical theatre: the only true operas among his later works, *Circe* (1902) and *Margarita la Tornera* (1909), show that characterization and dramatic force were not his strengths. His almost exact contemporary Tomás Bretón vehemently inveighed against the Italian influences which from Farinelli's day onwards, he declared, had 'stifled and degraded' native art. His *Los amantes de Teruel* to his own libretto (nevertheless given in Italian) was warmly received in Madrid in 1889 and later heard in Vienna and Prague: *Garín* (also played in Italian) was successful in Barcelona in 1892; but his most important opera was the veristic three-act *La Dolores* (1895), which received 175 performances in its first season alone – although this pales into insignificance beside the universal acclamation that greeted his *sainete* or zarzuela, *La verbena de la Paloma* (1894).

Much the most influential figure in Spanish music in the latter part of the century was Felipe Pedrell, who worked unceasingly as a historian, teacher and editor to persuade his countrymen of the value of their national heritage. Like Vaughan Williams later in England, he stressed the importance both of a nation's genuine folk music and of its past artistic masterpieces, and by his own example did much to make these generally available. In the theatrical sphere he strove for a lyric drama on the highest intellectual plane. After his first, frequently revised opera *El último Abencerraje* (1874, Barcelona), he set his ambitions on a trilogy which earned him the misleading soubriquet of 'the Spanish Wagner'. Its first part, *Els Pirineus* (composed in 1890–91 but not performed until 1902, Barcelona), suffers from its excessive stylistic diversity, with borrowings not only from Catalan, Moorish and troubadour melodies but also from 16th- and 17th-century composers: written with seriousness of purpose but lacking the vital spark of inspiration, it is significant primarily for its focussing of native aspirations. The second part, the dramatic *La Celestina* (completed in 1904 but not performed), based on a 15th-century literary classic, is perhaps more important. *El Conde Arnau* (1904) completes the trilogy. His pupil Albéniz was ill-advised enough to agree to a financially rewarding contract with an English banker and amateur writer, Francis Burdett Money-Coutts (Lord Latymer), to set his librettos exclusively: their collaboration produced the turgid historical *Henry Clifford* (1895, Barcelona) and a neo-Wagnerian Arthurian trilogy of which only the first part, *Merlin* (1906), was written; these and *The Magic Opal* (1893, London; to a libretto by Arthur Law) all found the composer uncertain in style and out of his depth. Only in *Pepita Jiménez* (1896, Barcelona), which was set on his home ground, was Albéniz able to rise above the stilted and feeble libretto to produce melodically convincing if indifferently orchestrated music; as a result it was presented in several European countries.

Spain's struggles to shake off the dead weight of Italian music were paralleled in Portugal. After writing some 20 successful operas in Italy since 1792, Marcos Portugal returned to Lisbon in 1800 to take over the direction of the S Carlos opera house from Moreira and wrote as many new operas again (his *Non irritar le donne*, 1798, was selected by Napoleon for the opening in 1801 of the Théâtre-Italien in Paris). In 1811 he followed the court to Rio de Janeiro, where it had fled four years previously, and there revived several of his earlier operas, such as *Merope* and *Artaserse*, and wrote more, including the Metastasian *Adriano in Siria* (1813, Padua); all these were in Italian except *A sàloia namorada* (1812, Rio).

Portugal's own list of his works names 35 Italian operas and 21 comic operas in Portuguese. The temporary exile of the court and the political upheavals that followed were naturally not conducive to artistic activity and, except for a few minor composers who pursued an entirely Italian style, native Portuguese opera languished until late in the century. The Viscount of Arneiro, Ferreira Veiga, had little response to his first opera in the vernacular, *Elixis da mocidade* (1876), until it was revised to include a ballet and given in Italian in Milan as *L'elisir di giovinezza* (1877). A momentary change from the Italian tradition was made by Augusto Machado: his *O cruz de ouro* had been produced in 1873, but ten years later, after being influenced in Paris by Massenet, he scored a success with *Lauriane*, to a libretto by Guiot after George Sand (presented in Marseilles in 1883 before reaching Lisbon or Rio). After this, however, he reverted to Italian opera and busied himself with operettas. A native Portuguese spirit is first unmistakably seen in the operas of the highly cultivated Alfredo Keil, who sought out national subjects: his successful *Donna Bianca* (1888) and *Irene* (1893, Turin) were nevertheless composed to Italian librettos and even his still popular three-act comic opera *Serrana* (1899), which was written to a Portuguese text, was first played in translation.

2. Scandinavia

In the last quarter of the 18th century, specifically Danish and Swedish traditions of theatre music had begun to develop, usually through collaboration between native librettists and composers of Italian, German or French origin in works exploiting Scandinavian history, legend, antiquities and folklore. Outstanding examples were the Singspiels *Balders Død* (1779) and *Fiskerne* (1780), both to texts by the Danish poet Johan Ewald and with music by the German-born J. E. Hartmann. In Sweden, King Gustav III had striven to foster serious spoken and music drama in the vernacular. He founded an academy for the purpose and himself wrote a scenario for J. G. Naumann's opera *Gustaf Wasa* (1786) whose libretto is by the Swedish poet J. H. Kellgren; he had also built in 1766 the court opera house at Drottningholm (the only 18th-century one to survive today with its original working machinery). The king's assassination in his own Stockholm opera house in 1792 brought to an untimely end the brilliant Gustavian era with its lofty aesthetic ideals.

By the beginning of the 19th century, Singspiel and vaudeville had become rooted in the affections of Danish middle-class society, lending themselves to homely sentiment and mild social satire. Both the popularity and the international provenance of Singspiel were exemplified in *Ungdom og Galskab* ('Youth and Folly', 1806), a Danish adaptation of a French libretto set to music by the Swiss Edouard Dupuy, a violinist, singer and composer in the Stockholm and Copenhagen courts. Hardly less successful in their day were the works of C. E. F. Weyse, all first given at the Copenhagen Royal Theatre, notably *Sovedrikken* ('The Sleeping Draught', 1809), *Faruk* (1812), *Ludlams Hule* ('Ludlam's Cave', 1816), which have texts by Adam Oehlenschlaeger, the dominant literary figure of Danish Romanticism, and *Et Eventyr i Rosenborg Have* ('An Adventure in Rosenborg Gardens', 1827). This last is to a text by J. L. Heiberg, whose *Elverhøj* ('The Fairy Mound') was set as a Singspiel by Friedrich Kuhlau, first produced at the Royal Theatre (1828), where it has remained the most frequently performed work in the repertory, making sensitive use of traditional Danish melodies. A Swedish counterpart is Andreas Randel's *Värmlänningarne* (1846), enshrining the national 'Song of Värmland', while a Norwegian one is Waldemar Thrane's music to Bjerregaard's *Fjeldeventyret* ('The Mountain Adventure', 1825). Finland acquired its first native opera with Fredrick Pacius's *Kung Karls Jakt*, 1852) to a Swedish-language libretto by Topelius.

For much of the 19th century, nationalist operatic ambitions in Scandinavia had to contend with the vogue for the lighter forms of Singspiel, vaudeville and operetta as well as the influx of more substantial works from the standard international repertory. Furthermore, the increasing vitality of spoken drama in the Nordic countries diverted the creative energies of composers towards the elaborate incidental music that 19th-century stage productions often called for. Grieg's hopes of writing a large-scale Norwegian opera were frustrated mainly by his failure to capture the interest of dramatists like Bjørnson or Ibsen except on such terms as relegated the composer to a subordinate position. Another potentially significant Norwegian composer of opera, Martin Andreas Udbye, was defeated when the score and parts of his *Fredkulla* ('The Peacemaker', 1858) were destroyed in 1877 in a theatre fire on the eve of a production. Among the Swedish composers who attempted opera, A. F. Lindblad (*Frondörerna*, 'The Rebels', 1835) and Franz Berwald (*Estrella di Soria*, composed in 1841, and given in 1862; and *Drottningen av Golconda*, composed in 1864, not given until 1968) had stronger talents in other fields – Lindblad in lyric song, Berwald in chamber and symphonic music.

Cultural links with the German-speaking countries, and the fact that a large number of Scandinavian musicians received their professional training in Leipzig, Berlin or Vienna, intensified the influence of Wagnerian music drama during the second half of the century and renewed the background of Nordic folklore that was already an integral part of the Scandinavian heritage. An opera by the Swedish composer Andreas Hallén, *Harald der Wiking*, was first produced in Leipzig in 1881 and adapted as *Harald Viking* for the Stockholm theatre in 1894; it was followed in 1896 by *Häxfällan* and, for the opening of the new Royal Theatre in 1899, by *Waldemarsskatten*, which Strindberg is said to have described as a combination of Skansen (the Stockholm folk museum), Wagner and Waldteufel. Ivar Hallström, his French sympathies notwithstanding, was deeply committed to Swedish nationalism; he collaborated with Prince Gustaf in *Hvita frun på Drottningholm* ('The White Lady of Drottningholm', 1847) and went on to set two librettos by Tor Hedberg, *Den Bergtagna* ('The Bewitched', 1874) and *Vikingarna* (1877), among other dramatic works. In the closing years of the century Stenhammar, a bridge figure between late Romanticism and the general Nordic reaction in favour of Beethoven, Berwald, Sibelius and Nielsen, still chose nationalist subjects for his two early music dramas, *Gildet på Solhaug* and *Tirfling*, composed in the 1890s.

In Denmark, J. P. E. Hartmann, grandson of the composer of *Balders Død* and *Fiskerne*, produced in the earlier years of his long life a series of Romantic Singspiels including *Ravnen* ('The Raven', after Gozzi, 1832) and *Liden Kirsten* (1846), both to texts by Hans Christian Andersen. Wagnerian traits begin to appear in such operatic works as Peter Heise's *Drot og Marsk* ('King and Marshal', 1878), based on the medieval Danish ballad of King Erik Glipping, and C. F. E. Horneman's *Aladdin* (1888), the libretto of which is derived from the allegorical verse-drama by Oehlenschlaeger. By far the most prominent Danish opera composer of the century was August Enna, whose Wagnerian *Heksen* ('The Witch', 1892) and *Den lille Pige med Svolvstikkerne* (1897), based on Andersen's story *The Little Match-girl*, won international though transient fame. Enna's eclectic and cosmopolitan outlook (he was of Italian descent) distanced him from Danish traditions, which were soon to find their true consummation in the operas of Carl Nielsen.

CHAPTER XIX

America

VICTOR YELLIN, MALENA KUSS

1. The USA and Canada

The first operas heard in America were of the English ballad opera type. *Flora, or, Hob in the Well*, a farcical tale of a country bumpkin, was given in Charleston in 1735. The earliest native American opera is probably *The Disappointment, or, The Force of Credulity*, to a text thought to be by Andrew Barton (published anonymously in Philadelphia in 1767, though the work was not performed then); based on ballad opera conventions, it reveals its American origins in its combination of a Pennsylvania-German dialect with the tune of *Yankee Doodle* to characterize a rascal.

Comic operas by 18th-century English composers such as Arne, Shield and Dibdin were also played, and provided the basis for native works. During the Revolution operatic activity, already inhibited by a congressional resolution of 1774 discouraging 'every species of extravagance and dissipation' and by religious objections, was largely suspended. Limited musical theatre continued; the religious objections were circumvented by the use of puppets or by the billing of productions as 'moral dialogues' or concerts. But a new period succeeded in which the foundations were laid for the institutions that were to shape operatic life until the mid-19th century. In the busy seaport cities (notably Boston, Newport, New York, Philadelphia, Charleston and New Orleans), theatres with facilities for opera were built, and trained and gifted musicians and singing actors were attracted. Among the entrepreneurs, composers, music directors and teachers were Rayner Taylor, Alexander Reinagle, Benjamin Carr, James Hewitt, Victor Pelissier and Gottlieb Graupner, who arranged and scored music for English comic operas, plays and melodramas and occasionally supplied original music. Among the early works in this American tradition were Hewitt's *Tammany, or, The Indian Chief* (1794, New York), Carr's *The Archers, or, The Mountaineers of Switzerland* (1796, New York), Pelissier's *Edwin and Angelina* (1796, New York), Reinagle's orchestral accompaniments based on Samuel Arnold's *The Mountaineers*

(1796, Philadelphia), John Bray's *The Indian Princess* (1808, Philadelphia) and Taylor's *The Aethiop* (1814, Philadelphia).

The existence of such scores as these, however, should not obscure the fact that the American musical theatre of the period was essentially a vibrant extension of the London stage. Not even the war of 1812 could interrupt this collaboration, as in the case of *The Aethiop* (1812, Covent Garden), a 'New grand Romantick Drama' (William Dimond), which crossed the sea without its original score by Henry Bishop to be produced first in New York (April 1813) and a little later in Philadelphia with completely new music by Taylor (January 1814), just after the British burnt down the White House.

Foreign-language opera had begun with the arrival in New Orleans of Louis Tabery, who in 1792 opened a theatre at which his troupe performed; in the 1805–6 season 16 operas by nine composers, including Monsigny, Grétry, Dalayrac, Boieldieu, Méhul and Paisiello, were given. A permanent opera company was established in the city in 1810. At the same period French opera was introduced in several east-coast cities, by the late 1820s as far north as Quebec. The first opera by a Canadian was Joseph Quesnel's *Colas et Colinette* (1790, Montreal), which follows the style of the 18th-century *comédie mêlée d'ariettes*. In the USA, Italian works given in English were more popular than French ones. Bishop's English adaptations of *Don Giovanni* and *Il barbiere di Siviglia* were given in New York in 1817 and 1819, and Rophino Lacy's of Rossini's *La Cenerentola* (1831) became so widely known that it was much parodied in the minstrel shows of the 1840s and 50s. *Il barbiere* was the first opera heard in Italian in New York, in 1825, given by a Spanish company under Manuel García. The success of works such as these as well as serious operas by Rossini and García himself created a new channel of American musical theatre; several troupes, visiting as well as resident, rode the wave of enthusiasm for early Romantic Italian opera. German opera in the original language gained a foothold only in the 1850s, but it too had been preceded by English adaptations, for example of *Der Freischütz* in 1825 and *Fidelio* in 1839. *Fidelio* was given in German, in New York, in 1856 and *Tannhäuser* three years later. Leading European singers, such as Jenny Lind, Maria Malibran, Adelina Patti and Christine Nilsson, paid regular visits, and travelling companies carried opera across the country. As support for opera increased, so did the building of well-equipped opera houses. The Metropolitan, in New York, built in rivalry with other houses, opened in 1883 with an Italian translation of Gounod's *Faust*; its first season of Italian productions was highly unsuccessful but this was followed by several much more successful seasons of German opera in which Wagner's music dramas were introduced to the USA.

Before the middle of the century, the first full-length American opera had been given, the Italianate *Leonora* of William Henry Fry (1845, Philadelphia; his two earlier operas remained unperformed). George Frederick Bristow's *Rip Van Winkle* (1855, New York) is the first American opera on an American subject. Several American composers followed their example in writing operas on English-language librettos, though with a marked lack of success; among them were Julius Eichberg (*The Doctor of Alcantara*, 1862, Boston), Max Maretzek (*Sleepy Hollow, or The Headless Horseman*, 1879, New York), Dudley Buck (*Deseret, or A Saint's Affliction*, 1880, New York), Silas G. Pratt (*Zenobia, Queen of Palmyra*, 1882, Chicago) and Frederick G. Gleason (*Otho Visconti*, composed 1876–7; posthumously produced 1907, Chicago). In Canada, the European operatic repertory had also taken root by the mid-century though performances of Canadian works remained limited; two of Calixa Lavallée's light operas, *The Widow* (1882) and *TIQ (The Indian Question Settled at Last*, 1883), had their premières in the USA. Among other Canadian operas of this period is Susie Harrison's three-act *Pipandor* (late 1880s), which incorporated French-Canadian folksongs.

Further impetus to opera in English was provided by the success in 1878 of Gilbert and Sullivan's *H.M.S. Pinafore* and their later operas, which rekindled the interest in opera in English of a kind conforming to Anglo-American dramatic sensibilities, and so reviving an earlier tradition. Several operatic enterprises tried, with varying success, to capitalize on this zeal for musical theatre in English. The most ambitious was the American Opera Company: begun in New York in 1886 to provide 'grand opera sung in our own language by the most competent artists', it engaged Theodore Thomas to conduct and assembled American singers to perform the standard foreign repertory in English and to encourage American works, but it lasted only up to the 1887–8 season.

Many composers of the Second New England School wrote operas or other large-scale works in what Fry would have identified as a dramatic – that is operatic – style. John Knowles Paine's only grand opera, *Azara* (composed 1883–98; concert performance 1903, Boston), was not completed until the end of his career and did not reach the stage, but his earlier works are suffused with operatic gestures. Younger than Paine, and quicker to follow a natural inclination towards dramatic music, was George Whitefield Chadwick, who wrote seven stage works. In these the influence of the Gilbert and Sullivan repertory can clearly be seen, especially in *The Peer and the Pauper* (1884, unperformed), *A Quiet Lodging* (1892, Boston), the burlesque opera *Tabasco* (1894, Boston) and the later Broadway extravaganza *Everywoman: her Pilgrimage in Quest of Love* (1911; also given in 1912 in London). Chadwick's two major theatre works – the 'lyric drama' *Judith* (1901, Worcester Festival) and *The Padrone* (composed 1912–13; see Chapter XXVIII), influenced by the Italian *verismo* school – reconcile a concern for correct English musical diction with the expressive aims of grand opera as found in such composers as Saint-Saëns, Massenet and Puccini.

Following in his footsteps, Chadwick's students and later his colleagues were also active composing operas. Frederick Shepherd Converse's *The Pipe of Desire* (1910, New York) was the first opera by an American produced at the Metropolitan; two years later Horatio Parker's *Mona* (1912, New York) won both production and a prize from the same company. Henry Kimball Hadley continued the stage activity of the New Englanders with such successful works as *Azora, Daughter of Montezuma* (1914, Chicago), *Bianca* (1917, New York) and *Cleopatra's Night* (1918, New York).

2. Latin America

Although the first New World operas were written in Peru and Mexico in the early 18th century (see Chapter XI), the composition of operas remained occasional in Latin America until about 1870. There is however evidence of some operatic output from early 19th-century composers. In Cuba, the lyric drama *Apolo y América*, to a libretto by Manuel de Zequeira y Arangú, was produced in 1807 (the music is now lost). In Brazil the most important composer of this period was José Mauricio Nunes Garcia, who wrote one Italian opera, *Le due gemelle* (1809, also lost); another early Brazilian opera is Bernardo José de Sousa Queirós's *Os doidos fingidos por amor* (1813). In the other countries operatic composition seems to have begun rather later.

Several factors contributed to this. After independence, declared in most Latin American countries between 1811 and 1825, cultural life in the cities was influenced by the influx of Italian, French and German immigrants; European forms of salon music were cultivated and Italian opera thrived at the public theatres. Regular opera seasons, including visits from foreign troupes, were given in Havana from 1810, in Buenos Aires from 1825, and soon thereafter in other cities. Local composers had to compete with the European repertory and met with little success. Early attempts to perform Italian operas in Spanish and Portuguese translations were often thwarted, though in observance of a royal ordinance issued in Mexico in 1799 such favourites as Cimarosa's *Il matrimonio segreto* and Paisiello's *Il barbiere di Siviglia* were sung in Spanish. While *sainetes, tonadillas* and zarzuelas remained in the Mexican repertory throughout the 19th century, a Spanish translation of Paisiello's *Il barbiere* was performed in Mexico City in 1806, with Mexican dances and popular songs during the intervals, in a tradition akin to that of the Italian intermezzo. The visit of Manuel García's opera company to Mexico City in 1827, however, popularized performance in the original language, which became standard after 1830. In Rio de Janeiro, the imperial Academia de Música e Ópera Nacional, managed by the versatile José Zapata y Amat (1857–60), trained local singers and produced foreign operas in Portuguese translation, a practice he continued at the Empresa de Ópera Lírica Nacional (1860–63); there, in 1860, the première of Elías Álvarez Lôbo's *A noite de São João* – the first opera on a Brazilian subject sung in Portuguese by Brazilian singers – was given under the direction of Carlos Gomes.

If the success of Italian opera inhibited the development of national styles before 1900, it also stimulated the composition of well-crafted Italianate operas. Early Mexican works include Manuel Covarrubias's *Reynaldo y Elina, o La sacerotisa pervana* (1838) and Luis Baca's *Leonor* and *Giovanna di Castiglia* (dates unknown). Among the most successful Italian operas by Mexicans were Cenobio Paniagua's *Catalina di Guisa* (written in 1845 but not produced until 1859), the first of his three operas, and *Ildegonda* (1865), the second of Melesio Morales's five. The first opera on a Puerto Rican subject was *Guarionex, o La palma del cacique* (c1856, lost) by Felipe Gutiérrez y Espinosa; his three-act *Macías*, based on a play by Mariano José de Larra, was written in 1871 but did not reach the stage until 1977. The earliest opera by a Venezuelan performed in the 19th century was José Angel Montero's *Virginia* (1873); the first documented opera from Argentina is Francisco Hargreaves's *La gatta bianca* (1877).

A number of 19th-century operas incorporate elements from traditional music within a predominantly Italian style. Representative examples are Aniceto Ortega del Villar's *Guatimotzín* (1871), one of several settings of the legend of Cuauhtémoc, the last Aztec ruler, in which the 'Marcha Tlaxcalteca' is an assemblage of popular Mexican tunes; *Atahulpa* (1877), the first opera on an Inca subject, by Carlo Enrico Pasta, an Italian resident in Peru; *Pampa* (1897), by the Argentine Arturo Berutti, discussed below; and *Yumurí* (1898), by the Cuban Eduardo Sánchez de Fuentes, which treats a subject from colonial history.

No 19th-century Latin American composer, however, enjoyed the reputation and international acclaim of the Brazilian Carlos Gomes. He was a protégé of Emperor Pedro II, an enthusiastic patron of Brazilian arts who subsidized the Rio Conservatory (1847) and the national opera house. After the Rio premières of Gomes's first two operas, the three-act *A noite do castelo* (1861) – his only setting of a Portuguese libretto – and *Joana de Flandres* (1863), Gomes went to Italy in 1863 where he studied in Milan under Lauro Rossi. His most popular opera, *Il Guarany*, based on the novel by José Martiniano de Alençar, portrays Portuguese characters and Guarani Indians as heroes and Spanish adventurers as villains. After its successful première at La Scala in 1870, it was given there 27 times in 1870–71, produced in Rio in 1870 and in many European cities during the next few years. Verdi heard it in Ferrara and praised it highly; he later chose the French baritone Victor Maurel, who had made his La Scala début as Cacique in *Il Guarany*, as his first Iago and Falstaff. The stage music for the 'Baccanale indiano' in Act 3 scene iii calls for such instruments as maracas, claves and *inubias* (war trumpets), but the score otherwise follows mid-19th-century Italian conventions. The effective polacca for coloratura soprano, 'Gentile di cuore', on Cecilia's entrance in Act 1 scene iv, is clearly reminiscent of Bellini, popular in Brazil during Gomes's formative years. While the nativism of *Il Guarany* is confined to its libretto and a few orchestration details, the overture (the 'Symphonia do

Guarany' or 'Protofonia', which in 1871 or 1872 replaced the original Preludio) has come to be as closely identified with Brazilian nationalism as the official national anthem.

Il Guarany was followed by *Fosca* (1873) and *Salvator Rosa* (1874), both to librettos by Ghislanzoni, and *Maria Tudor* (1879; libretto by Emilio Praga, after Victor Hugo); *Salvator Rosa* had its première in Genoa, the other two at La Scala. Gomes spent the next decade (1880–90) in Brazil, where he wrote *Lo schiavo* (1889, Rio). The popular aria 'Ciel di Parahyba' of Act 3 scene ii retains his polished and eclectic Italian style, though he enriched the orchestration of the Indian dances with indigenous rattles and trumpets and used a syncopated rhythm associated with Afro-Brazilian music in the Act 2 'Dansa dos Tamoyos'. More than through explicit means, however, the orchestration for oboe and high strings of the opening 'Alborada' conjures up the spirit of Brazil.

The first Argentine opera on a national subject to incorporate folkdances is Arturo Berutti's *Pampa* (1897), which treats the life and times of the outlawed hero Juan Moreira, the most significant subject in the history of Argentine opera. Eduardo Gutiérrez's original police drama (1874) is a character study of the gaucho and the adverse social conditions that surrounded him; Guido Borra's libretto for Berutti's opera is based on a dramatized version by the actor José J. Podestá, whose brother Antonio Podestá wrote *sainetes* caricaturing Italian and French opera convention, including *Otelo criollo*, *Fausto criollo* (1894) and *Moreira en ópera* (1897, a satire on *Pampa*).

CHAPTER XX

Operetta, musical comedy, zarzuela

ANDREW LAMB, LIONEL SALTER

Origins and development

During the second half of the 19th century operetta became the principal form of popular musical theatre. It was essentially a lighthearted form of entertainment with songs, ensembles and dances interspersed with spoken dialogue, incorporated into a comic, romantic or satirical dramatic framework. The term 'operetta', as a diminutive, had long been applied in a general way to stage works that were shorter or otherwise less ambitious than fully developed opera. In its late 19th-century usage it came to acquire a more specific connotation as the works to which it became attached enjoyed extensive international popularity.

As a specific artistic form, operetta evolved in Paris in the 1850s as an antidote to the increasingly serious and ambitious pretensions of *opéra comique*. The policy of the Théâtre de l'Opéra-Comique to favour works of a more ambitious kind left a gap between *opéra comique* and vaudeville; to fill this gap, various attempts were made to establish a home for short, lighthearted works in operatic style. The particular success of Offenbach and his Bouffes-Parisiens, offering programmes of two or three satirical one-act pieces, was such that it led to the extension of the format into full-length works and to the establishment of *opéra bouffe* as a separately identifiable form of full-length entertainment.

The success of Offenbach's works was not confined to France, and in due course other national schools of operetta came into being, each with its own national style. In Austria and Germany Offenbach's works fitted readily into the repertories of theatres whose productions ranged from lighter operatic works, as written by Lortzing, to comedies with interpolated songs. Composers who attempted native works in the Offenbach style were initially house composers for these theatres, but it was Johann Strauss the younger, the 'Waltz King', who gave Viennese operetta its characteristic romantic style and a strong dependence on dance rhythms, especially the waltz. In due course an English-language form of operetta flourished, most notably through the comic operas of Gilbert and Sullivan, with national characteristics owing something to the burlesque tradition, to English ballad opera, and even to Victorian church music. At the same time, in Spain, the strongly nationalistic zarzuela was enjoying a revival in popularity as the native counterpart of operetta.

As a popular form of entertainment, the operetta reflected contemporary taste in the nature of its plots and moral attitudes. As the predominant form of popular musical theatre entertainment of its time, it readily attracted composers, librettists, performers, managers and designers. Because of the importance of its dialogue and dramatic framework, operetta was even more dependent than opera upon a strong libretto, and some of its major successes involved recognized comic playwrights, among them Henri Meilhac and Ludovic Halévy in France and W. S. Gilbert in England. Operetta built up its own specialist performers who could combine singing with comic acting ability, notable among them being Offenbach's leading lady Hortense Schneider and the Viennese tenor Alexander Girardi. Although such composers as Bizet and Chabrier tried their hand at operetta in its early years, the most successful were generally specialists in lighter forms.

By the 1880s and 1890s, the expansion of the operetta form from its one-act origins had brought it to the point where it occupied much the same position as the *opéra comique* of 40 or 50 years earlier. With the passing of many of the leading major practitioners of operetta and the periodic quest for change that typifies the popular musical theatre, another fundamental change in the nature of operetta began during the 1890s. Elements of the contemporary variety theatre began increasingly to be incorporated, especially in works presented in London under the designation 'musical comedy'. Where previously the integrity of a score had been paramount, the musical comedy was concerned at least as much with the staging of individual song-and-dance numbers; where the logical development of the story had been of prime importance, it now became increasingly important to offer opportunities for displays of female glamour, fashionable dress and elaborate chorus routines. Though by the turn of the century the trend had only just begun, it provided a foretaste of developments that were to become of considerable importance in the 20th century.

France

Although it was not until the mid-1850s that what is now recognized as operetta began to emerge as a separately distinctive genre, works that would now be classed as such had been given in Paris before that time. Adam's *Le chalet* (1834) and *La poupée de Nuremberg* (1852), Massé's *Le noces de Jeannette* (1853) and Offenbach's *Pépito* (1853) had scores that were far more operatic in form than the collections of numbers provided for vaudevilles, but were none the less more modest and lighter than the works increasingly being accepted by the Théâtre de l'Opéra-Comique. Adam himself had opened an Opéra-National in 1847, but the venture proved short-lived. More successful was Hervé's Théâtre des Folies-

Nouvelles (opened initially as the Folies-Concertantes) in 1854. But it was only with the opening of Offenbach's Théâtre des Bouffes-Parisiens in 1855 that these foundations were firmly built upon. The works in Offenbach's repertory were initially little more than satirical sketches with a few musical numbers, as in *Les deux aveugles* (1855). However, the wit and sparkle of the theatre's productions, composed not always by Offenbach himself but by Adam, Emile Jonas, Delibes and others, made them the rage of Paris. Within a year or two Offenbach was able to tour not only in France but abroad.

With a small theatre licensed for only three or four stage performers, Offenbach's early *opéras bouffes* or *opérettes* remained for some time necessarily modest one-act pieces, satirical or farcical in tone and with scores of up to eight musical numbers (assorted solos, duets, trios and quartets) accompanied by an orchestra of up to 16 players. In 1858 the relaxation of restrictions on the number of stage performers enabled him to put on his first two-act *opéra bouffe*, the mythological satire *Orphée aux enfers*, which added enormously to his reputation at home and abroad. Although Offenbach continued to produce one-act works, the pattern for future operettas was set by his sequence of longer works – *Geneviève de Brabant* (1859), *La belle Hélène* (1864), *Barbe-bleue* (1866), *La vie parisienne* (1866), *La Grande-Duchesse de Gérolstein* (1867) and *La Périchole* (1868) – light-hearted, witty works with a full cast, chorus, orchestra of up to 30 musicians, and scores comprising some 20 or 30 musical numbers including elaborately constructed opening numbers and finales. Thus by the end of the 1860s operetta had grown into a fully-fledged genre with characteristics that firmly distinguished it not only from contemporary vaudeville but also, in its satirical wit and popular appeal, from *opéra comique*.

The Second Empire had fostered Offenbach's satirical flair and after its demise in 1870 his popularity began to wane. The French public came to prefer a more romantic, escapist form of entertainment, and it was through Charles Lecocq, whose *La fille de Madame Angot* (1872, Brussels) remains a classic of the genre, that French operetta retained its international appeal. Hervé, despite three big successes in the late 1860s, was destined to be eclipsed first by Offenbach and then by Lecocq, and his most lasting success was achieved only in 1883 with *Mam'zelle Nitouche*. By then Lecocq's pre-eminence had been challenged, first by Robert Planquette with the lively *Les cloches de Corneville* (1877), another outstanding and enduring international success, and then by Edmond Audran whose *La mascotte* (1880) was among several works of his that were internationally acclaimed. At the turn of the century French operetta could still be ranked as a worthy successor of the old *opéra comique* with works of the quality of Messager's *Véronique* (1898) and Louis Ganne's *Les saltimbanques* (1899), the former displaying an elegance and charm unsurpassed in operetta, the latter an irresistible spirit and élan. Among other eminent composers of French operetta in the 19th century were

Léon Vasseur (*La timbale d'argent*, 1872), Paul Lacome (*Jean, Jeannette et Jeanneton*, 1876), Gaston Serpette (*Le moulin du Vert-Galant*, 1876), Louis Varney (*Les mousquetaires au couvent*, 1880) and Victor Roger (*Les vingt-huit jours de Clairette*, 1892).

Austria, Germany, England

In the late 1850s Viennese theatres began staging Offenbach's *opéras bouffes*, at first in pirated versions, but in the 1860s under his own direction. These in turn inspired one-act comic and satirical operettas in similar style from local composers, notably Franz Suppé. His *Das Pensionat* (1860) is generally reckoned the first Viennese operetta, while his mythological satire *Die schöne Galathe* (1865) was the most distinguished of its one-act successors, several of which remain familiar through their overtures.

Offenbach's virtual monopoly of the larger-scale productions remained unchallenged in Vienna until the recruitment of Johann Strauss the younger from the dance hall. In 1871 the Theater an der Wien staged his first operetta, *Indigo und die vierzig Räuber*, which introduced the distinctively Viennese operetta style, with its more exotic settings, more romantic stories and scores built around dance forms, particularly the waltz. Strauss's *Die Fledermaus* (1874), which like many other Viennese works of the time was based on a French source, remains perhaps the most celebrated of all operettas, with its spirited music and its sophisticated, satirical libretto. The classical Viennese operetta went on to enjoy its richest period with works such as Suppé's *Fatinitza* (1876) and *Boccaccio* (1879), Strauss's *Eine Nacht in Venedig* (1883) and Carl Millöcker's *Der Bettelstudent* (1882) and *Gasparone* (1884). All five had librettos by the team of F. Zell (the pseudonym used by Camillo Walzel) and Richard Genée, the latter of whom also had some success as a composer with *Nanon* (1877). Strauss's *Der Zigeunerbaron* (1855) demonstrated ambitions towards full-scale opera, but the lighter Viennese style was continued to the end of the century through such works as Carl Zeller's *Der Vogelhändler* (1891) and *Der Obersteiger* (1894), Richard Heuberger's *Der Opernball* (1898) and C. M. Ziehrer's *Die Landstreicher* (1899).

In London, English versions of Offenbach's *opéras bouffes* began to appear during the 1860s. British composers proved slower than the Viennese to follow the example, but it was directly under the influence of Offenbach's *Les deux aveugles* that in 1866 Sullivan composed *Cox and Box*. As the larger-scale French and Viennese operettas caught hold in London, examples came from other native composers, such as Frederic Clay's *Princess Toto* (1876), Alfred Cellier's *Dorothy* (1886) and Edward Solomon's *The Nautch Girl* (1891). Though each of these achieved real success at the time, they were in the long run eclipsed by the series of comic operas on which Sullivan collaborated with Gilbert between 1871 and 1896 (see Chapter XVII); these swept the stages of the English-speaking world, though success in translation was limited by the distinctively British nature of the humour and music.

It was particularly in London during the 1890s, however, that a trend which was to have fundamental significance for the whole nature of operetta and the popular musical theatrical show became evident. At a time when imported French operettas and the native comic operas of Gilbert and Sullivan were losing their appeal, the London public took readily to the style of show loosely termed 'musical comedy'. While retaining the basic musical framework of the operetta, the musical comedy aimed for a wider, more immediate appeal, with an emphasis on contemporary fashion, glamorous female and male chorus lines, catchy interpolated numbers and specially staged song-and-dance routines. These elements were particularly noticeable in a string of shows with 'girl' titles, for example *The Shop Girl* (1894), with music by Ivan Caryll and additional numbers by Lionel Monckton. They were also evident to a lesser extent in such works as Sidney Jones's *The Geisha* (1896), whose designation 'musical play' indicated a more consistent story line and a work that was still basically comic opera; *The Geisha* had phenomenal success not only throughout the British Empire but around the world. Thanks to its oriental setting and greater absorption of continental European melodic styles, it became the most successful of all British operettas in translation, giving it a currency on the Continent that continues to this day.

By the end of the century the fashion for musical comedy had been confirmed through other highly successful works, such as Leslie Stuart's *Florodora* (1899). It had also begun to be developed in other countries, especially in capitals that had hitherto been of less significance in the development of operetta. Germany had already produced its own composers of works in the Viennese style, among them Rudolf Dellinger (*Don Cesar*, 1885) and Hermann Zumpe (*Farinelli*, 1886). In the USA, too, a significant body of indigenous works had begun to emerge in the 1890s under the influence of Gilbert and Sullivan, among them Reginald De Koven's *Robin Hood* (1890, Chicago), John Philip Sousa's *El Capitán* (1896, Boston) and Victor Herbert's *The Fortune Teller* (1898, Toronto). By the turn of the century, however, both New York and Berlin had produced works whose style paralleled developments in London, the former for instance in Gustave Kerker's *The Belle of New York* (1897), the latter in Paul Lincke's one-act revue-style operetta *Frau Luna* (1899). Both New York and Berlin were to become of increasing importance in the popular musical theatre during the 20th century, the former especially as developments in musical comedy and American popular song led to the evolution of a form of musical theatre radically different from that of the classical 19th-century operetta.

Spain

The roots of the indigenous Spanish form of light musical theatre, the zarzuela, go back to the mid-17th century (see Chapter V); but within a century its character had radically changed from the courtly to the popular. Even so, after about 1770 it was swept aside by the short *tona-dillas escénicas*, though this form too burnt itself out in less than 50 years (see Chapter XI). At the turn of the 18th century a royal decree requiring all opera to be sung in Spanish served, paradoxically, only to increase the already great hold of Rossini and Italian opera, and led many – musicians as well as cultural snobs – to disdain the native zarzuela as artistically inferior, plebeian and trivial. There were nevertheless pockets of resistance to Italian domination. In 1832 students at the Madrid Conservatory (where Italian was the language of instruction) staged a Spanish pasticcio, and in 1839 the poet Manuel Bretón de los Herreros, who had written a satire attacking Italian opera, collaborated with Basilio Basili (an Italian) in the one-act *El novio y el concierto*, which contained popular dance rhythms and was the first work since the time of de la Cruz to be described as a 'zarzuela-comedia'. Its success led them to write *El sentor-rillo de Crespo* (1841) and *Los solitarios* (1843) and other composers to write short farcical zarzuelas, mostly on Andalusian subjects. In 1849 Rafael Hernando produced the more ambitious two-act *Colegiales y soldados*, and as a result was commissioned to write 14 'actos de zarzuela'; his *El duende*, which appeared a mere ten weeks later, was a triumph and ran for 126 consecutive nights. That year Joaquín Gaztambide became director of the Teatro Español, where his *La mensajera* became the first zarzuela (its original appellation of 'ópera cómica' was altered after three nights) for which professional singers were engaged as distinct from theatrically agile but musically often illiterate stage artists.

This was the first surge in the history of the zarzuela. Basing itself on the depiction of lower-class life, customs and humour, and on the traditional songs and dances familiar from the *tonadilla*, it took shape as a popular entertainment, partly spoken, partly sung, with a distinct national character. Popular airs and dances were a permanent ingredient, audience participation was encouraged, and the colourful *costumbrista* plots (based on picturesque representations of regional characters, customs and scenes) ranged from farce to tragedy. Songs and dances from many zarzuelas were to become as familiar to the Spanish man-in-the-street as Gilbert and Sullivan numbers to his English counterpart.

F. A. Barbieri, a distinguished self-made musician and the most important figure in the zarzuela's history (he wrote over 70, alone or in partnership), had *Gloria y peluca* staged in 1850. He joined forces with Hernando, Gaztambide, Oudrid y Segura and others to take over the Teatro del Circo, which opened in 1851 with Gaztambide's *Tribulaciones*; this was poorly received, and the enterprise would have collapsed had not Barbieri saved the situation three weeks later with *Jugar con fuego*, notable for being in three acts (until then thought impracticable), which founded the *zarzuela grande* genre. Later successes by him include *Los diamantes de la corona* (1854), the musically and dramatically outstanding *Pan y toros* (1864), which put the figure of Goya on the stage and contained the widely known seguidilla 'Aunque soy de la Mancha', and that most celebrated classic in the repertory, *El barberillo de Lavapiés* (1874), whose subject was political intrigue under Carlos III.

In 1856 the Madrid writers who had formed a society for the furtherance of their art opened the Teatro de la Zarzuela. Leading composers of this time (who sometimes worked as a team) were the prolific but superficial Oudrid y Segura, whose biggest successes were *El postillón de la Rioja* (1856) and *El molinero de Subiza* (1870), the latter of which received over 300 performances in one year; the rhythmically vital and fierily dramatic Gaztambide, who had already enjoyed success with the three-act *Catalina* (1854) and whose *Los magyares* (1857) was exceptional in having four acts; and the cultivated Arrieta y Corera, educated in Milan, in whose first essay *El dómino azúl* (1853) every number was encored at its première and whose *Marina* (1855), performed all over Spain and Latin America, was revised and expanded into an opera with recitatives and a third act (1871). The public appetite was as voracious as it had earlier been for the *tonadilla*, and the one-act *género chico* became the rage: so great was the demand that in the last decade of the century 11 Madrid theatres were entirely devoted to this form and more than 1500 stage pieces were written.

Five composers in particular stood out. There was the popular, realistic but unrefined Federico Chueca, writer of over 35 zarzuelas, whose *La canción de la Lola* (1880) became so familiar that nearly 40 years later Falla could quote a phrase from it (at the constable's appearance in *El sombrero de tres picos*), confident that the allusion would be understood by everyone; his *La gran vía* (1886, with Valverde) had nearly 1000 consecutive performances and his *Agua, azucarillos y aguardiente* (1897) is a score of particular vitality. Arrieta's pupil Ruperto Chapí, a 'meteor' who wrote well over a hundred stage works, possessed style and rhythmic vivacity but was less effective in dramatic characterization; his best works were the serious *La tempestad* (1882), *La bruja* (1887, which might be called an opera of sorts), *El rey que rabió* (1891, termed an 'ópera cómica' in the score) and the one-act *La revoltosa* (1897). The libretto of this last was by Carlos Fernández Shaw, who with his son Guillermo and Miguel de Echegaray occupied the front rank of zarzuela authors. Manuel Fernández Caballero, who composed some 200 short zarzuelas, displayed his gift for melody in *El dúo de La Africana* (1893, about an Italian opera company playing Meyerbeer), *La viejecita* (1897), which has a slight affinity with Brandon Thomas's farce *Charley's Aunt* (1892), and *Gigantes y cabezudos* (1898). Tomás Bretón, another pupil of Arrieta and an essentially serious composer who contributed to the operatic repertory, marked the peak of the *género chico* with his immensely popular *La verbena de la Paloma* (1894; designated a 'sainete lírico'). Jerónimo Giménez, a stylish writer of the *género chico* who was responsible for over two dozen zarzuelas by the turn of the century, achieved fame with *La boda de Luis Alonso* (1897) and *La tempranica* (1900), a sentimental piece which held the stage uninterruptedly for three years.

CHAPTER XXI

Staging

MANFRED BOETZKES, ROGER SAVAGE

1. Design

The 19th-century theatre not only reflected the progress and social change of the Industrial Revolution but also based its organization and production on the governing principles of the industrial age. Encouraged by the suppression or relaxation of the previous rigid conventions, musical theatre in most of Europe was freed of its court associations. The more trivial genre of musical drama that now flourished in the cities was designed to cater for the expanding middle-class society as, increasingly, were opera and ballet productions.

The theatre's vital role in this society was expressed by its outward appearance, its characteristic architecture marking it out as a centre of bourgeois culture. The new class system (as the old had been) was manifested in most 19th-century theatres by hierarchical tiers of boxes. This kind of theatre, typified by Garnier's rebuilt Paris Opéra (1875), prevailed partly because the amphitheatre-type conception favoured by progressive architects could not be satisfactorily combined with the illusionist perspective stage before the construction of Wagner's Bayreuth Festspielhaus (1876). Bayreuth had few direct successors, but its example led late 19th-century theatre architects to strive for a combination of the tiered and amphitheatre style such as became obligatory in the 20th century.

The facilities offered by the 18th-century stage system were increased by the adoption of industrial techniques. Decisive factors in this process, besides the building of more spacious stage areas allowing greater mechanization (Drury Lane Theatre, London, 1812), were gas and electric lighting. Coal gas lighting was first used in London (Drury Lane and Lyceum, 1817) and was soon taken up by all the larger European theatres; it provided a relatively strong, controllable and safe light which not only made possible the introduction of the closed-in 'box set' (important in the evolution of realism) but also considerably enhanced the illusionist techniques of the Romantic musical theatre: the panorama (1785), the diorama (c1820) and the moving panorama (c1820). Particularly intense lighting effects could be produced by limelight (invented in 1826 but not generally used in theatres until the 1840s). The theatrical use of electricity began with the carbon arc (used for the sun in the première of Meyerbeer's *Le prophète* at the Opéra in 1849), installed during the second half of the 19th century primarily as a spotlight and projection lamp; the general electrification of the stage came about only after the invention of the dynamo (1866) and the incandescent lamp (1879). After the experimental electric illumination of the auditorium and foyer of the Opéra, in 1881, the large theatres of Europe all came to be fitted with electric stage lighting, beginning in the same year with the Savoy, London.

The integration of these new technologies into artistic production was possible only through the development of the art of stage management, which sprang both from the Enlightenment's desire to coordinate the production as a self-contained work of art and from the interest in local colour, styles and milieux. The idea of artistic stage production had already been apparent in the 18th-century *ballet d'action*, but in opera the concept was applied, first in France, only as a consequence of the economic pressures towards rationalization resulting from dependence on the public and from the introduction of commercial principles in opera management. However, since this practice was based on a 'common agreement between the egoisms' of the individual arts, in Wagner's view it resulted in only a 'pseudo-unification'; it was only in a *Gesamtkunstwerk*, akin to a Utopian model of society, that each art could be deployed to its fullest extent (*Das Kunstwerk der Zukunft*, 1849).

Theatrical production in the 19th century is marked by its attempts to standardize the theatrical work and so make it reproducible. By the late 18th century, commercial theatrical agencies in Paris were successfully publishing production books; this procedure, which became standard, gave Parisian box-office successes the status of model productions, to be copied by provincial and foreign theatres. The reproduction of sets, properties and costumes was taken over by scenic studios – workshops run as private enterprises by the designers of large theatres; the first of these was founded in 1822 by P.-L.-C. Ciceri, scenic director of the Opéra, whose historical sets for Meyerbeer's *Robert le diable* were remarkably detailed and accurate (see Plate 77). Within a few decades the production of sets was predominantly in the hands of workshops similar to Ciceri's in most of Europe and North America. Such technical and organizational innovations increased the stage's visual potential to a new degree and gave rise to a relatively uniform international style of staging, even if with specific national characteristics.

Aided by the survival of forms of *opera seria*, and influenced by the international success of Napoleonic grand opera, many stage designers of the early 19th century clung at first to the enlightened early bourgeois concept of an art raised above 'common reality' (F. C. Beuther: *Dekorationen für die Schaubühne*, 1824) and hence to the idealism of neoclassicism, even if, like Karl Friedrich Schinkel (see Plates 66 and 67), chief designer at the Berlin Royal Theatre from 1815 to 1828, they used new illusionist techniques. The other most important representatives of this movement were Ignazio Degotti and J.-B. Isabey (Paris), Paolo Landrini (Milan), Giuseppe Borsato (Venice), Giacomo Pregliasco (Milan), Giuseppe Quaglio and his son Angelo the elder (Munich) and Gaetano Marinari (London).

However, with the continuing decline of the distinct traditional genres and the emergence of Romantic opera, subjective tendencies began to dominate stage design, in reaction against early industrial society. For the designers of the early Romantic musical theatre – among them Giorgio Fuentes and Alessandro Sanquirico (see Plate 58) working in Milan and elsewhere, Antonio de Pian, Simon Quaglio (see Plate 68), and William Capon (London) – the formal rules of classicism, systematized in Lorenzo Sacchetti's *Quanto sia facile l'inventare decorazioni teatrali* (1830), were relevant. With the increasingly important medieval ('Gothick') and exotic themes, however, they were appropriated in a stock of motifs within a historic-idyllic style coloured by personal sentiment and characterized by atmospheric architecture, picturesque landscapes and genre scenes.

This subjective conception predominated until after the mid-century, though it was increasingly mixed with realistic tendencies. Triggered by social conflicts during the French Restoration, and stimulated by the rediscovery of national historical and cultural traditions, there was a revival of interest in primarily realistic art for historical subjects. Ciceri and his collaborators and pupils at the Opéra were responsible, from the late 1820s, for exploiting the most modern stage techniques to create, with the help of costume designers and a highly coordinated production method, effective historical paintings, precisely depicting the relevant milieu, for the grand operas of Auber, Halévy and Meyerbeer and the ballets of Taglioni and Coralli (see C. Séchan: *Souvenirs, d'un homme de théâtre 1831–55*, 1893). Historical depiction was achieved less through meticulous reconstruction than through the often purely formal use of familiar social elements: the revolutionary gesture, crowd scenes and crude effects were basic to set construction.

The production style of French grand opera achieved international dissemination, and its influence on stage design was to be found above all where opera was a vehicle for political ideas: in pre-1848 Germany (Wagner's *Rienzi*), in the Italy of the Risorgimento (Verdi) and in countries striving for independence, such as Belgium, Poland, Hungary and the Czech lands. However, the work of many stage designers, such as Giuseppe and Pietro Bertoja (Plate 60), Domenico Ferri, C. W. Gropius, Hermann Neefe, Joseph Mühldorfer, Antonio Sachetti and Andreas Roller, though formally dependent on the Paris school, remained in many respects within the bounds of idyllic early Romanticism.

In England early 19th-century stage designers such as John Henderson Grieve and his sons Thomas and William, as well as Robert C. Andrews, David Roberts and above all Clarkson Stanfield, linking up with the tradition of English landscape painting, were able with the aid of an accomplished stage technique to outdo anything on the Continent. Their technique was inseparable from genres (pantomime, extravaganza, burletta etc) that had increasingly sacrificed realism to colour, ostentation and triviality, and there developed a tendency to exploit effect for its own sake. This was to dominate European stage design during the second half of the century, and was characterized by a preoccupation with detail, a complacent bourgeois historicism and a flight into myth and an exotic dream-world perhaps to be seen as symptomatic of the diminished sense of purpose in life in an industrial society. The visual aspect of production thus acquired a still greater importance, but the integrated visual impact formerly sought in grand opera was lost in favour of academic virtuosity which, above everything else, demanded of a designer encyclopedic knowledge, as Théophile Gautier wrote (*Portraits contemporains*, 1874):

> He must have an intimate knowledge of every country, every period, every style; he must be acquainted with the geology, the flora and the architecture of the five continents . . . Lost civilizations, the splendours of the antediluvian world, the azure pastures of Paradise, the red blazes of Hell, the coral grottos of the ocean, Babel, Enochia, Nineveh, Tyre, Memphis, and the whole world of fairy lore, existent and non-existent things: the stage designer must be prepared to produce all this diversity of spectacles.

The most impressive contributions to this universal panorama reduced within the perspective of the bourgeois were provided by numerous stage designers associated with various scenic studios, among them Joseph Thierry in France (see Plate 74), Carlo Ferrario (Verdi's favourite designer; in Italy, and in Germany and Austria the court scene-painters Angelo Quaglio the younger (see Plate 69) and Heinrich Döll (see Plate 129) and the costume designers Franz Seitz (who worked at the Wagner premières in Munich) and Josef Flüggen (at the Bayreuth Festspielhaus).

In addition to this theatrical art, screening off or ignoring social realities of the time, there evolved other genres of musical theatre which approached reality either satirically, as did Offenbach and his followers, or in a critically descriptive way, as in *verismo*. While parodistic operettas caricatured conventional sets and costumes (as in the stage designs by Jules Draner and costumes by Alfred Grévin for the Théâtre des Variétés in Paris), *verismo* introduced objective, functional design placed wholly at the service of the drama, developed particularly by Georg von Meiningen the younger. However, apart from the stagings by von Meiningen and the Naturalist school, there was little unifying principle behind *verismo* stage designs. In the designs of Marcel Jambon, Bailly, Lucien Jusseaume, the former *féerie* specialist Amable, Adolf Hohenstein and Georg Hacker for the operas of Charpentier, Bizet, Mascagni, Puccini and others, and in the related work of Hawes Craven, Joseph Harker and Bruce Smith, there was an eclectic mixture of historical, naturalistic, impressionistic and neo-romantic elements. The novelty of the style lay in its preference for realistic, flexible pieces of décor to complement the illusionistic painting.

Descriptive realism made an even more important appearance in Russian musical theatre during the late 19th century, although it was basically restricted to the private opera productions of the magnate Vlassa Ivanovich Mamontov in Abramtsevo and Moscow (1885–7), apart from some naturalistic designs by Ivan Petrovich Andreyev (see Plate 83 above) for the Imperial Court Theatre in St Petersburg, which was otherwise dominated by the Romantic tradition of stage design associated with Andreas Roller. The painters in Mamontov's circle at Abramtsevo worked as his stage designers, and their work was inspired by the realism of Russian folk art; among those who were outstanding were Viktor Andreyevich Simov and Viktor Mikhailovich Vasnetzov (see Plate 86).

2. Production

If the operatic producer as an independent professional did not come into existence until the 20th century, the beginnings and early development of the art he would practice belong to the second half of the 19th, whose operas required his emergence. That the first half of the century did well enough without the producer is easy to understand: operatic plots to some extent resembled one another, with situations and dramatic scene-shapes based on well-established conventions and musical forms. One *aria d'entrata* or one *largo concertato* was doubtless like another as far as stage arrangement was concerned. But in theatre as in music the 19th century was characterized by the breakdown of widely shared assumptions as audiences broadened and became more diverse. It was central to the Romantic idea that the artist, and thus inevitably the particular work of art, should be individual. As it gradually became impossible to present operatic pasticcios or to interpolate arias by one composer into another's opera, so it became difficult to act one opera with the standard moves learnt in another.

Little is known about how operatic singers moved on the stage in the early years of the century. What little evidence exists for later decades has only recently come to be scrutinized. References to someone's 'staging', 'mounting', 'directing' or 'producing' an opera, often encountered, give little clear indication of that person's role in the preparation of the performance.

Two broad directorial functions, which eventually merged in the role of the 20th-century producers, can be distinguished. First, there is the job of the stage manager, directing traffic on the stage; Shaw described him, later in the century (in the course of calling for a different kind), as 'a person who arranged the few matters which cannot either be neglected or left to arrange themselves as best they may'. He would assign entrances, exits and rudimentary blocking – often in a very few rehearsals just before the opera was to open – but would not concern himself with artistic or interpretative questions. In many theatres the stage manager was a retired singer, or perhaps one still active in small or *buffo* parts. For a première, his duties might devolve on the librettist; for revivals, in the larger Italian houses, a staff librettist was often the stage manager. The English baritone Charles Santley left in his memoirs a rather disparaging account of Verdi's librettist Piave as an ineffective stage manager at La Scala (in fairness to Piave it should be said that Santley supposed him to have written the libretto of *Il trovatore*, which is by Cammarano, and to have forgotten his own work). It should also be noted that this method of operatic production has never entirely died out in practice; it remained common in provincial performances in the English-speaking world up to the 1960s, and given the participation of singers who had strong familiarity with and confidence in 'stock' operatic traditions it could yield persuasive results.

The other function, much more loosely defined and often left unfulfilled, had to do with explaining the work to the performers, guiding their interpretation of it and ensuring unity of approach to the drama. During most of the century this had more the character of advice and suggestion than actual direction in the modern sense (the person now known as a *Dramaturg* is something of a parallel). Goethe apparently interacted with his Weimar players in more or less this way:

> I attended the readings of plays, and explained to every one his part; I was present at the chief rehearsals, and talked with the actors as to any improvements that might be made; I was never absent from a performance, and pointed out the next day anything that did not appear to me to be right. By these means I advanced them in their art.

In the opera house these duties were occasionally assigned to someone engaged for that purpose; Weber hired the poet Ludwig Tieck in 1825 in Dresden as a 'Literator', with responsibilities that answer to Goethe's description, but this seems to have been unusual. More often the composer or librettist, occasionally with assistance from an impresario or (later) a publisher, carried out this role. At the turn of the century it was often filled by the conductor, notably by Toscanini and Mahler.

The history of 19th-century opera production is essentially a matter of the growing complexity and responsibility involved in the first of these functions (management of stage traffic), the consolidation and ascendance of the second (interpretative guidance) and their gradual intertwining. What cannot be gleaned directly from operatic scores must be viewed largely by extrapolation from the history of the spoken theatre, as there is a dearth of accounts specifically related to opera. Intercourse between theatre and opera was great. Goethe produced opera (Singspiel) at Weimar. Lucia Elizabeth Vestris (née Bartolozzi), widely credited as one of the first actor-managers to insist on thorough rehearsal and precision of ensemble acting, had been an opera singer of considerable attainments, appearing in many Rossini works at their London premières. The actor-producer Eduard Devrient, a leading figure in German theatrical reform in the mid-century, had also been a significant singer and was a member of a celebrated theatrical and musical family. As the century progressed composers and librettists eagerly adopted advances in theatrical production for their own works – and at its end, opera was central to the work of two seminal thinkers of the 20th-century theatre, Stanislavsky and Appia.

The rise of the régisseur in the theatre had largely to do with the growing concern for pictorial unity and elaboration, especially (as far as stage movement was concerned) the organized and convincing deployment of choruses and supernumeraries. Edmund Kean's touring company is said to have achieved impressive crowd scenes by placing a professional actor at the head of each of several groups into which the supernumeraries (amateurs gathered in each town) were divided. In the last quarter of the century the Meininger troupe astounded all Europe with the elaborate drill of its massed scenes; the Duke of Saxe-Meiningen had established rehearsal procedures of rigid discipline and required all his actors to take their turns as supernumeraries. Many accounts make it clear that the norm for crowds and choruses was near or complete immobility, as is implied in the set-piece approach that permeates much of even Wagner's treatment of the chorus.

The achievement of the Meininger troupe represented the traffic-director's craft raised to a high artistic pitch; at the same time the function of the Dramaturg as guide to interpretation grew with the increasing complexity and diversity of plots and became indispensable as pictorialism yielded to the naturalism of Antoine's Théâtre Libre (1887–94), Brahm's Freie Bühne (founded 1890) and Stanislavsky's Moscow Art Theatre (founded 1898).

Operatic production followed in rough concordance the same stages of development. Up to the middle of the century it seems to have gone nearly without question that the purpose of stage management was to arrive at a series of static tableaux corresponding to the musical set numbers. Within those, individually charismatic singing actors aspired to dramatic heights (Schröder-Devrient, Pasta, Malibran, Vogl and others were praised for their acting no less than their singing), but production was hardly in question.

Works demanding coordinated ensemble acting did, however, gain a foothold and increased, first in Paris, where preoccupation with *mise-en-scène* was in part a legacy of the *ballet d'action* (though the lengthy rehearsals of opera in Paris seem to have been concerned more with musical adjustments and special effects of scenery and machinery than with acting or stage direction as such). With Meyerbeer or Halévy, as later with

Verdi, crowd scenes became an element in the spectacle. The chorus was a notoriously weak and unprofessional component of most Italian companies; it was rarely called upon for any but the simplest movement and was generally ranged statically at the rear. But by 1851 in *Rigoletto* it could be asked to carry out an abduction; Donizetti and Bellini could rarely if ever have risked such a complication. (Perhaps this difficulty, not just censorship, was to blame for the occasional performances of *Rigoletto* in which the act ended with 'Caro nome' while the abduction was left to the imagination.)

During the third quarter of the century there was a rapid advance in composers' demands, especially Wagner's and Verdi's, that opera be taken as a theatrical, visual whole, with some kind of scenic director who would have the authority to command discipline. Naturalism, meanwhile, found its counterpart in the Italian *verismo* movement and in the works of the French composers who followed Massenet towards subjects of everyday life. The nature of rehearsal therefore needed reconsideration. Though Goethe had ordained early on that 'one should not permit oneself to do anything in rehearsal that one cannot do in the play', much time elapsed before performers – singers included – generally accepted the idea that rehearsals must be pre-creations of the dramatic experience rather than mere practical preparations for an emotional and theatrical encounter that could take place only in the presence of the public. This was especially true in England, according to the actor William Charles Macready's reminiscences:

> It was the custom of the London actors, especially the leading ones, to do little more at rehearsals than read or repeat the words of their parts, marking on them their entrances and exits, as settled by the stage manager, and their respective places on the stage. To make any display of passion or energy would be to expose oneself to the ridicule or sneers of the green-room.

It was some time before opera singers adopted different methods, and indeed many simply did not rehearse roles they already knew; in the last quarter of the century Patti could still send her répétiteur, and Sims Reeves his wife, to deputize at rehearsals and advise the rest of the company where the absent stars would stand (and what tempos they would require). The result was a level of operatic performance increasingly subject to criticism of production values, including caustic comparison with the spoken theatre and musical comedy.

The new works being created could not be adequately realized without jostling this system. As early as 1850, Wagner described part of the preparatory process now needed. He called on the stage manager to move towards his future role as producer, in a letter to Liszt about the *Lohengrin* stage manager Eduard Genast (a former singer), who, Wagner gathered:

> remained entirely on the proper standpoint of the stage manager, who arranges things in a general way, and justly leaves it to the individual actors to find out for themselves what concerns them only. In spite of this, I ask him now

to interfere even there, where the power and the natural activity of the stage manager ceases; let him be the trustee of infant actors. . . . Let Genast . . . call the whole personnel to a reading rehearsal; let the singers read their parts in connection, distinctly and expressively. . . . Let Genast take the score, and from the remarks therein inserted explain to the singers the meaning of the situations and their connection with the music bar by bar. . . . In that case he may boast of having been the chief participant in a revolution which will lift our theatrical routine out of its grooves.

How singers moved and acted, and how the traffic was directed in 19th-century operatic productions, can be gleaned from various blocking plans (*Regiebücher, mises-en-scène, disposizioni sceniche*) which explain the action verbally and represent it graphically. In France especially the *ballet d'action* had engendered a strong tradition, dating back to the late 18th century, of drawing up and even publishing such *mises-en-scènes*, many of which survive. It was apparently as a result of his Paris experience that Verdi initiated the series of *disposizioni sceniche* that appeared regularly with his new operas after *Les vêpres siciliennes*. Eight of these are known, including *Otello*; *Falstaff* was assigned plate numbers, but no copy has been found. They provide a clear and fascinating picture of the advances made during the second half of the century.

The first, for *Giovanna de Guzman* (1855, the initial Italian version of *Les vêpres*), runs to 38 pages and is in essence a clear, rudimentary traffic plan, in which set pieces are simply announced ('Aria', 'Duetto' etc), with directions for movement resumed afterwards. The chorus is arranged by voice category and given only the simplest movement. (This is representative, investigation suggests, of the French *mises-en-scène* up to that time, on which the early Ricordi ones are closely modelled.) Verdi was pleased with it ('any child could do the staging', he wrote), but successive *disposizioni* show a steady advance in the graphic representation of the blocking, in the sophistication of the movement (and thus of the rehearsal process) requires, and in the discussion of character and motivation. The 111-page *Otello* production book (1887), with its 100 pages of stage directions and 270 diagrams (the one for *Aida* had 92), is virtually a moment-by-moment dramatic analysis. By this time the most detailed directions for the exact composition of processions and scenes of pageantry are given, with stage movements and interpretative directions running right through the solo arias (even including the number of steps to be taken). The sophistication of choral movement is striking and requires the assumption that current innovations in the theatre had already begun to rub off in opera. Each chorister is exhorted to remember that he or she is an individual character with an individual personality; block movement and staring at the conductor are discouraged.

The detailed *disposizione* for *Aida* is essentially the work of Verdi himself, as may be seen by comparing it with the libretto annotated in his hand (facsimile and transcription in Busch, 1978; see Plate 63). So may others be, though Ricordi is listed as the compiler; for *Un ballo in maschera* it had been Giuseppe Cencetti, the house librettist and stage manager at the theatre of the première in 1858. Wagner exercised similarly direct control over the staging of his later operas; Porges's account (1877) of the rehearsals for the première of the *Ring* cycle is a valuable, if only fitfully specific, description of Wagner's directorial attitude. But the detailed approach these composers demanded for their premières was slow to penetrate the mounting of established works. At the end of the century in England Shaw could still complain:

> For want of a stage manager *Orfeo* was murdered. For want of a stage manager the first act of *Otello* was laid waste. For want of a stage manager *Tannhäuser* was made a laughing-stock to every German who went to see it, except in the one or two passages which Albani [the singer who played Elisabeth] stage-managed. . . . For want of a stage manager, no man in *Les Huguenots* knows whether he is a Catholic or a Protestant; and conversations which are pure nonsense except on the supposition that the parties cannot distinguish one another's features in the gloom are conducted in broad moonlight and gaslight.

To effect their newly specific marriage of music and drama within the natural conservatism of the operatic theatre, dominated as it was by older works which continued to fit satisfactorily into traditional concepts of production and routines of preparation, composers had to exercise to the fullest their hard-won personal authority – which was felt directly only at premières and supervised revivals. By the end of the century, a few leading operatic conductors had established their right to represent the composer's authority in his absence and to extend it to scenic questions. But such a procedure was inherently limited to the work of extraordinary individuals. In order that fulfilment of the emerging principles of music theatre might be counted on (or at least aspired to) when repertory operas were mounted in leading houses around the world, the emergence of a new kind of figure on the operatic scene was required.

A sobering look at the details of late 19th-century operatic acting comes from a small volume entitled *Acting in Opera* (1915), by G.E. Shea, a modestly successful American baritone. It gives the minutest particulars for achieving just the sort of melodramatic gesture and attitude from which later audiences have learnt to recoil, and has copious, similarly outmoded photographs. Hundreds of stock operatic utterances ('Never!'; 'Take him away!' or 'You shall perish!'; 'That is the villain!'; 'A treasure dearer than life!') as well as more general sentiments ('antipathetic refusal', 'meditating vengeance or dissimulating rage', 'insolent defiance') are supplied with precise descriptions showing the contribution of each limb and digit to the desired attitude. One shrinks from the thought that this typifies the work of the better actors in opera; but it does resemble, at least in surface attributes, the surviving film documentation of Shalyapin.

Entr'acte III

STANLEY SADIE

The most important harbinger of the 20th century and its attitudes to the arts, as far as opera was concerned, was the *verismo* movement. In almost all its earlier phases, opera had in some way been wedded to pleasurable illusion and the escape from reality. It might, and often did, carry social, political or symbolic meanings, but always within a fairly strictly stylized context. With the arrival in the opera house of *verismo*, introduced by Mascagni's *Cavalleria rusticana* in 1890, opera moved into line with the other arts of the late years of the 19th century in its readiness to accept the daily life of common people, even (indeed especially) at its most squalid, as apt material for treatment.

The chief European literary representative of the 'verist' movement was the French writer Emile Zola; its leading Italian figure, the novelist Giovanni Verga, was the writer of the story that served as Mascagni's basis for *Cavalleria rusticana*. That work was quickly followed into the repertory by Leoncavallo's *Pagliacci* (to provide that long-lasting favourite among operatic double bills, *Cav* and *Pag*); other operas concerned with the lower social strata, and dealing naturalistically with such topics as lust or murder, soon ensued. The use of the serving or menial classes for operatic treatment was not of course wholly new: it goes back to the maid and page in Monteverdi's *L'incoronazione di Poppea*, to Pergolesi's 'serva padrona', to Mozart's Susanna and the numerous others who can claim ancestry in *commedia dell'arte* models. But such characters were viewed by their creators largely as adjuncts to their aristocratic masters, and we are rarely asked to take their emotions wholly seriously. In *verismo* opera their passions and their violence are central. Opera is no longer an art about kings and heroes; the plight of the ordinary man in the modern world was now an appropriate topic for operatic treatment. The attitudes of *verismo* penetrated operas, like Puccini's *Tosca*, which do not deal with low life at all (Puccini's only true *verismo* opera is the one-act *Il tabarro*). The movement was strongest in Italy, with such composers as Cilea, Giordano and Zandonai, but was taken up too in France, with Bruneau (who wrote several operas based on works by Zola) and Gustave Charpentier, in England with Ethel Smyth and in Germany with d'Albert and Wolf-Ferrari, to name some of the more significant.

But in the German-speaking countries there was a parallel and more complex manifestation in the expressionist movement. Here is the same preoccupation with degradation and misery, conveyed in a tortured musical language that represents psychological agony as well as brutality. It has roots in (or shares roots with) Freudian psychology as well as the *fin de siècle* operas of Strauss, *Elektra* and *Salome*, with their representation in music of twisted sexuality and violence. By no means all the German or Austrian operas that fall under this heading deal with low-life subjects; the prototypical one, Schoenberg's *Erwartung*, depicts nothing but the state of mind of an anonymous woman *in extremis*, while what is arguably the greatest expressionist opera, Berg's *Wozzeck* – for all that its literary source comes from a century before – exemplifies outstandingly the figure of a 'hero' who is the epitome of ordinariness or worse, an inarticulate creature who is bullied, exploited, cuckolded and victimized and driven to murder and suicide, the impact enhanced by the use of such expressionist devices as the exaggerated violence of his surroundings and the use of symbols. This places *Wozzeck* (and the same is true to some extent of Berg's *Lulu*) apart from the many more purely naturalistic operas of the first two-thirds of the century, including several of Janáček's, Poulenc's *Dialogues des Carmélites*, in England works by Britten, and in the USA such operas as Copland's *The Tender Land* or Douglas Moore's *The Ballad of Baby Doe*, which look back on folk traditions, or Menotti's (which draw on Italian ones too).

It would have been unthinkable for an opera that concentrates on the plight of such a man as Wozzeck to reach the stage in the time of Handel or Mozart, or even Verdi or Wagner. The 20th century could consider and sympathize with central characters who were in no established sense conventionally heroic, and might show quite different aspects of individuality, such as creativity (Pfitzner's Palestrina, Krenek's Jonny, Hindemith's Mathis, Maxwell Davies's Taverner) or an incapacity to find a place in society (Janáček's Jenůfa or Katya, Britten's Grimes or Budd). A Russian tradition of epic opera continues, mainly in the vein of the Soviet interpretation of naturalism, that is, 'socialist realism'; by far its most distinguished creation is Prokofiev's *War and Peace*.

The diversity of this situation, produced by social and political changes of different kinds and different speeds in an industrial society, and accelerated by two world wars, was not of course particular to opera; it can be seen in all the arts of the time. Among its more direct causes was the changing basis of artistic patronage. In opera, such houses – that at Vienna, for example – as had continued through the 19th century under court patronage moved to national or municipal patronage and became increasingly dependent on a middle-class public, which had a social conscience and expected to be seriously addressed in the course of its entertainment. This was especially the case in central Europe, above all the German-speaking countries, during the 1920s, an era of experiment and increasing politicization in the arts. It is to this era that the concept of the *Zeitoper* – 'opera of the [present] time' – belongs, used by Krenek, Hindemith and, influenced by Brecht and Berlin cabaret music, Weill, who drew in his works of the late 1920s and early 1930s a picture of a society run by criminals and swindlers, a portrayal of the capitalist world as he then saw it, paralleling the work of the painters of the period who recorded human misery and degradation and moral ugliness. Such themes, though pursued by isolated figures (such as Marc Blitzstein in the USA, but not by Weill himself when later he was there), could not be followed up in the political circumstances of Europe in the 1930s. It was a sign of the times that the most progressive and experimental opera house of the period (in design and staging as well as repertory), the Kroll Opera in Berlin, which had opened in 1927, was forced to close down in 1931. It was only after World War II that a new generation of composers arose eager to embody social and political protest in their works, men such as Henze, Dallapiccola, Zimmermann, Nono and Goehr: all, it should be noted, working west of the 'iron curtain', where social protest had a purpose; east of it, in any case, the range of acceptable topics was long circumscribed by the dictates of Stalinist socialism.

But it is not only in the composition of new operas that one may find important symptoms of change. Indeed new operas have formed an increasingly small part of the business of an opera house during the 20th century – a symptom of change in itself. While the opera-house repertory, to meet the preferences of a conservative public drawn above all by its favourite operas and favourite singers, and not eager to listen to 'difficult' new works, has come increasingly to be based on a fairly modest number of standard works (those of Mozart, Verdi, Wagner, Puccini and Strauss, with a smaller number each by another dozen or so composers, form the core of the repertory), interest has tended to focus on their presentation and interpretation. It is in this context that the role of the opera producer or director has steadily come to assume greater prominence. The concept of a single person's exercising overall control of the dramatic aspects (and even having some say over the musical ones) in an opera performance was new with the post-Wagnerian era, that is to say the 20th century. To some extent it could be put down to Wagner himself, because of the symbolic richness of his operas and their susceptibility to a wide range of interpretations. As long as it had been supposed that an opera needed no unified interpretation – as long as, that is, it could be left to the singers, perhaps with a little advice from an impresario or a stage manager or a conductor, or as long as the concept of an alliance of the arts to a particular end had not come into being – there was no need for the producer.

After Wagner all this changed. The committed producer has come to see it as his role to look below the surface of a work, to consider something more than what the composer and librettist seem to be saying. He may try to discern sub- or unconscious elements in the music or the text, or in an earlier historical or literary source for the work, and use them as a basis for his decisions about the action or the characterization. He may aim to see the opera in terms of the psychology, as he understands it, of one or more of its characters. He may move its action from the period in which it was originally set, usually to a later period (often to the time when its music was composed, or to the present, or to the time of some particularly suggestive social or political situation), so as to lend new meanings to it. He may introduce deliberate clashes of style – a Brechtian 'alienation' device – to emphasize some aspect of the work or to identify a character with a current archetype (Wotan may be portrayed as a capitalist company director, Carmen as a gun-toting female guerrilla, Mozart's Belmonte as a selfish male chauvinist). Members of an audience may be forgiven for objecting if this results in an inconsistency between a character's new identity and what the composer has him sing, or indeed the librettist has him say; but producers, particularly those who have come to opera from the 'straight', spoken theatre, have claimed that the severing of traditional links, especially that between words and musical expression (which is anyway often ambiguous), may represent a creative and socially or psychologically aware way of viewing a 'museum art' – as opera has frequently been called because its stamping-ground is so largely from the past. Producers eager for novelty and fresh meaning, and understandably eager, too, to draw new, young and socially conscious audiences into the opera house, feel no need to be respectful of historical, still less of purist, sensibilities.

In spite of the hegemony of the producer in the middle and late 20th century, the role of the singer as a central attraction remains largely undisturbed. It is the appearance of a Sutherland or a Pavarotti – as it once was of a Farinelli, a Pasta, a Lind, or more lately a Melba, a Caruso or a Callas – that can be depended upon above all to draw audiences, especially in traditional Italian repertory where vocal prowess has the maximum scope. As in every other period in the history of opera, a large part of the audience is more concerned with singing than with anything else, and the era of jet air travel has provided them with opportunities as never before. For the singers, this has attendant dangers: many promising voices have become prematurely worn and faded when their owners have succumbed to the temptation of over-frequent appearances in too many roles, too little prepared, in houses too large for them.

Opera houses themselves, in the course of the 20th century, have grown in size and increased in number. Economics dictate the necessity for houses still larger than those of the previous century, while the rise in public interest coupled with awareness of local prestige has led to the establishment of many new ones, or of new opera companies that perform in existing theatres. The cost of their active maintenance, now that the rich or courtly patron has virtually disappeared, is another matter. In some countries, notably Germany, it falls primarily on municipal authorities, and is most often willingly borne, as a traditional facility ratified by longstanding custom and continuing use and an accepted enhancement of regional cultural life. In others, such as Britain, a large proportion of the funding is supplied by government through an agency, while in the USA the main role is provided by the private or corporate patron. Running an opera house – especially one with international pretensions, and accordingly expected to present the finest international artists and to pay them the highest fees – costs far more than any amount that can be taken at the box office. In the late 1980s, box office receipts at typical large European houses represented only about a quarter of the annual revenue, the remainder being supplied by grants. At such houses, opera is usually given during some ten months of the year, with performances most evenings; some theatres are shared with ballet companies, and in smaller towns with operetta, musicals and even spoken drama. Where operatic traditions are less firmly established, and in smaller towns, seasons may be shorter, anything from four- to ten-week ones two or three times a year down to the occasional season of a week or two. Some opera companies serve two houses, while others undertake regular tours that bring brief opera seasons to cities where it is otherwise unavailable.

The question of the language in which opera is performed often excites controversy. Composers have normally, but not always, expected that their works will be given in a language fully comprehensible to the audience – though the prevalence of Italian opera in the 18th century established a tradition of using Italian even as far from Italy as London, Stockholm or St Petersburg. Audiences then, as we have seen, could follow the sense, using a bilingual wordbook in a lighted house. Generally speaking, audiences in Italy and Germany have always taken for granted that they would hear opera in their own language; even the Italian operas of Mozart, composed for a court opera house in Vienna, were translated into German for performance in other German-speaking centres, just as Handel's Italian operas written for London had been heard in German in Hamburg. In some countries, such as England, traditions of vernacular opera and foreign-language opera developed in the 19th century with some degree of independence. But language was not a prime issue among opera audiences away from the main creative centres: London had its Royal Italian Opera, where all operas (including German ones) were given in Italian, while the Metropolitan Opera in New York began its main existence as a German opera house, where all operas (including Italian ones) were given in German. Even Paris had its Théâtre-Italien for nearly half a century.

With the widening public of the 20th century – serious-minded, middle-class, generally less readily able to understand foreign languages – the need for translation has come to be more widely accepted, and many companies (particularly those that specifically cater for this broader public) have preferred the vernacular as a matter of policy. But such a policy is excluded for the kind of house that calls on an international body of singers who can be expected to sing the repertory only in the languages in which it was written. Some houses have favoured the vernacular for Slavonic opera (unless performed by a guest cast) and sometimes for comic works; but there tends to be a clear division between original-language companies and vernacular ones. In the mid-1980s the practice of showing 'surtitles' – translations into the audience's native language of essential lines in the text, carefully synchronized with the performance, projected on to a screen just below the proscenium arch – has increasingly come to be accepted in original-language performances, and although they are sometimes regarded as offensive by those deeply familiar with the repertory they have led to a noticeable quickening of audience response.

The widespread acceptance of surtitles may be related to the longstanding use of sub-titles in films and television, media in which opera has been given and has reached a very much larger audience than ever before. Whether intended primarily for a large cinema screen or a small television one, filmed opera – whose traditions go back, perhaps surprisingly, to the times of silent films at the very beginning of the century – is now made in two basic ways. One simply involves the placing of cameras in an opera house and filming a performance (or a group of performances), cutting as appropriate between the cameras to provide different views. This is the procedure used, necessarily, in live transmissions such as the regular ones from the Metropolitan Opera House, New York, and in such films as those of the Russian repertory made at the Bol'shoy Theatre in Moscow and the Kirov Theatre in Leningrad. The other approach involves making a film of an opera rather than merely filming one – that is, using the techniques of film-making, including realistic outdoor scenes and rapid cutting, allusive shots involving images in the singer's mind, and so on, as was done in (for example) Joachim Herz's *Der fliegende Holländer*, Joseph Losey's *Don Giovanni*, Jean-Pierre Ponnelle's *La clemenza di Tito* and Franco Zeffirelli's *La traviata* and *Otello*. While the former type (which of course is very much cheaper to make) preserves the ambience of the opera house and some of its conventions – it can be argued that the habitual switching between cameras giving a wide view of the stage and those providing a close-up of a singer or a group of singers represents fairly the opera-goer's normal changes of visual focus – the latter type makes the full use of the film medium that television and cinema audiences instinctively expect from their experience of its naturalism and flexibility; any more conservative treatment, in fact, could be said to deny the essential nature of film as a medium.

Yet taking opera out of the opera house, away from the proscenium whose artificiality provides a framework for, and justifies, a world of convention in which people do not behave realistically (for example, they address each other and express their feelings plausibly in song), equally denies something of the essential nature of opera. Directors have sought to resolve the fundamental contradictions between the two media, film and opera, in various ways; one satisfactory compromise involves making a film by treating the opera house as a studio and filming what is visibly a stage performance (or in actuality a series of performances, section by section) from a much wider variety of angles and distances, and more effective dispositions of lighting, than would be feasible at a real stage performance. Ingmar Bergman's famous film of *Die Zauberflöte*, filmed partly inside a mock-up of the 18th-century Swedish court opera house at Drottningholm, near Stockholm, with glimpses behind the scenes, at the audience and at the countryside, implicitly acknowledges some of the contradictions.

But it is not only on the screen that the outlines of opera have become blurred. The nature of opera as a costly, formal entertainment for a socially limited audience has, especially in the period following World War II, rendered it alien to many composers, younger ones especially. One outcome of this was the rise of chamber opera, opera on a modest scale, suitable for touring companies with limited resources and facilities. There are of course earlier examples of the kind; much 18th-century opera can be regarded as 'chamber' in scale (and some duly found a place in the repertories of modern chamber opera companies) and there are precedents earlier in the 20th century, in composers as diverse as Stravinsky, Hindemith and Holst. The most important exponent of the chamber opera of the post-World War II period, however, was Benjamin Britten, with such works as *The Rape of Lucretia* and *The Turn of the Screw*.

The Rape of Lucretia includes singing parts, labelled 'Male Chorus' and 'Female Chorus', for narrators and commentators, external to the action, akin in function to a Greek chorus. This represents a break with operatic convention that is characteristic of the time and of the thinking of younger composers in response to the world of formal opera. This idea of a 'music theatre' that avoided not only the title 'opera' but also the accoutrements traditional to the genre had a strong appeal. And here too there were notable precedents for works that used elements of traditional opera in a selective or highly stylized way; the most often cited are Schoenberg's *Pierrot lunaire*, a concert work that lent itself to costume performance with appropriate lighting effects, and Stravinsky's *Histoire du soldat*, a theatre work using narration and mime. The further influence of John Cage and the concept of the 'happening' affected the generation of Berio, Ligeti, Kagel and Pousseur who, in the 1960s and 70s, wrote works for concert performance with theatrical elements (special lighting, speech, mime, projections etc), or for semi-theatrical performance, as well as Maxwell Davies whose specialist ensemble, the Fires of London, gave many performances of his own and other composers' works including elements of music theatre.

It is too early to discern any patterns in the history of opera into the 1980s. Composers remain eager to write for traditional opera houses, on the rare opportunities that the economic factors governing opera-house management permit them. Yet many senior figures, like Carter or Boulez, have stood aside from opera (though Boulez conducts it), while Messiaen has produced a single opera, profoundly religious in content, and Henze has given the form up altogether. Berio – an Italian – has retained his interest; and Stockhausen continues working on his mammoth, part-autobiographical, seven-night cycle, *Licht*. Minimalist composers, notably Glass, have found in their technique a framework for extended composition that many of their traditional colleagues lack, and have developed a new opera-going public that can accept it. Whatever the future of opera, it seems certain to reflect the diversities of the late 20th century.

PART FOUR

The 20th Century

CHAPTER XXII

Italy

JULIAN BUDDEN, JOHN C.G. WATERHOUSE

Puccini and the period 1890–1910

Operatic *verismo* became fashionable in Italy following the explosively successful première of Mascagni's *Cavalleria rusticana* (1890, Rome). Based on a short story and play by the realist novelist Giovanni Verga, the work had won a competition organized by the Milan publisher Sonzogno, owner of the Italian rights of *Carmen*. *Cavalleria* recalls that opera in its colourful depiction of uninhibited emotions in a southern European community and in the brutal terseness with which the final catastrophe is presented. Yet the effect is profoundly Italian, and despite the work's crude technique its compellingly sincere melodic expression has made a lasting impact on audiences all over the world. Imitations inevitably followed, most of which won only ephemeral acceptance. A few, like Spinelli's *A basso porto* (1894, Cologne), remained in the repertory for some decades; but only Leoncavallo's *Pagliacci* (1892, Milan) proved a match for *Cavalleria*, becoming its perennial companion piece. Leoncavallo's superior stagecraft and more sophisticated harmony and orchestration here compensate for his eclectic, commonplace melodic invention. Neither Mascagni nor Leoncavallo fully recaptured these first successes with their subsequent works, in which they tended to veer from one kind of subject to another, sometimes drastically overreaching their creative limitations. Yet their best later operas are not without merit: Mascagni in particular broadened his technical and expressive vocabulary considerably while retaining his individuality. This is notably the case in *Iris* (1898, Rome), despite Illica's pretentious, pseudo-symbolic libretto set in Japan.

Far more gifted, self-critical and purposeful in his evolution, Puccini was the only Italian composer of his generation (known collectively as the *giovane scuola*) who possessed the power of self-renewal with each successive opera. A pupil of Ponchielli and the violinist-composer Bazzini, he was first thought to show a specifically symphonic talent; and the subject chosen for his earliest opera, *Le villi* (1884, Milan), originally in one act but later expanded into two, appealed to him as belonging to the 'symphonic descriptive' genre. It is basically a 'number' opera, made up of arias, duets and larger ensembles, but among its more unusual features, deriving from the 'scapigliato' outlook of the librettist, Fontana, are an intermezzo mimed behind a gauze curtain and framed by recited poetry and direct participation by the corps de ballet in the dramatic action – hence the sub-title 'opera ballo'. Massenet's influence can be traced in the suppleness of the vocal line, together with a gentle melancholy redolent of Puccini's fellow-Luccan, Catalani. Individual traits, however, are already present, notably a fondness for sequences that move to the flat side of the key. In *Edgar* (1889, Milan), a full-length opera again to a Fontana text, the texture is more continuous and the craftsmanship surer, while further Puccinian fingerprints are discernible, such as a fondness for dissonant chords moving in parallel and for doubling the melody with the bass line. The villainess Tigrana is a lineal descendant of Bizet's Carmen, pinpointed by a similar orchestral motif.

However, the phenomenon of *Cavalleria rusticana* convinced Puccini that his true path lay in the direction of realism rather than in the fantastications of the 'scapigliatura'. 'Great sorrows in little souls' was from now on his professed ideal. Accordingly, in *Manon Lescaut* (1893, Turin), his first opera to show a fully integrated artistic personality, the Abbé Prévost's story is treated in the direct, emotional manner of Mascagni, coloured here and there by a certain Gallic refinement. The Wagnerian experience begins to bear fruit in the use of the developing motif, especially notable in the first act whose score is of an almost symphonic workmanship. It will be seen however that Puccini's use of recurring motifs is less explicitly referential than Wagner's, so that the same theme may take on different connotations according to its context; and that neither here nor in his subsequent operas does he disdain the detachable number. The most striking innovation of *Manon Lescaut* is to be found in the parade of the prostitutes that closes Act 3, where for the first time Puccini breaks the mould of the traditional 'pezzo concertato' with a grand, spectacular ensemble during which time is never for a moment suspended. Two flaws remain: a certain discontinuity in the action that precludes the establishment of the heroine's character, and a concentration of all the gaiety in the first two acts and all the gloom in Acts 3 and 4.

Both these faults are triumphantly remedied in *La bohème* (1896, Turin), the first of three highly successful collaborations with the poets Illica and Giacosa. Here the comic and tragic elements are held in perfect equilibrium, symbolized by the quartet that concludes Act 3. Leading themes are incorporated effortlessly into set numbers. Refinement in scoring and harmony goes hand in hand with a new boldness, as in the parallel brass triads that open the second act at the Café Momus and the open 5ths for flutes and harp that depict the falling snow at the Barrière d'Enfer. The text too offers a happy blend of the traditional high-flown operatic jargon, used parodistically, with the down-to-earth directness favoured by the 'veristi'. In Mimì we meet for the first time the typical Puccinian heroine – the frail, suffering victim, who has loved 'not wisely but too well'. In *Tosca* (1900, Rome), a grim, historical drama, Puccini adopts a more forceful manner; the aggressive 'Scarpia' chords, associated with the police chief, that open the work herald a tensely dramatic opera, showing his much-criticized streak of sadism. He makes powerful use of chromaticism and of harmony based on the whole-tone scale. Tosca – convent girl, professional singer, jealous lover and perforce murderess – herself remains the most various and interesting of Puccini's heroines and thus a rare challenge to a singer's dramatic ability. *Madama Butterfly* (1904, Milan) shows a still larger scale of musical thought (it contains the longest and most elaborate love duet Puccini wrote). Here Japanese melodies, suitably stylized, are used to colour the score. The heroine, who dominates the entire work, follows the pattern of Mimì, with the difference that by the end she attains a genuinely tragic dignity.

That Puccini felt the need to escape from this feminine stereotype is clear from the choice of his next subject. The protagonist of *La fanciulla del West* (1910, New York) is a strong-minded young woman of strict morality, capable of keeping order amongst a rough mining community but sufficiently tender-hearted to bend her high principles in order to save the life of the man she loves. A veneer of American folk melody replaces the Japanese colouring of *Madama Butterfly*, while the harmonic idiom is further enriched and diversified by influences from Richard Strauss and Debussy. If the lyrical flights are briefer and less frequent than in the earlier operas, they are often the more striking for their harsher context. *La rondine* (1917, Monte Carlo) originated in a commission from a Viennese publisher for an operetta with spoken dialogue; it was Puccini himself who insisted on turning it into a through-composed opera. The style, however, remains light and melodious throughout, with an abundance of dance-rhythms and little in the way of harmonic daring. Unhappily the theme of renunciation proved uncongenial to Puccini, who preferred a tragic dénouement; and the result is a weak final act. His powers are once again at full strength with *Il trittico* (1918, New York). The first of its three one-act 'panels', *Il tabarro*, ventures into the realm of Grand Guignol: its dark, brooding atmosphere is reinforced by occasional starkly 20th-century dissonances and lit by flashes of the old lyricism. The second 'panel', *Suor Angelica*, for women's voices only, evokes the serenity and innocence of life in a convent, using stylized elements of liturgical chant that have counterparts in Pizzetti, Malipiero and Respighi. Here tragedy obtrudes with lacerating force, culminating, however, on an unconvincing note of redemption. *Gianni Schicchi* is a work of robust high spirits, Puccini's only excursion into pure comedy. Totally distinct from one another in mood and language, all three operas bear witness to an ever-growing width of musical range.

Turandot (1926, Milan), whose ending was completed from the composer's sketches by Alfano, shows a massiveness of scale unprecedented in Puccini's operas. Here he re-creates the fantastic Orient of Gozzi with the aid of Chinese melodies, some authentic, some invented, but harmonized and developed far more adventurously than the Japanese elements in *Madama Butterfly*. Stravinskian (or Casella-like) bitonality and piled-up chords, the whole-tone scale and the pentatonic, all contribute threads to the rich tapestry without displacing the familiar Puccinian traits – the sequences that move stepwise, the phrases that end with a falling 5th, the pendulum-like alternation of dissonant chords. There is even a traditional Puccinian sub-heroine in the slave girl Liù, who sacrifices herself for the sake of the hero; some of her music, however, is formed entirely on the pentatonic scale. Thematic reminiscence is used sparingly; much of the score is built into broad slabs from varied repetitions of a single motif – a method already adumbrated in *Il tabarro* and clearly deriving from Stravinsky. No other score of Puccini's shows such a degree of orchestral imagination.

Yet for all the modernisms to be found in his late works Puccini remains spiritually a member of the generation of Italian composers that emerged during the 1890s to follow the trail blazed by *Cavalleria rusticana*. If Verdi's *oeuvre* mirrors the ideals of the Risorgimento and the liberal humanity of Manzoni without its Catholic overtones, Puccini's is the musical voice of the 'little Italy' ('Italietta') of the pre-1915 era. The wider horizons of moral, political or religious idealism lay outside his field of vision; hence, no doubt, his failure to end *Suor Angelica* on a suitable note of sublimity and to end *Turandot* at all. He excels in portraying the joys and sorrows of ordinary people and in evoking a particular ambience, whether the cheerful bustle of the Paris Quartier Latin (*La bohème*); dawn on the Roman Campagna (*Tosca*) or the River Seine flowing monotonously beneath leaden skies (*Il tabarro*).

As far as musical dramaturgy is concerned, Puccini has never been surpassed. In adapting his literary sources he frequently transformed them out of all recognition, adding incidents and characters that had never occurred to the original authors – in *Madama Butterfly* Cio-Cio-San's wedding, with its host of secondary roles, in *La fanciulla del West* the lynching scene, in *Turandot* the character of Liù. By basing the heroine of *La bohème* not so much on her counterpart in the novel as on the marginal character of Francine (the only one of Mürger's *grisettes* to be drawn in wholly romantic terms), he not only added a fresh dimension to the plot; he avoided the pitfall of Leoncavallo's opera on the same story (*La bohème*, 1897, Venice) where Mimì and Musetta, remaining true to Mürger's portrayal of them, become musically indistinguishable. All Puccini's operas are marked by a minute attention to detail; note, word, gesture and movement are integrated in such a way as to allow little room for the invention of a producer. His favourite method of dramatic exposition in the later operas is to open with a succession of apparently disconnected vignettes from which the tragedy gradually takes shape, gathering momentum as it proceeds. Except in the case of *La fanciulla del West*, in which soprano and tenor escape to freedom, the end is unrelieved by any hint of consolation. The hero and heroine of Giordano's *Andrea Chénier* face their execution convinced of the value of their sacrifice; no such faith inspires the doomed Cavaradossi, and the final curtain falls upon a cry of pain, which, however crude in its effect, at least testifies to the emotional honesty of a composer for whom death was simply the end of everything.

Among the composers whose careers partly paralleled Puccini's, the most important were Cilea and Giordano. Cilea gave of his best in *L'arlesiana* (1897, Milan) – a picturesque operatic version of Daudet's rustic tragedy, strongly influenced by Massenet – and in the eclectic *Adriana Lecouvreur* (1902, Milan), which provides plentiful scope for a *prima donna*'s histrionic talents. Giordano won his biggest success with *Andrea Chénier* (1896, Milan), in which the issues of the French Revolution loom larger than in *Tosca*: although the musical invention cannot match Puccini's, this hardly matters in, for example, the starkly dramatic confrontation between plebeians and aristocrats at the end of Act 1. Giordano's next two operas, *Fedora* (1898, Milan) and *Siberia* (1903, Milan), are set at least partly in Russia and sometimes reflect this in their music. Neither equals *Chénier* dramatically; yet they show that Giordano, too, broadened his stylistic horizons as time went on.

Two significant Italian opera composers of this period stand apart; they won little success in Italy, mainly because they did not share the ideals of the publishing magnates Sonzogno and Ricordi. Smareglia continued to develop his Italianized Wagnerian methods, reaching considerable heights of musical inspiration at (especially) the culmination of Act 2 in *Oceàna* (1903, Milan), with its haunting sirens' chorus and pervasive aura of the sea. Wolf-Ferrari excelled in operatic comedies evoking the spirit (rather than the letter) of 18th-century *opera buffa*: his imagination found an ideal stimulus in Goldoni's plays, on which *Le donne curiose* and *I quattro rusteghi* (1903 and 1906, Munich) are based. The latter, though unpretentious, is one of the most perfect Italian operas of its time: a hilarious, exquisitely polished comedy of manners, known in English as *School for Fathers*. Yet its success in Germany was exceedingly slow to percolate south of the Alps. Wolf-Ferrari's most frequently staged opera is the amiable one-act intermezzo *Il segreto di Susanna* (1909, Munich), which owes its popularity partly to its conveniently small cast and its gently parodistic story (Susanna's secret is the fact that she smokes).

1910–30

By 1910 opera was beginning to lose its dominant place in Italian musical life. Concert music was again coming to the fore, and most of the younger composers who nevertheless wrote operas usually differed from their immediate predecessors in writing many non-operatic works too. The conservative Montemezzi was an exception; and even his operatic output remained small. Yet his one big success, *L'amore dei tre re* (1913, Milan), has theatrical qualities which won it lasting favour in the USA – more, indeed, than in Italy. Montemezzi's music, indebted to Wagner and achieving real emotional power in the Act 2 love scene, on the whole commands respect rather than enthusiasm. Zandonai was more prolific and adventurous, although he too lacked originality of a deeper kind. In *Conchita* (1911, Milan) the *Carmen*-like subject provided opportunities for vivid Spanish local colour, and the idiom parallels the Debussian and Straussian tendencies in *La fanciulla del West*. Zandonai's most famous opera, *Francesca da Rimini* (1914, Turin), is based on D'Annunzio's play: although the music's response to the text's sumptuous decadence is at times crudely rhetorical, parts of Act 1 in particular have a memorable, radiantly archaic evocativeness.

Alfano came to prominence with *Risurrezione* (1904, Turin), whose treatment of a Russian subject (after Tolstoy) calls to mind Giordano as well as Puccini. While lacking the latter's melodic distinction, the work proved strong enough dramatically to win considerable success. Only after 1910, however, did Alfano turn to a less traditional operatic style, revealing a deepened understanding of (especially) Debussy. The result, in his masterpiece *La leggenda di Sakuntala* (1921, Bologna), based on a classic Sanskrit drama by Kalidasa, is more atmospheric than urgent, more distinguished orchestrally than vocally. Yet the work's highlights are fine enough to have won it an honourable place in the annals of interwar Italian opera, though it has never matched the popularity of *Risurrezione*. Respighi's stage works are a relatively minor branch of his output; yet the winsome children's opera *La bella dormente nel bosco* (1922, Rome), originally designed for puppets, is one of his best compositions. His most effective opera for adults is probably *La campana sommersa* (1927, Hamburg; after Hauptmann), whose supernatural elements provided opportunities for his well-known flair for the picturesque.

The most original newcomers to the Italian operatic scene during 1910–30 were, however, Pizzetti and G. F. Malipiero – the only significant Italians (apart from the expatriate Busoni: see below) to depart relatively thoroughly from established operatic methods at this time. Pizzetti's approach was conditioned by a musico-dramatic theory which outlawed self-sufficient lyricism except in special circumstances, replacing it with a continuous, usually rather rapid declamation, sensitive to every nuance of the text. Partial precursors for such methods range from the Florentine Camerata through Dargomïzhsky to Debussy; but the result in Pizzetti's operas is a distinctive, often modally tinged style that can be intensely expressive, despite a serious risk of monotony in the weaker scenes. The first fruit of these innovations was *Fedra* (1915, Milan), a setting of a shortened version of D'Annunzio's play, devised in collaboration with the poet himself. Although less colourful than *Francesca da Rimini*, this is an altogether deeper operatic response to the D'Annunzian ethos, notable for the powerful portrayal of the volatile heroine and for some sublime neo-madrigalian choral writing at the beginning of Act 3. In *Dèbora e Jaéle* (1922, Milan) the chorus has a still more important part, sometimes dwarfing the individual characters: this is especially the case in the darkly turbulent first half of Act 1, where a debt to *Boris Godunov* is

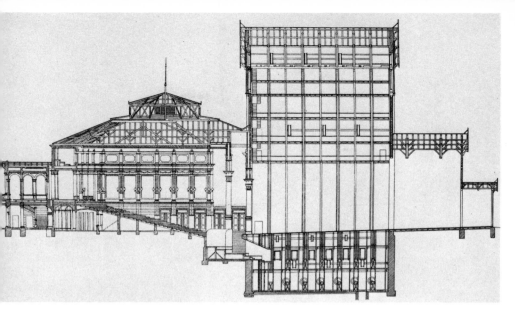

88. *Section of the Bayreuth opera house from Sachs and Woodrow, 'Modern Opera Houses and Theatres', i (1896)*

Rehearsal in the Bayreuth Festspielhaus conducted by ...ann Levi: drawing (1882) by Josef Grief in the ...rd Wagner Gedenkstätte, Bayreuth (Wagner is ...ng through the hole at the top of the pit)

90. *A scene from Wallace's opera 'Maritana', first performed at [?] London, 15 November 1845: engraving from the 'Illustrated Lo[?]* *(22 November 1845)*

91. *Playbill advertising a performance of Henry Bishop's arrangement of Mozart's 'Marriage of Figaro' at the Theatre Royal, Covent Garden, London, on 6 March 1819*

92. *Illustration showing scenes from the first performance of Gilber[?] van's opera 'Iolanthe' at the Savoy Theatre, London, 1882 (from [?] phic', 23 December 1882)*

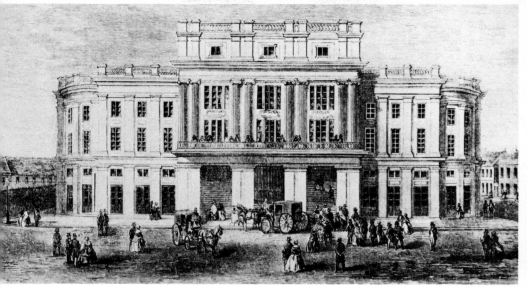

French Opera House, New Orleans: wood engraving by Fichot ...au from 'L'illustration' (10 December 1859)

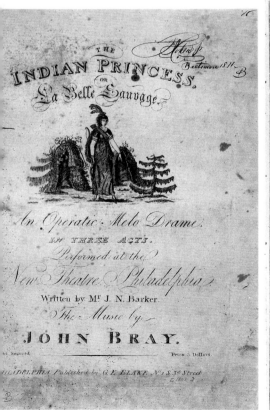

...page of the vocal score of 'The Indian Princess, or La belle ...y James Nelson Barker, with music by John Bray, first per-...Philadelphia in 1808

METROPOLITAN
OPERA HOUSE.

MR. HENRY E. ABBEY, · · · · · Director.
Acting Manager, · · · · · MR. MAURICE GRAU.

MONDAY EVENING, OCTOBER 22, 1883,

INAUGURAL NIGHT
AND
First Night of the Subscription,

WHEN GOUNOD'S OPERA OF

"FAUST."

Will be presented with the following Cast:

FAUST, · · · · · · ·	Sig. ITALO CAMPANINI
MEPHISTOPHELES, · · · ·	Sig. FRANCO NOVARA
VALENTINO, · · · ·	Sig. GIUSEPPE DEL PUENTE
WAGNER, · · · · · ·	Sig. CONTINI
SIEBEL, · · · · ·	Mme. SOFIA SCALCHI
MARTA, · · · · ·	Mlle. LOUISE LABLACHE

(Who has kindly consented to assume the part at short notice. Her first appearance.)
AND
MARGHERITA, · · · · · Mme. CHRISTINE NILSSON

Musical Director and Conductor, · Sig. VIANESI

WEBER PIANO USED.

Mason & Hamlin's Organ Used.

All the above Operas performed at this House can be had in every form, Vocal and Instrumental at G. SCHIRMER, No. 35 Union Square, Importer and Publisher of Music

The Scenery by Messrs. Fox, Schaefler, Maeder, and Thompson.
The Costumes are entirely new, and were manufactured at Venice by D. Ascoli.
The Appointments by Mr. Bradwell.
Machinists, Messrs. Lundy & Gifford.

NIGHTLY PRICES OF ADMISSION:

Boxes, holding six (6) seats..	$50
Orchestra Stalls..	6
Balcony Stalls..	3
Family Circle (reserved)..	2
Admission to Family Circle..	1

Seats and Boxes can be secured at the Box Office of the Metropolitan Opera House, which will remain open daily from 8 A. M. to 5 P. M.

Doors open at 7.15.   **Performances at 8 precisely.**

Generius Gabrielson & Son, Florists to the Metropolitan Opera House.

Opera Glasses on Hire in the Lobby.

L. F. Masotte, Caterer

Parties desiring Ices can be supplied by the Weber, in Corridor

Business Manager · · · · · · · Mr. W. W. TILLOTSON.
Treasurer · · · · · · · Mr. CHAS. H. MATHEWS.

95. Programme for the opening of the Metropolitan Opera House, New York, on 22 October 1883

96. Title-page of the piano score of Mascagni's opera 'Cavalleria rusticana' published in Milan by Sonzogno (1890)

97. Poster by L. Metlicovitz for the first performance of Puccini's opera 'Madama Butterfly'

Design by G. B. Santoni for Puccini's opera 'Il tabarro', with annotations by the composer (Museo Teatrale alla Scala, Milan)

Original sketch (1925–6) for a stage design for the first production of Puccini's opera 'Turandot' at La Scala, Milan

100. Strauss's 'Elektra', first production (Dresden, Court Opera, 1909): Elecktra offers to light Aegisthus's way into the palace

101. Costume designs by Alfred Roller for 'Der Rosenkavalier': Baron Ochs (left) and the Marschallin (right)

102. Design by Alfred Roller for Act 3 of Strauss' 'Der Rosenkavalier', first performed at the Dresden Opera on 26 January 1911

3. Berg's 'Wozzeck', first production (Berlin, Staatsoper, 1925): design by Panos Aravantinos for the Doctor's study (Act
scene iv)

4. Design by Casper Neher for the Act 3 finale of 'Die Dreigroschenoper' by Brecht and Weill, Cologne, Stadttheater,
30: pen, ink and watercolour

105. *Henze's 'König Hirsch': stage design by Jean Pierre Ponnelle for the first production (Berlin, 1956)*

106. *Mauricio Kagel (centre) in a scene from his 'Staatstheater' (Hamburg, Staatsoper, 1971)*

Scene from the first performance of Luigi Dallapicola's opera 'Ulisse', 29 September 1968, Deutsche Oper, Berlin

Collage of slide and film projections designed by Josef Svoboda for Nono's 'Intolleranza 1960', Venice, La Fenice, 1961

109. *Stage design by Jusseaume for the scene of the death of Pelléas in Debussy's 'Pelléas et Mélisande', first performed Paris, 30 April 1902*

110. *Scene from Act 3 of Messiaen's opera 'Sanit François d'Assise', first performed at the Paris Opéra, 28 November (Bibliothèque et Musée de l'Opéra, Paris)*

Stage design by I. Bilibin for Act 3 of Rimsky-Korsakov's opera 'Zolotoy petushok' ('The Golden Cockerel'), first performed *scow, 1909*

Scene from Act 1 of the first performance of Stravinsky's opera 'The Rake's Progress' at La Fenice, Venice, 11 September 1951

114. Set design by
Čapek for the first Prag
formance (1928) of Ja
opera 'Věc Makr
('The Makropulos Af

13. *Scene from the first complete performance of Prokofiev's opera 'Voyna i mir' ('War and Peace'), 8 November 1957,* *ol'shoy Theatre, Moscow*

15. *Scene from Penderecki's opera 'Diably z Loudun' ('The Devils of Loudun'): gala performance at the Grand Theatre of* *Opera and Ballet, Warsaw, 8 June 1975*

116. Peter Grimes (Peter Pears) and
Orford (Joan Cross) in a scene from th
production of Britten's opera, London,

117. Britten's 'Death in Venice', first p
tion at The Maltings, Snape, Suffolk,
English Opera Group, June 1973:
showing the end of the Games in Act
Peter Pears as Aschenbach (seated, far
and Robert Huguenin as Tadgio (carri

18. Scene from Act 3 of Tippett's opera 'The Knot Garden', first performed at Covent Garden, London, on 2 December 1970, with Jill Gomez as Flora, Thomas Hemsley as Mangus, Raimund Herinex as Faber, Thomas Carey as Mel and Robert Tear as Dov (design by Timothy O'Brien)

19. Scene from Harrison Birtwistle's opera 'The Mask of Orpheus', first performed by the English National Opera at the Coliseum, London, 21 May 1986

120. *The Santa Fe Opera Theater, Santa Fe, New Mexico*

121. *Aerial view of the manor and opera house at Glyndebourne*

evident. Though uneven, *Dèbora* remains the peak of Pizzetti's theatrical output and one of the outstanding Italian operas of its day: his subsequent stage works on the whole represent a disappointingly self-repetitive decline.

Malipiero's musico-dramatic innovations, unlike Pizzetti's, were not conditioned by any rigid theory: they arose, rather, from a fanatical urge to rebel against the Establishment, coupled (especially during 1918–29) with an eccentric desire to construct his librettos largely from fragments of old Italian poetry. The results, often hardly operas in the normal sense, can be regarded as anticipating postwar music theatre. In *Sette canzoni* (1920, Paris) seven tiny operatic vignettes, without any unifying plot and lasting 45 minutes in all, are threaded together like beads on a string. Each has a song as its musical nucleus but is otherwise largely mimed. The score combines Gregorian archaisms, Debussian refinements, Stravinskian acerbities and quintessentially Italian radiance in one of the most hauntingly individual musical works of the 20th century. Malipiero's subsequent stage pieces only intermittently rise to this level, for he was over-prolific, lacking in self-criticism and sometimes slapdash in his workmanship. Moreover, his freakish librettos can at times seem merely confused. Nevertheless, the *Tre commedie goldoniane* (1926, Darmstadt) have a captivating Venetian zest and freshness, and the outer 'panels' of the triptych *L'Orfeide* (1925, Düsseldorf) – in which *Sette canzoni* serves as centrepiece – have a wild, surrealistic inventiveness (the final panel even mingles singer-actors with marionettes). *Torneo notturno* (1931, Munich) is another of Malipiero's outstanding achievements, pervaded by an enigmatic, dream-like symbolism. It is a work to be experienced rather than intellectually understood – 'a phantom drama whose meaning is defined exclusively by the music' (Santi, 1960).

Hardly surprisingly, these recklessly unconventional pieces did not win easy acceptance in conservative, provincial Italy: most of them were first performed in pre-Nazi Germany. Meanwhile, the longer-established Italian opera composers, Puccini apart, were losing creative momentum. By 1910 Cilea had stopped writing operas, while Smareglia's final one broke little new ground. Wolf-Ferrari, in *I gioielli della Madonna* (1911, Berlin), tried his hand at post-Mascagnian *verismo*, to which his talents were ill suited; then during the war and immediately thereafter he went through a crisis which greatly reduced his productivity. Mascagni's most ambitious opera, the enormous, intermittently Wagnerian *Parisina* (1913, Milan), to a libretto by D'Annunzio, attempted far more than he could adequately realize; yet the work contains considerable bursts of inspiration amid the turgidity. Meanwhile Leoncavallo ended his career with the posthumously produced *Edipo re* (1920, Chicago), which pales beside the Oedipus operas of Stravinsky and Enescu, although it is by no means worthless. Giordano's last operas show a further decline in his lyrical invention, offset by a continuing interest in modernizing his language: *Il re* (1929, Milan) contains dissonances akin to those in Puccini's *Turandot*.

The expatriate Busoni, too, wrote a *Turandot* (1917, Zurich), which remains closer than Puccini's to the true Gozzian spirit with its undisguised *commedia dell'arte* characters mingling incongruously yet delightfully with the exotica. The libretto, however, is in German, as are those of all Busoni's completed operas: his long-cherished ambition to write a major work for the Italian stage remained unfulfilled. Of his other three operas *Die Brautwahl* (1912, Hamburg) proved too uneven and long-winded to win success, although the score contains much that is highly original. *Arlecchino* (1917, Zurich) is far more trenchant and concise: its *commedia dell'arte* figures are skilfully manipulated in a barbed, deliberately artificial satire, whose allusions to Mozart and to other past operatic styles are transformed by a pungently 20th-century harmonic idiom. Much more ambitious, and in some ways problematic, is *Doktor Faust* (1925, Dresden, completed after Busoni's death by Jarnach and revised in a more satisfactory version by Antony Beaumont, 1985, Bologna). Consciously planned by the composer as his crowning achievement, the work brings together materials from numerous preparatory non-operatic pieces. The result is an impressive re-creation of the Faust legend, rooted in the 16th-century puppet play rather than in Goethe, but elaborated in a quintessentially Busonian way. Despite much extremely fine, restrained yet intricately expressive music, however, the opera needs the help of an imaginative producer to make it work well in the theatre.

1930–50

In the 1930s only Wolf-Ferrari, among the more conservative composers already discussed, showed signs of renewed creative energies: after *Sly* (1927, Milan), the most convincing of his serious operas, he picked up the stylistic threads of his pre-war Goldoni comedies and recaptured much of their sparkle in *La vedova scaltra* (1931, Rome) and *Il campiello* (1936, Milan). Meanwhile, the more adventurous composers were inhibited by pressures from the Fascist regime. Italian Fascism never emulated Nazism's wholesale censorship of advanced trends: the Venice festival of 1937 could still feature music by Schoenberg, and the Italian première of *Wozzeck* took place, astonishingly, in Rome in 1942. Nevertheless, Italian composers were scarcely encouraged to follow such paths, and it was in opera (in which the regime took considerable interest, backed up by substantial subsidies) that such pressures were most likely to affect their artistic choices. Small wonder that Alfano, for example, retreated into unconvincing compromises with tradition; and Respighi, too, adopted a more conventionally melodramatic manner in *La fiamma* (1934, Rome), although the work contains fine things. Nor did the Fascist order discourage Pizzetti's growing tendency to repeat himself.

The case of Malipiero was more complex and (as always) more interesting. In 1932–3 he collaborated with Pirandello, with whose famous 'paradoxical' dramas he had a natural affinity. The resultant opera, *La favola del figlio cambiato* (1934, Brunswick), enjoyed considerable success in Germany in the months before Nazism closed the door on such unconventionalities; but after a single performance in Rome it was banned by Mussolini. Only in the 1980s has this vivid, thought-provoking work begun to emerge from near-oblivion. In the circumstances the composer can hardly be blamed for withdrawing into relatively safe territory: *Giulio Cesare* (1936, Genoa) is based on Shakespeare and contains a recognizable obeisance to the Duce. Malipiero's mercurially experimental side reasserted itself, however, in *I capricci di Callot* (1942, Rome), freely based on E. T. A. Hoffmann's *Prinzessin Brambilla*.

The most distinguished Italian newcomer to opera in the early 1930s was Casella, whose pungently radical non-operatic music of the World War I period had influenced Puccini. Hitherto he had avoided the opera house, though he had written two ballet scores; and his only full-length opera, *La donna serpente* (1932, Rome), was itself first planned as a choral ballet. Based on one of Gozzi's eccentric theatrical fantasies, the work is full of opportunities for diverting spectacle and has a typically trenchant and nimbly colourful score. Yet it was a failure when new and had to wait many years for recognition. A far more immediately fortunate newcomer to the operatic scene was Rocca, whose eclectic but highly dramatic *Il Dibuk* (1934, Milan), won what was then considered the biggest Italian success since Puccini's *Turandot*. The work is now seldom heard, and nor are most other Italian operas of the later Fascist years: pressures to conform were too strong, and the results tend to seem hollow and dated.

Nevertheless, the 1930s saw the emergence of at least three major Italian composers who proved that Fascism need not stifle originality. Dallapiccola, Petrassi and the late-developing Ghedini made their marks initially in the concert hall, where they had more freedom to develop in ways of their own. Although Ghedini wrote three operas in the late 1930s, full operatic self-realization came only in *Le baccanti* (1948, Milan), a ruggedly impressive adaptation of Euripides whose music has distant affinities with both Stravinsky and Frank Martin. Petrassi's two operas are not among his most important compositions, although they were undervalued when new (as, still more, was *Le baccanti*). More significant, however, was the emergence of Dallapiccola as an opera composer of international standing. His first operatic venture, *Volo di notte* (1940, Florence), suffers from a rather heterogeneous style and from an excess of offstage action. Yet it reveals a subtle musical imagination, and for the first time grafted prominent Bergian elements on to the Italian tradition. Dallapiccola's first major opera, and still arguably his finest, was *Il prigioniero* (1950, Florence), in which Fascism's degenerate last phase and World War II provoked an intense piece of protest music. Making free, rather unorthodox use of Schoenbergian dodecaphony, the opera again recalls Berg rather than his teacher; yet a recognizable heritage from Verdi and Puccini may be noted, and there are precedents in Malipiero too. The impact of *Il prigioniero* was such that it has become the most internationally admired Italian opera since Puccini's *Turandot*.

Since 1950

Pizzetti had by 1950 acquired 'grand old man' status – revered by the orthodox and resented by the rebellious young. His last few operas, though still breaking little new stylistic ground, have in some cases proved more vital than his weak middle-period works. *Assassinio nella cattedrale* (1958, Milan) was particularly successful, helped by the power of Eliot's great play. The quality of Malipiero's last-period stage works remains variable; too often they suffer from relatively undistinguished vocal writing which pales in comparison with that in his best earlier operas. Nevertheless *Il capitan Spavento* (1963, Naples) and *Il marescalco* (1969, Treviso) recapture the comic zest of the *Tre commedie goldoniane* in more spikily chromatic terms; and *Uno dei Dieci* (1971, Siena), composed at the age of 88, presents a grotesque yet touching picture of intolerant old age, in which many have recognized a caricatured self-portrait. Dallapiccola followed up *Il prigioniero* with *Job* (1950, Rome), a highly stylized *sacra rappresentazione* whose music shows his increasingly rigorous attitude to dodecaphony. Only after 1960, however, did he write the long-premeditated *Ulisse* (1968, Berlin), his largest and most ambitious composition. Less compelling dramatically than *Il prigioniero*, more refined and (in some ways) Webern-like in idiom, the work is essentially a restrained philosophical meditation on modern man's search for a meaning to existence; it is best served by relatively stylized, oratorio-like production.

The range of idioms and approaches current in postwar Italian opera is bewilderingly wide, and the works that have hitherto attracted most notice may not necessarily in the long run prove the most important. Attempts to revive the older Italian operatic tradition have not been lacking, even after 1950: most vociferous in this rearguard action was Rossellini, whose operas often reflect neo-realism in postwar Italian literature, art and cinema, and parallel the internationally far more successful achievements of the Americanized Menotti (see Chapter XXVIII.1 below). The most frequently performed ultra-conservative opera written in Italy since the war has been Rota's *Il cappello di paglia di Firenze* (1955, Palermo), whose music harks back, Wolf-Ferrari-like though with mildly Prokofievian twists, to Rossinian *opera buffa*: the result is slender but amiable, and well matched to a libretto based on Labiche's famous farce.

Among the operas of the early postwar years that emulate Dalla-piccola in using 12-note technique (at least intermittently), one of the most effective is Peragallo's *La gita in campagna* (1954, Milan). To a wryly comic neo-realist libretto by Moravia, the work combines suitably barbed orchestral imagery with vocal lines smooth enough to suggest, again, a kinship with Menotti. The independent-minded Bucchi has steered an enterprising zigzag course between opera and music theatre. His most widely known opera, *Il contrabbasso* (1954, Florence), matches Chekhov's amusing, mildly risqué story with witty music that mingles neo-medieval touches with passages whose pervasive false relations may remind British listeners of Rawsthorne. *Il coccodrillo* (1970, Florence) is more controversial: here Dostoyevsky's satire about a man swallowed alive by a crocodile provides the nucleus for an episodic extravaganza in which song, speech, dance, mime, film projections, note clusters, quarter-tones and electronic means all play their parts.

Il coccodrillo brought Bucchi unexpectedly close to the avant-garde composers who now dominate the Italian musical scene. The most influential figure in this movement's Darmstadt-inspired early stages was Maderna, whose refinedly sensuous radio opera *Don Perlimplin* (broadcast 1962), after Lorca's puppet play, whimsically represents the protagonist by a flute and his mother-in-law by a group of saxophones; the heroine is the only character who sings. *Hyperion* (first version 1964, Venice; subsequently revised) also has a flautist as protagonist. The dramatic realization is left largely at the producer's discretion, and the work belongs to the sphere of music theatre rather than opera. The principal stage works of Maderna's pupil Nono reflect his intense left-wing political commitment: *Intolleranza 1960* (1961, Venice; revised as *Intolleranza 1970*, 1974, Florence) is heavily loaded with scenes of political violence and 'projections of episodes of terror and fanaticism'. Musically the work is one of Nono's most striking, with forceful if seemingly fragmented choral textures and angular, pulseless yet often surprisingly lyrical solo lines. *Al gran sole carico d'amore* (1975, Milan) is political propaganda at its shrillest, presented in crudely black and white terms which are unlikely to persuade the unconverted. Yet there is no mistaking Nono's quasi-religious devotion to the cause, expressed in a musical language more miscellaneous than that of *Intolleranza*.

In the output of Berio (who has collaborated with such leading Italian writers as Sanguineti and Calvino) the distinction between dramatic and concert works is sometimes extremely fluid: even *Laborintus II* (1965, Paris) may be presented as a theatrical event, though hardly as an opera. *Passaggio* (1963, Milan) is more unambiguously dramatic: a lone soprano suffers the tortures and degradations of commercialized modern society while two choruses – one mostly singing, the other speaking and shouting – respond in drastically different ways. Berio's most complex theatre composition (1970, Sante Fé; revised in three acts, 1977) bears the austere title *Opera*, to be understood also in its original Latin sense. Elements relating to the Orpheus legend are juxtaposed with others centred on the terminal ward in a hospital and on the sinking of the *Titanic*, with quasi-cinematic cross-cutting. In *La vera storia* (1982, Milan) the juxtaposition is, rather, between radically different manners of presentation: the two acts set essentially the same libretto, which is realized first as a clear-cut number opera (using *Il trovatore* as archetype) and then as a dream-like music theatre piece. *Un re in ascolto* (1984, Salzburg) is enigmatically dream-like throughout, with its melancholy, moribund Prospero figure and its fragmentary allusions to *The Tempest* woven into the kaleidoscopic hurly-burly of an otherwise very un-Shakespearean theatrical rehearsal. In all these works Berio matches the ambiguous dramatic conceptions with comparably many-faceted music.

The most flamboyantly unconventional Italian composer who came forward in the 1950s and 60s was Bussotti, in whose notorious *La Passion selon Sade* (partial performance 1965, Palermo; complete, 1969, Stockholm) musical instruments are provocatively mingled with instruments of torture. The score is notable more for extraordinary calligraphic beauty than for precise intelligibility, and the whole culminates in an anarchic 'happening' involving audience participation. Such works may be far removed indeed from opera in the normally understood sense. Yet however bizarre some of the results, they prove that Italy's musico-dramatic inventiveness is still very much alive.

CHAPTER XXIII

Germany, Austria, Switzerland

DERRICK PUFFETT

The early years of the century

German opera around 1900 was dominated by the influence of Wagner. To describe a work such as Pfitzner's *Der arme Heinrich* (1895, Mainz) as 'post-Wagnerian' – a common term of abuse in the years immediately following World War I – is both to state the obvious and to deny the work its particularity. Wagner's purely musical influence – the expansion of tonal and harmonic resources, the vastly extended time-scale, the new orchestral possibilities, the formal and expressive significance of the leitmotif – was not of course confined to opera. But opera composers were also influenced by his choice of subject matter. *Tristan*, *Parsifal* and the *Ring* cycle inspired many works based on myth and legend, sometimes reaching into fairy-tale, as in the operas of Humperdinck; *Tannhäuser* and *Lohengrin* encouraged a passion for medieval costume drama; and *Die Meistersinger* became the most important single model for romantic comedies. Against the background of all this Wagnerizing, a work like Wolf's *Der Corregidor* (1896, Mannheim), even though written by one of Wagner's leading disciples, suggests the beginning of a reaction, a conscious 'Mediterraneanizing' which would have pleased Nietzsche. Later, with the influence of *verismo*, the reaction was to become stronger, in such works as d'Albert's *Tiefland* (1903, Prague) and more pervasively in the operas of Schreker and Korngold. All in all it was a time of immense productivity: with opera houses in most of the major cities, and with seemingly unlimited financial support, the art flourished as rarely before.

Richard Strauss's first opera, *Guntram* (1894, Weimar), fell firmly within the Wagnerian tradition. Its themes of chivalry and renunciation mix uneasily with Strauss's doggerel libretto, though the work contains one truly original character in the Fool, a prototype for similar characters in Schreker and Zemlinsky. The most eloquent music occurs in the final duet, which already shows Strauss's ability to think in long paragraphs and to devise musical material to suit (including a theme he thought worth quoting in *Ein Heldenleben*). He revised the work for revival in 1940 but it has never achieved widespread success. His next opera, *Feuersnot*

(1901, Dresden), was more original. Although its 'old German' setting owes much to *Die Meistersinger*, the comedy has a satirical edge, and the music a folklike quality, which Wagner's work lacks. The satirical element, which Strauss was simultaneously cultivating in his tone poems (an opera on the subject of Till Eulenspiegel was considered but abandoned), was to become a hallmark of the mature operas, even when suffused with the tenderness of *Capriccio*. The folklike quality is important too: Strauss's music is always fundamentally diatonic – more so than Wagner's – and is apt to keep returning to this bedrock even amid the wildest chromatic squalls.

Salome (1905, Dresden) presents some of the wildest of these squalls. Its text is a compressed German translation of Wilde's French original. The work was bound to cause a scandal, not just because of the lurid subject matter but because the music is some of Strauss's most extreme: in volume, in its vocal demands, in its contrasts between bland diatonicism (for Jokanaan, a character by whom the composer declared himself bored) and shrieking chromaticism. There is no all-embracing tonal scheme; keys are used for dramatic symbolism, as in Wagner. Again the final scene – Salome's monologue – is of crucial importance, with Strauss's long soprano lines supported by an orchestration of unprecedented (and sometimes inaudible) complexity. *Elektra* (1909, Dresden) took the composer even further down the same road. Another 'antique' setting, and again in a single act (Strauss was already worried about the danger of repeating himself), this study of an obsession with vengeance evoked music of astonishing imaginative power, the dissonances more excruciating than those of *Salome*, the climaxes heavier, the diatonic passages equally bland. The central monologue for Clytemnestra – perhaps Strauss's most original achievement – became the prototype for musical expressionism (though there is reason to think Berg was more influenced by it than Schoenberg) with its violent changes of mood, its 'realistic' declamation and its orchestral pictorialism. And the final pages are a purely orchestral apotheosis: an orgiastic Viennese waltz during which Electra dances herself to death, and the forerunner of many such climaxes in Strauss and others.

Elektra was Strauss's first collaboration with the poet Hugo von Hofmannsthal, whose correspondence with him forms a fascinating record of their 20-year partnership. Strauss's uncertainty about the direction his work should take, and Hofmannsthal's efforts to guide him, led to a series of uneven masterpieces which are still the subject of controversy. *Der Rosenkavalier* (1911, Dresden), set in the Vienna of Maria Theresa's time, has been considered by some critics a retreat from the 'radical' position of *Elektra*, by others the opera in which Strauss finally found his true gift; at any rate it marks a decisive change. Comedy and sentimentality are now the essence, dissonance subdued to the point where a Viennese waltz no longer seems incongruous (extreme dissonance is in fact reserved for mock expressionist outbursts, a case of Strauss amusedly turning his style back on itself). The psychological penetration, however, has deepened – especially in the characterization of the Marschallin, compelled to realize that she must yield her youthful lover to a younger woman – and this is due to the music as much as to the libretto. *Ariadne auf Naxos* (1912, Stuttgart; revised 1916, Vienna), the next collaboration, is based on a brilliant conceit, combining *opera seria* with *commedia dell'arte*; if something goes wrong in the working out, it has none the less provided much food for scholarly thought. By this time Strauss had evolved a fluid, 'conversational' style of declamation, most vividly seen in the Prologue to the second version, set backstage in an 18th-century court theatre. This too was to become a hallmark of the later operas (especially in *Intermezzo*, where the orchestra is again, as here, reduced to chamber size).

Guntram and *Feuersnot*, *Elektra* and *Rosenkavalier*: a pattern has been set for sudden contrasts, unexpected changes of direction. After *Ariadne* the collaborators began work on *Die Frau ohne Schatten* (1919, Vienna), a sprawling allegory in Strauss's Wagnerian manner. Nowadays its most modern feature might appear to be the contrast between upper and lower worlds, epitomized in the characters of the Empress and Barak's Wife; the oscillation between small and large orchestras, between translucent and dense textures, is an important means of formal articulation. Nevertheless the work as a whole seems a regression, a return to 19th-century values, an indulgence for both poet and musician. The next opera, *Intermezzo*, was to include a part for a telephone.

Schoenberg, Berg and their contemporaries

Expressionism has been such a vital force in 20th-century music that it comes as a shock to realize there was no tradition of expressionist opera before the 1920s, when expressionism in the other arts had largely exhausted itself. Schoenberg's one-act operas *Erwartung* (composed 1909) and *Die glückliche Hand* (composed 1910–13) – works central to any discussion of expressionism in music – were not staged until 1924, though they were known to musicians in the Schoenberg circle, notably Berg and Zemlinsky. Berg's *Wozzeck* (composed 1917–22), for many a more truly 'contemporary' piece than anything by Strauss, had its première (in Berlin) only in 1925. For the first two decades of the century, and indeed until the triumphant reception of *Wozzeck*, Schoenberg and Berg were overshadowed, as opera composers, not only by Strauss but by lesser men, Schreker, Pfitzner and Korngold.

Schreker is undoubtedly the most interesting of these. An exceptionally cultivated man – at the time of his birth, his father was court photographer at Monaco – he drew inspiration from the German fairy-tale tradition, now invested with a post-Freudian concern with sexuality and the bizarre, French naturalism and Italian *verismo*. He always wrote his own librettos. His first success, *Der ferne Klang*, was substantially composed in 1901–3 but not completed until 1910; its première was in Frankfurt in

1912. At this time Schreker was close to Schoenberg (he conducted the première of Schoenberg's *Gurrelieder* in 1913), but thereafter they began to move apart, though their careers continued to overlap in various ways. Schreker's two greatest successes, *Die Gezeichneten* (1918, Frankfurt) and *Der Schatzgräber* (1920, Frankfurt), combined fantastic plots, verging on the sentimental, with spectacular stage effects and music recalling such diverse models as Strauss, Debussy and Puccini. After 1920, however, Schreker's star waned. The new generation – composers such as Hindemith and Weill – had no time for his extravaganzas, which at a time of poverty and hardship seemed impossibly pretentious. The première of *Christophorus* (composed 1924–7), an allegory of the artist's role in society, was cancelled because of the threat of Nazi demonstrations; ironically, it was one of Schreker's most forward-looking works – not for nothing was it dedicated to Schoenberg.

Another distinguished treatment of the artist theme was Pfitzner's *Palestrina* (1917, Munich), to his own libretto. Pfitzner had moved from a position which could be described as vaguely progressive (he revered Wagner and had assisted Mahler) to one of extreme conservatism. This new position was embodied in his opera, a glowing tribute to the past as symbolized by the 16th-century composer. Music of astonishing vehemence invokes the Council of Trent, but the opera ends quietly and sadly, with Palestrina left alone: nostalgia is tempered with realism. Pfitzner's last opera, *Das Herz* (1931, Berlin and Munich), is an anti-climax by comparison.

The Austro-Hungarian Franz Schmidt, who lived in Vienna from 1888, produced two operas, *Notre Dame* (composed 1902–4; 1914, Vienna) and *Fredigundis* (1922, Berlin). Within the limitations of his essentially symphonic style – *Fredigundis* in particular is dramatically hopeless – both contain music of the utmost radiance, the cathedral scene from the latter recalling Act 2 of *Lohengrin*. *Notre Dame*, while a travesty of Hugo, is notable for its brilliant carnival scene and its vivid characterization of the gypsy girl (Schmidt's Hungarian background pays dividends here). 25 years younger, but of the same general sensibility, was the prodigy Erich Wolfgang Korngold. His one-act operas *Der Ring des Polykrates* and *Violanta* caused a critical sensation when they were given together in Munich in 1916; the style is a heady mixture of Strauss and Puccini, but with a rhythmic vitality unusual in German opera of this period. Four years later came *Die tote Stadt*, given a dual première in Hamburg and Cologne; this was similarly acclaimed. Its modern setting is noteworthy for anticipating the 'topical' works produced later in the 1920s, but its theatrical effects are more like Meyerbeer: in the last act a ghostly procession seems to penetrate the hero's room. In 1934 Korngold left Europe for Hollywood, where he made a successful career as a film composer.

In the context of such works Schoenberg's *Erwartung* seems more original than ever. Its expressionist aspects are now fairly well documented: the concentration on a single character (significantly labelled

'Frau'), the projection of the most intense emotions, the absence of any conventional structural device (no repetition, except on the smallest scale), the violent contrasts, the breathless delivery of the text. The music long resisted analysis; even the most sophisticated techniques seem inadequate when placed beside the extraordinary expressive power of the work. The most rewarding approach for the naive listener is through the text and the stage directions (which, as always in Schoenberg, are of fascinating detail); the music then makes its dream-like effect. The stage directions in *Die glückliche Hand* are even more fascinating: here is the perfect musical equivalent of Kokoschka and Kandinsky, complete with 'colour crescendo' (an effect fully notated in the score). Interestingly enough, its formal structure is more easily grasped than that of *Erwartung*; Schoenberg evidently felt that the earlier work, with its sense of continuous improvisation, was an unrepeatable experiment. From now on conventional structural devices return to his music with ever greater frequency.

The combination of apparent spontaneity and formal artifice is in fact as characteristic of expressionism as is spontaneity *tout court*. For this reason *Wozzeck*, a more universal work than *Erwartung*, may be considered the expressionist masterpiece. Berg's formal contrivances, which include a fugue, a sonata movement and a set of variations, have become a byword for musical constructivism and as such belong firmly in the 1920s. But the impact of the work – treating the victimization and degradation by society, and ultimately the death, of its 'hero' – is overwhelmingly emotional, a type of experience recognized by anyone familiar with Wagner and Strauss. So many scholarly words have been written about Berg, so much analytical ink spilt, that it is easy to forget that his operas have entered the repertory more securely than any since Puccini's. Schoenberg's reservations about *Wozzeck* may have been prompted partly by jealousy.

Another composer in the Schoenberg circle was Zemlinsky, whose operatic career spans a longer period than either Schoenberg's or Berg's. His first opera, *Sarema* (1897, Munich), has not held its place in the repertory, but the next 40 years saw a steady output of works, many of which have recently enjoyed critical acclaim. His most durable opera seems likely to be *Der Zwerg* (1922, Cologne).

Between the wars
The reaction against Romanticism that followed World War I had profound effects on German opera. Although houses continued to employ large orchestras, so that the works of Wagner and Strauss were never completely out of fashion, there was an increasing feeling that such extravagance went ill with the times. Composers like Schreker and Korngold lost their following; the new opera had to be tougher, more economical, more in tune with everyday events. Topicality became the order of the day; even Zemlinsky found himself writing jazz, or something

like it, as in *Der Kreidekreis* (1933, Zurich). Under the influence of Busoni (whose *Arlecchino* and *Turandot*, both written during the war and given in Zurich in 1917, introduced what he called a 'young classicism') and Stravinsky (whose *Histoire du soldat* reached Berlin in 1920, when it left an indelible impression on Weill), composers sought to instil into opera the values of 'absolute' music: from now on there would be as many passacaglias in the theatre as in the concert hall (Hindemith's *Cardillac* contains a good example). Another important figure – as much an impresario as a conductor – was Otto Klemperer; in his years at the Kroll Opera in Berlin (1926–31) he became almost synonymous with the modern movement, performing works by Schoenberg, Stravinsky, Hindemith, Weill and Janáček, among others.

Cardillac (1926, Dresden), for all its modernisms, is in fact simply another version of the artist theme, one which places Hindemith in the same idealistic tradition as Schreker and Pfitzner. This theme was to remain his lifelong preoccupation: *Mathis der Maler* (1938, Zurich), a study of the German Gothic painter Matthias Grünewald, and his much later opera about the Renaissance astronomer Kepler, *Die Harmonie der Welt* (1957, Munich), both return to it. Such works indeed tended to isolate Hindemith from his contemporaries. Those operas of his which received most publicity at the time were *Hin und zurück* (1927, Baden-Baden), a sketch in which the action proceeds to midpoint and then runs back on itself again – such constructivist conceits were the delight of the 1920s – and the 'topical opera' to end all topical operas, *Neues vom Tage* (1929, Berlin). Hindemith left Germany in 1938.

Another composer who achieved notoriety at this time, but later became a staunch upholder of tradition, was Krenek, a Viennese pupil of Schreker's. His *Der Sprung über den Schatten* (1924, Frankfurt) was the first German opera to use jazz; Schoenberg detested it. But the work with which Krenek made his name was *Jonny spielt auf* (1927, Leipzig), whose main character is a jazz musician. After these successes Krenek turned out a stream of dull, respectable works, including the operas *Leben des Orest* (1930, Leipzig), whose classical subject matter was influenced by Stravinsky's *Oedipus rex*, and *Karl V* (1938, Prague). Another admirer of *Oedipus* was Kurt Weill, who reviewed a performance under Klemperer at the Kroll Opera in 1928. Before that he had written two brilliant one-act operas, *Der Protagonist* (1926, Dresden) and *Der Zar lässt sich photographieren* (1928, Leipzig), which anticipate the busy contrapuntal manner of Hindemith as well as being 'topical' almost to excess. *Der Zar* also includes a tango, showing that Weill's popular style was not invented by Brecht (the crucial influence in fact seems to have been *Histoire du soldat*). The major Brecht collaborations were *Die Dreigroschenoper* (1928, Berlin), a social satire modelled on *The Beggar's Opera*, and *Aufstieg und Fall der Stadt Mahagonny* (1930, Leipzig), a satirical attack on some of the nastier manifestations of the capitalist system, specifically in America; their iron originality withstands any number of bad productions. *Mahagonny* is a full-length opera, sung virtually from beginning to end; *Die Bürgschaft* (1932, Berlin), to words by Caspar Neher, completes the process, and here the Stravinsky influence (but of the 'monumental' style of *Oedipus* rather than the dance-rhythms of *Histoire*) exerts full sway. Monumental and popular styles come together in Weill's last German opera, *Der Silbersee* (1933, Leipzig) – strictly, a 'play with music' – written in collaboration with Georg Kaiser. Weill left Germany for Paris in 1933.

Strauss's last 30 years were a story of increasing isolation. *Intermezzo* (1924, Dresden) was in fact the very first 'topical opera', a semi-autobiographical piece which had the fastidious Hofmannsthal reeling with horror. For this Strauss had to write his own words; and they are not bad, allowing a better balance of voice and orchestra than he sometimes achieved with Hofmannsthal. The operas of the next two decades show a familiar alternation between classical tragedy and romantic comedy, the comedies (*Arabella*, 1933, *Die schweigsame Frau*, 1935, both produced in Dresden) perhaps emerging as the more successful. When Hofmannsthal died in 1929, Strauss had to find another librettist, a problem exacerbated by his decision to stay in Germany during the Third Reich. His last opera, *Capriccio* (1942, Munich), is regarded by many critics as his finest. He wrote the words himself with the conductor Clemens Krauss; and here the conversational style achieves a subtlety only hinted at before. It is a commonplace to point out that *Capriccio* is an opera about opera, about the contending claims of words and music; but Strauss more than any other composer sums up the problems confronting the writer of German operas in the first half of the 20th century.

Schoenberg, in the 1920s, was planning his two operatic masterpieces, *Von heute auf morgen* (1930, Frankfurt), a biting satire on all things topical, and *Moses und Aron* (composed 1930–32; first performed, in concert form, 1954, and staged only in 1957, Zurich). The biblical work seems oddly removed from the typical operatic concerns of the time; but in fact it is yet another version of the artist theme, combined with Schoenberg's ever-increasing attraction to religion. Schoenberg the visionary (Moses) is here seen to be at odds with Schoenberg the composer (Aaron); it is almost as if his earlier fascination with technique had led him to distrust it. The work ends in silence, for Act 3 was never written; and Moses's last words in Act 2 are a howl of frustration, a lament at the inadequacy of human speech (or of music). It is a far cry from Berg's *Lulu*, another work of which Schoenberg disapproved. Berg began the composition in 1929 but had not finished the orchestration at the time of his death (1935); a two-act version was performed in Zurich in 1937, the complete score not until 1979, (when it could finally be completed, by Friedrich Čerha, in accordance with Berg's intentions). *Lulu*, like *Moses*, is a 12-note work, and between them these two operas bring the technique to new heights of complexity. *Lulu* is also a constructivist work: it uses the same schematic forms as *Wozzeck*, though even more elaborately. This is particularly clear, of course, in the complete opera; and it is hard to see how anyone made sense of the first two acts before Act 3 became available. Certainly no-one will again be satisfied with the two-act version.

The Swiss composer Schoeck was in many ways typical of the interwar period. He began with subjects from early Romanticism (*Venus*, 1922, Zurich; after Mérimée and Eichendorff), moved on to a classical theme (*Penthesilea*, 1927, Dresden; after Kleist), brushed with fairy-tale (*Vom Fischer un syner Fru*, 1930, Dresden; after Grimm) and achieved Straussian serenity (*Massimilla Doni*, 1937, Dresden; after Balzac). His last opera, *Das Schloss Dürande* (1943, Berlin), may or may not have been intended as a comment on the current political scene – an ambiguity of attitude which, again, is typical of many German composers at this time.

Since 1945

After World War II there was little money to spend on opera, though with Germany's economic recovery the situation improved. The period immediately after the war was one of caution and conservatism. Orff had already begun his search for a new form of 'total theatre', often drawing on Baroque models (as in *Orpheus*, 1925, Mannheim; based on Monteverdi). In practice this meant a style of extreme simplicity, as in *Der Mond* (1939, Munich) and *Die Kluge* (1943, Frankfurt), with their endless diatonic harmony and mechanically repetitive rhythms. The postwar years saw his adaptations of Sophocles and Aeschylus (notably *Oedipus der Tyrann*, 1959, Stuttgart) as well as his work in music education and broadcasting. His last opera was the apocalyptic *De temporum fine comoedia* (1973, Salzburg).

Commercially, the most successful German opera composer of this period has been Hans Werner Henze. After a string of neo-Straussian successes, including *Boulevard Solitude* (1952, Hanover), he collaborated with Auden and Kallman on *Elegy for Young Lovers* (1961, Schwetzingen) and *The Bassarids* (1966, Salzburg). His flirtation with revolutionary ideas led to *We Come to the River* (1976, London), written to words by Edward Bond; but Henze's recent work has been largely in the field of music theatre, opera now seeming to him a debased art.

Bernd Alois Zimmermann, who worked mainly in Cologne, is represented by one opera, *Die Soldaten* (1960, Cologne), his masterpiece. It has obvious affinities in its choice of subject and to some extent in its musical language with *Wozzeck*, but it is also a work of great originality, especially in its use of quotation. At times the texture achieves an almost Straussian opulence (as in the trio for three sopranos in Act 3), but more often the effect is of grinding intensity, with a complex 'layered' treatment of the orchestra. A second opera, *Medea*, was unfinished at Zimmermann's death.

Die Soldaten is an example of 'literary opera', a genre which has come to dominate postwar Germany and which may in retrospect appear a mistake. It rests on the assumption that significant works can be created by taking established classics of the theatre and setting them to music with as little alteration as possible. Cuts are unavoidable, but otherwise the composer's attitude is one of reverence – which can lead to a monotonous style of word-setting, with the orchestra kept in the background. *Die Soldaten* transcends these limitations because Zimmermann was a great composer. It is less certain whether the same can be said of his successors. Gottfried von Einem has produced many commercial successes, all modelled on literary classics, of which *Dantons Tod* (1947, Salzburg; after Büchner), *Der Prozess* (1953, Salzburg, Kafka) and *Der Besuch der alten Dame* (1971, Vienna; Dürrenmatt) are the best known. The Austrian Čerha has written only one opera, *Baal* (1981, Salzburg), based on the play by Brecht. Its idiom is extended expressionism with popular elements (shades of Weill in Baal's Act 2 song). Aribert Reimann (*b* 1936) produced a *Lear*, his third opera, for Munich in 1978. This too has been commercially successful, perhaps because the title role was written for Fischer-Dieskau. In Reimann's interpretation of 'literary opera', music assumes a humble role, being confined to the merest background.

Among these composers Stockhausen seems a veritable giant. Dwarfing anything conceived by the 'literalists', his *Licht* is a seven-part cycle with an opera for every day of the week, of which *Donnerstag* (1981, Milan), *Samstag* (1984, Milan) and *Montag* were the first completed. *Donnerstag* had its première at a conventional opera house (La Scala), but *Samstag* required a sports stadium, an indication of how the scope of the work has grown. Whether *Licht* is no more than a vast megalomaniac fantasy or whether it will turn out to have some as yet unsuspected inner coherence remains to be seen. But one thing is clear: the work marks a return to the seriousness and idealism of the earlier part of the century, qualities which were in danger of disappearing. Stockhausen, for all his 'modernity', may prove to be the most thorough traditionalist German opera has seen since the war.

CHAPTER XXIV

France

RONALD CRICHTON

No more in French musical life than in other branches of culture did the year 1900 bring a clean break. Yet the extent to which the later works of Wagner began to seep into the bloodstream of composers, and the improvement in quantity and quality of symphonic and instrumental music during the final decade or so of the old century, marked a new stage in the evolution of French opera, distinguished by a predominantly serious tone.

Some idea of the degree of absorption of Wagner in France towards 1900 may be gained by comparing the libretto for Reyer's *Sigurd* (see Chapter XV), in which Scandinavian myth is garnished with the trappings of grand opera (including an amount of the *merveilleux* worthy of Quinault and Lully), with d'Indy's text for his *Fervaal* (1897, Brussels), cogent and compact in d'Indy's efficient way. As librettist d'Indy is densely Wagnerian. As composer, even in episodes as derivative as the appearance of the Erda-figure Kaito, he had something of his own to offer. In his maritime *L'étranger* (1903, Brussels), an *action musicale* laid out on a more intimate scale than *Fervaal*, echoes in the story from *Der fliegende Holländer* are fainter than those from Ibsen's *Brand*: among the elements in the music are folksong and Gregorian chant. Chausson's scenario for his *Le Roi Arthus* (produced posthumously, 1903, Brussels) comes dangerously near *Tristan* in the Lancelot–Guinevere–Arthur triangle. There is *Tristan* in the music as well, but Chausson's distinct personality is not submerged. D'Indy's independent-minded pupil Magnard, as serious as Chausson but more austere, who described himself as 'straying between Gluck and Wagner', remained for his last opera, *Bérénice* (1911), within the classical world of Corneille and Racine. A neglected addition to the repertory of this period is the Swiss Ernest Bloch's *Macbeth* (1910, Opéra) to a French libretto based on Shakespeare by Edmond Fleg. Literary influence was not confined to adaptations from the classics but extended to the contemporary novel. The series of collaborations between Zola and Bruneau, including *Le rêve* (1891), *L'attaque du moulin* (1893) and *L'ouragan* (1901), all for the Opéra-Comique, shows few signs of revival, but

Gustave Charpentier's *Louise* (1900, Opéra-Comique), a *roman musical* which infuses working-class realism with an elaborate symbolization of the lures of Paris, won – and still has not entirely lost – success well beyond the borders of France.

The crown of this period was formed by three outstanding works: Debussy's *Pelléas et Mélisande* (1902), Dukas' *Ariane et Barbe-bleue* (1907) and Fauré's *Pénélope* (1913, Monte Carlo). *Pelléas*, the most original and individual of them, holds a special place in the history of 20th-century opera, a turning-point, connecting past and future. Unthinkable, in spite of Debussy's equivocal attitude to Wagner, without *Tristan* and *Parsifal*, there are yet traces of Gounod and Massenet. The outwardly seamless texture of the dream-like succession of short, shadowy, sometimes inconclusive scenes is a complex fabric. It embraces tenuous yet purposeful accompanied recitative (using the term in a comprehensive sense) reflecting, as Rolland (1908) noted, Rousseau's expressed desire of 150 years earlier for recitative written in small intervals, on a limited emotional and dynamic level, avoiding long notes. Debussy develops Gounod's and Massenet's art of setting conversation naturally and reveals his admiration for the rougher naturalism of Musorgsky. Although *Pelléas* may initially have appeared to sound a death-knell for number opera, submerged beneath the surface (for example in the greeting of Pelléas to the sun and in his last meeting with Mélisande at the fountain) one can discern the outline of closed lyrical forms, aria and duet. Debussy's texture is hypersensitively responsive to the suggestions of Maeterlinck's ambiguous exchanges, whose apparent preciosity veils sympathetic understanding of the stammerings, contradictions and repetitions of young people out of their emotional depth. As Debussy observed, *Pelléas* contains 'much more humanity than so-called documents of real life'. Lockspeiser (1962) attributed the violent hostility aroused by the work to 'the fact that the realities of the dream were brought to the surface . . . rather too alarmingly to be faced with comfort'. As one result of this hostility *Pelléas* became a rallying-ground for young musicians. It was slow however to gain general popularity and did not fully establish itself in France or abroad until after World War II.

Widespread recognition by the public has so far eluded *Ariane et Barbe-bleue* and *Pénélope*. Both operas have Wagnerian undercurrents: otherwise they have little in common. *Ariane* is linked on the one hand to the formal world of d'Indy ('Les cinq filles d'Orlamonde' is based on a folksong used by d'Indy in his Second Symphony) and on the other reflects the orchestral palette of Rimsky-Korsakov and Balakirev. The 'jewel' variations in Act 1 brilliantly (the adjective is justified) combine the two influences. Like *Pelléas*, *Ariane* has a text by Maeterlinck, but the tone is different – more positive, less pessimistic. Into *Pénélope*, for which René Fauchois provided a competent, uninspired libretto, Fauré in his autumn years poured his still vigorous genius. Compared with that of Debussy or Dukas the instrumental colour is sober. (It has been established that Fauré was responsible for two-thirds of the orchestration, entrusting the remainder, under his supervision, to Fernand Pécoud.) The taut reticence, the deep feeling elliptically expressed, share the lean, concentrated lyricism of Fauré's late songs. There was little, apart from Berlioz and Bizet at their best, in French 19th-century opera to foreshadow the riches of this period. But ironically the fame of Paris as the centre of the operatic world was being eclipsed by cities further east – for example Vienna, Munich and Berlin.

World War I and the subsequent shift of taste away from late Romanticism and Impressionism made a cleaner break than the turn of the century. Even so there were stragglers. The war interrupted the progress of two large-scale works by major composers. D'Indy's 'sacred drama' *La légende de Saint-Christophe*, composed in 1908–15 but not produced at the Opéra until 1920, has been described as 'an operatic compendium and a key to d'Indy's ideals and pet aversions' (Cooper, 1951). Since these aversions included 'atheists, freemasons, revolutionary socialists, Jews and . . . composers of modern music' (Vallas, 1950), the subsequent neglect of *Saint-Christophe* becomes comprehensible. A kinder fate was reserved for Roussel's *Padmâvatî*, finished in 1918 after a break for war service, produced at the Opéra in 1921, but remaining more often admired than performed. *Padmâvatî* is an *opéra-ballet* with a sombre subject, set in India (Roussel had first-hand experience of the East), a descendant of Lully and Rameau, exhibiting two permanent threads of the French tradition – exoticism and the dance. These had been refreshed some years before by the first Russian opera and ballet seasons (1907 onwards) of what became Dyagilev's Ballets Russes. With such stimulation the traditions of operatic spectacle and dancing could hardly wither away. More conventional approaches however persisted, for example in Rabaud's through-composed *opéra comique* derived from the Arabian Nights, *Marouf, savetier du Caire* (1914, Opéra-Comique).

As the prevailing tone became more serious, the rate of production decreased. Many front-rank composers completed only a single opera. Massenet was among those who maintained a 19th-century abundance. Having prolonged the natural life of Meyerbeerian grand opera (see Chapter XV), he kept discreetly in touch with later developments, evading more than an occasional skirmish with Wagner, sometimes advancing a catspaw to the future. His two-act *La navarraise* (1894, London) is a compressed *verismo* drama whose proportions are so skilfully calculated as to teach Massenet's Italian contemporaries a lesson in the avoidance of crudity. The fairy music of *Cendrillon* (1899, Opéra-Comique) looks as far ahead as the enchanted world of Ravel's *L'enfant et les sortilèges* (1925, Monte Carlo). Among Massenet's late operas, *Don Quichotte* (1910, Monte Carlo) contains fragile but effective invention with featherweight vocal scherzos and Spanish colour applied with as light a touch as Ravel's *L'heure espagnole* of the following year, though with less sharp irony. By this time the fusion of grand opera and *opéra comique* may be regarded as accomplished.

During the interwar years Paris remained the centre of operatic activity in France, although some works of an advanced nature for their time (e.g. Honegger's *Antigone*, 1927, Brussels; Milhaud's *Christophe Colomb*, 1930, Berlin) were first heard abroad. In the subsidized theatres there was little of more than local importance as far as new French operas were concerned. Reviewing the first Paris production of Ravel's *L'enfant et les sortilèges* at the Opéra-Comique in 1925, Prunières welcomed the work:

> at last... after more than 15 years, a new masterpiece at the theatre where *Pelléas*, *Ariane et Barbe-bleue* and *L'heure espagnole* were born. Oh! those *générales* at the Opéra-Comique, where one could not even admire the décors, productions or ballet, where one's senses, instead of being held as La Bruyère wished in equal enchantment, were equally offended by what they heard and saw! The boredom, the terrible boredom of those performances, the uselessness of music poured into outworn moulds. (*ReM*, vii/5, 1926, p.258)

Younger composers looked elsewhere. The French fondness for mixed genres (opera-ballets, opera-oratorios, spoken melodrama etc) ran riot in all sorts of places of entertainment. There was more vitality in the world of ballet (not only in Dyagilev's company, still a force even in its years of decline, but in the Swedish Ballet, Ida Rubinstein's seasons and other private enterprises) than in the opera houses. The literary background remained important. Poets as dissimilar as Claudel and Cocteau engaged with opera, and in the cases of Honegger and Milhaud, who may be taken as representative figures of the period, their spheres overlapped. Milhaud started work on music for Claudel's French version of the *Oresteia* of Aeschylus before World War I. The trilogy occupied him for a dozen years, music gradually asserting its rights against the spoken word. *Agamemnon* (1927) required comparatively little music; a larger amount was needed for *Les Choéphores* (1935, Brussels), while *Les Euménides* (concert performance, 1949, Brussels) became a three-act opera. Poet and composer worked together again on another grandiose project, *Christophe Colomb*. Cocteau provided a text for Milhaud's dirge *Le pauvre matelot* (1927) and, in the form of a 'bird's eye view' of the *Antigone* of Sophocles, a ready-made libretto for Honegger (1927, Brussels). Claudel and Honegger came together later, in the dramatic oratorio *Jeanne d'Arc au bûcher* (1938, Basle). From *Le Roi David* (1921, Mézières) onwards a number of Honegger's works were first staged in Switzerland. His output for France included a biblical opera, *Judith* (1926, Monte Carlo), two operettas for the Bouffes-Parisiens and an opera written in collaboration with Ibert, *L'aiglon* (1937, Monte Carlo), based on Rostand's play. Milhaud, whose *La brebis égarée* (1923), a setting of a play by Francis Jammes, was begun as far back as 1910, ranged still wider, from the three tiny *opéras minutes* on classical subjects (*Europa*, *Ariadne* and *Theseus*, 1927–8, Baden-Baden and Wiesbaden) through the pungently Provençal *La malheurs d'Orphée* (1925, Brussels) and *Esther de Carpentras* (written 1925, performed 1937, Opéra-

Comique) to the Latin-American frescoes *Maximilien* (1932, Opéra) and *Bolivar* (1950, Opéra). The extent and variety of Milhaud's operatic achievement (like Honegger he wrote a large quantity of ballets, incidental, film and radio music) have still to be recognized.

Poulenc, like Honegger and Milhaud a former member of the group Les Six, did not emerge as an opera composer until after World War II. *Les mamelles de Tirésias* (1947, Opéra-Comique) transforms into an *opéra bouffe* a play written by Apollinaire at an equivalent stage of the previous war. In 1944 Poulenc was isolated in the country during the Normandy landings: the outcome was a sudden release of creative high spirits and an instinctive return to the mood of sophisticated Paris between the wars. *La voix humaine* (1959, Opéra-Comique), a setting of Cocteau's dramatic monologue of 1930, also appears as a delayed interwar work. *Dialogues des Carmélites* (1957, Milan) stands on a higher level, at the head of Poulenc's religious work, barely conceivable from him before the war. More operas of literary origin came from Sauguet: *La chartreuse de Parme* (1939, Opéra, revised 1968) based on Stendhal and *Les caprices de Marianne* (1954, Aix-en-Provence) on Musset. Stravinsky's seminal opera-oratorio *Oedipus rex* (1927, staged 1928, Vienna), with a latinized Cocteau text, rates as Parisian if not strictly French. Another opera with the same tragic hero by a foreign composer familiar in Parisian musical circles was Enescu's *Oedipe* (written 1921, performed 1936, Opéra; French libretto by Fleg). *Socrate* (concert performance, 1920, Paris), a 'symphonic drama' after Plato by the inimitable Satie, remains in a class of its own.

Although Dyagilev substituted recitative for spoken dialogue in his revivals of Gounod's *Le médicin malgré lui* and *La Colombe* and Chabrier's *Une éducation manquée* (1924, Monte Carlo) and commissioned Satie and Milhaud to do the job, a few comic operas with spoken dialogue continued to be written. These included the *opéras bouffes* by Honegger referred to above and Roussel's *Le testament de la tante Caroline* (1936, Olomouc; the familiar reduction to one act from the original three was made by Marcel Mihalovici after Roussel's death). French operetta entered a silver age, graced by such composers as Messager and Hahn (see Chapter XXIX); it is an indication of the respectability the genre had acquired that both composers during their operatic careers held important administrative posts.

Although some middle-of-the-road composers, for example Delvincourt, Delannoy and Landowski, continued to write for the lyric stage, the temptation to do so cannot have been overwhelming during the postwar years; the 19th-century view that there must be something wrong with a French composer who failed to win success in the theatre had long died out. To many young progressives the traditional apparatus of the opera business was an irrelevant, useless survival. Boulez, who may be taken as their spokesman, expressed himself forcibly on the subject, and although he has conducted Wagner at Bayreuth and Berg's operas in Paris, he has not, apart from incidental theatre and radio music in his early days, attempted a dramatic work. Messiaen, on the other hand, accepted a commission from Liebermann, then director of the Opéra, and after several years produced a full-length three-act opera, *Saint François d'Assise* (1983, Opéra) to his own libretto based on the saint's writings. Whether *Saint François* will appear to the future as a grand gesture of renewed confidence in the form by one of the leading composers of the mid-century or as an isolated phenomenon it is early to say.

CHAPTER XXV

The Soviet Union and Eastern Europe

LAUREL FAY

1. Russia and the Soviet Union

Two of the most influential patrons and arbiters of musical taste in late 19th- and early 20th-century Russia, Mitrofan Belyayev and Sergey Dyagilev, shared a fundamental indifference to opera. Nevertheless, the genre continued to play a formative role in Russia after the turn of the century. In his last years Rimsky-Korsakov produced two of his most effective masterpieces – *Skazaniye o nevidimom grade Kitezhe i deve Fevronii* ('Legend of the Invisible City of Kitezh and the maiden Fevroniya'; 1907, St Petersburg) and *Zolotoy petushok* ('The Golden Cockerel'; 1909, Moscow). Both were brilliantly orchestrated, with the characteristically bold melodic and harmonic strokes which influenced Stravinsky and other young composers. Furthermore, both elevated the fairy-tale opera to the level of modern parable, the former concerning spiritual values and owing something to the influence of Wagner, and the latter a pointed satire of a foolish monarch. Production of *The Golden Cockerel* was prudently prevented by Russian censors until changes had been made to the libretto – posthumously and against the composer's express wishes; the original text was restored only after the Revolution.

At the beginning of the century, Rakhmaninov appeared to be poised to further the more strictly Romantic traditions of Russian opera deriving from Tchaikovsky, but after the premières of *Skupoy rïtsar* ('The Miserly Knight') and *Francesca da Rimini* (both 1906, Moscow), he did not complete another opera. The musical mantle of Rimsky-Korsakov, however, was taken up most immediately in the work of his pupil Igor Stravinsky, whose choice of fairy-tale subject for *Solovey* ('The Nightingale'; composed in 1908 and revised for its 1914 première, in Paris), his first operatic project, was made under the former's tutelage. Similarly, the use of pentatonic and artificial scales and the exotic scoring are reminiscent of his teacher. By the time Stravinsky came to write *Mavra* (1922,

Paris), an *opera buffa*, he was a leading light in the European musical avant-garde; but the subtle, understated (though typically Russian) humour of the score as well as its affectionate tribute to the great Russian eclectics Pushkin – from whom the story is taken – Glinka and Tchaikovsky confused and disappointed his Western followers. On the other hand, the opera-oratorio *Oedipus rex* (concert performance 1927, Paris; staged 1928, Vienna), which treats the classical subject in his mature neo-classical style and has a Latin text, was motivated at least in part by the desire to communicate with an increasingly cosmopolitan public.

Stravinsky's only full-length opera, *The Rake's Progress* (1951, Venice), owes little to his Slavonic heritage. It nevertheless owes many debts. The novel, non-native approach to the text-setting of the ingenious libretto by Auden and Kallman, after Hogarth, and the stylized, ironic treatment of Mozartian and Bellinian musical and dramatic traditions were greeted initially with some scepticism, but the opera has become one of the most popular and is certainly one of the most important English-language works of the 20th century.

Prokofiev's lifelong dedication to opera was in the best traditions of his 19th-century forebears – as was the limited success his works achieved during his lifetime. A planned production of his setting of Dostoyevsky's *Igrok* ('The Gambler'; composed 1915–17), a taut drama using continuous speech-song fleshed out by evocative orchestration, was a casualty of the 1917 revolutions; a revised version was given in Brussels in 1929 though the work had to wait until the 1970s to be appreciated by his countrymen. His most enduring success came with a comic opera written when he was in the West, *Lyubov' k tryom apel'sinam* ('The Love for Three Oranges'; 1921, Chicago), which is derived from the Russian tradition of fantasy opera but adds a veneer of urbane intellectual satire. The angular melodic lines, brash harmonic juxtapositions, clever word-play and dazzling orchestration spoke directly to postwar aesthetic sensibilities. The religious mysticism of his next operatic project, *Ognenniy angel* ('The Fiery Angel'; completed in 1923 and revised in 1927), was aesthetically more remote, as were the daunting demands of its musical realization: it was not staged until 1954, in Paris.

Despite the passing of most of the older generation of composers and the emigration of many leading younger ones, in the short term the watershed of 1917 scarcely disrupted Russian operatic life. In the longer term the new regime was forced to grapple with the social and political ramifications of the existing repertory and to encourage the production of works reflecting the new socialist order. Ambivalent attitudes towards tradition led to radical extremes in the 1920s, ranging from the ludicrous transformation of Western operatic classics into revolutionary tracts to Shostakovich's selfconscious experimentation. His *Nos* ('The Nose'; 1930, Leningrad), a delightfully bizarre work, drew inspiration from contemporary advances in the theatre and cinema, as well as from the Western musical avant-garde ranging from Prokofiev and Stravinsky to Berg and Krenek.

The flair for dramatic pacing and vivid, often grotesque musical characterization were retained in Shostakovich's second opera, the 'tragedy-satire' *Ledi Makbet Mtsenskovo uyezda* ('Lady Macbeth of the Mtsensk District'; 1934, Leningrad), but these were tempered by a realistic plot and a more accessible, though profoundly expressive, melodic and harmonic language. The work had been internationally acclaimed and was well on its way to becoming the first undisputed Soviet operatic classic when in 1936 it became the target of a vicious official campaign. It was unceremoniously removed from the boards, to be revived – in a revised version entitled *Katerina Izmaylova* – only in 1963, when it was staged in Moscow and its status as a masterpiece was decisively reaffirmed. Despite a later, unfinished attempt to pick up the thread of Musorgsky's musical 'realism' in a literal setting of Gogol's play *Igroki* ('The Gamblers'), on which he worked in 1941–2, Shostakovich's promising career as an operatic composer came to an abrupt halt.

The attack on *Lady Macbeth* put an end to the permissive period in Soviet music. Dzerzhinsky proffered a positive alternative to the Shostakovich work with *Tikhiy Don* ('Quiet Flows the Don'; 1935, Leningrad), an insipid medley of folksongs which was officially endorsed as a model Soviet opera. The 'song opera' – a primitive compilation of tuneful songs and dances, eschewing complexity of musical language or dramatic situation, usually glorifying revolutionary heroism and sacrifice and capped with an uplifting moral – was most convincingly realized in Tikhon Khrennikov's *V buryu* ('Into the Storm'; 1939, Moscow). It became the formulaic prototype for acceptable opera in the Stalinist period and spawned innumerable undistinguished clones, including ethnic variants in the non-Russian republics. Works which rose above the prevailing level of mediocrity were rare; Yury Shaporin's long-awaited *Dekabristï* ('The Decembrists', begun 1920; 1953, Moscow), whose musical style is redolent of Musorgsky and Tchaikovsky, managed at least to impart sincerity and genuine lyricism to its historical subject.

Prokofiev's fascination with the genre continued after his repatriation in the mid-1930s. For his first Soviet opera he chose the seemingly unobjectionable tale of a young Ukrainian partisan during the Civil War, *Semyon Kotko* (1940, Moscow). Although he drastically simplified his style as compared with his earlier efforts in the genre, especially *The Fiery Angel*, his pervasive use of melodic recitative to draw strong musical characterization and motivate the dramatic development and his avoidance of self-contained arias, folksongs and dances, found little support in the reactionary atmosphere of the period. A later attempt to enrich the topical repertory of socialist realism, *Povest' o nastoyashchem cheloveke* ('The Story of a Real Man'; 1948, not staged until 1960, Moscow), also missed its mark. The unpretentiously witty send-up of Sheridan's *The Duenna* in *Obrucheniye v monastïre* ('Betrothal in a Monastery'; 1941), in spirit a successor to *Love for Three Oranges*, received a more sympathetic reception (1946, Leningrad). The major preoccupation of the last years of his life, however, was the composition and laborious revisions, extending from 1941 for 12 years, of Tolstoy's epic *Voyna i mir* ('War and Peace'); despite Prokofiev's repeated attempts to secure performances, it was not staged complete until 1957, after his death. Its episodic nature, its vast panoramic scope and its stirring choral perorations hark back to *Prince Igor* and *Khovanshchina*, but these aspects are balanced by some of his most heartfelt lyrical inspiration.

Despite the instinctive Russian attraction to opera and its historical status as the testing ground for new musical ideas, the aesthetic repressions of the Stalinist period greatly stifled the vitality of opera composition in the USSR. Although the economic climate in the Soviet Union has been more favourable for opera than in many Western countries, commitment to the medium has not been fully regenerated among later composers. The gap has been bridged, in part, by such composers as Rodion Shchedrin, whose comic one-act opera *Ne tol'ko lyubov'* ('Not Love Alone'; 1961, Moscow) is a sophisticated musical treatment of life on a collective farm. In the more ambitious, full-length *Myortvïe dushi* ('Dead Souls'; 1977, Moscow) Shchedrin attempted a complex synthesis of eclectic musical and theatrical elements, both manner and substance of which are reminiscent of Shostakovich's *The Nose*. Shchedrin has not been alone in the resuscitation of the repressed past; Alfred Shnitke, for instance, paid tribute to the synaesthetic experiments of Kandinsky in his multi-media theatrical work *Zholtïy zvuk* ('Yellow sound'; 1974, Moscow).

2. Eastern Europe

Although *Její pastorkyňa* ('Her Foster-daughter'; known outside Czechoslovakia as *Jenůfa*) had been successfully produced in Brno in 1904, it was the Prague production of 1916 that stimulated the incredible operatic productivity of Leoš Janáček's last years. While the treatment of Moravian village life in *Jenůfa* seemed to evolve naturally from the Czech nationalistic tradition, Janáček had already begun to dispense with the conventions of the number opera and to pursue more intuitive and naturalistic musical solutions. His study of ordinary speech patterns (the basis of his 'speech-melody' theory) contributed increasingly to a distinctive style of detached vocal writing, unified and bolstered by luxurious orchestral development of repetitive motivic fragments – often using instruments at extremes of their compass to create an effect of high intensity – along with concise dramatic argument. *Kát'a Kabanová* (1921, Brno), based on a play by Ostrovsky, was the last of his conventional operatic subjects, a tale of adultery and family oppression in which Janáček's concentration on the emotions and fate of the protagonist firmly secures our sympathies. Quirkier ones were heralded by the comic-satirical *Mr Brouček's Excursions* – excursions to the moon and the 15th century, in companion works later made into a whole (1920, Prague); Brouček is a late 19th-century philistine, baffled by the aesthetes he discovers on the moon, who becomes involved with the fervedly patriotic Hussites (Janáček took the opportunity to include some thrilling settings of Hussite chorales). His choices continued to be decidedly singular: the interaction of human and animal characters and affectionate nature imagery in *Příhody Lišky Bystroušky* ('The Adventures of the Vixen Bystrouška', or *The Cunning Little Vixen*; 1924, Brno), with its opportunities for music portraying the forest and the sounds of the creatures that inhabit it; the legal and amorous intrigues surrounding the fate of a 300-year-old woman in *Věc Makropulos* ('The Makropulos Affair', after Karel Čapek; 1926, Brno), remarkable for the intensity of the depiction of its central character; and the slice-of-life portrayal of prison inmates in Dostoyevsky's *Z mrtvého domu* ('From the House of the Dead'; 1930, Brno), in which he achieved some of his most striking effects through sharp juxtapositions and an outstandingly original orchestral palette, often using three low trombones and three piccolos. Janáček's ability to realize this range of subject matter in powerful dramatic and musical terms makes him all the more impressive.

Among other Czech composers Alois Hába, a pioneer in the exploration of microtonal music, scored at least a *succès d'estime* with his quarter-tone opera *Matka* ('The Mother'; 1931, Munich). Bohuslav Martinů's numerous theatrical projects include radio and television operas. Although much of his work was rooted in his deep feeling for Czech folklore and music, his best-known works for the stage, *Julietta* (1938, Prague) and *Řecké pašije* ('The Greek Passion'; 1961, Zurich) drew on other sources, the former on surrealist fantasy and the latter on Greek folk melody and liturgical chant.

Martinů's residence in Paris and later the USA insulated him from the strictures of socialist realism, which crippled operatic innovation in Czechoslovakia as surely as they did in the USSR. By the late 1950s a new generation of composers had begun to emerge, schooled in the most advanced musical developments of the West. Ján Cikker's expressionistic opera *Vzkriesenie* ('Resurrection'; 1962, Prague) shows the influence of Alban Berg, while Josef Berg absorbed serial techniques in his satirical chamber operas.

Béla Bartók showed deep commitment to his Hungarian musical heritage, fusing the results of his ethnographic research with advanced contemporary techniques. *A Kékszakállú herceg vára* ('Duke Bluebeard's Castle'; 1918, Prague), his only opera, was a remarkable product of this synthesis. Its intense psychological depth, reminiscent of Debussy's *Pelléas*, is explored through the use of a style of vocal writing based on the metre and modality of the Hungarian language and its folk ballads; at the same time, the sophisticated harmonic language and exquisite symphonic fabric owe much to the example of Richard Strauss.

Bartók's masterpiece might have served as the basis for development of a distinctive Hungarian operatic style, but it met with little immediate understanding in his homeland. His friend and colleague Zoltán Kodály opted for a more direct application of the Hungarian musical legacy in such works as the Singspiel *Háry János* (1926, Budapest), which met with correspondingly greater success.

As Hungary was subject to severe social, political and economic upheavals, its musical life and operatic productivity suffered accordingly. The 1960s, nevertheless, heralded new accomplishments, such as Sándor Szokolay's *Vérnász* ('Blood Wedding'; 1964, Budapest), noteworthy for the stark brutality of its musical interpretation of Lorca's play, and *Az ajtón kívül* ('The Man Outside'; 1977, Budapest), a grim and powerful work by Sándor Balassa. György Ligeti left Hungary in 1956 and his subsequent style is more reflective of the international avant-garde than of his national roots; in 1974–7 he wrote a phantasmagoric and tantalizingly ambiguous opera on the commonplace theme of the approach of death, *Le grand macabre* (1978, Stockholm), influenced by such disparate traditions as mystery play, puppet theatre and surreal aspects of the fairground.

In Poland, as in other eastern European countries in the 20th century, the composition of opera has not been a focus of significant musical involvement. Ludomir Różycki attracted attention with *Eros i Psyche* (1917, Wrocław) and the comic opera *Casanova* (1923, Warsaw), but it is Szymanowski's *Król Roger* ('King Roger'; 1926, Warsaw) that stands out as the major accomplishment of the period. Szymanowski evoked vividly the exotic milieu of Norman Sicily, not excluding its oriental atmosphere, in a lush harmonic and symphonic framework which showed his interest in the music of Skryabin. Postwar composers in Poland have paid comparatively little attention to opera. Those by Penderecki, the expressionistic *Diably z Loudun* ('The Devils of Loudun'; 1969, Hamburg), the 'rappresentazione' *Paradise Lost* (1978, Chicago), neo-Romantic in spirit and Wagnerian in form, and *Die schwarze Maske* (1986, Salzburg) were aimed at the broader international community.

CHAPTER XXVI

Britain

PETER EVANS

The critical commonplace that a native tradition of opera became a realistic aspiration in Britain only with the production of *Peter Grimes* (1945) is serviceable enough, yet it encourages misrepresentation of the periods before and after that momentous event. British opera of one kind or another has rarely been in drastically short supply, but demand has been fitful and tastes fickle. After Sullivan's partnership with Gilbert foundered, that slender thread of consistency was lost, and the operas of the new century were remarkably heterogeneous. Comic operetta with spoken dialogue lost favour to grander projects. The search for a tradition to which composers could attach themselves may be seen in the many English operas originally set to foreign texts; both Ethel Smyth and Stanford were aided in rising above the common blend of sickly technique and Romantic pretensions by experience in working to the regulated standards of the German houses. Yet the finest of these export operas, Delius's *Romeo und Julia auf dem Dorfe* (completed 1901; 1907, Berlin; as *A Village Romeo and Juliet*, 1910, London), lacks the crafted quality of the good repertory piece, the sensuous abandon of its best music intermittently revealing the Tristanesque potentialities of the homespun story.

More calculated attempts to learn from Wagner were made by composers who saw in the Celtic revival appropriate mythological roots for indigenous music drama. Joseph Holbrooke's trilogy, *The Cauldron of Annwyn* (1912–29) was surpassed in scale by Rutland Boughton's five Arthurian music dramas (1920–45), though Boughton's Bayreuth at Glastonbury offered pitifully inadequate performing resources; only his early *The Immortal Hour* (1914, Glastonbury) achieved resounding popular success. That its pallid pentatonics, short-breathed melodic spans and choruses redolent of the festival cantata or the partsong spurn Wagner's polyphonically braced harmonic tensions no doubt contributed to the success, for the highly equivocal English response to Wagner was compounded of a willingness to plunge into absurdities of Druidic fantasy unsecured by any trace of Wagner's sinewy causality and a reluctance to surrender to the truly magical properties peculiar to music. Something of the embarrassment Wagner's musical language represented to the next generation can be seen in Holst's parody of it (and of the highflown alliterative style of Wagner's English translators) in *The Perfect Fool* (1923), yet in *Sāvitri*, composed in 1908 (1916), Holst had uninhibitedly juxtaposed a still chromatic idiom with the more ascetic language he was developing in response to Sanskrit texts; the sense of drama as ritual is far more compelling in this modest chamber opera than in the church-hall theatricalities of the Celtic sagas.

A characteristic postwar reaction to the whole concept of Romantic opera, not just its curious British progeny, may be seen in the reversion to ballad opera cultivated in the 1920s, in the wake of Frederic Austin's phenomenally successful prettification of *The Beggar's Opera* (1920). Vaughan Williams's *Hugh the Drover* of 1914 (performed 1924) used eight traditional tunes, though still relied on artful transition and conventionally 'expressive' climax, but Holst in *At the Boar's Head* (1925, Manchester) performed the questionable miracle of threading a text derived from *Henry IV* on to a vast compendium of English airs. Ambitious full-length operas could still be launched during the Depression – works by Albert Coates, Eugene Goossens and George Lloyd appeared in successive years at Covent Garden – but two one-acters, Holst's last (and still ballad-inspired) opera *The Wandering Scholar* of 1930 (1934, Liverpool) and Vaughan Williams's *Riders to the Sea* of 1932 (1937), seem the most durable salvage from a fallow decade, one that was followed by a famine during World War II.

The decision to reopen Sadler's Wells Theatre on 7 June 1945 with Britten's *Peter Grimes* was courageous not only in its timing and its choice of an untried opera composer but in its assumption that the future role of the revitalized company, to present a wide repertory in the vernacular, would naturally include the regular introduction of new British operas. Neither the British National Opera nor the Carl Rosa, the two companies most enterprising in the cause of native opera between the wars, had a permanent home, and the range of theatres, in London and the provinces, in which premières were mounted is bizarre. But now opera and ballet were to be served by establishments at two London theatres, and *Peter Grimes* appeared to define a house style for one of them. Certainly its many nimbly sketched minor characters made it an ideal company opera, and the crucial corporate role of the chorus at last gave overwhelming dramatic force to an element that, while much cultivated in earlier English operas, had too often subscribed, in its reiterated platitudes, to the festival cantata tradition. Word-setting of an idiomatic rhythmic cast rescued the English language from that strange operatic limbo in which even original texts could sound like translations, and the number-opera convention, with which audiences felt most at home, was skilfully absorbed into act-structures reflecting extended, and dramatically potent, tonal planning, while the whole opera was further braced by pervasive yet unobtrusive motivic usages. The musical language offered great subtlety of nuance around scalic and triadic norms that did not affront conservative tastes, yet such dramatic agencies as the orchestral interludes and the stage music showed clear debts to an opera as modern as *Wozzeck*. But above all it was in the nature of its parable that *Peter Grimes* associated British opera with some preoccupations of 20th-century culture: the character of Peter, more curiously compounded in its visionary aspirations and self-destroying resentments than the placarded heroes of much English Romantic opera, is made explicable only because his alienation from the society that has bred him is so painfully probed.

Many of Britten's later operas rework this theme, often directing the composer's passionate outrage against those social taboos of which the outsider may become a compliant victim; Philip Brett's identification of this obsession with Britten's homosexuality is convincing. Its relevance is no less clear to *The Rape of Lucretia* (1946, Glyndebourne), Britten's first chamber opera, than to *Billy Budd* (1951), his most ambitious full opera, written for Covent Garden, after Herman Melville. *Budd* exemplifies at its most lowering the conflict that characterizes Britten's operatic subjects, the background of naval warfare almost a diversion from foreground confrontations between good and evil that disconcertingly resist consistent black-and-white interpretation. Structures are more intensely organized than in *Grimes*, while the all-male vocal timbres against searing orchestral colourings create a darkly individual tonal world. *Lucretia* and its immediate successor, the comedy after Maupassant, *Albert Herring* (1947, Glyndebourne), became the foundation repertory of a new company, the English Opera Group, in establishing which Britten recognized that progress in Britain would be unconscionably slow if measured solely by the number of new operas the two permanent houses could present to their metropolitan audiences.

Unlike its distinguished English precursors (*Sāvitri*; Blow and Purcell), the new 'chamber opera' was to limit material resources (typically to an orchestra of a dozen and a handful of singers) but not necessarily time-scale: full-length works could be presented in modest provincial theatres, though with Britten's next venture, the Aldeburgh Festival, inaugurated in 1948, the new company's activities became regulated by festival planning. And what began as a response to domestic conditions soon attracted international attention: *The Turn of the Screw* (1954, after Henry James) was first performed in Venice. The confinements of Britten's chamber format here powerfully reinforce the mounting sense of isolation in which the Governess carries through her self-appointed task. Still tighter constraints are felt through the unusually schematic structuring of the whole opera around a tonally ordered arch of orchestral interludes, variations on a no less schematic 12-note theme that, patently symbolizing the inexorable process of the title, also generates the thematic material of the action. The consistent association of the tonal centre on A which frames the work with the Governess's resolve to save her charges, and of the A♭ of the two central scenes with the ghosts' corrupting will, provides a particularly clear (and finally momentous) example of Britten's tendency to realize in tonal dichotomy a fundamental dramatic opposition.

Even though the hopes raised by Britten's meteoric emergence, that British opera could become simply an accepted part of the repertory, were by now subdued, some of his older contemporaries were sufficiently encouraged to essay full-length works. In *The Pilgrim's Progress* (1951) Vaughan Williams expanded an earlier reverie around Bunyan to four acts without exchanging meditation for dramatic immediacy (he had worked intermittently on the opera for 40 years). Arthur Bliss and J. B. Priestley collaborated in a stolid view of *The Olympians* (1949), while Walton's retreat to a mildly piquant lyricism served him well in matching the rather glibly packaged sentiments of Christopher Hassall's book for *Troilus and Cressida* (1954, revised 1976). Walton's only return to opera was in a one-acter for the English Opera Group (*The Bear*, 1967, Aldeburgh). Lennox Berkeley's three-act *Nelson* (1954) was followed by several miniatures for the English Opera Group in which his nicely pointed observation found expression on a more appropriate scale. Indeed the gap between the apt sketch that could be sustained by wit and the full operatic canvas, with its demand for some consistent moral or social statement as well as for highly disciplined musical invention, was one that many composers never bridged: in a country so poor in operatic establishments, to write except on commission was likely to be futile idealism.

Like Walton, Tippett was able on the strength of his reputation as an instrumental composer to earn a Covent Garden début in opera. Whereas *Troilus* was instantly accessible to an audience with, say, some Puccini and a little Britten, the many-layered symbolism and the textural density of *The Midsummer Marriage* (1955) proved thickets that could be penetrated only slowly; the recognition of a complementary talent to Britten's was correspondingly slow to pass into general critical currency. The simplification that Britten's message is conveyed in parables, Tippett's in myths, at least highlights the contrast between Britten's practice of rounding out character in a compassionate awareness that unique foibles create unique fates, however symbolically apt, and Tippett's more commanding view of the *dramatis personae* as archetypal figures in which we do not recognize, but are helped to understand, ourselves. However much post-Freudian access to unconscious (and unnerving) levels of experience is afforded musically by *The Turn of the Screw*, the dramatic thrust is at the foreground level of cumulative incident, whereas the Jungian resonances of *The Midsummer Marriage*, its almost didactic confrontation and eventual reconciliation of opposing life-forces, are the opera's *raison d'être*. The orchestral interludes in *The Turn of the Screw* anticipate the emotional nuances of the following scenes, but the orchestral Ritual Dances of Tippett's second act exemplify a universal drama which makes the responses of the workaday couple, Jack and Bella, almost tiresomely specific. Charming though their music is, Tippett seems to be writing down to these earthbound natures; it is for the 'ideal' Mark and Jenifer that he released the floods of a visionary music that can aspire to ecstasy. A paradox is felt in the levitating quality of textures which yet seem to be weighed down by a surfeit of harmonic units and by attendant arabesque; indeed, the impression that more is sweeping by (characteristic also of the magnificently rich choral writing) than can be entirely assimilated gives a heady sensation at a vast remove from the limpid precision (which is not to rule out acute emotional ambiguity) of Britten's most penetrating moments.

Having devoted six years to the composition of *The Midsummer Marriage*, Tippett wrote his next opera, *King Priam* (1962), in half that time; the crude computation that it contains far fewer notes is relevant to the quality it conveys in the theatre, of a wiry, almost cryptic style. In adapting a familiar mythology rather than constructing his own, Tippett could sound its tragic resonances in the sparest terms, and his mosaic of characterizing materials produces contrasts that are dramatically immediate. He described the opera as being about the nature of choice, and in unwinding the chain of its consequences he achieved one of the most convincing translations of the spirit of classical tragedy into music. War has been divested of all romantic associations, yet he still probes into its nature with a cosmic pity wholly unlike Britten's compassion for the victim.

While Tippett was teaching audiences to see in opera a cathartic rite, Britten, whose early prodigality slackened markedly after *The Turn of the Screw*, produced only a miracle play for children, *Noyes Fludde* (1958, Orford), and a comedy, *A Midsummer Night's Dream* (1960, Aldeburgh). Music as a key to unlock that enchantment we otherwise experience only in dreams gives a new tone to a Shakespearean text retained in literal, if necessarily pruned, form. The danger avoided here, that music will fall away lifelessly from the familiar verse it has simply incommoded, had marred the 'ballad' Shakespeare settings of the 1920s, and was to make of Humphrey Searle's *Hamlet* (1968, Hamburg) an evident superfluity. But it is the radiantly simple music that justifies to children the stylized enactment of *Noyes Fludde*, and with this work (rather than the more parochially moralizing *The Little Sweep*; 1949, Aldeburgh) Britten devised a quasi-operatic medium for children, as participants and audience, that has remained influential, on composers as unlike as Malcolm Williamson, Gordon Crosse and Peter Maxwell Davies.

Their generation was the first to profit from the generally enhanced interest in native opera Britten had stimulated, and to embark on operatic enterprises early in their careers with good prospects for performance. Some of their elders, like Elisabeth Lutyens and Iain Hamilton, came late to opera; others, like Alan Bush and Searle, found openings more readily in Germany than at home. Bush's deflection from the mainstream of British operatic activity is particularly regrettable, since his works for East German stages (*Wat Tyler*, 1953, Leipzig; *Men of Blackmoor*, 1966, Weimar) appear to be so firmly rooted in an English ballad tradition in need of his sturdy revitalizing qualities, yet are estranged from it by the insistence on vehement political parable. Opera audiences who value the reassurance of so conservative a musical language usually expect it to say nothing in particular, with some degree of eloquence. Written against the background of that Schoenbergian tradition Bush had renounced, Searle's operas favoured a far more 'modern' language, yet without finding in it the range of acutely characterized music to equate potent literary material (*Diary of a Madman*, after Gogol, 1958, Berlin; *The Photo of the Colonel*, after Ionescu, 1964, Frankfurt). Britten's success in finding operatic potentialities in classic texts – and librettists, notably Myfanwy Piper, to realize them – may have encouraged other composers to underestimate the difficulty of the task: John Gardner's *The Moon and Sixpence* (after Maugham) and Arthur Benjamin's *A Tale of Two Cities* (after Dickens), both produced at Sadler's Wells in 1957, are well-made pieces that lack the vital imaginative leap beyond their sources.

Before Britten's own last two adaptations, in the 1970s, he forsook traditional operatic conventions in the three 'parables for church performance' (first given at Orford Church). *Curlew River* (1964) re-creates the story of a Japanese nō play to exemplify a medieval monastic homily, the consequent application of such oriental practices as heterophony to material audibly deriving from the framing plainsong hymn resulting in Britten's most pronounced stylistic shift. Instead of the miniature orchestra of the chamber operas, a few discrete instrumental colours suffice, and as the all-male cast sing in textures that float free from exact alignment, 'harmony' exchanges its traditional Western urge for the stasis of simple aggregates of melodic pitches. Stylizations accumulate, in gesture and staging as in music, and the retreat from all ambitions of realism enhances the moving dénouement, of healing miracle. In the two later parables, Britten turned to biblical sources (*The Burning Fiery Furnace*, 1966; *The Prodigal Son*, 1968), effectively introducing more garish colourings without quite matching the intense emotional impact of *Curlew River*.

The slender resources, the liberated time-flow and the exotic inspiration of the parables could be held to forge a link with more general European preoccupations of these years, though Britten's pitch organization retained its idiosyncratic tonal stamp. Surprisingly, the younger British generation showed a greater concern for cultivating more conventional operatic genres, often attempting to woo the equally conventional audiences these implied by eclecticism involving an element of pastiche (as in the versatile Richard Rodney Bennett's *The Mines of Sulphur*, 1965, and *Victory*, 1970). Despite its quotation of *The Cries of London* as period colour, Alexander Goehr's *Arden Must Die* (1967) more consistently forges an idiom that retains the subterranean organizing powers bred of his early serial experience while deploying a harmonic palette that, mordantly allusive to the tonal world it largely circumvents, points the irony of this deadpan social commentary; the tone is far removed from Bush's, but, despite obvious literary parallels with Brecht in Erich Fried's libretto,

Goehr also avoids the futile pursuit of Weill's caustic artlessness. Commissioned by the Hamburg Staatsoper, *Arden Must Die* was introduced to England the year after its première by the New Opera Company, which pioneered several other notable pieces, including Gordon Crosse's *Purgatory* (1966, Cheltenham), on Yeats's play, and unusual among one-acters of this period for its dramatic pungency, and Thea Musgrave's first full-length opera, *The Decision* (1967). By this date national companies had been established in Wales (1946) and Scotland (1962), and in expanding their scope they gave a cautious welcome to such local composers as Grace Williams (*The Parlour*, 1966, Cardiff) and Robin Orr (*Full Circle*, 1968, Perth). Even Glyndebourne ventured into the field, with Nicholas Maw's *The Rising of the Moon* (1970); if Maw's romantic comedy seems circumspectly tailored, it is carried through with a persuasive zest and a refined ear for beautiful sound.

Television also offered access to an audience with no predisposition towards operatic innovation (or indeed towards operatic commonplace either), though only Britten was entrusted with more than a one-act commission, and he ensured that *Owen Wingrave* (broadcast 1971) could be transplanted to the orthodox stage (1973, Covent Garden). This second opera after Henry James, while it permitted Britten to make an unusually direct declaration of his pacifist beliefs, lacks the harrowingly inevitable convergence on catastrophe of *The Turn of the Screw*. Its wide range of character parts elicited a rich retrospective of the composer's operatic techniques, for *Death in Venice* (1973, Snape) was to narrow the dramatic focus to the exterior and interior life of a single character, Thomas Mann's Aschenbach. This demanding tenor role was the last operatic tribute to Peter Pears, a decisive influence on Britten's musico-dramatic thinking, as well as his vocal style, since *Peter Grimes*. In charting the moral destruction of a proudly discriminating creative spirit by passionate frenzy, Britten was at the very heart of his expressive territory, where the corrupting power of beauty inspires an ambivalent response. Texturally thinner than all but the parables (and sharing their limited concern for harmonic phenomena), *Death in Venice* is the more palpably infected by its terse motivic cells. Yet apotheosis of a kind is not denied, the final desolation being illuminated by a memory of Aschenbach's most rarefied Apollonian transport.

Tippett's two operas of the 1970s seek to create a less unified impression not only than the cancerous obsession of this last Britten opera but also than his own earlier ones. In *The Knot Garden* (1970), the archetypal is rendered as the case study, and although transitional passages (known as 'dissolves' by an analogy with the technique used in filming) assist the shifts between prosaic and fantasy modes, the recurrences of musical material savour more of an intellectual puppet show than of the awesome inevitabilities of *King Priam*. The lyrical power of the first opera is recalled, but in lines far more tenuously related to tonal models, and something of its textural profusion is readmitted, even if, like so much else (beyond the obvious Schubert song, protest chorus and blues), it now seems to bear quotation marks. Whether self-knowledge is more certainly unlocked by the determined topicality of Tippett's characters (and their quickly dated speech) is not beyond dispute, but how important it had become to him to forge his symbols from the very raw materials of the time is clearer still in *The Ice Break* (1977). While the title's image of renewal is compellingly reiterated, the cliché nature of his chosen depictions of the modern predicament – the black boxing champion, the political dissident, the race riot – can blunt response to the darker reaches of Tippett's vision; similarly the musical range and the pacing of the shifts are more disconcerting than in *The Knot Garden*. Yet the passage of time has usually served to reinforce central meanings and reduce to insignificance the wilful gaucheries of Tippett's work.

Tippett's extension of sound sources in *The Ice Break* (chiefly to bludgeon the audience with the amplified noises of modern life) was little cultivated by younger composers. Musgrave used pre-recorded sound to dramatically crucial effect in *The Voice of Ariadne* (1974, Snape), but more commonly a distinction was observed between the limitations peculiar to traditional opera and the wider horizons of music theatre, totally freed from any blinkers of verisimilitude; Goehr and Maxwell Davies, for example, have worked in both fields. The challenge of a production at one of the London houses (in 1968 the Sadler's Wells company had moved to the Coliseum, being restyled the English National Opera six years later) remained irresistible: Maxwell Davies's *Taverner* (1972, Covent Garden) and David Blake's *Toussaint l'Ouverture* (1977, Coliseum) could typify not only the range, of treatment and of style, but also the tendency, so evident in Tippett's development, to see in operatic composition a peak of creative definition surrounded by necessary foothills. In at least one case, the final ascent was postponed: the brilliant savagery of Harrison Birtwistle's one-act *Punch and Judy* (1968, Aldeburgh) gave advance notice of an idiosyncratic talent which was harnessed to less quirky ends in the three-act *Mask of Orpheus* (1986, Coliseum). Blake's *Toussaint* keeps alive the overtly socio-political opera without recourse to the dulling certainties of Bush, and with no inhibitions about enlisting the aid of precisely imagined beauty of sound.

Taverner, by contrast, has considerable stretches in which the sound images appear merely generic, whatever the transformational subtleties of the underlying technical loom. But the wider correspondences, between dramatic and musical events of the two acts (Taverner's trial by the White Abbot is replayed, with reversed roles, as a parody) are pointed, while the internal ones are on a small enough time-scale to prompt recognition. The expressionistic element, of orgiastic blasphemy, is offset elsewhere by Davies's practised appropriation of liturgical musical controls, culminating in the recall of Taverner's own music (the original *In nomine* context), an artistic legacy renounced by the fanaticism which, abetted by political expediency, is the destructive force that racks this work. Animal violence erupts also in Maxwell Davies's chamber opera, *The Martyrdom of Saint Magnus* (1977, Kirkwall); the use of pastiche popular music and generally more lucid textures signals a clarification characteristic of his music written on (and often for) Orkney, and applied to powerfully dramatic ends in *The Lighthouse* (1980, Edinburgh).

CHAPTER XXVII

Iberia, Scandinavia, the Low Countries

LIONEL SALTER, JOHN HORTON, ELIZABETH FORBES

1. Spain and Portugal

Responding to Pedrell's campaign for authentic Spanish opera of a serious type, as distinct from zarzuelas, the Real Academia de Bellas Artes of Madrid held a competition in 1904 for the best one-act lyric drama by a Spanish composer. It was won the following year by *La vida breve*, a last-minute entry by Pedrell's pupil Manuel de Falla, who had hitherto written almost nothing but five zarzuelas, two of them in collaboration with Vives. No production followed, however, and the work, recast into two acts, was first heard only in 1913, and then in France (at Nice and Paris); its eventual presentation in Madrid in 1915 was a triumph. The dramatic structure of *La vida breve* is rudimentary, its characters pasteboard except for the heroine, but its music, despite some lapses into a Massenet-type idiom, is powerfully evocative of Andalusian atmosphere. A slightly older pupil of Pedrell, Enric Morera, had meanwhile created a stir in his native Barcelona with his three one-act operas *Emporium* (1906), *Bruniselda* and *Titania* (both 1908).

Many 20th-century Spanish opera composers also wrote zarzuelas, which stood a better chance of being performed. The new generation showed greater technical skill than their predecessors, and the level improved. A typical figure is Amadeo Vives, who composed about 70 *género chico* zarzuelas, two dozen *zarzuelas grandes* and six operettas, of which the most popular was *La generala* (1912), and five operas, of which the two most noteworthy are *Artus* (1897, Barcelona), a setting of the Arthurian legend which had but a *succès d'estime*, and the light 'lyric eclogue' *Maruxa* (1914), set in Galicia and introducing in the score the local *gaita* (bagpipe). Enrique Granados, like Vives a Pedrell pupil, had been decorated by the king for his zarzuela *María del Carmen* (1898), but his further zarzuelas made little mark and he did not taste acclaim again until his *Goyescas* had its première in New York in 1916. This was not so much a real opera as a series of tableaux strung together from his piano pieces, to which words had been added: as with Falla's *La vida breve*, it was its poetic atmosphere, largely arising from the orchestral writing, that made the deepest impression.

An interesting feature of Spanish opera in the 20th century has been the emergence of Basque composers, notably Jesús Guridi and José Usandizaga. The former first attracted attention with his Basque 'lyric idyll' *Mirentxu* (1910, Bilbao); his next stage work, *Amaya* (1920, Bilbao), is more Wagnerian in its orchestration and its use of leitmotifs. Thereafter he moved to the zarzuela repertory, bringing it distinction. Usandizaga also began with a Basque 'lyric pastoral', *Mendi mendiyan* ('High in the Mountains'; 1911, San Sebastián); his *Las golondrinas*, with a libretto by Martinez Sierra, which first won success in a zarzuela version (1914), was revised as an opera by the composer's brother (1929, Barcelona), who also completed the opera on which José was working at his death, *La llama* (1918, San Sebastián).

Almost all the above composers had spent some time in Paris; but Conrado del Campo, an influential post-Romantic writer, was inspired by the Wagner-Strauss tradition, which made itself felt even in the scoring of his popular zarzuelas. His operas include the passionate one-act *El final de Don Alvaro* (1911), the Goyesque three-act *El Avapiés* (1919), the graceful chamber opera *Fantochines* (1924) and *Lola la piconera* (1950). Standing almost by itself in this period is Falla's puppet opera *El retablo de Maese Pedro* of 1923 (concert performance Seville, staged in Paris), based on an episode from *Don Quixote*; Falla had by this time moved away from his early picturesque style to a crisper, more spare and incisive idiom owing something to the example of Stravinsky's *Histoire du soldat*. In 1932 Manuel Penella, hitherto known only in the lightest and most trivial sphere, produced in Barcelona a well-wrought three-act historical opera, *Don Gil de Alcalá*, which incorporates dances from the New World as well as Spanish Rococo music.

Most of the other notable Iberian operas have been written by Catalan composers (and given in Barcelona). Jaime Pahissa was best known for his writing about music, but he composed ten operas, of which the most striking are the abrasive *Gala Placidia* (1913), the more mellifluous *Marianela* (1923) and, particularly, *La Princesa Margarida* (1928), which dramatically and musically is derived from a Catalan folksong. It was also in 1928 that Barcelona saw the première of the lyrical comic opera *El giravolt de maig* by Eduardo Toldrá. The violinist Juan Manén, self-taught as a composer, was particularly successful with *Soledad* (1952), and Antonio Massana was much praised for his *Canigó* (1953, but written much earlier); but the most important Catalan composer of that period was one who went into voluntary exile after the Civil War, Roberto Gerhard. His only opera, *The Duenna* (composed 1947; 1951, Wiesbaden), despite its English libretto and freely employed serialism, has its roots deep in Spanish soil and has been called 'the greatest of all Spanish operas'.

Twentieth-century Portuguese opera has made little impact outside its own linguistic territories. The vastly prolific Rui Coelho wrote some two dozen operas, most of which have been staged in Lisbon. Though a pupil of Humperdinck and Schoenberg, he deliberately set out to use a nationalist idiom (sometimes drawing on folk themes) and nationalist subject matter; four of his stage works are based on works by the 16th-century dramatist Gil Vicente. Among his others are *Belkiss* (1924), *Ines de Castro* (1925) and *Orfeu em Lisboa* (1963), the last to his own libretto. Joly Braga Santos, also primarily active in Lisbon (after studies in Venice and Rome), has considerably deepened and developed his style since his early works: besides radio operas he has written two three-act operas, *Merope* (1959) and *Trilogia das barcas* (1970, after Vicente).

2. Scandinavia

Carl Nielsen's two operas, the psychologically complex *Saul og David* (1902) and the sparkling Holbergian comedy *Maskarade* (1906), are landmarks not only in Danish theatre music but also in modern Scandinavian opera as a whole. Written when Nielsen was in his 30s, these scores show impressive dramatic qualities and a mature, independent musical personality which acknowledged the revolutionary achievements of Wagner but was resistant to aspects of late German Romanticism alien to the Danish spirit. The most prominent Danish dramatic composer between the world wars was Ebbe Hamerik, whose *Stepan* (1924, Mainz) is set in the Russia of 1917. Hamerik's later works are based on Danish literature: *Marie Grubbe* (1940) on the historical novel by J. P. Jacobsen, *Reisekammeraten* (1946) on H. C. Andersen's tale *The Travelling Companion* and *Drømmerne* (composed 1949; 1974, Århus) to his own libretto after Karen Blixen's story. Hamerik's style ranges from lyrical simplicity (*Marie Grubbe*) to a polytonal freedom (*Drømmerne*) that recalls Nielsen and also Hindemith.

Other Danish operatic works of the years up to World War II include works by Finn Høffding, Hakon Børreson, Jørgen Bentzon and Knudåge Riisager. In the 1940s a marked adventurousness in Danish music theatre helped to generate such works as Niels Viggo Bentzon's *Faust III* (1964, Kiel), whose libretto links Goethe with Joyce's *Ulysses* and Kafka's *The Trial*. The stimuli of radio and television are apparent in Ib Nørholm's *Invitation til skafottet* ('Invitation to a Beheading', broadcast 1967), while continued demand for school opera was met by Per Nørgård in *Labyrinten* (1967) and *Gilgamesj* (1973, Århus). The wide range of Nørgård's interests is further revealed in *Siddharta* (1983, Stockholm), an opera-ballet on the life of the Buddha, and *Det gudommelige Tivoli* (1983, Århus), a study of the Swiss poet and painter Adolf Wölfli (1864–1930).

Romanticism continued to colour much of the output of a group of Swedish composers active principally in Stockholm during the first half of the century. These included Wilhelm Peterson-Berger, Ture Rangström,

Kurt Atterberg, Oskar Lindberg and Natanael Berg. A boundary between this period and the full dawn of Swedish modernism can be distinguished in the works of Hilding Rosenberg; his experiments with various dramatic forms include the Singspiel *Resa till Amerika* (1932, on the theme of emigration), the *opere buffe Marionetter* (1939) and *Lycksalightens ö* ('The Isle of the Blessed', 1945; after the early 19th-century epic by Per Atterbom) and the opera-oratorio *Josef och hans bröder* (after Thomas Mann's cycle of novels, broadcast 1946–8).

Neo-classical ideas permeated a younger generation in Sweden. Gunnar Frumerie's *Singoalla* (1940, based on a novel by Viktor Rydberg) and Lars-Erik Larsson's *Prinsessan av Cypern* (1937, after Topelius) reflect current eastern European styles, the former being orientated towards Sibelius, the latter towards Musorgsky. Sven-Erik Bäck, a pupil of Rosenberg, has specialized in chamber opera, for example in *Tranfjä-drarna* ('The Crane-Feathers', broadcast 1957), a delicate treatment of a Japanese legend. The most widely publicized of all modern Swedish operas, Karl-Birger Blomdahl's *Aniara* (1959), belongs to a period in the 1950s and 60s when the Stockholm Royal Opera was mounting its productions of such works as *Wozzeck*, *The Turn of the Screw*, *The Rake's Progress* and *The Makropulos Affair*. The impact of *Aniara* was however to be matched, if not eclipsed, by Johan Werle's opera-in-the-round *Drommen om Thérèse* (1964, based on Zola's *Pour une nuit d'amour*), the total theatre of *Resan* (1969, commissioned by Hamburg State Opera) and his two-act *Tintomara* (1973), a chamber opera derived from C. L. J. Almqvist's novel dealing with the assassination of Gustavus III.

Before the inauguration of the Norwegian Opera in Oslo in 1959, the works of Norwegian composers usually had to remain unperformed or to seek acceptance in German theatres. Of Sigwardt Asperstrund's eight operas, only *Sjömansbunden* (1907) reached the stage in his lifetime and of Ole Olsen's four, only *Lajla* (composed 1893), on Lapp themes, gained a hearing (1908). Christian Sinding composed a single opera, *Der heilige Berg*, produced in Dessau in 1914. Gerhard Schelderup, an ambitious writer for the stage, had better support in the German-speaking lands than in Norway. The ardent nationalist Geirr Tveitt wrote five operas, the last of which, based on Holberg's comedy *Jeppe paa Bjerget* (1966, Bergen) has also been staged in Paris. Probably the most successful Norwegian opera before the half-century was Arne Eggen's *Olav Liljenk-rans* (1940), based on Ibsen's early saga-drama. Edvard Fliflet Braein made a considerable impression with *Anne Pedersdotter* (1971), whose subject is the historical episode of the burning of a witch at Bergen in 1590.

Oskar Merikanto's *Pohjan neiti* ('Girl of the North', composed 1899, produced 1908) is the earliest opera to a Finnish text. His *Elinan surma* ('Elina's Death') appeared two years later, in the year that the Finnish National Opera was established. Sibelius, whose only opera *Jungfrun i tornet* ('The Maiden in the Tower') was composed in 1896 and virtually discarded, was a teacher of Leevi Madetoja, whose *Pohjalaisia* ('The Ostro-Bothnians', 1924) is now recognized as a Finnish classic. His *Juha* (1935) is derived from the same source, a novel (by Juha Aho) that had already served as a basis for Aarre Merikanto (son of Oskar) in an opera with the same title, written in 1922, but not staged until 1963. Armas Launis, a musicologist by training who moved to France in 1930, made use of Finnish and Lapp folk idioms, combined with late Romantic orchestration, in his eight operas including *Seitsemän veljestä* ('The Seven Brothers', 1913) and *Kullervo* (1917).

The two most active composers of Finnish opera in the mid-20th-century were Väinö Raitio and Tauno Pylkkänen. Raitio's five works, beginning with *Jeftan tytär* ('Jephtha's Daughter', 1929), show close attention to Finnish text declamation. Pylkkännen, the most productive of modern Finnish composers for the stage, progressively broke away from the Sibelius tradition in a series of operas beginning with *Mare ja hänen poikansa* ('Mare and her Son', 1945). The operas of Einojuhani Rautavaara, a pupil of Aarre Merikanto, include *Kaivos* ('The Mine', 1963), written for television, the comic opera *Apollon contra Marsyas* (1970) and *Runo 42* (1974), on an episode from the *Kalevala* epic. Two contemporary Finnish composers have gained international reputations with works produced at the Savonlinna Festivals: Joonas Kokkonen took as his subject for *Viimeiset kiusaukset* ('The Last Temptations', 1975) the life of the evangelist Paavo Routsalainen (1777–1852), and Aulis Sallinen, a pupil of Kokkonen and Aarre Merikanto, chose a historical episode, the full-suffrage elections of 1907, as the subject of his second opera, *Punainen viiva* ('The Red Line', 1978), which shows some indebtedness to Janáček, and also attracted considerable attention with *The King Goes Forth to France* (1984), which has been given in London as well as his native country.

3. The Low Countries

During the early years of the century, Belgian opera was dominated by three composers, two of them Flemish and one French-speaking. The first two, the exact contemporaries Paul Gilson and August de Boeck, were both influenced by the Russian 'Five', Rimsky-Korsakov in particular. Gilson wrote three operas first produced at the Royal Flemish Opera in Antwerp, *Prinses Zonneschijn* (1903), *Zeevolk* (1904) and *Rooversliefde* (1906). Boeck also composed three that were first performed in Antwerp, *Winternachtsdroom* (1903), *Rijndwergen* (1906) and *Reinaert de Vas* (1909), but his last and most successful opera, *La route d'émeraude* (or *Francesca*, in the Flemish version), had its première in Ghent (1921) before being given in Antwerp and Brussels.

Albert Dupuis, for some years conductor at the Théâtre de la Monnaie in Brussels, composed 13 operas in all; six, showing the influence of Massenet, from *Jean Michel* (1903) to *Un drame sous Philippe II* (1948), were produced at La Monnaie. Another French-speaking composer, Fernand Brumagne, a pupil of Vincent d'Indy, had three operas produced at La Monnaie, *L'invasion* (1919), *Le miracle de Saint Antoine* (1927) and *Le marchand de Venise* (1933) which, adapted from Shakespeare's play, was his most successful stage work and has frequently been revived. Two operas by Françoise Rasse, also a conductor at La Monnaie, had their premières there, *Deidamia* (1906) and *Soeur Béatrice* (1944), an adaptation of Maeterlinck's miracle play.

A pupil of Gilson, Marcel Poot, composed two operas to Flemish texts while still under 30: *Het ingebeeld eiland* ('The Fancy Isle', 1925) and *Het vrouwtje van Stavoren* ('The Little Woman of Stavoren', 1928). His chamber opera, *Moretus ou Le damné recalcitrant*, received a concert performance in Brussels in 1944 and was staged at La Monnaie in 1950. The founder of Les Synthétistes, a group of eight composers, all former pupils of Gilson, Poot was much influenced by Prokofiev and to a lesser extent the neo-classical works of Stravinsky. Gaston Brenta, another of the Synthétistes, wrote a comic opera, *Le Khadi dupé* (1929), that was successfully produced at La Monnaie. Jean Absil, also a pupil of Gilson (though not a Synthétiste), had a one-act comic opera, *Fansou* (1947), given at La Monnaie in a double bill with Britten's *Rape of Lucretia*. At first influenced by Schoenberg, Absil later evolved a serial method of his own which he used in his second opera, *Les voix de la mer* (1954). Another independent composer, Louis de Meester, wrote a successful radio opera, *De grote verzoeking van St Antonius* ('The Great Temptation of St Anthony', 1957), a television opera, *Twee is te weinig, drie is te veel* ('Two is not Enough, Three is too Many', 1965), and a stage work, *De Paradijsgeuzen* ('The Birds of Paradise', 1967), while directing the Belgian radio Institute for Psycho-acoustics and Electronic Music.

Possibly the most widely known Belgian opera of the century, however, is Henry Pousseur's *Votre Faust* (1969, Milan), 'une fantaisie variable genre opéra'. Pousseur, a pupil of Absil and at first greatly influenced by Webern, later worked extensively in electronic music; in *Votre Faust*, stimulated by Butor's use of literary excerpts, he saw in quotation a means of reintroducing ideas proscribed by classical serialism. His quotations, ranging from Monteverdi to his own music, are sometimes introduced in chronological order but elsewhere linked by technical devices; there is also scope for audience intervention. Frederic Devreese, a contemporary of Pousseur and who also employs electronic music, has written two television operas, *Willem van Saeflinge* (1964) and *Le cavalier bizarre* (1967); the former won the Italia Prize and was staged at Antwerp.

Several leading Dutch composers of the first half of the 20th century wrote operas that were subsequently staged at the Holland Festival in Amsterdam. One of the most interesting is Hendrik Andriessen's *Philomela*, based on an episode in Ovid's *Metamorphoses* (1950); it is notable for the detailed, symphonic working of its leitmotifs and for its finale, where the gods transform humans into birds, resolving conflicts in a triumph for eternal song which is realized in broad melody, individual modal harmony and colourful orchestral writing. Andriessen later wrote a one-act opera, *De spiegel van Venetie*, on an episode in the life of Sweelinck. Another primarily symphonic drama heard at the Holland Festival (1952) was Willem Pijper's single completed opera, *Halewijn* (composed in 1933). Sem Dresden's *François Villon* (1958) was given the year after the composer's death and Jan van Gilse's *Thijl* (1980; it was written in 1940) on the eve of the composer's centenary. More fortunate was Guillaume Landré, a pupil of Pijper and a more conventional composer, whose one-act *Jean Levecq* was given at the Holland Festival (1963); he also wrote a comic, surrealist opera in a colourful polytonal idiom, *De snoek* (1938, Amsterdam) and *La symphonie pastorale*, after the novel by André Gide (1968, Rouen). *Jean Levecq* was given with *De droom*, by Ton de Leeuw, which includes a striking dream scene, a dance accompanied by choral singing of *haiku*; his works include a television opera, *Alceste* (1963). Ton de Kruyf's *Spinoza*, also heard at the Holland Festival (1971), is in a decorative, atmospheric style, with individual instrumentation and, sometimes, composition technique assigned to each of the characters. Henk Badings's *Martin Korda D. P.*, given at the Holland Festival in 1960, includes an electronic sequence; his radio opera *Orestes* (1954), an Italia Prize winner, was among the first of his electronic works and includes a representation of the Eumenides, using a male chorus at accelerated speed. He wrote a further radio opera, *Asterion* (1957), for South African Radio, and a successful television opera, *Salto mortale* (1959); his earlier works include an opera on the life of Rembrandt, *De Nachtwacht* (1942, Antwerp).

Among the most sensational of opera premières at the Holland Festival was that of Peter Schat's *Labyrint* (1966), described as 'a conception of total theatre for orchestra, chorus, vocal and instrumental soloists, actors, dancers, film and electronic music': a work in which its components function independently, in contradictory and sometimes related ways. This experiment in music theatre was followed three years later by a collaboration with four other young Dutch composers, Louis Andriessen, Reinbert de Leeuw, Mischa Mengelberg and Jan van Vlijman: the result, a 'morality' called *Reconstructie*, concerns the destructive powers of world imperialism and takes the form of a reworking of the Don Juan legend (using material from Mozart's opera); it was performed in the round at the Carré Theatre, Amsterdam, at the 1969 Holland Festival. Schat's third 'alternative' opera, *Aap verslaat de Kneckelgest* ('Monkey Subdues the White-Bone Demon', 1980), was given in a tent in Amsterdam.

Dutch operas of the 1980s include a number of bilingual works: Reinbert de Leeuw and Jan van Vlijman collaborated on *Axel*, an adaptation of the play by Villiers de l'Isle Adam, whose first act is in French and the second and third in German, while Thoe Loevendie's *Naima*, in Latin and English, was performed at the 1985 Holland Festival.

Otto Ketting's *Ithaka*, a one-act opera based on a poem by Cavafy, was written for the opening in 1986 of Het Musiektheater, the new Amsterdam home of Netherlands Opera.

CHAPTER XXVIII

New Worlds

LEIGHTON KERNER, MALENA KUSS, THÉRÈSE RADIC

1. The USA and Canada

Although dozens of operas were composed, and a fair number of them produced, in the USA during the first third of the 20th century, it was not until the appearance of Virgil Thomson's *Four Saints in Three Acts* (1934, Hartford, Conn.) that a genuinely American opera could be said to exist. Before then such composers as Horatio Parker, Frederick Converse, Henry Hadley, Charles Wakefield Cadman and Deems Taylor had indeed written operas; but these bear the stamp of French, German, Italian or British culture. Borderline cases are Otto Luening's *Evangeline* (composed 1930–32; 1948, New York), Marc Blitzstein's *Triple Sec* (Philadelphia, 1929) and Chadwick's *The Padrone* (composed 1912–13). According to Chadwick's diary, *The Padrone* (which remains unperformed) was rejected by the Metropolitan Opera's general manager, Giulio Gatti-Casazza, because the story of Italian immigrants persecuted by the Mafia in an American city was 'too true to life'. Its Americanization of Italian *verismo* foreshadows Gian Carlo Menotti's relatively popular string of operas in that genre.

Plainly not 'too true to life' was Converse's *The Pipe of Desire* (1906, Boston), the first American opera to be staged by the Metropolitan, in 1910. Like almost every other opera produced by that company until Gershwin's *Porgy and Bess* eventually joined its repertory in 1985, it was not particularly true to an indigenously American musical language either. This is not to deny that many attempts were made to forge a distinctively American operatic style through drawing on indigenous traditions: Cadman's *Shanewis or The Robin Woman*, which the Metropolitan produced in 1918 and revived the next year, deals with American Indians but has an unconvincing varnish of European conservatory orthodoxy; Louis Gruenberg's *The Emperor Jones*, also given at the Metropolitan (1933), based on Eugene O'Neill's relentless drama, is set in the West Indies and uses tom-toms.

The first third of the century was notable primarily for the development of American operetta and musical comedy, and an important part of that achievement was the blurring – occasionally the dissolution – of boundaries between the types (see Chapter XXIX). In Canada too the foundation of the Société Canadienne d'Opérette (Montreal, 1921) encouraged lyric theatre for and by Canadians, notably J.-Ulric Voyer's *L'Intendant Bigot* (1929).

Of all the many Broadway composers, only Gershwin and Leonard Bernstein successfully moved into genuine opera; even the determinedly self-Americanizing Kurt Weill, who left Germany in 1933 and wrote eight shows for Broadway, used an essentially popular idiom although handling serious social issues. Blitzstein's similar political commitment was shown in *The Cradle Will Rock* (1937, New York), 'a play in music' dedicated to Brecht, followed by several other theatrically powerful works. Among the works left unfinished at his death in 1964 are fragments of *Sacco and Vanzetti*, which had been commissioned by the Metropolitan.

Apart from the developments on Broadway, American opera had not made itself felt aesthetically until the arrival of *Four Saints in Three Acts*. When Thomson had met Stein in Paris in 1927, the two expatriates laid plans for an opera that would celebrate not only the saintly life but also, according to the composer, the artistic life. There are actually four acts and a prologue, eleven named saints, a chorus of unnamed saints and two masters of ceremonies. The strings of words seldom make literal sense but abound in mystical, humanistic and even jocular references. Stein left little that is concrete for producers, performers or audiences, but the scenario (pageants, picnics and the like) which Maurice Grosser provided after the libretto and music were completed has prevailed so convincingly that it has been published with the score. That score firmly established the composer's language, which William Schuman described as 'simple but not simplistic'. The pandiatonic harmonies and tunes of rural Protestant churches (not pastiches but Thomson's own) are balanced against each other with shrewdly absorbed elements of French neo-classicism.

Thomson's other collaboration with Stein, *The Mother of us All* (1947, New York), can still be ranked, along with *Porgy and Bess*, as the most fully realized of American operas. Centred on Susan B. Anthony's struggle for women's rights, the libretto is more specific than that for *Four Saints* as regards characters and incidents, but its surrealistic and non-narrative aspects required Grosser's services once more as scene designer. Musically it resembles the previous opera in its exquisitely fashioned 'American' simplicity, but here Thomson allows himself even more soaring flights of lyricism, a more outgoing motivic humour and, most important, a deeply serious and moving vocal utterance in the crucial scenes. This is most remarkable in the final scene, where the heroine, from within her monument, challenges posterity to abide by her example. Thomson's third opera, *Lord Byron*, commissioned by the Metropolitan Opera but not performed there, was first performed in 1972 in New York by the professional wing of the Juilliard School, the American Opera Center; it was subsequently revised but has rarely been staged since. Thomson's most ambitious opera, *Lord Byron* is a work of emotional intensity as well as sometimes wicked wit.

Porgy and Bess has fared better than Thomson's operas with the New York companies. As an 'American folk opera', it was first produced as a Broadway musical in Boston in 1935 before moving to New York for 16 weeks and going on tour. This production, like several later ones, reduced the work's operatic character by cutting of the lyrical numbers and replacing much of the recitative with spoken dialogue. The 'operatic' *Porgy*, with recitatives restored, was produced in 1976 at Houston and in 1985 at the Metropolitan, for which Gershwin had intended it. The work is now recognized as a true music drama in which the recitatives serve a violent, genuinely American *verismo* narrative. The tragedy is both communal and individual: the black community of Catfish Row in Charleston, South Carolina, loses a beloved couple to a hurricane and Bess, former mistress of the murderous Crown, abandon's Porgy's redeeming love to embrace the glittering, drug-sustained career offered by Sportin' Life.

Seen alongside the humanity in the music and text of *Porgy and Bess*, many other American operas seem slight, but the theatrical effectiveness and abiding popularity of several of them cannot be ignored. Menotti's one-act marital farce, *Amelia al ballo*, was presented by the Metropolitan shortly after its première (1937, Philadelphia), and many smaller companies and school workshops welcomed it in its English version as *Amelia Goes to the Ball*, often on a double bill with *The Old Maid and the Thief* (broadcast 1939, staged 1941, Philadelphia). In both these pieces and in the even slighter *The Telephone* (1947, New York), the tunes are fluent and facile and the humour diligently arch. However, with *The Medium* (1946, New York), a concise two-acter, Menotti proved himself a theatre composer capable of instilling a Musorgskian pathos into a plot whose ingredients are akin to those of Grand Guignol (it concerns a charlatan necromancer whose conscience drives her to insanity and murder). *The Telephone* and *The Medium* are often presented as a double bill; with *The Consul* (1950, Philadelphia) and the one-hour television opera *Amahl and the Night Visitors* (1951), they clinched Menotti's domination of the American public's consciousness, such as it was, of indigenous contemporary opera. *The Consul*, which is about the plight of would-be refugees from European police states, has survived in the American repertory by virtue of its shrewdly plotted libretto (Menotti has written all his own) and its climactic, neo-Puccinian scena for the principal (soprano) victim, Magda Sorel. *Amahl*, about a crippled shepherd boy cured because he offers his crutches to the newborn Jesus, boasts an easy, unpretentious charm and pathos; it was the first opera composed for television (and is thought to have been heard by more people than any other opera). Unfortunately the many operas that succeeded *Amahl* (16 by 1986), for adults or children, tragic or comic, have declined in musical quality and increased in maudlin self-projection; the most recent is *Goya* (1986, Washington, DC).

Menotti's operas are conservative in idiom, avoiding such persuasions as atonality and serialism. Many other opera composers followed his example, some drawing on an Italian-derived *verismo* but more on American folk or pseudo-folk material though without Thomson's élan. One of the most popular among the latter type has been Douglas S. Moore's *The Ballad of Baby Doe* (1958, Central City, Colorado), an effectively sentimental tale based on the life of a Vermont stonecutter. Though not ambitious compositionally, it is notable for its evocation of atmosphere; the set pieces include a dialogue waltz for the stonecutter and Baby Doe and a parlour-ballad-style 'Willow Song' for Baby Doe. Of Moore's several other operas, the one-act *The Devil and Daniel Webster* (1939, New York), a transplantation of the Faust legend to 19th-century rural New England, is the only one to have taken hold. Puccini's influence is also evident in the works of Mark Bucci, who has written many musicals and received awards for his operas *Tale for a Deaf Ear* (1957, Berkshire Music Festival) and *The Hero* (broadcast 1965). The variety of idioms (especially jazz) assimilated by Gunther Schuller has made his works similarly appealing, as exemplified by *The Visitation* (1966, Hamburg) and his children's opera *The Fisherman and his Wife* (1970, Boston).

Not many operas by the best-known American composers have found permanent niches in the repertory. The complex, atonally lyrical score of Roger Sessions's *Montezuma* (1964, Berlin; American première 1976, Boston) requires an orchestra of Wagnerian dimensions; its powerful expression is marred by a turgid libretto and, like his one-act *The Trial of Lucullus* (1947, Berkeley), it is seldom performed. Of Hugo Weisgall's operatic ventures, the most notable are *The Stronger* (1955, New York), a 25-minute work for a single voice and eight instrumentalists, and *Six Characters in Search of an Author* (1959, New York). George Antheil's involvement with what he called 'a new theater movement – musical ballet-opera theater' resulted in several experimental dramatic works while he was in New York in 1933-6, an interest revived in the 1950s; his most successful opera is *Volpone* (1953, Los Angeles), whose lively rhythms and colourful orchestration expertly enhance Jonson's comedy. A similar interest in ballet-opera was shown by Jerome Moross, whose *Gentlemen, be Seated!* (composed 1955-6) sets episodes from the Civil War in the form of a minstrel show. Samuel Barber's *Vanessa* (1958, New York) and *Antony and Cleopatra*, the latter commissioned by the Metropolitan Opera to inaugurate the company's new house at the Lincoln Center in 1966, are attractive romantic throwbacks; the revised version of the latter (1975), a tidier score, was better received but omits some of the more interesting music. Leon Kirchner's *Lily* (1977, New York), based on Saul Bellow's novel *Henderson, the Rain King* (an earlier title of the opera was *Why we were in Vietnam*), shows his gift for shaping complex, potentially knotty structures of atonality into a directly appealing lyricism, an aspect of his work that is comparable to but not imitative of Dallapiccola; but the opera is hampered by too compressed a libretto.

Schuman's *The Mighty Casey* (1953, Hartford), revised as a cantata in 1976, has particular claims to an American flavour in that it concerns a baseball hero. Copland's only full-length opera, *The Tender Land* (1954, New York), was not well received and (ballets apart) he has produced only one other dramatic work, the 'school play-opera' *The Second Hurricane* (1937, New York). His pupil William Flanagan collaborated with Edward Albee on several projects, notably *Bartleby* (1961, New York). Louise Talma's *The Alcestiad*, completed in 1958, had its première in Frankfurt in 1962, the first opera by an American woman produced by a major European house.

In Canada, operatic activity began to flourish after 1940; the Canadian Broadcasting Corporation has been influential in commissioning new works and broadcasting their premières. Examples include Healey Willan's *Transit through Fire* (1942), about a young Canadian's reaction to war, followed by his grand opera *Deirdre* (1946), Barbara Pentland's chamber opera *The Lake* (1954) and John Beckwith's *Night Blooming Cereus* (1959). The celebration of Canada's centenary in 1967 stimulated new works, many of them on Canadian topics, notably Harry Somers's *Louis Riel* and Raymond Pannell's *The Luck of Ginger Coffey*. Later Canadian operas include Charles Wilson's *Héloise and Abelard* (1973) and *Kamouraska* (1979), Raymond Pannell's *Aberfan*, which won the Salzburg International Television Opera prize in 1977, and Beckwith's *The Shivaree* (1979).

The emergence of minimalism led to the creation of a new repertory of music characterized by metric manipulation and almost imperceptible change. One of its principal exponents (though he has disclaimed the term) is Philip Glass. His *Einstein on the Beach* (1976, Avignon), performed at the Metropolitan shortly after its première, has a surrealistic scenario by the producer and designer Robert Wilson; it is a dance-theatre work where singing is confined to voices in the pit singing numerals and whose stage utterances are spoken fragments of narration and comment, repeated at great length. With *Satyagraha* (1980, Rotterdam) and *Akhnaten* (1984, Stuttgart), Glass moved closer to operatic traditions, letting the singing act as the main medium for the drama. The former depicts Gandhi's years as a young lawyer and social activist in South Africa and progresses solely through mime; its sung text is derived from appropriately allusive passages from the *Bhagavad Gita*. *Akhnaten*, based on the rise and fall of the eponymous Egyptian pharaoh, is a more conventional narrative drama, but its musical style, if repetitious, shows a more exciting use of percussion and heavy brass than Glass had used in the theatre before as well as, in Akhnaten's long 'Hymn to the Sun', an authentic popular success.

The response to minimalism has ranged from enthusiasm to boredom; some composers initially attracted to the style have moved away, while others have chosen different paths altogether. Dominick Argento has proved in several of his stage works, especially the chamber opera *Postcard from Morocco* (1971, Minneapolis), the Chekhov-derived monodrama *A Water Bird Talk* (composed 1974; 1981, Minneapolis) and the compelling but not quite focussed *Miss Havisham's Fire* (1979, New York), that immediately accessible music theatre can exist without descending to Menotti's platitudes or to the cheap melodrama of Carlisle Floyd's persistently popular *Susannah* (1955, Tallahassee).

The tradition of opera's growing out of popular theatre has continued, occasionally with surprising results. Stephen Sondheim began his Broadway career as lyricist for Bernstein's *West Side Story* (1957) and has produced increasingly resourceful scores, the most 'operatic' of which is *Sweeney Todd* (although it is labelled an operetta). The fact that Bernstein's stage works have similarly encompassed popular and art music has enhanced his international reputation; the only ones to be designated operas have been the one-act *Trouble in Tahiti* (1952, Waltham, Mass.), with its intimately lyrical core surrounded by set pieces derived from nightclubs and the Broadway revue, and its longer, more powerful sequel, *A Quiet Place* (1983, Houston). *Candide* (1956, Boston) has undergone enough revisions to be considered the *Don Carlos* of operettas, while *West Side Story* remains a non-operatic Broadway musical. Not generally acknowledged as an opera but undeniably one in form and theatrical power is Bernstein's *Mass*. Written at the request of the Kennedy family to open the John F. Kennedy Center for the Performing Arts in Washington, DC (1971), it was perceived by most as a pretentiously multi-style setting of the Roman Catholic liturgy overloaded with contemporary political and social analogies, spanning nearly two hours (without interval). But the celebrant is a tragic hero whose religious faith is gradually shattered by his community's angry, mocking and despairing attitude to the church; after a mad scene, he wanders off but is accepted back into the now leaderless community though as an equal member, to share their unknown fate. Most of the singing is pop-style, with the use of microphones, and a full contingent of rock instruments joins an orchestra dominated by strings and percussion. With music ranging from the most raucous to knotty, muscular development of a 12-note row, and with its first performances at a time when America was cripplingly split over the Vietnam war, *Mass* became the most audacious American contribution to the tradition of political opera. Its political force is similar to that of Blitzstein's *The Cradle will Rock*. With *A Quiet Place*, however, the dramatic focus of Stephen Wadsworth's libretto is on not a nation but a family torn asunder by conflicting mores, but at least tentatively healed by abiding love. The fact that it is the first operatic portrayal of America in the 1980s induced Bernstein to compose music spiky and turbulent with layered serial implications, yet retaining his lyrical bent. Since its première *A Quiet Place* has been cut, with the musically simpler *Trouble in Tahiti* inserted as a flashback; the original double-bill format, with its stylistic separation and a fuller version of the later opera, may however be more successful.

Among younger American composers, Anthony Davis has had a notable success with his first opera, *X*, a subjective though powerful account of the events leading up to Malcolm X's assassination in 1960; it grew out of a series of workshops at the American Music Theater Festival and was given its first full production in Philadelphia in 1985, followed by a fruitfully revised version in 1986 for New York City Opera. The principal avant-garde innovation of John Eaton lies in his unprecedentedly extensive use of microtonal intervals to develop not only dissonance but also a satisfying sense of consonance derived from the emergence of natural pitches rather than tempered ones. His *Myshkin* (televised 1973), *Danton and Robespierre* (1973, Bloomington) and *The Cry of Clytaemnestra* (1980, Bloomington) make potent use of the device, but their more essential character involves a heightened use of vocal intensity. Less vehement but offering a heady mixture of grand-opera lyricism, roaring electronics and piquant pop-music effects is *The Tempest* (1985, Santa Fé) for which Andrew Porter deftly cut Shakespeare's play by two-thirds.

2. Latin America

During the first half of the 20th century many traditional elements of Ibero-American, Afro-American and American Indian origin began to surface in European forms of art music, opera among them. As in Europe, musical nationalism trailed behind similar impulses in literature. Several subjects from traditional 19th-century lyric and epic narrative were set by Argentine composers, including Juan Agustín García Estrada, Carlos López Buchardo and Arturo Berutti. While the use of rural folkdances in Berutti's *Pampa* (1897; see Chapter XIX) can be deduced from contemporary reviews, literal quotation of choral dances occupies almost half of Felipe Boero's *Raquela* (1923). This practice is particularly noteworthy in operas such as *Lázaro* (1929) by Constantino Gaito, the first composer to include the urban tango in an opera; *La ciudad roja* (1936) by Raúl H. Espoile, who used dances associated with the dictatorship of Juan Manuel de Rosas (Governor of Buenos Aires, 1829–32 and 1835–52); and Juan José Castro's *Proserpina y el extranjero* (1951), which includes a popular urban *milonga*. Dance also makes up an important part of Boero's *El matrero* (1929) – the best-known and most popular Argentine opera – and Gaito's *La sangre de las guitarras* (1932), whose first act closes with the national dance. Castro's opera won a Verdi Prize with a jury headed by Stravinsky in 1951 and consequently had its première at La Scala the following year. Of his other three operas, *La zapatera prodigiosa* (1943) and *Bodas de sangre* (1952) are settings of Lorca that reflect his Spanish roots, while *Cosecha negra* (1961), to his own libretto, is closer to the allegorical character of the neo-classical *Proserpina*. The only opera by the Argentine Valdo Sciammarella, *Marianita limeña*, was first given at the Brussels World Fair (1958) and is similarly neo-classical in its combination of formal clarity and emotional detachment; it concerns the first marital annulment case in the Spanish colonies and incorporates settings of traditional *coplas* from 18th-century Lima.

Melodic patterns in 4ths, derived from the tuning of the six-string guitar, are also characteristic of the rural folk tradition and can be traced in Argentine operas from Boero's *Raquela* and *El matrero* to Ginastera's *Don Rodrigo* (1964), where a transformation of the pattern surfaces in the 12-note row that regulates the pitch organization of the entire work. Commissioned by the municipality of Buenos Aires and chosen for the New York City Opera's first season at the Lincoln Center (1966), *Don Rodrigo* integrates gestures of 19th-century grand opera with a 12-note musical language. The Spanish dramatist Alejandro Casona produced a libretto that relies mostly on Christian versions of the Rodrigo legend. Ginastera's next two operas, *Bomarzo* (1967) and *Beatrix Cenci* (1971), were written for the Opera Society of Washington (the latter for the opening of the John F. Kennedy Centre for the Performing Arts). These are based on violent plots that deal with metaphysical anxiety (*Bomarzo*) and incest (*Cenci*), set in 16th-century Italy. Influenced by the dramatic theories of Antonin Artaud, Ginastera created them as theatre pieces of severed continuity and exaggerated theatricality that mark a significant breach with his earlier style. The surreal *Bomarzo* consists of 15 tableaux unfolding the inner life of Pier Francesco Orsini, Duke of Bomarzo: dramatic movement is abrogated as allegory replaces character and a play of sensory ideas replaces action, while the crystallization of pitch and the juxtaposition of static timbric blocks to portray the fragmentation of insanity suggest an affinity less with drama or the novel than with sculpture – an abstract version of the 16th-century mannerist grotesques built by Orsini in the gardens of Bomarzo, near Viterbo, that served as the opera's inspiration.

Characteristic traits of Afro-American music, notably the importance of percussion instruments and responsorial patterns, are prevalent in areas of Brazil, Cuba, Venezuela and Colombia. Brazilian composers in particular have selected and adopted rhythmic elements associated with Afro-American dances in their nationalistic works. The folkdance forms used by art music composers include the *batuque*, which as a choral dance closes Act 1 of Oscar Lorenzo Fernândez's four-act opera *Malazarte*, written in 1931–3 (1941, Rio de Janeiro). It is an adaptation of a play about a hero of Ibero-Brazilian folklore (called by Gilbert Chase the Lusitanian Till Eulenspiegel); the traditional rituals and supernatural legends drawn into the opera's simple plot provide a colourful setting for the re-creation of popular forms, including choral arrangements of well-known Luso-Brazilian tunes. Most of the opera's musical-dramatic motifs are derived from a popular anonymous *lundu* (another Luso-Brazilian folkdance form of African extraction), quoted in the *Preludio* and later restated, as Malazarte's motif, with the theme of the *batuque*. The same *lundu* tune is quoted in the preludio (1904) to the unfinished lyric comedy *O Garatuja* by Alberto Nepomuceno, a seminal figure in the formative phase of Brazilian musical nationalism. The legend also inspired a setting by Camargo Guarnieri and was considered by Villa-Lobos.

Heitor Villa-Lobos absorbed the pluralistic musical traditions of his country more exuberantly than any other Brazilian. Among his numerous compositions, however, his stage works have been the least successful. The four-act opera *Izath*, begun in 1912, is said to include material from earlier works; the last two acts were produced in Rio in 1921 and 1918 respectively and a concert version of the entire work was given in 1940, but it was not staged in complete form until 1958. *Magdalena*, a two-act musical comedy with libretto by F. H. Brennan and H. Curran and lyrics adapted by R. Wright and G. Forrest, had its première in Los Angeles in 1948 and ran on Broadway; it has been described as 'a crazy quilt of the best of Villa-Lobos's themes' (Mariz, 1963) extracted from his anthology of folk music (1932) and several instrumental works. He also wrote the three-act 'musical adventure' *A menina das núvens* (1960, Rio) and a three-act setting of Lorca's play *Yerma*, written in 1955–6 (1971, Santa Fé).

In Cuba, the most representative musical stage work is *Manita en el suelo* (1934), which synthesizes elements from the Iberian rural tradition (*guajiro*) and some of the most popular forms of Afro-Cuban music. A piece for puppets with only one live character, it was written by the novelist Alejo Carpentier with music by Alejandro García Caturla. The text draws on two popular Cuban sources: the legend of the apparition in the island of the Virgin Patron of Cuba and the *abakuá* and *lucumí* rituals practised by secret Afro-Cuban societies. The legendary Papá Montero sits on the stage and declaims the story to an accompaniment of claves, while puppets re-enact his narration on a small adjacent stage. The opera is virtually monothematic; its symmetrical arrangement comprises a central ballad (no.6), with unformulated melodic fragments converging on its theme (nos.1–5) and splintering into variants of it (nos.7–11). Caturla completed it in 1934 and had orchestrated most of it at his death (1940); a version following his specifications was given in Havana in 1985, with dancers replacing the puppets. Other significant Cuban works include the six operas by Eduardo Sánchez de Fuentes, from *Yumurí* (1898) to *Kabelia* (1942); *La esclava* (1921) by José Mauri Esteve, the composer of over 40 zarzuelas and two operettas; and Leo Brouwer's *Cantigas del tiempo nuevo* (1969) for actors, children's chorus, piano, harp and percussion.

The absence of notation in the Aztec and Inca cultures has hindered the reconstruction of aboriginal pitch systems. Composers attempting to create the sound-world of pre-Conquest music, to evoke a distant Amerindian past, have based their orchestration, which is percussive, reedy, and high-pitched, on a study of the many extant instruments (mainly flutes), supported by archaeological evidence and myths. The Amerindian literary movement initiated in Argentina by Ricardo Rojas found musical expression in the compositions of Pascual de Rogatis, who searched unsuccessfully for published collections of aboriginal melodies. Thus, in his first opera, *Huemac* (1916), based on the legend of the last Toltec king, Rogatis relied on anhemitonic pentatonic scales (long though inaccurately associated with the musics of pre-Columbian cultures), which produce pseudo-aboriginal themes such as that for the Chorus of Vestal Virgins. In his second opera, *La novia de hereje* (1935), based on a subject from Peruvian history, he also used pentatonic melodies.

The character of the sizeable repertory of Mexican operas shows that the genre was considered viable for the expression of nationalistic attitudes. Many composers favoured subjects from pre-Columbian history, notably Gustavo E. Campa in *Le roi poète* (1901), based on the legend of the 15th-century poet king Netzahualcoyótl, which has inspired three other Mexican operas. Paradoxically, the music for many settings of pre-Columbian subjects is derived from the traditional repertory of Mexican music of predominantly Ibero-American extraction. The country's most popular opera is Miguel Bernal Jiménez's *Tata Vasco* (1941, Patzcuaro), a 'symphonic drama in five scenes' to a Spanish libretto on the life of the first bishop of Michoacán. Other important Mexican works for the lyric stage include *La mulata de Córdoba* (1948) by José Pablo Moncayo García and *Carlota* (1948) by Luis Sandi, who also composed *La señora en su balcón* (1964).

Carlos Chávez, regarded as the leading Mexican composer of his generation, wrote only one opera – *The Visitors*, to a libretto by Chester Kallman (1957, Columbia University, New York). Another notable Mexican, Carlos Jiménez Mabarak, was a pupil of René Leibowitz, whose emphasis on the music of the Second Viennese School is manifest in Mabarak's work. His 12-note opera *Misa de seis*, for five characters, masquerades and small orchestra, is an expressionistic one-act work which contrasts the street crime and the pious innocence that coexist in the suburbs of Mexico City during the hours of the early Mass. Its successful première in 1962 led to a commission for Mabarak's second opera, the three-act *La güera* (1981).

Numerous experimental works have been written by younger Latin American composers, including the Argentine Mauricio Kagel, who moved to Cologne in 1957. Notable composers of multi-media works include the Brazilian Jorge Antunes, the Peruvians Cesar Bolaños and Pozzi Escot and the Uruguayan Sergio Cervetti.

3. Australia

Opera has been a relatively recent growth in Australia. In the first half of the 19th century indigenous theatre was hampered by government regulation, though imported entertainment from Britain flourished: two works by the English-born composer and singer Isaac Nathan, the comic opera *Merry Freaks in Troublous Times* on the life of Charles II (partly staged in 1844) and the historical Spanish romance *Don Juan of Austria* (1847, Sydney), are generally regarded as the earliest Australian operas, though claims have also been made on behalf of Stephen Hale Marsh's *The Gentleman in Black* (c1847, now lost). From this period onwards, a number of entrepreneurs took over the theatre circuits and established repertories on the English model, introducing new works soon after their European premières. The staging of Marsh's opera by W. S. Lyster's company (1861, Sydney) was an exception. Even in the early years of the 20th century such composers as G. W. L. Marshall-Hall, Alfred Hill and Fritz Hart had to resort to student performance to enable their operas to gain a hearing – an option not available to others without the backing of academia. Hill wrote his operas during the early part of his career, 1893–1923, treating not only traditional European subjects but also oriental, Maori and Australian themes and using indigenous materials towards the embellishment of a conservative Romantic style; Hart's 20 operas (1913–47), many to his own words, show the influence of his Celtic musical roots.

As recently as the generation of the mid- and middle-late 20th century, Australian composers such as Peggy Glanville Hicks (in the USA) and Arthur Benjamin and Malcolm Williamson (in England) have found it easier to gain hearings for their operas abroad than in Australia, and it was not until the 1970s that a renewed public interest in Australian contemporary music prompted composers to attempt the operatic form again. George Dreyfus's *Garni Sands*, to a libretto by the playwright and poet Frank Kellaway (1972, University of Sydney), was the first full-length opera on a local subject to be professionally performed since Alfred Hill's Maori opera *Tapu* in 1904 (it was also the first Australian opera performed in North America, in 1975 – the first overseas production of any major local work since Marshall-Hall's abbreviated *Stella* had its London début in 1914). The lyric flow of the music for *Garni Sands* stands in marked contrast to its sombre subject, the brutishness of early colonial life; scenes of violence, including cannibalism, remain firmly controlled and developed by Dreyfus's vocally and orchestrally assured score.

The year 1965 saw commissions for three small-scale operas by the Tasmanian Festival of Contemporary Opera and Music, at which all were performed. Margaret Sutherland's *The Young Kabbarli*, on an incident in the life of Daisy Bates, treats the inherent conflict between aboriginal and European cultures, using a spare instrumental texture that reflects Sutherland's lifelong involvement with chamber music; James Penberthy's *Ophelia of the Nine-Mile Beach*, a comedy, uses a traditional lyric and episodic style; and Larry Sitsky's *Fall of the House of Usher* is a surreal exposition of the Edgar Allan Poe story, built on ten 12-note rows and, though instrumentally imaginative, is vocally repressed.

The economics of the short form opera prevailed when the Australian Opera Company commissioned seven operas in 1970. Two of these, Sitsky's psycho-drama *Lenz*, based on Georg Büchner's novel and much influenced by Berg, and Felix Werder's highly political black comedy *The Affair*, which makes fractured use of words over an uncompromisingly arid score, were given as a double bill in the Opera Theatre of the newly completed Sydney Opera House in 1974. They fortuitously pre-empted the much-heralded commissioned work that was intended to open the Opera House, Peter Sculthorpe's *Rites of Passage*; sung in Latin and Southern Aranda (an aboriginal language), with emphasis on danced rituals, this piece aroused a storm of debate on the nature of opera. The repetitious music and the lack of communication between participants told against the work and Sculthorpe has yet to prove himself as an operatic composer.

With the advent of new arts centres and festivals, the popularization of opera through television and radio and the development of new companies (the Australian Opera and Victoria State Opera in particular), there has come a new wave of opera composers. Outstanding are Brian Howard, whose *Metamorphosis*, to a libretto by Steve Berkoff after Kafka (1983, Melbourne), is a compelling work with music described by the critics as empirical and direct and who wrote *Whitsunday* for the Australian Opera bicentenary celebrations (1988); Barry Conyngham, whose finely crafted *Fly* (1984, Melbourne), to a libretto by Murray Copeland on the life of Lawrence Hargreaves, provides accessible and attractive music with a well-judged orchestral score and sympathetic vocal lines; and Richard Meale, whose *Voss*, to an outstanding libretto by David Malouf from the novel by Patrick White (1986, Adelaide), is a lyrically rich work showing a clear sense of the stage and distinguished by its outstandingly beautiful scoring. The entry of *Metamorphosis* and *Voss* into the repertory of the Australian Opera suggests the beginnings of a new era for opera in Australia.

CHAPTER XXIX

The Lighter Forms

ANDREW LAMB, LIONEL SALTER

General developments

The 20th century has seen a movement in the popular musical theatre away from the traditional European operetta style, with the spread of American popular musical forms leading to the domination of the international musical theatre by the American musical. At least until the time of World War I, the operetta, along with the European style of musical comedy, retained something of its traditional contact with operatic forms. Indeed operetta enjoyed a powerful renaissance as a new school of sensuous Viennese works led by Lehár's *Die lustige Witwe* ('The Merry Widow', 1905) gave the genre its most glamorous international success. Lehár himself continued to maintain high standards of musicianship rooted in a European classical musical training; he could aspire to write for the opera house while Puccini (in *La rondine*) aimed to write operetta in Lehár's manner.

In the USA, however, the spread of new popular song styles led to a reaction against operatic-style singing, extended ensembles and romantic Ruritanian plots. The American musical comedy of the 1920s was peopled by American characters, with loose and improbable 'boy-meets-girl, boy-loses-girl, boy-regains-girl' plots designed primarily as pegs upon which to hang a series of catchy songs and striking production numbers. Viennese waltz and march rhythms gave way to the foxtrot, quickstep and slow waltz. Vocal ranges rarely exceeded an octave. Yet gifted composers, such as Jerome Kern and Vincent Youmans, and songwriting teams such as George and Ira Gershwin or Richard Rodgers and Lorenz Hart, were able to develop the theatre song into a vital new form, with clever shifts of rhythmic emphasis and melodic shape allied to lyrics that conveyed everyday feelings with witty turns of phrase.

Even in the America of the 1920s, however, there was considerable demand for works in the old-fashioned operetta style. More particularly, the older manner lingered on in Europe, though composers increasingly sought to integrate something of the new American dance styles into their scores. The result was often an uneasy compromise involving a substantial dilution of the operetta strain. There was a tendency for individual countries to produce their own works for their own star performers, and repertory came increasingly to be restricted within national or linguistic boundaries; few operettas since the early 1930s have enjoyed international currency. Although there have been phases of nostalgia for the older type of operetta in many countries, as a genre it was essentially defunct by the middle of the century.

In America, by contrast, there was a move in the 1930s towards more serious subject matter and a greater integration of music and plot, a move that reached fulfilment in the postwar 'musical'. Such conventions of the interwar musical comedy as the opening chorus number were abandoned in the interest of realism, while other conventions (such as the numbers for the secondary couple sung before a backcloth while the main scenery was changed) disappeared with developments in stagecraft. Since 1945 the American musical has achieved a position of dominance comparable with that enjoyed by operetta a century before. Its development has been advanced by the attentions of new generations of directors and choreographers; moreover, in the more profound dramatic and musical language exemplified by the works of Gershwin, Weill, Bernstein and Sondheim especially, it has achieved a renewed affinity with opera. The separation of musical numbers from dialogue has given way to a greater integration of song, ballet and movement, using the techniques of film music to underscore the action and vocal declamation by singing actors rather than lyrical outpourings by trained singers. Though the lighthearted musical comedy tradition has survived updated with the aid of brassy production numbers, the musical has also embraced works with a more serious message where a formal plot has been of less importance than the expounding of a concept.

The radical changes undergone in the popular musical theatre during the 20th century have been apparent not least in the mere sound of a theatre score and the techniques used to produce it. Whereas thoroughly trained theatre musicians such as Messager, Herbert, Jones or Lehár were fully capable of producing their works in full orchestral score, the specialist songwriter usually required someone to 'correct', harmonize and orchestrate his music. Moreover, changes in theatrical instrumentation and the use of electrical amplification since 1939 to enable performers untrained in singing to rise above increasingly loud orchestras have confirmed theatre orchestration as a specialist art. Many of the most famous musicals of the 1930s and 40s were orchestrated by Robert Russell Bennett. Weill and, later, Andrew Lloyd Webber have been exceptional in attending to their own orchestration.

Although the size of orchestra used for operetta and musicals has until recently remained fairly standard, its constitution has progressively changed. The conventional British, French or American operetta orchestra consisted of up to 30 players, namely strings, two flutes, oboe, two clarinets, bassoon, two trumpets, two horns, one or two trombones and percussion. The Viennese or German operetta orchestra was generally larger, with a second oboe and bassoon, four horns and three trombones. Influenced by the development of jazz and American dance bands, orchestrators began to include saxophones (first used in Kern's *Oh, I Say!*, 1913) and one or two pianos. The pit orchestra of Gershwin's *Girl Crazy* (1930) included the jazz musicians Benny Goodman, Red Nichols, Jimmy Dorsey, Glenn Miller, Jack Teagarden and Gene Krupa. Cole Porter's *Kiss Me, Kate!* (1948), a typical musical of the immediate postwar period, calls for a small body of strings supplemented by five reed players (each playing saxophone and one or two other instruments), two horns, three trumpets, trombone, percussion, harp, piano and guitar. The quest for originality of concept, combined with financial stringency, has since led to more varied combinations, including electric guitars and synthesizers.

Continental operetta

At the beginning of the 20th century the international position of French operetta continued to recede by comparison with that of other national schools. Prominent among composers to achieve local success was Claude Terrasse with a series of works in neo-Offenbachian vein, notably *Monsieur de la Palisse* (1904). Messager still upheld old-fashioned musical standards in his last stage work, *Coups de roulis* (1928), while another cultured musician who turned to operetta and produced work of commercial and artistic success was Reynaldo Hahn in *Ciboulette* (1923) and *Mozart* (1925). The progression of French operetta into the realm of the songwriter and dance band was led by Henri Christiné with such works as *Phi-Phi* (1918) and Maurice Yvain with *Là-haut* (1923). Other significant composers were Charles Cuvillier (more in the Viennese style), Jozef Szulc, Louis Beydts, Raoul Moretti and the prolific songwriter Vincent Scotto, whose most enduring success proved to be *Violettes impériales* (1948). Since World War II such works as *Irma la douce* (1956, music by Edith Piaf's songwriter Marguerite Monnot) have exemplified the move of the French theatre towards more modern themes, while Francis Lopez was responsible for a remarkable renewal of interest in the escapist operetta style in *La belle de Cadix* (1945) and a long series of subsequent works.

Heinrich Reinhardt's *Das süsse Mädel* (1901) exemplifies a type of early 20th-century Viennese musical comedy, but the typically Viennese operetta found a new lease of life when Lehár perfected his harmonically assured, sensuous musical style in *The Merry Widow* (1905). It achieved the most wide-ranging international success of any operetta and was followed by a succession of similar works including Lehár's own *Der Graf von Luxemburg* (1909), Oscar Straus's *Ein Walzertraum* (1907) and Leo Fall's *Die Dollarprinzessin* (1907). Before the international acceptability of central European operetta was temporarily restricted by World War I, these composers had been joined by Imre Kálmán, who fused the Viennese style with an individual Hungarian rhythmic quality, most notably in *Die*

Csárdásfürstin (1915). Other prominent exponents included Edmund Eysler (*Bruder Straubinger*, 1903), Georg Jarnó (*Die Försterchristl*, 1907) and Oskar Nedbal with the highly accomplished *Polenblut* (1913).

After World War I Vienna saw other notable premières, including Kálmán's *Gräfin Mariza* (1924). However, changes in popular music as well as in political structures helped to shift the centre of German-language operetta to Berlin, which saw the premières of works by Oscar Straus (*Der letzte Walzer*, 1920), Fall (*Madame Pompadour*, 1922) and Lehár (*Das Land des Lächelns*, 1929), as well as by other composers for whom Vienna had previously been the natural point of gravitation. Lehár's attempts to raise and diversify the status of operetta were by now an isolated phenomenon, and the production of his *Giuditta* at the Vienna Staatsoper in 1934 – ostensibly a mark of respect for his exceptional talent – can be seen in retrospect as an acknowledgment that operetta had become a form of the past. So, too, were subsequent sorties into the operetta form, for example Robert Stolz's *Frühjahrsparade* (1964), a stage version for the Vienna Volksoper of material already used in three musical films.

Meanwhile the spectacular revue style of operetta that had appeared in Berlin towards the end of the 19th century had been developed by Paul Lincke (*Lysistrata*, 1902) and Victor Hollaender (*Auf ins Metropol*, 1905), while a series of operettas in up-to-date musical comedy style was epitomized by the works of Walter Kollo (*Wie einst im Mai*, 1913) and above all Jean Gilbert, whose *Die keusche Susanne* (1910, Magdeburg) proved an international success. More in the mainstream operetta tradition was *Schwarzwaldmädel* (1917), with a rich score by Léon Jessel, and *Der Vetter aus Dingsda* (1921) which helped establish Eduard Künneke as Germany's leading operetta composer of the 1920s. At the end of the decade memories of older days were stirred with a number of pastiche operettas, notably *Casanova* (1928; music by Johann Strauss arranged by Ralph Benatzky) and *Die Dubarry* (1931; music by Millöcker arranged by Theo Mackeben). However, these works, with Benatzky's spectacular *Im weissen Rössl* (1930; with additional numbers by Stolz and others) and Paul Abraham's *Viktoria und ihr Husar* (1930), signalled the end of continental operetta as an international form. Subsequent works successful in German-speaking countries included Nico Dostal's *Clivia* (1933), Rudolf Kattnigg's *Balkanliebe* (1937, Leipzig), Fred Raymond's *Maske in Blau* (1937), Friedrich Schröder's *Hochzeitsnacht im Paradies* (1942) and Paul Burkhard's *Feuerwerk* (1950, Munich).

The political upheavals of the time helped to breed a profusion of other national schools. The Italian, which had enjoyed limited success before World War I and to which both Leoncavallo and Mascagni had turned in attempts to regain lost glories, achieved its most enduring successes in the 1920s through the works of Giuseppe Pietri (notably *Acqua cheta*, 1920, Rome) and Virgilio Ranzato (*Il paese dei campanelli*, 1923, Milan). A Hungarian school was at first little more than a branch of the Viennese tradition, with works such as Jenő Huszka's *Bob herceg* ('Prince Bob', 1902), Kálmán's *Tatárjárás* ('The Gay Hussars', 1908) and Viktor Jacobi's *Leányvásár* ('The Marriage Market', 1911) and *Szibill* (1914). A more nationalistic style was evident in Pongrác Kacsóh's *János vitéz* (1904), Albert Szirmai's *Mágnás Miska* (1916), Ferenc Farkas's *Csinom Palkó* (1950) and Lajos Lajtai's *Három tavasz* (1958). A Czech school of operetta included the works of Jára Beneš, notably *Na tý louce zelený* ('On that Green Meadow', 1935), a Yugoslav those of Ivo Tijardović (*Mala Floramye*, 1924), and a Soviet school those of Isaak Dunayevsky (*Zolotaya dolina*, 'The Golden Valley', 1937) and Yury Milyutin (*Devichiy perepolokh*, 'Girlish Commotion', 1945).

Britain

Sullivan's acknowledged successor in comic opera was Edward German, whose *Merrie England* (1902) and *Tom Jones* (1907, Manchester) enjoyed considerable success throughout the British Empire. Later isolated attempts at 'light opera' or 'comic opera' as opposed to 'musical comedy' or 'musical play' were made by Montague Phillips in *The Rebel Maid* (1921) and Walter Leigh in *The Pride of the Regiment* (1932). In commercial terms, however, it was the Edwardian musical comedies and musical plays that captured the public fancy with their light songs and dances, elaborate chorus routines and fashionable dress. Through them the British musical theatre product was for a few years at the beginning of the century the most internationally esteemed school of operetta. The scores were commonly collaborations of technically accomplished theatre musicians such as Ivan Caryll, Sidney Jones and Howard Talbot with specialists in catchy melodic songs such as Lionel Monckton and Paul Rubens, though both the latter also produced entire scores nominally their own.

Edwardian musical comedy reached its zenith in Rubens's *Miss Hook of Holland* (1907), Caryll's and Monckton's *Our Miss Gibbs* (1909), Monckton and Talbot's *The Arcadians* (1909) and Monckton's *The Quaker Girl* (1910). Thereafter the popularity of the genre faded rapidly in favour of, first, the Viennese operettas of Lehár, Straus and Fall, and then ragtime-inspired revue and song-and-dance musical comedy from the USA. Only in the special conditions of the war years did the glamorous Edwardian-style musical show enjoy a brief revival of fortune in *The Maid of the Mountains* (1916) with a score by Harold Fraser-Simson and additional numbers by James W. Tate; it ran in London for over three years, a record in turn exceeded by the 'spectacular musical tale of the East' *Chu Chin Chow* (1916, music by Frederic Norton), whose own five-year run was not to be exceeded in London for nearly 40 years.

In reaction to the war and the now old-fashioned romantic nature of these works, British taste readily embraced current American musical comedy during the 1920s. Among British theatre composers, Noël Coward was exceptional in the extent to which he captured some of the sophistication of American songwriting, both in his revue scores and the works in which he evoked older European influences, notably *Bittersweet* (1929) and *Operette* (1938). Other composers specializing in light musical comedies between the wars were Vivian Ellis – in *Mr Cinders* (1929, with Richard Myers) and *Jill Darling* (1934) – and Noel Gay, whose *Me and my Girl* (1939) ran for 1646 performances, thanks largely to the appeal of 'The Lambeth Walk'. Other musical plays, meanwhile, harked back to the Ruritanian operetta style, as in *Balalaika* (1936, music by George Posford and Bernard Grun) and above all in the romantic works of Ivor Novello, among them *Glamorous Night* (1935) and *The Dancing Years* (1939).

Developments in the American musical towards a more integrated dramatic style were largely passing the native British musical theatre by, though Harry Parr-Davies's *The Lisbon Story* (1943) broke new ground with an up-to-date spy story and the death of its leading female character. The most successful British works of the immediate postwar years continued to be those that looked back, whether to the English light opera style of half a century earlier, as in Ellis's *Bless the Bride* (1947), or to the Ruritanian operetta, as in Novello's *King's Rhapsody* (1949). While the postwar American musical was increasingly taking over the London musical theatre, the most successful British musicals of the 1950s were Sandy Wilson's *The Boy Friend* (1953), which provided a nostalgic look at the musical comedies of the 1920s, and Julian Slade's *Salad Days* (1954), which broke the long-running record of *Chu Chin Chow* with its simple, old-fashioned story, equally simple tunes and two-piano accompaniment.

The spirit of the times was, however, more accurately captured by Lionel Bart's *Fings ain't wot they used t'be* (1959), and its greater affinity with current popular song was continued in the same composer's *Oliver!* (1960, after Dickens) and in *Stop the World – I want to get off* (1961) by Leslie Bricusse and Anthony Newley. Other successes that sought stronger plots in classic stories included Cyril Ornadel's *Pickwick* (1963, after Dickens), David Heneker's *Half a Sixpence* (1963, after H. G. Wells's *Kipps*), Ron Grainer's *Robert and Elizabeth* (1964; based on the lives of the Brownings) and the rumbustious *Canterbury Tales* (1968, after Chaucer) with music by Richard Hill and John Hawkins. That since the 1970s the British musical has finally been able to match American developments in terms of strength of subject matter, use of modern production techniques and fusion of classical styles with current popular music is largely due to the remarkable sequence of works with scores by Andrew Lloyd Webber, including the rock musical *Jesus Christ Superstar* (1971), *Evita* (1978), *Cats* (1981, after T. S. Eliot) and *The Phantom of the Opera* (1986).

Spain
After the turn of the century Jerónimo Giménez, at the height of his popularity, wrote a further 70 zarzuelas, a dozen of them in collaboration with the versatile writer and sensitive orchestrator Amadeo Vives. The triumph of Vives's own three-act *Doña Francisquita* (1923), freely based on

Lope de Vega, which received over 5000 performances in 20 years, gave a new impetus to zarzuela composers (many however of inferior talent and technique). Rivalling Vives in the public's affection was the charming but facile José Serrano (*La reina mora*, 1903; *La alegría del batallón*, 1909; *Los de Aragón*, 1927). A highpoint in the repertory was *Las golondrinas* (1914), a score of some subtlety about circus folk by the Basque composer Usandizaga, who had studied at the Schola Cantorum in Paris.

Parisian and Viennese operetta had scarcely impinged on Spanish composers, but in the early part of the 20th century there was a move away from traditional local settings. Vives's *Bohemios* (1904) takes Paris as its scene, and more non-Spanish backgrounds were soon introduced. Lleó's *La corte de Faraón* (1910) is set in Egypt, Luna's *Molinos de viento* (1910, Seville) in the Netherlands, Serrano's *El carro del sol* (1911) in Venice and his *La canción del olvido* (1916) in Naples; Venice is also the setting of Millán's *La dogaresa* (1920), which played simultaneously in two Madrid theatres. This extension of scene inevitably marked some departure from the orthodox zarzuela towards operetta, but at the same time other musicians were attracted towards the *género ínfimo* (revue sketch) and the world of dance music. Padilla's *La bien amada* (1916), for example, was notable chiefly for the chorus later adapted as the hit song 'Valencia' and Penella's *El gato montés* (also 1916) for the *pasodoble* of the same name.

Counter-moves followed. Francisco Alonso determined to write a zarzuela set in each province of Spain, of which the most successful was *La Calesera* (1925), named after an early 19th-century Madrid singer of *tonadillas*. Jesús Guridi, who had been a fellow-pupil with Usandizaga in Paris, wrote *El caserío* (1926), a delicate score set in his native Basque country, and the excellent Galician *La meiga* (1928). Enric Morera furthered the cause of purely Catalan zarzuela with *Don Joan de Serrallonga* (1921) and *El castell dels tres dragons* (1924); Martinez Valls followed his lead with his *Cançó d'amor i de guerra* (1926) and *La legió d'honor* (1930). Jacinto Guerrero introduced the historical figure of Cervantes, as a character staying at an inn, in his *El huésped del Sevillano* (1926); but after his *La rosa del azafrán* (1930) he turned to revue and film music. Soutullo and Vert collaborated in many popular successes, including *La leyenda del beso* (1924) and *La del Soto del Parral* (1927).

Despite the contributions of such composers as Toldrá, Conrado del Campo and Manén, and the particular successes of Leoz's *La duquesa del Candil* (1947), which was awarded a national prize, and Arámbarri's *Viento sur* (1952), the zarzuela became outmoded, having succumbed to imported styles of commercial musical theatre. The composers that best represent the last chapter in its story are Pablo Sorozábal and Federico Moreno Torroba. Sorozábal's *Katiuska* (1931), set against the background of the Russian revolution, became extremely popular in spite of its feeble sentimental libretto; he followed it with the purely Spanish *La del manojo de rosas* (1934), a sparkling score, and *La tabernera del puerto* (1936), using more advanced tonal techniques. His later works, for instance *Black, el payaso* (1942) and *Don Manolito* (1943), were operettas rather than zarzuelas. A musician of considerable skill, taste and invention, Moreno Torroba (a pupil of del Campo) first achieved prominence with the three-act *Luisa Fernanda* (1932), a distinguished work set against the political upheavals of 1868. After the Civil War, in *La Maravilla* (1941) and *La Caramba* (1942), he took as his subjects two personalities in the early history of the zarzuela itself.

USA to 1940

During the early years of the century there was a significant development in the American theatre's output of native works, albeit initially primarily in the romantic European style by composers of European origin, including Gustav Luders (*The Prince of Pilsen*, 1903), Ludwig Englander (*The Rich Mr Hoggenheimer*, 1906) and above all Victor Herbert (*Mlle Modiste*, 1905; *The Red Mill*, 1906; *Naughty Marietta*, 1910; *Sweethearts*, 1913). However, the forerunners of an essentially American musical comedy style are best seen in the works of George M. Cohan. His earliest works were mere extensions of vaudeville routines, but *Little Johnny Jones* (1904) had all the elements of the future American musical in its simple story with American characters, lively dance routines and simply constructed songs such as 'Yankee Doodle Boy' and 'Give my regards to Broadway'. Around the same time Jerome Kern was attracting attention with his songs interpolated into European imports, notably 'They didn't believe me' for Jones's and Rubens's *The Girl from Utah* (1914). Progress towards a truly American musical comedy was furthered by series of intimate shows at the 299-seat Princess Theatre, New York, with music by Kern and book and lyrics by Guy Bolton and P. G. Wodehouse. The first big successes there were *Very Good, Eddie* (1915) and *Oh Boy!* (1917), both light situation comedies using functionally simple sets and costumes, a small orchestra and chorus, songs with witty lyrics and clever rhymes, as opposed to the high-flown concerted writing of many European works. Kern's next shows, notably *Sally* (1920) and *Sunny* (1925), exemplified the trend towards works that incorporated elements of the revue, but with songs such as 'Look for the silver lining' (from *Sally*) and 'Who?' (from *Sunny*) they also contributed to the establishment of a strong theatre song tradition.

The typical musical comedy of the 1920s was lightweight in plot, strong on spectacular staging and the charm of chorus girls, and noteworthy especially for its songs. Prominent among the teams of songwriters were George and Ira Gershwin; their *Lady, be Good!* (1924, including 'Fascinating rhythm' as well as the title song), with Fred and Adele Astaire in the leading roles, helped make tap dancing a popular feature. Another composer who contributed significantly was Vincent Youmans, whose *No, No, Nanette* (1924) and *Hit the Deck* (1927) contained such songs as 'Tea for two' and 'I want to be happy', which epitomize the decade of the charleston and the 'flapper'.

'Parisian Pierrot' from the revue 'London Calling' by Noël Coward (first produced in London in 1923): with Gertrude
rence (left)

Scene from Ivor Novello's musical comedy 'Glamorous Night' (1935) at the Theatre Royal, Drury Lane, London

124. Virgil Thomson's 'Four Saints in Three Acts': Prologue from the first production, Hartford, Connecticut, 1934

125. Sheet-music cover of the first edition of the song 'Bess you is my woman' from Gershwin's 'Porgy and Bess' (1935)

BESS YOU IS MY WOMAN

126. Stage design (1940) by Howard Marc Blitzstein's 'No for an Answer' (' Music', xviii/2, 1941)

127. Carol Laurence as Maria and Larry Tony (foreground) in the final scene of Bernstein's 'West Side Story' in the first tion at the Winter Garden, Broadway, Ne 1957

128. Marie Angel as Tye and Ch Robson in the title role (with moving figur ground) in a scene from Act 2 of 'Akhn Philip Glass, during the first performan joint production by the Houston Grand O the New York City Opera at Houston on ber 1984

26

27

28

129. *The grotto of Venus, design by Heinrich Döll for Act 1 scene i of Wagner's 'Tannhäuser', Munich, Hof- und Nationaltheater, 1867: gouache*

130. *Adolphe Appia's drawing of Mime's cave for Act 1 of Wagner's 'Siegfried', 1896: chalk*

Set designed by Benno von Arent for the
scene of Wagner's 'Die Meister-
, Berlin, Deutsches Opernhaus, 1936:
raph of stage model

Grail scene from Wagner's 'Parsifal',
signed by Wieland Wagner, Bayreuth,
ielhaus, 1954

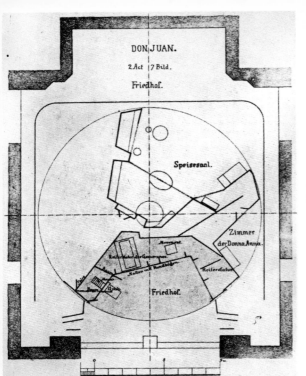

133. *Arrangement of a revolving stage by Karl Lautenschläger of scenery for Act 2 of Mozart's 'Don Giovanni', Munich, Residenztheater, 1896: heliogravure*

134. *Design by Alexandr Golovin for Act 1 of Gluck['s 'Orfe]ed Euridice', St Petersburg, Mariinsky Theatre[:] woodcut*

135. *Stravinsky's 'The Rake's Progress' (1951)[: design by] David Hockney for the Bedlam scene in Act 3 (Glyn[debourne], 1975)*

6. Design by László Moholy-Nagy for Act 1 of Offenbach's 'Les contes d'Hoffmann', Berlin, Kroll Opera, 1929: reprint with pen, ink and gouache

7. Set designed by Lila de Nobili for Act 2 scene ii of Verdi's 'Aida' in Franco Zeffirelli's production, Milan, La Scala, 1962

138. *Sketch for a set design by Joseph Urban for the first production (1927) of Jerome Kern's 'Show Boat'*

139. *Sheet-music cover of George M. Cohan's song 'Yankee Doodle Boy' from his 'Little Johnny Jones' (1904), published in New York by F. A. Mills*

140. *Ethel Merman as Annie Oakley, the role created in 1946 in Irving Berlin's 'Annie Get Gun': painting (1971) by Rosemarie Sloat in National Portrait Gallery, Smithsonian Institution, Washington DC*

Exactly contemporary with these works, however, shows that harked back to the Ruritanian, romanticized European operetta were also enjoying success. The American musical theatre could now offer not only a native type of musical show but also works in other national styles more distinguished than their models. Rudolf Friml's *Rose-Marie* (composed with Herbert Stothart, 1924) was, with *No, No, Nanette*, a considerable success in Europe, while scarcely less successful in the English-speaking world were his *The Vagabond King* (1925) and Sigmund Romberg's *The Student Prince in Heidelberg* (1924), *The Desert Song* (1926) and *The New Moon* (1928).

A landmark in the development of the American musical theatre tradition came in 1927 with *Show Boat*, with book and lyrics by Oscar Hammerstein II and music by Kern. By contrast with earlier works, in which an inconsequential story was written around songs, performers and production ideas, it boasted a cohesive story into which were woven songs that were not only noteworthy in themselves ('Ol' man river', 'Make-believe' and 'Can't help lovin' dat man', for instance) but contributed to the action by creating mood, revealing character and advancing the plot. The work pointed the way to further advances during the 1930s and, more particularly, to the development of the American musical play in the 1940s.

The song-and-dance musical comedy tradition, however, was continued into the 1930s, most notably by Cole Porter with his own brand of witty, sophisticated songs in *Gay Divorce* (1932), in which Fred Astaire introduced 'Night and day,' and *Anything Goes* (1934) – shows that provided lighthearted relief from the prevailing mood created by the Depression. But in general the 1930s were notable for the development of the American musical into material of greater substance. The Gershwins, for instance, contributed *Of Thee I Sing* (1931), which lampooned the American presidential system and became the first musical play to win a Pulitzer Prize for drama, while their final Broadway collaboration, *Porgy and Bess* (1935), brilliantly raised the genre to the level of opera (see Chapter XXVIII).

In its higher aspirations the American musical theatre was greatly aided by the contribution of Weill, whose *Knickerbocker Holiday* (1938) had a historical subject that drew analogies with Fascist oppression, while his *Lady in the Dark* (1941), which dealt with psychoanalysis, took an important step in the integration of plot and music. Another immigrant was Vernon Duke, whose black folk musical *Cabin in the Sky* (1940) was highly regarded artistically, if commercially unsuccessful. For the time being the most immediate pointer to the commercial development of the genre were provided by Rodgers and Hart in a series of works that retained much of the old musical comedy formula but took care to expand it in varied subject matter and up-to-date production techniques. Their topics ranged from ballet (*On your Toes*, 1936, including the song 'There's a small hotel' and a quasi-jazz ballet sequence 'Slaughter on Tenth Avenue') to political satire (*I'd Rather be Right*, 1937), while *Pal Joey* (1940) featured a cast of thoroughly disreputable characters and a story of blackmail, illicit love affairs and varied skulduggery.

The postwar American musical

The developments of the 1930s led to a period of maturity for the American musical, consolidated by the partnership of Rodgers and Hammerstein. Their first collaboration, *Oklahoma!* (1943), was notable not only for its well-developed story and the vitality of its musical numbers but for the way in which such musical comedy conventions as the opening chorus, the glamorous chorus line and set musical numbers were put aside in the interests of an integrated structure that carried the story along in extended vocal and ballet sequences. Weill's *One Touch of Venus* (1943) and Harold Arlen's *Bloomer Girl* (1944) during the same season confirmed the vogue for the logically constructed musical play and initiated a period of national and international acclaim for the American musical, helped by long-playing original-cast gramophone recordings and film versions.

Rodgers and Hammerstein themselves remained in the forefront with a string of successes from *Carousel* (1945) through *South Pacific* (1949) and *The King and I* (1951) to *The Sound of Music* (1959); they were also responsible as producers for *Annie get your Gun* (1946), a Wild West musical with a large number of hit songs by Irving Berlin. Cole Porter enjoyed his greatest stage success with *Kiss me, Kate* (1948), which, based on *The Taming of the Shrew*, developed the idea of a play within a play and appropriated some of Shakespeare's lines for its lyrics.

Whereas most of the musical comedies of the interwar years had contemporary American settings, the settings of postwar musicals ranged far wider in both period and location, as exemplified by *The King and I* (set in 19th-century Siam) and *The Sound of Music* (prewar Austria); Burton Lane's *Finian's Rainbow* (1947) concerned Irishmen in a southern American state, while *Brigadoon* (1947), with lyrics by Alan Jay Lerner and music by Frederick Loewe, featured American tourists in Scotland. Composers and producers were increasingly concerned not simply with writing appealing songs but with capturing the flavour of the setting and the viewpoint of the characters. Such was the case, for instance, with the most successful musical of the 1950s, Lerner's and Loewe's *My Fair Lady* (1956), an adaptation of Shaw's *Pygmalion* which variously evoked the dignity of the Edwardian aristocracy (the Ascot Gavotte) and the robustness of the English music hall ('I'm getting married in the morning').

The more essentially American style of musical comedy was currently being brought up to date in various star vehicles with big, brassy production numbers, notably *Gentlemen Prefer Blondes* (1949) and *Bells are Ringing* (1956), both with music by Jule Styne, who followed with the musical biographies *Gypsy* (1959) and *Funny Girl* (1964). Other works with thoroughly American subjects included *The Pajama Game* (1954), about trade unionism, and *Damn Yankees* (1955), about a baseball championship, both by Richard Adler and Jerry Ross. But, of all the works of the 1950s, those that most notably developed the musical as compulsive theatre were those of Frank Loesser and Leonard Bernstein. The former's vernacular verbal and musical language was used to best effect in the gangster fable *Guys and Dolls* (1956, after Damon Runyan), while the latter combined classical and jazz elements to remarkable effect in *West Side Story* (1957), which transformed Shakespeare's *Romeo and Juliet* into a tale of gang warfare in New York with a powerful fusion of singing, acting and dancing.

During the 1960s the musical developed in a very different financial, musical and technical environment. Provincial tours were no longer financially viable, and long Broadway runs were accordingly crucial; star names and big production numbers that could be taken up outside the theatre were increasingly required. The lively musical comedy with big production numbers achieved particular successes in Jerry Herman's *Hello, Dolly!* (1964) and Cy Coleman's *Sweet Charity* (1966). More thought-provoking in form were two works with scores by John Kander – *Cabaret* (1966), evoking Germany between the wars, and *Chicago* (1975), concerning American gang warfare of the 1920s presented through a series of vaudeville turns. The biggest international successes of the 1960s, however, were achieved by *Man of La Mancha* (1965), built around the characters of Don Quixote and Sancho Panza and with a score by Mitch Leigh, and *Fiddler on the Roof* (1964) with music by Jerry Bock. Concerned with the persecution of Jews in tsarist Russia, the latter epitomizes the trend towards the conceptualized musical in which stories and characters tended to be subservient to attitudes and perceptions.

Throughout this period the musical was increasingly subject to changing theatrical conventions and the influence of the director. In the rock musical *Hair* (1967), a look at hippies and dropouts, the first act ends with the cast totally nude, and its score, by Galt MacDermott, uses heavily amplified electronic sounds. Such efforts to incorporate current developments in popular music into the musical proved limited, however, because of the inability of rock music to express a wide range of moods. The developments of the 1970s were most immediately personified by Stephen Sondheim, whose witty but cynical lyrics are set to music that carries the action forward; set numbers are of comparatively little importance. His *Company* (1970) takes a cynical look at conventional sexuality; *A Little Night Music* (1972) is an adaptation of a screenplay by Ingmar Bergman and is composed entirely in waltz time or its derivatives; *Sweeney Todd* (1979) is a gruesome tale of throat-cutting; *Merrily we Roll Along* (1980) views the experiences of college graduates in a form in which the action unfolds in reverse; and *Sunday in the Park with George* (1984) is based on Seurat's execution of *La Grande Jatte* in appropriately pointillist music. All these works were directed by Harold Prince, whose bold ideas and stagecraft have made him one of the most influential forces in the modern musical. For all their intellectual and conceptual brilliance, Sondheim's works have not consistently achieved commercial success. Theatre parties seeking lighthearted relaxation have continued to welcome works in less demanding style, for instance Charles Strouse's *Annie* (1977), whose child lead is based on a comic-strip character, or the bright musical comedy style of Henry Krieger's *Dreamgirls* (1981). Increasingly, too, the public has welcomed revivals of works by Kern, Gershwin and Rodgers, suggesting that the best years of the American musical are in the past. Yet the genre continues to exercise a magnetic attraction for producers, writers, investors, performers and audiences alike, notwithstanding the rival attractions of radio, film, television and video.

CHAPTER XXX

Staging

MANFRED BOETZKES, PAUL SHEREN

1. Design

1900–45

In the early 20th century, the artist's traditional identification with the society around him came to be lost. The naturalists had been able to make their social criticism aristically fruitful; but the following generation, elevating its own lack of solutions into a principle, rejected confrontation with the inhuman and threatening world of industrial society and explored instead an 'inner world' of the soul and of dreams and the unscathed world of exoticism. Unlike Freud's attempts to form a theory of the unconscious mind, the artistic concepts of the symbolists and of their successors, the neo-romantics, were characterized by escapism, anti-realism and irrational, élitist mystical impulses. The resultant 'autonomous' art of the theatre would have remained without decisive influence on 20th-century stage design had it not contained vital progressive elements in its opposition to bourgeois décor and its demands that a style of staging contemporary and older dramatic works should be suitable to the works themselves.

Until then, works from the cultural heritage were performed in a way that attempted to bring the respected 'original conception' into a harmonious relationship with new emancipatory aims and theatrical conventions. The scenic interpretations of the neo-romantics, however, were achieved in ways implicit in the works being produced, expressing the attitude 'art for art's sake'. Under the influence of the 'vital philosophy' of Bergson, Nietzsche and Dilthey, and in particular through a trivialized application of hermeneutic method, the 'inner vision that a work awakens in its later re-creators' (R. Specht: *Gustav Mahler*, 1913) came to be a decisive criterion in performance. This conception inevitably led to a break with traditional stage production; staging no longer meant simply the coordination of the stage proceedings but rather the realization of an interpretation that applied to all aspects of the

343

production. Mahler's conception of stagecraft during his time at the Vienna court opera (1897–1907), developed through his contact with the Wagnerian *Gesamtkunstwerk*, was influenced (despite its neo-romantic individualism) by the reformative functionalism of *art nouveau* and in particular of the German and Austrian *Jugendstil*, which typified its era in striving towards a synthesis of the arts. However, its influence went beyond the neo-romantic movement and the concept of synthesis became the foundation of 20th-century opera and ballet production.

This concept also embraces functionally applied modern techniques which, although generally designed primarily to improve the historical and naturalistic theatre of illusion, were also essential elements in the evolution of modern theatrical art: the circular horizon, combined with a versatile lighting system (such as the cyclorama), facilitated an artistic stage structure largely free of top and side copings with soffits and wings. The bright metal filament lamp replaced arc lights, particularly for spotlights and projection lamps; the electrically driven rotating stage (developed in 1896 for the Munich Residenztheater, on the model of the Japanese kabuki; see Plate 133), the electric or hydraulic partly lowerable stage floor (1884) and the mechanically driven flies became normal resources of the modern operatic stage.

With the introduction at the beginning of the century of the movable proscenium modern opera linked up with the neo-romantic reform movement architectonically too. But, largely uninfluenced by the contemporary idea of a variable and multifunctional single arena and theatre area (projected as early as 1900), it maintained a strict distinction between the 'peepshow stage' and the wedge-shaped, sloping, amphitheatre-like auditorium (generally with galleries, as in the Metropolitan Opera House, 1966), even though the external appearance of the modern opera house has developed into the functional 'international style'.

During the years of radical change at the turn of the century producers sought help from the sister arts. It was avant-garde painters rather than professional stage designers who were looked to for the revitalization of stage design; they increased the artistic value of the setting of a dramatic work so that it became a component of a production that was the collective creation of an élite circle. This conception, expounded by the French symbolists and realized in the stage spectacles of Paul Fort (Théâtre d'Art, 1890–92) and Lugné-Poe (Théâtre de l'Oeuvre, from 1893) with painters such as Toulouse-Lautrec, Paul Serusier, Pierre Bonnard, Eduard Vuillard, Maurice Denis and others of the Nabis group, had been anticipated by the Mamontov Opera in Moscow in 1885–7. For a second cycle at the Mamontov Opera in 1896–9 stage designers included folk realists of the Abramtsevo circle, members of Princess Tenisheva's circle of artists and a group associated with the journal *Mir iskusstvo* ('World of art'), influenced by the *Jugendstil* and by the symbolism of the Nabis group, and including Mikhail Vrubel and Konstantin

Korovin. Under the influence of Dyagilev and Benois, S. M. Volkonsky, director of the Imperial Theatre from 1899, and his successor V. A. Telyakovsky followed Mamontov's lead and entrusted members of the *Mir iskusstvo* circle with the designs for numerous productions in St Petersburg and Moscow – notably Korovin, Alexandr Golovin, Alexandre Benois, Leon Bakst and Nikolay and Valentin Serov. From 1904 Mamontov's tradition was pursued by the Moscow opera impresario S. Zimin, using such painters as Fedor Fedorovsky and Ivan Bilibin, both closely linked with Russian folk art.

From about 1905 producers associated with symbolism in Russia – Vsevolod Meyerhold, Nikolay Evreynov, Fyodor Komisaryevsky and Konstantin Stanislavsky – also sought to collaborate with the *Mir iskusstvo* circle and associated artists, many of whom later became influential designers in opera and ballet. In his opera productions at the Mariinsky Theatre in St Petersburg from 1909, Meyerhold collaborated with Golovin in particular (Gluck's *Orfeo ed Euridice*, 1911; see Plate 134).

In the productions of Dyagilev's Ballets Russes, formed in Paris in 1909 from members of the imperial theatres of St Petersburg and Moscow, the principles of staging evolved in Russia were pursued. Their producers claimed to have realized the idea of the *Gesamtkunstwerk* (Benois), but it was the stage designs and costumes of the *Mir iskusstvo* painters that dominated these imaginative 'spectacles de rêve' of the *belle époque*. Their international success assured artistic scene painting a prominent place in musical theatre outside Russia and associated it more firmly with contemporary trends in the fine arts, an association strengthened by Dyagilev's collaboration with cubists such as Natalya Goncharova and Mikhail Laryonov. In Paris Jacques Rouché followed this example and, in operatic and balletic experiments at the Théâtre des Arts (1910–13) and in numerous productions at the Opéra (of which he was director, 1915–45), collaborated with such painters as Maxime Dethomas, René Piot, Jacques Drésa and Maurice Denis.

In German-speaking countries, too, cooperation between important conductors or producers and painters was decisive. In Berlin Max Reinhardt employed such painters as Lovis Corinth, Emil Orlik, Edvard Munch and Ernst Stern, while Mahler at Vienna favoured *Jugendstil* artists including Heinrich Lefler (1900–03) and Alfred Roller (1903–7); after Mahler's death Bruno Walter brought Koloman Moser and Joseph Urban to the Vienna Opera. Important work in Germany included the designs of Karl Walser for Hans Gregor's Berlin Komische Oper (1905–11), those of Bernhard Pankok for von Schillings's Mozart productions at the Stuttgart Hofoper (1909–11) and Max Slevogt's décor for Fritz Busch's Dresden production of *Don Giovanni* (1924). In the same spirit of revitalized stagecraft, Josef Wenig was active in Bohemia and Karol Frysz in Poland.

In England, deriving their inspiration from Edward Gordon Craig and stimulated by the Ballets Russes (from 1910), artists such as Charles

Ricketts, Norman Wilkinson, Glen Byam Shaw and Paul Nash reformed scenic design in the spirit of contemporary painting. In Boston and New York, Urban, influenced by the *Jugendstil*, became the pioneer of a new art of stage design (from 1912), further stimulated by visits of Anna Pavlova (from 1910) and the Ballets Russes (1916) and by Boris Anisfeld at the Metropolitan Opera (from 1919) and the Chicago Opera Company (from 1921).

The Swiss reformer Adolphe Appia (see p.354 and Plate 130) opposed the domination of the stage by painting, whether conventional or avant-garde, in the name of a musical theatre in which the actor should be the central mediator between author and public. He proposed a spatially structured stage for Wagner's works which would transcend external reality, rejecting Wagner's *Gesamtkunstwerk* as a 'dangerous aphorism' (*L'oeuvre d'art vivant*, 1921). The actor's plasticity demanded a three-dimensional stage which should manifest the dramatic 'vision issuing from the womb of music' corresponding to the stage action, using a rhythmically articulated architecture of cubes and surfaces, curtains and stairs; this should be effected by means of lighting set up according to dramatic requirements and only subordinately through painting (whose role as the medium of colour was now assigned to the lighting).

In some essentials Appia's abstract stages were close to the work of Craig (*The Art of the Theatre*, 1905), who constructed his poetic productions for the London Purcell Operatic Society (1900–03) mainly with the help of coloured curtains and atmospheric lights, but from about 1905 strove towards an architectonic structure whose functional problems he solved in a highly original way from about 1907 with the development of kinetic screens (*The Mask*, vii, 1914–15, p.139). With the development of the circular horizon and improved stage lighting, some theatres offered facilities for the application of the conceptions of Appia and Craig, but the established theatre shut itself off from their ideas even though a few experimental performances proved their practicability and attracted attention among artists and patrons during the *belle époque*.

In Vienna, possibly stimulated by these procedures, Roller developed a related architectonic structure from 1903 onwards for Mahler's Wagner and Mozart productions, but it incorporated elements of neo-romantic stage painting and assigned a vital role in conveying milieu and atmosphere to backcloths which, though stylized, were painted representationally. Through this modified 'stylized stage' Appia and Craig decisively influenced theatrical practice during the first two decades of the century, perhaps in the Munich Artists' Theatre (1908) and the Parisian Théâtre Vieux Colombier (1914) but particularly in German and American operatic stage design, for example Hans Wildermann's *Tristan und Isolde* (1911, Cologne), Kurt Kempin's *Iphigénie en Aulide* (1912, Darmstadt), Gustav Wunderwald's *Parsifal* (1914, Berlin) and Joseph Urban's *Parsifal* (1919, New York).

The neo-romantic dream of an aesthetic existence apart from reality was shattered first by increasingly acute social conflicts and eventually by the experience of World War I. Among progressive artists, the idealistic protest movement took on an activist guise, with expressionism, futurism and constructivism combating and destroying previous formal traditions. The passionate activism of expressionism did not conflict with its basis in the irrational: it dealt not with 'facts' but with 'human hearts', which the artist 'with a soul' renewed with the 'pathos of the unequivocal' and the 'melody of the grand gesture' (P. Kornfeld: 'Der beseelte und der psychologische Mensch', *Das junge Deutschland*, i, 1918, p.12). On the stage, taking the concepts of Appia and Craig to radical extremes, this occurred through a pathos-orientated arrangement of geometric basic forms and expressive colours, with a 'soul' instilled by lighting effects. In the symbolically designed, near-abstract spatial compositions of the most important representative of this tendency, Ludwig Sievert, there appeared from 1912 (*Das Rheingold*, Freiburg) a peculiarly suggestive visual manifestation of the intuitively conceived, subjective, emotional world of the expressionist drama and also of the freshly reappraised classical music drama. Essential contributions to expressionist design were made in Germany by Emil Pirchan, Hans Strohbach, Hein Heckroth (Handel festivals in Göttingen and Münster, from 1924), Panos Aravantinos (see Plate 103) and others; in Czechoslovakia by Vlastislav Hofmann, Bedřich Feuerstein and František Muzika; in Poland by Wincenty Drabik; in France by Andrée Parr and Gaston Baty; in Sweden by Isaac Grünewald; in England by Paul Shelving and Laurence Bradshaw; and in the USA by Robert Edmund Jones, Norman Bel Geddes, Lee Simonson and Donald Oenslager.

From about 1910 the Italian futurists, in numerous 'theatrical syntheses' primarily using burlesque, demonstrated their rejection of traditional forms, their irrational innovations and their desire for dynamism and activism at any price (including that of the war). Their aim of 'hurling the spectator through the labyrinth of sensory perceptions' (F. T. Marinetti and others: *Manifesto del teatro futurista*, 1915) was approached in the abstract, dynamic architectures of colours, light and space by Giacomo Balla (Stravinsky's *Fireworks*, Ballets Russes, 1917, Rome), Fortunato Depero (*Balli plastici* by Casella, Malipiero and others, 1918, Rome) and Enrico Prampolini.

While the futurists were celebrating the machine as a sort of blind Nemesis, the fascination with technique of Russian cubist futurism and of the constructivist movement which grew from it was more geared to reality and was marked by the desire to liberate Man from his dependence on Nature and traditional social structures with the aid of the machine. Kasimir Malevich's stage designs for the first manifestation of cubist futurism in the musical theatre – M. Matyushin's 'suprematist' Singspiel *Pobeda nad solnzem* ('The Victory over the Sun'; 1913, St Petersburg) – sought to treat this demand as its theme, though it was still under the imprint of a primarily painterly conception. The growing interest of progressive producers such as A. Tairov, Meyerhold and Nemirovich-Danchenko in the work of the constructivists played its part, after the October Revolution, in the emergence of a conception of a dynamic and technique-orientated spatial stage, whose partly strictly formal and partly frivolous functionalism exercised a lasting influence on the scenography of Soviet musical theatre. Constructivism was introduced to French musical theatre in the 1920s and had considerable influence in eastern Europe.

Similar social Utopianism was represented by the Bauhaus in Weimar, Dessau and Berlin (1919–33). After an early expressionist phase under Lothar Schreyer, stage design at the Bauhaus under Oskar Schlemmer (from 1923), in common with the Dutch *de stijl* movement (Piet Mondrian, Thee van Doesburg) and the Berlin G-Gruppe (Ludwig Mies van der Rohe, Friedrich Kiesler), successfully tackled the clarification of form and basic construction. Schlemmer took special interest in the relationship between Man and space. Bauhaus stage design sought to realize Walter Gropius's aim of 'a new unity of art with technique' by mechanizing not only the constructivist spatial articulation of the stage but all theatrical and musical means of expression. Some of its experiments influenced the progressive professional musical theatre, and in particular the productions of the Berlin Kroll Opera under Klemperer (1927–31). This applied less to the purist abstract constructions of Schlemmer (Hindemith's *Das triadische Ballett*, 1922, Stuttgart) and Vasily Kandinsky (Musorgsky's *Pictures at an Exhibition*, 1928, Dessau) than the creation of a functional constructional representation of reality by László Moholy-Nagy (Offenbach's *Les contes d'Hoffmann*, 1929, Berlin; see Plate 136) and Roman Clemens (Hindemith's *Neues vom Tage*, 1930, Dessau). The cubist stage areas of Klemperer's favoured designer Ewald Dülberg (*Fidelio*, 1927) also bore the imprint of Bauhaus ideas.

The experiences of revolution in Russia (1917) and Germany (1918) caused many artists to break with the idealism and romanticism of the expressionists and constructivists and to face economic reality. From the revolutionary socialist Berlin dadaists there grew a group of *verismo* artists among whom George Grosz and John Heartfield saw in the theatre, especially in the productions of Erwin Piscator, an instrument of aggressive and sometimes cynical social criticism. This type of realism influenced the early productions of Brecht – mostly realized in collaboration with the producer Erich Engel and the stage designer Caspar Neher – and was the basis of a critically realistic epic drama exhibiting the economic driving forces of its action partly through the reduction of its human terms and partly through commentary provided by banners, projections and film close-ups. Neher in particular realized this concept not only in the works of Brecht and Weill (see Plate 104) but occasionally also in repertory operas such as *Carmen* (1928, Berlin).

Alongside this socially committed art, which evolved in the late 1920s but was later suppressed by the Nazis, a further trend emerged in Germany in the mid-1920s which, though similarly geared to reality and objectivity, renounced the critical attitude and embraced a variety of formal trends linked by their aspiration towards objectivity. This is exemplified by the operatic stage constructions of Wilhelm Reinking, Lothar Schenk von Trapp and Gerd Richter, significant through their updated stagings of the classics, who renounced the Utopianism but not the formal techniques or the technological rationalism of constructivism and the Bauhaus. It shared this tendency towards the affirmative with the 'magical realism' of Cesar Klein and the surrealism of Heckroth, and also with the work of anti-modernists like the Wagner specialist Emil Preetorius, who expressed a preference for classical monumentality, or like Leo Pasetti and Josef Fenneker, who imprinted it with lyrical romantic features. Except for Heckroth these 'objective', monumental, romantic or surrealistic designers, together with former expressionists such as Sievert and Schröder, became after 1933 the most important German stage designers under fascism. Benno von Arent (who progressed from a revue painter to 'stage designer by order to the Reich') introduced a form of neo-historicism, his preference for a monumental neo-Baroque and neo-classical formal language typifying the ostentatiousness of the period (*Die Meistersinger*, 1936, Berlin; see Plate 131).

In Italy the experiments of the futurists and the *pittura metafisica* occasionally influenced musical theatre in the 1920s, but were unable to break the domination of 19th-century historicist painting. The pupils of Ferrario (particularly the 'Caramba' studio under Luigi Sapelli) set the style not only at La Scala but also in the provincial Italian and foreign theatres, including the Metropolitan Opera, well into the 1930s. Appia (*Tristan und Isolde*, 1923, La Scala) and N. A. Benois (at La Scala from 1926) introduced fresh, if dated, stimuli but (as later happened in Germany) the rise of fascism in 1923 resulted in a general architectonic monumentality of style. Only with the Maggio Musicale Fiorentino (1933) was an Italian forum created for modern design, which had, however, abandoned any formal radicalism. The designs of the former futurist Gino Severini for Florence, like those of the representatives of the *pittura metafisica*, were distinguished by clear, classicistic formal language. At the same time a picturesque neo-historicism developed.

In France, collaborations between producers and painters at the Ecole de Paris, initiated after the examples of Dyagilev and Rouché, affirmed the painterly conception and remained largely uninfluenced by isolated experiments along expressionist or constructivist lines. Furthermore the partly symbolist, partly romantic *belle époque* style long remained a vital force at the Opéra, extending into the 1930s and to some extent the 1940s. In the 1920s, under the influence of cubists such as Picasso, Léger and Braque and former fauvists such as Matisse, Rouault and Dufy, and above all in the productions of Dyagilev's Ballets Russes de Monte Carlo and R. de Maré's Ballet Suédois, there evolved an aesthetically independent and 'distant' décor, accompanying the production in an analytical or illustrative way and, in the work of André Derain and Hélène Perdriat, containing an element of the naive. After Chirico (J. Börlin's *La Jarre*, 1924, Paris), Max Ernst and Juan Mirò (C. Lambert's *Roméo et Juliette*, 1926, Monte Carlo), surrealism became the dominant tendency in French stage design in the early 1930s; vital contributions to its development in musical theatre were made by André Masson, Christian Bérard, Jean Cocteau and others.

In English musical theatre neo-romantic scene painting survived into the 1920s, as in the scenic work of George Sherringham and Adrian Allinson; and the nostalgic historicism of Cecil Beaton, Rex Whistler, Oliver Messel and the Motley studio and the personal 'impressions' of Sophie Fedorovich still showed strong elements of neo-romanticism during the 1930s and 1940s. During that period, however, surrealism also exerted a vital influence, notably on the ballet productions stimulated by the visits of the Ballets Russes and their successors, including the Camargo Society, the Ballet Club, the Ballet Rambert and the Vic-Wells Ballet. Designers such as the Fedoroviches, Gwendolin Raverat, William Chappell, Lesley Hurry and Roger Furse were influenced, at least for a time, by an art that evoked the 'surreal' or the 'magical' objectivity of the *pittura metafisica*, though for the most part in the 1940s they were already turning to a concrete representation of reality, even if without striving towards the authenticity of Tanya Moiseiwitsch's realistic stage constructions.

Under the influence of social drama and social comedy a realistic form of stage design evolved in the USA during the 1920s, further developing the formal heritage of the neo-romantics, expressionists and constructivists. During the Depression it was capable of strong social criticism (above all in the work of Mordechai Gorelik and Cleon Throckmorton), but with economic stability it followed objective if not affirmative trends. It came to exert a vital and lasting influence on American musical theatre, above all on musical comedy but also on opera and ballet, as stage designers of the expressionist generation (Bel Geddes, Jones, Simonson and Oenslager) and objective artists staged their varied musical-dramatic subjects through a rich diversity of forms, from naturalism through a selective form of realism to an ironic, romanticizing or historicizing manner, used in an eclectic yet effective way. Surrealism found its way into American stage design through Pavel Chelichev, Salvador Dali, Marc Chagall, Eugene Berman and Sergey Sudeykin during the 1930s and 1940s, yet Sudeykin's most successful work, the stage designs and costumes for Gershwin's *Porgy and Bess* (1935, New York), revealed an often naive, characteristically American realism.

In the USSR the consolidation of the Revolution provided a secure foundation for realistic stage design. Bearing the imprint of socialism's humanistic image of Man, there developed during the late 1920s and 1930s a scenic art of socialist realism, whose diverse influences include the tradition of neo-romantic painting, the constructivists' social-revolutionary functionalism, psychological realism (further developed by Stanislavsky's opera studio and its stage designers V. A. Simov and B. A.

Matrunin), the *verismo* stage production associated with the Jewish theatre in Moscow (whose grotesque comedy was introduced at the Bol'shoy Theatre in 1927 by Rabinovich in Prokofiev's *The Love for Three Oranges*) and, not least, folk art, already applied by the *Mir iskusstvo* circle. This polymorphic realism (not only folk art) was further developed by such artists as M. J. Kurilko (Glier's *Red Poppy*, 1927, Moscow) and P. V. Williams (Prokofiev's *Romeo and Juliet*, 1946, Moscow).

Since 1945

In many countries the political restoration after World War II was accompanied by regressive tendencies in the theatre. Many stage designers of the period renounced the objectivity of the previous decades in favour of approaching the content of a work through subjectivity and immanence and its form through eclecticism of a kind long practised in the USA. Arguing for an appropriate visual presentation of any specific work, the scenic interpreter – working on the basis of his emotional response, pragmatically rather than following any definite concept, and drawing on the abundant stock of available forms – 'assumes many styles, working in one production as a realist or a surrealist, in another as an expressionist' (Donald Oenslager: *Stage Designer and Teacher*, 1956, p.10). Within this concept, artists like John Piper, Georges Wakhevich, Teo Otto, Ita Maximowna, Rouben Ter-Arutunian, Nicholas Georgiadis, Jürgen Rose, Jörg Zimmermann and others were able to bring out their artistic individuality and to contribute significantly through their fertile imaginations to opera and ballet stage design. Since their eclecticism frequently involved not only the 'style' but also the constructional and material properties of the stage itself, and could draw on a constantly advancing technology, the conflict between painted and constructed décor was now largely a dramaturgical matter.

Eclecticism was spurned, however, by artists who had established a personal style outside the theatre, such as the painters Maurice Utrillo, Bernard Buffet or Oscar Kokoschka, the sculptors Alexander Calder, Barbara Hepworth and Fritz Wotruba, and more recently Giacomo Manzù, Victor Vasarely, Bernhard Schultze, Davic Hockney and Maurice Sendak. Another ostensible renunciation of the eclecticism was represented by the search for an operatic stage reduced to abstract, plastic formal components, a quest begun in the late 1940s in Kiel and Essen by Gustav Rudolf Sellner with the stage designers Franz Mertz and Paul Haferung and continued in Darmstadt by Michael Raffaeli.

Similar endeavours sustained the productions of Wieland and Wolfgang Wagner at Bayreuth (see Plate 132); from 1951 onwards they attempted to overcome the festival's traditional historicism, and by borrowing from Appia's formal language of symbolism and expressionism they worked out a form of Wagnerian stage that used lighting 'as an aid to dramaturgical expression, and deployed stylistic elements of contemporary art – visionary "symbols", geometric abstractions, symbolic colours and forms – in the articulation of the stage area' (Wieland Wagner: 'Denkmalsschutz für Wagner?', *Richard Wagner und das neue Bayreuth*, 1962, p.235). Wieland worked as his own producer and designer, paving the way for an increasing number of scene designers who have become their own producers, among them Franco Zeffirelli, Jean-Pierre Ponnelle and Pier Luigi Pizzi.

Bayreuth's modernistic symbolism, de-historicizing the work of Wagner and other composers with a considerable display of technique and, by stylization, rendering it into 'timeless', 'archetypal musical theatre' (Wieland Wagner), was represented outside Bayreuth by Wieland himself in Stuttgart and other German opera houses as well as by Heinrich Wendel, Alfred Siercke, Günther Schneider-Siemssen and (in most of his productions) Josef Svoboda (see Plate 108) who, reactivating the tradition of constructivism, has brought formal modernism and the technological performance (including shadowless laser lighting) to a new peak. He has been followed by Jan Brazda, Sean Kenny, Timothy O'Brien, John Bury and notably Ralph Koltai.

This emphatically subjective attitude of de-historicizing stands in opposition to the attempts by many designers to produce objective scenic re-creation, exemplified by the neo-historical movement which started in Italy and which aimed at scenic authenticity in re-creating the style of décor of the period in which the libretto is set or prevalent at the time of the work's composition. This movement, through the work of designers such as Zeffirelli, Lila de Nobili (see Plate 137), Filippo Sanjust, Salvatore Fiume, Fabrizio Clerici, Pier Luigi Samaritani, Desmond Heeley, Beni Montresor, Julia Trevelyan Oman and Terence Emery found a home in many of the world's leading opera houses.

In contrast with this decorative historicism, with its element of subjective nostalgia and spectacle for its own sake, Walter Felsenstein began working in 1947 at the Komische Oper in East Berlin with designers such as Heinz Pfeiffenberger, Rudolf Heinrich and Reinart Zimmermann to develop a musical theatre of the 'literal', a form of scenic art that did not 'accompany' but rather 'contained' the work being performed (W. Felsenstein: 'Der Weg zum Werk', *Musiktheater*, 1961, pp.50, 54). The work's visual presence could stretch over three interacting dimensions: the period of the action, the period of the music and the period of the interpretation. This framework, it was claimed, could 'release the historical proceedings from their context so that they could speak with a present-day voice', and thus 'actualize' them, presenting them 'in their historical clothing for comparison with present-day problems and proceedings', but also to 'leave them in their historicity, in the alien world of the historical, and by portraying this exactly 'present it to view in a distancing manner' (R. Zimmermann: 'Bühnenbild im Musiktheater', *Bühnenbildarbeit in der Deutschen Demokratischen Republik*, 1971, p.41).

Felsenstein's dialectical realism, founded partly on Brecht's theories of epic theatre and alienation, admitted philosophical and political ideas into the opera house and demanded dynamic collaborations between theatrical producers with a committed vision and their designers. This is particularly evident in the operatic work of Giorgio Strehler and his stage designers, including Luciano Damiani and Ezio Frigerio. Other notable collaborations between producer and designer in this Brechtian style have been between Felsenstein and N. Zolotaryov (*Carmen*, 1969, Moscow), Joachim Herz and Heinrich (*Ring*, 1973–4, Leipzig), Götz Friedrich and Svoboda (*Ring*, Covent Garden, 1974–6), Ponnelle (Mozart cycles, Cologne, Salzburg etc) and August Everding and Ming Cho Lee (*Boris Godunov*, 1974, New York).

Selected *Ring* cycles since the 1950s exemplify the prevalent style of post-war scene design for opera. Wieland Wagner's 1951 and 1965 Bayreuth productions were scenic abstractions painted with light. Schneider-Siemssen's version for Herbert von Karajan (1970, Salzburg) continued in that vein. Constructivist settings relying on stage technology and space age materials distinguished Svoboda's cycle at Covent Garden (1974–6) as well as Koltai's for the English National Opera (1973). Patrice Chéreau's iconoclastic Bayreuth production (1976) depended upon Richard Peduzzi's anti-romantic settings with their strong anachronistic elements, offset by the subsequent Bayreuth offering in 1983 in which William Dudley created eclectic picturesque décor. John Conklin returned to neo-romanticism for the San Francisco *Ring* (1985), while Ruth Berghaus's much acclaimed Frankfurt cycle was definitive poetic theatre with its powerful abstractions supported by the superb technical facilities of the Frankfurt opera house.

Opera scene design in the latter half of the 20th century has been influenced by a large number of new opera houses in Germany as well as the refurbishing of technical facilities elsewhere. Equipped with sophisticated machinery and advanced technology – stage elevators, concentric turntables, computerized lighting systems, multi-media capabilities – these facilities have themselves influenced choice and inspired complex spectacle. By reaction and sometimes because of management-imposed economies, austere minimalist productions on unit settings have also been produced. Lack of adventure on the part of major managements has led some houses to employ producers and designers to repeat productions worldwide, making 'stars' of individuals like Ponnelle or Zeffirelli. At the same time, star performers such as Joan Sutherland, Marilyn Horne, Luciano Pavarotti and Jon Vickers have commanded repertory choices as a vocal showcase rather than for their theatrical potential. In such cases works that in a modern sense are fundamentally non-dramatic, such as Handel's operas, have gained visual impact thanks to the contributions of their designers. Increasingly, the collaboration between producer and designer has become crucial. It may be arguable which artist has the greater responsibility for the success of a concept and the power and eloquence with which it is communicated in the opera house.

2. Production

Origins

The roots of 20th-century opera production can be found in the theories promulgated by Adolphe Appia and Edward Gordon Craig in the first quarter of the century; their work was complemented by the advances in stage practice of theatre directors such as Max Reinhardt (in the direction of romantic spectacle) and Konstantin Stanislavsky (in that of naturalism). These vastly different styles and new theories shared the requirement that a single individual control and unify the entire artistic enterprise; as these ideas were introduced to the opera house, it was inevitable that the producer (or stage director) for opera would assume greater prominence.

Appia first visited Bayreuth in 1882 and thereafter devoted himself to theatrical reform, focussing on Wagner's operas. He believed that the 19th-century production style prescribed by Wagner for his operas at Bayreuth was incompatible with the modernity of the music drama. In *La mise en scène du drame wagnérien* (1895) he called for radical reforms not only in lighting and scene designs (as we have seen, p.346) but also in costuming (to be as simple and stylized as possible) and stage movement, which was to be closer to true choreography than to realism (Appia even suggested a leitmotif of gesture and posture). In 1899 his most important book, *Die Musik und die Inszenierung* appeared; here he examined the problems of music drama and stage production, using *Tristan* and the *Ring* as illustrations. In the interest of serving the music, he proposed that actors be trained in rhythmic movement, arguing that, with movement dictated by the music, the actor surrounded by neutral symbolistic settings and costumes would be able to give the music physical form. Appia saw the producer as someone who would be a creative artist in his own right, but out of fidelity to the music he warned that the producer should not create a new fiction of his own. None the less, he recognized that the producer must be a despot, synthesizing all the elements of production, even at the actor's expense; for the first time he was to be equal to the conductor, and a counterpart to him.

Inspired by Wagner and believing that Bayreuth was the logical showcase for his innovations, Appia was disappointed when Cosima Wagner firmly rejected his ideas in favour of her husband's written dictates. It was not until the post-World War II Bayreuth of Wieland and Wolfgang Wagner that Appia's theories finally met acceptance and acclaim. His actual work in theatres and opera houses was limited and generally without widespread influence. In 1903, he staged scenes from *Carmen* and Schumann's *Manfred* in a private Paris theatre; from 1906 he worked closely with Emile Jaques-Dalcroze, the pioneer in rhythmic gymnastics, designing sets at Dalcroze's institute in Dresden, including a production of Gluck's *Orfeo ed Euridice* (1913). In 1923, he was invited to

La Scala to produce *Tristan und Isolde*, an extremely simplified and stark production; it was not universally popular, although Toscanini, who conducted, admired it. The Stadttheater in Basle invited him in 1924 to design a *Ring* cycle; the first two operas created such a scandal that the Bayreuth Festival Foundation of Switzerland forced the theatre to discontinue the cycle.

Like Appia, the English theatre designer, producer and actor Edward Gordon Craig was better known for his revolutionary theories and projects than for actual productions, although he travelled widely in Europe designing for major figures such as Isadora Duncan, Eleonora Duse and Konstantin Stanislavsky. Through his international theatre magazine, *The Mask* (1908–29), and his many books and articles, Craig's aesthetics were better publicized than Appia's, and they found more widespread acceptance among the theatrical avant-garde. As a producer he was, with his 'Über-Marionette' theory, the originator of the concept of the actor as a controlled instrument without egotism, the ideal tool of a higher directorial purpose; he differed from Appia in seeing the producer as a creative artist who may take liberties in interpreting the dramatic text.

Craig is most often associated with his famous production of *Hamlet* for the Moscow Art Theatre under Stanislavsky, but his earliest and arguably most artistically successful productions were those he directed in 1900–03 for the Purcell Operatic Society. These productions – Purcell's *Dido and Aeneas* and *The Masque of Love* (an adaptation of *Dioclesian*) and Handel's *Acis and Galatea* – marked the beginning of a revival of English opera. He used unusual textured materials in his designs and relied greatly upon light for illusion; the giant in *Acis* was suggested by the projected shadow of an offstage actor, moving in front of a naked electric light. Craig's techniques heralded the reform to be seen in opera over the next quarter-century. In the Purcell Operatic Society productions, soloists and chorus eschewed 19th-century acting conventions in favour of acting and moving in a style consistent with the mood of the operas.

In Russia, experiments in modern acting and production were successfully carried out by Konstantin Stanislavsky. A singer who turned to drama when he realized his voice was unsuitable for opera, he founded in 1898 the famous Moscow Art Theatre, where he and Vladimir Nemirovich-Danchenko experimented with naturalistic staging; from this distinguished ensemble came the Stanislavsky System or Method, the most widely followed approach to naturalistic acting and production. The actor prepares his role from within instead of concentrating on external presentation, determining his character's psychological and social background beyond the specific dramatic situation; combined with the actor's self-awareness and 'emotion memory', this leads to complete identification with the character, resulting in an intensely realistic performance. Stanislavsky approached setting, costume, movement, light and sound with similar concern for naturalistic detail. His early musical

355

training left him especially sensitive to tempo and rhythm: he proposed classes in music for his actors and was among the first to 'orchestrate' serious dramatic scenes with music and sound-effects to support underlying moods and ideas. He believed that dramatic art was moving towards a 'synthesis of music and drama, of words and sound'.

Stanislavsky turned specifically to opera in the last 20 years of his career. In 1918, he organized the Bol'shoy Theatre Opera Studio, which aimed to set up a laboratory for research in the art of lyric drama, to renovate archaic traditions of opera production, to apply the System to opera and to fuse music, singing, words and movement in performance. Stanislavsky maintained that the score, not the libretto, must be the point of departure in producing opera, and he depended upon the music to supply his motivation and truth as well as tempo and rhythm. Immediately successful and ultimately influential internationally, the studio productions were noted for narrative clarity and consistency, convincing acting and unmannered singing. By 1926 the studio, detached from the Bol'shoy, was renamed the Stanislavsky Opera Theatre. Stanislavsky continued planning and supervising opera until his death. His studio productions included Tchaikovsky's *Eugene Onegin* (1919–22), Massenet's *Werther* (1921), three Rimsky-Korsakov operas (1926–32), Musorgsky's *Boris Godunov* (1929), Rossini's *Il barbiere di Siviglia* (1933), Bizet's *Carmen* (1935) and, posthumously produced, Verdi's *Rigoletto* (1939).

Nemirovich-Danchenko, Stanislavsky's partner, founded in 1919 the Moscow Art Theatre Musical Studio, which was much more avant-garde and revolutionary. While Nemirovich-Danchenko shared Stanislavsky's basic concern for rhythm and internal truth in all aspects of production, he lost interest in pure naturalism and realism; inspired by Appia, he employed exercises and rehearsal techniques after Jaques-Dalcroze, creating a stylized 'Synthetic Theatre' and promoting the ideal of the 'singing actor'. Movement and gesture were strictly synchronized with the music and executed in abstract, spatial settings inspired by artistic movements such as expressionism and constructivism. The company was composed of young singers, and roles were rotated; no personality or voice was permitted to stand out.

Repertory included both opera and operetta, as well as new works such as Shostakovich's *Katerina Izmaylova*. Productions of standard repertory were controversial; librettos were rewritten in translation and scores were frequently altered. In *Carmen*, for example, Micaela's role was eliminated, and in *La traviata* a new chorus provided a running social commentary on Violetta's tragedy. Productions were generally mounted on constructivist unit sets. Both in Russia and abroad these productions were acclaimed for their daring and high standards of acting and staging, though musical standards were generally felt to be low and the altered scores to be intolerable. Stalin's conservative taste limited Nemirovich-Danchenko's influence in the USSR, but in the West he and Stanislavsky were important influences, seen especially in the work of directors like Walter

Felsenstein and Peter Brook.

It was in Germany and Austria that the stage director finally entered the opera house and remained to establish a strong tradition. The Austrian Max Reinhardt responded with enthusiasm and taste to new theatrical ideas; though generally associated with circus-like romantic spectacles, he was an entrepreneurial genius with the ability to bring together the ideal actors, designers, choreographers and musicians for each production. Although operettas were a staple of his repertory companies, he is best remembered on the opera stage for his collaborations with Richard Strauss and Hugo von Hofmannsthal. *Salome* and *Elektra* were both directly inspired by his stage productions of the dramas. Reinhardt was called in to direct the première in Dresden of *Der Rosenkavalier* when it became apparent that the original director was unable to work in this new form of music theatre. Strauss recalled that 'the result was a new style of opera and a perfect performance'. Details of Reinhardt's production are lost, but because the publisher forced opera houses to acquire the Alfred Roller sets and costumes along with the performing rights, the general shape of most early productions followed the Reinhardt-Roller original with little opportunity for reinterpretation. Reinhardt also staged the première of the original version of *Ariadne auf Naxos* (1912, Stuttgart). In 1920 Strauss, Hofmannsthal and Reinhardt together founded the Salzburg Festival; the idea, location and focus (Mozart and the Austrian dramatic tradition) were Reinhardt's; he remained active at Salzburg until forced into exile to America in 1937. Among his Salzburg accomplishments was his last opera production, Offenbach's *Les contes d'Hoffmann* (1931), a spectacular circus of a production; in the Giulietta act, Reinhardt and his designer, Oskar Strnad, used a revolving stage (a Reinhardt trademark) to treat the audience to a gondola ride past the decaying palaces of Venice.

Felsenstein and Wieland Wagner

Thanks to Reinhardt's lead, German opera houses began to give fuller rein to their producers. Between the two world wars, such men of the theatre as Jürgen Fehling, Gustaf Grundgens, Lothar Wallerstein and Heinz Tietjen (prominent at Bayreuth in the 1930s) achieved eminence. This tradition produced two major forces in 20th-century international opera production: Walter Felsenstein, the master of realistic opera theatre, and the symbolist Wieland Wagner, who finally established the aesthetics of Appia and Craig at Bayreuth.

Walter Felsenstein's most important work was in the German Democratic Republic where he was director of the Komische Oper, East Berlin, from 1947 until his death in 1975. He spurned 'singers' opera' and aspired to a dramatically logical realistic music theatre. His productions aimed to 'make the music and singing on the stage a credible, convincing, authentic and indispensable means of human expression'. The singer had to convince the audience that his part could be communicated only in song and that the notes sung had been discovered and improvised at the very moment of performance. In traditional opera, Felsenstein argued, 'the singing is done only with the empty voice, i.e. without concrete emotion. The notes are not fulfilled. Only fulfilled sound is real and thus dramatic'. He analysed librettos in terms of psychological and social issues, publishing copious programme notes. Turning to the music more than to the text, he came to conclusions such as that, in *Don Giovanni*, Donna Anna will not survive the year of mourning she and Don Ottavio have agreed upon – this is derived from the Larghetto of her aria 'Non mi dir' with its 'peculiar otherworldliness . . . more a farewell than a pledge', and from the subsequent Allegretto with its 'confident hope for release'.

Balanced against these subjective and often psychological readings of the score and the text (sometimes stressed in tailored German performance translations) was Felsenstein's powerful feeling for the music which he translated into movement and visual metaphor, especially for his choruses. His choruses moved as an acting ensemble – sometimes each supernumerary had a finely etched characterization – never relying upon eye contact with the conductor. In his 1959 *Otello*, the storm whipped the crowd across the stage until all members of the chorus were flat on their bellies; other theatrical devices used to heighten the dramatic spectacle in this production include the extending of the stage over one-third of the orchestra pit, to bring the action closer to the audience, and playing the final scene between Othello and Desdemona on this dark forestage, their figures silhouetted against the brilliant lighted background of the bed.

At an opposite pole to Felsenstein's realism is the symbolistic style of opera production exemplified by Wieland Wagner. A grandson of Richard Wagner, he was brought up to assume direction of the Bayreuth Festival and gained much experience working there before World War II, observing designers such as Alfred Roller and Emil Preetorius. He provided designs for Bayreuth productions such as *Parsifal* (1937) and *Die Meistersinger* (1943), and with his brother Wolfgang revived the Bayreuth Festival in 1951. His postwar productions were starkly modern and symbolistic, greatly at variance with the romantic production style dictated by his grandfather and instituted by Cosima Wagner, his widow. He produced and designed all his grandfather's operas, from *Rienzi* to *Parsifal*, according to the conviction that the music does not require the old-fashioned, explicit scenery and stage action prescribed by the composer, banishing from the *Ring* such elements as the rainbow bridge and shattering swords. He used reduced, stylized stage movement, and frequently imposed new images on the works – as with the 1954 Bayreuth *Tannhäuser* in which Act 2 was set on a chessboard, where the White Queen broke the rules by rushing forward to protect a threatened Black Knight.

Wieland Wagner's productions were characterized by the naked simplicity of his settings, most notably the tilted disc on which he staged the second of his three *Ring* cycles. He also stressed the importance of light to the extent that he considered the lighting technician as important as the conductor. Characterizations, always strongly defined, were sometimes built around the personality of a specific singer. In this he had much in common with Felsenstein, analysing obscure details of the libretto for psychological clues. Certain of his productions, such as the 1965 *Ring*, were received by some as highly political, even socialist, while others responded only to its highly mythical elements. He continually reworked his productions, so that many Bayreuth 'revivals' were in effect new productions. After Wieland Wagner's death in 1966, his brother Wolfgang became sole director at Bayreuth. Although clearly influenced by Wieland's reforms, Wolfgang's work shows neo-romantic and semi-naturalistic elements that offended Wieland's admirers. The basic concept of his 1970 *Ring* ranks as one of his most successful achievements: this too was set on a tilted disc, but in the early stages of the narrative the disc broke into fragments, to be restored at the end.

Felsenstein's disciples

Götz Friedrich and Joachim Herz are leading disciples and heirs of Walter Felsenstein. Friedrich worked with him at the Komische Oper, where he made his début in 1959. He left in 1973 for the Hamburg Staatsoper, and has produced opera widely throughout Europe, notably a *Ring* cycle at Covent Garden (1974–6) mounted on a mechanical unit setting by Josef Svoboda, remarkable for its use of Brechtian techniques.

A declared Marxist, Friedrich is committed to the social relevance of opera, and his most original and striking productions have been noteworthy for the social and philosophical perspective he introduced to otherwise 'uncommitted' narratives. His Bayreuth *Tannhäuser* (1972) portrayed an aesthete imprisoned by his art (he is first seen looking at the audience through the strings of his harp); Tannhäuser is ultimately rejected as a traitor by the sterile upper classes for challenging the traditions of the song contest. This production offended traditionalists by portraying the contest with Nazi overtones and ending with a clenched fist salute from a chorus dressed as modern workers (this was suppressed after the opening performances). Similarly, Friedrich's version of Schoenberg's *Moses und Aron* (1973, Vienna) illustrated the pain of captivity and the perils of liberty, with the physical influence of the orators over the crowd more dominant than the orgiastic images usually stressed by directors. His *Aida*, first produced at the Komische Oper in 1969 and then revised 'in the round' at the Carré Theatre, Amsterdam, a former circus, was an enactment of 'the collision between totalitarian, imperial power and the humane rebellion of the individual'; designed in cold metallic materials, it carried no visual reference to ancient Egypt.

Joachim Herz was Felsenstein's assistant at the Komische Oper (1953–6) and returned there after a period as director of opera at Leipzig (1959–76) to succeed him as Intendant (1976–81). In 1985 he became chief producer at the rebuilt Dresden Staatsoper; the inauguration was marked by his productions of *Der Freischütz* and *Der Rosenkavalier*. Although much of his earlier work was unknown in the West, the influence of his *Die Meistersinger* (1960) and of his film of *Der fliegende Holländer* (1963) may be detected in the stagings of Wieland Wagner and Harry Kupfer. The social criticism of his Leipzig *Ring* (1973–6) was similarly an important precursor of Chéreau's celebrated Bayreuth production. In recent years Herz's work has become more familiar in the West as he has fulfilled guest engagements at the English National Opera (*Salome*, 1975, *Fidelio*, 1980 *Parsifal*, 1986), Welsh National Opera (*Madama Butterfly*, 1978, *La forza del destino*, 1981), and in many other European cities. The political awareness of his *Fidelio* – in which the revolutionary resonances were shown to have a contemporary relevance – may be taken as characteristic.

The shock of iconoclasm

Jean-Pierre Ponnelle, the French producer (and generally designer of his own productions), was an idiosyncratic force in opera. The free play he allowed the imagination frequently resulted in charges of irrelevance and of disrespect for the originals from traditionalists, but neither was his work truly or consistently radical. Several of his productions, multi-faceted and teeming with detail, gained wide currency through film and television, notably his Mozart cycle (seen in Salzburg, Cologne, Paris, Washington and New York), unified by grey 'triumphal arches' with predominantly black and white costumes. He made his Metropolitan Opera début with a dizzy, farcical production of *L'italiana in Algeri* in 1973 and returned with his notorious, quirky *Der fliegende Holländer* (1979), conceived as the dream of the Steersman, who doubled as Erik. In a similar vein, his Bayreuth *Tristan* (1981) convincingly presented the final catastrophe (much of Act 3) as a projection of Tristan's: his death and Isolde's transfiguration take place only in his imagination.

Patrice Chéreau, an equally individualistic French director, with only two previous opera productions to his credit, created a demythologized and hugely influential *Ring* for the centenary of the Bayreuth Festival (1976). Drawing on an eclectic repertory of historical and cultural references, the settings and costumes explored parallels between the social and political conditions of Wagner's day and the modern era. Central to this Shavian allegory was the anti-heroic presentation of the gods and 'heroes'; the duplicity and savage violence that marked their corrupt, decadent world were graphically depicted.

Chéreau's *Ring* was not created in a vacuum: important antecedents were the *Ring* productions of Ulrich Melchinger in Kassel (begun 1970), with its visual references to science fiction and pop art among other styles, and of Herz in Leipzig (1973–6). Nevertheless, Chéreau's controversial achievement seemed to initiate a period in which innovatory directors turned increasingly from the spoken theatre to opera as the main focus of their activities. The ambiguities and contradictions inherent in Wagner's work encouraged Chéreau and others to explore a dialectic between visual and aural elements, and between text and music. Such a deconstructionist approach became common in other repertory works too, at least in certain houses, in the 1970s and 80s.

The East German tradition

After an association with the Berliner Ensemble (from 1964; director, 1971–7), Ruth Berghaus became director of the Berlin Staatsoper (1977–9). During the fruitful era of Michael Gielen (Opern- und Generalmusikdirektor) and Klaus Zehelein (chief Dramaturg) at the Frankfurt Opera (1977–87), she was one of a team of guest producers – also including Alfred Kirchner, Christof Nel and Hans Neuenfels – who presented a series of challenging, radical stagings that put the house in the front rank of innovation. Berghaus's demythologized, deconstructionist *Ring* (1985–7) was a thought-provoking confrontation with the Wagnerian ethos and legacy. Her repertory of frequently shocking images and bizarre gestures makes a subliminal appeal to the imagination; her stage conventions owe something to Brecht and something to Beckett and the Theatre of the Absurd. Her *Don Giovanni* for the Welsh National Opera (1984) was similarly notable for its arresting, if enigmatic, images and vibrant symbolism: crucifix-like swords shuddering in the ground fused the phallic with the religious. In a brilliant *coup de théâtre*, the swaddling clothes caressed by Elvira unravelled to reveal that her baby was but a phantom – they then became a nun's headdress: a telling combination of erotic longing and religious fervour. Ottavio's isolation and frigidity were neatly represented by a snowfall.

Harry Kupfer was director in Weimar (1966–72) and chief producer at Dresden (1972–81) before becoming chief producer at the Komische Oper, Berlin, in 1981. Although not a pupil of Felsenstein, he drew on such principles of his as realistic, motivated acting, as well as theories of the Brechtian theatre, in a large number of productions ranging from Handel and Mozart and Janáček and Puccini. He has staged all the mature Wagner operas, most notably *Der fliegende Holländer* (1978) – an incisive and dramaturgically potent socio-psychological exploration of the work – and the *Ring* (1988), both at Bayreuth. His multi-layered, densely symbolic *Ring* integrated mythological and contemporary planes so as to address the issues of accumulated wealth and power, ruination of the natural environment and global destruction while remaining faithful to the work's timeless universality. He has also produced *Elektra* (1978) and *Fidelio* (1981) for the Welsh National Opera and *Pelléas et Mélisande* (1981) for the English National Opera.

Spectacle and anti-spectacle

Not all modern opera producers are radical followers of Felsenstein and Wieland Wagner. The Austrian Otto Schenk is a more traditional man of the theatre, unencumbered by loyalties to opera-house routine, modern theatrical trickery for its own sake or socio-political ideology. His productions, realistic and faithful to the period and style of the opera, are generally marked by convincing delineations of character and high standards of acting, with any idiosyncratic devices and production ideas subtly applied. Schenk collaborates closely with his designers (usually Jürgen Rose and Günther Schneider-Siemssen) and builds productions around his cast. His *Der Freischütz* (1972, Vienna), which stressed the simplicity and naivety of the story, provoked reassessment of the opera. His 1967 production of Verdi's *Macbeth* in Munich responded to the Italian character in the music rather than Scottish or Shakespearean elements in the libretto; the result was a thrilling if melodramatic tragedy. His version of *Der Rosenkavalier* (1975, Munich) was a theatrical tour de force, an active production full of comic detail.

Luchino Visconti is typical of those opera producers who entered the opera house after achieving distinction in theatre and film. He came to opera largely because of his admiration for the musical and theatrical skill of Maria Callas, who sang in his first opera production, Spontini's *La vestale* (1954, La Scala, Milan). Subsequently he staged *La sonnambula*, *La traviata*, *Anna Bolena* and *Iphigénie en Tauride* at La Scala, all with Callas. If Visconti's films, such as *The Leopard*, have been described as 'operatic', it follows that his opera productions are intensely cinematic in their attention to detail in luxuriant style, taste and characterization. Thanks in part to his collaborations with Callas and the role he played in the rediscovery of neglected 19th-century operas, he revolutionized opera staging in Italy, investing production style with new standards of visual spectacle.

Franco Zeffirelli, who had served as Visconti's assistant, was greatly influenced by him. A protean talent who often serves as his own scene, costume and lighting designer, Zeffirelli came to opera after success in the theatre and has become a film director of equal distinction; his opera films include a widely admired *La traviata* (1982) and a more controversial *Otello* (1986). One of his early productions, with Maria Callas in *La traviata* (1958, Dallas), showed Violetta near death during the prelude with the rest of the action as a flashback. His *Alcina* (1960, Dallas; 1962, London), with Joan Sutherland, presented the work as if being performed before a courtly audience, onstage. Generally, however, visual elegance and tasteful, inventive detail have marked his productions.

With Visconti, Zeffirelli led the neo-romantic revival in opera staging and design in the early 1960s. Few contemporary designers and directors have so faithfully accommodated the realistic demands of romanticism and *verismo* without compromising theatrical integrity or audience credibility. Like Visconti's, Zeffirelli's productions have been marked by refined visual taste and by three-dimensional acting performances, equally from principal singers and chorus. No *coup de théâtre* has proved too extreme for him in the interest of bold Romantic spectacle.

The Italian theatre has also produced Giorgio Strehler, co-founder of the acclaimed Piccolo Teatro in Milan where he became famous as an interpreter of Bertolt Brecht's plays and theatrical style. He made his début as an opera producer with *La traviata* in 1947 at La Scala, where in 1955 he founded the Piccolo Scala, an experimental opera studio. Though less extreme than Felsenstein or Friedrich, Strehler has brought Brecht's political and theatrical sensibilities into the opera house. His La Scala production of Verdi's *Simon Boccanegra* stressed class struggle and political intrigue, to give the piece greater power and topicality; he also improved the pace and tension of the work by eliminating lengthy scene changes and reducing the intervals to one. One of his most distinctive productions is *Die Entführung aus dem Serail*, seen at La Scala and Salzburg (1965) and noted for the influence of *commedia dell'arte* on the rhythm and movement and for the original use of silhouette. More controversial was his 1974 *Die Zauberflöte* at Salzburg with settings by his frequent collaborator Luciano Damiani, a neo-classical production, not at all fanciful, set in a barren space: the visual emphasis on illusion, with settings appearing and disappearing as if by magic, supports Strehler's basic intepretation of the opera – that only wisdom is not an illusion.

The English theatre

In England, as elsewhere, major talents, both radical and traditional, from the spoken theatre have not infrequently been enticed into the opera house. Several leading producers in the postwar period deserve special mention. Peter Brook, who was producing Shakespeare at Stratford when barely 20, was appointed director of productions at Covent Garden at 23, in 1948. He was determined to rehearse an opera as he would a play and to create original productions with high standards of acting; he did not indulge fine singers who were poor actors. His version of Strauss's *Salome* (1949), with its unabashed response to the eroticism in both music and text (reflected in Salvador Dali's settings), created an outrage and was abandoned after six performances, marking the end of his association with Covent Garden. In the 1970s, at his theatre research institute in Paris, Brook and a permanent ensemble developed a radical but widely acclaimed adaptation of *Carmen*. Combining elements of the Prosper Mérimée story and the Bizet opera, and eliminating the chorus and most of the minor characters, Brook and his musical adapter, Marius Constant, reduced the spectacle to about 80 minutes with no interval. The result, presented by a remarkable ensemble of singing actors, was a fast-moving, tense and gritty theatre piece, stressing the eroticism and raw emotion of the relationships (a violent confrontation between Carmen and Micaela was introduced). Brook was criticized for his irreverence towards the score, which was re-orchestrated for a smaller ensemble, and the order of the musical numbers and even their sense in relation to the action was significantly altered. But the theatrical energy of the work and the quality of the dramatic performances Brook elicited from his singers were widely admired.

Peter Hall, director of the National Theatre from 1973 to 1988, is a theatrical producer who has established an international reputation staging opera along more conventional lines. He made his Covent Garden début with Schoenberg's *Moses und Aron* (1965), vividly remembered for the sensuous orgy sequences. Subsequent productions there included Tippett's *The Knot Garden* (1970), a naturalistic staging that aimed at sharply delineated character relationships, and a sensitive *Tristan und Isolde* (1971), sparsely set, emotionally strongly focussed. At the Glyndebourne Festival he has done arguably his best work in staging 17th-century Venetian operas and Mozart's three Da Ponte operas (1973, 1977–8), productions marked by an effort to clarify meaning and action and to make the archaic accessible to modern audiences. With John Bury, frequently Hall's designer, he alluded in the 17th-century works to the traditions of Baroque staging, reinterpreting stage machinery and cut-out painted scenery in terms of modern theatre with the machinery visible and the non-mortals treated with imaginative wit. In the Da Ponte operas the acting aimed at naturalism and humanity, with little stylization and a detailed characterization that drew its clues from both music and text. His staging of *Macbeth* (1982) and *Carmen* (1986) at the Metropolitan Opera and his *Ring* cycle at Bayreuth (1983) were less successful; in these he attempted to synthesize 19th-century theatrical cliché. *Macbeth* included a Cauldron Scene populated with flying witches on broomsticks, while the *Ring* was widely criticized for a too-respectful observance of Wagner's stage directions and a consequent lack of any contemporary interpretative view of the work.

Another National Theatre director to have made an impact on opera is Jonathan Miller. Armed with sound theatrical sense (though sometimes criticized for failure to respond to the music), his best work has been for the English National Opera, where his productions include *Le nozze di Figaro*, *Otello*, *The Turn of the Screw* and, most notably, *Rigoletto* (1982). He set the last in the Mafia-ruled Little Italy of New York in the 1950s, with the Duke of Mantua as 'Duke', a Mafia leader, Rigoletto as a hunchbacked bartender, the butt of everyone's jokes, and Gilda living in a tenement out of *West Side Story*. The production was invested with clever but rarely intrusive touches such as the Duke's putting a coin in a juke box at the beginning of 'La donna è mobile' and jiving to the musical introduction. The result was a stylish and remarkably serious approach, which gained strength from the analogies in power structure and the balance of relationships between a *mafioso* community and a late Renaissance court. He attempted something similar in his later *Tosca*, set in fascist Rome of the 1940s.

John Dexter is another product of the National Theatre to have met with success in opera. He worked first at Hamburg, where his productions included *Boris Godunov*, *Billy Budd* and *From the House of the Dead*, then at Covent Garden (*Benvenuto Cellini*, 1966) and the Metropolitan Opera (*I vespri siciliani*, 1974), where he became director of productions. He provided the Metropolitan with some of the most original productions in its repertory, such as Poulenc's *Dialogues des Carmélites, Billy Budd, Lulu,* Weill's *Rise and Fall of the City of Mahagonny,* a French triple bill (Satie's ballet *Parade,* Poulenc's *Les mamelles de Tirésias* and Ravel's *L'enfant et les sortilèges*) and a Stravinsky one (*The Rite of Spring, Le rossignol* and *Oedipus rex*). Under Dexter's regime, it was remarkable that the conservative Metropolitan's best productions were of 20th-century opera. *Dialogues des Carmélites,* staged with economy on a bare, cross-shaped platform, was visually and dramatically powerful; it opened during the prelude with the nuns prostrate on the platform, a foreshadowing of their deaths in Poulenc's harrowing finale. It was one of the Metropolitan's most successful forays into opera in English translation. *Billy Budd* was also distinguished for its rich theatrical values and fine acting. In *Les mamelles* and *Le rossignol,* vastly different in style, Dexter's clever and witty direction ideally complemented the moods established by David Hockney's original settings (his first for a large opera house).

Britain and the USA

David Pountney was director of productions at Scottish Opera (1976–80) and from 1982 at the English National Opera, where, in collaboration with the music director, Mark Elder, and the company ensemble, he has presented a succession of productions remarkable for the consistency of their imagination and stagecraft. Landmarks have been the British stage premières of Busoni's *Doktor Faust* (1986) and Shostakovich's *Lady Macbeth of the Mtsensk District* (1987), while Freudian insights into the world of dreams and fairy-tales have been fruitfully brought to bear on Tchaikovsky's *The Queen of Spades* (1983), Dvořák's *Rusalka* (1983) and Humperdinck's *Hänsel und Gretel* (1987).

The Australian Elijah Moshinsky worked with the Royal Shakespeare Company and the National Theatre before producing a series of operas for Covent Garden (including *Peter Grimes,* 1975, *Lohengrin,* 1978, *Tannhäuser,* 1984, Handel's *Samson,* 1985, *Otello,* 1987, and *Die Entführung,* 1987), as well as the English National Opera, the Metropolitan Opera, Australian Opera and elsewhere. Moshinsky's mainstream productions have frequently been praised for their imaginative deployment of minimal resources. Another Australian, David Freeman, who had initiated the Opera Factory Zurich to experiment with new musicodramatic performance techniques, using a small, highly trained ensemble operating outside the traditional theatre structure, founded a related enterprise called Opera Factory London; it has collaborated with the London Sinfonietta in a series of productions, notably a powerful realization of Birtwistle's *Punch and Judy* and a *Così fan tutte* rich in humour and psychological perception.

Because of the tendency of major American opera companies to import established European producers to repeat proven successes, American producers have had fewer opportunities to establish international reputations. Frank Corsaro and Peter Sellars are chief among the exceptions. While Corsaro is perhaps best known for his charming collaborations with the illustrator Maurice Sendak on *The Cunning Little Vixen* and *The Love for Three Oranges* he, as well as Sellars, has been responsible for transplanting operas into modern settings with strong social and political comment. While Corsaro has been the more traditional with a *Carmen* (1984) moved up to the Spanish Civil War, Sellars has been more imaginative and audacious. His *Giulio Cesare* (1985) portrayed a present-day American President being seduced by a Levantine *femme fatale* lounging seductively by a hotel swimming pool; *Così fan tutte* (1986) was enacted in a Cape Cod diner run by Don Alfonso; *Don Giovanni* was set in Spanish Harlem; and his Chicago *Tannhäuser* treated the plight of an erring television evangelist. Sellars sees his objective less as updating works of the past than as 'testing the present against them'.

Glossary

Act (Fr. *acte*; Ger. *Aufzug*; It. *atto*). One of the main divisions of a drama, opera or ballet, usually completing a part of the action and often having a climax of its own. Horace (*Epistle to the Pisos*) recommended five acts as the proper manner of dividing a play; this structure was adopted in early operas and usually preserved in serious French opera of the 17th and 18th centuries even when the three-act form predominated elsewhere. Rousseau (*Dictionnaire de musique*, 1768) insisted that the unities of time and place should be observed in each act, but there were already many exceptions and the development of techniques that afforded ways of presenting transformation scenes, together with the relaxation of the unities and the increasingly fluid requirements in the representation of time and place, meant that these principles were discarded. From the late 18th century, operas were written in anything from one act to five, with three the most common, though in *opera buffa* the third tended to become perfunctory and was often dropped: Mozart's *Don Giovanni* and *Così fan tutte* are in two, as is *Die Zauberflöte*. Wagner's ideal music drama was to consist of three acts; he adopted this division in his mature works, but other composers and librettists have remained unconvinced of the need for so restrictive a practice.

Action musicale (Fr.). A translation of Wagner's 'Handlung für Musik', his designation of the *Lohengrin* libretto, used by French Wagnerians (e.g. d'Indy, of his *Fervaal* and *L'étranger*) to suggest something more elevated than a mere opera.

Act tune. Term used in England mainly in the 17th and 18th centuries for a piece of music played between the acts of an opera or play.

Afterpiece. An English opera or pantomime of the 18th or early 19th century, usually about an hour long, designed for performance after a play or other theatrical work.

Air. Term used, in French and English, for 'song' or 'aria'. In French opera of the 17th and 18th centuries it was applied equally to unpretentious, brief pieces and to serious, extended monologues, comparable to arias in Italian opera. Some are accompanied by dancing, and some are purely instrumental (*airs de danse*). (See Chapter III.)

Alto. *See* CASTRATO; CONTRALTO; COUNTERTENOR; and HAUTE-CONTRE.

Aria (It.: 'air', 'style', 'manner'). A term normally signifying a closed, lyrical piece for solo voice. It had a central place in early opera. Most Venetian opera arias before 1660 are in triple time or a mixture of triple and duple; many early arias have four or more verses, though after 1650 two became the standard in opera. Most arias have continuo accompaniment, with instrumental ritornellos between verses; a few from the 1640s onwards have instrumental sections between vocal phrases, but these remain a minority until well into the 18th century.

Most later 17th-century arias are in the form *ABB'* (the last line or group of lines rendered twice to similar music, with a tonic cadence only the second time), or *ABA* (sometimes *ABA'*), where the first line or couplet is repeated at the end. This became the standard da capo aria, which was dominant by 1680. In the early 18th century the accompaniment could vary in texture and instrumentation; the aria with continuo only became increasingly rare after the 1720s.

By then, longer arias were favoured. With the composers regarded as originators of the modern 18th-century style (Vinci, Hasse, Pergolesi etc), the proportions of the da capo structure changed. The middle section became shorter and often contrasted in tempo and metre; the corresponding enlargement of the first section later led to the practice of replacing the da capo with the 'dal segno', indicating a return not to the beginning but to a later point. In the 1760s and 1770s this gave way to a scheme close in outline to the contemporary symphony or sonata first movement, with a first section ending in the dominant, a middle section as development or contrast and a restatement of the first section as tonic recapitulation. Other important types of this time were the rondeau, *ABACA*, and the so-called rondò, which began with a slow section and ended with an allegro (*AB* or *ABAB*). By 1780 the latter (prototype of the early 19th-century cantabile–cabaletta), at first reserved to the prima donna and primo uomo for a final, climactic number, was becoming increasingly popular in serious opera; arias in comic operas were more varied in form.

The last decade of the 18th century and the opening years of the 19th were a period of considerable freedom and experimentation in aria form. In *opera seria* the sonata form aria was becoming old-fashioned and dying out, replaced by multi-tempo forms. The slow–fast succession was highly favoured, although it had not yet achieved its later hegemony. Three- and four-tempo arias are also found, as are strophic romanzas and the like. By the 1820s the so-called cavatina–cabaletta (or 'cantabile–cabaletta'; 'cavatina' was used in this period for entrance arias) had become standard, as had the four-part scene format: a recitative (scena), establishing the dramatic situation and culminating in (second) a slow or moderate aria (the cantabile or *primo tempo*); then followed by (third) the *tempo di mezzo*, in recitative or *parlante*, often with choral or ensemble passages, and providing some dramatic turn to which there came, as reaction (fourth), the fast cabaletta (or *secondo tempo*), usually in two parts separated by a passage for the chorus. This pattern was much used by Bellini, Donizetti and their contemporaries.

19th-century operas show a continuing reduction in the number of arias and their increasing distance from the centre of musical-dramatic attention. This was hastened by the move away from *bel canto* singing towards a more dramatic style from the 1830s. The style centred on lyricism, ornamentation and agility, which lent itself to presentation in expansive, formal arias, was less in keeping with the changed relationship between music and drama and the new vocal style that it implied. The standard forms tended to disappear. Verdi's development exemplified the move towards free and fluid constructions, less readily extracted from their context. In *Rigoletto*, for example, the tenor has a conventional cantabile–cabaletta, 'Parmi veder le lagrime', while Rigoletto, an acting part, never sings an aria in a standard form and has, in 'Cortigiani, vil razza', a solo shaped to the scene's dramatic requirements, beginning 'agitato' as he denounces the courtiers and turning to 'cantabile' as he pleads with them (almost reversing the old pattern). There are few detachable arias in *Aida* (1871), none at all in *Otello* (1887) or *Falstaff* (1893). Iago's 'Credo' is not an aria in the traditional sense: an earlier age would have described it as a *recitativo stromentato*. Equally in Puccini an aria is part of the dramatic texture and cannot usually be extracted without fragmentation or mutilation. In Wagner's mature operas the same applies: the extended sections for a single voice are mostly narrative in character.

19th- and even 20th-century composers did, however, carry on the tradition of introducing songs, ballads and romances as such, either as a reflection of mood or state of mind or as a frankly undramatic divertissement (the tenor's song in *Der Rosenkavalier*, 1911, is a late example). Wagner turned this practice to strongly dramatic ends in Senta's Ballad and in the trial and prize songs in *Die Meistersinger* (1867).

Italian opera had a strong influence on most other contemporary operatic genres, including French grand opera and also *opéra comique*, for instance Hero's 'Je vais le voir' in Berlioz's *Béatrice et Bénédict* (1862), an example of the cavatina–cabaletta type. In the Slavonic countries, too, in spite of folk elements, the aria was accepted as a natural form of expression, for instance Lensky's aria in Act 2 of Tchaikovsky's *Eugene Onegin* (1878). Wagner's influence was so profound that by the 20th century the older aria, traditions had been almost entirely discarded, though Hindemith in *Cardillac* (1926) and Schoenberg in *Von heute auf morgen* (1929) reverted to the conception of an opera with separate 'numbers'. Stravinsky, in *The Rake's Progress* (1951), revived the form but not the substance of the 18th-century aria, in a neo-classical framework. More recent tendencies have been towards highly integrated forms of music-theatre from which the aria, as representing a formal or artificial element, has generally been excluded.

Arietta (It.). A song in an opera or similar work, shorter and less elaborate than a fully developed aria. In Landi's *Sant' Alessio* (1632), where 'arietta' is used apparently for the first time, it does not seem to have any special significance. In later usage it came to mean much the same as CAVATINA.

Ariette (Fr.). Strictly speaking, a short aria. In 18th-century French opera, however, it meant a vivacious piece with orchestral accompaniment, modelled on the style of the Italian da capo aria, e.g. 'Brillez, astres nouveaux' in Rameau's *Castor et Pollux* (1737); arias of this kind sometimes had Italian words. In the later 18th century the term changed its meaning. A COMÉDIE MÊLÉE D'ARIETTES consisted of dialogue interspersed with songs which might be long or short, fast or slow. The word thus became virtually synonymous with 'song'. Rosine's song in Act 3 of Beaumarchais' *Le barbier de Séville* (1775), with two stanzas and a *petite reprise*, is described in a footnote as an 'ariette, dans le goût espagnol' and in the stage directions as an 'air'; after she has sung it, Bartholo thinks she ought to study more lively things than 'ces grandes arias'.

Arioso (It.: 'like an aria'). A singing, as opposed to a declamatory, style of performance; a short passage in a regular tempo in the middle or at the end of a recitative; a short aria not so connected.

The introduction of arioso passages in recitative occurs first in Roman opera of the early 17th century. They are frequent in Venetian opera. In Monteverdi's *Il ritorno d'Ulisse* (1641) there is an example of an arioso developing into an aria; when Minerva assures Ulysses that he will return disguised to find the suitors impudent and Penelope faithful, he twice exclaims in arioso: 'O fortunato Ulisse', which at the end of the following scene becomes the opening phrase of an aria. Alessandro Scarlatti understood arioso to mean 'in a flowing melodic style'. Handel used 'arioso' to mean a short aria, e.g. Dorinda's 'Quando spieghi i tormenti' in *Orlando* (1733) or Melissa's 'Io già sento l'alma in sen' in *Amadigi* (1715), where it is preceded by a *recitativo accompagnato*. Many solos of the same kind are ariosos in this sense. Later composers generally preferred the term 'cavatina' for a short aria. Arioso, however, is still found occasionally in the 19th century, e.g. in Tchaikovsky's *Eugene Onegin* (1878) and *The Queen of Spades* (1890). Its use in Hindemith's *Cardillac* (1926) and Stravinsky's *The Rake's Progress* (1951) is a revival of 18th-century practice.

Appoggiatura (It.; Fr. *appoggiature*; Ger. *Vorschlag*). A 'leaning-note'. As a melodic ornament, it usually implies a note one step above or below the 'main' note. It usually creates a dissonance with the prevailing harmony, and resolves by step on the following weak beat. It may be notated as an ornament or in normal notation. In the Baroque and Classical periods, and the early Romantic period, the appoggiatura, even when not notated, was taken for granted in certain contexts, particularly in recitative to allow the music to fall in line with the natural enunciation of Italian words.

Azione teatrale (It.). A genre of music theatre, essentially a form of SERENATA, that enjoyed a brief vogue during the middle of the 18th century, particularly at the courts of Vienna and its environs. *Azioni teatrali* are almost invariably in a single act, with a cast of three to five characters. Intended for performance in private theatres, they are scored for a comparatively small orchestra. The term is found most often in the writings of Pietro Metastasio, who may have invented it; for all practical purposes it is identical with such terms as *azione scenica, festa teatrale* or *componimento da camera*.

Ballabile (It.: 'suitable for dancing'). A movement intended for dancing. In Act 3 of *Macbeth* Verdi termed the song and dance of the witches *ballabile*; the 'Galop con cori' that opens Act 2 of his *Ernani* is a *coro ballabile*; dance divertissements in Meyerbeer's operas are titled *1°, 2° ballabile* etc. The term is also used for instrumental pieces of a dance character; for example, the dances in Hans von Bülow's *Carnevale di Milano* are headed 'Ballabili'.

Ballad opera. English 18th-century form, consisting of a play, usually comic, in which spoken prose dialogue alternates with songs set mostly to traditional or currently popular melodies. Composers were rarely identified. The airs were derived from many sources, including song and dance collections popular at the time, the repertory of folk melodies and well-known theatre works. There are precedents for comedies with popular airs in the French THÉÂTRES DE LA FOIRE and in English 17th-century theatre, but John Gay was the first to blend English comedy with opera by inserting familiar tunes into spoken dialogue in *The Beggar's Opera* (1728). The first ballad opera of this nature, *The Beggar's Opera* treated low life in London, and satirized government, the legal profession and the Italian opera. Its phenomenal success inspired imitations; most were satirical, but some were on historical, patriotic, rural or sentimental topics. The genre was popular not only in London but in the provinces, Dublin and the American colonies, and one example, Coffey's *The Devil to Pay*, was a starting-point for the German SINGSPIEL. The form gave way around 1760 to the composed comic opera, but a few examples remained popular into the 19th century. (See Chapter X.)

Ballata (It.). A dance-song; although usually applied to a late medieval form, it was used in the 19th century for operatic songs in dance rhythm. Verdi used it for 'Questa o quella', in *Rigoletto*, sung by the Duke of Mantua, for 'Volta la terrea fronte alle stelle', sung by Oscar (Edgar) in *Un ballo in maschera*, and for Carlos's 'Son Pereda, son ricco d'onore' in *La forza del destino*.

Ballet. One of the principal ancestors of opera was the court *intermedio*, which involved much dance; in early Italian opera dance had an important role between the acts of court opera, but in a wider context its chief place was in final joyous scenes. Usually dances for use in such contexts were provided by a local composer attached to the theatre or the dance troupe rather than the composer of the opera itself. In France the place of dance was more central; French Baroque operas include numerous dances (some especially in the divertissements, with choral singing). Lully supplied the dance music to Cavalli's operas for Paris, just as local composers such as Schmelzer did for Cesti's operas for Vienna. Some of these dances were purely decorative, but others were integral to the drama, anticipating the concept of the *ballet d'action* (or *ballet en action*) which is generally credited to J. G. Noverre in the mid-late 18th century (it was also anticipated by John Weaver, in London, early in the century). Among leading French dancers in the early 18th century were Marie-Anne Camargo (1710–70), noted for her virtuosity, and her rival Marie Sallé (1707–56), noted for her expressiveness and imagination; both danced in operas by Rameau and Sallé also appeared in London in the few Handel operas that call for dance. Paris and Vienna, however, were the most important centres of dance (with Milan and Stuttgart also playing a significant role). It was in Vienna that Franz Hilverding van Wewen (1710–68) exercised much influence as a choreographer with his ballets for the Viennese theatres, usually to music by Joseph Starzer; Hilverding was in Vienna from 1762, except for a period (1745–62) in St Petersburg. He was succeeded by Noverre and later by Gasparo Angiolini, bitter rivals who simultaneously worked towards the *ballet d'action* and were both associated with Gluck's 'reform' operas in Vienna. Noverre's pupils, notably Jean Duberval (1742–1806) and Charles Louis Didelot (1767–1837), were influential in both aesthetic and technical developments, including the introduction of ballet into certain middle-class, vernacular opera forms as opposed to Italian *opera seria* and French *tragédie* where it had traditionally belonged.

Ballet retained a connection with certain types of opera throughout the 19th century. Weber included dance in a revival (1825) of *Euryanthe* and in *Oberon* (1826); Glinka's operas include dance scenes, calling for folkdance and growing out of the action, in his operas (*Ivan Susanin*, 1836; *Ruslan and Lyudmila*, 1842). Ballet was by 1820 an essential element of all productions at the Paris Opéra; Rossini, after incorporating dances from other sources in his earlier operas, provided dance sequences in *Guillaume Tell* (1829). Meyerbeer's and Donizetti's dance sequences were generally after the nature of divertissements (though in *Robert le diable* the ballet of spectral nuns has a dramatic function). Verdi's Opéra adaptations are of particular interest: he added a ballet to *I lombardi* for its production as *Jérusalem*, wrote a ballet of the Four Seasons into *Les vêpres siciliennes*, added Spanish gypsy dances to *Il trovatore*, wrote dances for Hecate and the witches in *Macbeth* and supplied a 'ballet de la reine' for *Don Carlos*. *La traviata* includes a ballet, as an entertainment at a party on the stage. He declined to add a ballet to *Rigoletto* for the Opéra but in 1894 provided a divertissement in *Otello*. Wagner added a substantial ballet to *Tannhäuser* for its Paris production, but so as to minimize its interference with the plot placed it at the beginning of Act 1 – where the fashionable latecomers missed it and in their irritation ensured the failure of the performance. French composers such as Berlioz, Gounod and Massenet took due care to provide for ballet sequences in their operas. Several Tchaikovsky operas include scenes that allow scope for dance: *Eugene Onegin* has both folkdance scenes and ballroom ones. Borodin's *Prince Igor* has a substantial folkdance scene (the Polovtsian Dances).

Prokofiev included a ballroom scene in *War and Peace*, and Schoenberg included a dance orgy in *Moses und Aron*. Dance is used by Strauss, in *Salome* and *Elektra*, almost as a kind of ritual, deeply laden with psychological significance. But in general it has been difficult for 20th-century composers to devise ways consistent with their musico-dramatic outlook that allow for stage dance sequences except in works, like

Britten's *Gloriana*, of special kinds.

Ballet de cour. A type of ballet popular at the French court in the late 16th and the 17th century. Its components were normally *récits* (*see* RÉCIT), *vers* (a form of libretto), entrées (*see* ENTRÉE) and a concluding *grand ballet* danced by the *grands seigneurs*. *Circé ou Le Balet comique de la Royne*, given at the Petit Bourbon palace in 1581, was the first in which poetry, music (by Jacques Salmon and Lambert de Beaulieu), décor and dance combined to support a single dramatic action; considered the earliest French work of consistent musical theatre, it stands first among the precursors of the TRAGÉDIE LYRIQUE. The *ballet de cour* suffered an eclipse when in 1670 Louis XIV ceased to dance and when Lully, with his *Triomphe de l'Amour* (1680), converted the court ballet into a stage ballet. It enjoyed a brief revival with the young Louis XV in the 1720s but was obsolescent by the mid-18th century. (See Chapter III.)

Ballet-héroïque (Fr.). A genre of the French lyric stage in the first half of the 18th century. It is a type of OPÉRA-BALLET, consisting of a prologue and three or four acts or entrées, each with a plot of its own. The *ballet-héroïque* substituted heroic or exotic characters for the *petits maîtres* and amorous ladies of the Regency that characterized the *opéra-ballet*. An early example is Collin de Blamont's *Les festes grecques et romaines* (1753); outstanding examples are Rameau's five *ballets-héroïques*, from *Les Indes galantes* (1735) to *Les surprises de l'amour* (1748). (See Chapter III.)

Baritone (from Gk. *barytonos*: 'deep-sounding'; Fr. *baryton*; Ger. *Bariton*; It. *baritono*). The most common category of male voice, normally written for within the range *A* to *f′*, which may be extended at either end, particularly in solo writing. In early opera the voice was little used, and it was first seriously explored by German composers. Mozart's use of it for principal roles was met elsewhere in Europe with surprise. In *De l'opéra en France* (1820) Castil-Blaze explained that 'the Italians dearly love high voices, the French seem to give the preference to the middle range, and the Germans to deep voices'; he found it extraordinary that in *Don Giovanni* and *Le nozze di Figaro* there should be four important roles for 'basses' and that the principal male should be a 'bass' (like others of the time, he did not distinguish between bass and baritone).

Baritone roles arrived late chiefly because so much emphasis had earlier been placed on florid singing, for which the higher voices had been better suited. The acceptance of the baritone for principal roles widened the range of male character types beyond those traditionally associated with the tenor (the hero and lover) and the bass (the monarch, high priest and old man). The baritone could project maturity in a young man (Wolfram) or youthfulness in an older man (the Dutchman). It became a vehicle of new manifestations of virility: the wooer in competition with the lover (Don Carlos in *Ernani*), the brother figure (Valentin), the less-than-sage father figure (Germont), the swashbuckler of the arena (Escamillo) and the lascivious villain (Scarpia). The ability of the baritone to project equally well such varied attributes as compassion, wisdom, authority, anger, anguish, malice, cynicism and wit makes this voice apt for some of the most complex and three-dimensional characters in opera: Sachs, Wotan, Rigoletto, Iago and Falstaff.

Associated with the rise to greater prominence of the baritone in the 19th century were Antonio Tamburini (1800–76), who sang florid parts in Italian opera early in the century, and Jean-Blaise Martin (1768–1837), one of the most admired singers at the Opéra-Comique, known for his falsetto singing: the designation 'baryton Martin' has been used to distinguish this type from the 'Verdi baritone', which carried the chest register further into the upper range, typified by Felice Varesi

(1813–89), the first Macbeth and Rigoletto. Other 19th-century baritones included Franz Betz (1835–1900), who won Wagner's admiration for his performance of the 'Hoher Bass' (or BASS-BARITONE) role of Wotan; Jean-Baptiste Faure (1830–1914), who created several roles including Nelusko in Meyerbeer's *L'africaine* and Posa in Verdi's *Don Carlos*, and whose fine singing and acting ability made him an unrivalled Don Giovanni; and Victor Maurel (1848–1923), for whom Verdi wrote Iago and Falstaff. Among more recent baritones Friedrich Schorr (1888–1953) was particularly noted for Wagner roles; Tito Gobbi (1915–84) combined a distinctive voice with rare acting ability, especially in Verdi roles and in Puccini characters as contrasted as Gianni Schicchi and Scarpia; and Dietrich Fischer-Dieskau (*b* 1925) has excelled both in lieder and in opera.

Bass (It. *basso*; Fr. *basse*; Ger. *Bass*). The lowest male voice, normally written for in the range *F* to *e'*, which may be extended at either end, particularly in solo writing. Although bass parts in Italian monodies of the 17th century were often florid, ornate writing was rare in opera, where the emphasis was on dramatic portrayal. In Monteverdi's operas, the bass already appears in what were to be some of its most important role types: as a god (particularly of the underworld) or as a sepulchral figure (Charon in *Orfeo*), and as a figure of authority (Seneca in *L'incoronazione di Poppea*) – though this last type of role vanished from serious opera or was reduced to secondary, comic status, typically a lecherous old tutor (Alfeo in A. Scarlatti's *Eraclea*, 1700). In serious Italian opera of the 18th century, the bass usually sang only minor roles: the father, the priest, the king, the military general, the confidant or adviser.

The bass however was important in opera in France. Cavalli's *Ercole amante*, written for Paris (1662), has a bass in the title role. Some of the most imposing French bass roles are by Rameau, for example Theseus in *Hippolyte et Aricie* (1733) and Castor in *Castor et Pollux* (1737), both first sung by Claude-Louis-Dominique de Chassée (1698–1786). This French tradition is further evident in Gluck's late operas for Paris, which include such roles as Agamemnon in *Iphigénie en Aulide* (1774).

In Italy, a special genre for the bass voice was the rage aria, parodied by such bellicose characters as Polyphemus ('O ruddier than the cherry' in Handel's *Acis and Galatea*, 1718) and the harem official Osmin (who sings two such arias in Mozart's *Die Entführung aus dem Serail*). The comic potential of the bass voice was also realized in the tradition of the *basso buffo*, whose spiritual ancestor was the *commedia dell'arte* character Pantalone. Such roles are sometimes at a pitch higher than that of a true bass (the word BARITONE was little used at the time). In early opera similar comic male characters appeared occasionally on the fringe of plots (e.g. Penelope's wooer, Antinous, in Monteverdi's *Il ritorno d'Ulisse*, 1641) and were called upon to perform exaggeratedly wide-spanning phrases. The comic bass as a central figure began to appear only in the last quarter of the 17th century (e.g. in Stradella's *Il Trespolo tutore*, 1679) but became virtually indispensable in 18th- and early 19th-century comic opera of which Pergolesi, Mozart, Piccinni, Cimarosa, Paisiello, Rossini and Donizetti are the chief representatives. The tradition inspired a battery of stock effects, including wide leaps, patter singing and long, violent crescendos.

The French and Italian traditions became universal in the 19th century. In the Romantic era the bass was chosen by Berlioz and Gounod to represent Mephistopheles and for an array of villains including Sparafucile in *Rigoletto* and Hagen in *Götterdämmerung*. The bass's resonance lends to the projection of authority, apt for the father (*Die Meistersinger*, *Mignon*), the king (*Tannhäuser*, *Lohengrin)* or the priest

(*La forza del destino*, *Don Carlos*). Its potential for tragic utterance is revealed in such roles as King Marke (*Tristan und Isolde*), Boris Godunov, Philip II (*Don Carlos*) and Arkel (*Pelléas et Mélisande*). The *buffo* tradition waned, but is still evident in various minor Puccini roles.

Operatic bass roles, and the types of voice that specialize in them, have often been designated by special terms such as *basso buffo* (see above), BASSE-CHANTANTE or BASSO CANTANTE, *basse-noble* and *basso profondo*. The *basse-noble* and *basso profondo* are heavy, deep voices, appropriate to a king, high priest or elderly father. *Basso profondo* roles are characterized more by their low tessitura than by the exploitation of extremely deep notes, since even when well sung these may be somewhat ludicrous: for example, the lengthy low *E* for Ochs that ends Act 2 of *Der Rosenkavalier* and the low *D* in Osmin's vengeance aria in *Die Entführung*. Other roles for *basso profondo* include Sarastro in *Die Zauberflöte*, Marcel in *Les Huguenots*, the King in Thomas' *Hamlet* and Balthasar in Donizetti's *La favorite*. Russian basses are noted for the strength and richness of their lower range; Ivan Mel'nikov (1832–1906) created roles in operas by Borodin, Rimsky-Korsakov, Musorgsky (including Boris) and others. Late singers in the same tradition include Fyodor Shalyapin (1873–1938) and Boris Christoff (*b* 1914). Alexander Kipnis (1891–1978), an American of Russian birth) also excelled in *basso profondo* roles, but his unusually wide repertory included Mozart and Wagner.

Bass-baritone. A male voice combining the compass and other attributes of the BASS and BARITONE. The term is probably derived from the German *Bassbariton*, and the voice itself is particularly associated with the German 19th-century upward development of the bass range. Wagner called the bass-baritone 'Hoher Bass' and used the term for the roles of Wotan, Alberich, Donner and Fasolt in *Das Rheingold* and *Die Walküre*. The most important, that of Wotan, requires a powerful upper register for phrases in the baritone range *e* to *f*♯', but Wagner also wrote numerous phrases in the range *A* to *a* which require the resonance of a bass voice if they are to be delivered with due authority.

Basse-chantante (Fr.: 'singing bass'). Term, originally meaning simply a vocal bass part, used in the 19th century for a BASS singer with a particularly high or light voice. The role of Max in Adam's *Le chalet* (1834) is described as for *basse chantante*; later roles include Escamillo in *Carmen* (1875).

Basse-noble (Fr.: 'noble bass'). A deep BASS voice.

Basso buffo (It.: 'comic bass'). Term, used in the 18th century, for a comic BASS role (or sometimes more exactly a low BARITONE one, such as Mozart's Figaro).

Basso cantante (It.: 'singing bass'). Term, first used in the late 18th century, for a BASS with a light, high voice. The Earl of Mount-Edgcumbe referred (1824) to the growing use of the bass voice: 'these new singers are called by the novel appellation of *basso-cantante* (which by-the-bye is a kind of apology, and an acknowledgment that they ought not to sing)'.

Basso profondo (It.: 'deep bass'). A deep BASS voice.

Bel canto (It.: 'fine singing'). A term loosely used and open to several interpretations. Though widely understood as indicating the elegant Italian vocal style of the 18th century and the early 19th, it entered the musical vocabulary well after that time (it does not appear in the important singing treatises of the 18th century), in the mid-19th century, when a weightier tone had come to be prized and there was less emphasis on a light, florid delivery. Rossini, in Paris in 1858, is reported to have inveighed against the decline of traditional Italian-style singing: 'Alas for us, we have lost our *bel canto*'. He went on to state the three requirements for a *bel canto* singer: a naturally beautiful voice, even in tone across its entire range; effortless delivery of florid music, acquired through careful training; and a mastery of style, assimilated from listening to the best singers rather than learnt. In the early 20th century German scholars applied the term anachronistically to the lyrical style called for in Venetian opera and the Roman cantata of the 1630s and 40s (Cesti, Carissimi, Luigi Rossi) in reaction to the text-dominated *stile rappresentativo*.

Breeches part [trouser role] (Fr. *travesti*). Term for a man's or boy's role sung by a woman. The central examples are Cherubino in *Le nozze di Figaro* and Oktavian in *Der Rosenkavalier*, but there are many more, among them Verdi's Oscar(Edgar) in *Un ballo in maschera* and Thibaut in *Don Carlos*, Ascanius in *Les troyens*, Nicklaus in *Les contes d'Hoffmann*, Fyodor in *Boris Godunov*, Hänsel, and the Composer in *Ariadne auf Naxos*. In Baroque opera numerous male parts were written for women (Sextus in Handel's *Giulio Cesare*, for example), but casting was then anyway less sexually specific, partly because the issue was confused by the castrato singers; and in Rome female parts were at some periods sung by male (castrato) singers.

Brindisi (It., ? from Sp. *brindis*, from Ger. *bring dir's*). An invitation to a company to raise their glasses and drink; a song to this effect. Such songs, usually solos with choral response, are common in 19th-century opera; well-known examples occur in Donizetti's *Lucrezia Borgia*, Verdi's *Macbeth*, *La traviata* and *Otello* and Mascagni's *Cavalleria rusticana*.

Burlesque (Fr.). A term for a musical work in which serious and comic elements were juxtaposed or combined to grotesque effect. In England the word denotes a dramatic production which ridicules stage conventions; in 19th- and 20th-century American usage its principal meaning is a variety show in which striptease is the chief attraction.

English plays called 'burlesques', which go back to 1671, mocked at the heroic tragedy, the pastorale, the pantomime, the Italian opera or even the ballad opera. In the operatic forms, music played a substantial part. J. Estcourt's *Prunella* (1708) was an early burlesque of Italian opera. *The Opera of Operas, or Tom Thumb the Great* (1733) was an operatic adaptation of Fielding's *The Tragedy of Tragedies*, a successful burlesque play of two years earlier. J. F. Lampe wrote music for one version, Arne for another (16 short songs with little trace of parody). Carey's *The Dragon of Wantley* (1737), on the other hand, was an all-sung burlesque of Italian opera, with songs, choruses and recitative by Lampe; the music as well as the text is satirical.

In the 19th century, every major opera was followed by a rash of burlesques at the minor theatres, such as *Der Freischütz, a New Muse-sick-all and See-nick Performance from the New German Uproar: by the Celebrated Funnybear* (1824); the musical part of the joke was to substitute familiar, commonplace music for the serious arias and recitatives of the original. There was rarely any effort at musical parody. W. S. Gilbert recovered real wit and pungency in his burlesques of the 1860s, and there is much burlesque in the Savoy operas, particularly *Trial by Jury*, *H.M.S. Pinafore*, *Ruddigore* and *Iolanthe*. But Sullivan's music, though often witty, is rarely a direct parody of serious operatic convention.

Burletta. A type of English operatic comedy of the late 18th century and the early 19th. The term was one of several used for Italian comic operas of the light intermezzo variety; Pergolesi's *La serva padrona* was so described at its London première (1750). Several Italian burlettas were played at Dublin in the 1750s, and an English imitation, *Midas*, performed privately near Belfast in 1760, with folksongs and tunes from Italian and English operas and recitative, was imitated in Dublin and London. These early burlettas, in verse and all sung, satirized the mythological and historical conventions of *opera seria*, though the music rarely participated in the joke. An example is Dibdin's *Poor Vulcan* (1778). The decline began with an adaptation of the BURLESQUE tragedy *Tom Thumb*, revived at Covent Garden in 1780, a play with added songs 'inadvertently announced . . . as a burletta'. Comedies, often with no burlesque element, were put on at the minor theatres under the title of 'burletta', but they departed further and further from the original model and ended up as spoken plays with a few ballads.

Cabaletta (It.). The word, of uncertain origin, originally meant a short aria with a persistent rhythm and a repeat which allowed the singer to improvise ornamentation. But it came to be applied to the concluding section, generally in a fairly rapid tempo and with mounting excitement, of an extended aria or duet, sometimes preceded by recitative, e.g. Amina's 'Sovra il sen la man mi posa' (the final section of 'Come per me sereno') in Act 1 of Bellini's *La sonnambula* (1831), where the soprano is joined by the chorus, and Violetta's 'Sempre libera degg'io' (the final section of 'Ah fors'è lui') in Act 1 of Verdi's *La traviata* (1853). The first section of an extended piece of this kind is often called 'cantabile' or 'cavatina'. In a letter to Giulio Ricordi in 1880 Verdi expressed himself in favour of cabalettas, which he preferred to 'realism' in opera. Stravinsky revived the term in *The Rake's Progress* (1951). *See also* ARIA.

Cadenza (from It.: 'cadence'). A virtuoso passage inserted near the end of an aria, usually indicated by a fermata over an inconclusive chord such as the tonic 6-4. Vocal cadenzas were most often improvised by the performer. The term can refer to simple ornaments on the penultimate note of a cadence, or to any accumulation of embellishments inserted near the end of a section or at fermata points.

The 'ornamented cadence' (*cadenza fiorita*) brought a certain brilliance to the ending of a piece; further, the inclusion of specific opportunities for virtuoso display permitted composers to avoid having the rest of their compositions spoilt by the liberties taken by performers. Many composers, unsure of performers' taste and improvisational skill, wrote out their own cadenzas. Caccini, as early as 1589, supplied an alternative version of a cadenza in an *intermedio*, *La Pellegrina*; he also wrote embellished endings for his own melodies in his *Euridice*. Peri praised Vittoria Archilei in the preface to his *Euridice* because she embellished his music 'with those attractive and gracious ornaments which cannot be written down'.

In the late 17th century and the early 18th, the popularity of virtuoso singing in opera increased and with it the importance of improvised embellishment. Final cadenzas became common towards the end of the 17th century, indicated by 'solo', 'tenuto', 'ad arbitrio', a rest or a fermata. In A. Scarlatti's early operas places for cadenzas can be found, but they are clearer after c1715. In da capo arias the usual place for the insertion of a cadenza was just before the final cadence of the first section; probably it was intended that a cadenza be performed only in the da capo, but often a cadenza is specified at the end of the middle section (and sometimes there only). P. F. Tosi, himself a virtuoso singer, described the excesses of cadenza performances in *Opinioni de' cantori antichi e moderni* (1723): 'The Presumption of some singers is not to be borne with, who expect that an whole Orchestra should stop in the midst of a well-regulated Movement, to wait for their illgrounded Caprices, learned by Heart, carried from one Theatre to another, and perhaps stolen from some applauded female singer.'

The rules for the construction of cadenzas given by Tartini (*Traité des agréments*, 1771) seem to have been widely followed and resemble in principle those given for singers: cadenzas should start with a swelling note (for singers, *messa di voce*), *passaggii* (ornamental passages) or a trill, succeeded by notes of smaller value, and then a high note, which may be identical with or followed by the highest note in the piece; the melodic peak is usually soon followed by the final trill. This basic form stood throughout the 18th century. According to the many complaints registered by 18th-century writers, it seems that singers in particular sometimes extended their final cadenzas to unbearable lengths. Tosi thought that a singer should never insert more than one cadenza into an aria, and then only towards the end of the da capo section, so that the audience would know when the aria was coming to an end. J. F. Agricola, his German translator (1757), commented in a footnote that Tosi's narrow restriction was usually ignored. J. A. Hiller was apparently the only well-known German theorist to abandon the basic principle that a singer's cadenza should never last longer than he or she can hold the breath. G. B. Mancini, singing teacher at the Vienna court and an important authority on singing traditions, demanded in his treatise (1774) that a singer have the 'correct judgment' to 'escape the embarrassment occasioned by shortness of breath . . . for he might find himself . . . . unable to perfect the cadenza with a trill'. He also touched on the relationship of improvised passages to thematic material: 'This same judgment should lead the singer to choose a motif from the cantilena of the . . . aria'. The Italian attitude becomes obvious later in Mancini's treatise: 'The cadenza is necessary to every appropriate finale, and whatever the aria written by a master with art, wisdom and taste, if a cadenza be not made by the singer, the whole remains imperfect and languid'. That is valid for Haydn's and Mozart's vocal works in the Italian tradition. Relatively few original vocal cadenzas by Haydn or Mozart survive, but the insertion of cadenzas in Mozart's *opera seria* arias, wherever indicating by fermata signs, is as necessary as it is in his concerto movements.

Italian operas of the early 19th century show many fermata signs indicating improvised embellishment, but such opportunities for display became rare in German or French music, and in Meyerbeer's operas cadenzas are asked for in Italian-style arias but not those in a German or French style. Only in Verdi's earliest operas did he allow singers to improvise their own cadenzas; his mature ones contain cadenzas he wrote himself (famous examples appear in 'Caro nome', in *Rigoletto*, and 'Ah fors è lui', in *La traviata*) or none at all, though that has not prevented singers from adding them or varying existing ones.

Camerata. A group of Florentine intellectuals, musicians and music-lovers who, meeting at Count Bardi's salon in the period *c*1573–*c*1587, were concerned with restoring music to the place it occupied in ancient Greek drama; they had some influence on the beginnings of opera. (See Chapter I.)

Cantabile (It.: 'singable'). Term used to mean 'in a singing style'. It is also applied, in opera, to an ARIA in slow or moderate tempo, with a broadly phrased vocal line. Verdi used the term for 'Alla vita che t'arride', sung by Anckarstroem (Renato) in *Un ballo in maschera*. The standard two-tempo aria is often described as 'cantabile–cabaletta'.

Canto fiorito. FIORITURA.

Canzone (It.: 'song'). The Italian word for any lyric or poetic expression. The term is used in opera for items presented as songs, sung outside the dramatic action, for example Cherubino's 'Voi che sapete' in *Le nozze di Figaro* (although Mozart called it simply 'Arietta'). Verdi used it twice in *Un ballo in maschera*, for 'Di' tu se fedele', sung by Gustavus (Riccardo) and 'Saper vorreste', sung by Oscar (Edgar); also for Preziosilla's 'Al suon di tamburo' in *La forza del destino* and, most famously, for Desdemona's Willow Song in *Otello*.

Canzonetta (It.: 'little song'). A diminutive of CANZONE, it is used in the same sense as that term in opera. An example is Don Giovanni's serenade, 'Deh vieni alla finestra', which recalls the amorous associations traditional to the term.

Castrato (It.). A male singer, castrated before puberty to preserve the soprano or contralto range of his voice. During the 17th and 18th centuries 'musico' usually referred to a castrato; the near-euphemism 'evirato' ('unmanned') has also had currency.

The castrato figured in the history of opera from its beginnings: Peri's *Euridice* (1600), Monteverdi's *Orfeo* (1607) and Vitali's *Aretusa* (1620) all included eunuchs in their casts. In the papal states, where a ban on women on stage was enforced with varying rigour, castratos sang female roles. There and elsewhere they performed the heroic male roles which until well past the middle of the 18th century were nearly always for high voices: Monteverdi's Nero, Cavalli's Pompey, Handel's Julius Caesar and Gluck's Orpheus were all sopranos or contraltos. Castrato roles were most common in Italian *opera seria*, except where women were banned from the stage; there were no castrato parts in French opera.

Castratos reached the pinnacle of their popularity between 1650 and 1750. They dominated the stage during the era of Metastasian *opera seria*, when the terms 'primo uomo' and 'primo musico' invariably referred to castratos. The singers were mostly Italian, but many achieved international reputations in England, the German-speaking lands and to a lesser extent in France. They often behaved with the capriciousness of prima donnas, in many cases commanded huge salaries and had a reputation as bad actors. Well-known castratos of the 17th century included Loreto Vittori, Baldassare Ferri and Siface (G. F. Grossi); among the most famous of the 18th century were Pier Francesco Tosi, Francesco Antonio Pistocchi, Farinelli (Carlo Broschi), Senesino (Francesco Bernardi), Nicolini (Nicolo Grimaldi), Caffarelli (Gaetano Majorano), Gioacchino Conti, Guadagni, Tenducci, Rauzzini, Millico, Pacchierotti, Marchesi, Rubinelli and Crescentini. Many, including most of those for whom Handel composed, were of contralto rather than soprano range; Senesino's was *g* to *e″*, Nicolini's *a* to *f″*.

The great demand for eunuchs in opera continued until the end of the 18th century. Mozart composed the roles of Idamantes (*Idomeneo*, 1781) and Sextus (*La clemenza di Tito*, 1791) for castratos. The French presence in Italy at the turn of the 19th century interrupted the production of castratos and largely succeeded in preventing their employment. In 1806 Joseph Bonaparte banned the entry of young eunuchs into the Naples conservatories, a principal source of castratos. After the Bourbon restoration in 1815 production for the choirs of the papal states resumed, and continued until the united Italian armies ended the temporal sovereignty of the popes in 1870.

In the early 19th century castrato roles appear in a few operas by Rossini and Meyerbeer; the latter's *Il crociato in Egitto* (1824) was the last important opera with one and Giovanni Battista Velluti (1780–1861), who sang the role of Armando, the last male soprano of major fame. The last known castrato was Alessandro Moreschi (1858–1922); in 1902–3 he made recordings in which, despite the embryonic recording technique, the passionate yet curiously disembodied quality of his voice is apparent.

The best castratos had high voices of great power, agility and penetration. Quality of voice varied enormously between singers, and to the ear of the hearer.

Burney referred to an aria as being 'rolled and thundered by the powerful voice and articulate execution' of Senesino. Gerber, quoting an Italian report, characterized the voice of Marchesi as 'pure and bright as the sound of silver'. According to Raguenet, the castrato sang no less sweetly and agreeably than a woman, but his voice was stronger, livelier and lasted longer. De Brosses described the castrato sound as 'clear and penetrating as that of choirboys and a good deal louder', with 'something dry and sour about it', yet 'brilliant, light, full of impact'. Other Frenchmen, from Voltaire to Bizet, spoke of it with distaste and scorn.

Cavata (It.: 'extraction'). A passage of particular significance at the end of a recitative text that is 'extracted' from the rest of the recitative and set in a regular tempo and metre as an arioso or short aria. The term was used in opera by the second half of the 17th century. Traetta used 'cavata' in the same sense as 'cavatina'.

Cavatina (It.: diminutive of 'cavata'). In 18th-century opera a short aria, without da capo, which may occur as an independent piece or as an interpolation in a recitative. Numerous such arias, though not described as cavatinas, occur in the operas of Handel, Keiser and their contemporaries. Graun's *Montezuma* (1755) has an unusually large number of cavatinas, apparently at the prompting of Frederick the Great, who wrote the original libretto. Mozart used the term three times in *Le nozze di Figaro* (1786), for Figaro's 'Se vuol ballare', the Countess's 'Porgi amor' and Barbarina's 'L'ho perduto'. The tradition was maintained in the 19th century by Weber, e.g. 'Glöcklein im Thale' in *Euryanthe* (1823), and by French composers, e.g. 'Salut! demeure chaste et pure' in Gounod's *Faust* (1859) and the Duke's 'Comme un rayon charmant' in Bizet's *La jolie fille de Perth* (1867). In 19th-century Italian opera, however, the name was given to an entrance aria, but could also serve for an elaborate aria demanding considerable virtuosity, e.g. Rosina's 'Una voce poco fà' in Rossini's *Il barbiere di Siviglia* (1816) and Lady Macbeth's 'Vieni! t'affretta' in Verdi's *Macbeth* (1847, rev. 1865). Such cavatinas often concluded with a CABALETTA.

Chaconne (Fr.; It. *ciaccona*). A Baroque dance in triple metre and moderate tempo which incorporated an element of continuous variation, usually involving a ground bass. It came into use in French ballet and opera, particularly as the final dance of a group (or of the entire work) in the late 17th century. Lully included short examples in the *Ballet d'Alcidiane* (1658) and the *comédie-ballet Pastorale comique* (1667). Longer chaconnes appeared in the 1680s, in works by Lully, Colasse and Lalande, in operas by Destouches (*Omphale*, 1701; *Les élémens*, written with Lalande, 1721), Campra (*Les fêtes vénitiennes*, 1710) and their contemporaries. These works are sectionalized by contrasting large groups of phrases by mode (usually major–tonic minor–major), or by instrumentation, with woodwind trios alternating with full orchestra (see Lully's *Roland*, 1685), or by choral sections (Lully's *Cadmus*, 1673, and *Amadis*, 1684). Rameau used the form in many operas, as did Grétry. Chaconnes continue to appear in French-influenced operas into the late 18th century (Gluck's *Orfeo ed Euridice*, 1762; Mozart's *Idomeneo*, 1781); in later examples the ground bass element becomes increasingly vestigial.

Chiamata (It.: 'call'). A 17th-century Italian term designating a military trumpet fanfare. Exampes are occasionally found in early 17th-century Italian operas, such as the five-part instrumental 'Chiamata alla caccia' from the first act of Cavalli's *Le nozze di Teti e di Peleo* (1639), a piece similar in style to the opening toccata of Monteverdi's *Orfeo* (1607).

Chorus (It. *coro*). As the creation of opera was partly motivated by a concern to re-create the musical practices of antiquity, the chorus was assigned an important part in early opera. The restoration of supposed Greek practices meant that the chorus was not merely decorative in its role, as it had been in the *intermedi*, but involved in the action as interlocutor and commentator. Choral passages do not appear frequently, and they are usually brief and simple, in Florentine operas, but in Monteverdi's early operas and those of Roman composers they assume greater significance. But with the rise of Venetian opera, in public theatres, the role of the chorus began to fade: partly because interest in reviving the music of the ancients had diminished, partly because the chorus's role in delineating musical structure had lessened with the development of other structural factors, and partly because public opera houses, run for profit, preferred not to have to pay for choral singers. The chorus virtually disappeared from Italian opera after *c*1640 except in special festal productions paid for by a munificent patron (usually at German or Austrian courts). In France, however, the chorus had an important role in Lully's *tragédies lyriques*, particularly in the divertissements, which were also a part of the various kindred French stage forms of the early 18th century. In the operas of Rameau the chorus often has a central role. It is also important in English theatrical music of the late 17th century, Purcell's in particular.

The chorus required for Marco da Gagliano's *Dafne* (1608) is specified as of 'no more than 16 or 18 singers'. This number seems to have been a rough norm, but later choruses were usually sung one to a part, except for lavish productions; the final 'coro' in the operas of Handel, for example, was to be sung by the assembled principals (including those 'killed' in the stage action). In France, the chorus was larger: Cambert's *Pomone* had a chorus of 15, but by 1713 the Opéra had a chorus of 34 (12 of them women), who could be reinforced by the principals, and by 1754 the figure was 38 (17 of them women).

With the late 18th century the chorus achieved its modern status in opera: a group, of a size appropriate to the theatre, that could play whatever role is required, and may also serve to provide commentary. Few operas dispense with a chorus; notable examples are the first three evenings of Wagner's *Ring*.

Coloratura (It.: 'colouring'). Florid figuration or ornamentation, particularly in vocal music. The term follows German usage, *Koloratur*, which is applied to all kinds of ornamentation; in English it is more often reserved to high-pitched florid writing, exemplified by such roles as the Queen of Night in Mozart's *Die Zauberflöte*, Violetta in Verdi's *La traviata* (especially the cabaletta 'Sempre libera') or Zerbinetta in Strauss's *Ariadne auf Naxos*, as well as many roles by Rossini and other early 19th-century Italian composers. The term 'coloratura soprano' signifies a singer of high pitch, lightness and agility, appropriate to such roles.

Comédie-ballet. A French musico-dramatic form of the late 17th century, devised by Molière and Lully, in which each ballet ENTRÉE is related to the main play, to 'make comedy and ballet one'. Their collaboration in this type of endeavour began in 1664 with *Le mariage forcé* and ended in 1670 with *Le bourgeois gentilhomme*; dramatist and composer were considered of equal importance. Molière saw music and dance as complementary to the comedy's main action; through *intermèdes* he introduced sub-plots that emphasized, mirrored or contrasted with the principal intrigue. This concept, first used as a dramatic principle in *La princesse d'Elide* (1664), was refined in *Le sicilien* (1667). Later, musical features tended to dominate and the link with dramatic action was compromised; *Le bourgeois gentilhomme* was even described as a 'ballet composed of six entrées accompanied by comedy' (*Gazette de Paris*, 1670). The antagonism between Molière and Lully, which ended their collaboration on *comédies-ballets*, began with the oppressive patents obtained by Lully from the king; Molière then worked briefly with Marc-Antoine Charpentier. The *comédie-ballet*, though sacrificed to Lully's ambition, was important in the development of the French lyric theatre. It is a compendium of musical forms and practices later adopted by Lully in his *tragédies lyriques*, and Quinault's poetry of his *livrets* for Lully was influenced by Molière's verses in the *comédies-ballets*; its basic format was taken over later by the *opéra comique*.

Comédie mêlée d'ariettes (Fr.: 'comedy mixed with little songs'). Term used in the 18th century for a type of opera that arose in France in the 1760s and 70s, with spoken dialogue and songs. As 'comédie' could mean 'play', it often designated more serious subjects. The generic term is Opéra comique. (See Chapter IX.)

Comédie lyrique. (Fr.). Term used for a French 18th-century theatre work, of the *opéra-ballet* type, in which the plot is continuous. (See Chapter IX.2.)

Comic opera. A term for a musico-dramatic work of a light or amusing nature. It does not have any precise historical meaning; it may, for example, be applied equally to an Italian *opera buffa*, a French *opéra comique* (though many *opéras comiques* are serious or tragic works), a German Singspiel, a Spanish zarzuela or an English opera of a light character. It is also often applied to operetta or *opéra bouffe* and even applied to musical comedy. Most comic operas have spoken dialogue rather than continuous music.

Commedia dell'arte (It.). A comic stage presentation characterized by the use of masks (or fixed parts), earthy buffoonery and improvisation. It developed in Italy in the first half of the 16th century, declined after about 1750 and was influential in the development of comic opera. Its stock characters (Harlequin, Scaramouche etc), or characters developed from them, have often been introduced into musical comedies such as Pergolesi's *La serva padrona*, Mozart's *Le nozze di Figaro*, Busoni's *Arlecchino* and Strauss's *Ariadne auf Naxos*.

Commedia per musica (It.: 'comedy through music'). A term used for comic opera, particularly in Naples, in the 18th century. Sometimes the form 'commedia in musica' was used. It seems to have indicated no nuance of genre as compared with 'opera buffa' or 'dramma giocoso'.

Comparse (It.). Supernumeraries, extras (who do not sing).

Componimento dramatico (It.: 'dramatic composition'). Term used for an operatic genre of the high Baroque period, cultivated mainly in Vienna. *See* Festa teatrale.

Comprimario (It.: 'with the principal'). Term used for the singer of secondary or minor roles in an opera.

Contralto (It.). A voice normally written for within the range g to e'', which may be extended at either end, particularly in solo writing. In modern English the term denotes the lowest female voice, but when the term was first used it would have denoted a male Falsetto singer, and later a Castrato.

In the 17th century, as castratos became more numerous in Italy, authors sometimes used 'contralto' for castratos as opposed to 'alti naturali' (falsettists); Burney, however, used 'contralto' for both castratos and women. In later English usage, 'contralto' came to refer always to a woman as distinct from a male alto (boy or falsettist).

In opera, true contralto (as distinct from mezzo-soprano) roles are exceptional. They occur in the 17th century for old women, almost invariably comic. In Cesti's *Orontea* (1649), for example, the contralto Aristea (range *e* to *g'*) is a crone who makes advances to a young man (in fact a woman in disguise). This stock use of the contralto became so popular that in A. Scarlatti's *Marco Attilio Regolo* (1719) the maid Eurilla (range *b* to *c"*) engages in burlesque pursuit of the servant Leonizio (a bass) in no fewer than five scenes.

In the 18th century composers came to appreciate the deep female voice for dramatic purposes. In Handel's operas several contralto roles stand in dramatic contrast to the prima donna, for example Cornelia, in *Giulio Cesare* (1724), a more mature woman than Cleopatra and a figure of tragic dignity. In *Rinaldo* (1711) the hero abandons the soprano Almirena for the enchantress Armida, also a soprano; in the 1731 revision Handel rewrote the part of Armida for contralto, emphasizing her supernatural, seductive character. Both roles were among those Handel composed for Antonia Merighi. Rossini's important contralto (or mezzo) roles include Cinderella in *La Cenerentola*, Rosina in *Il barbiere di Siviglia* (original version), both written for Geltrude Righetti (1793–1862), and the heroic part of Arsaces in *Semiramide*. Associated with Rossini's operas until about 1820 was the 'prima donna contralto' Marietta Marcolini, for whom he wrote several parts, including that of Isabella in *L'italiana in Algeri*. In later opera, contraltos were repeatedly cast as a sorceress-like figure (Azucena, Arvidson/Ulrica, Ortrud) or an oracle (Erda) and sometimes as an old woman (Mamma Lucia, La Cieca) or a trollop (Maddalena).

Coro (It.). CHORUS.

Countertenor. The English term for a male alto singer, normally a falsettist. It remains a matter of dispute whether the male alto and countertenor voices can be distinguished (the first as produced by a bass or baritone singing falsetto, the second as a natural voice with abnormally high tessitura). The voice has been only very rarely used in opera; the most important role is that of Oberon in Britten's *A Midsummer Night's Dream* (1960), written for Alfred Deller (1912–79).

Curtain tune. English 17th-century term for music played while the curtain was being raised at the beginning of a play or opera, usually after the prologue. It was increasingly cast in the form of a FRENCH OVERTURE. On occasion dramatists made the introductory music part of the opening scene; in the operatic *The Tempest* (1674), Locke's curtain tune depicts the storm with which the drama opens.

Da capo (It.: 'from the head'). An instruction (usually abbreviated D.C.) to return to the head of a piece of music and repeat the first section ('fine', end, or a pause sign indicates where to stop). The 'da capo aria' was the standard aria form of the late Baroque and early Classical periods, especially in *opera seria*; it was generally understood that the repeated section would be ornamented by the singer. When, around the middle of the 18th century, arias became very long, it was superseded by the 'dal segno aria' ('from the sign'), in which a sign part-way through the aria indicates the point at which the recapitulation should begin. The da capo aria, because it involved the repetition of music already heard, and invited indulgence on the singer's part, was seen as an obstacle to natural dramatic progress by operatic reformers of the time.

Dal segno (It.: 'from the sign'). *See* DA CAPO.

Dance. *See* BALLET.

Deus ex machina (Lat.: 'god from a machine'). Term for a dramatic device much used in Baroque opera, and often parodied, whereby a god (or a king or some other powerful being) arrives magically – or, at least figuratively, from a stage machine – and saves the situation, usually by an act of divine mercy in the light of the moral goodness of the person who is saved. Late examples are the appearance of Amor to restore Eurydice to Orpheus in Gluck's opera (1762) and that of the voice of Neptune to stay Idomeneus's hand as he is about to sacrifice his son Idamantes in Mozart's *Idomeneo* (1781); the parallel between the arrival of the Minister of State to free Florestan in Beethoven's *Fidelio* (1805) and these demonstrates a link between the early 19th-century 'rescue opera' and its predecessors.

Divertissement (Fr.). Term used since the 17th century, partly as an equivalent of the Italian 'divertimento' but also in wider senses for music, usually with spectacle, intended for entertainment or diversion. Two categories may be distinguished. The more important consists of a group of vocal solos, ensembles and dances within a larger stage work and often ancillary to the main action. Such are the divertissements found in pastorales, *tragédies lyriques*, *opéra-ballets*, productions of the Théâtres de la Foire, parodies and *opéras comiques* (in spoken drama, where they were sometimes called 'intermèdes', they were more closely related to the action, for example those by Lully and Charpentier for Molière's *comédies-ballets* and those by Lalande, Rameau and others for plays or by Campra, Clérambault and others for the Latin tragedies performed at the Jesuit College). Many divertissements of the Lully-Quinault *tragédies lyriques* show skilful liaison between dance and dramatic action. In the divertissement of Act 2 of *Roland*, for example, the bucolic levity of a village wedding offers contrast to the mounting anger of the distraught hero. In some of Rameau's operas the divertissement is fully integrated into the action, for example when, in Act 3 of *Hippolyte et Aricie* (1733), Theseus is welcomed with song and dance on his return to his kingdom. A different category includes the self-contained musical entertainments, usually on a pastoral or allegorical theme, in single or multiple acts, such as Campra's *Venus, feste galante* (1698), a divertissement in a prologue and one act. At the height of the *grand siècle*, this type marked such events as victories and royal births. Also in this category are the *grands divertissements* ordered by Louis XIV in 1664 and 1674, spectacles mounted at great expense and often lasting for days or even weeks.

Drame lyrique (Fr.: 'lyric drama'). A term used to distinguish a genre of late 19th- and early 20th-century French opera that is seen as having grown out of the more serious sort of *opéra comique*, though often with little or no spoken dialogue. Epitomized by many of the operas of Massenet, it encompassed a wide variety of subject matter from the contemporary to the historical. It was more intimate in scope and dramatic treatment than grand opera, and richer in musical style than the simpler and lighter *opéra comique*. The term was not widely used on librettos: of Massenet's operas only *Werther* is called a *drame lyrique*, but others have similar designations, such as *pièce lyrique*, *épisode lyrique*, *conte lyrique*, *comédie lyrique*, *drame musical* or *drame passionel* which reflect a closeness to the spoken drama and to other literary genres (Charpentier's *Louise* is called a *roman musical*).

Dramma eroicomico. (It.: 'heroic-comic drama'). Term used in the late 18th century for a comic opera with heroic elements (e.g. Haydn's *Orlando paladino*, 1782), akin to the *dramma giocoso* and a precursor of the OPERA SEMISERIA.

Dramma giocoso (It.: 'jocular drama'). A term used on Italian librettos in the second half of the 18th century to designate a particular type of comic opera. It was used, from 1748 onwards, by Carlo Goldoni for librettos in which character-types from serious opera ('parti serie') appeared alongside the standard peasants and servants of comic opera ('parti buffe'), sometimes with intermediate characters ('in mezzo carattere'). Notable early examples are *Il filosofo di campagna* (set by Galuppi in 1754) and *La buona figliuola* (1756, set by Piccinni in 1760); three further Goldoni *dramma giocoso* texts, *Il mondo della luna*, *Le pescatrici* and *Lo speziale*, were set by Haydn. The most famous example is Mozart's *Don Giovanni*, to a libretto by Da Ponte based on an earlier *dramma giocoso* by Giovanni Bertati. (See Chapter VII.)

Dramma [drama] **per musica** [dramma musicale] (It.: 'play for music'). A phrase found on the title-page of many Italian librettos; it refers to a text expressly written to be set by a composer. By some later writers, *dramma per musica* has been misinterpreted as 'drama *through* music' and applied to musico-dramatic effects.

Duet (It. *duetto*). An ENSEMBLE for two singers. It was used in opera almost from the outset. Monteverdi's *Orfeo* and *L'incoronazione di Poppea* both have them as concluding vocal items, the latter, a love duet for Poppaea and Nero, being the earliest significant example of a genre that persisted until the duet became merged in the general continuity of the music (Verdi, Puccini etc) or dissolved into a musical dialogue in which the voices no longer sang simultaneously (later Wagner, R. Strauss etc). Before that, in works of Bellini and others, the love duet had become characterized by a good deal of singing in 3rds or 6ths, acquiring a mellifluous quality of sound appropriate to shared emotion, in place of independent treatment of the voices. 'Fra gli amplessi' in Mozart's *Così fan tutte* provides an example of vocal textures changing to symbolize the flux of emotion. In some late Baroque *opere serie*, notably Handel's, duets appear mainly at act ends or when the principal lovers are united (or parted).

The diminutive *duettino* is sometimes used for a short duet of concise form. Mozart so described 'Via resti servita' in *Le nozze di Figaro* and 'Là ci darem' in *Don Giovanni*, though neither is particularly short.

Duodrama. A MELODRAMA (i.e. a work with spoken text and musical accompaniment) in which two principal characters are involved; an example is Georg Benda's *Ariadne auf Naxos* (1775).

Ensemble. In opera, the German 'das Ensemble' means the singing personnel of an opera house; the term is more often used, however, in the sense of the French 'morceau d'ensemble', a piece sung by more than one member of the cast. The most common kind of ensemble is the duet, which is used in opera of virtually all periods, especially for pairs of lovers when they are united, reconciled, forced to part, or placed in some other situation that gives natural rise to strong emotional expression. Larger ensembles are similarly used, as points at which several characters can give lyrical vent to their feelings – which may all be quite different – in reaction to the dramatic situation. Ensembles have long been traditional at the end of an opera, where the characters react to the outcome, or, at the end of an act, to some dramatic crux (as is usual at such a point, especially in comic opera). In some serious operas, the final ensemble is marked 'Coro' ('chorus') but sung by the assembled principals. In the ensemble act finales of 18th- and 19th-century comic operas, the plot is often carried forward, with the gradual assembly of characters on the stage, a series of clearly demarcated musical sections, and a general increase in both pace and confusion. A significant feature of operatic ensembles is the capacity of music to convey several different emotions, simultaneously expressed; usually the musical texture assigned to the various characters will differ according to the sense they are expressing, but there are examples of the powerful expression of distinct emotions to the same music, a notable one being the quartet 'Mir ist so wunderbar' in Beethoven's *Fidelio*, where to the same music, sung in canon, one person expresses love, another alarm at the developing situation, a third jealousy and a fourth benignity. In this case, as in others, the effect is as if the action momentarily halts – like a still in a moving film – while we are allowed to peer into the emotions of the characters.

See also CHORUS, DUET, QUARTET, QUINTET, SEPTET, SEXTET and TERZET.

Entr'acte (Fr.). A term for music or other events written for performance between the acts of a play or opera, like the earlier 'act music', 'act tune', 'first music' etc. It may refer to the *intermedi* performed between the acts of spoken comedies in the 16th century, to the *comédie-ballets* of Lully, or to the instrumental interludes between the acts of Bizet's *Carmen* or Debussy's *Pelléas et Mélisande*.

Entrée (Fr.). In the 17th-century French *ballet de cour*, a group of dances unified by subject. Entrées divided the acts of a ballet into scenes. The unifying plot of earlier *ballets de cour* gave way increasingly after 1620 to a varied choreographic spectacle in which each section, composed of several entrées, had its own subject matter. This genre, now known as the *ballet à entrées*, was the structural model for the late 17th- and 18th-century *opéra-ballet*, whose acts were normally called entrées.

'Entrée' had another meaning in the *opéra-ballet*: there, and in the *tragédie lyrique*, an 'entrée' marked the beginning of the divertissement of dances and songs found in most acts. It was an instrumental, march-like composition, an *air de danse* to which the 'corps d'entrée' entered.

Entremés (Sp.). A form of short Spanish scenic entertainment, usually comic, which flourished in the 17th century and was performed between the acts of a larger, more serious theatrical work. It was popular in character and commonly called for instrumentally accompanied songs and dances. Its traditional place was after the first act, though at other points similar forms were introduced – a *jácara* (picaresque interlude) or *baile* (dance scene with poetry and music) after the second and a *mojiganga* (burlesque) at the end.

Extravaganza. Term applied since the late 18th century to musical and dramatic works of a fantastic character. In England, theatrical entertainments similar to the 18th-century BURLESQUE, with exotic and fanciful plots often based on fairy-tales or myths and deriving their humour from exaggeration, became popular early in the 19th century; they were performed mainly to audiences of children. The success of Moncrieff's *Tom and Jerry, or, Life in London* (1821) was followed by 'a new, pedestrian, equestrian extravaganza and operatic burletta' of the same name by Pierce Egan (1822). These and their sequels contained many popular airs. A 'Chinese Extravaganza' by Hale and Talfourd called *The Mandarin's Daughter* (1851) was one of many exotic extravaganzas and may well have influenced Gilbert and Sullivan in works like *The Mikado*. Gilbert used the term more than once as a subtitle, e.g. *Trial by Jury: an Extravaganza*.

Falcon. A type of soprano voice, named after Cornélie Falcon (1814–97, but retired 1840), of strong dramatic character, particularly suited to the French grand opera repertory (Meyerbeer, Halévy).

Falsetto (It.; Fr. *fausset*; Ger. *Falsett, Fistelstimme*). The treble range produced by most adult male singers through a slightly artificial technique whereby the vocal cords vibrate in a length shorter than usual. It is modest in carrying power and rarely used in opera. *See also* COUNTERTENOR.

Farsa (It.: 'farce'). Term used in 18th-century Italy for works performed as intermezzos or, possibly, afterpieces to spoken comedies. Most early *farse* were in two parts, but some were in three acts. *Farsette* were being given at the Teatro delle Valle in Rome by the 1740s. In Venice a 'farsa ad uso francese', performed in 1768 by comedians without masks, consisted of spoken dialogue interspersed with arias. Similar pieces appeared in Venice regularly for several years; 'intermezzo' seems to have been used interchangeably with *farsa* for such works, still performed 'dopo la comedia', in the late 1770s and early 1780s. Existing *opere buffe* were also sometimes used in that context. In the same period a one-act *farsa* also sometimes formed the third act of an *opera buffa*. From the late 1780s *farsa* or *farsetta* was applied to works usually of one act or sometimes two, occasionally still with spoken prose dialogue. These seem to have been lighter and broader comedy than *opera buffa*, although short operas of a *semiseria* character were also sometimes given this designation. The *farsa* had a vogue in the 1790s which lasted into the 19th century. Two one-act *farse* were often performed together, sometimes separated by a ballet.

Favola in musica (It.: 'tale [told] in music'). The phrase, found on the title-pages of 17th-century scores and librettos, was perhaps intended to throw the composer's contribution into prominence as distinct from *favola per musica*, or a 'tale [written] for music'. The first is generally followed by the composer's name (e.g. *L'Orfeo: favola in musica da Claudio Monteverdi*), the other by the librettist's (e.g. Cavalli's *L'Ormindo: favola regia per musica. Di Giovanni Faustini*).

Festa teatrale (It.: 'theatrical festival'). A serenata-type genre of the high Baroque period, cultivated especially in Vienna. It was distinguished from the *dramma per musica* (as most operas were then called) in that the subject matter of the libretto was typically allegorical and the production was usually part of a celebration of an important marriage, birthday, name day or similar event at court. Similar but less common terms were *azione teatrale* and *componimento drammatico*. The first notable *festa teatrale* was Francesco Sbarra's sumptuous *Il pomo d'oro* (with music by Cesti), performed as part of Leopold I's wedding celebrations in 1668. During the next hundred years poets such as Nicolò Minato, Pietro Pariati, Apostolo Zeno and Giovanni Pasquini wrote many Viennese librettos in this genre, set to music by leading local composers, including Draghi, Fux, Caldara and J. A. Hasse. Although these musical *feste* were usually lavish, the more modest *festa di camera* became fashionable towards the middle of the 18th century as the *festa teatrale* went into decline. The last important poet of such works was Pietro Metastasio; about the time he ceased writing for the theatre (c1767) the *festa teatrale* virtually disappeared.

Finale (It.; Eng. and Ger. by usage; Fr. *final*). The concluding, continuously composed, section of an act of an opera. The ENSEMBLE finale developed, at the beginning of the second half of the 18th century, largely through the dramaturgical changes wrought in comic opera by Carlo Goldoni (1707–93), who in his librettos (especially for Galuppi) made act finales longer, bringing in more singers and increasing the density of the plot (see Chapter VII and especially XII, p.170). His developments represent an essential step from the late Baroque number opera to the continuous style of 19th-century post-Wagnerian music drama.

Fioritura [canto fiorito] (It.: 'flourish'). Embellishment of a melodic line, either improvised by a performer or written out by the composer. The use of words meaning 'flower' or 'florid' to refer to the process of ornamenting melodies has long been common in most European languages. Jerome of Moravia (13th century) listed melodic ornaments as 'flos harmonicus'. While 'fioritura' as a musical term would be understood by any Italian, it is (like 'coloratura') notably absent from Italian treatises, where ornamentation is elucidated with more precise terminology ('trillo', 'mordente', 'passaggi' etc).

Fredon (Fr). *See* TIMBRE.

French overture. A festive musical introduction for an opera or other work. The form combines a slow opening, marked by stately dotted rhythms and suspensions, with a lively fugal second section; one or more dances may follow. It originated with Lully's ballet overtures of the 1650s and quickly became the sole pattern for French opera and ballet overtures. It was much copied, borrowed and adapted, by composers of all nationalities, including Cesti, G. Bononcini, Handel, Keiser, Purcell and Boyce. In the mid-18th century it gave way to more flexible, energetic or dramatic approaches, particularly the rival Italian sinfonia, but vestiges of it are found up to the end of the 18th century (for example in Mozart's *La clemenza di Tito*, 1791). *See* OVERTURE.

Gebet (Ger.: 'prayer'). *See* PREGHIERA.

Gesamtkunstwerk (Ger.: 'total art work'). Term used by Wagner for his music dramas, in which all the arts (music, poetry, movement, design etc) should combine to the same artistic end. The concept was not original to Wagner, but the term was.

Grand opera. A term used particularly in French opera to signify both the Paris Opéra and the operas performed there. Later it tended to be applied more narrowly to the specially monumental works performed at the Opéra during its period of greatest magnificence, including Rossini's *Guillaume Tell* (1829) and several operas composed to librettos of Eugène Scribe by Meyerbeer and others during the 1830s (including *Les Huguenots*, 1836). The term may also be applied to operas by Donizetti, Gounod, Verdi and Massenet, and to non-French operas in a similar manner, including Wagner's *Rienzi* (1842). (See Chapter XV.)

Handlung für Musik (Ger.: 'action in music'). Term used by Wagner in the libretto for *Lohengrin*.

Haute-contre (Fr.). A high tenor or countertenor voice, cultivated in France until about the end of the 18th century. The *haute-contre* was the voice to which most of the important male roles in the operas of Lully and Rameau were entrusted. Among the finest *haute-contre* singers was Pierre de Jélyotte, who took the lead in most of Rameau's operas. The *haute-contre* normally sang in a natural voice, but occasionally used falsetto at the top of the range. As late as 1820 Castil-Blaze (*De l'opéra en France*) listed the *haute-contre* in his table of voices with the normal range *e* to *c″* (though extending as low as *c*), but by this time the elegant *haute-contre* voice was being displaced by the more robust variety of tenor represented by Adolphe Nourrit (1802–39).

Heldentenor (Ger.: 'heroic tenor'). A robust tenor voice of clarion timbre and unusual endurance, particularly suited to Wagner's heroic roles (Tannhäuser, Tristan, Siegmund, Siegfried); it was an extreme manifestation of the new dramatic tenor that appeared in the 1830s and 1840s. The term has become standard in the Wagner literature though not used by the composer himself. He did, however, reveal strong convictions as to the sort of tenor he considered appropriate for some of his roles, particularly in his essay in praise of Ludwig Schnorr von Carolsfeld

(*Prose Works*; Eng. trans., 1894, iv, 225ff) and in his commentary on performing *Tannhäuser* (ibid, iii, 167–205), where he complained that the singing and acting of most tenors was 'unmanly, soft, and completely lacking in energy'.

Hoher Bass (Ger.). BASS-BARITONE.

Interlude (Fr. *intermède*; Ger. *Zwischenspiel*; It. *intermedio*, *intermezzo*). Term for something played or sung between the main parts of a work or event. In theatrical performances they include instrumental items between the acts (*see* ACT TUNE, ENTR'ACTE, ZWISCHENSPIEL) or, on a more elaborate scale, entertainments such as the INTERMEDIO or INTERMEZZO. Some operas, such as Debussy's *Pelléas et Mélisande* and Berg's *Wozzeck*, include interludes that are dramatically related, indeed essential, to the whole. The two interludes of Britten's *The Rape of Lucretia* respectively tell of Tarquinius's ride to Rome and comment on the rape itself (episodes that cannot easily be represented on the stage); the six orchestral interludes that punctuate the action of his *Peter Grimes* either prepare for the music of the next scene or continue the development of material from the previous one.

Intermède [intermédie, intramède, entremets] (Fr.). 'Music and dance inserted between the acts of a larger production at the Opera and sometimes at the Comedy to amuse and relax the minds of the spectators' (J.-J. Rousseau, *Dictionnaire de musique*, 1768). The history of the *intermède* in France is complex, and the latitude over what constituted an *intermède* was wide. The earliest examples date from the 16th century. In the late 17th century, elaborate *intermèdes* were placed between the five acts of Latin tragedies, some of them closely aligned with the action they supplemented; some were extended compositions in their own right. From 1684 the concept of the *intermède* could embrace an entire opera, comparable with those of Lully and Quinault, then drawing crowds to the Académie Royale de Musique; a notable example is *David et Jonathas* by Charpentier (1688). Earlier, the French *intermèdes* performed between the acts of Mazarin's ill-fated Italian opera importations proved more popular than the operas themselves. The title-page of Caproli's *Le nozze di Peleo e di Theti* (1654) states that the opera was 'intermingled with a Ballet on the same subject'. In Cavalli's *Serse*, the six entrées of ballet by Lully written as *intermèdes* have nothing to do with the subject of the opera. The full range of possibilities inherent in French *intermèdes* may be seen in those by Lully (and later by Charpentier) for 14 of Molière's comedies.

Intermedio [intromessa, introdutto, tramessa, tramezzo, intermezzo] (It.). A form of musico-dramatic entertainment inserted between the acts of plays in the Renaissance. It could involve songs, madrigals, dance, spoken drama, instrumental music and lavish spectacle. The genre did not disappear after the birth of opera but became interwoven with it. *Intermedio* traditions furnished many of the themes and conventions of early opera: Rinuccini's libretto for *Dafne* is an expansion of an *intermedio* given in Florence in 1589, while Monteverdi's *Orfeo* (1607) draws heavily on the *intermedio* tradition in its scene changes, its use of instruments and its danced choruses and final *moresca*.

Operas, like spoken plays, were felt to need their own *intermedi* for contrast. Both genres continued to have *intermedi* written for them occasionally. Caccini's *Il rapimento di Cefalo* (1600, Florence) had *intermedi* devised by Giovanni de' Medici requiring 100 musicians and 1000 men to work the machines. Dances by courtiers could also serve as *intermedi*, as for Marco da Gagliano's opera *La Flora* (1628, Florence). Stefano Landi's *Il Sant'Alessio* (1631 or 1632, Rome) is one of the few printed scores with an *intermedio*, added after Act 1, to introduce dancing for the sake of diversity. Another Roman opera, *Chi soffre speri* (1639), by Virgilio Mazzocchi and Marco Marazzoli, has an *intermedio* after Act 2 using chorus and ballet, 'Alla fiera' ('At the fair'), for which Marazzoli wrote the music. In the latter half of the century, most Italian *intermedi* were composed for the public theatres, for the revivals of Venetian operas at the Teatro Tordinona, Rome, in the 1670s, Stradella composed *intermedi* for operas by Cavalli, Cesti, Sartorio and others. His insertions show the persistence of the mythological divertissement in the *intermedio* tradition, and perhaps a Roman fondness for pomp and splendour.

See also INTERMÈDE.

Intermezzo. Term used during the 18th century (generally in its plural form 'intermezzi') for comic interludes sung between the acts or scenes of an *opera seria*. (See Chapter VII.2)

Introduzione e cavatina (It.). A typical unit in a Rossinian opera, usually comprising a choral number followed by a two-tempo aria. (See Chapter XII.)

Italian overture. Term for the type of OVERTURE favoured in Italian operas from the 1680s and used into the second half of the 18th century. It is in three movements, fast–slow–fast (the last usually in dance rhythm), usually played without a break, and scored for strings, generally with pairs of oboes and horns (and occasionally a trumpet). It is usually thought to have originated with A. Scarlatti, in particular his overture (or *sinfonia avanti l'opera*) to *Tutto il mal non vien per nuocere* (1681, Rome; rev. as *Dal male il bene*, 1687, Naples). Such overtures were often detached from operas and used as concert pieces; they played an important role in the development of the symphony.

Largo concertato (It.). See PEZZO CONCERTATO.

Lehrstück (Ger.: 'teaching piece'). A 20th-century neologism associated with the work of Bertolt Brecht (who probably invented it); he used it for a theatrical genre for amateurs whose function was to teach the participants (through performance and discussion) rather than to engage the attention of an audience. Written when the Nazis were gaining power in Germany, Brecht's *Lehrstücke* attempt to teach political attitudes, often Marxist. Music plays an important part, and a dominant one in the *Lehrstücke* by Weill, Hindemith and Eisler, whose settings enlarged the boundaries of music theatre by integrating techniques from conventional opera and theatre with elements from oratorio, revue, dance and film.

Leitmotif (Ger. *Leitmotiv*: 'leading motif'). A theme, or other musical idea, that represents or symbolizes a person, object, place, idea, state of mind, supernatural force or some other ingredient in a dramatic work. It may recur unaltered, or it may be changed in rhythm, intervallic structure, tempo, harmony, orchestration or accompaniment, and may be combined with other leitmotifs. The concept is particularly associated with Wagner, but the term was invented by F. W. Jähns in his study of Weber. The allusive use of musical phrases is found in Baroque opera; a later example is Blondel's song in Grétry's *Richard Coeur-de-lion* (1784), where a character is recognized by a repetition of music he sang earlier; other composers went beyond this kind of 'reminiscence motif' (*Reminiszenzmotiv* or *Erinnerungsmotiv*) including Dalayrac, Catel and Méhul, in whose *Euphrosine* (1790) a motif stands not only for jealousy but also for its action and its object; Mozart (*Idomeneo*, 1781; *Don Giovanni*, 1787) also used motifs with consistent expressive reference, as did Lemoyne (*Electre*, 1782). Weber pursued this in *Der Freischütz* (1821) and especially *Euryanthe* (1823), where a theme takes different guises governed by dramatic factors.

Wagner took this further, using it in his mature works as the principal way of articulating the drama through the music. Characters, concepts, objects etc are associated with their own motifs. These not only serve to guide the listener in his understanding of the work (even of ideas unclear to the characters on the stage – for example where Sieglinde, in *Die Walküre*, tells of the stranger at her wedding feast: the orchestra identifies him for us) but also embody the dramatic development of what they symbolize. The perfect 4ths for Fafner in *Das Rheingold* become sinister augmented 4ths when, in *Siegfried*, he takes the form of a dragon; the carefree horn call of the young Siegfried becomes slower and more imposing, with its enriched harmony, as he becomes more mature. Note-patterns in common between different motifs may establish or suggest dramatic links. Most important, the symphonic development of motifs runs parallel to the dramatic developments, binding the music closely to the drama and giving it a coherence that is dramatically functional.

Leitmotif was taken up, after Wagner, by his disciples, such as Cornelius and Humperdinck, and by others, including Strauss, Debussy, Fauré and Janáček, some of them also being influenced by the slightly different technique of Lisztian thematic metamorphosis.

Libretto (It.: 'small book'; Fr. *livret*; Ger. *Textbuch*). A printed book containing the words of an opera or other extended work; by extension, the text itself. The earliest librettos, printed at the expense of the patron for whose entertainment the works were written, were mostly a little over 20 cm in height; when opera became a public spectacle the height was reduced to about 14 cm. In size and typographic style they have varied considerably. Most, produced for immediate performance rather than for posterity, use inferior paper and, produced in haste, abound in misprints. In the 17th and 18th centuries librettos were often read during performances, and contemporary annotations may often be of value and interest. When an opera was given in a language other than that of the audience, librettos were bilingual, with parallel texts on opposite pages. The sale of librettos was often a perquisite of the poet, and the poets regarded their texts as literary works in their own right. Passages not set to music or discarded before performance were often included and in Italy were distinguished by double commas (*versi virgolati*). Librettos may provide much valuable information for historians unavailable from other sources: stage directions, spoken texts, lists of characters, background to the plot (*argomento*), indications as to what versions were performed on what occasions etc. After about 1800 they ceased to be regularly produced, partly because theatres were often dimmed once gas (and later electric) light became available, and partly because works tended increasingly to have standard versions and were more often published.

Licenza (It.: 'licence'). In an opera, an epilogue inserted in honour of a patron's birthday or wedding, or for some other festive occasion. This usually consisted of recitatives and arias but choruses were sometimes included. It could be an integral part of the main work (as in Fux's *Costanza e fortezza*, 1723) or could be written later by a different composer and librettist; in 1667 the Emperor Leopold I composed his own *licenza* for the Viennese performances of Cesti's *Le disgrazie d'amore*. The term may also refer to a cadenza added at the performer's licence.

Lieto fine (It.: 'happy ending'). Term for the normal, almost obligatory happy ending found in virtually all serious operas of the late Baroque and the Classical periods (especially those to texts by Metastasio). Often it involved the appearance of a DEUS EX MACHINA. It was an integral part of the philosophy behind *opera seria* that it should end happily and reassure the audience that good behaviour and proper morality met their due rewards, thus reinforcing confidence in the accepted social and religious systems of the time.

Lirico spinto. *See* SPINTO.

Martin. The 'baryton Martin', named after Jean-Blaise Martin (1768–1837), is a high-lying BARITONE voice, passing easily into falsetto.

Mascherata (It.: 'masked', 'masquerade'). A type of Renaissance entertainment, popular in Florence, involving pantomimed action of a mythical or allegorical kind with music performed from floats; it is related to the INTERMEDIO and resembles the MASQUE.

Maestro concertatore (It.). In the early 19th century, the person on the opera-house staff with responsibility for rehearsing the singers.

Masque. A genre of entertainment that developed in England during the 16th and 17th centuries around a masked dance. Based on allegorical or mythological themes and involving poetry, music and elaborate sets, its finest achievement was in the court masques of the poet laureate Ben Jonson and stage architect Inigo Jones from 1605 to 1631. A lesser-noted but none the less important type was the theatre masque of the same period, which survived the demise of the court masque and reached its highest development in the dramas and semi-operas of the Restoration (1660–*c*1700), especially in the works of Dryden and Purcell. (See Chapter IV.)

Melodrama (from Gk. *melos, drama*; Fr. *mélodrame*; It. *melologo*; Ger. *Melodram*). A kind of drama, or a technique used with a drama, in which the action is carried forward by the protagonist speaking in the pauses of, or later during, a musical accompaniment. The orchestral passages that separate the speech are clearly related in style to those in operatic accompanied recitative.

J. E. Eberlin used the speaking voice against music in his Latin drama *Sigismund* (1753, Salzburg), but the invention of melodrama is usually dated to J.-J. Rousseau's *Pygmalion*, written in about 1762. It was first set by Coignet and Rousseau in 1770, then in German by Aspelmayr in 1772 (for the Vienna court opera) and by Schweitzer the same year for Weimar. French melodrama is generally divided into short musical numbers, between passages of spoken text; German composers preferred continuity of musical thought even with interruptions for the text.

Georg Benda was the chief exponent of the genre in Germany, with his *Ariadne auf Naxos* and *Medea* (both 1775) and *Pygmalion* (1779); the success of these works induced other composers, including Reichardt and Zumsteeg, to take it up. Mozart, enthusiastic about the genre, planned to write a *Semiramis*; there are melodrama sections in his unfinished *Zaide* and his music for *Thamos, König in Ägypten*. Some composers of the time wrote melodramas on biblical and comic topics. Beethoven used melodrama in the dungeon scene of *Fidelio*, in his music for *Egmont* and elsewhere; Weber used it, notably in *Der Freischütz*, Schubert in *Fierabras* and other works, and Marschner in *Hans Heiling* (1833). *Opéra comique* composers to use it include Méhul, Boieldieu and Cherubini (*Les deux journées*, 1800). Most 19th-century composers of opera have used it as a dramatic device, for example Verdi, for letter scenes in *Macbeth* and *La traviata*, and Smetana in *The Two Widows*. Among other composers to use it in Bohemia was Fibich, who wrote several full-length melodramas. The device has been much used by 20th-century composers, among them Puccini, Strauss, Berg, Britten and Henze.

Melodramma (It.). A dramatic text written to be set to music (*see* Dramma per musica), or the resultant opera. (It does not mean Melodrama, for which the Italian is *melologo*.) Verdi's second opera, *Un giorno di regno*, with a libretto by Felice Romani, was termed a *melodramma giocoso*; its successors were variously described as *tragedia lirica*, *dramma lirico*, *dramma tragico* and so on, but the term reappeared on two librettos of some literary pretension, *I masnadieri* and *Macbeth*, as well as *Rigoletto*, *Un ballo in maschera* and the revised *Simon Boccanegra*. It is hard to attach any special significance to the term; it alternated freely, often in successive editions of the same work, with the other terms mentioned above and also with *dramma* and *libretto composto per musica*. There is perhaps evidence that, unlike 'melodrama' in the popular English sense, *melodramma* was regarded as one of the more distinguished terms for a librettist's work.

Mezzo-contralto. Term used of the singer Rosine Stoltz (1815–1903), usually categorized as a mezzo-soprano or even soprano; it implied a specially strong lower register.

Mezzo-soprano (It.). A female voice, normally written for within the range *a* to *f ♯″*, which may be extended at either end, particularly in solo writing. The distinction between soprano and mezzo-soprano became common only towards the middle of the 18th century. Earlier, most music for 'soprano' had a range *c′* to *g″*, by later criteria a mezzo-soprano range. During the early 18th century, however, composers began writing soprano parts that not only extended the upper range, frequently reaching *a″*, but used a somewhat higher tessitura and were characterized by lengthy *fioriture* in the range *g′* to *g″*. With this trend towards more characteristic writing for soprano came an awareness of the somewhat weightier mezzo-soprano roles. This awareness was well expressed by J. J. Quantz, who described the castrato Senesino as having a 'penetrating, clear, even, and pleasant deep soprano voice (mezzo Soprano)' which he rarely used above *f″*. In comparing the soprano Cuzzoni (whose range was *c′* to *c‴*) with Faustina Bordoni, Quantz similarly reported that the latter had 'a less clear than penetrating mezzosoprano voice' with the range *b* to *g″*.

The distinction was more keenly sensed in the 19th century. Paradoxically, it became common to extend the mezzo-soprano range as high as *bb″* (even higher in the roles of Eboli and Amneris); and at the same time many sopranos cultivated their voices so as to be highly effective in producing the rich timbre required for mezzo-soprano roles. Mezzo-sopranos with an extended upper range tackled the lower of two soprano roles in such operas as Bellini's *Norma* (Adalgisa) and Donizetti's *Anna Bolena* (Jane Seymour); and mid-century singers at the Paris Opéra such as Rosine Stoltz and Pauline Gueymard resist strict classification as either dramatic sopranos or dramatic mezzos. Wagner's Ortrud, Fricka (described by Wagner as 'Sopran' in *Das Rheingold* and as 'tiefer Sopran' in *Die Walküre*) and Kundry are equally difficult to categorize; both sopranos and mezzo-sopranos sing them.

The mezzo-soprano is often assigned a Breeches part. In the era immediately after the demise of the Castrato, mezzos (or contraltos) were sometimes, for example by Rossini, given heroic male roles, such as Arsaces in *Semiramide*; but at all periods they have taken adolescent roles such as Cherubino (*Le nozze di Figaro*) or Oktavian (*Der Rosenkavalier*). The traditional casting however is as nurse or confidante (e.g. Brangäne in *Tristan und Isolde*, Magdalena in *Die Meistersinger*, Emilia in Verdi's *Otello* and Suzuki in *Madama Butterfly*) or as the mature married woman (e.g. Herodias in Strauss's *Salome*, Adelaide in *Arabella* and Kate Pinkerton in *Madama Butterfly*). Saint-Saëns's *Samson et Dalila* is one of the exceptions to the general rule that the heroine (particularly the beautiful maiden) is cast as a soprano.

Mezzo-tenor. Term occasionally used in the 18th century for what is now called a high BARITONE.

Monodrama. A MELODRAMA (i.e. a work with spoken text and musical accompaniment) for one character. The term is not strictly applied: Rousseau's *Pygmalion* (*c*1762) and Benda's setting of the same text (1779) are reckoned as monodramas, although Galatea speaks a few words at the close. Schoenberg called *Erwartung* (1909) a monodrama; despite the use of SPRECHGESANG, the notated vocal line and continuous score hardly accord with the original juxtaposition of speaking voice and orchestral commentary.

Musical comedy [musical]. Term for the chief form of popular musical theatre in the English-speaking world. It developed from comic opera and burlesque in London in the late 19th century and reached its most durable form in the 1920s and 30s, particularly in the USA. The term 'musical play' is sometimes used for works of a more substantial kind, but since World War II the most usual designation has been simply 'musical'. (See Chapter XXIX.)

Music drama [musical drama]. By the description 'A Musical Drama' Handel's *Hercules* (1745) was distinguished from, on the one hand, an opera and, on the other, 'An Oratorio, or Sacred Drama'. In more recent usage, the meanings attached to 'music drama' derive from the ideas formulated in Wagner's *Oper und Drama*; it is applied to his operas and to others in which the musical, verbal and scenic elements cohere to serve one dramatic end. In a letter of 1869, Verdi distinguished between a mere opera of the old sort and the *dramma musicale* that he believed his *La forza del destino* to be. English usage often hyphenates the words, music-drama, to stress the *Gesamtkunstwerk* conception that was Wagner's – and, for that matter, Verdi's – intention. Current theatrical practice tends to destroy this unity by performing music dramas with the original music and words but freshly invented scenic elements.

In the 17th century, *dramma musicale* was a term used to describe a play written for musical setting, for example Cicognini's texts for Cavalli's *Giasone* and Cesti's *Orontea* (both 1649). In this sense it means much the same as *dramma per musica, opera musicale, favola dramatica musicale* and other such terms. In 19th-century England, 'musical drama' could signify a work rather lighter than a true opera but more serious than a BURLETTA.

Musico (It.: 'musician'). Term applied, from the 17th century to the early 19th, usually in the form 'primo musico', to the leading male singer in an opera or an opera company. Normally it signified, like 'primo uomo', the principal castrato; later it could mean the tenor or, in the early 19th century, a female singer in a BREECHES PART, singing a heroic role at mezzo pitch of the type traditionally assigned to castratos.

Music theatre (Ger. *Musiktheater*). A catch-phrase that became common in the 1960s, particularly among composers, producers and critics who had artistic or social objections to the cost of traditional grand opera and the conservatism of grand opera companies and their audiences. It is used to designate musical works for small or moderate forces that involve a dramatic element in their presentation. Such works have included small-scale operas (e.g. Goehr's *Naboth's Vineyard*); song cycles with instrumental accompaniment that are 'staged' and enacted on a concert platform (e.g. Davies's *Eight Songs for a Mad King*); and pieces such as those by Ligeti (*Aventures* and *Nouvelles aventures*) and Kagel that resist precise definition.

Stravinsky's *Histoire du soldat* and *Reynard*, Weill's *Mahagonny-Songspiel* and Hindemith's *Wir bauen eine Stadt* (for children) – and, for that matter, Monteverdi's *Il combattimento di Tancredi e Clorinda* – are earlier examples.

The term 'music theatre' is also used to describe either an opera in which the theatrical element is deemed powerful enough to compensate for an indifferent or insubstantial score, or any uncommonly dramatic opera; or to describe a manner of performance in which the acting and staging are so vivid as to compensate for mediocre, or complement admirable, singing and playing (in this sense Felsenstein's carefully acted productions of the traditional operatic repertory are called 'music theatre').

Number opera. Term for an opera consisting of individual sections or 'numbers' which can easily be detached from the whole, as distinct from an opera consisting of continuous music. It is best applied to the various forms of 18th-century opera, including *opera seria*, *opera buffa*, *opéra comique*, ballad opera and Singspiel, as well as to some 19th-century grand operas. Under the influence of Wagner's ideas about the relationship between opera and drama, the number opera became distinctly unfashionable, and neither his operas nor those of late Verdi, Puccini and the *verismo* school can be so called. In spite of the general adherence to Wagner's aesthetic of continuous music drama, some notable 20th-century works can be considered number operas, such as Berg's *Wozzeck* (1925) and Stravinsky's deliberately archaic *The Rake's Progress* (1951).

Opéra-ballet (Fr.). A French genre of lyric theatre, cultivated in the period between the death of Lully in 1687 and the middle of the 18th century. The term is normally applied to works consisting of a prologue and three or four acts or entrées, each with its own set of characters and independent action but loosely related to a collective idea, which would be expressed in the work's title. Its creator was Campra; other leading exponents were Mouret, Montéclair and Rameau, whose *Les Indes galantes* (1735) is the outstanding example. The form was particularly popular in the declining years of Louis XIV and during the Regency; after the Regent's death, in 1723, it came to be superseded by the *ballet héroïque*, in which the *petits maîtres* and amorous ladies of its plots give way to heroic or exotic characters. (See Chapter III.)

Opéra bouffe (Fr.). A form of satirical operetta derived from the *opéra comique*; the earliest example is Offenbach's *Orphée aux enfers* (1858), written for the Théâtres des Bouffes Parisiens, opened in 1855. (See Chapters XV and XX.)

Opera buffa (It.: 'comic opera'). A term commonly used to signify Italian comic opera, principally of the 18th century, with recitative rather than spoken dialogue. Though now applied generically, it was one of several such terms used in the 18th century, including Dramma giocoso, 'commedia per musica', 'commedia in musica', 'burlesca', 'bernesca', 'grotesca' and 'operetta'; the choice of term was more a matter of local usage than of any attempt to classify sub-species of a particular genre. An *opera buffa*, usually a full-length work, should not be confused with the Intermezzo or the Farsa, which are short works generally designed as companion pieces to longer entertainments. (See Chapter VII.)

Opéra comique (Fr.). Term for French stage works with spoken dialogue interspersed with songs and other musical numbers; it does not necessarily imply a comic opera. The genre was specially associated with the Paris theatre, and the company connected with it, known as the Opéra-Comique. Some works to which it is now applied were at the time called 'comédie mêlée d'ariettes'. Early masters of the genre include Grétry and Philidor; the supreme *opéra comique* is by general consent Bizet's *Carmen*. (See Chapter IX.)

Opera semiseria (It.: 'half-serious opera'). A type of Italian opera falling into neither of the classical genres of tragedy or comedy. Derived from the 18th-century French *comédie larmoyante*, it used serious subject matter, treated with strong melo-dramatic and sentimental colouring, with subsidiary comic elements often pro-vided by servants, usually in a middle-class, and often contemporary, setting. Operas of the type began to appear in the 1780s; in the preface to *Il disertore* (1784), the librettist Benincasa wrote that he wished to create a 'musical drama between the grand heroic opera and the comic operetta'. Stimulus to the new genre was given by the phenomenal success of Paisiello's *Nina, o sia La pazza per amore* (1789), which dealt with a favourite theme of the *comédie larmoyante* – the thwarting of natural human urges (young love) by conventions and society (personified by tyrannical parents); the vaguely pastoral setting toned down the bourgeois aspect of the genre. It introduced spoken prose dialogue into Italian opera, where it continued to be used occasionally well into the 19th century in such works as Bellini's *Adelson e Salvini* (1825). The designation 'semiseria' became widespread only in the second decade of the 19th century; before that, terms such as 'dramma eroicomico', 'dramma tragicomico' and 'dramma di sentimento' were used. (See Chapter XIII.)

Opera seria (It.: 'serious opera'). Term applied to serious Italian operas, on a heroic or tragic subject, of the 18th century and the early 19th. It was rarely used at the time but can sometimes be found on scores of the late 18th century; 'dramma per musica' is however the more usual genre description, or in the early 19th century 'melodramma serio'. Defined primarily by music historians out of sym-pathy with the musical and dramatic principles by which the genre is governed, 'opera seria' has tended to be used in a derogatory sense. The classical *opera seria* is in three acts, has six or seven characters, consists primarily of arias in DA CAPO (or later dal segno) form in which characters express their emotional state, and recita-tive, in which the action takes place, with occasional orchestral recitatives at dramatic highpoints and sometimes duets; the topic traditionally involves a moral dilemma, typically a variant of 'love *v.* duty', and is resolved happily, with due reward for rectitude, loyalty, unselfishness etc. The most famous librettist was Pietro Mestastasio, whose texts were set many times over. (See Chapter VII.)

Operetta (It., diminutive of 'opera'; Fr. *opérette*; Ger. *Operette*; Sp. *opereta*). A light opera with spoken dialogue, songs and dances. The form flourished in Europe and the USA during the second half of the 19th century and the early part of the 20th. In the 17th and 18th centuries the term 'operetta' was applied in a more general way to a variety of stage works which were shorter or otherwise less ambitious than opera, such as vaudeville, Singspiel and ballad opera. It is still in use on the Continent for new works akin to the MUSICAL COMEDY, into which the operetta evolved in English-speaking countries. (See Chapters XX and XXIX.)

Overture (Fr. *ouverture*; Ger. *Ouvertüre*; It. *sinfonia*). A piece of orchestral music designed to precede a dramatic work (*see also* VORSPIEL).

Renaissance court entertainments frequently began with a flourish of trumpets, of the type that survives as the Toccata of Monteverdi's *Orfeo*. At the beginning of Landi's *Il Sant'Alessio* (1631 or 1632) there is a 'sinfonia' in three sections, fast–slow–fast, that seems to anticipate later Italian developments; but Venetian opera overtures of the mid-17th century typically consisted of a slow section in duple metre followed by a faster one in triple metre. It was from this that the French overture developed and became the normal type of overture for dramatic works. Handel preferred it but used it with freedom and added a variety of additional movements, sometimes linked with the ensuing action. In England a French overture was often used as a prelude to a spoken play, in which the only other music consisted of simple songs or dances (as in *The Beggar's Opera*). The scoring of French overtures was predominantly for strings, oboes and continuo.

The Italian overture, which emerged from Naples late in the 17th century, was in three short, simple sections, fast–slow–fast, often with a prominent trumpet part. By the mid-18th century this type prevailed for operas, even in France, and the first movement had become longer and more elaborate – generally in sonata form, sometimes with a slow introduction. After 1760 there was a tendency to drop the second and third movements. Mozart's last true three-movement opera overture dates from 1775, Haydn's from 1779. In serious opera there was sometimes an effort to set the mood of the coming drama, as in Gluck's *Alceste* and Mozart's *Idomeneo*; the famous preface to *Alceste* emphasizes the importance of relating the overture to the drama it precedes. In *Die Entführung* Mozart replaced the 'development' section with an Andante that anticipated the opening of the opera, and in several of his operas there is no formal ending to the overture, which runs straight into the first act. In *Don Giovanni*, *Così fan tutte* and *Die Zauberflöte* the overture quotes significant musical ideas from the opera. The overture along Mozartian lines was standard for operas between 1790 and 1820. There was usually a slow introduction; the fast movement was almost invariably in common time; the scoring was remarkably consistent (double woodwind, horns, trumpets, timpani and strings); and there was little thematic development. Rossini frequently omitted the 'development' altogether, as in *Il barbiere di Siviglia*; Schubert did the same.

The notion of tying the overture to the opera in mood and theme was further developed in France by Spontini and Méhul. It also appealed to the German Romantics. Beethoven made powerful use of dramatic motifs in his three *Leonore* overtures, while Weber in *Der Freischütz* and *Euryanthe* extended the method to a point where almost every theme, in both slow and fast sections, was to reappear at an important point in the drama. But the formal structure changed little. Composers of French grand opera, from *Guillaume Tell* onwards, tended to expand the traditional overture by means of a slow lyrical section preceding the loud, fast conclusion. Often they brought in important themes from the opera. Wagner in his early operas imitated this type, but in the *Ring* preferred a 'prelude' fully integrated into the drama, as did Richard Strauss. For Bellini, Donizetti and Verdi the prelude was always an alternative possibility, and it became normal in Italian opera after the mid-century, though *La forza del destino* (1862) has an extended overture. With Verdi the prelude to the first act may be no longer than those to the other acts; *Otello* has no overture or prelude at all. Puccini's preludes are brief and integrated into the drama; that to *Tosca* consists simply of three chords (associated with a particular character). Some 'nationalist' operas were conservative in their overtures, for instance *Prince Igor*, which has a full sonata-form movement complete with slow introduction.

In comic operas and operettas the independent overture lasted longer, and here the structure based on themes from the drama became a mere medley of tunes, with perhaps a short final sonata-form section as a link with the traditional form. The 'medley' or 'potpourri' overture was the pattern frequently chosen by Auber, Gounod, Thomas, Offenbach, Johann Strauss and Sullivan; it can still be traced in musical-comedy overtures of recent times.

Pantomime (from Gk. *pantomimos*: 'one who does everything by imitation'). The Latin *pantomimus* referred to a Roman actor who specialized in dumb show, supported by instrumental music and a chorus; by extension the word denotes a dramatic representation in dumb show. The term was used for a form of theatrical entertainment, primarily English, in the 18th century. Its origins lie in the *commedia dell'arte*, in its modified forms that became established north of the Alps, above all in Paris. From the beginning of the 18th century, when the earliest known pantomimes began to appear on the London stage, until the early 20th, the genre developed along fairly consistent lines. It was a mixed-medium entertainment, akin to the intermezzos performed between the acts of serious operas. Between the sung numbers were short instrumental pieces ('the comic turns') during which the action was mimed. Dialogue was introduced late in the 18th century. The subjects were usually mythological or exotic, and extravagant stage effects were important. John Weaver claimed that his *The Tavern Bilkers* (1702) or his *The Loves of Mars and Venus* (1717) was the first pantomime. But the genre, slow to take root, was established by John Rich, who managed the Lincoln's Inn Fields theatre and regularly played Harlequin. When David Garrick took over Drury Lane theatre, he tried to suppress pantomime; but he enjoyed great success with a pantomime series and even persuaded the ballet-master Noverre to come from Paris with his ensemble to take part in *Les fêtes chinoises* (1755). In time, the pantomime became a more fully integrated comic play, using the stock elements of Italian comedy. Vocal music dominated, and leading composers provided scores (Galliard and Pepusch in the early years, later the Arnes, Dibdin, Linley, Boyce, Shield and others). Instrumental music accompanied the elaborate transformation scenes, though as the emphasis shifted towards the spectacular elements of the age of the British melodrama, reputable musicians more rarely wrote pantomime scores.

On the Continent too the pantomime was popular in the 18th and 19th centuries. In France it tended to be a dignified form of danced entertainment. Rousseau (*Dictionnaire de la musique*, 1768) defines it as an 'Air to which two or more dancers execute in dance an action (itself also known under the same term). The pantomime airs . . . speak, as it were, and form images, in the situations in which the dancer is to put on a particular expression'. The French pantomimic tradition lived on in the famous mute title-role of Auber's *La muette de Portici* (1828); and though Wagner (who admired *La muette*) had completed the second act of *Rienzi* before he moved to Paris in autumn 1839 the ballet sequence in that act is often referred to as a pantomime because of the relevance of the dances to the story. The Olympia act of Offenbach's *Les contes d'Hoffmann* (1881) also has important pantomimic elements. Wagner may be held to have written the most successful of all pantomimic scenes in opera, in Act 3 of *Die Meistersinger von Nürnberg* in which Beckmesser, painfully reminded at every turn of his beating of the night before, visits Sachs's workshop and misappropriates Walther's Prize Song.

There was a strong pantomime tradition in 18th-century Vienna, where the presence of a vital popular theatre (including native elements, above all the character of Hanswurst) was combined with the south German tendency to use music in the theatre. The appellation 'Pantomime' was used by the 1720s. Among authors, Kurz-Bernardon is the most important, and Haydn's lost music for Kurz's *Der neue krumme Teufel* (*c*1758) included a pantomime. Mozart wrote a pantomime of his own (κ446/416*d*; only a fragment survives) in 1783. The tradition continued in Vienna roughly until the advent of the operetta; elements of its more elevated aspect live on in the Kessler–Richard Strauss *Josephslegende* (1912).

Parlando [parlante] (It.: 'speaking'). A direction requiring a singer to use a manner approximating to speech.

Pasticcio (It.: 'mess', 'hotch-potch'; Fr. *pastiche*). Term for a work made up, at least in part, from existing works by a variety of composers. The practice of putting operas, mainly serious operas, together in this way began in the late 17th century and persisted for most of the 18th; it arose from the need for commercial success in the public theatres, whch was better assured if singers could be given music they knew and liked and the public could be offered tried favourites. A pasticcio was normally put together by a 'house' composer and librettist. They might adapt an existing score, adding items from other sources or writing them afresh; they might start with an existing libretto and gather up arias from various sources to which it could be fitted; or they might put together a new libretto and recitatives around a collection of arias. The term is sometimes also applied to a work by several composers or a work (like a ballad opera) assembled from miscellaneous and popular sources. The process of preparing pasticcios, which was made much easier by the existence of multiple settings of the same libretto (those of Metastasio in particular), was widespread and indeed normal wherever Italian *opera seria* was performed in commercial opera houses. Many more pasticcios were performed than freshly composed operas. Virtually all composers accepted the practice and partook of it, including Vivaldi, Handel, Gluck, J. C. Bach and Haydn; Mozart too provided arias for other composers' operas. After his time, however, the opera repertory – a body of works widely known and performed – began to develop, and the idea of unity and originality as desirable features came to hold sway, so the days of the pasticcio were numbered. It would however be misguided to condemn pasticcios, in their heyday, because they did not conform to the dictates of a later aesthetic; and there is no reason to suppose, in a time of widely accepted musical styles, that a pasticcio was necessarily inferior to a newly composed opera in terms of characterization, unity of style, or balanced and coherent drama. (See Entr'acte II.)

Pastorale [pastoral]. A literary, dramatic or musical genre that depicts the characters and scenes of rural life or is expressive of its atmosphere. The pastoral tradition has served a variety of audiences and artistic purposes. Most of the early operas of the late 16th and early 17th centuries were based on pastoral material, favourite tales being *Dafne* (libretto by Rinuccini, 1597, set by Peri, Gagliano, Schütz and others) and *Euridice* (libretto by Rinuccini, 1600, set by Peri and Caccini). The latter is based on the Orpheus legend, also the subject of numerous operas (by Monteverdi, Landi, Sartorio, Draghi and many others up to the 20th century).

In the 17th and 18th centuries, however, Guarini's *Il pastor fido* remained the chief model for pastorales. It was translated into the principal European languages, and was often parodied, from *Il pastor infido* (a 'scherzo drammatico', 1715), and *Il pastor fido ridicolo* (1739) to 19th-century operettas such as Offenbach's *Orphée aux enfers* (1858) and Sullivan's *Iolanthe* (1882).

Pastoral operas declined in popularity towards the mid-17th century. Late 17th-century secular pastorales are usually small-scale, sometimes termed *favole boscareccie*, and often intended as occasional entertainments (e.g. *La Circe*, a two-act pastoral 'operetta' with music by Cesti and Stradella, 1668). The initial interest in the pastorale in Italy was followed by one in France. The *Pastorale d'Issy* of Perrin and Cambert (1659), cited as the first real French opera, was preceded by the pastorale *Le triomphe de l'Amour*, with music by Michel de la Guerre, performed in Mazarin's residence at the Louvre in 1655. Many pastoral operas followed, by Lully (*Les fêtes de l'Amour et de Bacchus*, 1672), Destouches (*Issé*, 1697), Rameau (*Zaïs*, 1748) and others. Pastoral scenes and characters were common in various kinds of opera, for example Rousseau's *Le devin du village* (1752). In England such works as Handel's *Il pastor fido* (1712) and *Acis and Galatea* (1718) and Boyce's *The Shepherd's Lottery* (1751) belong to the tradition. In the 20th century the pastorale's aesthetic appeal to neo-classical composers is reflected in such works as Casella's opera *La favola d'Orfeo* (1932) and Stravinsky's ballet *Orpheus* (1948).

Patter song. A comic song in which the humour derives from having the greatest number of words uttered in the shortest possible time. The technique was foreshadowed by such composers as A. Scarlatti (the duet 'Non ti voglio' from *Tiberio imperatore d'Oriente*, 1702) but was not in common use until the second half of the 18th century, when composers often introduced the idea into *buffo* solos (e.g. Bartolo's aria 'La vendetta' in Mozart's *Le nozze di Figaro*). Other examples are found in the works of Logroscino, Piccinni, Paisiello, Haydn, Rossini (notably the 'confusion' ensemble in the Act 1 finale of *Il barbiere di Siviglia*), Donizetti (whose patter duet 'Chieti, chieti' in *Don Pasquale* is a classic example) and Sullivan – whose patter song in *Ruddigore* includes the lines: 'this particularly rapid, unintelligible patter isn't generally heard and if it is it doesn't matter'.

Pertichini (It.). Term for the characters who enter during a musical number and, by their actions or the news they bring, affect the progress of the drama and give rise to a musical contrast; most commonly they enter towards the end of the slow section (the cantabile or cavatina) of a two-part aria and provoke the fast part (cabaletta).

Pezzo concertato (It.: 'piece in concerted style'). A section within a finale in Italian 19th-century opera in which several characters express divergent emotions simultaneously, a 'multiple soliloquy' (as it were). It is usually in slow tempo and is sometimes called 'largo concertato').

Pièce de sauvetage (Fr.). RESCUE OPERA.

Preghiera (It.: 'prayer'; Ger. *Gebet*). A term used of the number common in 19th-century opera in which a character prays for divine assistance in his plight. Moses's 'Dal tuo stellato soglio' in Rossini's *Mosè in Egitto* (1818) is perhaps the best-known *preghiera* actually so titled in early editions of an opera. Desdemona's 'Ave Maria' in Verdi's *Otello* is a late example of the traditional gentle *preghiera*, and Tosca's 'Vissi d'arte' may be considered a *verismo* development of the tradition.

Prelude. *See* OVERTURE and VORSPIEL.

Prima donna (It.: 'first lady'). The principal female singer in the cast of an opera or in the roster of an opera company. The expression 'prima donna' seems to have come into use around the middle of the 17th century, with the opening of public opera houses; in Venice, where several theatres were in competition, the ability of a leading lady to attract audiences became a matter of economic importance, and this served to feed the vanity of singers and led to the cult of the prima donna. The nature of the cult is evident from 18th-century terminology. Virtually every singer who gained the status of prima donna insisted on keeping that title; when conflicts arose, managerial ingenuity devised such expressions as 'altra prima donna', 'prima donna assoluta' and even 'prima donna assoluta e sola'.

In some cases prima donnas made it a point of status to be difficult. Adelina Patti (1843–1919), at the height of her career, stipulated that her name appear on posters in letters at least one-third larger than those used for other singers' names and that she be excused from attending rehearsals. The need to meet a prima donna's demands, however, shaped many librettos and opera scores, particularly because her status was reflected in the number and character of the arias allotted to her.

Primo musico (It.: 'first musician'). *See* Musico.

Primo violino direttore (It.: 'first violin director'). In Italian opera houses of the early 19th century, the leading violinist in the orchestra, responsible for giving the beat.

Primo uomo (It.: 'first man'). The principal male singer in the cast of an opera or in the roster of an opera company. After about 1650 a trend developed towards opera plots in which the protagonists were historical heroes (Xerxes, Scipio Africanus, Alexander the Great etc); this was due partly to papal decrees forbidding women performers in the theatre and to the appearance of excellent castrato singers. Just as a leading lady had been given the title 'prima donna', so a famous castrato now claimed the title 'primo uomo'. His importance is evident in the roles he sang, which were occasionally as extensive as those created for the prima donna herself. For example, in Handel's *Giulio Cesare* (1724) Cleopatra and Julius Caesar each have eight arias. At first the term 'primo uomo' normally referred to a castrato, but during the 18th century it came also to be applied to leading tenors.

Prologue. The introductory scene to a dramatic work, in which the author explains, either directly or indirectly, the context and meaning of the work to follow. Less commonly, the prologue may simply pay homage to the author's patron.

Prologues, a usual feature of Baroque opera, were generally either literary or topical in content. Literary prologues reflected the neo-classical aims of Renaissance drama, showing mythological figures whose relationships and potential conflicts constituted an allegory of the action to follow. The first opera prologues were for only one character, usually Tragedia (Rinuccini's *Euridice*) or Musica (*L'Orfeo*). By the middle third of the 17th century, particularly at Venice, it became customary for several allegorical characters to appear. They normally represented forces at work in the ensuing drama; thus Fortuna, Virtù and Amor dispute their respective powers over men's fates in the prologue to Monteverdi's *L'incoronazione di Poppea* (1642), Amor's boasts being subsequently borne out in the opera. With the growing complexity of plots, prologues came to be integrated ingeniously into the main opera; thus the prologue to Cavalli's *Pompeo Magno* (text by Minato, 1666) ends with Fama hearing the crowd chorus 'Viva Pompeo', which begins the action.

Topical prologues were most often political allegories designed to show the ruler's actions in a favourable light. Quinault's for Lully's *Alceste* (1674), for example, depicts the nymphs of the Seine and the Marne being consoled by La Gloire, who brings news of Louis XIV's defeat of a rival river, the Rhine (his recent military victory). New topical prologues were normally added to revivals in the 17th century.

Prologues became less common in the 18th century, partly because of libretto reforms, partly because of the changing character of audiences. Naples had an important tradition of operatic prologues during the monarchy (1734–82); these were usually written for three characters, whose parts were sung by the prima donna, primo uomo and tenor and used allegory to praise the ruler or to refer to the festivity for which the opera was commissioned. Handel wrote only one prologue for an opera, a ballet for the 1734 revival of *Il pastor fido* that represents Terpsichore required to depict human emotions (later integral to the plot) in dance to qualify as a muse. In the late 18th century and the early 19th, prologues were rare. Wagner's *Das Rheingold* may be seen as a prologue to the *Ring* since it presents the background to the plot. The prologue to Gounod's *Roméo et Juliette* (1867) is similarly literary in purpose; a chorus at the end of the overture gives a synopsis of the Capulet-Montague tale. Boito's *Mefistofele* (1868) was originally introduced by a 'Prologo in cielo' conceived as a four-movement symphony for orchestra and chorus; for the 1875 revival he wrote a 'Prologo in teatro' but eventually returned to the more popular 'Prologo in cielo'. Leoncavallo's *Pagliacci* opens with a prologue explicitly modelled on those of ancient drama; Tonio, having declared himself to be 'Prologo', addresses the audience with an exposition of the dramatic theory of *verismo*. In the 20th century various kinds of literary prologue have preceded operas, from the brief spoken prologue to Stravinsky's *Oedipus rex*, through the allegorical competition for theatrical supremacy among 'tragedies', 'comedies', 'lyrics', 'empty heads' and 'ridiculousnesses' that precedes Prokofiev's *Love for Three Oranges*, to the famous lion-taming scene that sets the horrific tone for Berg's *Lulu*.

Puppet opera. Because of the caricature nature of puppets, most works for them have been comic adaptations, mock-heroic dramas or satires of popular dramas. The earliest known Italian puppet operas were burlesques staged in Venice at the Teatro S Moisè by the Florentine nobleman Filippo Acciaiuoli (1637–1700) in the period 1679–82; they were given in carnival season by wooden or wax figures while the music was performed behind the stage. In France, the puppet theatre was closely linked with the Parisian THÉÂTRES DE LA FOIRE; about 40 puppet *opéras comiques* have survived. A puppet theatre opened in London in 1710 and gave satires, opera burlesques and mock-heroic tragedies; ballad operas later made up the bulk of the repertory. Puppets were displayed in operettas in a special theatre at the summer palace of Prince Nikolaus Esterházy, which flourished in 1773–83 under Haydn's musical direction; at least two of Haydn's own works were given, *Philemon und Baucis* and *Die Feuersbrunst*. Interest in puppets faded in the late 18th century but revived late in the 19th, and several 20th-century composers, including Britten, Copland, Hindemith, Malipiero and Satie have contributed to the repertory, in which Falla's *El retablo de Maese Pedro* is the best-known item.

Quartet (It. *quartetto*). An ENSEMBLE for four singers. Quartets appear in opera as early as the 17th century; Cavalli's *Calisto* ends with one and A. Scarlatti wrote quartets in some of his late Roman operas. There are quartets in Handel's *Radamisto* and *Partenope*. They appear in many *opéras comiques*. In *opera buffa* of the Classical era, when ensembles are sometimes used to further the dramatic action (as opposed simply to expressing different emotions simultaneously), quartets sometimes occupy that role: examples are the Act 2 finale of Mozart's *Die Entführung aus dem Serail*, where the sequence of sections shows the consolidation of the relationships between the two pairs of lovers, and in Act 1 of his *Don Giovanni*, where 'Non ti fidar' draws together the dramatic threads. The great quartet in the last act of *Idomeneo*, the musical climax of the work, is however more a series of statements by the four characters of their emotional positions, as too is the quartet for the 'wedding' toast in the finale of *Così fan tutte* – this is in a tradition of canonic ensembles, and it is significant that Mozart turns to dramatic advantage the necessity (because a baritone cannot repeat music at the same pitch as sopranos and a tenor) of having Guglielmo sing different music, expressing his disgust at his beloved's lack of fidelity. Another canonic quartet is 'Mir ist so wunderbar' from Beethoven's *Fidelio*. Verdi wrote a quartet in *Otello*, but his best-known example is the one from *Rigoletto*, an inspired piece of simultaneous expression of feeling, the Duke lightheartedly wooing Maddalena, who is laughing at his protestations, while Gilda (who loves him) pours out her anguish, with her father's voice moving in parallel rhythms to hers, establishing their mutual sympathy.

Quintet (It. *quintetto*). An ensemble for five singers. Quintets, except within ensemble finales, are rare in the operatic repertory. Several appear in Philidor's *opéras comiques*. Notable examples are the two in Mozart's *Così fan tutte*, where the 'farewell' quintet depicts two characters saying what they suppose to be a genuine farewell and two saying a feigned one to similar music while the fifth character in the background is suppressing his laughter. The only substantial ensemble – in the sense of a number where the characters sing simultaneously – in Wagner's late operas is the famous quintet in *Die Meistersinger von Nürnberg*, a rare moment in his operas where the dramatic action is suspended and the characters take emotional stock.

Rappresentazione sacra [sacra rappresentazione]. Term used in the 15th and 16th centuries for a religious play with music, in Italian, cultivated chiefly in Florence; the plays were performed by boys in costume on a stage with sets and in some cases elaborate machinery. The *rappresentazione sacra* is a significant forerunner of opera and oratorio. Emilio de' Cavalieri apparently intended his opera *Rappresentatione di Anima, et di Corpo* (1600) as a renewal of the genre, by then outmoded.

Récit (Fr.). Term used in the 17th and 18th centuries for a piece, independent or within a larger work, for solo voice (commonly a soprano) with instruments; it could be of any length, from very brief to an extended air. In the BALLET DE COUR, one usually began each act and served as commentary.

Recitative (Fr. *récitatif*; Ger. *Rezitativ*; It. *recitativo*). A type of vocal writing, normally for a single voice, which follows closely the natural rhythm and accentuation of speech, without necessarily being governed by a regular tempo or organized in a specific form.

The *stilo recitativo* derived from the Florentine Camerata's development, in the late 16th century, of a declamatory narrative style with a precise rhythmic notation, harmonic support, a wide melodic range and affective (emotionally charged) treatment of the words. During the 17th century, as the aria increasingly became the dominant element in opera, recitative came to be the vehicle for dialogue, so providing a connecting link between arias. Nevertheless, it had some expressive devices of its own, notably the trailing off of the voice before the expected cadence (representing the singer's being overcome with emotion), leaving the accompaniment to provide the harmonic closure. This became a convention, as did the addition of an appoggiatura to the final note or notes, at any cadence point, to follow the natural inflection of Italian words. Later it became usual – though probably this applied little if at all to opera – to delay the two final chords of the accompaniment until the singer had finished, which he habitually did to either a 4–3–(2)–1 descent or with a falling 4th.

By the late 17th century the carefully notated declamation of the rhythm in early recitative had given way to a more rapid, even delivery, notated largely in quavers, a trend taken still further in *opera buffa* of the middle and late 18th century. Clearly, however, recitative was sung in a free and conversational manner. This kind of plain or simple recitative, accompanied only by continuo, is known as *recitativo semplice* or *recitativo secco* (or simply *secco*), to distinguish it from accompanied or orchestral recitative (*recitativo accompagnato*, *recitativo stromentato*), which came into use in the late 17th century and grew, in the 18th, increasingly important for dramatic junctures in an opera, where it might include violent or pathetic orchestral writing to reflect the turbulent emotions of the singer (this is sometimes called *recitativo obbligato*). The orchestra accompanies throughout, to sustain the drama and avoid changes of texture, in certain 'reform' works such as Gluck's *Orfeo ed Euridice* (1762) and his Paris operas (1774–9).

Italian-style recitative came, after some resistance, to be used in Germany and England; in France, because of the nature of the language, its qualities and its rhythms, a different style of recitative, slower-moving, more lyrical and (through frequent changes of metre) more flexible, came to be developed.

In *Orfeo*, Monteverdi prescribed three keyboard instruments – harpsichord, organ and regal – as well as plucked string instruments to supply accompaniment in the recitatives. When opera became a public spectacle, such variety was precluded and the harpsichord became standard; the player was expected to support the voice, arpeggiate the chords when there is time to do so, and generally to help the singer. A sustaining instrument, most often the cello, generally lent weight to the bass line; there is some evidence that later a double bass was also used.

Recitative with keyboard accompaniment fell out of use (except for the revival of older works) during the second decade of the 19th century. Recitative-like declamation, however, remained an essential means of expression, with orchestral support or punctuation. Even late in the 19th century, when operas written with spoken dialogue were given in houses where speech was not acceptable (like the Paris Opéra), recitatives were written by house composers or hacks (or sometimes the composer himself, for example Gounod with his *Faust*) to replace the dialogue: the most famous example is Guiraud's long-used set of recitatives for Bizet's *Carmen*. With the more continuous textures generally favoured in the 20th century, the concept of recitative has disappeared (as indeed it did in Wagner's mature works), to be replaced by other kinds of representation of speech where that is called for. Schoenberg's SPRECHGESANG may be seen as an Expressionist equivalent of recitative.

Reform. Term applied to Gluck's operas, from *Orfeo ed Euridice* (1762) onwards, in which he applied, influenced by the librettist Raniero de' Calzabigi, the choreographer Angiolini and French musico-dramatic traditions, new principles to Italian (and later to French) opera, to rid it of what he saw as abuses; these principles are fully stated in the preface to his *Alceste* (1767; score published 1769). Several other composers, notably Jommelli and Traetta, had already worked along similar lines. (See Chapters VII and VIII.)

Rescue opera (Fr. *pièce de sauvetage*). Term for a type of opera, very popular in France during the years after the 1789 Revolution, in which the hero or heroine is delivered at the last moment either from the cruelty of a tyrant or from some great natural catastrophe (or both), not by a *deus ex machina* but by heroic human endeavour. It reflected the secular idealism of the age and often carried a social message. The genre was anticipated in Grétry's *Richard Coeur-de-lion* (1784), but its earliest true representative is Berton's *Les rigueurs du cloître* (1790), in which the inhabitants of a nunnery are rescued from the 'tyranny' of the church and sent into the world to rear families. Some rescue operas were based on contemporary real-life incidents, among them Gaveaux's *Léonore, ou l'amour conjugal* (1798) and Cherubini's *Les deux journées* (1800), both to librettos by J. N. Bouilly. The former was the source of Beethoven's *Fidelio* (1805), the most famous example of the class. The rescue opera was imitated in Italy by Mayr, Paer and others, who often used librettos translated or adapted from the French, and became a major influence on the *opera semiseria*. (See Chapter XV.)

Romance (Fr. and Sp.; It. *romanza*; Ger. *Romanze*). Term used in Spain and Italy for a narrative ballad, dating back to the 15th century; in France and Germany, it implied an extravagant, sentimental or romantic tale, in prose or strophic verse. An early example in opera appears in Rousseau's *Le devin du village* (1752), its style reflecting the naivety of the young peasant who sings it. The *romance* suited the vein of sentimentalism in *opéra comique*, with its strophic form, unadorned melody and simple accompaniment; there are examples by Philidor (one showing characteristic shifts between major and minor), Monsigny and Grétry, and in the next generation Méhul (two in *Joseph*, 1807), Cherubini and Auber. In Germany, there are many examples in the Singspiel, notably by Hiller, Mozart (Pedrillo's 'Im Mohrenland' in *Die Entführung aus dem Serail*, 1782) and later Weber ('Nero, dem Kettenbund' in *Der Freischütz*, 1821); Italian examples are more uncommon but include several by Verdi, notably Manrico's 'Deserto sulla terra' (*Il trovatore*, 1853) and Radamès's 'Celeste Aida' (*Aida*, 1871).

Rondò. Term for a type of ARIA popular in the late 18th century, marginally related to rondo form (*A-B-A-C-A* etc). Arteaga (1783), after mentioning that the term was loosely used, described the rondò as an extended and sublime aria, containing two sections, one slow and one fast, each repeated just twice; he claimed that such arias were 'certainly better than the so-called old-fashioned aria cantabile, because more natural, more truthful and more expressive'. As Framery stated, the form originated in the 1760s in the arias of Piccinni, and many examples, following Piccinni's practice, are in gavotte rhythm. Sarti was another notable user of the form. The best-known examples are by Mozart, who did not always observe the rule about repeating each section; they include 'Non temer, amato bene' (K490, written for *Idomeneo* in 1786), 'Non mi dir' (*Don Giovanni*, K527) and 'Per pietà' (*Così fan tutte*, K588). The rondò is an important precursor of the cantabile–cabaletta scheme of the early 19th century.

The spelling 'rondò' was commonly used for this form; but as other spellings (rondo, rondeau) are also found, and as 'rondò' was sometimes used in other contexts, it would be mistaken to regard it as prescriptive.

Sainete (Sp.: 'farce', 'titbit'). A type of one-act dramatic vignette which from the mid-18th century was often played at the end of Spanish theatrical entertainments. Similar to the *entremés*, it was quite comic and popular in character, drawing on incidents and situations of everyday life. Music formed an important element. It included dances, songs, vocal quartets, choruses and instrumental pieces. The *sainete* is particularly associated with Ramón de la Cruz, but Antonio Soler, Blas de Laserna and most of the *tonadilla escénica* composers contributed to its repertory. In the second half of the 18th century some 500 examples were performed in Madrid alone; later the form developed (e.g. in Bretón's *Verbena de la Paloma*) into the *género chico* of the ZARZUELA. (The term was also used by Massenet for his *Bérangère et Anatole*, 1876.) (See Chapters XI and XX.)

Scapigliatura (It.: 'dishevelment'). Term for a group of avant-garde Italian composers of the mid-late 19th century. (See Chapter XII.)

Scena (It.; Fr. *scène*; Ger. *Szene*, formerly *Scene*). The word is derived from the Latin *scaena*, which in turn comes from the Greek *skēnē*, 'tent', 'hut', 'booth' and hence 'stage', 'décor'. It is used in opera, as in drama generally, to mean (1) the stage (e.g. 'sulla scena', on the stage; 'derrière la scène', behind the stage), (2) the scene represented on the stage, (3) a division of an act.

In Italian opera it also has the specific meaning of an episode which has no formal construction but may be made up of diverse elements. The 'Scena e duetto' is a typical unit in opera of the Rossinian period (see Chapter XII). The opening of Act 3 of Verdi's *Ernani* (1844) is described as 'Preludio, Scena e Cavatina'. The 'Preludio' is for orchestra. The 'Scena' consists of recitative for the king, with interpolations by his squire. A scena is frequently more extended than this and may include, in addition to recitative, arioso passages and one or more arias, duets etc. A scena of a particularly dramatic character, often (though not invariably) for a single character, may be described as a 'gran scena', e.g. 'Gran scena del sonnambulismo', the sleepwalking scene in Verdi's *Macbeth* (1847, rev. 1865). The word was also used to describe a setting for concert performance of a scene from an opera libretto, e.g. Mozart's *Misera, dove son* K369 (1781), for soprano and orchestra, to a text from Metastasio's *Ezio*. In French and German opera 'scène' and 'Szene' are used much like 'scena', but generally to describe quite short sections of a work, e.g. no.11bis in Act 2 of Bizet's *La jolie fille de Perth* (1867), an accompanied recitative for the duke and Mab.

Scene (Fr. *scène*; Ger. *Szene*; It. *scena*). The location of an opera, or an act or part of an act of an opera. By extension, the term is used for any part of an opera in one location. In earlier usage, a scene was a section of an act culminating in an aria (or occasionally an ensemble); any substantial (in some operas, any at all) change in the characters on the stage was reckoned a change of scene, and the scenes were numbered accordingly.

Schuldrama (Ger.: 'school drama'). *See* SCHULOPER.

Schuloper (Ger.: 'school opera'). A German opera written for didactic use in schools; its suitability for performance by children is a secondary consideration. Early examples, which belong more strictly to the category of *Schuldrama* ('school drama'), derived from 15th-century humanism and concentrated on religious training and the teaching of Latin, undertaken particularly by the Jesuits and prevalent in central Europe; music was confined to choruses and short interludes. Although Singspiels were written for children during the 18th and 19th centuries, the *Schuloper* belongs to the 20th century. Interest in the idea was reawakened in the late 1920s through the influential musical Jugendbewegung and through the concern for amateur music shown by leading contemporary composers. The pedagogic content concentrated on the teaching of music, drama and a community spirit. Important examples are Weill's *Der Jasager* (1930), which also encouraged political thinking, and Hindemith's *Wir bauen eine Stadt* (1930), the latter suited to performance by children in junior and middle schools.

Secco (It.: 'dry'). Short for *recitativo secco*. A 19th-century term for recitative with continuo accompaniment. See RECITATIVE.

Semi-opera. A type of English Restoration drama, spectacularly staged and with extensive musical scenes, often masque-like in character, which were performed only by subsidiary characters, mainly supernatural beings, their worshippers or servants; the main action was carried out in speech. It was developed by Thomas Betterton, first with a version of Shakespeare's *The Tempest* (1674, music by Humfrey, Locke and others) and Shadwell's *Psyche* (1675, set by Locke and G. B. Draghi). The next true examples were the highly successful series set by Purcell: *Dioclesian* (1690), *King Arthur* (1691), *The Fairy Queen* (1692) and *The Indian Queen* (1695). Of these, only *King Arthur* was actually designed as a semi-opera; the others were adaptations of earlier plays. Seven more, set mainly by Daniel Purcell and

Jeremiah Clarke, were produced between 1696 and 1701. Two more, *The British Enchanters* (set by Eccles) and D'Urfey's *Wonders in the Sun* (a pasticcio), were staged in 1706, but all-sung Italianate opera had caught public attention and soon superseded the native type.

Septet (It. *septetto*). An ENSEMBLE for seven singers. Septets are rare in the operatic repertory; one in A. Scarlatti's *Eraclea* is not a true septet in that the characters do not sing together but rather sing a short melody in turn. There is one in Philidor's *Le boucheron* (1763). A famous septet is 'Par une telle nuit', from Berlioz's *Les troyens*, based on a text from Shakespeare's 'On such a night as this' (*The Merchant of Venice*).

Serenata [serenada] (It.). In the most general sense, a dramatic cantata given in honour of a person or an occasion. From *sereno* (It.), 'a clear night sky', referring to the usual performance circumstances, the term was used in the 17th and 18th centuries for large cantata-like works usually performed in courtly or aristocratic surroundings and in a quasi-dramatic manner to celebrate dynastic occasions or political events. From about the mid-17th century the term was often found on the title-pages of extended cantatas, though *azione teatrale, componimento musicale, favoletta drammatica, applauso genetliaco, festeggio armonico* and *festa teatrale* were more often used in printed librettos. The title 'serenata' seems to have implied outdoor performance: in Venice, an important centre of the serenata where Vivaldi produced several examples, they were often performed from gondolas. In Rome, the most important centre of serenata composition because of its concentration of political and diplomatic dignitaries, temporary theatres were sometimes erected, often in courtyards, for such performances. The serenata was widely used in courtly and aristocratic circles outside Italy. Fux, Caldara and Ercole Bernabei composed them for Vienna and Munich, Heinichen and Mattheson for Dresden.

The serenata normally has at least two characters, typically pastoral, allegorical or mythological figures or the personifications of places, rivers or natural objects. The plot usually involves an encomium of the person being honoured. Shorter than an opera, it is often divided into two or three parts, consisting of recitatives and arias, sometimes with a chorus. Often given in an elaborate scenic setting and with rich costumes, it was performed without stage action or movement and without change of scene.

Progressive orchestration characterizes the genre. Stradella's *Qual prodigio è ch'io miri* contains early examples of the division of the orchestra into concertino and concerto grosso, and has more expansive and forward-looking arias than contemporary operas or cantatas. The last of A. Scarlatti's *c*25 serenatas, *Erminia, Tancredi, Polidoro e Pastore* (1723), uses an orchestra of much more modern proportions than any found in his operas: flutes, oboes, bassoons, horns and trumpets in pairs, first and second violins, violas, cellos, at least two double basses and a harpsichord.

Set piece. Term sometimes used in opera for an aria or other number clearly demarcated from its context.

Sextet (It. *sestetto*). An ENSEMBLE for six singers. Sextets are rare in the operatic repertory, except within act finales, but there are two notable Mozart examples: the recognition scene in Act 3 of *Le nozze di Figaro* and the central scene of Act 2 of *Don Giovanni* (which may originally have been planned as an act finale). The most celebrated operatic sextet however is that at the grand dramatic climax of Donizetti's *Lucia di Lammermoor*.

Simile aria [metaphor aria]. An aria in which the text makes a comparison between the singer's situation or thoughts and some natural phenomenon or activity in the world at large, and the music provides appropriate illustration. Its literary origins are found in the elaborate metaphorical style of Giambattista Marino (1569–1625), whose influence on 17th-century Italian literature extended to the opera libretto; aria texts using conceits broadly similar to those favoured by Metastasio are common in the 17th century. Such arias offered composers an opportunity to introduce a wide variety of imagery. An example from Handel is Caesar's aria 'Va tacito e nascosto' in *Giulio Cesare* (1724), where a solo horn alludes to the hunter who must go cautiously in pursuit of his prey and the text makes a comparison with the intriguer who conceals his real intentions. In Gay's *The Beggar's Opera* (1728) the beggar claims to have 'introduc'd the similes that are in all your celebrated *Operas*', and the texts include several parodies of the type, e.g. 'I'm like a skiff on the Ocean tost'. The convention was increasingly criticized during the 18th century and had nearly died out by the end of it. (See Chapter VII.)

Sinfonia avanti l'opera (It.: 'symphony before the opera'). *See* ITALIAN OVERTURE.

Singspiel (Ger.: 'sing-play', 'play with singing'). A German play with music. In a precise and limited sense, the term, which was used as early as the 16th century, normally covers dramatic works with a liberal infusion of song (and occasionally of more ambitious musical forms) and which, following the success of the English ballad opera, from the time of Standfuss in the 1750s and Hiller in the 1760s, offered a popular and vernacular alternative to the operas (of the court and permanent public opera houses) that were sung throughout. The Singspiel in this sense was frequently referred to by its authors and their contemporaries as 'komische Oper' or 'Operette', and indeed, in the 1860s and 70s, it merged with the operetta proper. The Singspiel as a mainly lighthearted and popular form of theatrical entertainment had by then disappeared.

More generally, 'Singspiel' has been applied to virtually any stage work that includes vocal music, from medieval and Renaissance dramas, sacred and secular, and the works performed by the wandering troupes of Englische Comödianten in the late 16th and 17th centuries, to the Italian operas of Mozart which, when first performed at the Vienna court opera, were announced on the bilingual playbills as 'Neues Singspiel', 'Ein italiänisches Singspiel' and so on. (See Chapter VIII.)

Soprano (It.). The highest female voice, normally written for within the range *c'* to *a''*, which may be extended at either end, particularly in solo writing; the word is also used for a boy's treble voice and was used in the 17th and 18th centuries for a CASTRATO of high range. Sopranos were used in the earliest opera: Vittoria Archilei, who had sung in the Florentine *intermedi* of 1589, took the title role in Peri's *Euridice* (1600), and was called by the composer 'the Euterpe of our age', while after Virginia Andreini's performance of the lament in Monteverdi's *Arianna* (1608) 'there was not a woman who did not shed tears'. In the course of the Baroque period the soprano was also found to be particularly suited to brilliant vocal display, and when a singer achieved fame in the first half of the 18th century it was usually because of an ability to perform elaborate, difficult music with great technical precision as well as tonal beauty. The role of the heroine was sung by the most skilful soprano, the 'prima donna'; to her were assigned the greatest number of arias and the most difficult and expressively widest-ranging music. In this period music for soprano normally observed *a''* as the top note and little merit was placed on the ability to sing higher.

During the 18th century, composers came to appreciate essential differences among female voices in the soprano range that had to do not only with technical facility and compass but with timbre and character as well. Mozart, above all, created soprano roles of notable variety: bravura roles in the grand tradition (Fiordiligi, Constanze, Donna Elvira and Donna Anna), serious roles of a pathetic character with less bravura display (Ilia, the Countess, Pamina), primary roles of a soubrette character (Susanna, Zerlina) and secondary roles of even lighter character (Despina, Papagena, Marcellina). Type casting was not however as rigid as it is today: the singer of Susanna at the 1789 Vienna revival of *Figaro* sang Fiordiligi shortly afterwards. Although in bravura roles Mozart usually demanded *a"* or *bb"* as the highest note, in the unusually brilliant role of the Queen of Night (written for the soprano Josepha Hofer) the voice is carried as high as *f'''*.

In the early 19th century the coloratura requirements that composers such as Bellini, Rossini and Donizetti placed on the soprano voice reached a peak. Such roles as Amina in *La sonnambula*, Elvira, Norma and Lucia provided the basis for the careers of a remarkable generation of singers that included Giuditta Pasta (1797–1865), Wilhelmine Schröder-Devrient (1804–60), Henriette Sontag (1806–54), and Giulia Grisi (1811–69). At the same time, however, different qualities of tone and projection came to be called for by German composers, for example with Beethoven's Leonore and Weber's Agathe and Reiza. By the mid-19th century larger opera houses and the increased size of orchestras had led to a demand for greater volume from all singers and for sopranos in particular it was difficult to ride the sound of a full orchestra. In the Wagner repertory the need was especially great. Not surprisingly, as soprano voices were developed for maximum power less emphasis was placed on coloratura singing and in the second half of the century many sopranos appeared who were associated chiefly with dramatic roles, an early example being Amalie Materna (1845–1918), the first Brünnhilde and Kundry. More recent Wagner sopranos have included Kirsten Flagstad (1895–1962) and Birgit Nilsson (*b*1918). Verdi too came increasingly to demand a powerful, dramatic soprano, for such works as *Aida* and *Otello*, as opposed to the lighter, more lyrical soprano capable of florid singing which had served for *La traviata* or *Rigoletto*.

Some modern sopranos, notably Maria Callas (1923–77), have shown themselves to be equally at home in all Italian music from Bellini to Verdi and Puccini; others, such as Joan Sutherland (*b*1926), sing primarily the earlier 19th-century repertory and go back to the florid music of the 18th. Recent developments in soprano singing included the coming of the avant-garde specialist, with perfect pitch and extraordinary agility, and the growth of the period specialist who uses lighter tone and a fluent command of florid writing, and little or no vibrato, to sing music of the 17th and 18th centuries in period style, notably Emma Kirkby (*b*1949).

Spieloper (Ger.). Term for a type of German 19th-century comic opera with spoken dialogue between set musical numbers. Examples include Kreutzer's *Das Nachtlager von Granada* (1834), Lortzing's *Zar und Zimmermann* (1839) and *Der Wildschütz* (1842), Flotow's *Martha* (1847), Nicolai's *Die lustigen Weibern von Windsor* (1849) and Cornelius's *Der Barbier von Baghdad* (1858); similar in type are Berlioz's *Béatrice et Bénédict* (1862) and Smetana's *The Bartered Bride* (1866). The term has also been used for an all-sung opera as opposed to one (a *Sprechoper*) with spoken dialogue.

Spinto (It.: 'pushed'). Term for a lyric voice, usually soprano or tenor, that is able to sound powerful and incisive in dramatic climaxes. The full expression is 'lirico spinto'. The term is used also to describe operatic roles that require voices of this character, for example Mimì in Puccini's *La bohème* and Alfredo in Verdi's *La traviata*.

Sprechgesang [Sprechstimme] (Ger.: 'speech-song' ['speech-voice']). A type of vocal enunciation intermediate between speech and song. Notated Sprechgesang was introduced by Humperdinck in his opera *Königskinder* (1897), though in the edition of 1910 he replaced it by conventional singing. It was exploited most extensively by Schoenberg in *Die glückliche Hand* and *Moses und Aron*. Schoenberg wrote that Sprechgesang should 'give [the pitch] exactly, but then immediately leave it in a fall or rise'; the performer is also instructed that Sprechgesang should neither resemble natural speech nor recall true singing. These directions have given rise to various interpretations, largely because of the difficulty in speaking the range and exactness of pitch required. Berg used Sprechgesang in *Wozzeck* and *Lulu*, and at the same time introduced a new shade, 'half sung', between Sprechgesang and song.

Stile rappresentativo (It.: 'theatrical style'). Term for the solo vocal style employed in the earliest theatrical pieces set completely to music. It was first used publicly by Giulio Caccini in the title and dedication (1600) of his *Euridice* to describe its music. It includes a variety of styles: the narrative, using repeated notes and fast speech-like rhythm over static harmony; the expressive, with a more marked melodic profile, free dissonances and more frequent changes of harmony; and the recitation, with melodic formulae of narrow compass strophically repeated or varied, and cadences at the ends of lines (the 'strophic aria'). Dance songs also appeared in the pastorals. The earliest surviving music in this style is some fragments by Peri from *Dafne* (1598, Florence) and the *Rappresentatione di Anima, et di Corpo* by Cavalieri (1600, Rome).

Stretta [stretto] (It.). Term used to indicate a faster tempo at the climactic concluding section of a piece. It is common in Italian opera: examples include the end of the Act 2 finale of Mozart's *Le nozze di Figaro* and Violetta's aria at the end of Act 1 of Verdi's *La traviata*.

Strophic. Term for songs or arias in which all stanzas of the text are set to the same music. The term 'strophic variations' is used of songs where the melody is varied from verse to verse while the bass remains unchanged or virtually so. The form was popular in early 17th-century Italy; the aria 'Possente spirto', sung by Monteverdi's Orpheus, is an example, and Cavalli occasionally used the form in his operas.

Tenor (From Lat. *tenere*: 'to hold'). The highest natural male voice, normally written within the range *c* to *a'*, which may be extended, particularly at the upper end in solo writing. The word, from the structurally fundamental, 'holding' voice in early polyphony, came in the 15th century to refer to the male voice that sang such parts.

Although the tenor voice was valued in early opera – a tenor, Francesco Rasi (1574–after 1620), sang Monteverdi's Orpheus (1607), and it was at first the normal voice for the hero-lover – the heroic roles in middle and late Baroque opera were assigned to the castrato. Tenors took minor roles, such as the old man (sometimes with comic overtones), the lighthearted confidant, the mischievous schemer or the messenger, or even a travesty role of the old nurse. By the 1720s, important roles were occasionally given to tenors (for example in Handel's *Tamerlano* and *Lotario*), and by the Classical era the voice was more regularly used in central roles although the castrato retained his dominance in serious opera to the end of the century. Such roles as Mozart's Basilio, Ottavio, Ferrando and Titus – comic, docile lover, more virile lover, benevolent monarch – define the scope of the voice at this period; a type he did not use in a mature work was the *tenore buffo*. It is a matter of dispute whether the very high French tenor roles of the 18th century, written for the HAUTE-CONTRE voice, were sung with a falsetto or with an extension of the natural tenor.

A creation of the early 19th century was the *tenore di grazia*, a light, high voice moving smoothly into falsetto up to *d″*, called for by many Rossini roles and typified by Manuel García (1775–1832), Giovanni Davide (1790–1864) and Andrea Nozzari (1775–1832), or half a generation on by Giovanni Battista Rubini (1790–1854), creator of several Bellini roles. With the increasing size of opera houses, and the changes in musical style, the *tenore di forza* was called for: Domenico Donzelli (1790–1873) bridges the gap, while Adolphe Nourrit (1802–39) and Gilbert-Louis Duprez (1806–96) typify the new, stronger voice. The tendency continued as, with Verdi's operas, the *tenore robusto* developed; the name speaks for itself. For the German heroic tenor roles of the 19th century, especially Wagner's, a more weighty and durable type was needed, the HELDENTENOR, typified by Joseph Tichatschek (1807–86), the first Tannhäuser and Lohengrin, and the first Tristan, Ludwig Schnorr von Carolsfeld (1836–65). The lighter tenor continued to be cultivated for the more lyrical roles in French opera. A special type is the *tenor-altino* (or *-contraltino*), a very high, light voice, called for by Rimsky-Korsakov for the Astrologer in *The Golden Cockerel*, where he is expected to sing up to *e″* without falsetto (an alternative is offered if a tenor using falsetto takes the part). Many of the great tenors of the 20th century have been Italians, and made their names in Italian music, from Enrico Caruso (1873–1921), Beniamino Gigli (1890–1957) and Giovanni Martinelli (1885–1969) to Luciano Pavarotti (*b*1935) (the Spaniard Plácido Domingo, *b* 1937, should be added); Jussi Björling (1911–60), however, was greatly admired as a stylist in any repertory, Lauritz Melchior (1890–1973) and Max Lorenz (1901–75) were perhaps the most famous Wagner tenors, Peter Pears's (1910–86) individual voice and partnership with Britten gave rise to a new English tenor repertory, and Jon Vickers (*b*1926) has shown himself a leading interpreter equally of Italian, German, French and English roles.

Tenor-altino [tenor-contraltino] (It.). A high, light tenor voice; *see* TENOR.

Tenore di forza (It.: 'forceful tenor'). A type of TENOR voice, developed in the early 19th century for roles of the era of Donizetti and early French grand opera.

Tenore di grazia (It.: 'tenor of grace'). A type of TENOR voice, developed at the beginning of the 19th century for high, florid roles such as those of Rossini.

Tenore robusto (It.: 'robust tenor'). A type of TENOR voice, developed in the early to mid-19th century, for roles such as Verdi's that call for vigorous singing.

Terzet (It. *terzetto*). An ENSEMBLE for three singers; the term is generally preferred, in vocal music, to 'trio'. Terzets have been used throughout the history of opera. An early example is the item for Seneca's *famigliari* in Monteverdi's *L'incoronazione di Poppea*; there are also terzets in two Cavalli operas (*Rosinda* and *Eliogabalo*) and in some of A. Scarlatti's late Roman operas. Handel used the terzet several times, notably in *Tamerlano*, *Orlando* and *Alcina*; Gluck wrote terzets in the closing scenes of his Italian reform operas. Many terzets are for a pair of lovers with an outsider (a rival in love, a despotic king); in such cases the composer often uses musical means to establish the relationships, having the lovers sing in 3rds or 6ths while the third person's music has a quite different character and rhythm. Mozart's however vary widely in type. Notable are those in Act 1 of *Le nozze di Figaro*, where the action unfolds, propelled by the music; in *Così fan tutte*, which begins with a sequence of three, with a further one (a *terzettino*, a miniature example) soon following; in *Die Zauberflöte*, where they are for the Three Ladies or the Three Boys; and in *La clemenza di Tito*, where one is a violent outburst of anguish with uncomprehending commentary from two other characters. There are two examples in Weber's *Der Freischütz* and a notable one for three very high tenors in Rossini's *Armida*. The form was much used by the Romantics, among them Verdi, who wrote three terzets in *Un ballo in maschera*.

Tessitura [testura] (It.: 'texture'). Term for the part of a vocal compass in which a piece of music lies – whether high or low, etc. The tessitura of a piece is decided not by the extremes of its range but rather by which part of the range is most used. The role of Siegfried in Wagner's *Ring*, for example, ranges from $c\sharp$ to c'', but its tessitura would be described as high because the tenor is required to sing a great deal in the range c' to a'.

Testo (It.: 'text'). Term used in 17th-century Italian oratorio settings for the narrative portions of the text; by extension, the role of the narrator. In secular music the term was occasionally used for the narrator in dramatic dialogues and similar works; Monteverdi used a tenor for the *testo* in *Il combattimento di Tancredi e Clorinda* (1624).

Théâtres de la Foire (Fr.: 'fair theatres'). Term used of the theatres at the two Paris fairs, the Foire St Germain (held between 3 February and Palm Sunday) and the Foire St Laurent (held in the summer). The fair theatres, which traditionally housed popular entertainment, took over the Comédie-Italienne repertory in 1697 when that institution was closed down; they were involved in disputes with the Comédie-Française and the Opéra, but were later permitted to give dramatic entertainments with songs under the title Opéra-Comique. The fair theatres performed this repertory in 1715–18, 1724–44 and 1752–8; in 1762 Opéra-Comique performances moved to the Hôtel de Bourgogne. The fair theatres represent an important stage in the early history of the OPÉRA COMIQUE genre. (See Chapter IX.)

Timbre (Fr.). The opening words or the refrain from a vaudeville tune, by which it was known and which permitted deft allusion to it. The music to it was called *fredon*.

Tonadilla (Sp., diminutive of *tonada*: 'song'). Originally a song, usually topical, with guitar, appended to Spanish theatrical interludes; later, a short stage piece. By the early 1750s the type was developing, in the hands of Antonio Guerrero, into a sung sketch in one act (akin to the Italian intermezzo), referred to as the *tonadilla escénica*. Usually satirical or political, it was either for a single character (frequently a woman) or for up to about five; Valledor's *La plaza de palacio de Barcelona* (1774) calls for 12 singers. The usual duration of a solo *tonadilla* in 1791 was 10–12 minutes, for a dialogue 15, and for one with four characters 20–25. The genre exploited national dances and melodies of folk type, and dealt mainly with lower-class popular life. It was colourful, broad in humour and predominantly picaresque, though a romantic element was also common.

From about 1770 to 1810 a spate of *tonadillas* were produced in Madrid. But by the end of the first decade of the 19th century it was in decline; the treatment of its subjects, once natural and unpretentious, was turning towards allegory, a moralizing tone was creeping into its texts, and musically its nationalistic character had been diluted through the influence of Italian opera, reinstated in Madrid in 1787. By the middle of the 19th century it had given way to the ZARZUELA. (See Chapter XI.)

Tragédie lyrique (Fr.). Name given to serious, though not necessarily tragic, French opera of the 17th and 18th centuries. As a term it was favoured more by aestheticians than by composers, who often preferred the terms 'opéra', 'tragédie en musique' and 'tragédie opéra'. The form was inaugurated by Lully and Quinault (*Cadmus*, 1673), who collaborated on 11 such works, all on subjects from mythology or medieval chivalry; each had a prologue and five acts. It was pursued by Campra and, particularly, Rameau (his first was *Hippolyte et Aricie*, 1733); and its last great exponent was Gluck, whose French reform operas, like his rival Piccinni's, belong in the same tradition. The term was used for several kinds of work in the late 18th century including, in the operas of Gluck, Lemoyne, Salieri and Sacchini, works based on Greek tragedy, operatic treatments of Corneille's plays, historical operas and revisions of earlier *tragédies lyriques*. (See Chapters III and IX.)

Travesti (Fr.). *See* BREECHES PART. 'Travesty' is sometimes used of a role in which a singer wears the clothes of the opposite sex.

Trial. A type of tenor singer, named after Antoine Trial (1736–95), specializing in comedy and dramatic skill rather than vocal accomplishment.

Vaudeville (Fr.). A French poem or song of satirical or epigrammatic character common in the 17th and 18th centuries. Comedy using vaudeville tunes with new words was one of the theatrical styles that caught the imagination of the Paris public at that time. The theatres at the annual Paris fairs of St Germain and St Laurent (*see* THÉÂTRES DE LA FOIRE) experimented with acrobatic shows, plays with songs and dances, monologues, pantomimes, poster plays and marionettes, centred on the use of vaudevilles. Originally vaudevilles made up the bulk of the music, supplemented by short opera excerpts which quickly invaded the vaudeville repertory, dances and instrumental interludes. Attempts were made to select vaudevilles that best represented the emotional state of the play at the point they were to be introduced, either through the tune or by recalling or re-using part of the original text. A clever choice could underscore a situation forcefully, or even contradict it in a humorous way. As the *opéra comique* developed from these ventures, more original music was added, beginning with the finales. The French *comédie en vaudeville* had an international influence: it spread to England as the ballad opera and to Germany as the early Singspiel.

In the 19th century, 'vaudeville' or 'pièce en vaudeville' was applied to a stage work using pre-existing airs.

See also VAUDEVILLE FINAL.

Vaudeville final (Fr.). Placed at the end of an act or play, the *vaudeville final* reassembled on stage all the important characters and required each to sing one or more verses of a vaudeville. At times the strophic form was emphasized by having a chorus repeat a refrain line. This style was common to French opera and *opéra comique*. Rousseau's *Le devin du village* has a *vaudeville final*; Rameau, along with Mouret, Duni, Monsigny and Philidor, wrote them for the Théâtres de la Foire and the Opéra-Comique. Normally the words of the *vaudeville final* were still in keeping with the characters singing them, each of whom usually presented some moral. Attempts to make the final scene more impressive soon led composers to write an original *vaudeville final*, chorus and dance music; with this as its starting-point, original music then gradually infiltrated the entire play. The influence of the *vaudeville final* may also be seen in other genres, and it continued into later periods, as in Gluck's *Orfeo*, Mozart's *Die Entführung aus dem Serail*, Rossini's *Il barbiere di Siviglia*, Verdi's *Falstaff*, Ravel's *L'heure espagnole* and Stravinsky's *The Rake's Progress*.

Verismo (It.: 'realism'). Name for the Italian version of the late 19th-century movement towards naturalism in European literature, of which Emile Zola in France was the dominant figure. In Italy the novelist Giovanni Verga occupied a similar position; his *Cavalleria rusticana* was the basis for Mascagni's opera (1889), whose tremendous success spawned a series of similar one-act *verismo* operas in Italy and outside (e.g. Massenet's *La Navarraise*, 1894), of which only Leoncavallo's *Pagliacci* (1891) remains in the repertory. These followed the general naturalistic tendencies towards introducing characters from the lower social strata, strong local colour and situations centring on the violent clash of fierce, even brutal passions, particularly hatred, lust, betrayal and murder. The term has been used more broadly to include Italian operas of the same period that strictly belong to other genres but which have elements in common with true *verismo* operas or were written by the same composers. (See Chapter XXII.)

Voce di testa (It.: 'head voice'). Term used in singing to denote the head register, as distinct from the chest and throat registers. In the 17th and 18th centuries it was often used to denote the falsetto voice.

Voix sombrée (Fr.: 'darkened voice'). A technique of voice production, made famous by the singing of the tenor Gilbert Duprez during the 1830s; it was probably produced by Duprez's keeping his larynx at a low level even in the upper range. It was highly controversial. Even the voice of Duprez is reported to have tired easily because of his use of the *voix sombrée*.

Vorspiel (Ger.). Prelude. The term appears frequently in German operatic scores from Wagner's *Lohengrin* (1846–8) onwards. Following Wagner's prescriptions in *Oper und Drama* it was closely linked with the musical and dramatic events of the opera. The two that function as symphonic prologues to Acts 1 and 3 of *Die Walküre*, for instance, depict respectively the storm which drives Siegmund to seek shelter in Hunding's hut and the ride of the Valkyries before their assembly. The Vorspiel was not necessarily purely orchestral; the Prologue to Act 1 of *Götterdämmerung*, marked 'Vorspiel', embraces two extended scenes, and may have been influenced by the opening of Marschner's *Hans Heiling* (1833), where the Vorspiel, consisting of choruses flanking a solo for Heiling, precedes the overture.

Zarzuela (Sp., from *zarza*: 'bramble bush'). A Spanish dramatic form, characterized by the alternation of singing and dancing with spoken dialogue. It reached its peak of popularity in the second half of the 19th century. (See Chapters V, XI, XX and XXIX.)

Zauberoper (Ger.: 'magic opera'). Term, used more often by historians than composers, for the kind of opera that relies to an unusual extent on stage machinery and spectacular effects. In practice its use is normally restricted to the kind of 'magic' Singspiel given with success in Vienna during the 18th and early 19th centuries; Mozart's *Die Zauberflöte* is the most famous example. Hafner's *Megära, die förchterliche Hexe* (a 'Zauberlustspiel', 1763) is an earlier example. The genre continued to be popular in Vienna at least until the time of Ferdinand Raimund and Wenzel Müller (whose setting of Perinet's adaptation of Hafner's *Megära* in 1806 is actually sub-titled 'Zauberoper').

Zwischenspiel (Ger.). An interlude or intermezzo. The term has been applied to interludes that serve simply to entertain between the acts of operatic works of the 19th and 20th centuries; even in German-speaking countries, however, 'entr'acte' or 'Entrakt' has often been preferred. It has also been used of interludes which contribute to the essential dramatic structure of the whole, e.g. the Zwischenspiel between Acts 1 and 2 of Schoenberg's *Moses und Aron*; 'Siegfrieds Rheinfahrt' is described as a Zwischenspiel in some editions of *Götterdämmerung*, though it is doubtful whether Wagner himself so described it.

Bibliography

This bibliography begins with general sections, followed by sections devoted to librettos and periodicals. Then follow sections corresponding to the main parts of the book – that is, organized first by period and then by country (or group of countries); there is a final section dealing with aspects of staging.

Items that are appropriate for citation in two or more successive period sections are, unless there are strong reasons otherwise, cited only in the earlier; a few are cited twice, and a very few only in the later. Discussions of librettos are cited in the specific national and period section to which they apply unless they are of a more general character, in which case they are noted in the 'Libretto' section. Works of theatrical history are normally cited in the national/period section where they are first relevant.

GENERAL

Histories, General and Miscellaneous Studies

P. Lohmann: *Über die dramatische Dichtung mit Musik* (Leipzig, 1861, 3/1886 as *Das Ideal der Oper*)

H. S. Edwards: *History of the Opera from Monteverdi to Donizetti* (London, 1862, 2/1862/R1977)

H. M. Schletterer: *Die Entstehung der Oper* (Nördlingen, 1873)

A. A. Regnard: *La renaissance du drame lyrique 1600–1876: essai de dramaturgie musicale* (Paris, 1895)

R. A. Streatfeild: *The Opera* (London, 1897, rev., enlarged 2/1902, rev. 5/1925 by E. J. Dent)

W. F. Apthorp: *The Opera Past and Present* (New York, 1901)

A. Elson: *A Critical History of Opera: giving an Account of the Rise and Progress of the Different Schools, with a Description of the Master Works in Each* (Boston, Mass., 1901)

E. Istel: *Die komische Oper: eine historisch-ästhetische Studie* (Stuttgart, 1906)

J. Combarieu: 'Histoire du théâtre lyrique', *RHCM*, vii (1907), 581; viii (1908), 1–594 passim; ix (1909) passim; x (1910) passim

L. Aubin: *Le drame lyrique: histoire de la musique dramatique en France* (Tours, 1908)

H. de Curzon: *L'évolution lyrique au théâtre dans les différents pays: tableau chronologique* (Paris, 1908)

J. Goddard: *The Rise and Development of Opera* (London, 1912)

O. Bie: *Die Oper* (Berlin, 1913, 10/1923)

K. M. Klob: *Die Oper von Gluck bis Wagner* (Ulm, 1913)

H. Kretzschmar: *Geschichte der Oper* (Leipzig, 1919/R1970)

H. F. Peyser: 'Some Observations on Translation', *MQ*, viii (1922), 353

M. Steidel: *Oper und Drama* (Karlsruhe, 1923)

G. Adler: *Handbuch der Musikgeschichte* (Frankfurt, 1924, 2/1930/R1961)

E. Bücken: *Der heroische Stil in der Oper* (Leipzig, 1924)

A. Aber: *Musik im Schauspiel* (Leipzig, 1926)

H. Abert: *Grundprobleme der Operngeschichte* (Leipzig, 1926)

E. Rabich: *Die Entwicklung der Oper* (Langensalza, 1926)

F. Haböck: *Die Castraten und ihre Gesangkunst* (Stuttgart, 1927)

A. Bonaventura: *L'opera italiana* (Florence, 1928)

G. Bustico: *Bibliografia delle storie e cronistorie dei teatri italiani* (Milan, 1929)

History of Opera

D. Hussey: *Eurydice: or, The Nature of Opera* (London, 1929)
R. Capell: *Opera* (London, 1930, enlarged 2/1948)
P. Bekker: *Wandlungen der Oper* (Zurich, 1934; Eng. trans., 1936)
E. J. Dent: 'The Translation of Operas', *PMA*, lxi (1934–5), 81
W. Götze: *Studien zur Formbildung der Oper* (Frankfurt, 1935)
A. Capri: *Il melodramma dalle origini ai nostri giorni* (Modena, 1938)
A. Della Corte: *Tre secoli di opera italiana* (Turin, 1938)
H. Closson: *Musique et drame* (Brussels, 1939)
E. J. Dent: *Opera* (Harmondsworth, 1940, rev. 5/1949)
M. A. Barrenechea: *Historia estética de la música, con dos estudios mas sobre consideraciones históricas y técnicas acerca del canto y la obra maestra del teatro melodramático* (Buenos Aires, 1941)
W. Brockway and H. Weinstock: *The Opera: a History of its Creation and Performance, 1600–1941* (New York, 1941, 2/1962)
J. Gregor: *Kulturgeschichte der Oper: ihre Verbindung mit dem Leben, den Werken des Geistes und der Politik* (Vienna, 1941, 3/1950)
J. Loschedler: *Die Oper als Kunstform* (Vienna, 1941)
I. Pizzetti: *Musica e dramma* (Rome, 1945)
O. Riemer: *Musik und Schauspiel* (Zurich, 1946)
I. Gundry: 'The Nature of Opera as a Composite Art', *PRMA*, lxxiii (1946–7), 25
D. J. Grout: *A Short History of Opera* (New York and London, 1947, rev. 3/1988)
A. Matthis: 'A Survey of Opera between the Two World Wars', *HMYB*, iv–v (1947–8), 85–124
M. Doisy: *Musique et drame* (Paris, 1949)
E. Wellesz: *Essays on Opera* (London, 1950)
W. H. Auden: 'Some Reflections on Opera as a Medium', *Tempo*, no.20 (1951), 6
M. Geisenheymer: *Kulturgeschichte des Theaters: Volk und Drama* (Berlin, 1951)
A. A. Abert: *Die Oper von den Anfängen bis zum Beginn des 19. Jahrhunderts* (Cologne, 1953; Eng. trans., 1962)
R. Dumesnil: *Histoire illustrée du théâtre lyrique* (Paris, 1953; Sp. trans., 1957)
G. Gavazzeni: *La musica e il teatro* (Pisa, 1954)
A. Hostomská: *Opéra* (Prague, 1955, 3/1958)
D. de Paoli: *L'opera italiana dalle origini all'opera verista* (Rome, 1955)
A. Heriot: *The Castrati in Opera* (London, 1956)
J. Kerman: *Opera as Drama* (New York, 1956, rev. 2/1988)
H. Kindermann: *Theatergeschichte Europas* (Salzburg, 1957–)
R. Leibowitz: *Histoire de l'opéra* (Paris, 1957)
N. Loeser: *De opera: haar wezen en haar ontwikkeling* (Haarlem, 1958)
P. Hope-Wallace: *A Picture-History of Opera* (London, 1959)
K. V. Burian: *Die Oper: ihre Geschichte in Wort und Bild* (Prague, 1961)
A. Khokhlovina: *Istoriya zapadno-evropeyskoy oper* [History of western European opera] (Moscow, 1962)
G. R. Marek: *Opera as Theater* (New York, 1962/R1977)
K. Pahlen: *Oper der Welt* (Zurich, 1963)
H. Schmidt-Garre: *Oper: eine Kulturgeschichte* (Cologne, 1963)
C. Rezzonico: *Il melodramma* (Como, 1964)
H. H. Stuckenschmidt: *Oper in dieser Zeit* (Hanover, 1964)
U. Weisstein, ed.: *The Essence of Opera: the Creative Process of Opera Revealed by Librettists and Composers in Original Writings from 1600 to the Present* (New York and London, 1964)
A. S. Garlington: *The Concept of the Marvelous in French and German Opera, 1770–1840: a Chapter in the History of Opera Esthetics* (diss., U. of Illinois, 1965)
W. Mellers: *Harmonious Meeting: a Study of Music, Poetry and Drama in England, 1600–1900* (London, 1965)
C. Hamm: *Opera* (Boston, Mass., 1966)
M. F. Robinson: *Opera before Mozart* (London, 1966, 2/1972)
R. Hofmann: *Histoire de l'opéra* (Paris, 1967)
F. H. Tørnbloom: *Operans historia* (Stockholm, 1967)
J. Elsendoorn: *Vier eeuwen opera van Monteverdi tot Nono* (Haarlem, 1968)
New Looks at Italian Opera: Essays in Honor of Donald J. Grout (Ithaca, NY, 1968)
H. C. Wolff: *Oper, Szene und Darstellung von 1600 bis 1900*, Musikgeschichte in Bildern, iv/1 (Leipzig, 1968)
H. Becker, ed.: *Beiträge zur Geschichte der Oper* (Regensburg, 1969)
H. Krause-Graumnitz: *Vom Wesen der Oper: Opernkomponisten in Autobiographien, Vorreden und Briefen,*

416

Werk-Erläuterungen und anderen Dokumenten über die Oper (Berlin, 1969)
R. Berges: *The Backgrounds and Traditions of Opera* (Cranbury, NJ, and London, 1970)
E. Brody: *Music in Opera: a Historical Anthology* (Englewood Cliffs, NJ, 1970)
L. Orrey: *Opera: a Concise History* (London, 1972, rev. 2/1987)
P.-A. Gaillard: 'Les compositeurs suisses et l'opéra', *SMz*, cxiv (1974), 219, 280
Essays on Opera and English Music in Honour of Sir Jack Westrup (Oxford, 1975)
E. J. Dent: *The Rise of Romantic Opera*, ed. W. Dean (Cambridge, 1976)
A. Basso and G. Barblan, eds.: *Storia dell'opera* (Turin, 1977–)
J. and H. LaRue: 'Trade Routes and Time Lag in the Export of Late Eighteenth-Century Opera',
   A Musical Offering: Essays in Honor of Martin Bernstein (New York, 1977)
R. Donington: *The Opera* (London, 1978)
J. Gourret: *Histoire de l'Opéra de Paris* (Paris, 1978)
E. Mordden: *Opera in the Twentieth Century: Sacred, Profane, Godot* (New York, 1978)
H. E. Smither: 'Oratorio and Sacred Opera, 1700–1825: Terminology and Genre Distinction',
   PRMA, cvi (1979–80), 88
D. Altenburg, ed.: *Ars musica, musica scientia: Festschrift Heinrich Hüschen* (Cologne, 1980) [see
   articles by H. Becker, G. Heldt, R. Jackson and F. Noske]
J. Drummond: *Opera in Perspective* (London, 1980)
G. Martin: *A Companion to Twentieth Century Opera* (London, 1980)
P.-J. Salazar: *Idéologies de l'opéra* (Paris, 1980)
S. Wiesmann, ed.: *Werk und Wiedergabe: Musiktheater exemplarisch interpretiert* (Bayreuth, 1980)
H. Mayer: *Versuche über die Oper* (Frankfurt, 1981)
H. C. Wolff: *Geschichte der komischen Oper: von der Anfängen bis zur Gegenwart* (Wilhelmshaven, 1981)
E. Fischer: *Zur Problematik der Opernstruktur: das künstlerische System und seine Krisis im 20. Jahrhundert*
   (Wiesbaden, 1982)
A. S. Garlington: 'Opera', *MQ*, lxviii (1982), 238 [review of 'Opera', *Grove 6*]
R. Martorella: *The Sociology of Opera* (New York, 1982)
J. Schläder and R. Quandt, eds.: *Festschrift Heinz Becker* (Laaber, 1982) [§I: 'Opernforschung',
   incl. articles by R. Brinkmann, W. Osthoff, M. Rühnke, M. Staehelin, H. C. Wolff and others]
S. Wiesmann: *Für und wider die Literaturoper* (Laaber, 1982)
L. K. Gerhartz: *Oper: Aspekte der Gattung* (Laaber, 1983)
E. Surian: 'Musical Historiography and Histories of Italian Opera', *CMc*, no.36 (1983), 167
N. John: *Opera* (Oxford, 1984)
H. Lindenberger: *Opera: the Extravagant Art* (Ithaca, NY, 1984)
W. Oehlmann: *Oper in vier Jahrhunderten* (Stuttgart, 1984)
J. M. Fischer, ed.: *Oper und Operntext* (Heidelberg, 1985)
J. Herz: *. . . und Figaro lasst sich scheiden: Oper als Idee und Interpretation* (Munich, 1985)
R. Kloiber: *Handbuch der Oper* (Munich and Kassel, 1985)
P. Robinson: *Opera and Ideas: from Mozart to Strauss* (New York, 1985)
G. Wickham: *A History of the Theatre* (London, 1985)
R. Blanchard and R. de Condé: *Dieux et divas de l'opéra*, i: *Des origines au romantisme* (Paris, 1986)
J. L. DiGaetani: *An Invitation to the Opera* (New York, 1986)
M. and S. Harries: *Opera Today* (New York, 1986)
R. Katz: *Divining the Powers of Music: Aesthetic Theory and the Origins of Opera* (New York, 1986)
G. Marchesi: *L'opera lirica: guida storico-critica dalle origini al Novecento* (Milan, 1986)
A. Seebohm, ed.: *Die Wiener Oper: 350 Jahre Glanz und Tradition* (Vienna, 1986) [Eng. trans. S. Nye
   as *The Vienna Opera* (New York, 1987)]
L. Bianconi and G. Pestelli, eds.: *Storia dell'opera italiana*, iv: *Il sistema produttivo e le sue competenze*
   (Turin, 1987)
P. Conrad: *A Song of Love and Death: the Meaning of Opera* (London, 1987)
S. Corse: *Opera and the Uses of Language: Mozart, Verdi and Britten* (London and Toronto, 1987)
N. Fortune, ed.: *Music and Theatre: Essays in Honour of Winton Dean* (Cambridge, 1987)
C. Headington, R. Westbrook and T. Barfoot: *Opera: a History* (London, 1987)
N. Pirrotta: *Scelte poetiche di musicisti: teatro, poesia e musica da Willaert a Malipiero* (Venice, 1987)
J. Tambling: *Opera, Ideology and Film* (New York, 1987)
J. Webster: 'To Understand Verdi and Wagner we must Understand Mozart', *19th-Century Music*,
   xi (1987–8), 175
L. Bianconi and G. Pestelli, eds.: *Storia dell'opera italiana*, v: *La spettacolorita* (Turin, 1988)
R. Christiansen, ed.: *The Grand Obsession: a Collins Anthology of Opera* (London, 1988)
J. Rosselli: 'The Castrati as a Professional Group and a Social Phenomenon, 1550–1850', *AcM*, lx
   (1988), 143–79

C. Abbate and R. Parker, eds.: *Analyzing Opera: Verdi and Wagner* (Berkeley, in preparation)
R. Parker and A. Groos, eds.: *Reading Opera* (in preparation)

Catalogues, Dictionaries, Guides

F. Clément and P. Larousse: *Dictionaire lyrique, ou Histoire des opéras* (Paris, 1867–9, 4 suppls. to 1881, 2/1897 ed. A. Pougin, suppl. 1904, 3/1905/*R*1969)
T. de Lajarte: *Bibliothèque musicale du Théâtre de l'Opéra: catalogue historique, chronologique, anecdotique* (Paris, 1878/*R*1969)
H. Riemann: *Opern-Handbuch* (Leipzig, 1887–93, 2/1893 with suppl. by F. Stieger)
C. Dassori: *Opere e operisti (dizionario lirico 1541–1902): elenco nominativo universale dei maestri compositori di opere teatrali* (Genoa, 1903/*R*1979, 2/1906)
J. Towers, ed.: *Dictionary-Catalogue of Operas and Operettas* (Morganstown, 1910/*R*1967)
J. Kapp: *Das Opernbuch: eine Geschichte der Oper und ein musikalisch-dramatischer Führer* (Leipzig, 1922, rev. 2/1939)
G. Kobbé: *Kobbé's Complete Opera Book* (London, 1922, rev. 10/1987 by the Earl of Harewood)
E. Newman: *Opera Nights* (London, 1943)
A. Loewenberg: *Annals of Opera, 1597–1940* (Cambridge, 1943, rev. 3/1978 by H. Rosenthal)
E. Newman: *More Opera Nights* (London, 1954)
F. D'Amico, ed.: *Enciclopedia dello spettacolo* (Rome and Florence, 1954–62; suppl. 1966)
U. Manferrari: *Dizionario universale delle opere melodrammatiche* (Florence, 1954–5)
D. Ewen: *Encyclopedia of the Opera* (New York, 1955, rev. 4/1971 as *The New Encyclopedia of the Opera*)
H. Schnoor: *Oper, Operette, Konzert* (Gütersloh, 1955; rev. by S. Pflicht as *Mosaik-Opernfährer*, 1979)
P. Czerny, ed.: *Opernbuch* (Berlin, 1958, 5/1961)
R. Bauer: *Oper und Operetta: ein Führer durch die Welt der Musikbühne* (Berlin, 1959)
A. Ross: *The Opera Directory* (London, 1961)
M. Ōtaguro: *Kageki daijiten* [Dictionary of opera] (Tokyo, 1962)
A. Jacobs and S. Sadie: *The Pan Book of Opera* [also pubd as *The Opera Guide* and *Opera: a New Guide*] (London and New York, 1964, enlarged 2/1986)
H. Rosenthal and J. Warrack: *Concise Oxford Dictionary of Opera* (London, 1964, rev. 3/1978)
T. Besterman: *Music and Drama: a Bibliography of Bibliographies* (Totowa, NJ, 1971)
F. Stieger: *Opernlexikon* (Tutzing, 1975–83)
L. Orrey, ed.: *The Encyclopaedia of Opera* (London, 1976)
Who's Who in Opera (New York, 1976)
L'opera: repertorio della lirica dal 1597 (Milan, 1977; Eng. trans. as *Simon and Schuster Book of the Opera/Phaidon Book of the Opera*, 1977, 1979)
C. M. Gruber, ed.: *Opern-Uraufführungen: ein internationales Verzeichnis von der Renaissance bis zur Gegenwart* (Vienna, 1978–)
H. Seeger: *Opern Lexikon* (Berlin, 1978, rev. 1987)
F. von Stranz: *Der grosse Opernführer* (Munich, 1978)
A. Blyth, ed.: *Opera on Record*, [i], ii, iii (London, 1979–85)
P. Gammond: *Illustrated Encyclopedia of Recorded Opera* (New York, 1979)
A. Payne: *Grands opéras du repertoire: résumés des livrets, analyses musicales, discographie* (Paris, 1979)
F. Endler: *Endlers Opern-Führer* (Vienna and Stuttgart, 1980)
B. Reger-Bellinger and others: *Knaurs grosser Opernführer* (Munich, 1983)
E. W. White: *A Register of First Performances of English Operas and Semi-Operas from the Sixteenth Century to 1980* (London, 1983)
G. A. Marco: *Opera: a Research and Information Guide* (New York, 1984)
C. Osborne: *Dictionary of Opera* (London, 1983)
S. Pitou: *The Paris Opera: an Encyclopedia of Operas, Ballets, Composers and Performers* (Westport, Conn., 1985)
C. Dahlhaus, ed.: *Pipers Enzyklopädie des Musiktheaters: Oper, Operette, Musical, Ballett* (Munich and Zurich, 1986–)
P. Korenhof: *Winkler Prins Encyclopedie van de Opera* (Amsterdam, 1986)
C. H. Parsons, ed.: *Opera Composers and their Works* (Lewiston, NY, 1986)
D. Hamilton; ed.: *The Metropolitan Encyclopedia of Opera* (London and New York, 1987)
J. Lazarus: *The Opera Handbook* (Harlow, 1987)
E. Mordden: *A Guide to Opera Recordings* (New York, 1987)

THE LIBRETTO

E. H. de Bricqueville: *Le livret d'opéra français de Lully à Gluck, 1672–1779* (Brussels, 1887)

E. Istel: *Das Libretti: Wesen, Aufbau und Wirkung des Opernbuchs* (Berlin, 1914, 2/1915; Eng. trans., rev., as *The Art of Writing Opera Librettos*)

O. G. T. Sonneck: *Catalogue of Opera Librettos Printed before 1800* (Washington, DC, 1914/R1967)

H. Child: 'Some Thoughts on the Opera Libretto', *ML*, ii (1921), 244

A. de Ternant; 'French Opera Libretti', *ML*, xi (1930), 172

M. Kraussold: *Geist und Stoff der Operndichtung* (Vienna, 1931)

A. Della Corte: *Le relazioni storiche della poesia e della musica italiana* (Turin, 1936)

E. Closson: 'Les livrets d'opéra', *Cahiers de la musique*, i (Brussels, 1938), 193

G. Gavazzeni: 'La poesia dell'opera in musica', *RaM*, xi (1938), 137

E. Valentin: 'Dichtung und Oper', *AMf*, iii (1938), 138–79

F. Vatielli: 'Operisti e librettisti dei secoli XVII e XVIII', *RMI*, xliii (1939), 1–16, 315–32, 605–21

C. Culcasi: *Musica e poesia: rappporti estetici e storici* (Verona and Milan, 1940)

A. Della Corte: *La 'poesia per musica' ed il libretto d'opera* (Turin, 1950)

——: *Il libretto e il melodramma* (Turin, 1951)

U. Rolandi: *Il libretto per musica attraverso i tempi* (Rome, 1951)

L. Schrade: 'Das Libretto der modernen Oper', *Melos*, xx (1953), 312

A. Scherle: *Das deutsche Opernlibretto von Opitz bis Hofmannsthal* (Munich, 1954)

U. Weisstein: *The Libretto as Literature* (Norman, Oklahoma, 1961)

R. Müller: *Das Opernlibretto im 19. Jahrhundert* (Winterthur, 1966)

L. Bragaglia: *Storia del libretto* (Rome, 1970–)

P. J. Smith: *The Tenth Muse: a Historical Study of the Opera Libretto* (New York, 1970)

E. Fisher: *Die Texte der Oper: Studien zur Struktur einer Gattung* (diss., Ruhr U., Bochum, 1974)

A. Fraser: 'Truth and Reality in Operatic Librettos', *Opera*, xxv (1974), 9

Opernlibretti vor 1800 (Leipzig, 1982)

J. J. Fuld: *The Book of World-Famous Libretti: the Musical Theater from 1598 to Today* (New York, 1985)

D. Goldin: *La vera Fenice: librettisti e libretti tra sette e ottocento* (Turin, 1985)

A. Gier, ed.: *Oper als Text: Romantische Beiträge zur Libretto-Forschung* (Heidelberg, 1986)

C. H. Parsons, ed.: *Opera Librettists and their Works* (Lewiston, NY, 1987)

PERIODICALS

Abbreviations: B – bi-monthly; F – fortnightly; H – half-yearly; M – monthly; O – occasional; Q – quarterly; S – semi-monthly; Y – yearly

General

(alphabetically by title)

About the House: the Magazine of the Friends of Covent Garden (London, 1962/53–) 3–4 p.a., from 1970 3 p.a.

Cambridge Opera Journal; (Cambridge, 1989–) 3 p.a.

Central Opera Service Bulletin (New York, 1959–) 5–7 nos. Y, from 1965/6 no.3, B, from 1971/2 no.4, Q

Entr'acte: la revue des théâtres lyriques (Paris, 1955–) S

Jahrbuch für Opernforschung (Frankfurt, 1985–) O

Oper heute: ein Almanach der Musikbühne (Berlin, 1978–) Y [superseded *Jahrbuch der Komischen Oper Berlin* and *Musikbühne: Probleme und Informationen*]

Oper und Konzert (Munich, 1963–) M

Opera (London, 1950–) M [13 p.a. with festival no.] [continuation of *Ballet and Opera*, 1948–50, which divided into two]

L'Opera: a Magazine dedicated to the International Lyric Theatre (Milan, 1966) Q

Opéra: la revue française de l'art lyrique (Paris, ?1983–) M [superseded *Opéra 61: la revue de l'art lyrique* (Paris, 1961–73) which, March 1973 to Aug 1974, was incorporated into *Le guide du concert*; from

1974 called *Opéra: théâtre musical, danse, disque, variétés*, from 1977/8 *Opéra international: le magazine de l'art lyrique*]
Opera Australia (Sydney, 1978) Y
Opera Companion (San Francisco, 1978–) 10 p.a.
Opera in Canada (Toronto, 1960–) 6 p.a.; from 1975 5 p.a.; from 1976 Q [until July 1963 *Opera Canada*]
Opera Journaal (Amsterdam, 1972/3–) M [continuation of *Opera: periodiek voor muziedramatische kunst*, Amsterdam, 1967/8–1971/2, 5 vols.]
Opera Journal (Columbia, MS, 1968–) Q
Opera News (New York, 1936–) M out of season, F in season (Dec–April)
Opera Quarterly (Chapel Hill, 1983–) Q
Opera Review (Arlington, VA, 1977–) B
Opernwelt: die internationale Opernzeitschrift (Stuttgart, 1960–62: Velber bei Hanover, 1963–) M, with yearbook, *Oper*
Scottish Opera News (Glasgow, 1976–) 6 p.a. [originally M] [supersedes *Scottish Opera News* (Glasgow, 1964–9), M; then *Scottish Opera Magazine* (Glasgow, 1970–75), M]
Sydney Opera House Diary (Sydney, 1973–) B

Composers

(alphabetically by composer)

Donizetti Society Journal (London, 1974–) Y
Donizetti Society Newsletter (London, 1973–) H
Göttinger Händel-Beiträge (Kassel, 1984–) O
Händel-Jahrbuch (Leipzig, 1928–33; 1955–) Y
Haydn-Studien (Munich and Duisburg, 1965/7–) O
The Haydn Yearbook/Das Haydn-Jahrbuch (Bryn Mawr, PA, and Vienna, 1962–71; Eisenstadt, 1975–8; Cardiff, 1980–) O
Mozart-Jahrbuch (Munich, 1923–24, 1929 only) Y
Neues Mozart-Jahrbuch (Regensburg, 1941–3) Y
Mozart-Jahrbuch (Salzburg, 1950–) Y
Bollettino del Centro rossiniano di studi (Pesaro, 1955–60, 1967–) 3 p.a.
AIVS Newsletter (New York, 1976–) (from 1976 no.2 entitled *Verdi Newsletter*) H
Bollettino dell' Istituto di studi verdiani (Parma, 1960–) O
Quaderni dell' Istituto di studi verdiani (Parma, 1963–) O
Studi verdiani (Parma, 1982–) Y
The Wagner Society Newsletter (London, 1965–) [from 1971 *Wagner: the Magazine of the Wagner Society*; from June 1980 divided into *Wagner* (London) Q, and *Wagner News*, 8 p.a.]

BAROQUE

Italy

B. Croce: *I teatri di Napoli dal Rinascimento alla fine del secolo decimottavo* (Naples, 1891)
H. Kretzschmar: 'Die Venetianische Oper und die Werke Cavallis und Cestis', *VMw*, viii (1892), 1
H. Goldschmidt: *Studien zur Geschichte der italienischen Oper im 17. Jahrhundert* (Leipzig, 1901–4/ R1967)
A. Solerti, ed.: *Gli albori del melodramma* (Milan, 1904–5/R1969)
E. J. Dent: *Alessandro Scarlatti: his Life and Works* (London, 1905, rev. 2/1960 by F. Walker)
H. Kretzschmar: 'Beitrage zur Geschichte der Venetianischen Oper', *JbMP*, xiv (1907), 71 [see also xvii (1910), 61, and xviii (1911), 49
H. Prunières: *L'opéra italien en France avant Lulli* (Paris, 1913/R1975)
E. Wellesz: 'Zwei Studien zur Geschichte der Oper im 17. Jahrhundert', *SIMG*, xv (1913–14), 124–54
G. Bustico: 'Bibliografia delle storie e cronistorie dei teatri italiani', *RMI*, xxvi (1919), 36–65
B. Brunelli: *I teatri di Padova dalle origini alla fine del secolo XIX* (Padua, 1921)

H. Neitan: *Die Buffoszenen der spätvenezianischen Oper (1680 bis 1710)* (diss., U. of Halle, 1925)

H. Prunières: 'I libretti dell'opera veneziana nel secolo xvii', *RaM*, iii (1930), 441

G. Norman: *A Consideration of Seicento Opera with Particular Reference to the Rise of the Neapolitan School* (diss., Columbia U., 1937)

H. C. Wolff: *Die venezianische Oper in der zweiten Hälfte des 17. Jahrhunderts* (Berlin, 1937, 2/1975)

R. Giazotto: *Il melodramma a Genova nel XVII e nel XVIII secolo* (Genoa, 1942)

S. T. Worsthorne: 'Venetian Theatres: 1637–1700', *ML*, xxix (1948), 263

R. Giazotto: *Poesia melodrammatica e pensiero critico nel settecento* (Milan, 1952)

'La scuola romana: G. Carissimi – A. Cesti – M. Marazzoli', *Chigiana*, x (1953) [whole issue]

A. A. Abert: *Claudio Monteverdi und das musikalische Drama* (Lippstadt, 1954)

N. Pirrotta: 'Temperaments and Tendencies in the Florentine Camerata', *MQ*, xl (1954), 169

S. T. Worsthorne: *Venetian Opera in the Seventeenth Century* (Oxford, 1954, 2/1968)

N. Burt: 'Opera in Arcadia', *MQ*, xli (1955), 145

N. Pirrotta: 'Commedia dell'arte and Opera', *MQ*, xli (1955), 305

A. Della Corte: *Drammi per musica dal Rinuccini allo Zeno* (Turin, 1958)

R. L. Weaver: *Florentine Comic Operas of the Seventeenth Century* (diss., U. of North Carolina, 1958)

J. E. Rotondi: *Literary and Musical Aspects of Roman Opera, 1600–1650* (diss., U. of Pennsylvania, 1959)

L. Schrade: *La représentation d'Edipo tiranno au Teatro Olimpico (Vicenze 1585)* (Paris, 1960)

J. O. DeLage jr: *The Overture in Seventeenth-century Italian Opera* (diss., Florida State U., 1961)

J. Golos: 'Italian Baroque Opera in Seventeenth-Century Poland', *Polish Review*, viii (1963), 67

D. J. Grout: 'The Chorus in Early Opera', *Festschrift Friedrich Blume* (Kassel, 1963), 151

R. T. Katz: *The Origins of Opera: the Relevance of Social and Cultural Factors to the Establishment of a Musical Institution* (diss., Columbia U., 1963)

R. L. Weaver: 'The Orchestra in Early Italian Opera', *JAMS*, xvii (1964), 83

W. C. Holmes: *Orontea: a Study of Change and Development in the Libretto and Music of Mid-Seventeenth-Century Italian Opera* (diss., Columbia U., 1968)

C. V. Palisca: 'The First Performance of "Euridice"', *The Department of Music, Queens College . . . 25th Anniversary Festschrift*, ed. A. Mell (New York, 1964), 1

P. Petrobelli: 'L'*Ermiona* di Pio Enea degli Obizzi ed i primi spettacoli d'opera veneziani', *Quaderni della Rassegna musicale*, iii (1965), 125

R. Giazotto: 'La guerra dei palchi: documenti per servi'e alla storia del teatro musicale a Venezira come istituto sociale e initiativa privata nel secoli XVII e XVIII, *NRMI*, i (1967), 245–86, 465–508; iii (1969), 906–33

D. Arnold and N. Fortune, eds.: *The Monteverdi Companion* (London, 1968, rev. 2/1984)

C. Molinari: *Le nozze degli dei: un saggio sul grande spettacolo italiano nel Seicento* (Rome, 1968)

R. Monterosso, ed.: *Claudio Monteverdi e il suo tempo: Venezia–Mantova–Cremona 1968*

S. Reiner: 'Vi sono molt'altre mezz'arie', *Studies in Music History: Essays for Oliver Strunk* (Princeton, 1968), 241

R. Freeman: 'Apostolo Zeno's Reform of the Libretto', *JAMS*, xxi (1968), 34

N. Pirrotta: 'Early Opera and Aria', *New Looks at Italian Opera: Essays in Honor of Donald J. Grout* (Ithaca, NY, 1968), 39–107

W. P. Stalnaker: *The Beginnings of Opera in Naples* (diss., Princeton U., 1968)

B. R. Hanning: *The Influence of Humanist Thought and Italian Renaissance Poetry on the Formation of Opera* (diss., Yale Y., 1969; Ann Arbor, 1980 as *Of Poetry and Music's Power: Humanism and the Creation of Opera*)

N. Pirrotta and E. Povoledo: *Li due Orfei* (Turin, 1969, 2/1978; Eng. trans., 1982 as *Music and Theatre from Poliziano to Monteverdi*)

R. L. Weaver: 'Opera in Florence: 1646–1731', *Studies in Musicology: Essays . . . in Memory of Glen Haydon* (Chapel Hill, 1969), 60

H. M. Brown: 'How Opera Began: an Introduction to Jacopo Peri's Euridice (1600)', *The Late Italian Renaissance, 1525–1630*, ed. E. Cochrane (New York, 1970), 401–43

C. M. Gianturco: *The Operas of Alessandro Stradella (1644–1682)* (diss., Oxford U., 1970)

O. Termini: *Carlo Francesco Pollarolo: his Life, Time, and Music with Emphasis on the Operas* (diss., U. of Southern California, 1970)

W. Witzenmann: *Domenico Mazzocchi, 1592–1665: Dokumente und Interpretationen (Cologne, 1970)* [= *Analecta musicologica*, no.8]

M. T. Muraro, ed.: *Studi sul teatro veneto fra Rinnascimento ed età barocca* (Florence, 1971)

L. Zorzi, M. T. Muraro, G. Prato and E. Zorzi, eds.: *I teatri pubblici di Venezia (secoli XVII–XVIII)* (Venice, 1971)

R. Pagano: *Alessandro Scarlatti* (Turin, 1972)

Venezia e il melodramma nel seicento: Venezia 1972

B. Corrigan: 'All Happy Endings: Libretti of the Late Seicento', *Forum italicum*, vii (1973), 250

C. B. Schmidt: *The Operas of Antonio Cesti* (diss., Harvard U., 1973)

L. Bianconi: *Francesco Cavalli und die Verbreitung der venezianischen Oper in Italien* (diss., Heidelberg U., 1974)

N. Mangini: *I teatri di Venezia* (Milan, 1974)

F. W. Sternfeld: 'Aspects of Italian intermedi and Early Operas', *Convivium musicorum: Festschrift Wolfgang Boetticher* (Berlin, 1974), 359

L. Bianconi and T. Walker: 'Dalla *Finta pazza* alla *Veremonda*: storie di Febiarmonici', *RIM*, x (1975), 379–454

L. Bianconi: 'Funktionen des Operntheaters in Neapel bis 1700 und die Rolle Alessandro Scarlattis', *Colloquium Alessandro Scarlatti: Würzburg 1975*, 13

C. Gianturco: 'Evidence for a Late Roman School of Opera', *ML*, lvi (1975), 4

G. Tomlinson: 'Ottavio Rinuccini and the "Favola affettuosa"', *Comitatus*, vi (1975), 1

H. C. Wolff: 'Italian Opera from the later Monteverdi to Scarlatti', *NOHM*, v (1975)

M.-T. Bouquet: *Il Teatro di Corte dalle origini al 1788* [Turin] (Turin, 1976)

E. Rosand: 'Comic Contrast and Dramatic Continuity: Observations on the Form and Function of Aria in the Operas of Francesco Cavalli' *MR*, xxxvii (1976), 92

C. B. Schmidt: 'Antonio Cesti's "Il pomo d'oro": a Reexamination of a Famous Hapsburg Court Spectacle', *JAMS*, xxix (1976), 381–412

A. Szweykowska: *Dramma per musica w teatrze Wazów* (Kraków, 1976)

L. Bianconi and others: 'Seventeenth-Century Music Drama', *IMSCR*, xii Berkeley 1977, 680

H. M. Brown, ed.: *Italian Opera, 1640–1770: Major Unpublished Works in a Central Baroque Tradition* (New York, 1977–) [facs. ser.]

R. D. Covell: *Monteverdi's 'L'incoronazione di Poppea': the Musical and Dramatic Structure* (diss., New South Wales U., 1977)

L. Lindgren: 'Il trionfi di Camilla', *Studi musicali*, vi (1977), 89–159

L. Zorzi: *Il teatro e la città: saggi sulla scena italiana* (Turin, 1977)

J. Glover: *Cavalli* (London, 1978) [see also *JAMS*, xxxiii (1980), 196]

R. L. and N. W. Weaver: *A Chronology of Music in the Florentine Theater 1590–1750* (Detroit, 1978)

B. R. Hanning: 'Glorious Apollo: Poetic and Political Themes in the First Opera', *Renaissance Quarterly*, xxxii (1979), 485

M. Murata: 'The Recitative Soliloquy', *JAMS*, xxxii (1979), 45

E. R. Rutschmann: 'Minato and the Venetian Opera Libretto', *CMc*, no.27 (1979), 84

F. W. Sternfeld: 'The Birth of Opera: Ovid, Poliziano, and the *Lieto fine*', *AnMc*, no.19 (1979), 30

T. Carter: 'Jacopo Peri', *ML*, lxi (1980), 121

E. Rosand: 'In Defense of the Venetian Libretto', *Studi musicali*, ix (1980), 271

H. Becker, ed.: *Quellentexte zur Konzeption der europäischen Oper im 17. Jahrhundert* (Kassel, 1981)

E. Cross: *The Late Operas of Antonio Vivaldi* (Ann Arbor, 1981)

R. Donington: *The Rise of Opera* (London, 1981)

R. S. Freeman: *Opera without Drama: Currents of Change in Italian Opera, 1675–1725* (Ann Arbor, 1981)

S. Leopold: 'Die Hierarchie Arkadiens: soziale Strukturen in den frühen Pastoralopern und ihre Ausdrucksformen', *Schweizerisches Jb für Musikwissenschaft*, new ser., i (1981), 71

M. Murata: *Operas for the Papal Court 1631–1668* (Ann Arbor, 1981)

L. Bianconi: *Il seicento* (Turin, 1982; Eng. trans., 1987, as *Music in the Seventeenth Century*)

L. Bianconi and G. Morelli, eds.: *Antonio Vivaldi: teatro musicale, cultura e società* (Florence, 1982)

T. Carter: 'Jacopo Peri's *Euridice* (1600): a Contextual Study', *MR*, xliii (1982), 83

C. Gianturco: 'Nuove considerazioni su "il tedio del recitativo" delle prime opere romane', *RIM*, xviii (1982), 212

G. Morelli: *Scompiglio e lamento (simmetrie dell'incostanza e incostanza delle simmetrie): l'"Egisto" di Faustini e Cavalli* (Venice, 1982)

R. L. Weaver: 'The State of Research in Italian Baroque Opera', *JM*, i (1982), 44

A. L. Bellina and T. Walker: 'Il melodramma: poesia e musica nell'esperienza teatrale', *Storia della cultura veneta: il Seicento* (Vicenza, 1983), 409

W. C. Holmes: *'La Statira' by Pietro Ottoboni and Alessandro Scarlatti: the Textual Sources with a Documentary Postscript* (New York, 1983)

G. Morelli, R. Strohm and T. Walker, eds.: *Drammaturgia musicale veneta* (Milan, 1983–)

L. Bianconi and T. Walker: 'Production, Consumption and Political Function of Seventeenth-Century Opera', *EMH*, iv (1984), 209–96

I. Fenlon: 'Monteverdi's Mantuan *Orfeo*: some New Documentation', *EM*, xii (1984), 163

Il tranquillo seren del secol d'oro: musica e spettacolo musicale a Venezia e Vienna fra Seicento e Settecento (Milan, 1984)

F. A. D'Accone: *The History of a Baroque Opera: Alessandro Scarlatti's 'Gli equivoci nel sembiante'* (New York, 1985)

P. Fabbri: *Monteverdi* (Turin, 1985)

B. L. Glixon: *Recitative in Seventeenth-Century Venetian Opera: its Dramatic Function and Musical Language* (diss. Rutgers U., 1985)

C. Monson: *'Giulio Cesare in Egitto*: from Sartorio (1677) to Handel (1724)', *ML*, lxvi (1985), 313–43

E. Rosand: 'Seneca and the Interpretation of *L'incoronazione di Poppea*', *JAMS*, xxxviii (1985), 34

H. S. Saunders: *The Repertoire of a Venetian Opera House (1678–1714): the Teatro Grimani di San Giovanni Grisostomo* (diss., Harvard U., 1985)

E. Selfridge-Field: *Pallade veneta: Writings on Music in Venetian Society, 1650–1750* (Venice, 1985)

M. Schwager: 'Public Opera and the Trials of the Teatro San Moisé', *EM*, xiv (1986), 387

J. Whenham, ed.: *Claudio Monteverdi: Orfeo* (Cambridge, 1986)

H. Leclerc: *Venise et l'avènement de l'opéra publique à l'âge baroque* (Paris, 1987)

B. W. Pritchard, ed.: *Antonio Caldara: Essays on his Life and Times* (Aldershot, 1987)

G. Tomlinson: *Monteverdi and the End of the Renaissance* (Berkeley and Los Angeles, 1987)

S. Harris: 'The Significance of Ovid's *Metamorphoses* in early Seventeenth-Century Opera', *MR*, xlviii (1988), 12

F. W. Sternfeld: 'Orpheus, Ovid and Opera', *JRMA*, cxiii (1988), 172–202

Germany and Austria

J. C. Gottsched: *Versuch einer critischen Dichtkunst* (Leipzig, 1730, enlarged 4/1751/*R*1962)

L. Schneider: *Geschichte der Oper und des königlichen Opernhauses in Berlin* (Berlin, 1852)

M. Fürstenau: *Zur Geschichte der Musik und des Theaters am Hofe zu Dresden* (Dresden, 1861–2/*R*1971)

K. F. F. Chrysander: 'Geschichte der Braunschweig-Wolfenbüttelschen Capelle und Oper vom sechzehnten bis zum achtzehnten Jahrhundert', *Jb für musikalische Wissenschaft*, i (Leipzig, 1863), 147–286

H. M. Schletterer: *Das deutsche Singspiel von seinen ersten Anfängen bis auf die neueste Zeit* (Augsburg, 1863/*R*1975)

F. M. Rudhart: *Die italienische Oper von 1654–1787*, Geschichte der Oper am Hofe zu München, i (Freising, 1865)

O. Teuber: *Geschichte des Prager Theaters* (Prague, 1883–5)

J. Sittard: *Zur Geschichte der Musik und des Theaters am Württembergischen Hofe* (Stuttgart, 1890/*R*1970)

O. Teuber and A. von Weilen: *Die Theater Wiens* (Vienna, 1896–1909)

F. Walter: *Geschichte des Theaters und der Musik am kurpfälzischen Hofe* (Leipzig, 1898)

H. Leichtentritt: *Reinhard Keiser in seinen Opern* (diss., U. of Berlin, 1901)

A. von Weilen: *Zur Wiener Theatergeschichte: die vom Jahre 1629 bis zum Jahre 1740 am Wiener Hofe zur Aufführung gelangten Werke theatralischen Charakters und Oratorien* (Vienna, 1901)

C. Sachs: *Musik und Oper am kurbrandenburgischen Hof* (Berlin, 1910)

A. Werner: *Städtische und fürstliche Musikpflege in Weissenfels* (Leipzig, 1911)

A. von Weilen: *Das Theater: 1529–1740* (Vienna, 1917)

E. Wellesz: 'Die Opern und Oratorien in Wien von 1600–1708', *SMw*, vi (1919), 5–138

A. W. Bartmuss: *Die Hamburger Barockoper und ihre Bedeutung für die Entwicklung der deutschen Dichtung* (diss., U. of Jena, 1926)

E. Rosendahl: *Geschichte der Hoftheater in Hannover und Braunschweig* (Hanover, 1927)

G. F. Schmidt: *Neue Beiträge zur Geschichte der Musik und des Theaters am herzoglichen Hofe zu Braunschweig-Wolfenbüttel* (Munich, 1929)

L. Schiedermair: *Die deutsche Oper: Grundzüge ihres Werdens und Wesens* (Leipzig, 1930, 3/1943)

G. F. Schmidt: *Die frühdeutsche Oper und die musikdramatische Kunst Georg Caspar Schürmanns* (Regensburg, 1933–4)

F. Brüggemann: *Bänkelgesang und Singspiel vor Goethe* (Leipzig, 1937)

W. Schulze: *Die Quellen der Hamburger Oper: 1678–1738* (Hamburg and Oldenburg, 1938)

A. Bauer: *Opern und Operetten in Wien* (Graz and Cologne, 1955)

F. Hadamowsky: 'Barocktheater am Wiener Kaiserhof: mit einem Spielplan (1625–1740)', *Jb der Gesellschaft für Wiener Theaterforschung, 1951–2* (Vienna, 1955), 7–117

H. C. Wolff: *Die Barockoper in Hamburg, 1678–1738* (Wolfenbüttel, 1957)

R. Alewyn and K. Sälzle: *Das grosse Welttheater: die Epoche der höfischen Feste in Dokument und Deutung* (Hamburg, 1959)

H. Kindermann: *Theatergeschichte Europas* (Salzburg, 1957–74 [esp. vols. iii–v, 1959–62]
R. Brockpähler: *Handbuch zur Geschichte der Barockoper in Deutschland* (Emsdetten, 1964)
D. I. Lindberg: *Literary Aspects of German Baroque Opera: History, Theory and Practice* (diss., U. of California, Los Angeles, 1964)
R. D. Brenner: *The Operas of Reinhard Keiser in their Relationship to the Affektenlehre* (diss., Brandeis U., 1968)
A. A. Abert: 'Die Barockoper: ein Bericht über die Forschung seit 1945', *AcM*, xii (1969), 121
M. A. Peckham: *The Operas of Georg Philipp Telemann* (diss., Columbia U., 1969)
G. J. Buelow: 'An Evaluation of Johann Mattheson's Opera, *Cleopatra* (Hamburg, 1704)', *Studies in 18th Century Music: a Tribute to Karl Geiringer* (London, 1970) 92
R. D. Brenner: 'Emotional Expression in Keiser's Operas', *MR*, xxxiii (1972), 222
J. D. Lindberg: 'The German Baroque Opera Libretto', *The German Baroque: Literature, Music, Art*, ed. G. Schulz-Behrend (Austin, Texas, 1972), 89–122
J. A. Westrup: 'Opera in England and Germany', *NOHM*, v (1975), 267–323
K. Zelm: *Die Opern Reinhard Keisers* (Munich, 1975)
G. Flaherty: *Opera in the Development of German Critical Thought* (Princeton, NJ, 1978)
H. J. Marx: 'Geschichte der Hamburger Barock-Oper: ein Forschungsbericht', *Hamburger Jb für Musikwissenschaft*, iii (1978), 7
J. E. Wenzel: *Geschichte der Hamburger Oper 1678–1978* (Hamburg, 1978)
K. Zelm: 'Die Sänger der Hamburger Gänsemarkt-Oper', *Hamburger Jb für Musikwissenschaft*, iii (1978), 35
R. D. Lynch: *Opera at Hamburg, 1718–1738: a Study on the Libretto and Musical Style* (diss., New York U., 1979)
R. Meyer, ed.: *Die Hamburger Oper: eine Sammlung von Texten der Hamburger Oper aus der Zeit 1678–1730*, i–iii (Munich, 1980), iv (Millwood, NY, 1984)
B. Baselt: 'Bemerkungen zum Opernschaffen Georg Philipp Telemanns', *Musica*, xxxv (1981), 19
S. Dahms: 'Salzburger Barockoper an der Komischen Oper Berlin', *ÖMz*, xxxvi (1981), 29
W. Braun: '"Die drey Töchter Cecrops": zur Datierung und Lokalisierung von Johann Wolfgang Francks Oper', *AMw*, xl (1983), 102
G. J. Buelow and H. J. Marx, ed.: *New Mattheson Studies* (Cambridge, 1984)
H. Seifert: *Die Oper am Wiener Kaiserhof im 17. Jahrhundert* (Tutzing, 1985)
H. Watanabe-O'Kelly: 'Barthold Feind, Gottsched, and *Cato* – or Opera Reviled', *Proceedings of the English Goethe Society*, new ser., lv (1986), 107
R. Strohm: 'Italienische Barockoper in Deutschland: eine Forschungsaufgabe', *Festschrift Martin Ruhnke zum 65. Geburtstag* (Stuttgart, 1986), 348
J. D. Arnn: *Text, Music and Drama in Three Operas by Reinhard Keiser* (diss., Rutgers U., 1987)
S. R. Huff: 'The Early German Libretto: some Considerations based on Harsdörffer's "Seelewig"', *ML*, lxix (1988), 345

France

C.-F. Menestrier: *Des représentations en musique anciennes et modernes* (Paris, 1681/*R*1972)
F. Raguenet: *Paralèle des italienes et des françois, en ce qui regarde la musique et les opéra* (Paris, 1702/*R*1976, 3/*c*1710); Eng. edn. (London, 1709/*R*1968; repr. in *MQ*, xxxii (1946), 411)
Receuil général des opéra (Paris, 1703–46/*R*1971)
J. L. Le Cerf de la Viéville: *Comparaison de la musique italienne et de la musique françoise* (Brussels, 1704–6/*R*1972)
J. L. le Gallois: *Traité du récitatif* (Paris, 1707, 2/1740)
N. Boindin: *Lettres historiques sur tous les spectacles de Paris* (Paris, 1719)
J.-B. Dubos: *Réflexions critiques sur la poésie et la peinture et la musique* (Paris, 1719, 7/1770/*R*1972; Eng. trans. of 5/1748, 1748/*R*1978)
E. Titon du Tillet: *Le Parnasse françois* (Paris, 1732–60)
Maupoint: *Bibliothèque des théâtres* (Paris, 1733)
C. and F. Parfaict: *Histoire de l'Académie royale de musique* (MS, 1741, Bibliothèque nationale, Paris; also annotated copy, 1835, by Beffara)
T. Rémond de Saint-Mard: *Réflexions sur l'Opéra* (The Hague, 1741/*R*1972)
J. B. Durey de Noinville: *Histoire du Théâtre de l'Opéra en France* (Paris, 1753/*R*1958, 2/1757/*R*1972)
[A. de Leris]: *Dictionnaire portatif des théatres . . . de Paris* (Paris, 1754, 2/1763)
[C. and F. Parfaict]: *Dictionnaire des théâtres de Paris* (Paris, 1756/*R*1967, 2/1767)

[Louis, Duke of La Vallière]: *Ballets, opéra, et autres ouvrages lyriques par ordre chronologique* (Paris, 1760/R1967)

J. B. Durey de Noinville: *Histoire du théâtre de l'Académie royale de musique* (Paris, 1776/R1969)

J. de La Porte and S. R. N. Chamfort: *Dictionnaire dramatique* (Paris, 1776/R1967)

J. P. Lacroix, ed.: *Notes et documents sure l'histoire des théâtres de Paris an XVIIe siècle, par Jean Nicolas de Tralage* (Paris, 1880)

C. Nuittier and E. Thoinan: *Les origines de l'opéra français* (Paris, 1886/R1977)

J. Ecorcheville: *De Lulli à Rameau* (Paris, 1906/R1970)

H. Prunières: *Lully* (Paris, 1909, 2/1927)

P.-M. Masson: 'Lullistes et ramistes', *Année musicale*, i (1911), 187

H. Prunières: *L'opéra italien en France avant Lulli* (Paris, 1913)

J. G. Prod'homme: *L'Opéra (1669–1925)* (Paris, 1925/R1972)

H. Prunières: 'Lully and the Académie de Musique et de Danse', *MQ*, xi (1925), 528

E. Gros: *Philippe Quinault* (Paris, 1926)

P.-M. Masson: 'Les fêtes venitiennes de Campra', *RdM*, xiii (1932), 127, 214

P. Melèse: *Le théâtre et le public à Paris sous Louis XIV* (Paris, 1934)

M. Barthélemy: *André Campra* (Paris, 1957)

J. R. Anthony: *The Opéra Ballets of André Campra: a Study of the First Period of French Opéra-Ballet* (diss., U. of Southern California, 1964)

——: 'The French Opéra Ballet in the Early 18th Century', *JAMS*, xviii (1965), 197

N. Wild: 'Aspects de la musique sous la régence, les Foires: naissance de l'Opéra-Comique', *RMFC*, v (1965), 129

J. R. Anthony: 'Thematic Repetition in the Opéra-Ballets of André Campra', *MQ*, lii (1966), 209

——: 'Some Uses of the Dance in the French Opéra-Ballet', *RMFC*, ix (1969), 75

——: 'Printed Editions of André Campra's *L'Europe galante*', *MQ*, lvi (1970), 54

C. Girdlestone: *La tragédie en musique, considérée comme genre littéraire (1673–1750)* (Geneva, 1972)

J. R. Anthony: *French Baroque Music from Beaujoyeulx to Rameau* (London, 1973, rev. 2/1978, rev. Fr. trans., 1981)

G. E. Barksdale: *The Chorus in French Baroque Opera* (diss., U. of Utah, 1973)

R. M. Isherwood: *Music in the Service of the King: France in the Seventeenth Century* (Ithaca, NY, and London, 1973)

R. Scott: *J.-B. Lully: the Founder of French Opera* (London, 1973)

XVIIe siècle, no.98 (1973) [Molière-Lully issue]

A. I. Borowitz: 'Lully and the Death of Cambert', *MR*, xxxv (1974), 231

P. Howard: *The Operas of Lully* (diss., U. of Surrey, 1974)

M. Seares: 'Aspects of Performance Practice in the Recitatives of Jean-Baptiste Lully', *SMA*, viii (1974), 8

M. M. McGowan: 'The Origins of French Opera', *NOHM*, v (London, 1975), 169

P.- M. Masson: 'French Opera from Lully to Rameau', *NOHM*, v (London, 1975), 206

C. Massip: *La vie des musiciens de Paris au temps de Mazarin* (Paris, 1976)

H. Schneider: *Die Rezeption der Lully-Oper im 17. und 18. Jahrhundert in Frankreich* (Mainz, 1976)

E. Lemaitre: *L'orchestre dans le théâtre lyrique français chez les continuateurs de Lully, 1687–1715* (diss., Conservatoire national de Paris, 1977)

L. E. Brown: *The tragédie lyrique of Andrá Campra and his Contemporaries* (diss., U. of North Carolina, 1978)

R. Fajon: 'Proposition pour une analyse rationalisée du récitatif de l'opéra lullyste', *RdM*, lxiv (1978), 55

J. de La Gorce: *L'Opéra sous le règne de Louis XIV: le merveilleux ou les puissances surnaturelles, 1671–1715* (diss., U. of Paris-Sorbonne, 1978)

R. P. Wolf: 'Metrical Relationships in French Recitative of the Seventeenth and Eighteenth Centuries', *RMFC*, xviii (1978), 29

J. de La Gorce: 'L'Académie Royale de Musique en 1704, d'après des documents inédits conservés dans les archives notarials', *RdM*, lxv (1979), 160

J. E. W. Newman: *Jean-Baptiste de Lully and his tragédies lyriques* (Ann Arbor, 1979)

L. E Brown: 'Oratorical Thought and the *tragédie-lyrique*: a Consideration of Musical-Rhetorical Figures', *Symposium*, xx (1980), 99

W. Hilton: *Dance and Music of Court and Theatre: the French Noble Style, 1690–1725* (Princeton, 1980)

D. Muller: 'Aspects de la déclamation dans le récitatif de Jean-Baptiste Lully', *Basler Studien zur Interpretation der alten Musik*, ii (Winterthur, 1980), 244

G. Sadler: 'The Role of the Keyboard Continuo in French Opera, 1673–1776', *EM*, viii (1980), 148

M. Turnbull: 'Ercole and Hercule: les goûts désunis?' *MT*, cxxi (1980), 303
D. Barnett: 'La rhétorique de l'opéra', *XVIIe siècle*, no.132 (1981), 336
J. de La Gorce: 'L'Opéra et son publique au temps de Louis XIV', *Bulletin de la Société de l'histoire de Paris et de l'Ile-de-France*, cviii (1981), 27
L. Rosow: *Lully's 'Armide' at the Paris Opéra: a Performance History, 1686–1766* (diss., Brandeis U., 1981)
H. Schneider: 'Dokumente zur Französichen Oper von 1659 bis 1699', *Quellentexte zur Konzeption der europäischen Oper in 17. Jahrhundert* (Kassel, 1981)
C. Wood: 'Orchestra and Spectacle in the *tragédie en musique*, 1673–1715: Oracle, *Sommeil* and *Tempête*', *PRMA*, cviii (1981–2), 25
H. Schneider: *Die Rezeption der Opern Lullys' im Frankreich des Ancien Régime* (Tutzing, 1982)
E. Lemaitre: 'Le premiér opéra-ballet et la première tempête, deux originalités de l'oeuvre de Pascal Colasse', *XVIIe siècle*, no.139 (1983), 242
S. Pitou: *The Paris Opéra: an Encyclopedia of Operas, Ballets, Composers and Performers*, i: *Genesis and Glory, 1671–1715* (Westport, Conn., 1983)
L. Rosow: 'French Baroque Recitative as an Expression of Tragic Declamation', *EM*, xi (1983), 468
J. de La Gorce: 'L'opéra français à la cour de Louis XIV', *Revue d'histoire du théâtre* (1983–4), 387
L'avant scène opéra, no.68 (Oct 1984) [*Médée* issue]
L. E. Brown: 'Departure from Lullian Convention in the *tragédie lyrique of the preramiste* Era', *RMFC*, xxii (1984), 59
——: 'The *Récit* in the Eighteenth-Century *tragédie en musique*', *MR*, xlv (1984), 96
R. Fajon: *L'Opéra à Paris du Roi-Soleil à Louis le Bien-aimé* (Geneva, 1984)
H. W. Hitchcock: 'Charpentier's "Médée"', *MT*, cxxv (1984), 563
N. S. Beagle: *The Théâtres de la Foire in Early Eighteenth-Century France: Analysis of 'La Ceinture de Venus' by Lesage* (diss., Stanford U., 1985)
P. Cabrie: *Etude du caractère héroïque dans 'Armide' de J. B. Lully* (diss., U. of Paris, 1985)
J. Gourret: *Histoire des salles de l'Opéra de Paris* (Paris, 1985)
H. Lagrove, C. Mazover and M Regaldo: *La vie théâtrale à Bordeaux des origines à 1789* (Paris, 1985)
A. Parmley: *The Secular Stage Works of Marc-Antoine Charpentier* (diss., U. of London, 1985)
M. Aranda: *Iphigénie de Racine à Du Roullet: illustration concrète d'une confrontation tragédie/opéra* (diss., U. of Paris-Sorbonne, 1986)
L. E. Auld: *The Lyric Art of Pierre Perrin, Founder of French Opera* (Henryville, PA, 1986)
A. Ghazala: *Spectacles et divertissements à la cour de France 1661–1680* (diss., U. of Paris-Sorbonne, 1986)
C. Kintzler: 'Essai de définition du récitatif, *le chainon manquant*', *RMFC*, xxiv (1986), 128
——: 'De la pastorale à la tragédie lyrique: quelques éléments d'un système poétique', *RdM*, lxxii (1986), 67
E. Lemaitre: 'L'orchestre dans le théâtre lyrique français chez les continuateurs de Lully, 1687–1715', *RMFC*, xxiv (1986), 107
M. Pineda: *Magie et phénomènes surnaturels dans l'opéra lullyste* (diss., U. of Paris-Sorbonne, 1986)
J. S. Powell: 'Charpentier's Music for Molière's *Le malade imaginaire* and its Revisions', *JAMS*, xxxix (1986), 87
L'avant scène opéra, no.94 (Jan 1987) [*Atys* issue]
J. R. Anthony, 'Lully's airs – French or Italian?', *MT*, cxxviii (1987), 126
J. de La Gorce: 'Lully's First Opera', *EM*, xv (1987), 308
C. Perrault, Saint-Evremond and A. L. LeBrun, eds.: *Textes sur Lully et l'opéra français* (Geneva, 1987)
L. Rosow: 'Performing a Choral Dialogue by Lully', *EM*, xv (1987), 325
——: 'From Destouches to Berton: Editorial Responsibility at the Paris Opéra', *JAMS*, xl (1987), 285
P. Russo: 'L'isola di Alcina: funzioni drammaturgiche del *divertissement* nella *tragédie lyrique* (1699–1735)', *NRMI*, xxi (1987), 1
D. M. Powers: *The Pastorale héroïque: Origin and Development of a Genre of French Opera in the Seventeenth and Eighteenth Centuries* (diss., U. of Chicago, 1988)
XVIIe siècle, no.161 (Oct–Dec 1988) [Lully issue]
J. Hajdu-Heyer, ed.: *Studies on Jean-Baptiste Lully and the Music of the French Baroque: Essays in Honor of James R. Anthony* (Cambridge, 1989)

England

E. J. Dent: *Foundations of English Opera* (London, 1928/*R*1965)

D. Arundell: *The Critic at the Opera* (London, 1957/*R*1980)

K. Sasse: 'Opera Register from 1712 to 1734 (Colman-Register)', *HJb 1959*, 199

E. W. White: 'New Light on "Dido and Aeneas"', *Henry Purcell 1659–1695*, ed. I Holst (London, 1959), 14

The London Stage 1660–1800 (Carbondale, 1960–68)

A. M. Laurie: *Purcell's Stage Works* (diss., U. of Cambridge, 1961)

R. E. Moore: *Henry Purcell and the Restoration Theatre* (London, 1961)

J. Buttrey: *The Evolution of English Opera between 1656 and 1695: a Re-investigation* (diss., U. of Cambridge, 1967)

W. Dean: *Handel and the Opera Seria* (Berkeley and Los Angeles, 1969)

E. Haun: *But Hark! More Harmony: the Libretti of Restoration Opera in English* (Ypsilanti, 1971)

L. Lindgren: *A Bibliographic Scrutiny of Dramatic Works Set by Giovanni and his Brother Antonio Maria Bononcini* (diss., Harvard U., 1972)

R. Fiske: *English Theatre Music in the Eighteenth Century* (Oxford, 1973, 2/1986)

W. Dean: 'A French Traveller's View of Handel's Operas', *ML*, lv (1974), 172

R. Strohm: 'Händel's Pasticci', *AnMc*, no.14 (1974), 209–67

L. Lindgren: 'I trionfi di Camilla', *Studi musicali*, vi (1977), 89

R. Luckett: 'Exotick but Rational Entertainments: the English Dramatick Operas', *English Drama: Forms and Development*, ed. M. Axton and R. Williams (Cambridge, 1977), 123

C. A. Price: 'The Critical Decade for English Music Drama, 1700–1710', *Harvard Library Bulletin*, xxvi (1978), 38

M. Lefkowitz: 'Shadwell and Locke's *Psyche*: the French Connection', *PRMA*, cvi (1979–80), 42

M. Chan: *Music in the Theatre of Ben Jonson* (Oxford, 1980)

L. Lindgren: 'Ariosti's London Years, 1716–29', *ML*, lxii (1981), 331

J. MacDonald: 'Matthew Locke's *The English Opera* and the Theatre Music of Purcell', *Studies in Music*, xv (1981), 62

J. Milhous and R. D. Hume: *Vice Chamberlain Coke's Theatrical Papers* (Carbondale, 1982)

R. Luckett: 'Music', *The Companion to The Diary of Samuel Pepys*, ed. R. Latham and W. Matthew, x (London, 1983)

E. W. White: *A History of English Opera* (London, 1983)

R. D. Hume: 'Opera in London, 1695–1706', *British Theatre and the Other Arts*, ed. S. S. Kenny (Washington, DC, 1984), 67

J. Milhous: 'The Multimedia Spectacular on the Restoration Stage', *British Theatre and the Other Arts*, ed. S. S. Kenny (Washington, DC, 1984), 41

C. A. Price: *Henry Purcell and the London Stage* (Cambridge, 1984)

G. Bimberg: *Dramaturgie der Händel-Opern* (Halle, 1985)

D. Burrows: 'Handel's London Theatre Orchestra', *EM*, xiii (1985), 349

T. N. McGeary: *English Opera Criticism and Aesthetics 1685–1747* (diss., U. of Illinois, 1985)

R. Strohm: *Essays on Handel and Italian Opera* (Cambridge, 1985)

R.D. Hume: 'Handel and Opera Management in London in the 1730s', *ML*, lxvii (1986), 347

H. Meynell: *The Art of Handel's Operas* (Lewiston, NY, 1986)

C. A. Price: *Purcell: Dido and Aeneas*, Norton Critical Score (New York, 1986)

W. Dean and J. M. Knapp: *Handel's Operas 1704–1726* (Oxford, 1987)

E. T. Harris: *Henry Purcell's 'Dido and Aeneas'* (Oxford, 1987)

J. H. Roberts: 'Handel and Vinci's *Didone abbandonata*: Revisions and Borrowings', *ML*, lxviii (1987), 141

S. Sadie and A. Hicks, eds.: *Handel Tercentenary Collection* (London, 1987) [incl. section 'The Dramatic Music and its Background']

R. D. Hume: 'The Sponsorship of Opera in London, 1704–1720', *Modern Philology*, lxxxv (1988), 420

Spain

F. Pedrell: *Teatro lirico español anterior al siglo xix*, iii–v (La Coruña, 1897–8)

E. Cotarelo y Mori: *Origenes y establecimiento de la ópera en España hasta 1800* (Madrid, 1917)

——: *Historia de la zarzuela, ó sea el drama lirico* (Madrid, 1934) [also in *Boletin de la Real Academia Española*, xix–xxiii (1932–6)]

J. Subirá: *'Celos aun del aire matan': ópera del siglo xvii* (Barcelona, 1933)

G. Chase: 'Origins of the Lyric Theater in Spain', *MQ*, xxv (1939), 292

——: *The Music of Spain* (New York, 1941, rev. 2/1959)

J. Subirá: *Historia de la música teatral en España* (Barcelona, 1945)

J. Sage: 'Calderón y la música teatral', *Bulletin hispanique*, lviii (1956), 275

J. Subirá: 'Calderón de la Barca, libretista de ópera: consideraciones literario-musicales', *AnM*, xx (1965), 59

——: 'La ópera "castellana" en los siglos xvii y xviii', *Segismundo*, i (1965), 23

N. D. Shergold: *A History of the Spanish Stage from Medieval Times until the End of the Seventeenth Century* (Oxford, 1967)

R. E. L. Pitts: *Don Juan Hidalgo, Seventeenth-Century Spanish Composer* (diss., George Peabody College, Nashville, Tenn., 1968)

A. M. Pollin: 'Calderón's "Falerina" and Music', *ML*, xlix (1968), 317

J. Sage: 'Texto y realización de *La estatua de Prometeo* y otros dramas musicales de Calderón', *Hacia Calderón: Exeter 1969*, 37

——: 'La música de Juan Hidalgo para *Los celos hacen estrellas*', *Juan Vélez de Guevara: 'Los celos hacen estrellas'*, ed. J. E. Varey and N. D. Shergold (London, 1970), 169–273

——: 'Nouvelles lumières sur la genèse de l'opéra et la zarzuela en Espagne', *Baroque: revue internationale*, v (1972), 107

——: 'Seventeenth-Century Spanish Music Drama and Theatre', *IMSCR, xii Berkeley 1977*, 701

L. F. Rebello: *Historia do teatro de revista em Portugal* (Lisbon, 1984)

D. Becker: 'La *Plática sobre la música* en toscano, y los principios del teatro musical barroco en España', *RdMc*, x (1987), 501

Staging

Il corago, o vero Alcune osservazioni per metter bene in scena le composizioni drammatiche (MS, c1630, Modena, Biblioteca Estense; ed. P. Fabbri and A. Pompilio, Florence, 1983)

L. Celler [pseud. of L. Leclerc]: *Les décors, les costumes et la mise en scène au XVIIᵉ siècle: 1615–1680* (Paris, 1869)

A. Nicoll: *The Development of the Theatre* (London, 1927, rev. 5/1966)

A. Tessier: 'La décoration théâtrale à Venise à la fin du XVIIe siècle', *Revue de l'art ancien et moderne*, liv (1928), 181, 217

F. Rapp: 'Ein Theaterbauplan des Giovanni Battista Aleotti', *Neues Archiv für Theatergeschichte*, ii (1930), 95

E. Boswell: *The Restoration Court Stage (1660–1702)* (Cambridge, Mass., 1932/R1966)

G. Schöne: *Die Entwicklung der Perspektivbühne von Serlio bis Galli-Bibiena nach den Perspektivbüchern* (Leipzig, 1933)

H. Tintelnot: *Barocktheater und barocke Kunst* (Berlin, 1939)

J. Eisenschmidt: *Die szenische Darstellung der Opern Händels auf der Londoner Bühne seiner Zeit* (Wolfenbüttel, 1940–41/R1987)

H. Leclerc: *Les origines italiennes de l'architecture théâtrale moderne* (Paris, 1946)

T. Cole and H. Krich Chinoy, eds.: *Actors on Acting* (New York, 1949, rev. 1970)

G. Guerrieri and E. Povoledo: *Il secolo dell'invenzione teatrale* (Venice, 1951)

A. M. Nagler, ed.: *Sources of Theatrical History* (New York, 1952/R1959 as *A Source Book in Theatrical History*)

H. Krich Chinoy: 'The Emergence of the Director', *Directing the Play: a Source Book of Stagecraft*, ed. T. Cole and H. Krich Chinoy (Indianapolis, 1953, rev. 1963, 2/1976 as *Directors on Directing*)

T. E. Lawrenson: *The French Stage in the 17th Century: a Study in the Advent of the Italian Order* (Manchester, 1957)

G. Wickham: *Early English Stages 1300 to 1660* (London, 1959–72)

E. Battisti: *Rinascimento e Barocco* (Turin, 1960), 96ff

L. Schrade: *La représentation d'Edipo tiranno au Teatro Olimpico (Vincenza, 1585)* (Paris, 1960)

P. Bjurström: *Giacomo Torelli and Baroque Stage Design* (Stockholm, 1961, rev. 2/1962)

I. Lavin: 'Lettres de Parmes (1618, 1627–28) et débuts du théâtre baroque', *Le lieu théâtral à la Renaissance: CNRS Royaumont 1963*, 106

M. McGowan: *L'art du ballet de cour en France, 1581–1643* (Paris, 1963)

W. F. Michael: *Frühformen der deutschen Bühne* (Berlin, 1963)

A. Jackson: 'Restoration Scenery 1586–1680', *Restoration and 18th Century Theatre Research*, iii (1964), Nov, 25

A. M. Nagler: *Theatre Festivals of the Medici 1539–1637* (New Haven, 1964)

A. Parronchi: *Studi su la dolce prospettiva* (Milan, 1964)

M. Baur-Heinhold: *Theater des Barock* (Munich, 1966; Eng. trans., 1967), 3

M.-F. Christout: *Le ballet de cour de Louis XIV 1643–1672: mise en scène* (Paris, 1967)

C. Molinari: *Le nozze degli dei: un saggio sul grande spettacolo italiano nel seicento* (Rome, 1968)

N. Pirrotta: *Li due Orfei: da Poliziano a Monteverdi* (Turin, 1969; Eng. trans., 1975)

A. Cavicchi: 'Scenotecnica e macchinistica teatrale in un tratto inedito di Fabrizio Carini Motta (Mantova, 1688)', *Venezia e il melodramma nel seicento: Venezia 1972*, 359

R. A. Griffin: *High Baroque Culture and Theater in Vienna* (New York, 1972)

F. Marotti: 'Lo spazio scenico del melodramma, esaminato sulla base della trattatistica teatrale italiana', *Venezia e il melodramma nel seicento: Venezia 1972*, 349

F. Marotti, ed.: *Lo spettacolo dall'umanesimo al manierismo* (Milan, 1974)

R. Savage: 'Producing *Dido and Aeneas*: an Investigation into Sixteen Problems', *EM*, iv (1976), 393

G. A. Bergman: *Lighting in the Theatre* (Stockholm, 1977)

C. J. Day: 'The Theater of SS. Giovanni e Paolo and Monteverdi's *L'incoronazione di Poppea*', xxv *CMc*, no.25 (1978), 22

C. MacClintock, ed.: *Readings in the History of Music in Performance* (Bloomington, Ind., 1979)

J. Milhous: *Thomas Betterton and the Management of Lincoln's Inn Fields, 1695–1708* (Carbondale, 1979)

I. Lavin: *Bernini and the Unity of the Visual Arts* (New York, 1980) [incl. 'Bernini and the Theater', p.146]

L. Rosow: *Lully's 'Armide' at the Paris Opéra: a Performance History 1686–1766* (diss. Brandeis U., 1981)

A. F. Ivaldi: 'Giovanni Battista Olivieri scnografo nel Teatro Romano di Tordinona (1737)', *NRMI*, xviii (1984), 376

J. Milhous: 'The Multimedia Spectacular on the Restoration Stage', *British Theatre and the Other Arts, 1660–1800*, ed. S. S. Kenny (Washington, DC, 1984), 41

N. Pirrotta: *Music and Culture in Italy from the Middle Ages to the Baroque* (Cambridge, Mass., 1984) [incl. 'Monteverdi and the Problems of Opera', p.235; 'Theater, Sets, and Music in Monteverdi's Operas', p.254; and *Commedia dell' Arte* and Opera' p.343]

J. Powell: *Restoration Theatre Production* (London, 1984)

R. W. Vince: *Renaissance Theatre: a Historiographical Handbook* Westport, Conn., 1984)

E. Povoledo: 'Incontri romani: Francesco Bibiena e Giovanni Paolo Pannini (1719–1721)', *RIdM*, xx (1985), 296

J. Milhous and R. D. Hume: 'A Prompt Copy of Handel's "Radamisto"', *MT*, cxxvii (1986), 316

L. Lindgren: 'The Staging of Handel's Operas in London', *Handel Tercentenary Collection*, ed. S. Sadie and A. Hicks (London, 1987), 93

PRE-CLASSICAL AND CLASSICAL

Italy

B. Marcello: *Il teatro alla moda, o sia Metodo sicuro e facile per il ben comporre ed eseguire l'opere italiane in musica all'uso moderne* (Venice, c1720; abridged Eng. trans. in O. Strunk, ed.: *Source Readings in Music History*, New York, 1950/R1965)

P. F. Tosi: *Opinioni de' cantori antichi e moderni* (Bologna, 1723/R1968; Eng. trans., 1742, 2/1743/R1969 as *Observations on the Florid Song*)

L. Riccoboni: *Réflexions historiques et critiques sur les différens théâtres de l'Europe* (Paris, 1738; Eng. trans. 1741)

F. S. Quadrio: *Della storia e della ragione d'ogni poesia* (Bologna and Milan, 1739–52)

C. G. Krause: *Abhandlung von der musikalischen Poesie* (Berlin, 1752)

F. Algarotti: *Saggio sopra l'opera in musica* (Bologna, 1755/R1975, 2/1763; Eng. trans., 1767)

[G. Durazzo]: *Lettre sur le méchanisme de l'opera italien* (Florence and Paris, 1756)

G. Ortes: *Riflessioni sopra i drammi per musica* (Venice, 1757)

L. Garcin: *Traité du mélo-drame, ou Réflexions sur la musique dramatique* (Paris, 1772)

A. Planelli: *Dell'opera in musica* (Naples, 1772)

A. Eximeno y Pujades: *Dell'origine e delle regole della musica* (Rome, 1774)

C. Burney: *A General History of Music* (London, 1776–89; ed. F. Mercer, New York, 1935/R1957)

A. Goudar: *Le brigandage de la musique italienne* (Venice, 1777)

A. M. Beloselsky: *De la musique en Italie* (The Hague, 1778/R1969)

S. Arteaga: *Le rivoluzioni del teatro musicale italiano dall sua origine fino al presente* (Bologna, 1783–8, rev. and enlarged 2/1785)

C. Goldoni: *Mémoires* (Paris, 1787; Eng. trans., 1814)

C. Burney: *Memoirs of the Life and Writings of the Abate Metastasio* (London, 1796/*R*1971)

C. de Brosses: *Lettres historiques et critiques sur l'Italie* (Paris, 1799); ed. Y. Bezard as *Lettres familières sur l'Italie* (Paris, 1931), [written 1739–40]

V. Lee [pseud. of V. Paget]: *Studies of the Eighteenth Century in Italy* (London, 1880, 2/1907)

F. Florimo: *La scuola musicale di Napoli e i suoi conservatorii*, iv (Naples, 1881/*R*1969)

M. Scherillo: *Storia letteraria dell'opera buffa napolitana dalle origini al principio del secolo XIX* (Naples, 1883, enlarged 2/1916/*R*1969 as *L'opera buffa napolitana durante il settecento: storia letteraria*)

B. Croce: *I teatri di Napoli del seccolo XV–XVIII* (Naples, 1891/*R*1968)

N. D'Arienzo: 'Origini dell'opera comica', *RMI*, ii (1895), 597; iv (1897), 421; vi (1899), 473; vii (1900), 1

T. Wiel: *I teatri musicali veneziani del settecento* (Venice, 1897/*R*1975)

E. J. Dent: 'Leonardo Leo', *SIMG*, viii (1906–7), 550

H. Abert: *Niccolo Jommelli als Opernkomponist* (Halle, 1908)

E. J. Dent: 'Ensembles and Finales in 18th Century Italian Opera', *SIMG*, x (1908–9), 543; xi (1909–10), 112

O. G. Sonneck: 'Ciampi's *Bertoldo, Bertoldino e Cacasenno* and Favart's *Ninette à la cour*: a Contribution to the History of *Pasticcio*', *SIMG*, xii (1910–11), 525–64

E. J. Dent: 'Italian Opera in the Eighteenth Century, and its Influence on the Music of the Classical Period', *SIMG*, xiv (1912–13), 500

——: 'Notes on Leonardo Vinci', *MA*, iv (1912–13), 193

J. Pulver: 'The Intermezzi of the Opera', *PMA*, xliii (1916–17), 139

A. Della Corte: *L'opera comica italiana del '700* (Bari, 1923)

E. Bücken: *Der heroische Stil in der Oper* (Leipzig, 1924)

H. Nietan: *Die Buffoszenen der spätvenezianischen Oper* (diss., U. of Halle, 1924)

R. Gerber: *Der Operntypus Johann Adolf Hasses und seine textlichen Grundlage* (Leipzig, 1925)

U. Prota-Giurleo: *La grande orchestra del Teatro S. Carlo nel settecento* (Naples, 1927)

R. Giazotto: *Poesia melodrammatica e pensiero critico nel settecento* (Milan, 1952)

F. Walker: '*Orazio*: the History of a Pasticcio', *MQ*, xxxviii (1952), 369

A. Yorke-Long: *Music at Court: Four Eighteenth-Century Studies* (London, 1954)

N. Burt: 'Opera in Arcadia', *MQ*, xli (1955), 145

E. O. D. Downes: *The Operas of Johann Christian Bach as a Reflection of the Dominant Trends in Opera Seria 1750–1780* (diss., Harvard U., 1958)

——: 'The Neapolitan Tradition in Opera', *IMSCR, viii New York 1961*, i, 277

H. Hucke: 'Die Neapolitanische Tradition in der Oper', *IMSCR, viii New York 1961*, i, 253

W. Binni: *L'Arcadia e il Metastasio* (Florence, 1963)

W. Vetter: 'Italienische Opernkomponisten um Georg Christoph Wagenseil', *Festschrift Friedrich Blume* (Kassel, 1963), 363

K. Hortschansky: 'Gluck und Lampugnani in Italien: zum Pasticcio *Arsace*', *AnMc*, no.3 (1966), 49

H. Hucke: 'Vinci, Leonardo', *MGG*

D. Heartz: 'Opera and the Periodization of 18th-century Music', *IMSCR, x Ljubljana 1967*, 160

R. Freeman: 'Apostolo Zeno's Reform of the Libretto', *JAMS*, xxi (1968), 34

V. Monaco: *Giambattista Lorenzi e la commedia per musica* (Naples, 1968)

L. Bianconi: 'Die pastorale Szene in Metastasios "Olimpiade"', *GfMKB, Bonn 1970*, 185

G. Lazarevich: *The Role of the Neapolitan Intermezzo in the Evolution of Eighteenth-Century Musical Style: Literary, Symphonic and Dramatic Aspects, 1685–1735* (diss., Columbia U., 1970)

E. Surian: *A Checklist of Writings on 18th Century French and Italian Opera (excluding Mozart)* (Hackensack, NJ, 1970)

K. Hortschansky: '*Arianna* – ein Pasticcio von Gluck', *Mf*, xxiv (1971), 407

J. Rushton: 'Theory and Practice of Piccinnisme', *PRMA*, xcviii (1971–2), 31

L. Zorzi, M. T. Muraro, G. Prato and E. Zorzi, eds.: *I teatri pubblici di Venezia (secoli XVII–XVIII)* (Venice, 1971)

M. F. Robinson: *Naples and Neapolitan Opera* (Oxford, 1972)

O. Landmann: *Quellenstudien zum 'intermezzo comico per music' und zu seiner Geschichte in Dresden* (diss., U. of Rostock, 1972)

I. Mamczarz: *Les intermèdes comiques italiens au XVIIIᵉ siècle en France et en Italie* (Paris, 1972)

A. A. Abert and H. C. Robbins Landon: 'Opera in Italy and the Holy Roman Empire', *NOHM*, vii (1973), 1–199

H. Becker: 'Opern-Pasticcio und Parodie-Oper', *Musicae scientiae collectanea: Festschrift Karl Gustav Fellerer* (Cologne, 1973), 40

F. Degrada: 'Origini e sviluppi dell'opera comica napoletana', *Venezia e il melodramma nel settecento: Venezia 1973*, i, 149

D. Heartz: 'Hasse, Galuppi and Metastasio', *Venezia e il melodramma nel settecento: Venezia 1973*, i, 309

——: 'Vis comica: Goldoni, Galuppi and *L'Arcadia in Brenta*', *Venezia e il melodramma nel settecento: Venezia 1975*, ii, 33

M. F. Robinson: 'Three Versions of Goldoni's *Il filosofo di campagna*', *Venezia e il melodramma nel settecento: Venezia 1975*, ii, 75

G. Lazarevich: 'Eighteenth-Century Pasticcio: the Historian's Gordian Knot', *AnMc*, no.17 (1976), 121

R. Strohm: 'Italienische Opernarien des frühen Settecento', *AnMc*, no.16 (1976) [whole issue, incl. sources for 61 pasticcios and similar works, *c*1715–40]

F. Degrada: *L'opera a Napoli nel settecento* (Turin, 1977)

D. Heartz: 'The Creation of the Buffo Finale in Italian Opera', *PRMA*, civ (1977–8), 67

R. L. and N. W. Weaver: *A Chronology of Music in the Florentine Theater 1590–1750* (Detroit, 1978)

F. J. Millner: *The Opera of Johann Adolf Hasse* (Ann Arbor, 1979)

C. E. Troy: *The Comic Intermezzo: a Study in the History of Eighteenth-Century Italian Opera* (Ann Arbor, 1979)

P. Gallarati: 'L'estetica musicale di Ranieri de' Calzabigi: il caso Metastasio', *NRMI*, iv (1980), 497

J. Jorgenson: *Metastasio: Revaluation and Reformulation* (diss., U. of Minnesota, 1980)

M. P. McClymonds: *Niccolò Jommelli: the Last Years 1769–1774* (Ann Arbor, 1980)

——: 'The Evolution of Jommelli's Operatic Style', *JAMS*, xxxiii (1980), 326

R. Angermüller: 'Grundzüge des nachmetastasianische Librettos', *AnMc*, no.21 (1982), 192–235

'Crosscurrents and the Mainstream of Italian Serious Opera, 1730–1790', *Studies in Music*, vii (1982) [incl. N. Pirrotta: 'Metastasio and the Demands of his Literary Environment', p.10; D. Neville: 'Moral Philosophy in the Metastasian Dramas', p,28: M. F. Robinson: 'How to Demonstrate Virtue: the Case of Porpora's Two Settings of *Mitridate*, p.47; D. Heartz: 'Traetta in Vienna', p.65; M. F. Robinson: 'The Ancient and the Modern: a Comparison of Metastasio and Calzabigi', p.137]

F. Lippmann: 'Über Cimarosas Opere serie', *AnMc*, no.21 (1982), 21–59

N. Morea: *Tommaso Traetta: riformatore del melodramma* (Bitonto, 1982)

F. Piperno: 'Buffe e buffi (considerazioni sulla professionalità degli interpreti di scene buffi ed intermezzi)', *RIM*, xviii (1982), 240

M. Ruhnke: 'Opera semiseria und dramma eroicomico', *AnMc*, no.21 (1982), 263

P. Weiss: 'Metastasio, Aristotle, and the *Opera seria*', *JM*, i (1982), 385

G. Cummings: 'Reminiscence and Recall in Three Early Settings of Metastasio's *Alessandro nell'Indie*', *PRMA*, cix (1982–3), 80

H. Lühning: '"Titus" Vertonungen im 18. Jahrhundert: Unter suchungen zur Tradition der Opera seria von Hasse bis Mozart', *AnMc*, no.20 (1983) [whole issue]

P. Rigoli: *Tre teatri per musica a Verona nella prima metà del Settecento: cronologie e documenti* (Verona, 1983)

R. Wiesend: 'Il giovane Galuppi el l'opera: materiali per gli anni 1722–1741', *NRMI*, xvii (1983), 383

F. Blanchetti: 'Tipologia musicale dei concertati nell'opera buffa di Giovanni Paisiello', *RIM*, xix (1984), 234

P. Gallarati: *Musica e maschera: il libretto italiano del settecento* (Turin, 1984)

G. Gronda: 'Metastasiana', *RIM*, xix (1984), 314

E. Weimer: *Opera Seria and the Evolution of Classical Style, 1755–72* (Ann Arbor, 1984)

P. Weiss: 'Venetian commedia dell'arte "Operas" in the Age of Vivaldi', *MQ*, lxx (1984), 195

R. Wiesend: *Studien zur Opera Seria von Baldassare Galuppi* (Tutzing, 1984)

F. Dorsi: 'Un intermezzo di Niccolò Jommelli: *Don Falcone*', *NRMI*, xix (1985), 432

Galuppiana: Venice 1985

M. N. Massaro: 'Il ballo pantomimo al Teatro Nuovo di Padova (1751–1830)', *AcM*, lvii (1985), 215

M. P. McClymonds: 'Jommelli's Last Opera for Germany: the Opera Seria-Comica *La schiava liberata* (Ludwigsburg, 1768)', *CMc*, no.39 (1985), 7

R. Verti: 'L'indice de "teatrali spettacoli", Milan, Venise, Rome 1764–1823: une source pour l'histoire de l'opéra italien', *FAM*, xxxii (1985), 209

T. Bauman: 'The Society of La Fenice and its First Impresarios', *JAMS*, xxxix (1986), 332

S. Henze-Döhring: 'Opera serie, Opera buffa und Mozarts "Don Giovanni": zur Gattungskonvergenz in der italienischen Oper des 18. Jahrhunderts', *AnMc*, no.24 (1986) [whole issue]

M. Hunter: 'The Fusion and Juxtaposition of Genres in opera buffa 1770–1800: Anelli and Piccinni's *Griselda*', *ML*, lxvii (1986), 363

431

M. T. Muraro, ed.: *Metastasio e il mondo musical* (Florence, 1986)

J. A. Rice: 'Sense, Sensibility, and Opera Seria: an Epistolary Debate', *Studi musicali*, xv (1986), 101–38

G. Rotondella: 'Giovanni Battista Pergolesi: fra leggenda e realtà', *Rassegna musicale curci*, xxxix (1986), 17

F. Lippmann, ed.: 'Johann Adolf Hasse und die Musik seiner Zeit: Siena 1983', *AnMc*, no.25 (1987) [whole issue.]

Germany and Austria

J. C. Gottsched: *Versuch einer critischen Dichtkunst* (Leipzig, 1730, enlarged 4/1751/*R*1962), esp. 731–55

J. Mattheson: *Die neueste Untersuchung der Singspiele* (Hamburg, 1744/*R*1975)

J. F. Reichardt: *Ueber die deutsche comische Oper* (Hamburg, 1774/*R*1974)

G. J. Vogler: *Betrachtungen der Mannheimer Tonschule* (Mannheim, 1778–81/*R*1974)

C. D. von Dittersdorf: *Lebensbeschreibung* (Leipzig, 1801; Eng. trans., 1896/*R*1970); ed. N. Miller (Munich, 1967)

Stendhal: *Lettres . . . sur le célèbre compositeur Haydn: suivies d'une vie de Mozart et considérations sur Métastase* (Paris, 1814, rev.2/1817 as *Vies de Haydn, de Mozart et de Métastase*; Eng. trans., 1972)

L. Schneider: *Geschichte der Oper und des Königlichen Opernhauses in Berlin* (Berlin, 1852)

M. Fürstenau: *Zur Geschichte der Musik und des Theaters am Hofe zu Dresden* (Dresden, 1861–2/*R*1971)

H. M. Schletterer: *Das deutsche Singspiel von seinen ersten Anfängen bis auf die neueste Zeit* (Augsburg, 1863/*R*1975)

O. Teuber: *Geschichte des Prager Theaters* (Prague, 1883–5)

W. Creizenach, ed.: *Die Schauspiele der englischen Komödianten* (Berlin and Stuttgart, *c*1889)

R. Eitner: 'Die deutsche komische Oper', *MMg*, xxiv (1892), 37–92

J. Bolte: *Die Singspiele der englischen Komödianten und ihrer Nachfolger in Deutschland, Holland und Skandinavien* (Hamburg and Leipzig, 1893)

O. Teuber and A. von Weilen: *Die Theater Wiens* (Vienna, 1896–1909)

F. Brückner: 'Georg Benda und das deutsche Singspiel', *SIMG*, v (1903–4), 571–621; also pubd separately (Leipzig, 1904)

K. M. Klob: *Beiträge zur Geschichte der deutschen komischen Oper* (Berlin, 1903)

G. Calmus: *Die ersten deutschen Singspiele von Standfuss und Hiller* (Leipzig, 1908/*R*1973)

A. Weissmann: *Berlin als Musikstadt: Geschichte der Oper und des Konzerts von 1740–1911* (Berlin and Leipzig, 1911)

E. J. Dent: *Mozart's Operas: a Critical Study* (London, 1913, 2/1947)

E. Lert: *Mozart auf dem Theater* (Berlin, 1918)

H. Abert: *W. A. Mozart: neu bearbeitete und erweiterte Ausgabe von Otto Jahns 'Mozart'* (Leipzig, 1919–21, rev. 3/1955–66, 10/1983)

T. Krogh: *Zur Geschichte des dänischen Singspiels im 18. Jahrhundert* (Copenhagen, 1924)

K. Lüthge: *Die deutsche Spieloper* (Brunswick, 1924)

R. Haas: *Gluck und Durazzo im Burgtheater: die Opera Comique in Wien* (Zurich, Vienna and Leipzig, 1925)

———: 'Die Musik in der Wiener deutschen Stegreifkomödie', *SMw*, xii (1925–6), 1–64

L. Schiedermair: *Die deutsche Oper: Grundzüge ihres Werdens und Wesens* (Leipzig, 1930, 3/1943)

W. Flemming, ed.: *Das Schauspiel der Wanderbühne* (Leipzig, 1931/*R*1965)

F. Hadamowsky: *Das Theater in der Wiener Leopoldstadt* (Vienna, 1934)

D. F. Tovey: 'Christoph Willibald Gluck (1714–1887) and the Musical Revolution of the Eighteenth Century', *The Heritage of Music*, ii, ed. H. J. Foss (Oxford, 1934), 69–117; repr. in *Essays and Lectures on Music* (London, 1949)

M. Cooper: *Gluck* (London, 1935)

A. Einstein: *Gluck* (London, 1936/*R*1964)

F. Brüggemann: *Bänkelgesang und Singspiel vor Goethe* (Leipzig, 1937)

H. Wirth: *Joseph Haydn als Dramatiker: sein Bühnenschaffen als Beitrag zur Geschichte der deutschen Oper* (Wolfenbüttel and Berlin, 1940)

R. Gerber: *Christoph Willibald Gluck* (Potsdam, 1941, 2/1950)

A. Einstein: *Mozart: his Character, his Work* (New York, 1945; Ger. orig., 1947, 4/1960)

A. H. King: 'The Melodic Sources and Affinities of Die Zauberflöte', *MQ*, xxxvi (1950), 241

S. Levarie: *Mozart's 'Le nozze di Figaro': a Critical Analysis* (Chicago, 1952/*R*1977)

A. A. Abert: 'Der Geschmackswandel auf der Opernbühne am Alkestis-Stoff dargestellt', *Mf*, vi (1953), 214

W. Hess: *Beethovens Oper Fidelio und ihre drei Fassungen* (Zurich, 1953)

H. Engel: 'Die Finali der Mozartschen Opern', *MJb 1954*, 113

A. Bauer: *Opern und Operetten in Wien* (Graz and Cologne, 1955)

K. Wesseler: *Untersuchungen zur Darstellung des Singspiels auf der deutschen Bühne des 18. Jahrhunderts* (diss., U. of Cologne, 1955)

A. Greither: *Die sieben grossen Opern Mozarts: Versuche über das Verhältnis der Texte zur Musik* (Heidelberg, 1956, enlarged 2/1970)

H. Kindermann: *Theatergeschichte Europas* (Salzburg, 1957–74) [esp. vols. iii–v, 1959–62]

H. Kunz: 'Höfisches Theater in Wien zur Zeit der Maria Theresia', *Jb der Gesellschaft für Wiener Theaterforschung, 1953–4* (1958), 3–113

A. A. Abert: *Christoph Willibald Gluck* (Munich, 1959)

D. Bartha and L. Somfai: *Haydn als Opernkapellmeister: die Haydn-Dokumente der Esterházy Opernsammlung* (Budapest, 1960) [corrections and updating in *New Looks at Italian Opera: Essays in Honor of Donald J. Grout* (Ithaca, NY, 1968), 172–219]

W. Hess: *Beethovens Bühnenwerke* (Göttingen, 1962)

P. Howard: *Gluck and the Birth of Modern Opera* (London, 1963)

A. R. Neumann: 'The Changing Concept of the Singspiel in the 18th Century', *Studies in German Literature*, ed. C. Hammer (Baton Rouge, 1963), 63

B. Brophy: *Mozart the Dramatist: a New View of Mozart, his Operas and his Age* (London, 1964, enlarged 2/1988)

E. M. Batley: 'The Inception of Singspiel in 18th Century Southern Germany', *German Life and Letters*, xix (1965–6), 167

P. Branscombe: '"Die Zauberflöte"; some Textual and Interpretative Problems', *PRMA*, xcii (1965–6), 45

D. Heartz: 'The Genesis of Mozart's Idomeneo', *MJb 1967*, 150; repr. in *MQ*, lv (1969), 1

R. B. Moberly: *Three Mozart Operas: Figaro, Don Giovanni, The Magic Flute* (London, 1967)

D. Heartz: 'From Garrick to Gluck: the Reform of Theatre and Opera in the Mid-Eighteenth Century', *PRMA*, xciv (1967–8), 111

E. M. Batley: *A Preface to The Magic Flute* (London, 1969)

G. Feder: 'Einige Thesen zu dem Thema: Haydn als Dramatiker', *Haydn-Studien*, ii (1969), 126

K. Kawada: *Studien zu den Singspielen von Johann Adam Hiller* (diss., U. of Marburg, 1969)

A. A. Abert: *Die Opern Mozarts* (Wolfenbüttel, 1970; abridged Eng. trans., *NOHM*, vii (1973), 97–171)

O. Michtner: *Das alte Burgtheater als Opernbühne: von der Einführung des deutschen Singspiels (1778) bis zum Tod Kaiser Leopolds II. (1792)* (Vienna, 1970)

G. Zechmeister: *Die Wiener Theater nächst der Burg und nächst dem Kärntnerthor von 1747 bis 1776* (Vienna, 1970)

P. Branscombe: 'The Singspiel in the Late 18th Century', *MT*, cxii (1971), 226

W. Dean: 'Beethoven and Opera', *The Beethoven Companion*, ed. D. Arnold and N. Fortune (London, 1971), 331–86

P. Branscombe: 'Music in the Viennese Popular Theatre of the Eighteenth and Nineteenth Centuries', *PRMA*, xcviii (1971–2), 101

S. Kunze: *Don Giovanni vor Mozart: die Tradition der Don Giovanni-Opern im italienischen Buffo-Theater des 18. Jahrhunderts* (Munich, 1972)

A. A. Abert and H. C. Robbins Landon: 'Opera in Italy and the Holy Roman Empire', *NOHM*, vii (1973), 1–199

R. Monelle: 'Gluck and the "Festa teatrale"', *ML*, liv (1973), 308

H. Federhofer and others: 'Tonartenplan und Motivstruktur (Leitmotivtechnik?) in Mozarts Musik', *MJb 1973–4*, 82–143

D. Heartz: 'Tonality and Motif in Idomeneo', *MT*, cxv (1974), 2

H.-A. Koch: *Das deutsche Singspiel* (Stuttgart, 1974)

N. Schiørring and N. M. Jensen: *Deutsch-dänische Begegnungen um 1800: Kunst, Dichtung, Musik* (Copenhagen, 1974)

Chigiana, xxix–xxx (1975) [Gluck issue]

G. Feder: 'Opera seria, opera buffa und opera semiseria bei Haydn', *Opernstudien: Anna Amalie Abert zum 65. Geburtstag* (Tutzing, 1975), 37

P. Gallarati: *Gluck e Mozart* (Turin, 1975)

R. Hughes: *Haydn* (London, 5/1975), chap.16

D. Koenigsberger: 'A New Metaphor for Mozart's *Magic Flute*', *European Studies Review*, v (1975), 229–75

A. Tyson: '"La clemenza di Tito" and its Chronology', *MT*, cxvi (1975), 221

P. Branscombe: *The Connexions between Drama and Music in the Viennese Popular Theatre* (diss., London U., 1976)

C. Gianturco: *Le opere del Giovane Mozart* (Pisa, 1976, enlarged 2/1978, Eng. trans., enlarged, 1981)

H. C. Robbins Landon: *Haydn: Chronicle and Works* (London, 1976–80)

T. Baumann and others: 'Opera and Enlightenment', *IMSCR*, xii *Berkeley 1977*, 212

W. Mann: *The Operas of Mozart* (London, 1977)

D. Neville: 'Idomeneo and La clemenza di Tito: Opera seria and "vera opera"', *SMA*, ii (1977), 138; iii (1978), 97; v (1980), 99; vi (1981), 112; viii (1983), 107

F. Noske: *The Signifier and the Signified: Studies in the Operas of Mozart and Verdi* (The Hague, 1977)

G. Flaherty: *Opera in the Development of German Critical Thought* (Princeton, NJ, 1978)

'Mozart und Italien: Rom 1974', *AnMc*, no.18 (1978) [whole issue]

C. Osborne: *The Complete Operas of Mozart* (London, 1978)

S. Vill, ed.: *Così fan tutte: Beiträge zur Wirkungsgeschichte von Mozarts Oper* (Bayreuth, 1978)

P. Gossett: 'The Arias of Marzelline: Beethoven as a Composer of Opera', *BeJb 1978–81*, 141–84

D. Heartz: 'Mozart and his Italian Contemporaries: La clemenza di Tito', *MJb 1978–9*, 275

——: 'Goldoni, Don Giovanni and the dramma giocoso', *MT*, cxx (1979), 993

G. Feder: 'Haydns Opern und ihre Ausgaben', *Musik, Edition, Interpretation: Gedenkschrift Günter Henle* (Munich, 1980)

D. Heartz: 'The Great Quartet in Mozart's Idomeneo', *Music Forum*, v (1980), 233

R. Schusky, ed.: *Das deutsche Singspiel im 18. Jahrhundert: Quellen und Zeugnisse zur Ästhetik und Rezeption* (Bonn, 1980)

C. Ballantine: 'Social and Philosophical Outlook in Mozart's Operas', *MQ*, lxvii (1981), 507

T. Bauman: 'Benda, the Germans, and Simple Recitative', *JAMS*, xxxiv (1981), 119

'Die frühdeutsche Oper und ihre Beziehungen zu Italien, England und Frankreich', *Hamburger Jb für Musikwissenschaft*, v (1981), 9–111 [8 essays, chiefly on Hamburg operas]

R. Gruenter, ed.: *Das deutsche Singspiel im 18. Jahrhundert* (Heidelberg, 1981)

P. Howard: *C. W. von Gluck: Orfeo* (Cambridge, 1981)

'Mozart und die Oper seiner Zeit', *Hamburger Jb für Musikwissenschaft*, v (1981), 115–226 [10 essays]

MT, cxxii/7 (1981) [Mozart issue]

J. Rushton: *W. A. Mozart: Don Giovanni* (Cambridge, 1981)

A. Steptoe: 'The Sources of "Così fan tutte": a Reappraisal', *ML*, lxii (1981), 281

A. Tyson: 'Le nozze di Figaro: Lessons from the Autograph Score', *MT*, cxxii (1981), 456

E. Badura-Skoda, ed.: *Haydn: Wien 1982* [incl. section on the operas, 248–415]

D. Heartz: 'Mozart's Tragic Muse', *Studies in Music*, vii (1982), 183

R. Würtz: 'Ignaz Holzbauer and *Das teutsche*', 'Anton Schweizer and Christoph Martin Wieland: the Theory of the Eighteenth-Century Singspiel', *Studies in Music*, vii (1982), 89, 148

W. J. Allenbrook: *Rhythmic Gesture in Mozart: 'Le nozze di Figaro' and 'Don Giovanni'* (Chicago, 1983)

D. Heartz: 'La clemenza di Sarastro: Masonic Benevolence in Mozart's Last Operas', *MT*, cxxiv (1983), 152

F. Lippmann: 'Haydn e l'opera buffa: tre conforti con opere italiane coeve sullo stesso testo', *NRMI*, xvii (1983), 223

——: 'Haydns Opere serie: Tendenzen und Affinitäten', *Studi musicali*, xii (1983), 301–32

H. Lühning: '"Titus" Vertonungen im 18. Jahrhundert: Untersuchungen zur Tradition der Opera seria von Hasse bis Mozart', *AnMc*, no.20 (1983) [whole issue]

'Haydn e il suo tempo: Siena 1979', *Chigiana*, xxxvi (1984) [whole issue]

S. Kunze: *Mozarts Opern* (Stuttgart, 1984)

J. Platoff: *Music and Drama in the 'Opera buffa' Finale: Mozart and his Contemporaries in Vienna, 1781–1790* (diss., U. of Pennsylvania, 1984)

J. A. Rice: 'Sarti's Giulio Sabino, Haydn's Armida, and the Arrival of Opera seria at Eszterháza', *Haydn Yearbook*, xv (1984), 181

G. Thomas: 'Zur Frage der Fassungen in Haydns Il mondo della luna', *AnMc*, no.22 (1984), 405

A. Tyson: 'Notes on the Composition of Mozart's Così fan tutte', *JAMS*, xxxvii (1984), 356–401

T. Bauman: *North German Opera in the Age of Goethe* (Cambridge, 1985)

C. Dahlhaus: 'Idylle und Utopie zu Beethovens Fidelio', *NZM*, xi (1985), 4

H. Goertz: *Mozarts Dichter Lorenzo da Ponte, Genie und Abenteurer* (Vienna, 1985)

S. Hodges: *Lorenzo da Ponte: the Life and Times of Mozart's Librettist* (London, 1985)

I. Nagel: *Autonomie und Gnade: über Mozarts Opern* (Munich, 1985)

M. Slevogt: *Die Zauberflöte: Randzeichnungen zu Mozarts Handschrift*, ed. B. Roland (Edenkoben, 1985)

M.-C. Benard: *Orphée de Gluck: naissance d'une esthétique* (diss., U. of Paris-Sorbonne, 1986)

B. A. Brown: *Christoph Willibald Gluck and opéra-comique in Vienna, 1754–1764* (diss., U. of California, Berkeley, 1986)

——: 'Beaumarchais, Mozart and the Vaudeville: Two Examples from "The Marriage of Figaro"', *MT*, cxxvii (1986), 261

B. Cooper: 'The Composition of "Und spür' ich" in Beethoven's *Fidelio*', *MQ*, xlvii (1986–7), 231

J. A. Eckelmeyer: 'Structure as Hermeneutic Guide to *The Magic Flute*', *MQ*, lxxii (1986), 51

M. Freyhan: 'Toward the Original Text of Mozart's *Die Zauberflöte*', *JAMS*, xxxix (1986), 355

D. Heartz: 'Setting the Stage for Figaro', *MT*, cxxvii (1986), 256

S. Henze-Döhring: 'Opera seria, Opera buffa und Mozarts 'Don Giovanni': zur Gattungskonvergenz in der italienischen Oper des 18. Jahrhunderts', *AnMc*, no.24 (1986) [whole issue]

W. Hess: *Das Fidelio-Buch: Beethovens Oper Fidelio, ihre Geschichte und ihre drei Fassungen* (Winterthur, 1986)

D. J. Neville: *Mozart's La clemenza di Tito and the Metastasian opera seria* (diss., U. of Cambridge, 1986)

A. Steptoe: 'Mozart, Mesmer and *Così fan tutte*', *ML*, lxvii (1986), 248

D. Heartz: 'Constructing *Le nozze di Figaro*', *JRMA*, cxii (1986–7), 77

A. Tyson: 'Some Problems in the Text of *Le nozze di Figaro*: did Mozart have a Hand in Them?', *JRMA*, cxii (1986–7), 99–131

H. Geyer-Kiefl: *Die heroïsch-komische Oper, ca 1770–1820* (Tutzing, 1987)

P. Howard: *Christoph Willibald Gluck: a Guide to Research* (New York, 1987)

J. Kristek, ed.: *Mozarts 'Don Giovanni' in Prague* (Prague, 1987)

J. Rice: *Emperor and Impresario: Leopold II and the Transformation of Viennese Musical Theater, 1790–1792* (diss., U. of California, Berkeley, 1987)

J. Rushton: 'The Musician Gluck', *MT*, cxxviii (1987), 615

J. Webster: 'To Understand Verdi and Wagner we must Understand Mozart', *19th-Century Music*, xi (1987–8), 175

T. Bauman: *W. A. Mozart: Die Entführung aus dem Serail* (Cambridge, 1988)

T. Carter: *W. A. Mozart: Le nozze di Figaro* (Cambridge, 1988)

H. C. Robbins Landon: *1791: Mozart's Last Year* (London, 1988)

A. Tyson: 'The 1786 Prague Version of Mozart's *Le nozze di Figaro*', *ML*, lxix (1988), 321

A. Steptoe: *The Mozart–Da Ponte Operas* (Oxford, 1988)

France

C. Parfaict and F. Parfaict: *Mémoires pour servir à l'histoire des spectacles de la Foire* (Paris, 1743)

J.-J. Rousseau: *Lettre sur la musique française* (Paris, 1753, 2/1753); Eng. trans., abridged, in O. Strunk, ed.: *Source Readings in Music History*, New York, 1950/R1965)

A. G. Contant d'Orville: *Histoire de l'opéra bouffon* (Amsterdam and Paris, 1768)

J. A. Jullien: *Histoire anecdotique et raisonnée du Théâtre Italien* (Paris, 1769/R1968)

——: *Histoire du Théâtre de l'Opéra-Comique* (Paris, 1769/R1968)

P. J. B. Nougaret: *De l'art du théâtre* (Paris, 1769)

B. Farmian de Rosoy: *Dissertation sur le drame lyrique* (The Hague and Paris, 1775)

J. M. Marmontel: '*Opéra*': Eléments de littérature, Oeuvres complettes, ix (Paris, 1787), 47–114

A. J. B. d'Origny: *Annales du Théâtre Italien* (Paris, 1788/R1970)

A. E. M. Grétry: *Mémoires, ou Essais sur la musique* (Paris, 1789, enlarged 2/1797/R1973)

N. E. Framery: *De l'organisation des spectacles de Paris* (Paris, 1790)

Castil-Blaze: *Histoire de l'Opéra Comique* (MS, c1840, Bibliothèque de l'Opéra, Paris)

G. Desnoiresterres: *Gluck et Piccinni* (Paris, 1872)

E. and J. de Goncourt: *L'art du dix-huitième siècle* (Paris, enlarged 2/1873, 4/1884)

E. Campardon: *Les spectacles de la Foire* (Paris, 1877)

A. Jullien: *La cour et l'opera sous Louis XVI* (Paris, 1878/R1976)

——: *L'Opéra secret au XVIIIᵉ siècle (1770–1790)* (Paris, 1880)

E. Campardon: *Les comédiens de la troupe italienne pendant les deux derniers siècles* (Paris, 1880)

——: *L'Académie royale de musique au XVIIIᵉ siècle* (Paris, 1884/R1971)

V. Barbaret: *Le Sage et l'histoire le Théâtre de la Foire* (Nancy, 1887)

E. H. de Bricqueville: *Le livret d'opéra français de Lully à Gluck 1672–1779* (Brussels, 1887)

A. Font: *Favart: L'opéra-comique et la comédie-vaudeville au XVIIᵉ et XVIIIᵉ siècles* (Paris, 1894/R1970)

M. Albert: *Les Théâtres de la Foire (1660–1789)* (Paris, 1900)

E. Hirschberg: *Die Encyclopädisten und die französische Oper* (Leipzig, 1903)

G. Cucuel: *Les créatures de l'opéra-comique français* (Paris, 1914)
P.-M. Masson: 'Le ballet héroïque', *ReM*, ix/8 (1928), 132
——: *L'opéra de Rameau* (Paris, 1930/R1972)
J. Tiersot: 'Gluck and the Encyclopedists', *MQ*, xvi (1930), 336
F. J. Carmody: *Le répertoire de l'opéra-comique en vaudevilles de 1708 à 1764* (Berkeley, 1933)
L. P. Arnoldson: *Sedaine et les musiciens de son temps* (Paris, 1934)
R. Guiet: *L'évolution d'un genre: le livret d'opéra en France de Gluck à la révolution (1774–1793)*, Smith College Studies in Modern Languages, xviii (Northampton, Mass., 1936–7)
L. Richebourg: *Contribution à l'histoire de la 'Querelle des Bouffons'* (Paris, 1937)
D. Grout: *The Origin of the Opéra-Comique* (diss., Harvard U., 1939)
E. Kisch: 'Rameau and Rousseau', *ML*, xxii (1941), 97
N. Boyer: *La Guerre des Bouffons et la musique française (1752–1754)* (Paris, 1945)
M. Cooper: *Opéra-Comique* (London, 1949)
R. Viollier: *Jean-Joseph Mouret* (Paris, 1950)
C. Girdlestone: *Jean-Philippe Rameau* (London, 1957, rev. 2/1969)
C. D. Brenner: *The Théâtre Italien: its Repertory 1716–1793, with a Historical Introduction* (Berkeley and Los Angeles, 1961)
A. S. Garlington: '*Le merveilleux* and Operatic Reform in 18th Century French Opera', *MQ*, xlix (1963), 484
A. M. Whittall: *La Querelle des Bouffons* (diss., U. of Cambridge, 1963)
C. E. Koch: 'The Dramatic Ensemble Finale in the Opéra-Comique of the Eighteenth Century', *AcM*, xxxix (1967), 72
J. Rushton: *Music and Drama at the Académie Royale de Musique 1774–1789* (diss., U. of Oxford, 1969)
O. F. Saloman: *Aspects of 'Gluckian' Operatic Thought and Practice in France: the Musico-dramatic Vision of Le Sueur and La Cépède (1785–1809) in Relation to the Aesthetic and Critical Tradition* (diss., Columbia U., 1970)
E. Surian: *A Checklist of Writings on 18th Century French and Italian Opera (excluding Mozart)* (Hackensack, NJ, 1970)
J. Rushton: 'An Early Essay in "Leitmotiv": J. B. Lemoyne's "Electre"', *ML*, lii (1971), 387
H. Lagrave: *Le théâtre et le public a Paris de 1715 à 1750* (Paris, 1972)
A. McConnell: *The Opera Ballet: Opera as Literature* (diss., U. of Arizona, 1972)
J. Rushton: '"Iphigénie en Tauride": the Operas of Gluck and Piccinni', *ML*, liii (1972), 411
M. Cooper: 'Opera in France', *NOHM*, vii (London, 1973), 200
D. Launay, ed.: *La Querelle des Bouffons* (Geneva, 1973) [facs. of 61 pamphlets pubd 1752–4]
M. Lütolf: 'Zur Rolle der Antike in der musikalischen Tradition der französischen Epoque Classique', *Studien zur Tradition in der Musik: Kurt von Fischer zum 60. Geburtstag* (Munich, 1973), 145
C. Dahlhaus: 'Ethos und Pathos in Glucks Iphigenie auf Tauris', *Mf*, xxviii (1974), 289
D. Charlton: 'Motive and Motif: Méhul before 1791', *ML*, lvii (1976), 362
K. S. Pendle: 'The Opéras Comiques of Grétry and Marmontel', *MQ*, lxii (1976), 433
G. Sadler: *Rameau's Last Opera: Abaris ou Les Boréades'*, *MT*, cxvi (1975), 327
K. S. Pendle: '*Les philosophes* and *opéra comique*: the Case of Grétry's *Lucile*', *MR*, xxxviii (1977), 177
L'opéra au XVIIIe siècle: Aix-en-Provence 1977
J. Gourret: *Histoire de l'Opéra-Comique* (Paris, 1978)
H. C. Wolff: 'Voltaire und die Oper', *Mf*, xxx (1978), 257
M. Cyr: 'Eighteenth Century French and Italian Singing: Rameau's Writing for the Voice', *ML*, lxi (1980), 318
L. Rosow: 'Lallemand and Durand; Two Eighteenth-Century Music Copyists at the Paris Opéra', *JAMS*, xxxiii (1980), 142
G. Sadler: '*Naïs*, Rameau's "Opéra pour la paix"', *MT*, cxxi (1980), 431
——: 'The Role of the Keyboard Continuo in French Opera, 1673–1776', *EM*, viii (1980), 148
K. M. Smith: *Egidio Duni and the Development of the Opéra-Comique from 1753 to 1770* (diss., Cornell U., 1980)
G. Sadler: 'Rameau and the Orchestra', *PRMA*, cviii (1981–2), 47
M. Cyr: 'Basses and Basse-continue in the Orchestra of the Paris Opéra, 1700–1764', *EM*, x (1982), 155
J. Hayes: 'Armide: Gluck's most French Opera?', *MT*, cxxiii (1982), 408
J. B. Kopp: *The 'Drame Lyrique': a Study in the Esthetics of opéra comique, 1762–1791* (diss., U. of Pennsylvania, 1982)
H. Schneider: 'Tragédie et tragédie en musique: querelles autour de l'autonomie d'un nouveau genre', *Komparatistische Heft* (1982), 43

EM, xi (1983) [Rameau issue, incl. G. Sadler: 'Rameau's Singers and Players at the Paris Opéra', p.453; L. Sawkins: 'New Sources for Rameau's *Pigmalion* and Other Works', p.490; R. P. Wolf: 'Rameau's *Les Paladins*: from Autograph to Production', p.497]

Jean-Philippe Rameau: Dijon 1983

P. F. Rice: 'Mid-Eighteenth Century Change in French Opera: the Two Versions of Rameau's *Zoroastre*', *RMFC*, xxi (1983), 128

G. Sadler: 'Rameau, Pellegrin and the Opéra', *MT*, cxxiv (1983), 533

M. E. C. Bartlet: 'Politics and the Fate of *Roger et Olivier*, a Newly Recovered Opera by Grétry', *JAMS*, xxxvii (1984), 98

——: 'Grétry, Marie-Antoinette and *La rosière de Salency*', *PRMA*, cxi (1984–5), 92

L. E. Brown: 'Metaphor and Music: the Landscape Garden in Eighteenth-Century Operatic Sets', *OQ*, ii (1984), 37

——: 'The Récit in the Eighteenth-Century tragédie en musique', *MR*, xlv (1984), 96

R. Angermüller: 'Gluck oder Piccinni: Padre Martinis Urteil über französische und italienische Musik', *Mitteilungen der Internationalen Stiftung Mozarteum*, xxxiii (1985), 50

V. N. Briantseva: *Frantsuzskaya komicheskaya opera XVIII veka: puti stanovleniya i razvitiya zhanra* (Moscow, 1985)

D. Charlton: 'Orchestra and Chorus at the Comédie-Italienne (Opéra-Comique), 1755–1799', *Slavonic and Romantic Music: Essays for Gerald Abraham* (Oxford, 1985), 87

E.-T. Forsius: *Der 'gout français' in den Darstellungen des coin du roi: Versuch zur Rekonstrucktion einer 'Laienasthetik' wahrend des Parisier Buffonsitenstreites 1752–1754* (Tutzing, 1985)

D. Heartz: 'Opéra Comique and the Théâtre Italien from Watteau to Fragonard', *Music in the Classic Period: Essays in Honor of Barry S. Brook* (New York, 1985), 69

M. Lecrivain: *L'esprit de réforme dans l'opéra français de 1750 à 1790* (diss., U. of Paris-Sorbonne, 1985)

R. Legrand: *Chaconnes et passacailles dansées dans l'opéra français de Lully à Le Sueur* (diss., U. of Paris, 1985)

F. Lesure, ed.: *Querelle des Gluckistes et des Piccinnistes* (Geneva, 1985)

S. Pitou: *The Paris Opéra: an Encyclopedia of Operas, Ballets, Composers and Performers, ii: Rococo and Romantic, 1715–1815* (Westport, Conn., 1985)

C. Pré: 'L'opéra-comique à la cour de Louis XVI', *XVIIIᵉ siècle*, xvii (1985), 221

A. L. Ringer: 'A German Gluckist in Pre-Revolutionary France: Johann Christoph Vogel as an Opera Composer in the 1780s', *Music in the Classic Period: Essays in Honor of Barry S. Brook* (New York, 1985), 221

L. Sawkins: 'Rameau's Last Years: some Implications of Re-Discovered Material at Bordeaux, Orchestral Parts for Late Operas', *PRMA*, cxi (1984–5), 66

L. M. Stones: *Musical Characterization in Eighteenth-Century opéra comique: Tom Jones, Le Deserteur, and Richard Coeur-de-Lion* (diss., U. of Illinois, 1985)

X. Testot: *La Querelle des Bouffons: querelle musicale et querelle littéraire* (diss., U. of Paris-Sorbonne, 1985)

D. Charlton: *Grétry and the Growth of Opéra-comique* (Cambridge, 1986)

J. Mongrédien: *La musique en France des lumières au romantisme* (Paris, 1986)

D. Charlton: ' "L'art dramatico-musical": an Essay', *Music and Theatre: Essays in Honour of Winton Dean* (Cambridge, 1987), 229

M. E. C. Bartlet: 'A Musician's View of Rameau after the Advent of Gluck: Grétry's *Les trois âges de l'opéra* and its Background', *Studies on Jean-Baptiste Lully and the Music of the French Baroque: Essays in Honor of James R. Anthony* (Cambridge, 1989)

England

See and Seem Blind: or, A Critical Dissertation on the Publick Diversions (London, 1732/R1986)

J. Brown: *Letters upon the Poetry and Music of the Italian Opera* (Edinburgh, 1789, 2/1791)

R. Mount-Edgcumbe: *Musical Reminiscences, Containing an Account of the Italian Opera in England from 1773* (London, 1824, 4/1834/R1973)

M. Kelly: *Reminiscences* (London, 1826, 2/1826); ed. R. Fiske (London, 1975)

J. Ebers: *Seven Years of the King's Theatre* (London, 1828/R1972)

W. T. Parke: *Musical Memoirs* (London, 1830)

F. Kidson: *The Beggar's Opera: its Predecessors and Successors* (Cambridge, 1922)

W. C. Smith: *The Italian Opera and Contemporary Ballet in London 1789–1820* (London, 1955)

E. O. D. Downes: *The Operas of Johann Christian Bach as a Reflection of the Dominant Trends in Opera Seria 1750–1780* (diss., Harvard U., 1958)

H. Rosenthal: *Two Centuries of Opera at Covent Garden* (London, 1958)
The London Stage 1660–1800 (Carbondale, 1960–68)
F. H. W. Sheppard, ed.: *The Parish of St. James Westminster: Survey of London*, xxix–xxxi (London, 1960–63)
E. Warburton: 'J. C. Bach's Operas', *PRMA*, xcii (1965–6), 95
G. E. Dorris: *Paolo Rolli and the Italian Circle in London 1715–1744* (The Hague and Paris, 1967)
E. Warburton: *A Study of Johann Christian Bach's Operas* (diss., U. of Oxford, 1969)
D. Nalbach: *The King's Theatre, 1704–1867* (London, 1972)
M. F. Robinson: 'Porpora's Operas for London, 1733–1736', *Soundings*, ii (1971–2), 67
R. Fiske: *English Theatre Music in the Eighteenth Century* (London, 1973, 2/1986)
T. J. Walsh: *Opera in Dublin 1705–1797: the Social Scene* (Dublin, 1973)
W. Rubsamen, ed.: *The Ballad Opera: a Collection of 171 Original Texts of Musical Plays printed in Photo-facsimile* (New York, 1974)
H. C. Robbins Landon: *Haydn: Chronicle and Works*, iii: *Haydn in England 1791–1795* (London, 1976)
J. W. Hill: *The Life and Works of Francesco Maria Veracini* (Ann Arbor, 1979)
R. D. Hume, ed.: *The London Theatre World 1660–1800* (Carbondale, 1980)
C. Kephart: 'An Unnoticed Forerunner of "The Beggar's Opera"', *ML*, lxi (1980), 266
F. C. Petty: *Italian Opera in London 1760–1800* (Ann Arbor, 1980)
C. Chapman: 'A 1727 Pantomime: The Rape of Proserpine', *MT*, cxxii (1981), 807
R. D. Hume: 'The London Theatre from *The Beggar's Opera* to the Licensing Act', *The Rakish Stage* (Carbondale, 1983), 270
E. W. White: *A History of English Opera* (London, 1983)
D. Martin: *The Operas and Operatic Style of John Frederick Lampe* (Detroit, 1985)
L. V. Troost: *The Rise of English Comic Opera: 1762–1800* (diss., U. of Pennsylvania, 1985)
E. Gibson: 'Earl Cowper in Florence and his Correspondence with the Italian Opera in London', *ML*, lxviii (1987), 235

Spain and Portugal

L. Carmena y Millán: *Crónica de la ópera italiana en Madrid desde el año 1738 hasta nuestros dias* (Madrid, 1878; suppls. 1879, 1880)
———: *Origenes y establecimiento de la ópera en España hasta 1800* (Madrid, 1917)
F. Pedrell: *Teatro lírico español anterior al siglo XIX* (La Coruña, 1897–8)
J. Subirá: *La tonadilla escénica* (Madrid, 1928–30)
———: *La tonadilla escénica, sus obras y sus autores* (Barcelona, 1933)
———: 'La ópera castellana en los siglos XVII y XVIII', *Segismundo*, i (1965), 23
G. Chase: 'Origins of the Lyric Theater in Spain', *MQ*, xxv (1939), 292
M. N. Hamilton: *Music in 18th-Century Spain* (Urbana, 1937)
M. de Sampayo Ribeiro: *A música em Portugal nos séculos XVIII e XIX* (Lisbon, 1938)
J. de Freitas Branco: *Historia da música portuguesa* (Lisbon, 1959)
R. Stevenson: *Foundations of New World Opera* (Lima, 1973)
M. C. de Brito: *Opera in Portugal in the Eighteenth Century (1708–1793)* (diss., U. of London, 1986)
X. M. Carreira: 'Orígenes de la ópera en Cádiz: un informe de 1768 sobre el coliseo de operas', *RdMc*, x (1987), 581
———: 'La tasa de regulación del coliseo de óperas y comedias fabricado por Setaro (*La Coruña*, 1772)', *RdMc*, x (1987), 601

Staging

F. Galli-Bibiena: *L'architettura civile* (Parma, 1711)
B. Marcello: *Il teatro alla moda, o sia Metodo sicuro e facile per il ben comporre ed eseguire l'opere italiane in musica all'uso moderno* (Venice, c1720); Eng. trans., *MQ*, xxxix (1948), 222, 371; xxxv (1949), 85, and, abridged, in *Source Readings in Music History*, ed. O. Strunk, New York, 1950/R1965)
F. Algarotti: *Saggio sopra l'opera in musica* (Bologna, 1755/R1975, 2/1763; Eng. trans., 1767)
J. Noverre: *Lettres sur la danse et sur les ballets* (Lyons and Stuttgart, 1760, 2/1783; Eng. trans., 1783, enlarged 1803, and 1930)
J. C. Le Vacher de Charnois: *Costumes et annales des grands théâtres* (Paris, 1786–9)
Boullet: *Essai sur l'art de construire les théâtres, leurs machines et leurs mouvemens* (Paris, 1801)
C. F. D. Schubart: *Ideen zu einer Ästhetik der Tonkunst* (Vienna, 1806/R1969)
E. Cotarelo y Mori: *Estudios sobre la historia del arte escénico en España* (Madrid, 1896–1902)

A. Beijer: *Slottsteatrarna & Drottningholm och Gripsholm* (Stockholm, 1937)

B. Brunelli, ed.: *P. Metastasio: Tutte le opere* (Milan, 1943–54)

A. Downer: 'Nature to Advantage Dressed: 18th Century Acting', *Proceedings of the Modern Language Association of America*, lviii (1943), 1002

A. H. Mayor: *The Bibiena Family* (New York, 1945)

M. S. Konopleva: *Giuseppe Valeriani* (Leningrad, 1948)

J. Scholz, ed.: *Baroque and Romantic Stage Design* (New York, 1949/R1962)

C. Varese: *Saggio sul Metastasio* (Florence, 1950) [esp. appx, 'La regia dal dramma Metastasiano']

E. Povoledo: 'La scenografia architettonica del XVIII secolo a Venezia', *Arte veneta*, v (1951), 126

E. Croft-Murray: *John Devoto: a Baroque Scene Painter* (London, 1953)

G. M. Bergman: 'Les agences téâtrales et l'impression des mises en scène aux environs de 1800', *Revue de la Société d'histoire du théâtre*, viii (1956), 228

A. Blunt and E. Croft-Murray: *Venetian Drawings of the XVII and XVIII Centuries in the Collection of Her Majesty the Queen at Windsor Castle* (London, 1957)

M. Horányi: *Eszterházi vigasságok* (Budapest, 1959; Eng. trans., 1962)

M. Kindermann: *Theatergeschichte Europas*, iv–v (Salzburg, 1961–2)

M. Viale Ferrero: *La scenografia del '700 e i fratelli Galliari* (Turin, 1963)

F. Mancini: *Scenografia napoletana dell'età barocca* (Naples, 1964)

A. Boll: 'L'oeuvre théatrale de Rameau: sa mise en scène', *ReM*, no.260 (1965), 13

S. Rosenfeld and E. Croft-Murray: 'Checklist of Scene Painters Working in Great Britain and Ireland in the 18th Century', *Theatre Notebook*, xix (1964–5), 6, 49, 102, 133; xx (1965–6), 36, 69, 113

M. T. Muraro: *Scenografie di Pietro Gonzaga* (Venice, 1967)

D. Heartz: 'From Garrick to Gluck: the Reform of Theatre and Opera in the Mid-18th Century', *PRMA*, xciv (1967–8), 111

J. M. da Silva Correira: 'Teatros regios do seculo xviii', *Boletim do Museo nacional de arte antiga*, iii–iv (Lisbon, 1969)

F. Lesure: *L'opéra classique français: XVIIe et XVIIIe siècles* (Geneva, 1972)

S. Hansell: 'Stage Deportment and Scenographic Design in the Italian *Opera Seria* of the *Settecento*', *IMSCR* xi: *Copenhagen 1972*, i, 415

A. M. Nagler: 'J. N. Servandonis und F. Bouchers Wirken an der Pariser Oper', *Bühnenformen– Bühnenräume–Bühnendekorationen . . .: Herbert A. Frenzel zum 65. Geburtstag* (Berlin, 1974), 64

D. Barnett: 'The Performance Practice of Acting: the 18th Century', *Theatre Research International*, ii (1976–7), 157; iii (1977–8), 1, 79; v (1979–80), 1

J. de la Gorce: 'Décors et machines à l'Opéra de Paris au temps de Rameau', *RMFC*, xxi (1983), 145

G. Sadler: 'Rameau's Singers and Players at the Paris Opéra', *EM*, xi (1983), 453

R. Fajon: *L'Opéra à Paris du Roi-Soleil à Louis le Bien-Aimé* (Geneva, 1984)

B. Cohen-Stratyner: *Scenes and Machines from the Eighteenth Century: the Stagecraft of Jacopo Fabris and Citoyen Boullet* (New York, 1986)

D. Barnett: *The Art of Gesture: the Practices and Principles of Eighteenth-Century Acting* (Heidelberg, 1987)

ROMANTIC

Italy

G. B. Rinuccini: *Sulla musica e sulla poesia melodrammatica italiana nel secolo XIX* (Lucca, 1843)

P. Beltrame: 'Della poesia lirico-musicale odierna'; 'Come si diventa librettista', *Componimenti editi e inediti* (Venice, 1847), 43, 232

A. Basevi: *Studio sulle opere di Giuseppe Verdi* (Florence, 1859)

G. Pacini: *Le mie memorie artistiche* (Florence, 1865, rev. 2/1872)

E. Hanslick: *Die moderne Oper* (Berlin, 1875/R1971)

L. Schiedermair: *Simon Mayr* (Leipzig, 1907–19/R1973)

F. Torrefranca: *Giacomo Puccini e l'opera internazionale* (Turin, 1912)

G. M. Gatti: 'Gabriele d'Annunzio and the Italian Opera Composers', *MQ*, x (1924), 263

A. Bonaccorsi: *Giacomo Puccini e i suoi antenati musicali* (Milan, 1950)

M. Carner: *Puccini: a Critical Biography* (London, 1958, rev. 2/1974)

F. Walker: *The Man Verdi* (London, 1962)

G. Martin: *Verdi: his Music, Life and Times* (New York, 1963, 2/1964)

H. Weinstock: *Donizetti and the World of Opera in Italy, Paris, and Vienna in the First Half of the Nineteenth Century* (New York, 1963)

L. Dallapiccola: 'Parole e musica nel melodramma', *Quaderni della RaM*, ii (1965), 117; repr. in *Appunti, incontri, meditazioni* (Milan, 1970)

M. Rinaldi: *Felice Romani* (Rome, 1965)

F. Lippmann: 'Verdi e Bellini', *1° congresso internazionale di studi verdiani: Venezia 1966*, 184: Ger. trans., *Beiträge zur Geschichte der Oper*, ed. H. Becker (Regensburg, 1969), 77

F. L. Arruga: *Incontri fra poeta e musicisti nell'opera romantica italiana* (Milan, 1968)

R. Celletti: 'Il vocalismo italiano da Rossini a Donizetti', *AnMc*, no.5 (1968), 267; no.7 (1969), 214–47

——: 'Origini e sviluppi della coloratura rossiniana', *NRMI*, ii (1968), 872–919

F. Lippmann: 'Vincenzo Bellini und die italienische Opera seria seiner Zeit', *AnMc*, no.6 (1969), 1–104

C. Osborne: *The Complete Operas of Verdi* (London, 1969, 3/1985)

G. Baldini: *Abitare la battaglia: la storia di Giuseppe Verdi* (Milan, 1970; Eng. trans., 1980 as *The Story of Giuseppe Verdi: 'Oberto' to 'Un ballo in maschera'*)

P. Gossett: 'Gioachino Rossini and the Conventions of Composition', *AcM*, xlii (1970), 48

——: *The Operas of Rossini: Problems of Textual Criticism in 19th-Century Opera* (diss., Princeton U., 1970)

F. Lippmann: 'Zum Verhältnis von Libretto und Musik in der italienischen Opera seria der 1. Hälfte des 19. Jahrhunderts', *GfMKB, Bonn 1970*, 162

P. Petrobelli: 'Note sulla poetica di Bellini: a proposito de *Il puritani*', *MZ*, viii (1972), 70

J. Budden: *The Operas of Verdi*, i: *From Oberto to Rigoletto* (London, 1973); ii: *From Il trovatore to La forza del destino* (London, 1978); iii: *From Don Carlos to Falstaff* (London, 1981)

D. Lawton: *Tonality and Drama in Verdi's Early Operas* (diss., U. of California, Berkeley, 1973)

W. Dean: 'Donizetti's Serious Operas', *PRMA*, c (1973–4), 123

M. Mila: *La giovinezza di Verdi* (Turin, 1974)

F. Lippmann: 'Der italienische Vers und der musikalische Rhythmus: zum Verhältnis von Vers und Musik in der italienischen Oper des 19. Jahrhunderts, mit einem Rückblick auf die 2. Hälfte des 18. Jahrhunderts', *AnMc*, no.12 (1973), 253–369; no.14 (1974), 324–410; no.15 (1975), 298–333

G. Bezzola: 'Aspetti del clima culturale italiano nel periodo donizettiano', *1° convegno internazionale di studi donizettiani: Bergamo 1975*

V. Godefroy: *The Dramatic Genius of Verdi: Studies of Selected Operas*, i: '*Nabucco*' to '*La traviata*' (London, 1975); ii: '*I vespri siciliani*' to '*Falstaff*' (London, 1977)

F. Lippmann: 'Donizetti und Bellini: ein Beitrag zur Interpretation von Donizettis Stil', *Studi musicali*, iv (1975), 193–243 [shorter original in *1° convegno internazionale di studi donizettiani: Bergamo 1975*]

——: 'Verdi und Donizetti', *Opernstudien: Anna Amalie Abert zum 65. Geburtstag* (Tutzing, 1975), 153

F. Noske: *The Signifier and the Signified: Studies in the Operas of Mozart and Verdi* (The Hague, 1977)

G. Pestelli, ed.: *Il melodramma italiano dell'Ottocento: studi e ricerche per Massimo Mila* (Turin, 1977)

W. Weaver: *Verdi; a Documentary Study* (London, 1977)

H. Busch: *Verdi's Aida: the History of an Opera in Letters and Documents* (Minneapolis, 1978)

M. Conati: 'Italian Romantic Opera and Musicology', *CMc*, no.27 (1979), 65

M. Mila: *L'arte di Verdi* (Turin, 1980)

J. Nicolaisen: *Italian Opera in Transition, 1871–93* (Ann Arbor, 1980)

W. Weaver: *The Golden Century of Italian Opera from Rossini to Puccini: a Documentary Study* (London, 1980)

M. R. Adamo and F. Lippmann: *Vincenzo Bellini* (Turin, 1981)

D. R. B. Kimbell: *Verdi in the Age of Italian Romanticism* (Cambridge, 1981, 2/1985)

M. de Angelis: *La carte dell'impresario* (Florence, 1982)

W. Ashbrook: *Donizetti and his Operas* (Cambridge, 1982)

J. Black: *Donizetti's Operas in Naples 1822–1848* (London, 1982)

W. Dean: 'Italian Opera', *NOHM*, vii (1982), 376–451

H. Gál: *Giuseppe Verdi und die Oper* (Frankfurt, 1982)

D. Goldin: 'Aspetti della librettistica italiana fra 1770 e 1830', *AnMc*, no.21 (1982), 128

H. Lühning: 'Die Cavatina in der italienischen Oper um 1800', *AnMc*, no. 21 (1982), 333–68

V. Scherliess: '*Il barbiere di Siviglia*: Paisiello und Rossini', *AnMc*, no.21 (1982), 100

P. Weiss: 'Verdi and the Fusion of Genres', *JAMS*, xxv (1982), 138

W. Witzenmann: 'Grundzüge der Instrumentation in italienischen Opern von 1770 bis 1830', *AnMc*, no.21 (1982), 276

G. Barblan and B. Zanolini: *Gaetano Donizetti: vita e opere di un musicista romantico* (Bergamo, 1983)

M. Conati: *La bottega della musica: Verdi e la Fenice* (Milan, 1983)

J. Hepokoski: *Giuseppe Verdi: Falstaff* (Cambridge, 1983)

N. Till: *Rossini: his Life and Times* (New York, 1983)

G. Tintori: *Bellini* (Turin, 1983)

A. L. Ringer: 'Some Socio-economic Aspects of Italian Opera at the Time of Donizetti', *AnMc*, no.22 (1984), 229

D. Rosen and A. Porter, eds.: *Verdi's 'Macbeth': a Sourcebook* (New York, 1984)

J. Rosselli: *The Opera Industry in Italy from Cimarosa to Verdi: the Role of the Impresario* (Cambridge, 1984)

R. Alier: 'Giovanni Pacini: un compositor ja no oblidat del tot', *Revista musical Catalana*, v (1985), 5

S. L. Balathazar: *Evolving Conventions in Italian Serious Opera: Scene Structure in the Works of Rossini, Bellini, Donizetti and Verdi, 1810–1850* (diss., U. of Pennsylvania, 1985)

J. Black: *The Italian Romantic Libretto: a Study of Salvatore Cammarano (1801–52)* (Edinburgh, 1985)

J. Budden: *Verdi* (London, 1985)

P. Gossett: *'Anna Bolena' and the Artistic Maturity of Gaetano Donizetti* (Oxford, 1985)

N. John, ed.: *Gioachino Rossini: The Barber of Seville/Moses* (London, 1985)

R. Verti: 'Dieci anni di studi sulle fonti per la storia materiale dell'opera italiana nell' Ottocento', *RIM*, xx (1985), 124–63

'Vincenzo Bellini', *Musik-Konzepte*, no.46 (1985) [whole issue]

D. Danzuso, F. Gallo and R. Monti: *Omaggio a Bellini* (Milan, 1986)

A. Duault: *Verdi, la musique et le drame* (Paris, 1986)

U. Günther: 'La genèse de *Don Carlos* de Verdi: nouveaux documents', *RdM*, lxxii (1986), 104

G. W. Harwood: 'Verdi's Reform of the Italian Opera Orchestra', *19th-Century Music*, x (1986–7), 108

R. Osborne: *Rossini* (London, 1986)

D. Pistone: *L'opéra italien au XIXe siècle: de Rossini à Puccini* (Paris, 1986)

G. Tomlinson: 'Italian Romanticism and Italian Opera: an Essay in their Affinities', *19th-Century Music*, x (1986–7), 108

M. di Gregorio Casati and M. Pavarini, eds.: *Nuove prospettive nella ricerca verdiano: Vienna 1983* (Parma and Milan, 1987)

J. Hepokoski: *Giuseppe Verdi: Otello* (Cambridge, 1987)

G. Morelli, ed.: 'Tornando a Stiffelio: popolarità, rifacimenti, messinscena, effettismo e altre "cure" nella drammaturgia del Verdi romantico: Venice 1985', *Quaderni della RIM*, xiv (Florence, 1987)

S. L. Balthazar: 'Rossini and the Development of the Mid-Century Lyric Form', *JAMS*, xli (1988), 102

H. Busch, ed.: *Verdi's 'Otello' and 'Simon Boccanegra' in Letters and Documents* (Oxford and New York, 1988)

G. Martin: *Aspects of Verdi* (New York, 1988)

Germany and Austria

W. R. Griepenkerl: *Die Oper der Gegenwart* (Leipzig, 1847)

J. Cornet: *Die Oper in Deutschland und das Theater der Neuzeit* (Hamburg, 1849)

R. Wagner: *Oper und Drama* (1851), *Gesammelte Schriften und Dichtungen*, iii, iv (Leipzig, 1871–3; 2/1887/R1976, Eng. trans., ii, 1892, 2/1895)

J. C. Lobe: *Fliegende Blätter für Musik* (Leipzig, 1855–7)

L. Rellstab: *Die Gestaltung der Oper seit Mozart* (Sondershausen, 1859)

E. Hanslick: *Die moderne Oper* (Berlin, 1875–1900/R1970)

G. B. Shaw: *The Perfect Wagnerite: a Commentary on the Nibelung's Ring* (London, 1898, 4/1923/R1972)

K. M. Kolb: *Beiträge zur Geschichte der deutschen komischen Oper* (Berlin, 1902)

E. Schmitz: *Zur Geschichte des Leitmotivs in der romantischen Oper* (Hochland, 1907)

V. E. Frensdorf: *Peter Winter als Opernkomponist* (diss., U. of Munich, 1908)

G. R. Kruse: 'Otto Nicolais italienische Opern', *SIMG*, xii (1910–11), 267–96

M. Ehrenhaus: *Die Operndichtung der deutschen Romantik* (Breslau, 1911)

A. Weissmann: *Berlin als Musikstadt: Geschichte der Oper und des Konzerts von 1740–1911* (Berlin and Leipzig, 1911)

H. Gaartz: *Die Opern Heinrich Marschners* (Leipzig, 1912)

L. Krauss: *Das deutsche Liederspiel in den Jahren 1800–1830* (diss., U. of Halle, 1921)

A. Lorenz: *Das Geheimnis der Form bei Richard Wagner* (Berlin, 1924–33/R1966)

K. Lüthge: *Die deutsche Spieloper* (Brunswick, 1924)

G. Abraham: 'The Leit-motif since Wagner', *ML*, vi (1925), 175

R. Hänsler: *Peter Lindpaintner als Opernkomponist* (diss., U. of Munich, 1928)

W. H. Riehl: *Zur Geschichte der romantischen Oper* (Berlin, 1928)

L. Schiedermaier: *Die deutsche Oper* (Leipzig, 1930, 2/1940)

K. Wörner: *Beitrage zur Geschichte des Leitmotivs in der Oper* (diss., U. of Berlin, 1931; extracts in *ZMw*, xiv, 1931–2, p.151

A. Buesst: *The Nibelung's Ring* (London, 1932)

H. Laue: *Die Operndichtung Lortzings* (Würzburg, 1932)

E. Newman: *The Life of Richard Wagner* (London, 1933–47/R1976)

S. Goslich: *Beiträge zur Geschichte der deutschen romantischen Oper* (Leipzig, 1937, rev. 2/1975 as *Die deutsche romantische Oper*)

R. Butschek: *Die musikalischen Ausdrucksmittel in den Opern Lortzings* (diss., U. of Vienna, 1938)

K. Reiber: *Das Volkstümliche in der deutschen romantischen Oper* (Würzburg, 1942)

H. Schnoor: *Weber auf dem Welttheater: ein Freischützbuch* (Dresden, 1942, 5/1985)

E. Hofer: *Die Entwicklung des Musikdramas in der Romantik* (diss., U. of Vienna, 1943)

E. Newman: *Wagner Nights* (London, 1949/R1961 and 1977); as *The Wagner Operas* (New York, 1949/R1963)

E. Sanders: '*Oberon* and *Zar und Zimmermann*', *MQ*, xl (1954), 521

M. Hoffmann: *Gustav Albert Lortzing, der Meister der deutschen Volksoper* (Leipzig, 1956)

V. Köhler: *Heinrich Marschners Bühnenwerke* (diss., U. of Göttingen, 1956)

D. Greiner: *Louis Spohrs Beiträge zur deutschen romantischen Oper* (diss., U. of Kiel, 1960)

J. Lodemann: *Lortzing und seine Spielopern: deutsche Bürgelichkeit* (diss., U. of Freiburg, 1962)

E. N. McKay: *The Stage Works of Schubert, Considered in the Framework of Austrian Biedermeier Society* (diss., U. of Oxford, 1962–3)

R. Donington: *Wagner's 'Ring' and its Symbols: the Music and the Myth* (London, 1963, enlarged, 3/1974)

H. Becker: 'Die historische Bedeutung der Grand Opéra', *Beiträge zur Geschichte der Musikanschauung im 19. Jahrhundert*, ed. W. Salmen (Regensburg, 1965), 151

E. N. McKay: 'Schubert's Music for the Theatre', *PRMA*, xciii (1966–7), 51

A. A. Abert: 'Webers "Euryanthe" und Spohrs "Jessonda" als grosse Opern', *Festschrift für Walter Wiora* (Kassel, 1967), 35

B. Magee: *Aspects of Wagner* (London, 1968, rev. 3/1988)

J. Warrack: *Carl Maria von Weber* (London, 1968, 2/1976)

C. von Westernhagen: *Wagner* (Zurich, 1968; Eng. trans., 1979)

C. Dahlhaus, ed.: *Das Drama Richard Wagners als musikalisches Kunstwerk* (Regensburg, 1970)

M. J. Citron: *Schubert's Seven Complete Operas: a Musico-Dramatic Study* (diss., U. of North Carolina, 1971)

C. Dahlhaus: *Die Musikdramen Richard Wagners* (Velber, 1971; Eng. trans., 1979, 2/1985)

——: *Wagners Konzeption des musikalischen Dramas* (Regensburg, 1971)

——: 'Zur Geschichte der Leitmotivtechnik bei Wagner': *Richard Wagner: Werk und Wirkung* (Regensburg, 1971)

J. W. Klein: 'Verdi and Nicolai: a Strange Rivalry', *MR*, xxxii (1971), 63

G. Jones: *Backgrounds and Themes of the Operas of Carl Maria von Weber* (diss., Cornell U., 1972)

M. Gregor-Dellin: *Die Revolution als Oper* (Munich, 1973)

A. S. Garlington jr: 'German Romantic Opera and the Problem of Origins', *MQ*, lxiii (1977), 247

J. Warrack: 'German Operatic Ambitions at the Beginning of the 19th Century', *PRMA*, civ (1977–8), 79

D. Cooke: *I Saw the World End* (London, 1979) [on the *Ring* cycle]

A. D. Palmer: *Heinrich August Marschner: his Life and Stage Works* (Ann Arbor, 1980)

P. Ackermann: *Richard Wagners 'Ring des Nibelungen' und die Dialektik der Aufklärung* (Tutzing, 1981)

L. Beckett: *Richard Wagner: Parsifal* (Cambridge, 1981)

W. Dean: 'German Opera', *NOHM*, viii (1982), 452–522

P. McCreless: *Wagner's Siegfried: its Drama, History and Music* (Ann Arbor, 1982)

'Richard Wagner: Parsifal', *Musik-Konzepte*, no.25 (1982) [whole issue]

C. Dahlhaus: 'Tonalität und Form in Wagners "Ring des Nibelungen"', *AMw*, xl (1983), 165

——: 'Webers "Freischütz" und die Idee der romantischen Oper', *ÖMz*, xxxviii (1983), 381

F. Oberkogler: *Parsifal: der Zukunftsweg des Menschen in Richard Wagners Musikdrama* (Stuttgart, 1983)

J. Rohr: 'Wenn Sprache und Handlung Musik werden: E. T. A. Hoffmanns Begriff der "romantischen Oper"', *Festschrift Hans Conradin* (Berne, 1983)

M. Tusa: *Carl Maria von Weber's 'Euryanthe': a Study of its Historical Context, Genesis, and Reception* (diss., Princeton U., 1983)

L. Finscher: 'Weber's *Freischütz*: Conceptions and Misconceptions', *PRMA*, cx (1983–4), 79

C. Brown: *Louis Spohr* (Cambridge, 1984)

A. Fecker: *Sprache und Musik: Phänomenologie der Deklamation in Oper und Lied des 19. Jahrhunderts* (Hamburg, 1984)

P. Franklin: '*Palestrina* and the Dangerous Futurists', *MQ*, lxx (1984), 499

S. Gozzi: 'Nuovi orientamenti della critica wagneriana', *RIM*, xix (1984), 147

G. Haffner: *Die Wagner-Opern* (Munich, 1984)

B. Millington: *Wagner* (London, 1984)

R. Bailey, ed.: *Wagner: Prelude and Transfiguration from Tristan und Isolde*, Norton Critical Scores (New York, 1985)

C. Dahlhaus: 'Wagner, Meyerbeer und der Fortschritt', *Festschrift Rudolf Elvers* (Tutzing, 1985)

O. Fambach: *Das Repertorium des Koniglichen Theaters und der italienischen Oper zu Dresden 1814–1832* (Bonn, 1985)

N. John, ed.: *Richard Wagner: Götterdämmerung* (London, 1985)

——: *Richard Wagner: Das Rheingold* (London, 1985)

W. Kinderman: 'Wagner's *Parsifal*: Musical Form and the Drama of Redemption', *JM*, iv (1985), 431

T. Mann: *Pro and Contra Wagner* (Chicago, 1985)

A. D. McCredie: 'Leitmotive: Wagner's Points of Departure and their Antecedents', *MMA*, xiv (1985), 1

M. C. Tusa: 'Richard Wagner and Weber's *Euryanthe*', *19th-Century Music*, ix (1985–6), 206

I. Capelle: 'Albert Lortzing und das norddeutsche Singspiel: zu Lortzings Bearbeitung von Johann Adam Hillers Singspiel *Die Jagd* (1829–1830)', *Mf*, xxxix (1986), 123

A. Csampai and D. Holland, eds.: *Richard Wagner: 'Tannhauser'; Texte, Materialien, Kommentare* (Reinbeck bei Hamburg, 1986)

N. John, ed.: *Richard Wagner: Parsifal* (London, 1986)

U. Müller and P. Wapnewski, eds.: *Richard-Wagner-Handbüch* (Stuttgart, 1986)

E. Roch: 'Akkumulative Rhetorik: Die Kunst, zu "revolutionieren" in Richard Wagners Sprache und Musik', *BMw*, xxviii (1986), 284

F. Ferlan: *Le thème d'Ondine dans la littérature et l'opéra allemande au XIXème siècle* (Berne, 1987)

J. Liebscher: 'Biedermeier-Elemente in der deutschen Spieloper: zu Otto Nicolais *Die lustigen Weiber von Windsor*', *Mf*, xl (1987), 229

J. Maehder: 'Studi sul rapporto testo-musica nell'*Anello de Nibelungo* di Richard Wagner', *NRMI*, xxi (1987), 43

H.-M. Palm: *Richard Wagner's 'Lohengrin': Studien zur Sprachbehandlung* (Munich, 1987)

L. R. Shaw, N. R. Cirillo and M. S. Miller, eds.: *Wagner in Retrospect: a Centennial Reappraisal* (Amsterdam, 1987)

S. Spencer and B. Millington, eds.: *Selected Letters of Richard Wagner* (London, 1987)

W. Darcy: '"Everything that is, ends!": the Genesis and Meaning of the Erda Episode in *Das Rheingold*', *MT*, cxxix (1988), 443

M. H. Schmid: 'Metamorphose der Themen Beobachtungen an den Skizzen zum *Lohengrin* "-Vorspiel"', *Mf*, xli (1988), 105

France

J. D. Martine: *De la musique dramatique en France* (Paris, 1813)

Castil-Blaze: *De l'opéra en France* (Paris, 1820)

V. E. de Jouy: *Essai sur l'opéra français*, Oeuvres complètes, xxii (Paris, c1828)

J. d'Ortigue: *Le balcon de l'Opéra* (Paris, 1833)

L. Véron: *Mémoires d'un bourgeois de Paris*, iii (Paris, 1854)

Castil-Blaze: *Sur l'opéra français, vérités dures mais utiles* (Paris, 1856)

P. C. B. de Boigne: *Petits mémoires de l'Opéra* (Paris, 1857)

T. Gautier: *Histoire de l'art dramatique en France* (Paris, 1858–9/R1968)

J. Moynet: *L'envers du théâtre: machines et décorations* (Paris, 1873/R1972)

O. Fouqué: *Histoire du Théâtre-Ventadour 1829–1879* (Paris, 1881)

H. Blaze de Bury: 'The French Opera', *Nineteenth Century* (1890), no.2, p. 39
A. Soubies: *Histoire du Théâtre-lyrique, 1850–1870* (Paris, 1899)
P.-L. Hillemacher: *Charles Gounod* (Paris, n.d. [?1905])
E. Wahl: *Nicolo Isouard: sein Leben und sein Schaffen auf dem Gebiet der Opéra Comique* (Munich, 1906)
L. Schneider: *Massenet: l'homme et le musicien* (Paris, 1908)
A. Jullien: *Ernest Reyer: sa vie et ses oeuvres* (Paris, n.d. [?1909], 2/1914)
J. Loisel: *Manon de Massenet: étude historique et critique* (Paris, 1922)
L. Schneider: *Offenbach* (Paris, 1923)
J. Loisel: *Lakmé de Léo Delibes* (Paris, 1924)
G. Fauré: *Opinions musicales* (Paris, 1930)
S. Kracauer: *Jacques Offenbach und das Paris seiner Zeit* (Amsterdam, 1937, 2/1962; Eng. trans., 1937)
M. A. Allévy: *La mise en scène en France dans la première moitié du dix-neuvième siècle* (Paris, 1938)
W. L. Crosten: *French Grand Opera: an Art and a Business* (New York, 1948/R1972)
M. Cooper: *Opéra Comique* (London, 1949)
——: *French Music from the Death of Berlioz to the Death of Fauré* (London, 1951)
M. S. Selden: *The French Operas of Luigi Cherubini* (diss., Yale U., 1951)
M. Cooper: 'Giacomo Meyerbeer', *Fanfare for Ernest Newman* (London, 1955)
R. Longyear: *D. F. E. Auber: a Chapter in French Opéra Comique 1800–1870* (diss., Cornell U., 1957)
R. Pitrou: *De Gounod à Debussy* (Paris, 1957)
M. Curtiss: *Bizet and his World* (London, 1958)
R. M. Longyear: 'Notes on the Rescue Opera', *MQ*, xlv (1959), 49
H. Becker, ed.: *Giacomo Meyerbeer: Briefwechsel und Tagebücher* (Berlin, 1960–)
S. Wolff: *L'Opéra au Palais Garnier, 1875–1962* (Paris, 1963)
E. R. Hotaling: *Nineteenth-Century Opera Adaptations of Shakespeare's Romeo and Juliet* (diss., Northwestern U., 1964)
H. Kirchmeyer: 'Die deutsche Librettokritik bei Eugène Scribe und Giacomo Meyerbeer', *NZM*, Jg.-cxxv (1964), 372
H. Becker: 'Die historische Bedeutung der Grand Opéra', *Beiträge zur Geschichte der Musikanschauung im 19. Jahrhundert*, ed. W. Salmen (Regensburg, 1965), 151
W. Dean: 'The True Carmen?', *MT*, cvi (1965), 846
J. Harding: *Saint-Saëns and his Circle* (London, 1965)
W. Dean: 'Opera under the French Revolution', *PRMA*, civ (1967–8), 77
R. Myers: *Chabrier and his Circle* (London, 1969)
A. Ringer: 'Cherubini's *Médée* and the Spirit of French Revolutionary Opera', *Essays in Musicology in Honor of Dragan Plamenac* (Pittsburgh, 1969/R1977), 281
J. Harding: *Massenet* (London, 1970)
H. R. Cohen: *Berlioz and the Opera (1829–1849)* (diss., New York U., 1973)
J. Harding: *Gounod* (London, 1973)
K. S. Pendle: 'Scribe, Auber and the Count of Monte Cristo', *MR*, xxxiv (1973), 210
T. J. Walsh: *Monte Carlo Opera 1879–1909* (Dublin, 1975)
D. Charlton: 'Ossian, Le Sueur and Opera', *SMA*, xi (1977), 37
K. S. Pendle: *Eugène Scribe and French Opera of the Nineteenth Century* (Ann Arbor, 1979)
A. Faris: *Jacques Offenbach* (London, 1980)
J. Harding: *Jacques Offenbach* (London, 1980)
D. Rissin: *Offenbach* (Paris, 1980)
MT, cxxi (Oct 1980) [Offenbach issue]
'Jacques Offenbach', *Musik-Konzepte*, no.13 (1980) [Offenbach issue]
J. F. Fulcher: 'Meyerbeer and the Music of Society', *MQ*, lxvii (1981), 213
J. Langford: 'Berlioz, Cassandra, and the French Operatic Tradition', *ML*, lxii (1981), 310
T. J. Walsh: *Second Empire Opera: the Théâtre Lyrique in Paris 1851–1870* (London and New York, 1981)
Auber et l'opéra romantique: Paris 1982
M. E. C. Bartlet: *Etienne-Nicolas Méhul and Opera during the French Revolution, Consulate, and Empire: a Source, Archival, and Stylistic Study* (diss., U. of Chicago, 1982)
W. Dean: 'French Opera', *NOHM*, viii (1982), 26–119
L. Finscher: 'Aubers *La muette de Portici* und die Anfänge der Grand-Opéra', *Festschrift Heinz Becker* (Laaber, 1982)
J. F. Fulcher: 'French Grand Opera and the Quest for a National Image: an Approach to the Study of Government-Sponsored Art', *CMc*, no.35 (1983), 34
O. Salzer, ed.: *The Massenet Compendium* (Fort Lee, NJ, 1984)

J. M. Bailbé: '*Polyeucte* de Donizetti à Gounod', *Revue d'histoire littéraire de la France*, lxxxv (1985), 799

S. E. Huebner: *The Second Empire Operas of Charles Gounod* (diss., Princeton U., 1985)

W. Kirsch and R. Dietrich, eds.: *Jacques Offenbach: Komponist und Weltburger* (Mainz, 1985)

L. C. Shulman: *Music Criticism of the Paris Opéra in the 1830s* (diss., Cornell U., 1985)

K. S. Pendle: 'A Night at the Opera: the Parisian prima donna, 1830–1850', *OQ*, iv/1 (1986), 77

C. J. Robinson: *One-act 'Opéra-Comique' from 1800 to 1810: Contributions of Henri-Montan Berton and Nicolo Isouard* (diss., U. of Cincinnati, 1986)

A. Spires: *French Opera during the Belle Epoque: a Study in the Social History of Ideas* (diss., U. of North Carolina, Chapel Hill, 1986)

P. Barbier: *À l'Opéra au temps de Rossini et de Balzac: Paris, 1800–1850* (Paris, 1987)

P. Blom, ed: *Music in the Eighteen-Thirties* (Stuyvesant, NY, 1989)

V. Deschamps: *Histoire de l'administration de l'Opéra de Paris (Second Empire – Troisième République)* (diss., U. of Paris-Sorbonne, 1987)

J. F. Fulcher: *The Nation's Image: French Grand Opera as Politics and Politicized Art* (Cambridge and New York, 1987)

T. Schacher: *Idee und Erscheinungsformen des Dramatischen bei Hector Berlioz* (Hamburg, 1987)

W. E. Studwell: *Adolphe Adam and Léo Delibes: a Guide to Research* (New York, 1987)

E. Brody: *Paris: the Musical Kaleidoscope: 1870–1925* (New York, 1988)

I. Kemp: *Hector Berlioz: Les troyens* (Cambridge, 1988)

N. Wild: *Dictionnaire des théâtres lyriques à Paris au XIX siècle* (New York, in preparation)

Russia and Eastern Europe

Dramaticheskiy slovar', ili pokazaniya po alfabitu vsekh rossiyskikh teatral'nikh sochineniy [A dictionary of the theatre, or an alphabetical list of all Russian theatrical works] (Moscow, 1787, repr. 1881)

V. E. Cheshikin: *Istoria russkoy operï* (Moscow, 1902, enlarged 2/1905)

N. Nejedlý: *Zpěvohry Smetanovy* [Smetana's operas] (Prague, 1908, 3/1954)

N. Findeyzen: 'The Earliest Russian Operas', *MQ*, xix (1933), 331

G. Abraham: *Studies in Russian Music* (London, 1935)

———: *On Russian Music* (London, 1939)

S. L. Ginzburg: *Russkiy muzïkal'nïy teatr 1700–1833* (Leningrad and Moscow, 1941)

A. S. Rabinovich: *Russkaya opera do Glinki* (Leningrad, 1948)

I. F. Belza; *Cheshkaya opernaya klassika* (Moscow, 1951)

M. Cooper: *Russian Opera* (London, 1951)

J. Maróthy: *Erkel Ferenc opera-dramaturgiája* (Budapest, 1954)

K. Michalowski: *Opery Polski* (Krakow, 1954)

A. A. Gozenpud: *Muzïkal'nïy teatr v Rossii ot istokov do Glinki: ocherk* (Leningrad, 1959)

D. Lloyd-Jones: 'The Bogatyrs: Russia's First Operetta', *MMR*, lxxxix (1959), 123

G. Abraham: 'Tchaikovsky's First Opera', *Festschrift Karl Gustav Fellerer* (Regensburg, 1962), 12

G. B. Bernandt: *Slovar' oper, upervïye portavlennïkh ili izdannïlch v dorevolyutsionnoy Rossii i v SSSR (1736–1962)* ([A dictionary of operas first performed and published in pre-Revolutionary Russia and the USSR] (Moscow, 1962)

V. A. Pankratova and L. V. Polyakova: *Opernïye libretto: russkaya opera i opera narodov SSSR* (Moscow, 1962, enlarged 2/1970)

F. Bónis: 'Erkel über seine Oper *Bánk ban*', *SM*, xi (1969), 69

A. A. Gozenpud: *Russkiy opernïy teatr XIX veka 1836–56* (Leningrad, 1969)

T. Kaczyński: *Dzieje sceniczne 'Halki' Stanisława Moniuszki* [Performance history of Moniuszko's *Halka*] (Kraków, 1969)

R. Taruskin: 'Realism as Preached and Practiced: the Russian Opera Dialogue', *MQ*, lvi (1970), 431

A. A. Gozenpud: *Russkiy opernïy teatr XIX veka 1857–72* (Leningrad, 1971)

V. Hudeč: *Zdeněk Fibich* (Prague, 1971)

J. Clapham: *Smetana* (London, 1972)

J. Warrack: *Tchaikovsky* (London, 1973)

D. Brown: *Glinka: a Biographical and Critical Study* (London, 1974/R1985)

J. Baker: 'Dargomïzhsky, Realism and *The Stone Guest*', *MR*, xxxvii (1976), 193

G. Véber: *Ungarische Elemente in der Opernmusik Ferenc Erkels* (Bilthoven, 1976)

R. Taruskin: 'Glinka's Ambiguous Legacy and the Birth Pangs of Russian Opera', *19th-Century Music*, i (1977–8), 142

D. Brown: *Tchaikovsky: a Biographical and Critical Study* (London, 1978–)

B. Large: 'Smetana's Brandenburgers', *MT*, cxiv (1978), 329
J. Clapham: *Dvořák* (Newton Abbot and London, 1979)
I. Berlin: 'Tchaikovsky, Pushkin and Onegin', *MT*, cxxi (1980), 163
R. Tedeschi: *I figli di Boris: l'opera russa da Glinka a Stravinskij* (Milan, 1980)
'Modest Musorgskij: Aspekte des Opernwerks', *Musik-Konzepte*, no.21 (1980) [whole issue]
Musorgski: l'opera, il pensiero: Milan 1981, ed. A. M. Morazzoni (Milan, 1985)
R. Taruskin: *Opera and Drama in Russian as Preached and Practiced in the 1860s* (Ann Arbor, 1981)
M. Bobeth: *Borodin und seine Oper 'Fürst Igor': Geschichte–Analyse–Konsequenzen* (Munich and Salzburg, 1982)
G. Norris: 'An Opera Restored: Rimsky-Korsakov, Shostakovich and the Khovansky Business', *MT*, cxxiii (1982), 672
J. Smaczny: 'The Operas and Melodramas of Zdeněk Fibich', *PRMA*, cix (1982–3), 119
G. Abraham: 'The Operas of Alexei Verstovsky', *19th-Century Music*, vii (1983–4), 326
R. Taruskin: '"The Present in the Past": Russian Opera and Russian Historiography, ca. 1870', *Russian and Soviet Music: Essays for Boris Schwarz* (Ann Arbor, 1984), 77
P. Taylor: *Gogolian Interludes: Gogol's Story 'Christmas Eve' as the Subject of the Operas by Tchaikovsky and Rimsky-Korsakov* (London and Wellingborough, 1984)
R. Taruskin: 'Musorgsky vs. Musorgsky: the Versions of *Boris Godunov* (ii)', *19th-Century Music*, viii (1984–5), 245
G. Abraham: *Essays on Russian and East European Music* (Oxford, 1985)
M. H. Brown and J. Wiley, eds.: *Slavonic and Romantic Music: Essays for Gerald Abraham* (Ann Arbor and Oxford, 1985)
A. Csampai and D. Holland, eds.: *Peter Tschaikowsky, 'Eugen Onegin': Texte, Materialien, Kommentare* (Reinbek bei Hamburg, 1985)
A. B. Yakovlevich, B. G. Ivanovna and B. M. Shlemovich, eds.: *Teatre v zhizni i tvorchestve P. I. Chaikovskogo* (Izhevsk, 1985)
G. Abraham: 'The Operas of Zdeněk Fibich', *19th-Century Music*, ix (1985–6), 136
C. Emerson: *'Boris Godunov': Transpositions of a Russian Theme* (Bloomington and Indianapolis, 1986)
L. Krasinskaia: *Opernaya melodika P.I. Chaykovskogo: k voprosu o vzaimodeistviy melodiy i rechevoy intonatsiy: issledovaniye* (Leningrad, 1986)
M. H. S. Woodside: *Western Models for a Russian Opera: Glinka's 'Ruslan and Ludmilla'* (diss., U. of Chicago, 1987)
K. Bumpass and G. J. Kauffman: 'Nationalism and Realism in Nineteenth-Century Russian Music: "The Five" and Borodin's *Prince Igor*', *MR*, xlviii (1988), 43
N. John, ed.: *Pyotr Tchaikovsky: Eugene Onegin* (London, 1988)
J. Tyrrell: *Czech Opera* (Cambridge, 1988)

Britain

G. Hogarth: *Memoirs of the Opera* (London, 1851, rev. 2/1870)
B. Lumley: *Reminiscences of the Opera* (London, 1864)
W. A. Barrett: *Balfe: his Life and Work* (London, 1882)
H. C. Banister: *George Alexander Macfarren: his Life, Works and Influence* (London, 1891)
P. H. Fitzgerald: *The Savoy Operas and the Savoyards* (London, 1894, 2/1899)
J. F. Barnett: *Musical Reminiscences and Impressions* (London, 1906)
C. Forsyth: *Music and Nationalism: a Study of English Opera* (London, 1911)
R. Northcott: *The Life of Sir Henry R. Bishop* (London, 1920)
T. F. Dunhill: *Sullivan's Comic Operas: a Critical Appreciation* (London, 1928/R1981)
G. B. Shaw: *Music in London 1890–94* (London, 1932)
P. A. Scholes: *The Mirror of Music 1844–1944* (London, 1947), chap.6
W. C. Smith: *The Italian Opera and Contemporary Ballet in London, 1789–1920* (London, 1955)
F. Howes: *The English Musical Renaissance* (London, 1966)
N. Temperley: 'Raymond and Agnes', *MT*, cvii (1966), 307
——: 'The English Romantic Opera', *Victorian Studies*, ix (1966), 293
G. Hughes: *Sidelights on a Century of Music 1825–1924* (London, 1969)
P. M. Young: *Sir Arthur Sullivan* (London, 1971)
T. Fenner: *Leigh Hunt and Opera Criticism* (Lawrence, Kansas, 1972)
B. Carr: 'The First All-Sung English 19th-Century Opera', *MT*, cxv (1974), 125
J. W. Klein: 'Tragic, Forgotten Pioneer: Arthur Goring Thomas', *MR*, xxxvi (1975), 180
N. Temperley, ed.: *Athlone History of Music in Britain*, v: *The Romantic Age 1800–1914* (London, 1981)

E. W. White: *A History of English Opera* (London, 1983)

R. Bledsoe: 'Henry Fothergill Chorley and the Reception of Verdi's Early Operas in England', *Victorian Studies*, xxviii (1984–5), 631

S. Banfield: 'British Opera in Retrospect', *MT*, cxxvii (1986), 205

A.-M. H. Forbes: 'Celticism in British Opera: 1878–1938', *MR*, xlvii (1986–7), 176

A. Jacobs: *Arthur Sullivan: a Victorian Musician* (Oxford, 1987)

N. Temperley: 'Musical Nationalism in English Romantic Opera', *The Lost Chord*, ed. N. Temperley (Bloomington, Ind., 1989)

Spain and Portugal

A. Peña y Goñi: *La ópera española y la música dramática en España en el siglo XIX* (Madrid, 1881, 2/1967 as *España desde la ópera a la zarzuela*)

F. A. Barbieri: *La ópera española* (Madrid, 1880)

G. Chase: 'Barbieri and the Spanish Zarzuela', *ML*, xx (1939), 32

M. de Sampayo Ribeiro: *A música em Portugal nos séculos XVIII e XIX* (Lisbon, 1938)

J. Subirá: *Historia de la música teatral en España* (Barcelona, 1945)

———: *La ópera en los teatros de Barcelona* (Barcelona, 1946)

———: *Historia y anecdotario del Teatro Real* (Madrid, 1949)

J. de Freitas Branco: *Historia da música portuguesa* (Lisbon, 1959)

M. A. Palacios: '*El mozo de mulas*': una ópera inédita de Antonio José', *Monsalvat*, cxv (1984), 16

X. Aviñoa: *El barberillo de Lavapiés – Francisco A. Barbieri* (Barcelona, 1985).

———: *La Revoltosa – Ruperto Chapí* (Barcelona, 1985)

D. Fernando II e a ópera no século XIX: Exposição (Lisbon, 1985)

M. del Campo: 'Federico Chueca, y le Centenario de *La Gran Via*', *Tempo*, xxxix (1986), 19

M. A. Virgili: 'Música y teatro en Valladolid en el siglo XIX', *RdMc*, x (1987), 653

Scandinavia

A. Aumont and. E. Collin: *Det danske Nationaltheater 1748–1889* (Copenhagen, 1896–9)

T. H. Blanc: *Christiania theaters historie i tidsrummet 1827–77* (Kristiania, 1899)

L. Swendsen: *De kobenhavnske privattheaters repertoire (1847–1919)* (Copenhagen, 1907–19)

R. Engländer: *Johann Gottlieb Naumann als Opernkomponist (1741–1801), mit neuen Beiträgen zur Musikgeschichte Dresdens und Stockholms* (Leipzig, 1922/R1970)

T. Krogh: 'Det første forsøg paa at skabe en opera i det danske sprog' [The first attempt to create an opera in the Danish language], *Aarbog for Musik 1922*, 123–58

———: 'Aeldre dansk Teatermusik', *Musikhistorisk archiv*, i (1931), 1–100

A. Beijer: *Slottsteatrarna på Drottningholm och Gripsholm* [Palace theatres of Drottningholm and Gripsholm] (Stockholm, 1937)

I. E. Kindem: *Den norske operas historie* (Oslo, 1941)

Ø. Anker: *Christiania Theaters repertoire 1827–99* (Oslo, 1956)

———: *Kristiania Norske Theaters repertoire 1852–63* (Oslo, 1956)

G. Hilleström: *Drottningholmsteatern förr och nu* [The Drottningholm Theatre past and present] (Stockholm, 1956), [in Swed. and Eng.]

R. Engländer: 'Die Gustavianische Oper', *AMw*, xvi (1959), 314

B. Wallner: *Vår tids musik i Norden* (Stockholm, 1968)

K. Ralf, ed.: *Operan 200 år: Jubelboken* (Stockholm, 1973)

A. Aulin and H. Connor: *Svensk musik, i: Från Vallåi till Arnljot* (Stockholm, 1974)

A. Holmquist: *Från signalgivning till regionmusik* (Stockholm, 1974)

K Ralf, ed.: *Kungliga Teatern i Stockholm, repertoar 1773–1973* (Stockholm, 1974)

G. Leicht and M. Haller: *Det Kongelige Teaters Repertoire 1889–1975* (Copenhagen, 1977)

A. Johnson: 'Berwald and the Queen of Golconda', *MT*, cxxiii (1982), 17

F. H. Törnblom: *Operans Historia* (Stockholm, 1984)

G. Busk: *F. Kuhlau: en Biografi og en Kritisk Analyse of hans Musikdramatiske Produktion* (Århus, 1986)

L. Johansson: *Resa med Jenny Lind: Sällskapsdamen Louise Johanssons Dagböcker* (Stockholm, 1986)

North America

W. Dunlap: *A History of the American Theatre* (New York, 1832/R1963)

J. N. Ireland: *Records of the New York Stage* (New York, 1866–7/R1968)

W. G. Armstrong: *A Record of the Opera in Philadelphia* (Philadelphia, 1884/*R*1976)
J. H. Mapleson: *The Mapleson Memoirs* (New York, 1888, rev. 2/1966, ed. H. Rosenthal)
G. O. Seilhamer: *History of the American Theatre: New Foundations* (Philadelphia, 1891/*R*1968)
H. C. Lahee: *Grand Opera in America* (Boston, 1902/*R*1973)
O. G. T. Sonneck: 'Early American Operas', *SIMG*, vi (1904–5), 428–95
H. E. Krehbiel: *Chapters of Opera* (New York, 1908, rev. 2/1909/*R*1980, rev. 3/1911)
J. C. Baroncelli: *L'Opéra français de la Nouvelle Orléans* (New Orleans, 1914)
O. G. T. Sonneck: *Early Opera in America* (New York, 1915/*R*1963)
H. E. Krehbiel: *More Chapters of Opera* (New York, 1919/*R*1980)
H. C. Lahee: *Annals of Music in America* (Boston, 1922/*R*1969)
A. H. Quinn: *A History of the American Drama from the Beginning of the Civil War* (New York, 1923, 2/1943/*R*1951)
E. E. Hipsher: *American Opera and its Composers* (Philadelphia, 1927/*R*1978)
J. Mattfeld: *A Hundred Years of Grand Opera in New York, 1825–1925* (New York, 1927/*R*1976)
G. C. D. Odell: *Annals of the New York Stage* (New York, 1927–49/*R*1970)
R. D. James: *Old Drury of Philadelphia: a History of the Philadelphia Stage, 1800–1835* (Philadelphia, 1932/*R*1968)
I. Kolodin: *The Metropolitan Opera* (New York, 1936, rev. and enlarged 4/1966/*R*1967)
G. Gatti-Casazza: *Memories of the Opera* (New York, 1941/*R*1973)
J. Mates: *The American Musical Stage before 1800* (New Brunswick, NJ, 1962)
H. E. Johnson: *Operas on American Subjects* (New York, 1964)
R. L. Davis: *A History of Opera in the American West* (Englewood Cliffs, NJ, 1965)
————: *Opera in Chicago: a Social and Cultural History, 1850–1965* (New York, 1966)
H. A. Kmen: *Music in New Orleans: the Formative Years, 1791–1841* (Baton Rouge, 1966)
L. M. Lerner: *The Rise of the Impresario: Bernard Ullman and the Transformation of Musical Culture in Nineteenth Century America* (diss., U. of Wisconsin, 1970)
A. Stoutamire: *Music of the Old South: Colony to Confederacy* (Rutherford, NJ, 1972)
E. I. Zimmerman: *American Opera Librettos, 1767–1825* (diss., U. of Tennessee, 1972)
M. Nelson: *The First Italian Opera Season in New York City: 1825–1826* (diss., U. of North Carolina, Chapel Hill, 1976)
K. E. Gombert: *Leonora by William Henry Fry and Rip Van Winkle by George Frederick Bristow: Examples of Mid-nineteenth-century American Opera* (diss., Ball State U., 1977)
H. F. Jennings: *Grand Opera in Kansas in the 1880s* (diss., U. of Cincinnati, 1978)
O. E. Albrecht: 'Opera in Philadelphia, 1800–1830', *JAMS*, xxxii (1979), 499
P. H. Virga: *The American Opera to 1790* (Ann Arbor, 1982)
J. Mates: 'The First Hundred Years of the American Lyric Theater', *American Music*, i/2 (1983), 22
L. R. Wolz: *Opera in Cincinnati: the Years before the Zoo, 1801–1920* (diss., U. of Cincinnati, 1983)
P. E. Eisler: *The Metropolitan Opera: the First Twenty-Five Years* (Croton-on-Hudson, NY, 1984)
C. Macdonald: *Emma Albani: Victorian Diva* (Toronto, 1984)
D. McKay: 'Opera in Colonial Boston', *American Music*, iii (1985), 133
T. G. Kaufman: 'The Arditi Tour: the Midwest gets its First Real Taste of Italian Opera (1853–54)', *OQ*, iv/4 (1986), 39
M. F. Rich, V. F. Yellin and others: 'Opera', *The New Grove Dictionary of American Music* (London and New York, 1986)
I. Sablosky, ed.: *What they Heard: Music in America, 1852–1881: From the Pages of 'Dwight's Journal of Music'* (Baton Rouge, 1986)
D. Watmough: *The Unlikely Pioneer: Building Opera from the Pacific through the Prairies* (Oakville, 1986)
V. B. Lawrence: *Strong on Music: the New York Music Scene in the Days of George Templeton Strong, 1836–1875*, i: *Resonances, 1836–1850* (New York, 1988)
K. K. Preston: *Traveling Opera Troupes in the United States, 1830–1860* (diss., City U. of New York, 1988)
B. A. McConachie: 'New York Operagoing, 1825–50: Creating an Elite Social Ritual', *American Music*, vi (1988), 181

Latin America

E. de Olavarría y Ferrari: *Reseña histórica del teatro en México* (Mexico City, 1880–84, rev. 3/1961)
A. Fiorda Kelly: *Cronología de las óperas . . . cantadas en Buenos Aires* (Buenos Aires, 1934)
Revista brasileira de música, iii/2 (1936) [Gomes issue]

L. H. Corrêa de Azevedo: *Relação das óperas de autores brasileiros* (Rio de Janeiro, 1938)
O. Mayer-Serra: *Panorama de la música mexicana* (Mexico City, 1941)
R. Stevenson: *Music in Mexico* (New York, 1952)
L. H. Corrêa de Azevedo: *150 anos de música no Brasil (1800–1950)* (Rio de Janiero, 1956)
J. A. Calcaño: *La ciudad y su música* (Caracas, 1958)
R. Stevenson: 'Opera Beginnings in the New World', *MQ*, xlv (1959), 8
———: *The Music of Peru, Aboriginal and Viceroyal Epochs* (Washington, DC, 1959)
R. Rojas: 'Los gauchescos', *Historia de la literature argentina* (Buenos Aires, 1960)
C. Salas and E. F. Calcaño: *Sesquicentenario de la ópera en Caracas (1808–1958)* (Caracas, 1960)
V. Gesualdo: *Historia de la música en la Argentina* (Buenos Aires, 1961, rev. 2/1978)
J. A. González: 'La composición operática en Cuba', *Música*, no.20 (1972), 1
R. Stevenson: *Foundations of New World Opera* (Lima, 1973)
———: 'The South American Lyric Stage (to 1800)', *Inter-American Music Bulletin*, no.87 (1973), 1
M. Cánepa Guzmán: *La ópera en Chile (1839–1930)* (Santiago, 1976)
M. Conati: 'Formazione e affermazione di Gomes nel panorama dell'opera italiana: apunti e considerazioni', *Antonio Carlos Gomes: carteggi italiani*, ed. G. N. Vetro (Milan, 1976), 33
M. Kuss: *Nativistic Strains in Argentine Operas Premiered at the Teatro Colón (1908–1972)* (diss., U. of California, Los Angeles, 1976)
G. Béhague: *Music in Latin America: an Introduction* (Englewood Cliffs, NJ, 1979)
J. I. Pérdomo Escobar: *La ópera en Colombia* (Bogotá, 1979)
G. Doderer, ed.: *Modinhas Luso – Brasileiras* (Lisbon, 1984)
G. Batista: 'Felipe Gutiérrez y Espinosa y el ambiente musical en el San Juan de su época', *Revista: Centro de Investigaciones Folklóricas* (Ponce, Puerto Rico, 1986)
J. Peñín: *José María Osario: autor de la primera opera venezolana* (Caracas, 1985)
R. A. Zondergeld: 'Der Nachfolger Verdis? Vor 150 Jahren wurde Antonio Carlos Gomes geboren', *NZM*, x (1986), 49
V. Salles and others, eds.: *Carlos Gomes: uma obra – em foco* (Rio de Janeiro, 1987)

Staging

C. Brühl: *Neueste Kostume auf beiden königlichen Theatern in Berlin* (Berlin, 1822)
H. Porges: *Bühnenproben zu den Bayreuther Festspielen des Jahres 1876* (Leipzig, 1877, repr. 1896; Eng. trans., 1983, as *Wagner Rehearsing the Ring*)
G. E. Shea: *Acting in Opera* (New York, 1915/R1980)
J. Doin: 'Charles Séchan et son atelier de décoration théâtrale pendant le romantisme', *Gazette des beaux arts*, 5th ser., xi (1925), 344
A. Winds: *Geschichte der Regie* (Stuttgart, 1925)
C. Fischer: *Les costumes de l'Opéra* (Paris, 1931)
M. A. Allévy: *La mise en scène en France dans la première moitié du dix-neuvième siècle* (Paris, 1938)
T. Cole and H. Krich Chinoy, eds.: *Directing the Play: a Sourcebook of Stagecraft* (Indianapolis, 1953, rev. 1963/R1973, as *Directors on Directing: a Sourcebook of the Modern Theater, with an Illustrated History of Directing*)
A. Appia: 'Notes de mise en scène pour l'Anneau de Nibelungen (1891–1892)', *Revue d'histoire du théâtre*, vi/1–2 (1954), 46
G. Kernodle: 'Wagner, Appia and the Idea of Musical Design', *Education Theatre Journal*, vi (1954), 223
B. Król: 'Antoni Sacchetti – dékorator romantyczny: dziafainosc w latach 1829–1845', *Pamietnik teatralny*, viii (1959), 219–60
G. Schöne and H. Vriesen: *Das Bühnenbild im 19. Jahrhundert* (Munich, 1959)
G. Damerini: *Scenografi veneziani dell'ottocento: Francesco Bagnara, Giuseppe e Pietro Bertoja* (Venice, 1962)
M. Dietrich: 'Rottonara, un scénographe autrichien d'influence mondiale', *Anatomy of an Illusion: 4th International Congress on Theatre Research: Amsterdam 1965*, 19
E. Povoledo: 'Les premières représentations des opéras de Rossini et la tradition scénographique italienne de l'époque', *Anatomy of an Illusion: 4th International Congress on Theatre Research: Amsterdam 1965*, 31
S. Rosenfeld: 'The Grieve Family', *Anatomy of an Illusion: 4th International Congress. on Theatre Research: Amsterdam 1965*, 39
G. Schöne: 'Trois mises en scène de la "Flûte enchantée" de Mozart: Berlin 1816, Weimar 1817 et Munich 1818', *Anatomy of an Illusion: 4th International Congress on Theatre Research: Amsterdam 1965*, 54

D. Steinbeck: 'Die Bildinventare des Münchner Hoftheaters: zur Ausstattungspraxis der Oper im späten 19. Jahrhundert', *Maske und Kothurn*, xiii (1967), 141

F. Mancini: 'La scenografia romantica', *Critica d'arte*, xv (1968), no.96, p.45; no.98, p.65; xvi (1969), no.104, p.55

D. and M. Petzet: *Die Richard Wagner-Bühne König Ludwigs II.* (Munich, 1970)

G. Zeh: *Das Bayreuther Bühnenkostüm* (Munich, 1973)

H. C. Wolff: 'Das Bühnenbild um die Mitte des 19. Jahrhunderts', *Bühnenformen–Bühnenräume–Bühnendekorationen . . .: Herbert A. Frenzel zum 65. Geburtstag* (Berlin, 1974), 148

H. R. Cohen: 'La conservation de la tradition scénique sur la scène lyrique en France au XIXe siècle: les livrets de mise en scène et la Bibliothèque de l'Association de la Régie Théâtrale', *RdM*, lxiv (1978), 253

D. Coe: 'The Original Production Book for Otello: an Introduction', *19th-Century Music*, ii (1978–9), 148

H. Barth, ed.: *Bayreuther Dramaturgie: 'Der Ring des Nibelungen'* (Stuttgart, 1980)

C. Baumann: *Bühnentechnik im Festspielhaus Bayreuth* (Munich, 1980)

H. J. Gund: *Die Wagner-Bühnenbilder der Pariser Oper von 1891 bis 1914* (diss., U. of Freiberg, 1980)

R. Hartford, ed.: *Bayreuth: the Early Years* (London and New York, 1980)

L. Zeppegno: *Il manuale di Verdi* (Rome, 1980)

A. Tubeuf: *Bayreuth et Wagner: cent ans d'images, 1876–1976* (Paris, 1981)

D. Borchmeyer: *Das Theater Richard Wagners: Idee, Dichtung, Wirkung* (Stuttgart, 1982)

E. Braun: *The Director and the Stage* (London, 1982)

M. Mila: *I costumi della Traviata* (Pordenone, 1984)

H. R. Cohen: 'A Survey of French Sources for the Staging of Verdi's Operas: "Livrets de mise en scène", Annotated Scores and Annotated Libretti in Two Parisian Collections', *Studi Verdiani*, iii, (1985), 11

M. Ottlova and M. Popisil: 'Oper und Spektakel im 19. Jahrhundert', *Mf*, xxxviii (1985), 1

P. Trarieux: *L'Opéra-Comique de Paris et son décor* (diss., U. of Paris-Sorbonne, 1985)

H. R. Cohen and M. O. Gigou: *Cent ans de mise en scène lyrique en France (env. 1830–1930)* (Paris, 1986)

C. Dahlhaus: 'Operndramaturgie im 19. Jahrhundert', *AcM*, lix (1987), 32

20TH CENTURY

Italy

L. Torchi: 'Oceàna', *RMI*, x (1903), 309–66

G. Bastianelli: *Pietro Mascagni* (Naples, 1910)

F. Torrefranca: *Giacomo Puccini e l'opera internazionale* (Turin, 1912)

G. M. Gatti: *Dèbora e Jaéle di I. Pizzetti* (Milan, 1922)

———: 'Franco Alfano', *MQ*, ix (1923), 556

G. Pannain: *La leggenda di Sakuntala di Franco Alfano* (Milan, 1923)

G. M. Gatti: 'Gabriele d'Annunzio and the Italian Opera Composers', *MQ*, x (1924), 263

V. Levi: 'Un grande operista italiano: Antonio Smareglia', *RMI*, xxxvi (1929), 600

G. Adami: *Giulio Ricordi e i suoi musicisti* (Milan, 1933)

E. J. Dent: *Ferruccio Busoni* (London, 1933, 2/1974)

G. M. Gatti: *Ildebrando Pizzetti* (Turin, 1934, 2/1955; Eng. trans., enlarged, 1951)

D. de'Paoli: *La crisi musicale italiana (1900–1930)* (Milan, 1939), esp. pp. 177–285

L. Tomelleri and others: *Gabriele D'Annunzio e la musica* (Milan, 1939)

P. Mascagni: *Cinquantenario della 'Cavalleria rusticana': le lettere ai librettisti* (Milan, 1940)

RaM, xiii (1940) [Pizzetti issue]

F. Ballo: *Arlecchino di Ferruccio Busoni, Volo di Notte di Luigi Dallapiccola, Coro di Morti di Goffredo Petrassi* (Milan, 1942)

M. Mila: *La donna serpente di Alfredo Casella* (Milan, 1942)

W. Pfannkuch: *Das Opernschaffen Ermanno Wolf-Ferraris* (diss., U. of Kiel, 1952)

G. Scarpa, ed.: *L'opera di Gian Francesco Malipiero* (Treviso, 1952)

L. Dallapiccola: 'The Genesis of the Canti di prigionia and Il prigioniero', *MQ*, xxxix (1953), 355

E. Respighi: *Ottorino Respighi* (Milan, 1954)

A. Lualdi: *Tutti vivi* (Milan, 1955), 377–426 [on Wolf-Ferrari]

M. Carner: *Puccini: a Critical Biography* (London, 1958, rev. 2/1974)

T. d'Amico: *Francesco Cilea* (Milan, 1960)

P. Santi: 'Il teatro di Gian Francesco Malipiero', *Approdo musicale*, no.9 (1960), 19–112 [Malipiero issue]

A. M. Bonisconti: 'Il teatro musicale di Giorgio Federico Ghedini', *Musica d'oggi*, new ser., iv (1961), 194

L. Pestalozza: 'Luigi Nono e "Intolleranza 1960"', *Biennale di Venezia*, xi/43 (1961), 18

F. D'Amico: *I casi della musica* (Milan, 1962)

A. Porter: 'Coventry and London: Murder in the Cathedral', *MT*, ciii (1962), 544 [on Pizzetti's *Assassinio nella cattedrale*]

M. Morini, ed.: *Pietro Mascagni* (Milan, 1964)

J. C. G. Waterhouse: 'Puccini's Debt to Casella', *Music and Musicians*, xiii/6 (1965), 18, 44

Approdo musicale, no.21 (1966) [Pizzetti issue]

Approdo musicale, no.22 (1966) [Busoni issue]

W. Ashbrook: *The Operas of Puccini* (London, 1968, rev. 2/1985)

L. Dallapiccola: 'Nascita di un libretto d'opera', *NRMI*, ii (1968), 605 [on *Ulisse*]

M. Morini, ed.: *Umberto Giordano* (Milan, 1968)

J. C. G. Waterhouse: *The Emergence of Modern Italian Music (up to 1940)* (diss., U. of Oxford, 1968)

C. Annibaldi: 'Musica gestuale e nuovo teatro: ritorno alla teatralità', *Musica moderna*, iii/106 (1969), 145

J. C. G. Waterhouse: 'Malipiero's *Sette canzoni*', *MT*, cx (1969), 826

F. D'Amico: 'Petrassi operista', *Teatro alla Scala: la stagione lirica 1970–71* (Milan, 1971), 533

T. Lerario: 'Ruggero Leoncavallo e il soggetto dei "Pagliacci"', *Chigiana*, xxvi–xxxvii (1971), 115

G. Vigolo: *Mille e una sera all'opera e al concerto* (Florence, 1971)

F. Degrada, ed.: *Bussottioperaballet: Sylvano Bussotti e il suo teatro* (Milan, 1976)

M. Mila: *Maderna, musicista europeo* (Turin, 1976)

L. Pannella: *Valentino Bucchi* (Florence, 1976)

R. Brown: *Continuity and Recurrence in the Creative Development of Luigi Dallapiccola* (diss., U. of Wales, Cardiff, 1977)

M. Messinis, ed.: *Omaggio a Malipiero*, Studi di Musica Veneta, iv (Venice, 1977) [incl. L. Alberti: 'L'interpretazione registica e scenografica', p.55]

B. Cagnoli: *Riccardo Zandonai* (Trent, 1978)

C. Castini: *Giacomo Puccini* (Turin, 1978)

C. Sartori: *Puccini* (Milan, 1978)

M. Girardi: *Turandot: il futuro interrotto del melodramma italiana* (diss., U. of Venice, 1980); extracts in *RIM*, xvii (1982), 155

B. Pizzetti, ed.: *Ildebrando Pizzetti, cronologia e bibliografia* (Parma, 1980)

C. Osborne: *The Complete Operas of Puccini* (London, 1981)

S. Sablich: *Busoni* (Turin, 1982)

M. Zurletti: *Catalani* (Turin, 1982)

R. Chiesa, ed.: *Riccardo Zandonai* (Milan, 1984)

D. Kämper: *Gefangenschaft und Freiheit: Leben und Werk des Komponisten Luigi Dallapiccola* (Cologne, 1984; It. trans., 1985)

F. Nicolodi: *Musica e musicisti nel ventennio fascista* (Fiesole, 1984)

OQ, ii/3 (1984) [Puccini issue]

L. Pestalozza, ed.: *G. F. Malipiero e le nuove forme della musica europea*, Quaderni di Musica/Realtà, iii (Milan, 1984)

L. Baldacci: 'I libretti di Mascagni', *NRMI*, xix (1985), 395

A. Beaumont: *Busoni the Composer* (London, 1985)

M. Carner, ed.: *Giacomo Puccini: Tosca* (Cambridge, 1985)

M. Kaye: *The Unknown Puccini* (London and New York, 1985)

E. Krause: *Puccini* (Leipzig, 1985)

D. A. Martino: *Metamorfosi del femminino nei libretti per Puccini* (Turin, 1985)

D. Osmond-Smith, ed. and trans.: *Luciano Berio: Two Interviews, with Rossana Dalmonte and Bálint András Varga* (London, 1985)

D. Rubboli: *Ridi pagliaccio* (Lucca, 1985) [on Leoncavallo]

M. Venuti: *Il teatro di Dallapiccola* (Milan, 1985)

A. Groos and R. Parker, eds.: *Giacomo Puccini: La bohème* (Cambridge, 1986)

L. Chailly: *Buzzati in musica: l'opera italiana nel dopo-guerra* (Turin, 1987)

J. L. DiGaetani: *Puccini the Thinker: the Composer's Intellectual and Dramatic Development* (New York, 1987)

M. Kaye: *The Unknown Puccini* (New York, 1987)

E. Leoni: *Un medico e un teatro: mezzo secolo all'Opera di Roma* (Milan, 1987)
M. Sansone: *Verismo: from Literature to Opera* (diss., U. of Edinburgh, 1987)
R. Shackelford, ed. and trans.: *Dallapiccola on Opera* (London, 1987)
R. Tedeschi: *D'Annunzio e la musica* (Scandicci, 1988)
M. Girardi: *Puccini: La vita e l'opera* (Rome, 1989)
J. C. G. Waterhouse: 'Between Opera and Music Theatre: Gian Francesco Malipiero's Rebellion against the Italian Operatic Establishment, 1917–29', *Journal of the Association of Teachers of Italian*, no.56 (1989)
——: *La musica di Gian Francesco Malipiero* (Turin and Rome, 1989)

Germany, Austria, Switzerland

E. Krenek: 'Opera Between the Wars', *MM*, xx (1943), 102
E. Wellesz: *Essays on Opera* (London, 1950)
W. Schuh, ed.: *Richard Strauss und Hugo von Hofmannsthal: Briefwechsel* (Zurich, 1952, enlarged 2/1955, 4/1970; Eng. trans., 1961)
——: *Richard Strauss, Stefan Zweig: Briefwechsel* (Frankfurt am Main, 1957; Eng. trans., 1977)
E. Stein, ed.: *Arnold Schoenberg: Briefe* (Mainz, 1958; Eng. trans., enlarged, 1964)
J. Rufer: *Das Werk Arnold Schoenbergs* (Kassel, 1959, rev. 2/1975: Eng. trans., rev., 1962)
D. Drew: 'Musical Theatre in the Weimar Republic', *PRMA*, lxxxviii (1961–2), 89
N. Del Mar: *Richard Strauss: a Critical Commentary on his Life and Works* (London, 1962–72, 2/1978)
K. H. Wörner: *Karlheinz Stockhausen: Werk und Wollen* (Rodernkirchen, 1963; Eng. trans., enlarged, 1973)
——: *Gotteswort und Magie* (Heidelberg, 1959; Eng. trans., rev., 1963 as *Schoenberg's 'Moses and Aron'*)
W. Mann: *Richard Strauss: a Critical Study of the Operas* (London, 1964)
W. Schuh: *Hugo von Hofmannsthal und Richard Strauss: Legende und Wirklichkeit* (Munich, 1964)
H. H. Stuckenschmidt: *Oper in dieser Zeit* (Hanover, 1964)
K.-R. Danler: 'Gespräch mit Bernd Alois Zimmermann', *Musica*, xxi (1967), 180
D. Hartmann: *Gottfried von Einem* (Vienna, 1967)
L. Knessl: *Ernst Krenek* (Vienna, 1967)
H. Rectanus: *Leitmotivik und Form in den musikdramatischen Werken Hans Pfitzners* (Würzburg, 1967)
T. W. Adorno: *Alban Berg* (Vienna, 1968, rev. 2/1978)
E. Padmore: 'German Expressionist Opera', *PRMA*, xcv (1968–9), 41
H. Bures-Schreker: *El caso Schreker* (Buenos Aires, 1969; Ger. trans., rev., 1970 as *Franz Schreker*)
I. Kemp: *Hindemith* (London, 1970)
R. Münster, ed.: *Carl Orff: das Bühnenwerk* (Munich, 1970)
W. Rogge: *Ernst Kreneks Opern: Spiegel der zwanziger Jahre* (Wolfenbüttel, 1970)
H. W. Schmidt, ed.: *Carl Orff: sein Leben und sein Werk in Wort, Bild und Noten* (Cologne, 1971)
H. H. Stuckenschmidt: *Die grossen Komponisten unseres Jahrhunderts* (Munich, 1917; Eng. trans., 1971)
——: 'Von Einem's "Der Besuch der alten Damen"', *Tempo*, no.98 (1971–2), 28
G. Neuwirth: *Die Harmonik in der Oper 'Der ferne Klang' von Franz Schreker* (Regensburg, 1972)
E. Padmore: 'Hindemith and Grünewald', *MR*, xxxiii (1972), 190
N. Tschulik: *Franz Schmidt* (Vienna, 1972; Eng. trans., 1979)
J. Crawford: '"Die glückliche Hand": Schoenberg's Gesamtkunstwerk', *MQ*, lx (1974), 583
F. C. Heller, ed.: *Arnold Schoenberg–Franz Schreker: Briefwechsel* (Tutzing, 1974)
H. H. Stuckenschmidt: *Schoenberg: Leben, Umwelt, Werk* (Zurich, 1974; Eng. trans., 1978)
B. G. Carroll: *The Operas of Erich Wolfgang Korngold* (diss., U. of Liverpool, 1975)
D. Drew, ed.: *Kurt Weill: ausgewählte Schriften* (Frankfurt, 1975)
——: *Über Kurt Weill* (Frankfurt, 1975)
E. Hilmar: *Wozzeck von Alban Berg* (Vienna, 1975)
I. Scharberth: *Musiktheater mit Rolf Liebermann* (Hamburg, 1975)
G. Skelton: *Paul Hindemith: the Man behind the Music* (London, 1975)
O. Brusatti, ed.: *Studien zu Franz Schmidt*, i (Vienna, 1976)
H. W. Henze: *Musik und Politik: Schriften und Gespräche 1955–1975* (Munich, 1976: Eng. trans., 1982)
O. Kolleritsch, ed.: *Alexander Zemlinsky: Tradition im Umkreis der Wiener Schule* (Graz, 1976)
R. Maconie: *The Works of Karlheinz Stockhausen* (London, 1976)
W. Schuh: *Richard Strauss: Jugend und Meisterjahre: Lebenschronik 1864–98* (Zurich, 1976; Eng. trans., 1982)

H. Weber: *Alexander Zemlinsky* (Vienna, 1977)

R. Blackburn: 'Franz Schreker', *MT*, cxix (1978), 224

O. Kolleritsch, ed.: *Franz Schreker am Beginn der neuen Musik* (Graz, 1978)

————: *50 Jahre Wozzeck von Alban Berg* (Graz, 1978)

R. Stephan: *Alexander Zemlinsky: ein unbekannter Meister der Wiener Schule* (Kiel and Vienna, 1978)

D. Jarman: *The Music of Alban Berg* (London, 1979)

K. H. Kowalke: *Kurt Weill in Europe* (Ann Arbor, 1979)

A. P. Lessem: *Music and Text in the Works of Arnold Schoenberg* (Ann Arbor, 1979)

K. Achberger: *Literatur als Libretto: das deutsche Opernbuch seit 1945* (Heidelberg, 1980)

B. Adamy: *Hans Pfitzner: Literatur, Philosophie und Zeitgeschehen in seinem Weltbild und Werk* (Tutzing, 1980)

B. G. Carroll: 'Korngold's "Violanta"', *MT*, cxxi (1980), 695

G. Perle: *The Operas of Alban Berg*, i: *Wozzeck* (Berkeley, 1980)

A. L. Ringer: 'Schoenberg, Weill and Epic Theater', *Journal of the Arnold Schoenberg Institute*, iv (1980), 77

R. Stephan and E. Budde, eds.: *Franz Schreker Symposium* (Berlin, 1980)

C. Pangels: *Eugen d'Albert: Wunderpianist und Komponist* (Zurich, 1981)

A. Clayton: *The Operas of Alexander Zemlinsky* (diss., U. of Cambridge, 1982)

E. Fischer: 'Bernd Alois Zimmermanns Oper *Die Soldaten*: zur Deutung der dramatische-musikalischen Struktur', *Festschrift Heinz Becker* (Laaber, 1982), 268

R. Hilmar: 'Die Bedeutung der Textvorlagen für die Komposition der Oper *Lulu* von Alban Berg', *Festschrift Othmar Wessely* (Tutzing, 1982), 265

O. Kolleritsch, ed.: *Ernst Krenek* (Vienna and Graz, 1982)

S. Mauser: *Das expressionistische Musik-Theater der Wiener Schule* (Regensburg, 1982) [on *Erwartung*, *Die glückliche Hand* and *Wozzeck*]

D. Puffett: *The Song Cycles of Othmar Schoeck* (Berne and Stuttgart, 1982)

F. Saathen: *Einem Chronik: Dokumentation und Deutung* (Vienna, 1982)

P. Franklin: 'Style, Structure and Taste: Three Aspects of the Problem of Franz Schreker', *PRMA*, cix (1982–3), 134

A. Clayton: 'Zemlinsky's One-act Operas', *MT*, cxxiv (1983), 474

P. Heyworth: *Otto Klemperer: his Life and Times*, i: *1885–1933* (Cambridge, 1983)

R. Ermen, ed.: *Franz Schreker (1878–1934) zum 50. Todestag* (Aachen, 1984)

G. Huwe, ed.: *Die Deutsche Oper Berlin* (Berlin, 1984)

D. Puffett: 'Schoecks Opern', *Musiktheater: Schweizer Theaterjahrbuch*, xlv (1984), 43

K. Schultz, ed.: *Aribert Reimanns 'Lear': Weg einer neuen Oper* (Munich, 1984)

N. Tschulik: *Musiktheater in Österreich: die Oper im 20. Jahrhundert* (Vienna, 1984)

J. Williamson: 'Eugen d'Albert: Wagner and *Verismo*', *MR*, xlv (1984), 26

'Alban Berg: Wozzeck', *Musik-Konzepte*, Sonderband (1985) [whole issue]

P. Britton: 'Stockhausen's Path to Opera', *MT*, cxxvi (1985), 515

A. Csampai and D. Holland, eds.: *Lulu: Texte, Materialen, Kommentare* (Reinbeck bei Hamburg, 1985)

A. Jefferson: *Richard Strauss: Der Rosenkavalier* (Cambridge, 1985)

G. Perle: *The Operas of Alban Berg*, ii: *Lulu* (Berkeley, 1985)

R. Sanders: *The Days Grow Short: the Life and Music of Kurt Weill* (New York, 1985)

R. Schlötterer: *Musik und Theater im 'Rosenkavalier' von Richard Strauss* (Vienna, 1985)

P. C. White: *Schoenberg and the God-Idea: the Opera 'Moses und Aron'* (Ann Arbor, 1985)

B. Gilliam: 'Strauss's Preliminary Opera Sketches: Thematic Fragments and Symphonic Continuity', *19th-Century Music*, ix (1985–6), 176

A. Beaumont: 'Busoni's *Doctor Faust*', *MT*, cxxvii (1986), 196

C. Bennett: 'Maschinist Hopkins: a Father for Lulu?', *MT*, cxxvii (1986), 481

K. H. Kowalke, ed.: *A New Orpheus: Essays on Kurt Weill* (New Haven, 1986)

A. Laubenthal: *Paul Hindemiths Einakter-Triptychon: 'Mörder, Hoffnung der Frauen', 'Das Nusch-Nuschi' und 'Sancta Susanna'* (Tutzing, 1986)

S. Stompor: 'Oper in Berlin von 1933 bis 1945', *BMw*, xxviii (1986), 23

J. Williamson: 'Pfitzner and Ibsen', *ML*, lxvii (1986), 127

D. Fanning: 'Berg's Sketches for *Wozzeck*: a Commentary and Inventory', *PRMA*, cxii (1986–7), 280

D. Drew: *Kurt Weill: a Handbook* (London, 1987)

H.-U. Fuss: 'Richard Strauss in der Interpretation Adornos', *AMw*, xlv (1988), 67

S. C. Cook: *Opera for a New Republic: the 'Zeitopern' of Krenek, Weill and Hindemith* (Ann Arbor, 1988)

G. Hiss: *Korrespondenzen: Zeichenzusammenhänge im Sprech-und-Musiktheater mit einer Analyse des*

'*Wozzeck*' *von Alban Berg* (Tübingen, 1988)
D. Puffett: 'Berg and German Opera', *The Berg Companion*, ed. D. Jarman (London, 1989)
———: *Richard Strauss: Salome* (Cambridge, 1989)
———: *Richard Strauss: Elektra* (Cambridge, 1989)
D. Jarman: *Alban Berg: Wozzeck* (Cambridge, 1989)

France

Rolland: *Musiciens d'aujourd'hui* (Paris, 1908)
M. Emmanuel: *Pelléas et Mélisande: étude historique et critique: analyse musicale* (Paris, 1926)
Roland-Manuel: *Maurice Ravel et son oeuvre dramatique* (Paris, 1928)
ReM, no.178 (1937) [Roussel issue]
A. Hoérée: *Albert Roussel* (Paris, 1938)
ReM, no.187 (1938) [Ravel issue]
P. Coppola: *Dix-sept ans de musique à Paris 1922–1939* (Lausanne, 1944)
P. Collaer: *Darius Milhaud* (Antwerp and Paris, 1947; Eng. trans. 1987)
G. Beck: *Darius Milhaud* (Paris, 1949)
D. Milhaud: *Notes sans musique* (Paris, 1949; Eng. trans., 1952) [autobiography]
L. Vallas: *Vincent d'Indy*, ii: *La maturité et la vieillesse* (Paris, 1950)
M. Augier-Laribé: *Messager: musicien de théâtre* (Paris, 1951)
M. Cooper: *French Music from the Death of Berlioz to the Death of Fauré* (London, 1951)
A. Goléa: *Pelléas et Mélisande* (Paris, 1952)
Francis Poulenc: entretiens avec Claude Rostand (Paris, 1954)
W. D. Halls: 'Les débuts du théâtre nouveau', *Annales de la Fondation Maeterlinck*, iii (1957)
L. Vallas: *Claude Debussy et son temps* (Paris, 1958)
E. Lockspeiser: *Debussy: his Life and Mind* (London, 1962)
J. Roy: *Francis Poulenc* (Paris, 1964)
'Sprengt die Opernhäuser in die Luft!', *Der Spiegel* (1967), no.40; Eng. trans., in *Opera*, xix (1968), 440 [interview with Boulez]
M. Landowski: *Honegger* (Paris, 1967)
R. Crichton: 'Roussel's Stage Works', *MT*, cx (1969), 729
Earl of Harewood: 'Whither Opera?', *Opera*, xx (1969), 992 [interview with Boulez]
V. Jankélévitch: *Ravel* (Paris, 1969)
F. Lesure, ed.: *Monsieur Croche et autres écrits* (Paris, 1971; Eng. trans., 1976, as *Debussy on Music*)
B. Gavoty: *Reynaldo Hahn: le musicien de la Belle Epoque* (Paris, 1976)
R. Nichols: *Ravel* (London, 1977)
R. Orledge: *Gabriel Fauré* (London, 1979)
J.-M. Nectoux, ed.: *Gabriel Fauré: correspondance* (Paris, 1980; Eng. trans., 1984, as *Gabriel Fauré: his Life through his Letters*)
F. Nicolodi: 'Parigi e l'opera verista: dibattiti, riflessioni, polemiche', *NRMI*, xv (1981), 577
C. Vital: *Studien zur Debussys Skizzen zu 'Rodrigue et Chimène' und 'Pelléas'* (diss., U. of Zurich, 1981)
R. Orledge: *Debussy and the Theatre* (Cambridge, 1982)
C. Dupêchez: *Histoire de l'Opéra de Paris: un siècle au Palais Garnier, 1875–1980* (Paris, 1984)
S. Kunze: 'Der Sprechgesang und das Unsagbare: Bemerkungen zu "Pelléas et Mélisande" von Debussy', *Analysen, Beiträge zu einer Problemgeschichte des Komponierens: Festschrift für Hans Heinrich Eggebrecht* (Stuttgart, 1984)
M.-D. Bobin: *Les livrets d'opéras français créés au Palais Garnier entre 1919 et 1939* (diss., U. of Paris-Sorbonne, 1985)
E. Goulon-Querel: *Le thème de l'eau dans 'Pelléas et Mélisande' de Debussy* (diss., U. of Paris-Sorbonne, 1986)
D. A. Grayson: *The Genesis of Debussy's 'Pelléas et Mélisande'* (Ann Arbor, 1986)
J. Pasler: 'Pelléas and Power: Forces behind the Reception of Debussy's Opera', *19th-Century Music*, x (1986–7), 243
D. Pistone, ed.: *Le théâtre lyrique français 1945–1985* (Paris, 1987)
G. K. Spratt: *The Music of Arthur Honegger* (Cork, 1988)
R. Nichols and R. Langham Smith: *Claude Debussy: Pelléas et Mélisande* (Cambridge, 1989)

Russia and Eastern Europe

I. F. Belza, ed.: *S. V. Rakhmaninov i russkaya opera* (Moscow, 1947)

M. Lederman, ed.: *Stravinsky in the Theatre* (London and New York, 1949/*R*1975)

G. Kroó: 'Duke Bluebeard's Castle', *SM*, i (1961), 251–340

V. A. Pankratova and L. V. Polyakova: *Opernïye libretto: russkaya opera i i opera narodov SSSR* [Opera librettos: Russian opera and the operas of the Soviet peoples] (Moscow, 1962, enlarged 2/1970)

A. Porter: 'Prokofiev's Early Operas', *MT*, ciii (1962), 528

L. Dan'ko: *Operï S. Prokofyeva* (Leningrad, 1963)

A. A. Gozenpud: *Russkiy sovetskiy opernïy teatr (1917–1941)* (Leningrad, 1963)

P. Eckstein: *Die tschechoslowakische zeitgenössische Oper/The Czechoslowak Contemporary Opera* (Prague and Bratislava, 1967)

R. Pečman, ed.: *The Stage Works of Bohuslav Martinů* (Prague, 1967)

A. Porter: 'Prokofiev's Late Operas', *MT*, cviii (1967), 312

R. McAllister: *The Operas of Sergei Prokofiev* (diss., U. of Cambridge, 1970)

E. Chisholm: *The Operas of Leoš Janáček* (Oxford, 1971)

B. Schwarz: *Music and Musical Life in Soviet Russia, 1917–70* (London, 1972, enlarged [*1917–81*], 2/1983)

T. Kneif: *Die Bühnenwerke von Leoš Janáček* (Vienna, 1974)

H. Seeger, ed.: *Musikbühne 74: Probleme und Informationen* (Berlin, 1974) [incl. essays on Soviet opera, pp.157, 174]

A. A. Gozenpud: *Russkiy opernïy teatr mezhdu dvukh revoliutsiy (1905–1917)* [Russian opera theatre between the two revolutions] (Leningrad, 1975)

B. Large: *Martinů* (London, 1975)

A. Volkov: '*Voyna i mir' Prokof'eva* [Prokofiev's *War and Peace*] (Moscow, 1976)

M. H. Brown: 'Prokofiev's *War and Peace*: a Chronicle', *MQ*, lxiii (1977), 297–326

S. Campbell: 'The "Mavras" of Pushkin, Kochno and Stravinsky', *ML*, lviii (1977), 304

L. Dan'ko: '*Mavra* Stravinskovo i *Nos* Shostakovicha', *Muzïkal'nïy sovremennik*, ii (Moscow, 1977), 73

M. Ewans: *Janáček's Tragic Operas* (London, 1977; Ger. trans., 1981)

A. Bogdanova: *Operï i baletï Shostakovicha* (Moscow, 1979)

H. Robinson: *The Operas of Sergei Prokofiev and their Russian Literary Sources* (diss., U. of California, Berkeley, 1980)

G. Kroó: 'Data on the Genesis of Duke Bluebeard's Castle', *SM*, xxiii (1981), 79

D. Möller: *Jean Cocteau und Igor Strawinsky: Untersuchungen zur Ästhetik und zu Oedipus Rex* (Hamburg, 1981)

P. Griffiths: *Igor Stravinsky: The Rake's Progress* (Cambridge, 1982)

G. Norris: 'The Operas', *Shostakovich: the Man and his Music*, ed. C. Norris (London, 1982), 105

A. Schouvaloff and V. Borovsky: *Stravinsky on Stage* (London, 1982)

J. Tyrrell, ed.: *Leoš Janáček: Kát'a Kabanová* (Cambridge, 1982)

A. Bretanitskaya: '*Nos' D. D. Shostakovicha* (Moscow, 1983)

B. S. Shteynpress: *Opernïe prem'erï XX veka, 1901–1940: slovar* [Dictionary of 20th-century opera premières] (Moscow, 1983)

L. E. Fay: 'The Punch in Shostakovich's *Nose*', *Russian and Soviet Music: Essays for Boris Schwarz* (Ann Arbor, 1984), 229

I. A. Pekker: *Uzbekskaya opera: ot vozniknoveniya do kontsa shestidesiatykh godov XX veka* (Moscow, 1984)

G. Abraham: *Essays on Russian and East European Music* (Oxford, 1985)

S. Neef: *Handbuch der russischen und sowjetischen Oper* (Berlin, 1985)

J. Bajer: 'Opera druhe poloviny 20. stoleti', *HR*, xxxviii (1985), 452

R. Biks: *Bulgarski operen teatur*, ii: *1944–1980* (Sofia, 1985)

A. Fodor: 'Musical Life: a New Hungarian Opera (*Csongor* and *Tuende*)', *New Hungarian Quarterly*, xxvi (1985), 183

J. Fukac: 'Musiktheaterbilanz 1945 bis 1985 in Prag', *ÖMZ*, xl (1985), 530

N. John, ed.: *Leos Janáček: Jenůfa/Katya Kabanova* (London, 1985)

E. Kröplin: *Frühe sowjetische Oper: Schostakowitsch, Prokofjew* (Berlin, 1985)

C. Susskind: *Janáček and Brod* (New Haven and London, 1985)

S. V. Tsirkunova, ed.: *Is istoriy musykal'nogo teatra XX veka* (Kishinev, 1985)

J. Tyrrell: *Czech Opera* (Cambridge, 1988)

Britain

E. Crozier, ed.: *Peter Grimes* (London, 1945)

———: *The Rape of Lucretia: a Symposium* (London, 1948)

I. Holst: *The Music of Gustav Holst* (London, 1951, rev. 3/1985)
Opera, ii/6 (1951) [Britten issue: chamber operas]
D. Arundell: 'Benjamin's Operas', *Tempo*, no.15 (1951–2), p.15
D. Mitchell and H. Keller, eds.: *Benjamin Britten: a Commentary on his Works* (London, 1952)
A. Porter: 'Britten's "Billy Budd"', *ML*, xxxiii (1952), 111
Tempo, no.21 (1952) [Britten issue on *Billy Budd*]
A. Porter: 'Britten's "Gloriana"', *ML*, xxxiv (1953), 277
E. Stein: '"The Turn of the Screw" and its Musical Idiom', *Tempo*, no.34 (1954–5), 6
H. Lindlar, ed.: *Benjamin Britten: das Opernwerk* (Bonn, 1955)
M. Tippett: *Moving into Aquarius* (London, 1958, 2/1974)
J. Warrack: 'Vaughan Williams and Opera', *Opera*, ix (1958), 698
M. Hurd: *Immortal Hour: the Life and Period of Rutland Boughton* (London, 1962)
M. Kennedy: *The Works of Ralph Vaughan Williams* (London, 1964, rev. 2/1980)
I. Kemp, ed.: *Michael Tippett: a Symposium on his Sixtieth Birthday* (London, 1965)
S. Walsh: 'A Memory of Violins', *Opera*, xvii (1966), 851 [Williamson]
G. Crosse: 'Birtwistle's *Punch and Judy*', *Tempo*, no.85 (1968), 24
M. Kingsbury: 'Humphrey Searle's "Hamlet"', *MT*, cx (1969), 369
P. Howard: *The Operas of Benjamin Britten* (London, 1969)
S. Walsh: 'Nicholas Maw's New Opera', *Tempo*, no.92 (1970), 2
J. Warrack: 'The Knot Garden', *MT*, cxi (1970), 1092
E. W. White: *Benjamin Britten: his Life and Operas* (London, 1970, rev. 2/1983)
H. Ottaway: 'Holst as an Opera Composer', *MT*, cxv (1974), 465
L. Foreman, ed.: *British Music Now* (London, 1975)
M. A. Sheppach: *The Operas of Michael Tippett in the Light of Twentieth-Century Opera Aesthetics* (diss., U. of Rochester, NY, 1975)
J. Agar: *An Approach to the Operas of Michael Tippett* (diss., U. of East Anglia, 1976)
P. Brett: 'Britten and Grimes', *MT*, cxviii (1977), 995
R. E. Jones: *The Operas of Michael Tippett* (diss., U. of Wales, Cardiff), 1977
G. N. Odam: *Michael Tippett's Knot Garden: an Exploration of its Musical, Literary and Psychological Construction* (diss., Southampton U., 1977)
G. Larner: 'Toussaint', *MT*, cxviii (1977), 721 [interview with David Blake]
R. Threlfall: 'Delius's Unknown Opera: The Magic Fountain', *SMA*, xi (1977), 60
J. Warrack: 'The Ice Break', *MT*, cxviii (1977), 553
P. Evans: *The Music of Benjamin Britten* (London, 1979)
P. Pirie: *The English Musical Renaissance* (London, 1979)
E. W. White: *Tippett and his Operas* (London, 1979)
M. Boyd: *Grace Williams* (Cardiff, 1980)
D. Matthews: *Michael Tippett: an Introductory Study* (London, 1980)
B. Northcott, ed.: *The Music of Alexander Goehr* (London, 1980)
F. Sternfeld and D. Harvey: 'A Musical Magpie: Words and Music in Michael Tippett's Operas', *Parnassus: Poetry in Review*, x/2 (1982), 188
P. Griffiths; *Peter Maxwell Davies* (London, 1982)
A. Whittall: *The Music of Britten and Tippett: Studies in Themes and Techniques* (Cambridge, 1982)
P. Brett, ed.: *Benjamin Britten: Peter Grimes* (Cambridge, 1983)
E. W. White: *A History of English Opera* (London, 1983)
M. Hall: *Harrison Birtwistle* (London, 1984)
I. Kemp: *Tippett: the Composer and his Music* (London, 1984, rev. 2/1987)
C. Palmer, ed.: *The Britten Companion* (London, 1984)
N. Tierney: *William Walton: his Life and Music* (London, 1984)
P. Howard, ed.: *Benjamin Britten: Turn of the Screw* (Cambridge, 1985)
N. John, ed.: *Operas of Michael Tippett* (London, 1985)
S. Banfield: 'British Opera in Retrospect', *MT*, cxxvii (1986), 205
P. Brett: 'Character and Caricature in *Albert Herring*', *MT*, cxxvii (1986), 545
J. Evans: '*Death in Venice*: the Apollonian/Dionysian Conflict', *OQ*, iv/3 (1986), 102
R. Fawkes: *Welsh National Opera* (London, 1986)
J. Evans, P. Reed and P. Wilson, comps.: *A Britten Source Book* (Aldeburgh, 1987)
D. Mitchell, ed.: *Benjamin Britten: Death in Venice* (Cambridge, 1987)
C. Oliver: *It is a Curious Story: the Tale of Scottish Opera, 1962–1987* (Edinburgh, 1987)
R. Travis: 'The Recurrent Figure in the Britten/Piper Opera *Death in Venice*', *Music Forum*, vi (1987), 129
P. Brett: '*Grimes* and *Lucretia*', *Music and Theatre: Essays in Honour of Winton Dean*

(Cambridge, 1987)
F. Donaldson: *The Royal Opera House in the Twentieth Century* (London, 1988)

Spain and Portugal

F. Sopeña: *Historia de la música española contemporánea* (Madrid, 1958, 2/1976)
M. Valls Gorina: *La música española después de Manuel de Falla* (Madrid, 1962)
L. Arrones Peón: *Historia de la ópera en Oviedo*, i: *1948–1957*; ii: *1958–1969* (Oviedo, 1981–5)
X. Avinõa: 'Enrique Morera, compositor lírico', *Monsalvat*, cxviii (1984), 20
A. Sagardia: 'Entorno al maestro Jose Serrano', *Monsalvat*, cxix (1985), 22
X. M. Carreira; 'El nacionalismo operístico en Galicia', *RdMc*, x (1987), 667
T. Marco: 'El teatro musical en España hoy', *RdMc*, x (1987), 653

Scandinavia

G. Lynge, ed.: *Danske Komponister i det 20. aarhundredes begyndelse* (Århus, 1917)
R. Neiiendam: *Det Kongeliges Teaters historie* (Copenhagen, 1921–70)
G. Lehrmann: 'Stepan', *Dansk musiktidsskrift*, i (1925–6) [Hamerik]
R. Hove: 'Finn Høffding: "Kilderejsen"', *Dansk musiktidsskrift*, xiii (1938), 6
F. Nygaard: *Den virkelige Marie Grubbe* (Copenhagen, 1940) [Hamerik]
H. Tomasi: *Armas Launis: notes biographiques* (London, 1940)
I. E. Kindem: *Den norske operas historie* (Oslo, 1941)
K. Atlung: *Det Kongelige Teater 1889–1939* (Copenhagen, 1942)
B. Hjelmborg: 'Jorgen Bentzons opera "Saturnalia"', *Dansk musiktidsskrift*, xx (1945), 6
V. Kappel: 'Ebbe Hameriks opera *Rejsekammeraten*', *Dansk musiktidsskrift*, xxi (1946)
A. Rundberg: *Svensk operakonst* (Stockholm, 1952)
B. Wallner: 'Hilding Rosenberg och teatern', *Operan* (26 Oct 1956)
J. Horton: *Scandinavian Music: a Short History* (London, 1963)
J. Balzar: *Carl Nielsen: the Dramatic Music* (London, 1966)
A. Thoor: 'Opera in Space and in the Round', *Musikrevy international* (1967), 45
R. Aiken: *Karl-Birger Blomdahl* (diss., U. of Cincinnati, 1968)
K. Ralf, ed.: *Operan 200 år. Jubelboken* (Stockholm, 1973) [incl. L. Sjöberg: 'Nittiotalisterna och musikdramat – Stenhammar och Peterson-Berger', p.120]
————: ed.: *Kungliga Teatern i Stockholm, repertoar 1773–1973* (Stockholm, 1974)
E. Nordsjø: *Fra drøm til virkelighet: norsk operasangerforbund 1926–1976* (Oslo, 1975)
E. Tawaststjerna: *Esseitä ja arvosteluja* [Essays and criticism] (Helsinki, 1976) [incl. essays on Kokkonen and Sallinen]
D. Fog: *Kompositionen von Fridr. Kuhlau* (Copenhagen, 1977)
G. Leicht and M. Haller: *Det Kongelige Teaters repertoire 1889–1975* (Copenhagen, 1977)
D. Fog: *Kompositionen von C. E. F. Weyse* (Copenhagen, 1979)
L. Reitan: 'A Norwegian Opera Composer on the International Scene (Antonio Bibalo)', *Nordic Sounds*, iv (1984), 3
J. Fornäs: *Tältprojektet: musikteater som manifestation* (Stockholm, 1985)
R. Henderson: 'Aulis Sallinen: Singing of Man', *MT*, cxxviii (1987), 189

Low Countries

A. de Gers: *Théâtre Royale de la Monnaie 1856–1926* (Brussels, 1926)
L. Renieu: *Histoire du théâtre à Bruxelles* (Paris, 1928)
S. A. M. Bottenheim: *De opera in Nederland* (Amsterdam, 1946)
E. Reeser: *Een eeuw Nederlandse muziek* (Amsterdam, 1950)
K. P. Bernet Kempers: *Inleiding tot de opera Halewijn van Willem Pijper* (Rotterdam, n.d.)
E. Reeser: *Music in Holland* (Amsterdam, 1959)
R. Wangermée: *La musique belge contemporaine* (Brussels, 1959)
Music in Belgium (Brussels, 1964) [CeBeDeM publication]
R. de Leeuw: 'Schat's *Labyrinth*: an Opera of Sorts', *Sonorum speculum* (1966), no.27, p.19
P. Schat: '*Labyrinth*: a Kind of Opera', *Opera 66*, ed. C. Osborne (London, 1966), 250
C. Mertens: *Hedendaagse muziek in België* (Brussels, 1967)
J.-Y. Bosseur: 'Votre Faust: fantaisie variable genre opera', *Cahiers du Centre d'études et de recherches marxistes* (1968), no.62

L. Berio: 'Notre Faust', *NRMI*, iii (1969), 275
D. and J.-Y. Bosseur: 'Collaboration Butor/Pousseur', *Musique en jeu* (1971), no.4, p.83
J. Wouters: 'Guillaume Landré', *Dutch Composers' Gallery* (Amsterdam, 1971), 88
——: *Hendrik Andriessen* (Amsterdam, 1971)
——: *Henk Badings* (Amsterdam, 1971)
——: 'Ton de Leeuw', *Dutch Composers' Gallery* (Amsterdam, 1971), 17–19
J.-Y. Bosseur: 'Les scènes de foire dans Votre Faust', *Obliques*, iv (1974), 135
C. Gantelme and F. Michielsen: *Théâtre Royal de la Monnaie* (Brussels, 1981)
M. Reybrouck: 'De Koninklijke Vlaamse Opera te Antwerpen (1907–1914) en de Vlaamse Muziek', *Mededelingen van de Koninklijke Academie voor Wetenschappen, Letteren, en Schone Kunsten van Belgie*, Klasse der Schone Kunsten, xlii/1 (1981), 35–96
J.-P. Muller: 'L'opéra au Théâtre de Mons sous la regne de Leopold Ier', *Mémoires et publications de la Société des Sciences, des Arts et des Lettres du Hainaut*, lxxxix (1978), 51–93, and xci (1980), 1–78
A. Rousseau: *Van De Stomme van Portici tot De Lentewijding* [From *La muette de Portici* to *The Rite of Spring*] (Brussels, 1979)

North America

H. Charlesworth: 'Grand Opera in Canada', *Canadian Courier*, xii (12 Oct 1912)
E. C. Moore: *Forty Years of Opera in Chicago* (New York, 1930)
M. S. Teasdale: *20th Century Opera at Home and Abroad: 1900 through Season 1937/8* (New York, 1938)
H. Graf: *The Opera and its Future in America* (New York, 1941)
W. H. Seltsam, ed.: *Metropolitan Opera Annals* (New York, 1947, suppls., 1957, 1968, 1978; rev. edn., 1989)
E. Helm: 'Virgil Thomson's Four Saints in Three Acts', *MR*, xv (1954), 127
Q. Eaton: *Opera Caravan: Adventures of the Metropolitan on Tour, 1883–1956* (New York, 1957/R1978)
V. F. Yellin: *The Life and Operatic Works of George Whitefield Chadwick* (diss., Harvard U., 1957)
J. Beraud: *350 ans de théâtre au Canada français* (Montreal, 1958)
R. Jackson: *The Operas of Gertrude Stein and Virgil Thomson* (diss., Tulane U., 1962)
H. E. Johnson: *Operas on American Subjects* (New York, 1964)
H. Kallmann: 'History of Opera in Canada', *Opera in Canada*, v (1964)
R. L. Davis: *A History of Opera in the American West* (Englewood Cliffs, NJ, 1965)
Q. Eaton: *The Boston Opera Company* (New York, 1965/R1980)
E. C. Laufer: 'Roger Sessions: *Montezuma*', *PNM*, iv/1 (1965), 95
R. L. Davis: *Opera in Chicago: a Social and Cultural History, 1850–1965* (New York, 1966)
C. Hamm: 'Opera and the American Composer', *The American Composer Speaks*, ed. G. Chase (Baton Rouge, 1966), 284
R. J. Dietz: 'Marc Blitzstein and the "Agit-prop Theatre" of the 1930s', *Yearbook for Inter-American Musical Research*, vi (1970), 51
——: *The Operatic Style of Marc Blitzstein* (diss., U. of Iowa, 1970)
R. L. Larsen: *A Study and Comparison of Samuel Barber's 'Vanessa', Robert Ward's 'The Crucible', and Gunther Schuller's 'The Visitation'* (diss., Indiana U., 1971)
L. Grieb: *The Operas of Gian Carlo Menotti, 1937–1972: a Selective Bibliography* (Metuchen, NJ, 1974)
J. Harbison: 'Roger Sessions and Montezuma', *New Boston Review*, ii/1 (1976), 5; repr. in *Tempo*, no.121 (1977), 2
C. Northouse: *Twentieth Century Opera in England and the United States* (Boston, 1976)
E. Scott: *The First Twenty Years of the Santa Fé Opera* (Santa Fé, 1976)
A. Bloomfield: *The San Francisco Opera, 1922–1978* (Sausalito, 1978)
Q. Eaton: *Opera Caravan: Adventures of the Metropolitan Opera on Tour, 1883–1956* (New York, 1978)
C. Cassidy: *Lyric Opera of Chicago* (Chicago, 1979)
R. Crawford: 'Gershwin's Reputation: a Note on Porgy and Bess', *MQ*, lxv (1979), 257
G. Potvin: 'A Short History of Opera in Canada', *MusiCanada*, liv (fall 1980), 4
M. L. Sokol: *The New York City Opera* (New York, 1981)
C. N. Mason: *A Comprehensive Analysis of Roger Sessions' Opera Montezuma* (diss., U. of Illinois, Urbana, 1982)
J. F. Cone: *First Rival of the Metropolitan Opera* (New York, 1983)
M. Mayer: *The Met: One Hundred Years of Grand Opera* (New York, 1983)
L. Starr: 'Toward a Reevaluation of Gershwin's Porgy and Bess', *American Music*, ii/2 (1984), 25
J. Ardoin: *The Stages of Menotti* (Garden City, NY, 1985)
J. P. Baillie, ed.: *Look at the Record: an Album of Toronto's Lyric Theatres 1825–1984* (Oakville, 1985)
J. Mates: *America's Musical Stage: Two Hundred Years of Musical Theatre* (Westport, Conn., 1985)

R. P. Morgan: 'John Eaton and *The Tempest*', *MT*, cxxvi (1985), 397
P. Glass: *Music by Philip Glass* (New York, 1987; also pubd. as *Opera on the Beach*, 1988)

Latin America

E. T. Tolón and J. A. González: *Óperas cubanas y sus autores* (Havana, 1943)
A. Carpentier: *La música en Cuba* (Mexico City, 1946)
L. H. Corrêa de Azevedo: *150 anos de música no Brasil (1800–1950)* (Rio de Janeiro, 1956)
C. Salas and E. F. Calcaño: *Sesquicentenario de la ópera en Caracas (1808–1958)* (Caracas, 1960)
V. Mariz: *Heitor Villa-Lobos, Brazilian Composer* (Gainsville, 1963)
J. Orrego-Salas: 'The Young Generation of Latin American Composers: Backgrounds and Perspectives', *Inter-American Music Bulletin*, no.38 (1963), 1
R. Stevenson: *Music in Aztec and Inca Territory* (Berkeley, 1968, 2/1976)
R. Caamaño, ed.: *La historia del Teatro Colón (1908–1968)* (Buenos Aires, 1969)
G. Béhague: *The Beginnings of Musical Nationalism in Brazil* (Detroit, 1971)
E. Martín: *Panorama histórico de la música cubana* (Havana, 1971)
M. Kuss: *'Huemac'* by Pascual de Rogatis: Native Identity in Argentine Lyric Theater', *Yearbook for Inter-American Musical Research*, x (1974), 68
——: *Nativistic Strains in Argentine Operas Premiered at the Teatro Colón (1908–1972)* (diss., U. of California, Los Angeles, 1976)
I. Aretz, ed.: *América latina en su música* (Paris, 1977)
M. A. Marcondes, ed.: *Enciclopédia da música brasileira: erudita, folclórica, popular* (São Paulo, 1977)
K. Nketia: 'African Roots of Music in the Americas', *IMSCR*, xii *Berkeley 1977*, 82
M. A. Henríquez, ed.: *Alejandro García Caturla: Correspondencia* (Havana, 1978)
G. Béhague: *Music in Latin America* (Englewood Cliffs, NJ, 1979)
Z. Gómez, ed.: *Alejo Carpentier: ese músico que llevo adentro* (Havana, 1980)
M. Kuss: 'Type, Derivation, and Use of Folk Idioms in Ginastera's *Don Rodrigo* (1964)', *Latin American Music Review*, i/2 (1980), 176
L. M. Peppercorn: 'Villa-Lobos's Stage Works', *RBM*, xxxvi–xxxviii (1982–4), 175
M. Kuss: 'Symbol und Phantasie in Ginasteras *Bomarzo* (1967)', *Alberto Ginastera*, ed. F. Spangemacher (Bonn, 1984), 88
J. Peñín: *José Mariá Osario: autor de la primera opera venezolana* (Caracas, 1985)
Palacio de Bellas Artes: 50 años de opera (Mexico City, 1986)
M. Kuss: 'Native Idioms in 20th-Century Operas from Argentina, Brazil and Mexico: Towards a Comparative Chronology of Stylistic Change', *MMA*, xii (1987), 54

Australia

F. C. Brewer: *The Drama and Music in New South Wales* (Sydney, 1893)
C. H. Bertie: *Isaac Nathan: Australia's First Composer* (Sydney, 1922)
——: *The Story of the Royal Hotel and the Theatre Royal* (Sydney, 1927)
D. Arundell: 'Benjamin's Operas', *Tempo*, no.15 (1951–2), 15
C. Mackerras: *The Hebrew Molodist* (Sydney, 1963) [on Issac Nathan]
A. Bagot: *Coppin the Great* (Melbourne, 1965) [early entrepreneur]
S. Walsh: 'A memory of Violins', *Opera*, xvii (1966), 851 [Williamson]
R. Covell: *Australia's Music* (Melbourne, 1967)
B. and F. MacKenzie: *Singers of Australia* (Melbourne, 1967)
H. Hort: 'The First of our Operas', *Masque*, no.12 (1969), 8 [Marsh's *The Gentleman in Black*]
A. McCredie: *Musical Composition in Australia* (Canberra, 1969)
T. Radic: 'Italian Opera in Nineteenth-Century Melbourne', *Quaderni*, no.4 (Melbourne, 1971)
J. Murdoch: *Australia's Contemporary Composers* (Melbourne and Sydney, 1972)
K. Lucas: 'George Dreyfus's Garni Sands: a Forward Step for Australian Opera', *SMA*, vii (1973), 78
Opera and the Australian Composer: Melbourne 1973
I. G. Dicker: *J. C. W.: a Short Biography of James Cassius Williamson* (Sydney, 1974)
J. Cargher: *Opera and Ballet in Australia* (Sydney, 1977)
T. Radic: *Some Historical Aspects of Musical Associations in Melbourne* (diss., U. of Melbourne, 1977)
A. Hubble: *More than an Opera House* (Sydney, 1978)
D. Tunley and F. Callaway, eds.: *Australian Composition in the Twentieth Century* (London, 1979)
E. Wood: *Australian Opera, 1842–1970: a History of Australian Opera with Descriptive Catalogues* (diss., U. of Adelaide, 1979)

459

History of Opera

J. M. Thomson: *A Distant Music: the Life and Times of Alfred Hill* (Auckland, 1980)
H. Love: *The Golden Age of Australian Opera* (Sydney, 1981)
T. Radic: *G.W.L. Marshall-Hall: Portrait of a Lost Crusader* (Nedlands, 1982)
————: *Melba: the Voice of Australia* (Melbourne, 1986)
J. Cargher: *Bravo! Two Hundred Years of Opera in Australia* (Sydney, 1989)

Staging

A. Appia: *La mise en scène du drame wagnérien* (Paris, 1895; Eng. trans., 1982)
————: *Die Musik und die Inszenierung* (Munich, 1899; Eng. trans., 1962; Fr. orig., 1963)
C. Hagemann: *Oper und Szene: Aufsätze zur Regie des musikalischen Dramas* (Berlin and Leipzig, 1905)
K. MacGowan and R. E. Jones: *Continental Stagecraft* (New York, 1922)
W. R. Fuerst and S. J. Hume: *Twentieth-Century Stage Decoration* (London, 1928, 3/1967)
L. Moussinac: *Tendances nouvelles du théâtre* (Paris, 1931; Eng. trans., 1931/R1967)
V. I. Nemirovich-Danchenko: *Iz proshlovo* (Moscow, 1936; Eng. trans., 1936 as *My Life in the Russian Theatre*)
C. Niessen: *Die deutsche Oper der Gegenwart* (Regensburg, 1944)
D. Magarschack, ed.: *Stanislavsky on the Art of the Stage* (London, 1950)
O. F. Schuh: *Salzburger Dramaturgie* (Vienna, 1951)
G. Frette: *Scenografia teatrale* (Milan, 1954; Eng. trans., 1955)
R. Cogniat: *Cinquante ans de spectacle en France; les décorateurs du théâtre* (Paris, 1955)
R. Hainaux, ed.: *Le décor de théâtre dans le monde depuis 1935* (Brussels, 1956; Eng. trans., 1956)
W. Felsenstein and S. Melchinger: *Musiktheater* (Bremen, 1961)
H. Graf: *Producing Opera for America* (New York, 1961)
M. Koerth: *Felsenstein auf der Probe* (Berlin, 1961)
V. Jindra, ed.: *Le théâtre en Tchécoslovaquie: la scénographie* (Prague, 1962)
W. E. Schafer: *Gunther Rennert, Regisseur in dieser Zeit* (Bremen, 1962)
F. Hadamowsky, ed.: *Max Reinhardt: Ausgewählte Briefe, Reden, Schriften und Szenen aus Regiebüchern* (Vienna, 1963)
O. F. Schuh and F. Willnaeur: *Bühne als geistiger Raum* (Bremen, 1963)
Z. Strzelecki: *Polska plastyka teatralna* (Warsaw, 1963)
R. Hainaux, ed.: *Le décor de théâtre dans le monde depuis 1950* (Paris, 1964; Eng. trans., 1964)
W. Panofsky: *Wieland Wagner* (Bremen, 1964)
D. Bablet: *Esthétique générale du décor de théâtre de 1870 à 1914* (Paris, 1965)
G. Friedrich: *Walter Felsenstein: Weg und Werk* (Berlin, 1967)
G. N. Smith: *Luchino Visconti* (London, 1967)
A. Goléa: *Gespräche mit Wieland Wagner* (Salzburg, 1968)
H. Rischbieter and W. Storch: *Bühne und bildende Kunst im XX. Jahrhundert* (Velber, 1968)
K. Rowell: *Stage Design* (London, 1968)
W. R. Volbach: *Adolphe Appia: Prophet of the Modern Theatre* (Middletown, Conn., 1968)
F. Hodge, ed.: *Innovations in Stage and Theatre Design: 6th International Congress on Theatre Research: New York 1969*
N. I. Sokolova, V. F. Rïndyn and B. I. Volkov, eds.: *50 let sovyetskogo iskusstva: Khudozniki teatra* (Moscow, 1969)
W. R. Volbach, ed.: *Adolphe Appia: Essays and Scenarios* (Amherst, Mass., 1970)
H. Schubert: *Moderner Theaterbau: internationale Situation, Dokumentation, Projekte, Bühnentechnik* (Stuttgart, 1971; Eng. trans., 1971)
G. Skelton: *Wieland Wagner: the Positive Sceptic* (London, 1971)
U. Artioli: *Teorie della scena dal naturalismo al surrealismo* (Florence, 1972)
P. Baldelli: *Luchino Visconti* (Milan, 1973)
R. Hainaux and Y. Bonnat: *Le décor de théâtre dans le monde depuis 1960* (Brussels, 1973: Eng. trans., 1973)
E. B. Burdick, P. C. Hansen and B. Zanger, eds.: *Contemporary Stage Design: U.S.A.* (Middletown, Conn., 1974)
H. Fetting, ed.: *Max Reinhardt: Briefe, Reden, Aufsätze, Interviews, Gespräche, Auszüge aus Regiebüchern* (Berlin, 1974)
G. Strehler: *Per un teatro umano* (Milan, 1974)
J. Fiebach: *Von Craig bis Brecht: Studien zu Künstlertheorien in der ersten Hälfte des 20. Jahrhunderts* (Berlin, 1975)
P. P. Fuchs, ed.: *The Music Theatre of Walter Felsenstein* (New York, 1975)

G. Giertz: *Kultus ohne Götter: Emile Jaques-Dalcroze und Adolphe Appia: Versuch einer Theaterreform auf der Grundlage der rhythmischen Gymnastik* (Munich, 1975)

E. R. Hapgood, ed.: *Stanislavsky on Opera* (New York, 1975)

W. Felsenstein: *Schriften zum Musiktheater* (Berlin, 1976)

D. Kranz: *Gespräche mit Felsenstein* (Berlin, 1976)

D. Mack: *Der Bayreuther Inszenierungstil 1876–1976* (Munich, 1976)

R. Hartmann: *Opera* (New York, 1977) [on production techniques]

A. Rood: *Gordon Craig on Movement and Dance* (New York, 1977)

P. Barz: *Götz Friedrich* (Bonn, 1978)

C. d'Amico de Carvalho, ed.: *Album Visconti* (Milan, 1978)

C. d'Amico and R. Renzi, eds.: *Luchino Visconti: Il mio teatro* (Bologna, 1979)

D. Herbert, ed.: *The Operas of Benjamin Britten: the Complete Librettos Illustrated with Designs of the First Productions* (London and New York, 1979)

A. M. Nagler: *Malaise in der Oper: Opernregie in unseren Jahrhundert* (Rheinfelden, 1980; Eng. trans., 1981, as *Misdirection: Opera Production in the Twentieth Century*)

H. Christian: *Die Wiener Staatsoper 1945–1980: eine Dokumentation* (Vienna, 1981)

R. Hartmann: *Richard Strauss: the Staging of his Operas and Ballets* (New York, 1981)

S. Hughes: *Glyndebourne: a History of the Festival Opera* (Newton Abbot, 1981)

L. van Witsen: *Costuming for Opera* (Bloomington, Ind., 1981)

O. Bauer: *Richard Wagner: Die Bühnenwerke von der Uraufführung bis heute* (Fribourg, 1982; Eng. trans., 1982)

J. Kaut: *Die Salzburger Festspiele, 1920–1981* (Salzburg, 1982)

J. L. Styan: *Max Reinhardt* (Cambridge, 1982)

M. Friedman: *Hockney Paints the Stage* (Minneapolis, 1983)

C. Innes: *Edward Gordon Craig* (Cambridge, 1983)

J. M. Walton, ed.: *Craig on Theatre* (London, 1983)

R. Strong: 'The Rule of Taste: Design at Glyndebourne, 1935–84', *MT*, cxxv (1984), 258

I. Bontinck: *Angebot, Repertoire und Publikum des Musiktheaters in Wien und Graz* (Vienna, 1985)

A. Aronson: *American Set Design* (New York, 1985)

M. Ewans: 'Two Centenary Productions of *The Ring* at Bayreuth: the Bayreuth Centenary *Ring* by Patrick Chéreau and Pierre Boulez', *Miscellanea musicologica: Adelaide Studies in Musicology*, xiv (1985), 167

J. Gaulme: *Architectures scénographiques et décors de théâtre* (Paris, 1985)

R. M. Jacobson: *Magnificence: Onstage at the Met – Twenty Great Opera Productions* (London, 1985)

L. Morini and A. Premoli: *Träume in Samt und Seide: Mystik und Realität in den Opernkostümen des Sylvano Bussotti* (Munich, 1985)

C. Skulski: *Chagall et l'Opéra de Paris* (diss., U. of Paris-Sorbonne, 1985)

E. Burzawa: '*Walkiria* Sergiusza Eisensteina (Proba rekonstrukcji)', *Ruch Muzyczny*, xxx (1986), 10

P. Byrde: *A Visual History of Costume: the Twentieth Century* (New York, 1986)

F. Peixoto: *Opera e encenacão* (Rio de Janeiro, 1986)

J. Willett: *Caspar Neher: Brecht's Designer* (London and New York, 1986)

J. M. Gillette: *Theatrical Design and Production: an Introduction to Scene Design and Construction, Lighting, Sound, Costume and Make-up* (Palo Alto, 1987)

M. Eggert and H. K. Jungheinrich, eds.: *Durchbrüche: Die Oper Frankfurts* (Weinheim, 1987)

D. Harris: 'Full Cycle: how the *Ring* has been Staged since Wagner's Day', *Opera News*, li (1987), 12

B. Millington: '*The Ring* according to Berghaus', *MT*, cxxviii (1987), 491

S. Neef: 'Ein Anfang und kein Ende: Bühnenwerke des 20. Jahrhunderts an der Deutschen Staatsoper Berlin', *Musik und Gesellschaft*, xxxvii (1987), 252

D. Kranz: *Der Regisseur Harry Kupfer: 'Ich muss Oper machen'* (Berlin, 1988)

LIGHTER FORMS

Operetta

J. Scholtze: *Vollständiger Operettenführer* (Berlin, c1906)

C. Preiss: *Beiträge zur Geschichte der Operette* (1908)

L. Melitz: *Führer durch die Operetten* (Berlin, 1911, rev. 2/1933 by R. Kastner)

E. Rieger: *Offenbach und seine Wiener Schule* (Vienna, 1920)

———: *Die gute alte Zeit der Wiener Operette* (Vienna, 1922)
A. Orel: 'Wiener Tanzmusik und Operette', *Handbuch der Musikgeschichte*, ed. G. Adler (Frankfurt am Main, 1924, rev. 2/1930/R1961)
J. Brindejont-Offenbach: 'Cinquante ans de l'opérette française', *Cinquante ans de musique française*, ed. L. Rohozinski (Paris, 1925), 199
O. Keller: *Die Operette in ihrer geschichtlichen Entwicklung* (Leipzig, 1926)
M. S. Mackinlay: *The Origin and Development of Light Opera* (London, 1927)
K. Westermeyer: *Die Operette im Wandel des Zeitgeistes* (Munich, 1931)
C. Altmann: *Der französische Einfluss auf die Textbücher der klassischen Wiener Operette* (diss., U. of Vienna, 1935)
Anon: 'Histoire de l'opérette française au XIXe siècle', *Le théâtre lyrique en France*, ii (Paris, c1938), 265–325
S. Czech: *Das Operettenbuch* (Dresden, 1938, 4/1960)
F. Hadamowsky and H. Otte: *Die Wiener Operette* (Vienna, 1947)
A. M. Rabenalt: *Operette als Aufgabe* (1948)
R. Holzer: *Die Wiener Vorstadtbühnen: Alexander Girardi und das Theater an der Wien* (Vienna, 1951)
A. Bauer: *150 Jahre Theater an der Wien* (Vienna, 1952)
———: *Opern und Operette in Wien* (Graz, 1955)
H. Kaubisch: *Operette* (Berlin, 1955)
P. E. M[arkus]: *Und der Himmel hängt voller Geigen* (Berlin, 1955)
O. Schneidereit: *Operettenbuch* (Berlin, 1955)
H. Steger and K. Howe: *Operettenführer* (Frankfurt am Main, 1958)
O. S. Gál and V. Somogyi: *Operettek könyve* (Budapest, 1959)
B. Grun: *Kultergeschichte der Operette* (Munich, 1961, 2/1967)
O. Schumann: *Ich weiss mehr über die Operette und das Musical* (Stuttgart, 1961)
J. Bruyr: *L'opérette* (Paris, 1962)
D. Ewen: *European Light Opera* (New York, 1962)
G. Hughes: *Composers of Operetta* (London, 1962)
M. Lubbock and D. Ewen: *The Complete Book of Light Opera* (London, 1962)
O. Schneidereit: *Operette von Abraham bis Ziehrer* (Berlin, 1966)
A. Witeschnik: *Dort wird champagnisiert: Anekdoten und Geschichten zur Geschichte der Operette* (Vienna, 1971)
F. Bruyas: *Histoire de l'opérette en France, 1855–1965* (Lyons, 1974)
O. Schneidereit: *Berlin wie es weint und lacht* (Berlin, 1976)
A. Hyman: *Sullivan and His Satellites: a Survey of English Operettas, 1860–1914* (London, 1978)
J. Harding: *Folies de Paris: the Rise and Fall of French Operetta* (London, 1979)
G. Bordman: *American Operetta: from 'H.M.S. Pinafore' to 'Sweeney Todd'* (New York, 1981)
C. Dufresne: *Histoire de l'opérette* (Paris, 1981)
R. Traubner: *Operetta: a Theatrical History* (New York, 1983)
L. Garinei and M. Giovannini: *Quarant' anni di teatro musicale all' italiana* (Milan, 1985)
E. Oppicelli: *L'operetta: da Hervé al musical* (Genoa, 1985)
A. Würz: *Reclams Operettenführer* (Stuttgart, 18/1985)
D. Zöchling: *Operette: Meisterwerke der leichten Muse* (Vienna, 1985)
K. Gänzl and A. Lamb: *The British Musical Theatre*, i: *1865–1914*; ii: *1915–1984* (London, 1986)
K. Gänzl: *Gänzl's Book of the Musical Theatre* (London, 1988)
A. Jacobs: 'Cradled among the Reeds: two Victorian Operettas', *MT*, cxxix (1988), 234

Musical Comedy, the Musical

D. Forbes-Winslow: *Daly's: the Biography of a Theatre* (London, 1944)
J. W. McSpadden: *Operas and Musical Comedies* (New York, 1946, rev. 2/1951)
E. Short: *Fifty Years of Vaudeville* (London, 1946)
B. Atkinson: *Broadway Scrapbook* (New York, 1947)
W. J. Macqueen-Pope: *Gaiety: Theatre of Enchantment* (London, 1949)
C. Smith: *Musical Comedy in America* (New York, 1950, rev. 2/1981 by Glenn Litton)
A. E. Wilson: *Edwardian Theatre* (London, 1951)
J. Burton: *The Blue Book of Broadway Musicals* (New York, 1952, 2/1969)
J. Mattfeld: *Variety Music Cavalcade* (New York, 1952, rev. 3/1971)
P. G. Wodehouse and G. Bolton: *Bring on the Girls!* (New York, 1953)
W. J. Macqueen-Pope: *Nights of Gladness* (London, 1956)
D. Ewen: *Complete Book of the American Musical Theater* (New York, 1958, rev. 3/1976)

B. A. L. Rust: *London Musical Shows on Records, 1894–1954* (London, 1958, rev. 2/1977)
D. Blum: *A Pictorial History of the American Theatre, 1860–1960* (Philadelphia, 1960)
S. Green: *The World of Musical Comedy* (New York, 1960, rev. 4/1980)
D. Ewen: *The Story of America's Musical Theater* (Philadelphia, 1961, rev. 2/1968)
R. Lewine and A. Simon: *Encyclopedia of Theater Music* (New York, 1961)
A. Churchill: *The Great White Way* (New York, 1962)
H. Taubman: *The Making of the American Theater* (New York, 1965, 2/1967)
L. Engel: *The American Musical Theater: a Consideration* (New York, 1967)
D. Ewen: *Composers for the American Musical Theater* (New York, 1968)
A. Laufe: *Broadway's Greatest Musicals* (New York, 1969, rev. 4/1977)
R. Mander and J. Mitchenson: *Musical Comedy: a Story in Pictures* (London, 1969)
B. Atkinson: *Broadway* (New York, 1970)
T. Vallance: *The American Musical* (New York, 1970)
S. Green: *Ring Bells! Sing Songs! Broadway Musicals of the 1930s* (New York, 1971)
L. Engel: *Words with Music* (New York, 1972)
A. Wilder: *American Popular Song: the Great Innovators, 1900–1950* (New York, 1972)
R. Lewine and A. Simon: *Songs of the American Theater* (New York, 1973)
M. Wilk: *They're Playing Our Song: from Jerome Kern to Stephen Sondheim* (New York, 1973)
S. Green: *Encyclopedia of the Musical* (New York, 1976)
E. Mordden: *Better Foot Forward: the History of American Musical Theater* (New York, 1976)
D. Ewen: *All the Years of American Popular Music* (Englewood Cliffs, NJ, 1977)
A. Jackson: *The Book of Musicals from 'Show Boat' to 'A Chorus Line'* (London, 1977, rev. 2/1979)
G. Bordman: *The American Musical Theatre: a Chronicle* (New York, 1978, 2/1986)
D. and J. Parker: *The Story and the Song: a Survey of English Musical Plays, 1916–78* (London, 1979)
M. Gottfried: *Broadway Musicals* (New York, 1979)
T. Riis: *Black Musical Theater in New York, 1890–1915* (diss., U. of Michigan, 1981)
G. Bordman: *American Musical Comedy* (New York, 1982)
G. Loney, ed.: *Musical Theater in America* (Westport, Conn., 1984)
K. Bloom: *American Song: the Complete Musical Theater Companion* (New York, 1985)
G. Bordman: *American Musical Revue: from 'The Passing Show' to 'Sugar Babies'* (New York, 1985)
A. Lamb: *Jerome Kern in Edwardian London* (Brooklyn, 1985)
———: 'From *Pinafore* to Porter: United States–United Kingdom Interactions in Musical Theater, 1879–1929', *American Music*, iv (1986), 34
A. J. Lerner: *The Musical Theatre: a Celebration* (London, 1986)
G. Mast: *Can't help singin': the American Musical on Stage and Screen* (Woodstock, 1987)
S. Morley: *Spread a Little Happiness: the First Hundred Years of the British Musical* (New York, 1987)
R. Simas: *The Musicals No one Came to See: a Guidebook to Four Decades of Musical-Comedy Casualties on Broadway, off-Broadway and in Out-of-town Try-outs, 1943–1983* (New York, 1987)

Zarzuela

E. Cotarelo y Mori: *Historia de la zarzuela, ó sea El drama lírico* (Madrid, 1934)
M. Muñoz: *Historia de la zarzuela y el género chico* (Madrid, 1946)
J. Deleito y Piñuela: *Origen y apogeo del género chico* (Madrid, 1949)
A. Salazar: 'Zarzuela', *International Cyclopedia of Music and Musicians*, ed. O. Thompson (London, 1964)
R. Mindlin: *Die Zarzuela* (Zurich, 1965)
A. Fernández-Cid: *Cien años de teatro musical en España (1875–1975)* (Madrid, 1975)
J. Arnau and C. M. Gomez: *Historia de la zarzuela* (Madrid, 1979)
R. and C. Alier and others: *El libro de la zarzuela* (Barcelona, 1982)
A. Sagardia: 'Seminario de zarzuela', *Monsalvat*, cxix (1984), 19
R. Alier, X. Avinoa and F. X. Mata: *Diccionario de la zarzuela* (Barcelona, 1986)
R. Gilleron: *Approche musicale de la zarzuela chica* (diss., U. of Paris-Sorbonne, 1987)

Index